INDEX TO AMERICAN WOMEN SPEAKERS 1828-1978

Beverley Manning

The Scarecrow Press, Inc.
Metuchen, N.J., & London
1980

Library of Congress Cataloging in Publication Data

Manning, Beverley, 1942-
Index to American women speakers, 1828 to 1978.

1. American orations--Women authors--Indexes.
I. Title.
Z1231.07M36 [PS400] 016.815'00809287 79-26928
ISBN 0-8108-1282-7

Manufactured in the United States of America

Dedicated to

Edward and Flora Manning

TABLE OF CONTENTS

Introduction	vii
List of Books Indexed	1
Author Index	23
Subject Index	323
Title Index	515

INTRODUCTION

In recent years the interest in women and their problems in society has risen rapidly. This index is intended to assist college and high school students in locating women's speeches, both historical and contemporary. Women's rights and the struggle for education and employment are a major part of this index, but the full range of women's interests from the arts to world politics is covered.

The volumes selected for indexing include proceedings of conferences and symposia, anthologies, documentary histories, government documents, and periodicals. These were indexed for speeches by American women only. The majority of the speeches are listed in their entirety. On a few occasions the address was given by someone other than the author. The person reading the speech is noted in parentheses after the author entry. Susan B. Anthony frequently read Elizabeth Cady Stanton's speeches, especially in the later years, and a few other women were hesitant to give their own speeches, because public speaking was socially unacceptable for women in the nineteenth century. When a speech has been reprinted under several different titles, cross-references are noted after the author entry.

The index is divided into four sections: the List of Books Indexed and the Author, Subject, and Title indexes.

The Cumulative Book Index and the National Union Catalog were used to verify the List of Books Indexed. This list gives a complete bibliographical entry.

The Author Index contains two types of entries. Most of the author entries list the name of the speaker, title of the speech, and a brief bibliographical entry of author, title, and inclusive page numbers, referring to the complete bibliographical entry in the List of Books Indexed. The second type of author entry--used for periodicals, newspapers, pamphlets, and several books that contain only one speech--gives the full bibliographical statement.

The Author Index contains an alphabetical listing of all speakers under their popular name, e.g. Woodhull, Victoria, not Martin, Victoria Woodhull. Speakers are listed under their own names, e.g. Constance A. Sporburg, not Mrs. William Sporburg. The names were verified and completed by consulting the following: Dictionary of American Biography, Who's Who in America, Who Was Who in America, Who's Who of American Women, Woman's

Who's Who of America, A Biographical Dictionary of Contemporary Women of the United States and Canada, 1914-1915, American Women, by Willard and Livermore, and Notable American Women, by James.

The Subject Index lists the name of the speaker and title of speech under subject headings selected from the Library of Congress Subject Headings (8th edition and supplements). The Title Index lists title of speech and name of speaker. The Subject and Title indexes refer back to the Author Index.

The Connecticut State Library collection proved to have great value for research; it has an excellent collection of historical and contemporary sources. The following libraries have also been useful: the Sophia Smith Collection of Smith College Library, University of Hartford Library, Trinity College Library, Pope Pius XII Library of St. Joseph's College, Central Connecticut State College Library, and the libraries of the University of Connecticut/Storrs, School of Business Administration and School of Social Work.

The compiler wishes to express her appreciation for the assistance of the following: Sylvia H. Lazar, retired Head Branch Librarian, for suggesting the project and for her encouragement in seeking publication; Daniel P. Bogey, Easton (Connecticut) Town Librarian, for calling attention to a number of sources of material on black women; to Marilyn Noronha, present Head Branch Librarian for her continued support; Robert Vracenak and the staff of the Inter-Library Loan Department of the University of Connecticut/Storrs Library; the University of Connecticut Research Foundation, for financial assistance in preparing the manuscript; and Linda Medbury for the typing of the final manuscript.

Beverley Manning
University of Connecticut
Hartford Branch Library

LIST OF BOOKS

INDEXED

Abbott, Grace. From Relief to Social Security; The Development of the New Public Welfare Services and Their Administration. Edited by Edith Abbott. Chicago, University of Chicago Press, 1941.

Adams, Henry C., ed. Philanthropy and Social Progress; Seven Essays. Delivered before the School of Applied Ethics at Plymouth, Mass., during the Session of 1892, with an Introduction by Prof. Henry C. Adams. New York, Crowell, 1893.

Addams, Jane. A Centennial Reader. New York, Macmillan, 1960.

________. Democracy and Social Ethics. Edited by Anne Firor Scott. Cambridge, Mass., Belknap Press of Harvard University, 1964.

________. The Excellent Become the Permanent. New York, Macmillan, 1932.

________. Jane Addams on Peace, War, and International Understanding, 1899-1932. Edited by Allen F. Davis. New York, Garland, 1976.

________. The Second Twenty Years at Hull-House, September 1909 to September 1929, with a Record of a Growing World Consciousness. New York, Macmillan, 1931.

American Anti-Slavery Society. Proceedings of the American Anti-Slavery Society, at Its Third Decade, Held in the City of Philadelphia, Dec. 3d and 4th, 1864. New York, Negro Universities Press, 1969.

American Civil Liberties Union. The Trial of Elizabeth Gurley Flynn by the American Civil Liberties Union. Edited by Corliss Lamont. New York, Horizon, 1968.

American Home Economics Association. The Adventure of Change. Selected Speeches from the 57th Annual Meeting. New York, American Home Economics Association, 1966.

American Peace Congress, 1st (New York, 1907). Proceedings. New York, American Peace Society, 1907. (Also called National Arbitration and Peace Congress).

American Peace Congress, 2nd (Chicago, 1909). Proceedings. Edited by Charles E. Beals. Chicago, American Peace Society, 1909.

American Peace Congress, 3rd (Baltimore, 1911). Proceedings. Edited by Eugene A. Noble. Baltimore, American Peace Society, 1911.

American Peace Congress, 5th (San Francisco, 1915). Proceedings. Edited by H. H. Bell and Robert C. Toot. New York, American Peace Society, 1915.

Angeles, Philip, ed. Challenge to American Youth. Philadelphia, Macrae Smith, 1963.

Anthony, Katharine Susan. Susan B. Anthony: Her Personal History and Her Era. Garden City, N.Y., Doubleday, 1954.

Apthekar, Herbert, ed. A Documentary History of the Negro People in the United States from Colonial Times through the Civil War. New York, Citadel, 1951.

Arling, Emanie Nahm Sachs. "The Terrible Siren"; Victoria Woodhull (1838-1927). New York, Harper & Brothers, 1928.

Associated Country Women of the World. Proceedings of the Third Triennial Conference Held at Washington, May 31--June 11, 1936. Washington, D.C., U.S. Government Printing Office, 1937.

Association for the Advancement of Women. Papers and Letters Presented at the First Woman's Congress Held in the Union League Theatre, October, 1873. New York, Mrs. Wm. Ballard, Book and Job Printer, 1874.

________. Papers Read at the Third Congress of Women, Syracuse, October 13, 14, and 15, 1875. Chicago, Fergus Printing Company, n.d.

________. "Truth, Justice, and Honor." Papers Read before the Association for the Advancement of Women at its Eleventh Annual Congress, held at Chicago, Illinois, October, 1883. Buffalo, N.Y., Peter Paul & Bros., 1884.

Atkinson, Dorothy, ed. Women in Russia. Edited by Dorothy Atkinson, Alexander Dallin, and Gail Warshofsky Lapidus. Stanford, Calif., Stanford University Press, 1977.

Atkinson, Ti-Grace. Amazon Odyssey. New York, Links Books; distributed by Quick Fox, 1974.

Barbour, Floyd B., ed. The Black Seventies. Boston, Sargent, 1970.

Barton, Clara Harlowe. *The Red Cross; A History of This Remarkable International Movement in the Interest of Humanity.* Washington, D.C., American National Red Cross, 1898.

Baxandall, Rosalyn, ed. *America's Working Women.* Compiled and Edited by Rosalyn Baxandall, Linda Gordon, and Susan Reverby. New York, Vintage, 1976.

Beard, Mary Ritter, ed. *America through Women's Eyes.* New York, Macmillan, 1933.

________. *Mary Ritter Beard: a Sourcebook.* Edited by Ann J. Lane. New York, Schocken, 1977.

Bier, William Christian, ed. *Woman in Modern Life.* New York, Fordham University Press, 1968.

Blatch, Harriot Stanton. *Challenging Years; The Memoirs of Harriot Stanton Blatch,* by Harriot Stanton Blatch and Alma Lutz. Westport, Conn., Hyperion, 1976. (Reprint of the edition published by Putnam in 1940.)

Blaxall, Martha, ed. *Women and the Workplace; The Implications of Occupational Segregation.* Edited by Martha Blaxall and Barbara Reagan. Chicago, University of Chicago Press, 1976.

Bloomer, Dexter C. *Life and Writing of Amelia Bloomer.* With a New Introduction by Susan J. Kleinberg. New York, Schocken, 1975. (Originally published by Arena in 1895.)

Bosmajian, Hamida, ed. *This Great Argument: The Rights of Women.* Edited by Hamida Bosmajian and Haig Bosmajian. Reading, Mass., Addison-Wesley, 1972.

Brooks, Paul. *The House of Life: Rachel Carson at Work; With Selections from Her Writings Published and Unpublished.* Boston, Houghton Mifflin, 1972.

Brownlee, W. Elliot. *Women in the American Economy: A Documentary History, 1675 to 1929.* New Haven, Conn., Yale University Press, 1976.

Bryn Mawr College. *Carola Woerishoffer, Her Life and Work.* Published by the Class of 1907 of Bryn Mawr College. Bryn Mawr College, 1912.

Burton, Margaret Ernestine. *Mabel Cratty, Leader in the Art of Leadership.* New York, The Woman's Press, 1929.

Cade, Toni, comp. *The Black Woman; An Anthology.* New York, New American Library, 1970.

Cannon, James P. *Speeches for Socialism.* New York, Pathfinder, 1971.

Cantor, Milton, ed. Class, Sex, and the Woman Worker. Edited by Milton Cantor and Bruce Laurie. Westport, Conn., Greenwood, 1977.

Carroll, Berenice A. Liberating Women's History: Theoretical and Critical Essays. Urbana, University of Illinois Press, 1976.

Catt, Carrie Lane Chapman. Woman Suffrage and Politics; The Inner Story of the Suffrage Movement, by Carrie Chapman Catt and Nettie Rogers Shuler. Introduction by T. A. Larson. Seattle, University of Washington Press, 1969.

Chisholm, Shirley. The Good Fight. New York, Harper & Row, 1973.

Chmaj, Betty E., ed. American Women and American Studies. Pittsburgh, Know, 1971.

Clemens, Lois Gunden. Woman Liberated. Scottdale, Pa., Herald, 1971.

Conference for the Study of Negro Problems, 1st (Atlanta, 1896). Mortality among Negroes in Cities; Proceedings of the Conference for Investigation of City Problems, Held at Atlanta University, May 26-27, 1896. Atlanta, Atlanta University Press, 1896. (Reprinted by Arno Press and the New York Times, 1968, as Atlanta University Publications, nos. 1, 2, 4, 8, 9, 11, 13, 14, 15, 16, 17, 18.)

Conference for the Study of Negro Problems, 2nd (Atlanta, 1897). Social and Physical Condition of Negroes in Cities. Report of an Investigation under the Direction of Atlanta University and Proceedings of the Second Conference for the Study of Problems Concerning Negro City Life, Held at Atlanta University, May 25-26, 1897. Atlanta, Atlanta University Press, 1897. (Reprinted by Arno and the New York Times in Atlanta University Publications, 1968.)

Conference of Charities, 5th, 6th. Proceedings. American Social Science Association, Cincinnati, May 1878. Boston, A. William, September 1878, 1879.

Conference of Charities and Correction, 7th, 8th. Proceedings, 1880, 1881. New York, (etc.), 1880-81.

Conference of Professional and Academic Women. Sixteen Reports on the Status of Women in the Professions; Originally Presented April 11, 1970, New York University Law School. New York, Professional Women's Caucus, 1970.

Conference on Feminist Perspectives on Housework and Child Care. Feminist Perspectives on Housework and Child Care; Transcript of a Conference Sponsored by Sarah Lawrence College

Women's Studies Program, October 22, 1977. Edited by Amy Swerdlow. Bronxville, N.Y., Sarah Lawrence College, 1978.

Conference on Labor Market Segmentation (Harvard University, 1973). Labor Market Segmentation. Edited by Richard C. Edwards, Michael Reich, and David M. Gordon. Lexington, Mass., D.C. Heath, 1975.

Conference on the Present Status and Prospective Trends of Research on the Education of Women (Rye, N.Y., 1957). The Education of Women; Signs for the Future; Report. Edited by Opal D. David. Washington, D.C., American Council on Education, 1959.

Conference on the Universities and the Gay Experience. Proceedings of the Conference, Sponsored by the Women and Men of the Gay Academic Union, November 23 and 24, 1973. New York, Gay Academic Union, 1974.

Conference on Woman's Destiny--Choice or Chance? Report. Held at University of Washington, Seattle, Washington, November 21-22, 1963. Washington, D.C., U.S. Women's Bureau, 1963.

Conference on Women in the Defense Decade (New York, 1951). Women in the Defense Decade; Report ... of a National Conference of Persons Representing Schools, Colleges, Universities, Government Agencies, and Selected National Organizations, New York City, September 27-28, 1951. Edited by Raymond F. Howes. Washington, D.C., American Council of Education, 1952.

Conference on Women in the War on Poverty (1967). Proceedings. Washington, D.C., Office of National Councils and Organizations, Office of Economic Opportunity, 1967.

Conference on Women in the War on Poverty, 2nd (1968). Proceedings. Washington, D.C., Women's Advisory Council on Poverty and the Office of Economic Opportunity, 1968.

Conference on Women's Challenge to Management (Arden House, 1971). Corporate Lib: Women's Challenge to Management. Edited by Eli Ginzberg and Alice M. Yohalem. Baltimore, Johns Hopkins University Press, 1973.

Congress on Africa (Atlanta, 1895). Africa and the American Negro; Addresses and Proceedings of the Congress, Held under the Auspices of the Stewart Missionary Foundation for Africa of Gammon Theological Seminary in Connecticut with the Cotton States and International Exposition, December 13-15, 1895. Edited by J.W.E. Bowen. Miami, Mnemosyne, 1969.

Cott, Nancy Falik, comp. Root of Bitterness; Documents of the Social History of American Women. New York, Dutton, 1972.

Cross, Barbara M., ed. The Educated Woman in America; Selected Writings of Catharine Beecher, Margaret Fuller, and M. Carey Thomas. New York, Teachers College Press, 1965.

Danvers (Mass.) Historical Society. Old Anti-Slavery Days. Proceedings of the Commerative Meeting, Held by the Danvers Historical Society, at the Town Hall, Danvers, April 26, 1893, with Introduction, Letters and Sketches. Danvers, Danvers Mirror Print, 1893.

Davis, Angela Yvonne. If They Come in the Morning: Voices of Resistance. New York, The Third Press, 1971.

Davis, Paulina W. A History of the National Woman's Rights Movement, for Twenty Years, with the Proceedings of the Decade Meeting Held at Apollo Hall, October 20, 1870. New York, Kraus Reprint, 1971. (Reprint of the 1871 edition.)

Douglass, Frederick. Frederick Douglass on Women's Rights. Edited by Philip S. Foner. Westport, Conn., Greenwood, 1976.

Duniway, Abigail Scott. Path Breaking: An Autobiographical History of the Equal Suffrage Movement in Pacific Coast States. With a New Introduction by Eleanor Flexner. 2nd ed. New York, Schocken, 1971.

Dworkin, Andrea. Our Blood; Prophecies and Discourses on Sexual Politics. New York, Harper & Row, 1976.

Economic Problems of the Caribbean Area. Speeches, Addresses and Abstracts of Papers Delivered at the Public Conference Held in New York City Jointly with the Women's International League for Peace and Freedom on May 1, 1943. New York, Latin America Economic Institute, 1943.

Eddy, Mary Baker. Miscellaneous Writings, 1883-1896. Boston, Allison V. Stewart, 1917.

________. Retrospection and Introspection. Christian Healing. Rudimental Divine Science. Published by the Trustees under the Will of Mary Baker G. Eddy. Boston, 1968.

Epstein, Laurily, ed. Women in the Professions. Lexington, Mass., Lexington Books, 1975.

Farber, Seymour M., ed. Man and Civilization: The Potential of Woman; A Symposium. Edited by Seymour M. Faber and Roger H. L. Wilson. New York, McGraw-Hill, 1963.

Flexner, Eleanor. Century of Struggle; The Woman's Rights Movement in the United States. Cambridge, Mass., Belknap Press of Harvard University, 1959.

Fremon, Suzanne, ed. Women and Men: Traditions and Trends. New York, Wilson, 1977.

Frenz, Horst, ed. Nobel Lectures, 1901-1967; Including Presentation Speeches and Laureates' Biographies: Literature. New York, Elsevier, 1969.

Friedan, Betty. It Changed My Life; Writings on the Women's Movement. New York, Random House, 1976.

Furniss, Warren Todd, ed. Women in Higher Education. Edited by W. Todd Furniss and Patricia Albjerg Graham. Washington, D. C., American Council on Education, 1974.

Gardener, Helen Hamilton Chenoweth. Men, Women, and Gods, and Other Lectures. With an Introduction by Robert G. Ingersoll. New York, The Truth Seeker Company, 1885.

General Federation of Women's Clubs. Biennial Convention, 9 (1908, Boston). Official Report Compiled and Edited by the Retiring Recording Secretary, Mrs. John Dickinson Sherman. Chicago, 1908.

________. Biennial Convention, 16 (1922, Chautauqua, N. Y.). Official Report Compiled and Edited by the Recording Secretary Mrs. Adam Weiss. Washington, D. C., 1922.

Goldman, Emma. Red Emma Speaks; Selected Writings and Speeches. Compiled and Edited by Alix Kates Shulman. New York, Random House, 1972.

Goldman, George D., ed. Modern Woman; Her Psychology and Sexuality. Edited by George D. Goldman and Donald S. Milman. Springfield, Ill., Charles C Thomas, 1969.

Gordon, Anna Adams. The Beautiful Life of Frances E. Willard; A Memorial Volume. Chicago, Woman's Temperance Publishing Association, 1898.

________. The Life of Frances E. Willard. With an Introduction by Lady Henry Somerset. Evanston, Ill., National Woman's Christian Temperance Union, 1912.

Gordon, Francine E. Bringing Women into Management. Edited by Francine E. Gordon and Myra H. Strober. New York, McGraw-Hill, 1975.

Hallowell, Anna Davis, ed. Life and Letters of James and Lucretia Mott. Boston, Houghton Mifflin, 1884.

Hammond, Nancy, ed. Women and Children in Contemporary Society. Proceedings of a Conference at Kellogg Center, Michigan State University, November 22, 1975. Lansing, Michigan Women's Commission, 1976.

Harper, Ida Husted. The Life and Work of Susan B. Anthony; Including Public Addresses, Her Own Letters and Many from Contemporaries during Fifty Years.... New York, Arno, 1969. (Reprinted from the 1898-1908 edition.)

Harris, Dorothy V., ed. Women and Sport: A National Research Conference. Pennsylvania State University, College of Health, Physical Education, and Recreation, 1972.

Harris, Theodore F. Pearl S. Buck; A Biography. New York, John Day, 1969.

Howe, Julia Ward. Is Polite Society Polite? And Other Essays. Boston, Houghton Mifflin, 1899.

_______. Julia Ward Howe and the Woman Suffrage Movement. New York, Arno and the New York Times, 1969.

Illinois Farmers' Institute (Bloomington, 1934). Addresses, 40th Annual Meeting. Springfield, Illinois Department of Household Science, 1934.

Institute of Women's Professional Relations. War and Post-War Employment and Its Demands for Educational Adjustments; Proceedings of the Conference Held at the Mayflower Hotel, Washington, D.C., May 4 and 5, 1944. New London, Connecticut College, The Institute, 1944.

International Conference of Women Engineers and Scientists, 1st (New York, 1964). Focus for the Future; Developing Engineering and Scientific Talent. Proceedings. New York, Society of Women Engineers, 1964.

International Conference on Women in Health (Washington, D.C., 1975). Proceedings. Washington, D.C., U.S. Health Resources Administration, 1976.

International Congress of Women (London, 1899). The International Congress of Women of 1899. Edited by the Countess of Aberdeen. London, T.F. Unwin, 1900.

International Congress of Women (Toronto, 1909). Report of the International Congress of Women Held in Toronto, Canada, June 24-30, 1909, under the Auspices of the National Council of Women of Canada. Toronto, G. Parker & Sons, Printers, 1910.

International Congress of Women (Chicago, 1933). Our Common Cause, Civilization. Report of the International Congress of Women, Including the Series of Round Tables, July 16-22, 1933, Chicago, Illinois. New York, National Council of Women of the U.S., 1933.

International Council of Women (1888). Report of the International

Council of Women, Assembled by the National Woman Suffrage Association, Condensed from the Stenographic Report Made by Mary F. Seymour and Assistants, for the Women's Tribune, Published Daily During the Council, Washington, D.C., U.S. of America, March 25 to April 1, 1888. Washington, D.C., R.H. Darby, Printer, 1888.

Irwin, Inex Haynes. Angels and Amazons: A Hundred Years of American Women. Garden City, N.Y., Doubleday, 1933.

________. The Story of the Woman's Party. New York, Harcourt, Brace, 1921.

Itasca Conference on the Continuing Education of Women (Itasca State Park, Minn., 1962). Education and a Woman's Life; Proceedings. Edited by Lawrence E. Dennis. Washington, D.C., American Council of Education, 1963.

Jaquette, Jane S. Women in Politics. New York, Wiley, 1974.

Jewish Women's Congress. Papers. Held at Chicago, September 4, 5, 6, and 7, 1893. Philadelphia, Jewish Publication Society of America, 1894.

Josephson, Hannah Geffen. Jeannette Rankin; First Lady in Congress; A Biography. Indianapolis, Bobbs-Merrill, 1974.

Katzell, Mildred E., ed. Women in the Work Force; Proceedings of Conference Sponsored by the Division of Personnel Psychology of the New York State Psychology Association, New York, 1970. Edited by Mildred E. Katzell and William C. Byham. New York, Behavioral Publications, 1972.

Keller, Helen Adams. Helen Keller: Her Socialist Years; Writings and Speeches. Edited with an Introduction by Philip S. Foner. New York, International Publishers, 1967.

________. The Story of My Life, With Her Letters (1887-1901) and a Supplementary Account of Her Education, Including Passages from the Reports and Letters of Her Teacher, Anne Mansfield Sullivan, by John Albert Macy. Garden City, N.Y., Doubleday, 1954.

King, Coretta Scott. My Life with Martin Luther King, Jr. New York, Holt, Rinehart and Winston, 1969.

Kingman, Lee, ed. Newbery and Caldecott Medal Books: 1956-1965, with Acceptance Papers, Biographies & Related Material Chiefly from the Horn Book Magazine. Boston, Horn Book, 1965.

________. Newbery and Caldecott Medal Books: 1966-1975, with Acceptance Papers, Biographies and Related Material Chiefly from the Horn Book Magazine. Boston, Horn Book, 1975.

Kornbluh, Joyce L., ed. Rebel Voices, An I. W. W. Anthology. Ann Arbor, University of Michigan Press, 1964.

Kraditor, Aileen S., ed. Up from the Pedestal; Selected Writings in the History of American Feminism. Chicago, Quadrangle, 1968.

League of Women Voters of the U. S. Proceedings of the 2nd Annual Convention Held at Cleveland, Ohio, April 11-18, 1921. Peru, Indiana, N. L. W. V., 1921.

________. Yearbook and Proceedings of the 3rd Annual Convention, and Pan-American Conference of Women Held at Baltimore, Maryland, April 20-29, 1922. N. L. W. V., 1922.

________. Proceedings of the 4th Annual Convention Held at Des Moines, Iowa, April 9-14, 1923. Washington, D. C., N. L. W. V., 1923.

________. Proceedings of the 7th Annual Convention Held at St. Louis, Missouri, April 14-21, 1926. Washington, D. C., N. L. W. V., 1926.

________. Proceedings of the 8th National Convention Held at Chicago, Illinois, April 23-28, 1928. Washington, D. C., N. L. W. V., 1928.

Lerner, Gerda, ed. Black Women in White America; A Documentary History. New York, Pantheon, 1972.

________. The Female Experience; An American Documentary. Indianapolis, Bobbs-Merrill, 1977.

Leuchtenburg, William Edward, ed. The New Deal; A Documentary History. New York, Harper & Row, 1968.

Libraries and the Life of the Mind in America; Addresses Delivered at the Centennial Celebration of the American Library Association. Chicago, A. L. A., 1977.

Loewenberg, Bert James. Black Women in Nineteenth-Century American Life: Their Words, Their Thoughts, Their Feelings. Edited with an Introduction by Bert James Loewenberg and Ruth Bogin. University Park, Pennsylvania State University Press, 1976.

Lutz, Alma. Created Equal; A Biography of Elizabeth Cady Stanton, 1815-1902. New York, John Day, 1940.

M. I. T. Symposium on American Women in Science and Engineering (1964). Women and the Scientific Professions. Edited by Jacquelyn A. Mattfeld and Carol G. Van Aken. Cambridge, Mass., M. I. T. Press, 1965.

McGuigan, Dorothy Gies. New Research on Women at the University of Michigan. Ann Arbor, University of Michigan, Center for Continuing Education of Women, 1974.

________. A Sampler of Women's Studies. Ann Arbor, University of Michigan, Center for Continuing Education of Women, 1973.

Martin, George Whitney. Madam Secretary, Frances Perkins. Boston, Houghton Mifflin, 1976.

Martin, Wendy, ed. The American Sisterhood; Writings of the Feminist Movement from Colonial Times to the Present. New York, Harper & Row, 1972.

Michigan State University, East Lansing, School of Home Economics. Potentialities of Women in the Middle Years, by Robert O. Havinghurst and Others. Edited by Irma Hannah Gross. East Lansing, Michigan State University Press, 1956.

Miller, Bertha E. Mahony, ed. Caldecott Medal Books: 1938-1957, with the Artists' Acceptance Papers & Related Material Chiefly from the Horn Book Magazine. Boston, Horn Book, 1957.

________. Newbery Medal Books: 1922-1955, with Their Authors' Acceptance Papers & Related Material Chiefly from the Horn Book Magazine. Boston, Horn Book, 1955.

Millstein, Beth. We, the American Women; A Documentary History. By Beth Millstein and Jeanne Bodin. New York, Jerome S. Ozer, 1977.

Moquin, Wayne, comp. A Documentary History of the Italian Americans. Edited by Wayne Moquin with Charles Van Doren. New York, Praeger, 1974.

________. Great Documents in American Indian History. Edited by Wayne Moquin with Charles Van Doren. New York, Praeger, 1973.

Morgan, Robin, comp. Sisterhood Is Powerful; An Anthology of Writings from the Women's Liberation Movement. New York, Vintage, 1970.

Myers, Margaret, ed. Women in Librarianship: Melvil's Rib Symposium; Proceedings of the Eleventh Annual Symposium Sponsored by the Alumni and the Faculty of the Rutgers University Graduate School of Library Science. Edited by Margaret Myers and Mayra Scarborough. New Brunswick, N.J., Rutgers University Graduate School of Library Service, Bureau of Library and Information Science Research, 1975.

National American Woman Suffrage Association. Proceedings of the 39th Annual Convention Held at Chicago, February 14th to 19th, inclusive, 1907. Warren, Ohio, N.A.W.S.A., 1907.

National Conference of Charities and Correction (9th-43rd). Proceedings, 1882-1916. New York, 1882-1916.

National Conference of Social Work (44th-75th). Proceedings, 1917-1948. New York, 1917-1948.

National Congress of Mothers. The Work and Words of the National Congress of Mothers (First Annual Session) Held in the City of Washington, D.C., February 17, 18, and 19, 1897. New York, Appleton, 1897.

National Council of Women of the United States (Washington, D.C., 1891). Transactions of the National Council of Women of the United States, Assembled in Washington, D.C., February 22 to 25, 1891. Published by Order of the Executive Board of the National Council of Women. Edited by Rachel Foster Avery, Corresponding Secretary. Philadelphia, Lippincott, 1891.

National Council of Women of the United States of America. Yearbook and Directory, Including the Proceedings of the 14th Convention. New York, 1928.

National League of Cities. Women in Municipal Government. Washington, D.C., 1974.

National Negro Conference (New York, 1909). Proceedings of the National Negro Conference, Held May 31 and June 1, 1909. New York, Arno and the New York Times, 1969.

National Purity Congress, 1st (Baltimore, 1895). The National Purity Congress; Its Papers, Addresses, Portraits. An Illustrated Record of the Papers and Addresses of the First National Purity Congress, Held under the Auspices of the American Purity Alliance, Baltimore, October 14, 15, and 16, 1895. Edited by Aaron M. Powell. New York, American Purity Alliance, 1896.

New York (City). Commission on Human Rights. Women's Role in Contemporary Society; The Report of the Hearings ..., September 21-15, 1970. New York, Avon, 1972.

N.Y. Herald Tribune. Report of the 2nd Women's Conference on Current Problems. New York, 1932.

________. Report of the 3rd Women's Conference on Current Problems. New York, 1933.

________. Report of the 4th Annual Women's Conference on Current Problems. New York, 1934.

________. Report of the Annual Forum on Current Problems, 5th, 6th, 8th-21st, 1935, 1936, 1938-1952.

Noun, Louise R. Strong-minded Women: The Emergence of the Woman-Suffrage Movement in Iowa. Ames, Iowa State University Press, 1969.

O'Neill, William L. The Woman Movement: Feminism in the United States and England. New York, Barnes & Noble, 1969.

Palmer, George Herbert. The Teacher: Essays and Addresses on Education. By George Herbert Palmer and Alice Freeman Palmer. Boston, Houghton Mifflin, 1908.

Papachristou, Judith. Women Together: A History in Documents of the Women's Movement in the U.S. New York, Knopf, 1976.

Rosaldo, Michelle Zimbalist. Woman, Culture, and Society. Edited by Michelle Zimbalist Rosaldo and Louise Lamphere. Stanford, Calif., Stanford University Press, 1974.

Rossi, Alice S., ed. The Feminist Papers: From Adams to De Beauvoir. New York, Columbia University Press, 1973.

Salper, Roberta, ed. Female Liberation; History and Current Politics. New York, Knopf, 1972.

Sanger, Margaret Higgins. My Fight for Birth Control. New York, Farrar & Rinehart, 1931.

Schappes, Morris Urman, ed. A Documentary History of the Jews in the United States: 1654-1875. 3rd ed. New York, Schocken, 1971.

Schneiderman, Rose. All for One. By Rose Schneiderman and Lucy Goldthwaite. New York, Paul S. Eriksson, 1967.

Schneir, Miriam, comp. Feminism; The Essential Historical Writings. New York, Random House, 1972.

Scott, Anne Firor, ed. The American Women: Who Was She? Englewood Cliffs, N.J., Prentice-Hall, 1971.

________. One Half the People: The Right for Woman Suffrage. By Anne F. Scott and Andrew M. Scott. Philadelphia, Lippincott, 1975.

Smith, Fred B., ed. Law vs. Lawlessness; Addresses, Delivered at the Citizenship Conference, Washington, D.C., October 13-15, 1923. New York, Revell, 1924.

Smith, Julia E. Abby Smith and Her Cows. New York, Arno, 1972. (Reprint of the 1877 edition.)

Smith, Margaret Chase. Declaration of Conscience. Edited by William C. Lewis, Jr., Garden City, N.Y., Doubleday, 1972.

Spieler, Carolyn, ed. Women in Medicine--1976; Report of a Macy Conference. New York, Josiah Macy, Jr. Foundation, 1977.

Stanton, Elizabeth Cady, ed. History of Woman Suffrage. 2nd ed. New York, Arno, 1969. (V. 1-3 edited by Elizabeth Cady Stanton, Susan B. Anthony, Matilda Joslyn Gage. V. 4 edited by Susan B. Anthony and Ida Husted Harper. V. 5 & 6 edited by Ida Husted Harper.)

Stein, Leon, ed. Out of the Sweatshop; The Struggle for Industrial Democracy. New York, Quadrangle/The New York Times, 1977.

Stevens, Doris. Jailed for Freedom. Introduction by Janice Law Trecker. New York, Schocken, 1976.

Suhl, Yuri. Ernestine L. Rose and the Battle for Human Rights. New York, Reynal, 1959.

Tanner, Leslie Barbara, ed. Voices from Women's Liberation. New York, New American Library, 1970.

Theobald, Robert, ed. Dialogue on Women. Indianapolis, Bobbs-Merrill, 1967.

Tolchin, Susan. Clout: Womanpower and Politics. New York, Coward, McCann & Geoghegan, 1974.

U.S. Congress. House. Committee on Armed Services. Subcommittee No. 2. Hearings on H.R. 9832 to Eliminate Discrimination Based on Sex with Respect to the Appointment and Admission of Persons to the Service Academics and H.R. 10705, 11267, H.R. 11268, H.R. 11711, and H.R. 13729 to Insure That Each Admission to the Service Academies Shall Be Made without Regard to a Candidate's Sex, Race, Color, or Religious Beliefs. Washington, D.C., U.S. Government Printing Office, 1975.

________. ________. Committee on Education and Labor. Select Subcommittee on Labor. Equal Pay for Equal Work. Hearings on H.R. 8898; H.R. 10226 and Various Bills to Prohibit Discrimination on Account of Sex in the Payment of Wages by Employers Engaged in Commerce or the Production of Goods for Commerce, or to Provide for the Restitution of Wages Lost by Employees by Reason of Any Such Discrimination. 87th Cong., 2nd sess., pt. 1, March 26, 27, and 28, 1962; pt. 2, April 27, and 28, 1962. Washington, D.C., U.S. Government Printing Office, 1962.

________. ________. ________. Special Subcommittee on Education. Discrimination against Women: Congressional Hearings on Equal Rights in Education and Employment. Edited by Catharine R. Stimpson in Conjunction with the Congressional Information Service, Washington, D.C. New York, Bowker, 1973.

________. ________. ________. Special Subcommittee on Labor.

Equal Pay Act. Hearings on H.R. 3861 and Related Bills to Prohibit Discrimination, on Account of Sex, in the Payment of Wages by Employers Engaged in Commerce, or in the Production of Goods for Commerce and to Provide for the Restitution of Wages Lost by Employees by Reason of Any Such Discrimination, Washington, D.C., March 15, 25, 26, and 27, 1963. Washington, D.C., U.S. Government Printing Office, 1963.

———. ———. ———. Subcommittee on Employment Opportunities. Legislation to Prohibit Sex Discrimination on the Basis of Pregnancy. Hearings before the Subcommittee on Employment Opportunities, 95th Cong., 1st sess. on H.R. 5055 and H.R. 6075 to Amend Title VII of the Civil Rights Act of 1964 to Prohibit Sex Discrimination on the Basis of Pregnancy, April 6, 1977. Pt. 2, Hearing of June 29, 1977. Washington, D.C., U.S. Government Printing Office, 1977.

———. ———. ———. Subcommittee on Equal Opportunities. The Equal Opportunity for Displaced Homemakers Act. Hearing on H.R. 10272 to Provide for the Establishment of Multipurpose Service Programs for Displaced Homemakers, and for Other Purposes. Los Angeles, Calif., November 18, 1976. Washington, D.C., U.S. Government Printing Office, 1976.

———. ———. Committee on Government Operations. Subcommittee. National Women's Conference. Hearings, 94th Cong., 1st sess. on H.R. 8903 to Direct the National Commission on the Observance of International Women's Year, 1975, to Organize and Convene a National Women's Conference and for Other Purposes, September 30, 1975. Washington, D.C., U.S. Government Printing Office, 1975.

———. ———. Committee on Small Business. Subcommittee on Minority Enterprise and General Oversight. Women in Business: Hearings, 95th Cong., 1st sess., Washington, D.C., April 5, May 24, and June 7, 1977. Washington, D.C., U.S. Government Printing Office, 1977.

———. ———. Committee on the Judiciary. Equal Rights Amendment to the Constitution. Hearing, 72nd Cong., 1st sess. on H. J. Res. 197 Proposing an Amendment to the Constitution of the United States Relative to Equal Rights for Men and Women, March 16, 1932. Washington, D.C., U.S. Government Printing Office, 1932.

———. ———. ———. Equal Rights Amendment to the Constitution and Commission on the Legal Status of Women. Hearings, 80th Cong., 2nd sess., March 10 and 12, 1948. Serial No. 16. Washington, D.C., U.S. Government Printing Office, 1948.

———. ———. ———. Subcommittee No. 4. Equal Rights for Men and Women 1971; Hearings, 92nd Cong., 1st sess., on H.J. Res 35, 208 and Related Bills Proposing an Amendment to the Constitution of the United States Relative to Equal Rights for Men and Women, and H.R. 916 and Related Bills Concerning the Recommendations of the Presidential Task Force on Women's Rights and Responsibilities, March 24, 25, 31; April 1, 2, and 5, 1971. Serial No. 2. Washington, D.C., U.S. Government Printing Office, 1971.

________. ________. Select Committee on Aging. Subcommittee on Retirement Income and Employment. Social Security Inequities against Women; Hearings, 94th Cong., 1st sess., September 11 and 29, 1975. Washington, D.C., U.S. Government Printing Office, 1975.

________. ________. Select Committee on Crime. Drugs in Our Schools; Hearings before the Select Committee on Crime; 92nd Cong., 2nd sess., Miami, Fla., July 5, 6, 7, 1972. Washington, D.C., U.S. Government Printing Office, 1972.

U.S. Congress Joint Economic Committee. Economic Problems of Women; Hearings, 93rd Cong., 1st sess. Pt. 1, July 10, 11, and 12, 1973; Pt. 2, July 24, 25, 26, and 30, 1973; Pt. 4, July 17, 1974. Washington, D.C., U.S. Government Printing Office, 1973, 1976.

U.S. Congress. Senate. Committee on Human Resources. Nomination Hearing on Eleanor Holmes Norton, of New York, to be a Member of the Equal Employment Opportunity Commission, 94th Cong., 1st sess., May 24, 1977. Washington, D.C., U.S. Government Printing Office, 1977.

________. ________. ________. Nomination Hearings on Mary E. King, of the District of Columbia, to be Deputy Director of the ACTION Agency, 95th Cong., 1st sess., March 4, 1977. Washington, D.C., U.S. Government Printing Office, 1977.

________. ________. ________. Subcommittee on Labor. Discrimination on the Basis of Pregnancy, 1977; Hearings before the Subcommittee on Labor..., 95th Cong., 1st sess., on S. 995 to Amend Title VII of the Civil Rights Act of 1964 to Prohibit Sex Discrimination on the Basis of Pregnancy, April 26, 27, and 29, 1977. Washington, D.C., U.S. Government Printing Office, 1977.

________. ________. Committee on Labor and Public Welfare. Subcommittee on Alcoholism and Narcotics. Alcohol Abuse among Women; Special Problems and Unmet Needs, 1976. Hearing, 94th Cong., 2nd sess. on Examination of the Special Problems and Unmet Needs of Women Who Abuse Alcohol, September 29, 1976. Washington, D.C., U.S. Government Printing Office, 1976.

________. ________. ________. Subcommittee on Children and

Youth. *White Conference on Children--Child Development Recommendations; Hearings, 92nd Cong., 1st sess., April 26, and 27, 1971.* Washington, D.C., U.S. Government Printing Office, 1971.

________. ________. ________. ________. *White Conference on Youth--Examination of Recommendations; Hearing, 92nd Cong., 1st sess., August 2, 1971.* Washington, D.C., U.S. Government Printing Office, 1971.

________. ________. ________. Subcommittee on Labor. *Equal Pay Act of 1963; Hearings, 88th Cong., 1st sess. April 2, 3, and 16, 1963, on S. 882 and S. 910 to Amend the Equal Pay Act of 1963.* Washington, D.C., U.S. Government Printing Office, 1963.

________. ________. Committee on the Judiciary. Subcommittee on Constitutional Amendments. *Abortion; Hearings, 93rd Cong., 2nd sess. on S.J. Res. 119 Proposing an Amendment to the Constitution of the United States for the Protection of Unborn Children and Other Persons and S.J. Res. 130 Proposing an Amendment to the Constitution of the United States Guaranteeing the Right of Life to the Unborn, the Ill, the Aged, or the Incapacitated.* 4 volumes. Washington, D.C., U.S. Government Printing Office, 1974-76.

________. ________. ________. ________. *Equal Rights Amendment; Hearings, 70th Cong., 2nd sess. on S.J. Res. 64. A Joint Resolution Proposing an Amendment to the Constitution of the United States Relative to Equal Rights for Men and Women. February 1, 1929.* Washington, D.C., U.S. Government Printing Office, 1929.

________. ________. ________. ________. *Equal Rights; Hearing, 71st Cong., 3rd sess., on S.J. Res. 52. A Joint Resolution Proposing an Amendment to the Constitution of the United States Relative to Equal Rights for Men and Women, January 6, 1931.* Washington, D.C., U.S. Government Printing Office, 1931.

________. ________. ________. ________. *Equal Rights for Men and Women; Hearing, 73rd Cong., 1st sess. on S.J. Res. 1. A Joint Resolution Proposing an Amendment to the Constitution of the United States Relative to Equal Rights for Men and Women, May 27, 1933.* Washington, D.C., U.S. Government Printing Office, 1933.

________. ________. ________. ________. *Equal Rights for Men and Women; Hearings, 75th Cong., 3rd sess. on S.J. Res. 65. A Joint Resolution Proposing an Amendment to the Constitution of the United States Relative to Equal Rights for Men and Women, February 7, 8, 9, and 10, 1938.* Washington, D.C., U.S. Government Printing Office, 1938.

______. ______. ______. ______. Equal Rights Amendment; Hearing, 79th Cong., 1st sess. on S. J. Res. 61. A Joint Resolution Proposing an Amendment to the Constitution of the United States Relating to Equal Rights for Men and Women, September 28, 1945. Washington, D.C., U.S. Government Printing Office, 1945.

______. ______. ______. ______. Equal Rights; Hearings, 84th Cong., 2nd sess. on S. J. Res. 39 Proposing an Amendment to the Constitution of the United States Relative to Equal Rights for Men and Women, April 11 and 12, 1956. Washington, D.C., U.S. Government Printing Office, 1956.

______. ______. ______. ______. Equal Rights 1970; Hearings 91st Cong., 2nd sess. on S.J. Res. 61 and S.J. Res. 231 Proposing an Amendment to the Constitution of the United States Relative to Equal Rights for Men and Women, September 9, 10, 11, and 15, 1970. Washington, D.C., U.S. Government Printing Office, 1970.

______. ______. ______. ______. Women and the "Equal Rights" Amendment; Senate Subcommittee Hearings on the Constitutional Amendment, 91st Congress. Edited by Catharine Stimpson in Conjunction with the Congressional Information Service. New York, Bowker, 1972.

______. ______. Select Committee on Small Business. Women and the Small Business Administration; Hearing, 94th Cong., 2nd sess. on Women and the Small Business Administration, February 24, 1976. Washington, D.C., U.S. Government Printing Office, 1976.

______. ______. ______. The Effect of Government Regulations on Small Business and the Problems of Women and Minorities in Small Business in the Southwestern United States; Hearing, 94th Cong., 2nd sess., Oklahoma City, Oklahoma--October 8, 1976. Washington, D.C., U.S. Government Printing Office, 1977.

______. ______. Special Committee on Aging. Future Direction in Social Security; Hearing, 94th Cong., 1st sess., Pt. 18--Washington, D.C. Women and Social Security, October 22, 1975; Pt. 19, October, 23, 1975. Washington, D.C., U.S. Government Printing Office, 1976.

U.S. Equal Employment Opportunity Commission. Hearings on Discrimination in White Collar Employment, Held in New York, N.Y., January 15-18, 1968. Washington, D.C., U.S. Government Printing Office, 1968.

U.S. National Center for Health Services Research. Women and Their Health: Research Implications for a New Era. Proceedings of a Conference Held at University of California, San

Francisco, San Francisco, California, August 1-2, 1975. Edited by Virginia Olesen. Washington, D.C., National Center for Health Services Research, 1977.

U.S. Women's Bureau. Today's Woman in Tomorrow's World. Report of a Conference Commemorating the 40th Anniversary of the Women's Bureau, June 2 and 3, 1960. Washington, D.C., U.S. Government Printing Office, 1960.

________. Proceedings of the Women's Industrial Conference; Called by the Women's Bureau of the U.S. Department of Labor, Washington, D.C., January 11, 12, and 13, 1923. Washington, D.C., U.S. Government Printing Office, 1923.

U.S. Women's Bureau Conference, 1948. The American Woman--Her Changing Role, Worker, Homemaker, Citizen; Report on 1948 Women's Bureau Conference, Feb. 17, 18, 19. Washington, D.C., U.S. Women's Bureau, 1948.

Washington, Booker Tallafero. The Booker T. Washington Papers, v. 2, 1860-1889. Edited by Louis R. Harlan. Urbana, University of Illinois Press, 1972.

Weinberg, Arthur Myron, ed. Passport to Utopia; Great Panaceas in American History. Chicago, Quadrangle, 1968.

Willard, Frances Elizabeth. Glimpses of Fifty Years; The Autobiography of an American Woman. Written by Order of the National Woman's Christian Temperance Union. Introduction by Hannah Whitall Smith. Chicago, H.J. Smith, 1889.

Woman's Rights Convention (Akron, Ohio, 1851). Proceedings. New York, Burt Franklin, 1973. (Reprint of the 1851 edition.)

World's Congress of Representative Women, Chicago, 1893. Congress of Women, Held in the Woman's Building, World's Columbian Exposition, Chicago, U.S.A., 1893. With Portraits, Biographies, and Addresses. Edited by Mary Kavanaugh Oldham Eagle. Official Edition. Philadelphia, International Publishing Co., 1895.

World's Congress of Representative Women, Chicago, 1893. A Historical Resume for Popular Circulation of the World's Congress of Representative Women, Convened in Chicago on May 15, and Adjourned on May 22, 1893, under the Auspices of the Woman's Branch of the World's Congress Auxiliary. Edited by May Wright Sewall. Chicago, Rand, McNally, 1894.

Wright, Frances. Course of Popular Lectures, with Three Addresses, on Various Public Occasions. And a Reply to the Charges Against the French Reformers of 1789. 4th ed. New York, Office of the Free Enquirer, 1831. Supplement. Course of Lectures, Continuing the Last Four Lectures Delivered in the United States. New York, Wright and Owen, 1831.

AUTHOR INDEX

Abbott, Alice Asbury. "Compensation." In World's Congress of Representative Women, Chicago, 1893. *Congress of Women*, pp. 645-8.

Abbott, Edith. "Discussion of Immigration Under The Percentus Limit Law." In National Conference of Social Work. *Proceedings* (1922), pp. 464-6.

________. "The Experimental Period of Widow's Pension Legislation." In National Conference of Social Work. *Proceedings* (1917), pp. 154-64.

________. "Field Work and the Training of the Social Worker." In National Conference of Charities and Correction. *Proceedings* (1915), pp. 615-21.

________. "Immigration Legislation and the Problems of Assimilation." In National Conference of Social Work. *Proceedings* (1924), pp. 82-91.

________. "Introductory Statement of Chairman of Committee on Pensions, Insurance and the State." In National Conference of Social Work. *Proceedings* (1918), pp. 388-9.

________. "Public Assistance--Wither Bound?" In National Conference of Social Work. *Proceedings* (1937), pp. 3-25.

________. "Public Welfare and Politics." In National Conference of Social Work. *Proceedings* (1936), pp. 27-45.

________. "Relief, the No Man's Land, and How to Reclaim It." In National Conference of Social Work. *Proceedings* (1940), pp. 187-98.

________. "Remarks at Jane Addams Memorial Service." In National Conference of Social Work. *Proceedings* (1935), pp. 3-5.

________. "The Social Case Worker and the Enforcement of Industrial Legislation." In National Conference of Social Work. *Proceedings* (1918), pp. 312-18.

________. "Work of Maintenance?" In National Conference of Social Work. *Proceedings* (1940), pp. 332-43.

Abbott, Grace. "Address at Conference Dinner." In National Conference of Social Work. *Proceedings* (1932), pp. 45-51.

________. "Address at the Women's Industrial Conference." In U.S. Women's Bureau. *Proceedings of the Women's Industrial Conference*, pp. 91-3.

________. "Case Work Responsibility of Juvenile Courts." In National Conference of Social Work. *Proceedings* (1929), pp. 153-62.

________. "The Children's Bureau." In National Council of Women of the U.S. *Proceedings of the 14th Convention*, pp. 61-2.

________. "The County Versus the Community as an Administrative Unit." In Abbott, G. From Relief to Social Security, pp. 370-8.

________. "Developing and Protecting Professional Standards in Public Welfare Work." In Abbott, G. From Relief to Social Security, pp. 327-45.

________. "Developing Standards of Rural Child Welfare." In National Conference of Social Work. Proceedings (1927), pp. 26-37.

________. "The Government and Youth in a Troubled World." In National Conference of Social Work. Proceedings (1933), pp. 291-300.

________. "How Secure Administrative Skill With Professional Competence for State and Local Public Welfare Service?" In National Conference of Social Work. Proceedings (1936), pp. 494-508.

________. "The Need of Federal Aid for Relief in the Winter 1932-33. Testimony Before a United States Senate Committee." In Abbott, G. From Relief to Social Security, pp. 121-56.

________. "Neglected Fundamentals in Children's Work: Fundamental Question Now Before Us." In National Conference of Social Work. Proceedings (1922), pp. 21-4.

________. "The Public Protection of Children; A First Part of the Public Welfare Program." In Abbott, G. From Relief to Social Security, pp. 305-26. Also in National Conference of Social Work. Proceedings (1924), pp. 3-14.

________. "The Public Welfare Administrator and Civil Service in State and Local Services." In Abbott, G. From Relief to Social Security, pp. 346-63.

________. "The Responsibility of Club Women in Promoting the Welfare of Children." In General Federation of Women's Clubs. Biennial Convention, 16 (1922), pp. 509-15.

________. "Social Standards in Industry: Child Labor." In National Conference of Social Work. Proceedings (1923), pp. 109-10.

________. "Testimony Before the United States Senate Committee During the "Hearing" on the Economic Security Bill." In Abbott, G. From Relief to Social Security, pp. 201-25. Also in U.S. Congress. Senate. Hearings on S. 1130, A Bill to Alleviate the Hazard of Old Age, Unemployment, Illness, and Dependency, To Establish a Social Insurance Board in the Department of Labor, To Raise Revenue, And for Other Purposes, 74th Cong., 1st sess., January 22 to February 20, 1935, pp. 1076-91.

________. "Toward Health Security: Economic Security Against Illness." In Abbott, G. From Relief to Social Security, pp. 290-301.

________. "The Tragedy of Transients; A Statement Before a United States Senate Committee." In Abbott, G. From Relief to Social Security, pp. 49-68.

Abel, Mary Hinman. "Clean Food." In General Federation of Women's Clubs. Biennial Convention 9 (1908), pp. 155-8.

Abzug, Bella Savitsky. "The Abortion Rights Act." Congressional Record, 92nd Cong., 2nd sess., 1972, 118, pt. 12, 15327-32.

______. "Address to National Farmers Union Women Fly-In." Congressional Record, 93rd Cong., 1st sess., 1973, 119, pt. 17, 21272-3.

______. "The Conduct of the President." Congressional Record, 93rd Cong., 1st sess., 1973, 119, pt. 15, 19264-7.

______. "The Equal Rights Amendment." Congressional Record, 92nd Cong., 1st sess., 1971, 117, pt. 15, 19402.

______. "Nixon and Welfare for the Rich." Congressional Record, 93rd Cong., 1st sess., 1973, 119, pt. 10, 26030-1.

______. "Opening Statement." In U.S. Congress. House. Committee on Government Operations. National Women's Conference, pp. 1, 7.

______. "Should Auto Emission Controls Be Removed in Low-Pollution Areas to Help Conserve the U.S. Supply of Motor Fuels?" Congressional Digest, 53 (1974), 93.

______. "Should Congress Limit the Present Scope of the Federal Food Stamp Program?" Congressional Digest, 54 (1975), 157-9.

______. "Should "Conditional Amnesty" Be Granted to Vietnam War Draft Evaders?" Congressional Digest, 53 (1974), 235-9.

______. "Should Federal Subsidies Be Provided for Congressional Election Campaigns?" Congressional Digest, 56 (1977), 88-90.

______. "Speech by Congresswoman Bella S. Abzug at Inaugural Day Peace Demonstration in Washington--January 20, 1973." Congressional Record, 93rd Cong., 1st sess., 1973, 119, pt. 2, 1756-7.

______. "Statement." In U.S. Congress. House. Committee on the Judiciary Subcommittee #4. Equal Rights for Men and Women 1971, pp. 111-22.

______. "Statement." In U.S. Congress. Senate. Committee on the Judiciary. Subcommittee on Constitutional Amendments. Abortion, pt. 1, 100-10.

______. "Statement." In U.S. Congress. Senate. Committee on Human Resources. Subcommittee on Labor. Discrimination on the Basis of Pregnancy, 1977, pp. 307-10.

______. "Statement." In U.S. Congress. Senate. Special Committee on Aging. Future Directions in Social Security, pt. 18, 1669-72.

______. "The Vice-Presidency and the Order of Succession." Congressional Record, 93rd Cong., 1st sess., 1973, 119, pt. 26, 33779-80.

______. "Women in Elective Office." In N.Y. (City). Commission on Human Rights. Women's Role in Contemporary Society, pp. 635-9.

______. "Women's Political Power." Congressional Record, 92nd Cong., 1st sess., 1971, 117, pt. 19, 24787-9.

Ackerman, Jessie A. "Plan of Work Along Social Purity Lines." In National Purity Congress, 1st, Baltimore, 1895. National Purity Congress, pp. 332-5.

Ackerman, Judy. "Our Union Has Kept Faith With Us." In Stein, L. Out of the Sweatshop, pp. 343-4.

Ackroyd, Margaret F. "Remarks on Hours Limitation Law, Administrative and Technical Problems." In U.S. President's National Conference of Commissions on Status of Women, 3rd. Panel on Labor Standards and Equal Employment Opportunity for Women, June 29, 1966, Washington, D.C., U.S. Government Printing Office, 1966. 5 p.

Acton, Amy F. "Chartering and Supervision by State Authority." In National Conference of Charities and Correction. Proceedings (1916), pp. 316-21.

Adams, Mary Mathews. "The Highest Education." In World's Congress of Representative Women, Chicago, 1893. A Historical Resume, pp. 131-4.

Adams, Mary Newbury. "Influence of Great Women." In World's Congress of Representative Women, Chicago, 1893. Congress of Women, pp. 342-7.

________. "The Influence of the Discovery of America on the Jews." In Jewish Women's Congress. Papers, pp. 77-90.

________. "The Struggle and Reconciliation of the Ideal and the Practical in America." In Association for the Advancement of Women. Congress of Women, 3rd. Papers, pp. 117-26.

Addams, Jane. "Address." In National Society for the Promotion of Industrial Education. Bulletin, 1 (January, 1907), 37-44.

________. "Address." Playground, 2 (April, 1908), 25-8.

________. "Address, City Club, 1926." In Addams, J. Jane Addams On Peace, War, and International Understanding, pp. 195-9.

________. "Address of Miss Jane Addams, Delivered at Carnegie Hall, Friday, July 9, 1915." Christian Work, 99 (July 31, 1915), 145-8.

________. "Address WILPF, Washington 1924." In Addams, J. Jane Addams On Peace, War, and International Understanding, pp. 184-7.

________. "Alice Kellogg Tyler." In Addams, J. The Excellent Becomes The Permanent, pp. 51-8.

________. "At A Memorial Meeting for Henry Demarest Lloyd Held Under the Auspices of United Mine Workers of America..." In Addams, J. The Excellent Becomes The Permanent, pp. 39-48.

________. "The Attack On War." Christian Century, 38 (October 13, 1921), 10-2.

________. "Breadgivers." In Addams, J. A Centennial Reader, pp. 103-4.

________. "The Call of the Social Field." In Addams, J. A Centennial Reader, pp. 88-9. Also in National Conference of Charities and Correction. Proceedings (1911), pp. 370-2.

________. "Canon Samuel A. Barnett. Memorial Address Given

To The American Federation of Settlements." In Addams, J. The Excellent Becomes The Permanent, pp. 123-41.

________. "Charitable Effort." In Addams, J. Democracy and Social Ethics, pp. 13-70.

________. "Charity and Social Justice." In Addams, J. A Centennial Reader, pp. 85-7. Also in National Conference of Charities and Correction, Proceedings (1910), pp. 1-18. Also North American Review, 192 (July, 1910), 68-81. Also Survey, 24 (June 11, 1910), 441-9.

________. "Child at the Point of Greatest Pressure." In National Conference of Charities and Correction. Proceedings (1912), pp. 26-30.

________. "Child Labor and Education." In National Conference of Charities and Corrections. Proceedings (1908), pp. 364-9.

________. "Child Labor and Pauperism." In National Conference of Charities and Correction. Proceedings (1903), pp. 114-21.

________. "Child Labor Legislation: A Requisite for Industrial Efficiency." In National Child Labor Committee, New York. Child Labor; The Proceedings of the First Annual Conference, New York City, February 14-16, 1905 (New York, 1905), pp. 128-36.

________. "Child Labor on the Stage." Annals, 37, Supplement (July, 1911), 60-5. Also in National Child Labor Committee, New York. Uniform Child Labor Laws, The Proceedings of the 7th Annual Conference of the National Child Labor Committee, Birmingham, Alabama, 9-12 March 1911 (New York, 1911), pp. 60-5.

________. "Class Conflict in America." In American Sociological Society. Papers and Proceedings, 2 (1907), 152-5.

________. "Count Tolstoy." In Addams, J. Jane Addams on Peace, War, and International Understanding, pp. 26-33.

________. "Disarmament and Life." In Addams, J. Jane Addams on Peace, War, and International Understanding, pp. 173-8.

________. "Domestic Service and the Family Claim." In World Congress of Representative Women, Chicago, 1893. A Historical Resume, 2, 626-31.

________. "Education." In Addams, J. A Centennial Reader, pp. 145-50.

________. "Educational Methods." In Addams, J. Democracy and Social Ethics, pp. 178-220. (Same as "Education" above.)

________. "Excerpt from Address at the Organizational Meeting of the National Women's Trade Union League, Boston, 1903." In Schneiderman, R. All For One, p. 75.

________. "Family Affection." In Addams, J. A Centennial Reader, pp. 144-5. Also in Addams, J. Democracy and Social Ethics, pp. 77-82.

________. "The Federal Children's Bureau--A Symposium." Annals, 33, Supplement (March, 1909), 28-30. Also in National Child Labor Committee, New York. Child Workers of the Nation, The Proceedings of the 5th Annual Conference, Chicago, Illinois, January 21-23, 1909 (New York, 1909), pp. 28-30.

________. "Filial Relations, 1902." In Addams, J. Democracy and Social Ethics, pp. 71-101. Also in Martin, W. The American Sisterhood, pp. 211-5.

________. "Foreign-born Children in the Primary Grades." In National Education Association. Journal of Proceedings and Addresses (1897), pp. 104-12.

________. "A Function of the Social Settlement." Annals, 12 (May, 1899), 33-55.

________. "Gordon Dewey." In Addams, J. The Excellent Becomes The Permanent, pp. 61-9.

________. "The Home and the Special Child." In National Education Association. Journal of Proceedings and Addresses (1908), pp. 1127-31.

________. "Household Adjustment." In Addams, J. Democracy and Social Ethics, pp. 102-36.

________. "The Housing Problem in Chicago." Annals, 20 (July, 1902), 99-107.

________. "How Much Social Work Can a Community Afford? From the Ethical Point of View." In National Conference of Social Work. Proceedings (1926), pp. 108-13. Also Survey, 58 (November 15, 1926), 199-201.

________. "How Shall We Approach Industrial Education?" Educational Bi-Monthly, 1 (February, 1907), 183-90.

________. "The Immigrant and Social Unrest." In National Conference of Social Work. Proceedings (1920), pp. 59-62.

________. "The Immigrant Woman as She Adjusts Herself to American Life." In General Federation of Women's Clubs. Biennial Convention, 12 (1914), 370-4.

________. "Immigrants." Survey, 22 (June 26, 1909), 453-4.

________. "Industrial Amelioration." In Addams, J. Democracy and Social Ethics, pp. 137-77.

________. "The Interests of Labor in International Peace." In Universal Peace Congress, Official Report, 13 (New York, 1904), 145-7.

________. "International Co-operation for Social Welfare." In National Conference of Social Work. Proceedings (1924), pp. 107-13.

________. "Introduction to Forum." In International Congress of Women, Chicago, 1933. Our Common Cause, Civilization, p. 185.

________. "Italian Children in the Primary Grades." In Moquin, W. A Documentary History of the Italian American, pp. 306-12. Also in National Education Association. Journal of Proceedings and Addresses (1897), pp. 104-12.

________. "Jenny Dow Harvey." In Addams, J. The Excellent Becomes The Permanent, pp. 17-25.

________. "Joseph Tilton Bowen. At the Opening of the Joseph Tilton Bowen Country Club." In Addams, J. The Excellent Becomes The Permanent, pp. 83-93.

________. "Judge Murray F. Tuley." In Addams, J. The Excellent Becomes The Permanent, pp. 73-80.

________. "Labor as a Factor in the Newer Conception of International Relationships." In Academy of Political Science. Proceedings, 7 (July, 1917), 282-8.

________. "Lydia Avery Coonley-Ward." In Addams, J. The Excellent Becomes The Permanent, pp. 113-20.

______. "Mary Hawes Wilmarth." In Addams, J. The Excellent Becomes The Permanent, pp. 97-109.

______. "Maturing Concepts of Peace." In Addams, J. A Centennial Reader, pp. 252-3.

______. "The Modern City and the Municipal Franchise for Women." Woman's Journal, 37 (April 7, 1906), 53-5.

______. "Modern Devices for Minimizing Dependencies." In U.S. Congress. Senate. Proceedings of the Conference on the Care of Dependent Children, Washington, 25-26 January 1909, Senate Document 721, 60th Cong., 2nd sess., 1909, pp. 99-101.

______. "A Modern Lear." Survey, 29 (November 2, 1912), 131-7.

______. "National Protection for Children." Annals, 29 (January, 1907), 57-60. Also in National Child Labor Committee, New York. Child Labor and the Republic, The Proceedings of the Third Annual Conference, Cincinnati, Ohio, 13-15 December 1906 (New York, 1907), pp. 57-60.

______. "Neighborhood Improvement." In National Conference of Charities and Correction. Proceedings (1904), pp. 456-8, 560-2.

______. "New Ideals of Peace." In Addams, J. Jane Addams on Peace, War, and International Understanding, pp. 51-5. Also in American Peace Congress, 1st, New York, 1907. Proceedings, pp. 106-10.

______. "New Internationalism." In Addams, J. Jane Addams on Peace, War, and International Understanding, pp. 56-9. Also in American Peace Congress, 1st, New York, 1907. Proceedings, pp. 213-6.

______. "New Methods of Procedure." Unity, 98 (September 6, 1926), 15.

______. "The Newer Ideals of Peace." In Addams, J. Jane Addams on Peace, War, and International Understanding, pp. 19-25.

______. "The Objective Value of a Social Settlement." In Adams, H. Philanthropy and Social Progress, pp. 27-56.

______. "Operation of the Illinois Child Labor Law." Annals, 27 (March, 1906), 327-30. Also in National Child Labor Committee, New York. Child Labor, A Menace to Industry, Education, and Good Citizenship, The Proceedings of the 2nd Annual Conference, Washington, December 8-10, 1905 (New York, 1906), pp. 69-72.

______. "Patriotism and Pacifists in War Time." In Addams, J. Jane Addams on Peace, War, and International Understanding, pp. 140-8.

______. "The Philosophy of a New Day." In International Congress of Women, Chicago, 1933. Our Common Cause, Civilization, pp. 65-8.

______. "Political Reform." In Addams, J. Democracy and Social Ethics, pp. 221-77.

______. "Presidential Address." In International Congress of Women, Vienna, 1921. Report, 3 (1921), 1-3.

______. "Presidential Address, International Congress, The Hague." In Addams, J. Jane Addams on Peace, War, and International Understanding, pp. 67-71.

________. "Presidential Address, Women of the Pacific." In Addams, J. *Jane Addams on Peace, War, and International Understanding*, pp. 200-4.

________. "The Public School and the Immigrant Child." In National Education Association. *Journal of Proceedings and Addresses* (1908), pp. 99-102.

________. "Remarks." In U.S. Congress. House. Committee on the Judiciary, *Hearings on Woman Suffrage*, 13 March 1912, Serial 2, 62nd Cong., 2nd sess., 1912, pp. 7-8.

________. "Remarks as Chairman of Discussion (The Standing Committee on Neighborhood Improvements.) In National Conference of Charities and Correction. *Proceedings* (1904), pp. 608-17.

________. "Report of the Committee on Immigrants." In National Conference of Charities and Correction. *Proceedings* (1909), pp. 213-5. (Same as "Immigrants.")

________. "Response." In International Congress of Women, Chicago, 1933. *Our Common Cause, Civilization*, pp. 242-4.

________. "The Responsibilities and Duties of Women Toward the Peace Movement." In Universal Peace Congress. *Official Report*, 13 (1904), 120-2.

________. "The Revolt Against War" In Addams, J. *Jane Addams on Peace, War, and International Understanding*, pp. 72-90. Also *Survey*, 34 (July 17, 1915), 355-9.

________. "Sarah Rozet Smith. At the Dedication of the Hull-House Organ." In Addams, J. *The Excellent Becomes The Permanent*, pp. 29-36.

________. "Summary of An Address on Settlements." In International Congress of Women, Toronto, 1909. *Report*, 1, 9-11.

________. "Social Consequences of the Immigration Law." In National Conference of Social Work. *Proceedings* (1927), pp. 102-6.

________. "Social Settlements." In National Conference of Charities and Corrections. *Proceedings* (1897), pp. 338-46.

________. "Social Workers and Other Professions." In Addams, J. *A Centennial Reader*, pp. 94-7. Also in National Conference of Social Work. *Proceedings* (1930), pp. 50-4.

________. "Some Reflections on the Failure of the Modern City to Provide Recreation for Young Girls." *Charities and the Commons*, 21 (December 5, 1908), 365-8.

________. "Speech." *Woman's Journal*, 42 (June 17, 1911), 185-6.

________. "Speech at the Abraham Lincoln Center." *Unity*, 61 (July 2, 1908), 280.

________. "Speech at the Civic Dedication of the Abraham Lincoln Center." *Unity*, 55 (May 27, 1905), 364-5.

________. "Speech Seconding Theodore Roosevelt's Nomination for President at the Progressive Convention." *Congressional Record*, 62nd Cong., 2nd sess., 1912, 47, pt. 12, Appendix, 564-5.

________. "The Spirit of Social Service." In National Conference of Social Work. *Proceedings* (1920), pp. 41-3.

________. "Standards of Education for Industrial Life." In National Conference of Charities and Correction. *Proceedings* (1911), pp. 162-4.

_______. "Statement." In U.S. Congress. House. Committee on Military Affairs. Selective-Service Act, Hearings on the Bill Authorizing the President to Increase Temporarily the Military Establishment of the United States, 65th Cong., 1st sess., 1917, pp. 238-40.

_______. "Statement." In U.S. Congress. House. Committee on Military Affairs. Volunteer and Conscription System, 65th Cong., 1st sess., 1917, pp. 20-2.

_______. "Street Trading." Annals, 33, Supplement (March, 1909), 232-3. Also in National Child Labor Committee, New York. Child Workers of the Nation, the Proceedings of the 5th Annual Conference, Chicago, Illinois, January 21-23, 1909 (New York, 1909), pp. 28-30.

_______. "Struggle for Life Above the Poverty Line." In National Federation of Settlement. Conference, 3 (1913), 16-9.

_______. "The Subjective Necessity for Social Settlements." In Adams, H. Philanthropy and Social Progress, pp. 1-26. Also in Addams, J. A Centennial Reader, pp. 9-10. Also in Addams, J. Twenty Years at Hull-House, pp. 115-27.

_______. "Ten Years Experience in Child Labor Legislation in Illinois." Annals, 38, Supplement (July, 1911), 144-8. Also in National Child Labor Committee, New York. Uniform Child Labor Laws, The Proceedings of the 7th Annual Conference, Birmingham, Alabama, 9-12 March 1911 (New York, 1911), pp. 144-8.

_______. "Testimony." In U.S. Congress. Senate. Committee on Banking and Currency. Rehabilitation and Provision for European Countries; Hearings Relative to Need of Assistance in Exporting Our Goods and Rendering Financial Aid Generally in Rehabilitating European Countries, 66th Cong., 3rd sess., 1921.

_______. "Testimony." In U.S. Congress. House. Committee on Foreign Affairs. Commission for Enduring Peace, Hearings on H.R. 6921 and H.J. Resolution 32, 11 January 1916, 64th Cong., 1st sess., 1916, pp. 3-17.

_______. "Testimony." In U.S. Congress. House. Committee on Foreign Affairs. United States and the Orient, Hearing on H.R. 16661 to Provide for a Commission on Relations Between the U.S. and the Orient, 12 December 1916, 64th Cong., 2nd sess., 1916, pp. 10-2.

_______. "Testimony." In U.S. Congress. House. Committee on the Judiciary. Espionage and Interference with Neutrality, Hearings on H.R. 291, April 9 and 12, 1917, Serial 53, Pt. 2, 6th Cong., 1st sess., 1917, pp. 50-2.

_______. "Testimony." In U.S. Congress. House Committee on Rules. Subcommittee on Woman Suffrage. Hearing on Resolution Establishing a Committee on Woman Suffrage. House Document 754, 63rd Cong., 2nd sess., 1914, pp. 13-8.

_______. "Testimony Before Committee on Military Affairs." In Addams, J. Jane Addams on Peace, War, and International Understanding, pp. 113-7.

_______. "Tolstoy's Theory of Life." In Addams, J. Jane Addams on Peace, War, and International Understanding, pp. 34-43.

________. "Three Addresses, Thirteenth Universal Peace Congress." In Addams, J. Jane Addams on Peace, War, and International Understanding, pp. 44-50.

________. "What Peace Means." In Addams, J. Jane Addams on Peace, War, and International Understanding, pp. 11-4.

________. "What War is Destroying." In Addams, J. Jane Addams on Peace, War, and International Understanding, pp. 62-6.

________. "Woman's Peace Meeting--Jane Addams's Address." Woman's Journal, 35 (October 22, 1904), 337, 340-1.

________. "Woman's Special Training for Peacemaking." In American Peace Congress, 2nd, Chicago, 1909. Proceedings, pp. 252-4.

________. "Women's Clubs and Public Policies." In General Federation on Women's Clubs. Biennial Convention, 12 (1914), 24-30.

________. "The World Court." In Addams, J. Jane Addams on Peace, War, and International Understanding, pp. 188-94.

________. "World's Food Supply and Woman's Obligation." In General Federation of Women's Clubs. Biennial Convention, 15 (1918), 251-63. Also General Federation Magazine, 17 (July, 1918), 11-5. Also Journal of Home Economics, 10 (September, 1918), 389-400. Also in National Education Association. Journal of Addresses and Proceedings (1918), pp. 108-13.

________. "World's Food and World Politics." In National Conference of Social Work. Proceedings (1918), pp. 650-6.

Additon, Henrietta. "Community Responsibility for Preventing Crime." In International Congress of Women, Chicago, 1933. Our Common Cause, Civilization, pp. 626-34.

________. "The Responsibility of the Police for Preventing Crime." In New York. Herald Tribune. Report of the 4th Annual Women's Conference on Current Problems, pp. 45-8.

Adickes, Sandra. "Public Testimony." In New York (City). Commission on Human Rights. Women's Role in Contemporary Society, pp. 441-4.

Adkins, Frances L. "Reporting Activities of Group-Work Agencies." In National Conference of Social Work. Proceedings (1936), pp. 219-25.

Adler, Helen G. "Working Man's School of New York City." (Read by Sadie American.) In International Congress of Women, London, 1899, 2, 90-2.

Adrian, Marlene. "Sex Differences in Biomechanics." In Harris, D. Women and Sport, pp. 389-97.

Ahlgren, Mildred Carlson. "Challenge of Democracy. Build World Peace in Your Own Community." Vital Speeches, 18 (October 1, 1952), 756-7.

Aikers, Charlotte A. "The Educational Opportunity of the Visiting Nurse in the Prevention of Disease." In National Conference of Charities and Correction. Proceedings (1906), pp. 185-95.

Albee, Helen. "Value of Encouraging Handicrafts and Home Industries." In International Congress of Women, Toronto, 1909. Report, 1, 166-74.

Albert, Ethel M. "The Roles of Women: A Question of Values." In Farber, S. Man and Civilization: The Potential of Woman, pp. 105-15.

Alden, Cynthia Westover. "The Economic Position of Women as Journalists." In International Congress of Women, London, 1899, 465-7.

Alden, Margaret Hamilton. "The Responsibility of Women to the Press." In International Congress of Women, Toronto, 1909. Report, 1, 400-4.

Aleshire, Ruth Cory. "Problems of Adoption in Rural Areas." In National Conference of Social Work. Proceedings (1942), pp. 416-25.

Alexander, Elreta. "Reflections For a Graduate. Dare to be Your Creative Self." Vital Speeches, 42 (August 1, 1976), 628-32.

Alexander, Margaret Walker. "Religion, Poetry, and History. Foundations for a New Educational System." Vital Speeches, 34 (October 1, 1968), 760-3.

Alexander, Ruth. "Formula For Freedom. Attack Subversives Wherever Found." Vital Speeches, 20 (December 15, 1953), 150-3.

________. "Mid-century World. Whose World Has It Turned Out To Be?" Vital Speeches, 17 (February 1, 1951), 242-5.

________. "Post-war America That America Does Not Want. A Fair Trade Act Needed For Ideas." Vital Speeches, 9 (January 1, 1943), 171-4.

________. What Price The Fatted Calf? Juvenile Delinquency Approaching Epidemic Proportions." Vital Speeches, 22 (May 15, 1956), 460-7.

________. "What Price the Welfare State? Government--The Guardian or Master?" Vital Speeches, 18 (January 15, 1952), 199-203.

________. "Which Way America? What Businessmen Can Do About It." Vital Speeches, 15 (March 1, 1949), 301-3.

Allan, Virginia Rachel. "Statement." In U.S. Congress. House. Committee on Education and Labor. Special Subcommittee on Education. Discrimination Against Women, pp. 130-7.

________. "Statement." In U.S. Congress. House. Committee on the Judiciary. Subcommittee no. 4. Equal Rights For Men and Women 1971, pp. 125-37.

________. "Statement." In U.S. Congress. Senate. Committee on the Judiciary. Subcommittee on Constitutional Amendments. Women and the "Equal Rights" Amendment, pp. 172-80.

Allen, Dorothy. "Self Concept and the Female Participant." In Harris, D. Women and Sport, pp. 35-52.

Allen, Elizabeth. "Discussion of the Evolution of Psychiatric Social Work--From the Viewpoint of the Psychiatric Social Worker." In National Conference of Social Work. Proceedings (1930), pp. 396-403.

Allen, Florence Ellinwood. "Address." In International Congress of Women, Chicago, 1933. Our Common Cause, Civilization, pp. 11-2.

________. "Adventures in Understanding." In National Conference of Social Work. Proceedings (1937), pp. 84-94.

________. "Bridge to the Future. Have We Here and Now the Intelligence and Devotion to Cross Over?" Vital Speeches, 11, (April 15, 1945), 390-3.

________. "How Can We Put Our Living Traditions to Work?" In National Conference of Social Work. Proceedings (1938), pp. 51-7.

Allen, Lucile. "The Council's Interest." In Conference on the Present Status and Prospective Trends of Research on the Education of Women, Rye, N.Y., 1952. The Education of Women, pp. 3-5.

Allen, Nancy R. "Testimony at a Hearing of the Senate Committee on the Judiciary, January 23, 1880." In Stanton, E. History of Woman Suffrage, 3, 160.

Alper, Minnie. "Supervision as One Method of Staff Development: In a Rural Setting." In National Conference of Social Work. Proceedings (1939), pp. 294-303.

Alsberg, Elsa. "The Immigrant. Means of Using National and Racial Customs and Organizations in Relating Isolated Groups to General Community Movements." In National Conference of Social Work. Proceedings (1924), pp. 386-92.

Alschuler, Rose H. "Chairman's Introduction. Foundations of Education." In International Congress of Women, Chicago, 1933. Our Common Cause, Civilization, pp. 715-6.

Alvarado, Ernestine M. "Mexican Immigration to the United States." In National Conference of Social Work. Proceedings (1920), pp. 479-80.

American, Sadie. "The Child or Girl Without A Mother and Mother Without a Child." In International Council of Women, Toronto, 1909. Report, 2, 428-34.

________. "Play and Playgrounds." In International Congress of Women, Toronto, 1909. *Report*, 1, 32-8.

________. "Play and Playgrounds." In General Federation of Women's Clubs. *Biennial Convention*, 9 (1908), 135-8.

________. "Organization." In Jewish Women's Congress. *Papers*, pp. 218-62.

________. "Vocation Schools." In *International Congress of Women*, London, 1899, 2, 92-6.

Ames, Fanny B. "Care of Dependent Children." In National Council of Women of the U.S., Washington, 1891. *Transactions*, pp. 69-80.

Amigh, Ophelia L. "Alcoholism as a Case of Degeneracy." In National Conference of Charities and Correction. *Proceedings* (1901), pp. 282-3.

Anastasi, Anne. "Psychological Differences Between Men and Women." In Bier, W. *Woman in Modern Life*, pp. 42-54.

Anderson, Bette. "Customs Reorganization and Modernization. The Procedures Which Affect International Trade." *Vital Speeches*, 43 (August 1, 1977), 621-3.

Anderson, Harriet E. "Cooperation of the Home Service Department of the American Red Cross with Other Social Agencies." In National Conference of Social Work. *Proceedings* (1918), pp. 343-6.

________. "Training." In National Conference of Charities and Correction. *Proceedings* (1913), pp. 376-9.

Anderson, Jean. "Should Congress Enact Proposed Legislation to Require Mandatory Deposits on Beverage Containers?" *Congressional Digest*, 57 (March, 1978), 84-8.

Anderson, Mary. "Closing Statement at the Women's Industrial Conference." In U.S. Women's Bureau. *Proceedings of the Women's Industrial Conference*, pp. 188-90.

________. "Post-war Role of American Women." Washington, D.C., U.S. Women's Bureau, 1944. 7 p.

________. "Recent Industrial Investigations: Recent Investigations by Government Bureaus." In National Conference of Social Work. *Proceedings* (1923), pp. 140-2.

________. "Statement." U.S. Congress. Senate. Committee on the Judiciary. Subcommittee on Constitutional Amendments. *Equal Rights* (1956), pp. 54-6.

________. "Welcoming Address." In U.S. Women Bureau. *Proceedings of the Women's Industrial Conference*, pp. 1-2.

________. "The Women's Bureau and Standards of Women's Work." In National Conference of Social Work. *Proceedings* (1921), pp. 285-7.

Anderson, Meta L. "Community Control of the Feeble-Minded Instruction." In National Conference of Social Work. Proceedings (1918), pp. 536-43.

________. "Mental Hygiene Problems of Subnormal Children: In the Public Schools." In National Conference of Social Work. Proceedings (1921), pp. 363-7.

Andrew, Elizabeth Wheeler. "The Origin, History and Development of the World's Woman's Christian Temperance Union." In World's Congress of Representative Women, Chicago, 1893. A Historical Resume, pp. 400-12.

Andrews, Fannie Fern. "The American School Peace League." In American Peace Congress, 2nd Chicago, 1909. Proceedings, pp. 46-50, 378-82.

________. 'Education and International Peace." In American Peace Congress, 3rd, Baltimore, 1911. Proceedings, pp. 267-75.

Andrews, Judith Walker. "The Ramabai Association." In National Council of Women of the U.S., Washington, 1891. Transactions, pp. 325-30.

Anerdson, Eva. "Teacher on a Tightrope. Wither Your Goal?" Vital Speeches, 17 (January 1, 1951), 186-9.

Angell, Bee. 'Why Do New Products Fail: Mini-Market Tests." Vital Speeches, 35 (November 15, 1968), 91-6.

Anneke, Mathilde Franziska Giesler. "Address to the 3rd Annual Meeting of the American Equal Rights Association, New York, May 1869." In Stanton, E. History of Woman Suffrage, 2, 392-4.

Anthony, Susan Brownell. "Abolitionist Speech." In Anthony, K. Susan B. Anthony, pp. 151-2.

________. "Address." In National Council of Women of the U.S., Washington, 1891. Transactions, pp. 227-30.

________. "Address on the Amendment of the Rochester, New York City Charter, December 12, 1892." In Harper, I. The Life and Work of Susan B. Anthony, 2, 731-2.

________. "Address to a Convention in Hartford, Conn., October 1869." In Harper, I. The Life and Work of Susan B. Anthony, 1, 333.

________. "Address to a Convention of Bricklayers' and Masons' International Union, Rochester, N.Y., January 13, 1900." In Harper, I. The Life and Work of Susan B. Anthony, 3, 1161-2.

________. "Address to a Congressional Hearing, March 1884." In Harper I. The Life and Work of Susan B. Anthony, 2, 588-90.

________. "Address to a Hearing of the Joint Committee of Congress of the District of Columbia, January 22, 1870." Revolution, 5 (January 27, 1870), 60-1. Also in Stanton, E. History of Woman Suffrage, 2, 414-5.

________. "Address to a Senate Committee, February 1900." In

Harper, I. The Life and Work of Susan B. Anthony, 3, 1167-8.

_______. "Address to an Equal Rights Meeting, Albany, N. Y., November 21, 1866." In Harper, I. The Life and Work of Susan B. Anthony, 1, 263-4.

_______. "Address to Congress, Read at the 1866 Woman's Rights Convention." In Catt, C. Woman Suffrage and Politics, p. 39. Also in Harper, I. The Life and Work of Susan B. Anthony, 2, 968-71. Also in Stanton, E. History of Woman Suffrage, 2, 168-71.

_______. "Address to Celebration of Her 80th Birthday, February 15, 1900." In Harper, I. The Life and Work of Susan B. Anthony, 3, 1187-8. Also in Stanton, E. History of Woman Suffrage, 4, 403-4.

_______. "Address to Judiciary Committee of the House, March 8, 1884." In Stanton, E. History of Woman Suffrage, 4, 42-3.

_______. "Address to President Lincoln. Adopted by the Women's National Loyal League, May 14, 1863." In Harper, I. The Life and Work of Susan B. Anthony, 2, 957-9.

_______. "Address to the National Delegates, Before the First Joint Convention with the American Woman Suffrage Association, 1890." In Harper, I. The Life and Work of Susan B. Anthony, 2, 631.

_______. "Address to the National Woman Suffrage Convention, May 10, 1870." Revolution, 5 (May 19, 1870), 307-8.

_______. "Address to the New York State Assembly, February 1854." In Harper, I. The Life and Work of Susan B. Anthony, 1, 109-10.

_______. "Address to the Second National Woman Suffrage Association Convention, January 19, 1870." In Harper, I. The Life and Work of Susan B. Anthony, 1, 338.

_______. "Address to the Senate Committee on Woman Suffrage, March 7, 1884." In Stanton, E. History of Woman Suffrage, 4, 40. (Same as "Address to a Congressional Hearing, March 1884.")

_______. "Address to the Senate Judiciary Committee, January 12, 1872." In Harper, I. The Life and Work of Susan B. Anthony, 1, 410-1. Also in Stanton, E. History of Woman Suffrage, 2, 513-4.

_______. "Address to the 3rd Anniversary Meeting of the Equal Rights Association Meeting, May 12, 1869." In Harper, I. The Life and Work of Susan B. Anthony, 1, 323-4.

_______. "Address to the 31st Annual Convention of the National American Woman Suffrage Association, April 27, 1899." In Harper, I. The Life and Work of Susan B. Anthony, 3, 1127-8.

_______. "Address to the 33rd Annual Convention of the National American Woman Suffrage Association, May 30, 1901." In Harper, I. The Life and Work of Susan B. Anthony, 3, 1232.

_______. "Address to the Women's National Loyal League Convention, May 14, 1863." In Harper, I. The Life and Work of Susan B. Anthony, 1, 227-8, 229.

_______. "Address to the Woman's Rights Convention, New York,

May 10, 1866." In Harper, I. The Life and Work of Susan B. Anthony, 1, 260.

________. "Anthony Explains the National's Strategy." In Papachristou, J. Women Together, p. 99. (Same as "Address to a Congressional Hearing, March 1884.")

________. "Anthony on the Ballot and Women's Wages." In Papachristou, J. Women Together, pp. 148-9.

________. "Anthony's Remarks." In Papachristou, J. Women Together, pp. 86-7.

________. "Anthony's Speech." In Papachristou, J. Women Together, p. 149. (Same as "Address to a Convention of Bricklayers' and Masons' International Union, Rochester, N.Y. January 13, 1900.")

________. "Closing Address at the 17th Annual Convention of the National Woman Suffrage Association, March 1884." In Stanton, E. History of Woman Suffrage, 4, 27-8.

________. "Comments on Divorce Resolutions at 10th National Woman's Rights Convention, May 11, 1860." In Harper I. The Life and Work of Susan B. Anthony, 1, 194. Also in Lutz, A. Created Equal, pp. 116-7. Also in Stanton, E. History of Woman Suffrage, 1, 735.

________. "Constitutional Argument." In Harper, I. The Life and Work of Susan B. Anthony, 2, 977-92. Also in Kraditor, A. Up From The Pedestal, pp. 243-52.

________. "Debate at the 1893 Convention of the National American Woman Suffrage Association." In Harper, I. The Life and Work of Susan B. Anthony, 2, 738.

________. "Debate on the Bible Resolution at the National American Woman Suffrage Association Convention, November, 1895." In Harper, I. The Life and Work of Susan B. Anthony, 2, 853-4. Also in Stanton, E. History of Woman Suffrage, 4, 263-4. (Same as "Anthony's Remarks.")

________. "Debate With Judge Hunt at Her Trial For Voting, June, 1873." In Harper, I. The Life and Work of Susan B. Anthony, 1, 439-41. Also in Stanton, E. History of Woman Suffrage, 2, 687-9.

________. "Declaration of Rights For Women, Read at Independence Hall, Philadelphia, July 4, 1876." In Stanton, E. History of Woman Suffrage, 3, 31-4.

________. "Demand For Party Recognition. Delivered in Kansas City at the Opening of the Campaign, May 4, 1894." In Harper, I. The Life and Work of Susan B. Anthony, 2, 1015-21. Also in Martin, W. The American Sisterhood, pp. 93-100.

________. "Discussions of Resolutions at the 11th National Woman's Rights Convention, May 10, 1866." In Stanton, E. History of Woman Suffrage, 2, 171-2.

________. "1873 Trial For Voting, Rochester, N.Y." In Stevens, D. Jailed For Freedom, pp. 4-6. (Same as "Debate With Judge Hunt at Her Trial For Voting, June, 1873.")

________. "Failure Is Impossible, Last Public Address at Her 86th Birthday Celebration, February 15, 1906." In Harper, I. The Life and Work of Susan B. Anthony, 3, 1409.

________. "First Address at a Daughters of Temperance Supper,

March 1, 1849." In Anthony, K. Susan B. Anthony, pp. 89-90. Also in Harper, I. The Life and Work of Susan B. Anthony, 1, 53-5.

________. "History of the Fourteenth Amendment. Address to the National Woman Suffrage Convention of 1889." In Stanton, E. History of Woman Suffrage, 4, 152-3.

________. "Homes of Single Women." In Harper, I. The Life and Work of Susan B. Anthony, 1, 359.

________. "Is It a Crime for a United States Citizen to Vote?" In Stanton, E. History of Woman Suffrage, 2, 630-47. (Same as "Constitutional Argument.")

________. "Last Address to the 1906 National American Woman Suffrage Association Convention." In Harper, I. The Life and Work of Susan B. Anthony, 3, 1397. Also in Stanton, E. History of Woman Suffrage, 5, 185.

________. "The Loyal Women of the Country to Abraham Lincoln, President of the United States." In Stanton, E. History of Woman Suffrage, 2, 67-9. (Same as "Address to President Lincoln.")

________. "Marriage Has Ever Been a One-Sided Affair." In Tanner, L. Voices From Women's Liberation, p. 79.

________. "Opening Address." In International Council of Women, 1888. Report, p. 31.

________. "Opening Address at the National American Woman Suffrage Association Convention of 1900." In Stanton, E. History of Woman Suffrage, 4, 351.

________. "Opening Address at the National Woman Suffrage Association Convention, January 16, 1873." In Harper, I. The Life and Work of Susan B. Anthony, 1, 431.

________. "Organization Among Women as an Instrument in Promoting the Interests of Political Liberty." In World's Congress of Representative Women, Chicago, 1893. A Historical Resume, pp. 463-6.

________. "Plea on Behalf of Elizabeth Stanton at the National American Woman Suffrage Association Convention, January, 1896." In Lutz, A. Created Equal, pp. 303-5. (Same as "Anthony's Remarks.")

________. "Political Economy of Women." In Tanner, L. Voices From Women's Liberation, p. 57.

________. "Political Enfranchisement of Women." In International Congress of Women, London, 1899, 5, 125-9.

________. "Position of Women in the Political Life of the United States." In Harper, I. The Life and Work of Susan B. Anthony, 3, 1137. Also in International Congress of Women, London, 1899, 5, 3-8.

________. "Presentation of Carrie Chapman Catt as Her Successor to the National American Woman Suffrage Association Convention, February, 1900." In Harper, I. The Life and Work of Susan B. Anthony, 3, 1171-2. Also in Stanton, E. History of Woman Suffrage, 4, 388.

________. "President's Address at the National American Woman Suffrage Association Convention of 1896." In Stanton, E. History of Woman Suffrage, 4, 252.

________. "President's Address to the National American Woman Suffrage Association Convention of 1897." In Stanton, E. History of Woman Suffrage, 4, 272-3.

________. "President's Address to the National American Woman Suffrage Association Convention of 1899." In Stanton, E. History of Woman Suffrage, 4, 325-7. (Same as "Address to the 31st Annual Convention of the National American Woman Suffrage Association.")

________. "President's Address to the National Woman's Suffrage Association of January, 1873." In Stanton, E. History of Woman Suffrage, 2, 521.

________. "Public Address, 1894 on Political Parties Support For Suffrage." In Harper, I. The Life and Work of Susan B. Anthony, 2, 793.

________. "Reconstruction. Address Delivered at Ottumwa, Kansas, July 4, 1865." In Harper, I. The Life and Work of Susan B. Anthony, 2, 960-7.

________. "Remarks at a Meeting of the Cuban League in Rochester, N.Y., February, 1897." In Harper, I. The Life and Work of Susan B. Anthony, 2, 908.

________. "Remarks at a Woman's Christian Temperance Union Convention in Cleveland, November, 1895." In Harper, I. The Life and Work of Susan B. Anthony, 2, 800-1.

________. "Remarks at the 1894 Convention of the National American Woman Suffrage Association." In Harper, I. The Life and Work of Susan B. Anthony, 2, 757.

________. "Remarks at Her 70th Birthday Celebration, February 15, 1890." In Harper, I. The Life and Work of Susan B. Anthony, 2, 668.

________. "Remarks at State Teachers' Convention, Rochester, New York, August 3, 1853." In Harper, I. The Life and Work of Susan B. Anthony, 1, 98-9.

________. "Remarks Before a Senate Committee, 1902." In Stanton, E. History of Woman Suffrage, 5, 47.

________. "Remarks During Debate on Resolution Denouncing Dogmas and Creeds at the 17th National Convention of the National Woman Suffrage Association, January, 1885." In Harper, I. The Life and Work of Susan B. Anthony, 2, 595.

________. "Remarks on Divorce at the 1905 Meeting of the National Council of Women." In Harper, I. The Life and Work of Susan B. Anthony, 3, 1356-7.

________. "Remarks on Women in Industry." In International Council of Women, 1888. Report, pp. 162-3.

________. "Report on the International Council of Women in London to the 32nd Annual Convention of the National American Woman Suffrage Association, February, 1900." In Harper, I. The Life and Work of Susan B. Anthony, 3, 1166-7. Also in Stanton, E. History of Woman Suffrage, 4, 353-4.

________. "Report on Year's Activities of the Woman's National Loyal League at the Anniversary Meeting, May 12, 1864." In Stanton, E. History of Woman Suffrage, 2, 81-6.

________. "Report to the 10th National Woman's Rights Convention, N.Y., May 10-11, 1860." In Stanton, E. History of Woman Suffrage, 1, 689-92.

______. "Resolution for a Federal Amendment at the May, 1863 Meeting of the Women's Loyal League." In Beard, M. America Through Women's Eyes, p. 227. Also in Stanton, E. History of Woman Suffrage, 2, 57-8, 61, 66.

______. "Response to Greeting of South Carolina at the National American Woman Suffrage Association Convention of 1894." In Stanton, E. History of Woman Suffrage, 4, 224.

______. "Response to Tribute at Reception in Honor of Her 63rd Birthday, Philadelphia, February 15, 1883." In Harper, I. The Life and Work of Susan B. Anthony, 2, 547.

______. "Resignation Speech at the 32nd Annual Convention of the National American Woman Suffrage Association, February, 1900." In Harper, I. The Life and Work of Susan B. Anthony, 3, 1163. Also in Stanton, E. History of Woman Suffrage, 4, 386-7.

______. "Secretary's Report at the 1st Annual Meeting of the American Equal Rights Association, May, 1867." In Stanton, E. History of Woman Suffrage, 2, 183-4.

______. "Social Purity. First Delivered at Chicago in the Spring of 1875, in the Sunday Afternoon Dime Lecture Course." In Harper, I. The Life and Work of Susan B. Anthony, 2, 1004-12. Also in Kraditor, A. Up From the Pedestal, pp. 159-67. Also in Martin, W. The American Sisterhood, pp. 88-92.

______. "Speech of Susan B. Anthony." In American Anti-slavery Society. Proceedings at Its Third Debate, pp. 73-5.

______. "Statement of Support for the Populists at Their 1894 Convention." In Harper, I. The Life and Work of Susan B. Anthony, 2, 788.

______. "Woman Wants Bread, Not The Ballot! Delivered in Most of the Large Cities of the United States, Between 1870 and 1880." In Harper, I. The Life and Work of Susan B. Anthony, 2, 996-1003. Also in Schneir, M. Feminism, pp. 137-42.

______. "Women's Declaration of Rights." In Scott, A. One Half the People, pp. 90-5. (Same as "Declaration of Rights For Women, Read at Independence Hall, Philadelphia, July 4, 1876.")

Anthony, Susan Brownell, II. "Statement." In U.S. Senate. Committee on Labor and Public Welfare. Subcommittee on Alcoholism and Narcotics. Alcohol Abuse Among Women, pp. 13-4.

Anton, Mary. "Russia." O'Neill, W. The Woman Movement, pp. 164-7.

Apter, Julia T. "Increasing The Professional Visibility of Women in Academe: A Case Study." In Furniss, W. Women in Higher Education, pp. 104-9.

Armer, Laura Adams. "Acceptance Paper--Newbery Medal 1931." In Miller, B. Newbery Medal Books: 1922-1955, pp. 105-6.

Armstrong, Anne. "America's Bicentennial: Crisis and Challenge." Vital Speeches, 40 (March 15, 1974), 341-4.

Armstrong, Belle Grant. "The New England Woman's Press Association." In World's Congress of Representative Women, Chicago, 1893. A Historical Resume, pp. 806-10.

Armstrong, Florence A. "Statement." In U.S. Congress. Senate. Committee on the Judiciary. Subcommittee on Constitutional Amendments. Equal Rights Amendment (1945), pp. 42-4.

Arnold, Bertha. "Appeal to Lafayette at a Demonstration at the Lafayette Monument, September 16, 1918." In Irwin, I. Story of the Woman's Party, p. 364.

Arnold, Margaret Long. "Statement." In U.S. Congress. Senate. Special Committee on Aging. Future Directions in Social Security, pt. 19, 1752-5.

Arnold, Mildred. "The Growth of Child Welfare Services in Rural Areas." In National Conference of Social Work. Proceedings (1937), pp. 216-25.

________. "The Specialized Consultant in Child Welfare Services." In National Conference of Social Work. Proceedings (1941), pp. 426-39.

Arnold, Sarah Louise. "Industrial Education." In General Federation of Women's Clubs. Biennial Convention, 9 (1908), 307-12.

Aronoff, Rose. "Public Testimony." In New York (City). Commission on Human Rights. Women's Role in Contemporary Society, pp. 561-3.

Aronovici, Carol. "Organized Leisure as a Factor in Conservation." In National Conference of Social Work. Proceedings (1918), p. 464.

________. "Wider Use of Case Records." In National Conference of Charities and Correction. Proceedings (1916), pp. 468-71.

Astin, Helen S. "Where Are All the Talented Women?" In Furniss, W. Women In Higher Education, pp. 95-9.

Atkins, Ruth. "Address." Conference on Women in the War on Poverty, 1967. Proceedings, pp. 46-8.

Atkinson, Dorothy. "Society and the Sexes in the Russian Past." In Atkinson, D. Women in Russia, pp. 3-38.

Atkinson, Mary Irene. "Administration of Child Welfare Services from the Federal Level." In National Conference of Social Work. Proceedings (1938), pp. 551-8.

________. "Demonstration as Part of the Survey Process." In National Conference of Social Work. Proceedings (1930), pp. 438-47.

________. "The Relation of State Institutions and Agencies to Private Institutions: The Ohio Plan." In National Conference of Social Work. Proceedings (1921), pp. 230-3.
________. "The Rural Community Program of Relief." In National Conference of Social Work. Proceedings (1934), pp. 166-77.

Atkinson, Ti-Grace. "Catholic University." In Atkinson, T. Amazon Odyssey, pp. 191-7.
________. "The Equality Issue." In Atkinson, T. Amazon Odyssey, pp. 65-75.
________. "Individual Responsibility and Human Oppression (Including Some Notes on Prostitution and Pornography)." In Atkinson, T. Amazon Odyssey, pp. 117-30.
________. "Lesbianism and Feminism." In Atkinson, T. Amazon Odyssey, pp. 83-8.
________. "Metaphysical Cannibalism or Self-Creativity." In Atkinson, T. Amazon Odyssey, pp. 77-81.
________. "Movement Politics and Other Sleights of Hand." In Atkinson, T. Amazon Odyssey, pp. 95-108.
________. "The Older Woman: A Stockpile of Losses." In Atkinson, T. Amazon Odyssey, pp. 223-6.
________. "On 'Violence in the Women's Movement': Collaborators." In Atkinson, T. Amazon Odyssey, pp. 199-211.
________. "The Political Woman." In Atkinson, T. Amazon Odyssey, pp. 89-93.
________. "The Sacrificial Lambs." In Atkinson, T. Amazon Odyssey, pp. 25-37.
________. "Strategy and Tactics: A Presentation of Political Lesbianism." In Atkinson, T. Amazon Odyssey, pp. 135-89.
________. "Vaginal Orgasm as a Mass Hysterical Survival Response." In Atkinson, T. Amazon Odyssey, pp. 5-7.

Austin, Inez P. "Statement." In U.S. Congress. Senate. Select Committee on Small Business. Women and the Small Business Administration, pp. 76-8.

Austin, Jean. "Alone Together." Vital Speeches, 3 (November 15, 1936), 80-3.

Austin, Lucile Nickels. "Evolution of Our Case-Work Concepts." In National Conference of Social Work. Proceedings (1938), pp. 99-111.
________. "Trends in Differential Treatment in Casework." In National Conference of Social Work. Proceedings (1948), pp. 271-83.

Austin, Marianne. "Women Into Management: Vignettes." In Gordon, F. Bringing Women Into Management, pp. 139-42.

Avery, Nina Horton. "Statement." In U.S. Congress. House. Committee on the Judiciary. Subcommittee No. 1. Equal Rights Amendment (1948), pp. 23-27.
________. "Statement." In U.S. Congress. Senate. Committee on

the Judiciary. Subcommittee on Constitutional Amendments. Equal Rights Amendment (1945), pp. 28-30.

Avery, Rachel Foster. "Organization and Its Relation to the International and National Councils of Women." In World's Congress of Representative Women, Chicago, 1893. A Historical Resume, pp. 924-6.

________. "Reminiscence of Susan B. Anthony at Berkshire Historical Society Meeting, July, 1897." In Harper, I. The Life and Work of Susan B. Anthony, 2, 943.

Aves, Geraldine M. "Potentialities of Social Service to Children." In National Conference of Social Work. Proceedings (1948), pp. 324-30.

Aviel, JoAnn. "Changing the Political Role of Women: A Costa Rican Case Study." In Jacquette, J. Women in Politics, pp. 281-303.

Ayala, Angelina. "Statement." In U.S. Congress. House. Committee on Education and Labor. Subcommittee on Equal Opportunity. Equal Opportunity for Displaced Homemakers Act, pp. 61-2.

Babey-Brooke, Anna. "Patterns of Discrimination and Discouragement in Higher Education." In New York (City). Commission on Human Rights. Women's Role in Contemporary Society, pp. 590-602.

Bache, Louise Franklin. "The Value of Parades in an Educational Program." In National Conference of Social Work. Proceedings (1927), pp. 196-8.

Bacon, Alice Mabel. "The Study of Folk-lore." In Congress on Africa, Atlanta, 1895. Africa and the American Negro, pp. 187-94.

Bacon, Albion Fellows. "Housing: Its Relation to Social Work." In National Conference of Social Work. Proceedings (1918), pp. 194-200.

________. "How to Get Housing Reform." In National Conference of Charities and Corrections. Proceedings (1911), pp. 319-26.

Bacon, Georgia. "Report of the Local Biennial Board." In General Federation of Women's Clubs. Biennial Convention, 9 (1908), 48-50.

Bacon, Josephine Dodge Daskan. "Girl Scouts." In General Federation of Women's Clubs. Biennial Convention, 16 (1922), 113-4.

Bacon, Susan A. "Military Service--Bridge or Gap? Panel Discussion." In New York Herald Tribune. Report of the 20th Annual Forum on Current Problems, pp. 73-4.

Bagg, Mary E. "Historic Art." In Association for the Advancement of Women. "Truth, Justice and Honor," pp. 52-60.

Bailey, Carolyn Sherwin. "Acceptance Paper--Newbery Medal 1947. Miss Hickory: Her Genealogy." In Miller, B. Newbery Medal Books: 1922-1955, pp. 296-9.

Bailey, Ellen H. "Country Homes for Dependent Children." In National Conference of Charities and Corrections. Proceedings (1890), pp. 202-8.

________. "The Management of Tenement-houses." In National Conference of Charities and Corrections. Proceedings (1902), pp. 351-5.

Bailey, Hannah Clark Johnston. "The Woman's Foreign Missionary Union of Friends." In National Council of Women of the U.S., Washington, 1891. Transactions, pp. 132-3.

________. "Women's Place in the Peace Reform Movement." In American Peace Congress, 1st, New York, 1907. Proceedings, pp. 271-5.

Bailey, Kay. "Remarks Before the 1977 National Conference on Railroad-Highway Crossing Safety, Salt Lake City, Utah, August 23, 1977." Washington, U.S. National Transportation Safety Board, 1977. 5 p.

________. "Remarks at the First Houston Regional Transportation Conference, Whitehall Hotel, September 23, 1976, Houston, Texas." Washington, U.S. National Transportation Safety Board, 1976. 6 p.

________. "Remarks Before the Association of American Railroads Annual Safety Section Meeting, Duluth, Minn., June 22, 1977." Washington, U.S. National Transportation Safety Board, 1977. 4 p.

________. "Remarks Before the Air Transport Association, 1977 Airlines Operations Forum, Tampa, Florida, October 19, 1977." Washington, U.S. National Transportation Safety Board, 1977. 5 p.

Bailey, Mildred C. "Communication: Alternative Points of View." Vital Speeches, 39 (July 1, 1973), 565-7.

Bainbridge, Lucy S. "Mothers of the Submerged World. Day Nurseries." In National Congress of Mothers. Work & Words, pp. 47-55.

Baird, Priscilla. "Aesthetic Culture." In World's Congress of Representative Women, Chicago, 1893. Congress of Women, pp. 414-5.

Baker, Edith M. "The Contribution of Hospital Social Service to

Health Conservation." In National Conference of Social Work. Proceedings (1923), pp. 27-30.

________. "How Social Case Work Meets Individual Problems of Public Relief Clients From the Point of View of Medical Social Case Work." In National Conference of Social Work. Proceedings (1935), pp. 166-78.

Baker, Sybil M. "Alcoholism." In National Conference of Social Work. Proceedings (1942), pp. 499-517.

Balkany, Caron. "Statement." In U.S. Congress. Senate. Committee on Labor and Public Welfare. Subcommittee on Children and Youth. White House Conference on Youth--Child Development Recommendations, pp. 29-30.

Bamber, Goldie. "Woman's Place in Charitable Work--What It Is and What It Should Be." In Jewish Women's Congress. Papers, pp. 157-62.

Bamberger, Joan. "The Myth of Matriarchy: Why Men Rule in Primitive Society." In Rosaldo, M. Woman, Culture, and Society, pp. 263-80.

Bancroft, Margaret. "Classification of the Mentally Deficient." In National Conference of Charities and Correction. Proceedings (1901), pp. 191-200.

Bane, Geneva M. "The Home Teacher Experiment in Springfield, Illinois." In National Conference of Social Work. Proceedings (1921), pp. 477-80.

Banning, Margaret Culkin. "The Facts, the Hopes, and the Possibilities." In Itasca Conference on the Continuing Education of Women, Itasca State Park, Minnesota, 1962. Education and a Woman's Life, pp. 143-9.

________. "Points of General Agreement." In Conference on Women in the Defense Decade, New York, 1951. Women in the Defense Decade, pp. 15-7.

________. "Test of an Education." In Angeles, P. Challenge to American Youth, pp. 50-8.

________. "Today's Woman--Her Future Role in a Changing Society." In U.S. Women's Bureau. Today's Woman in Tomorrow's World, pp. 35-9.

________. "War and the Family. The Unit for 'A Better World.'" Vital Speeches, 9 (May 1, 1943), 442-4.

Bardwick, Judith. "The Dynamics of Successful People." In McGuigan, D. New Research on Women at the University of Michigan, pp. 86-104.

Barker, E. Florence. "The Woman's Relief Corps." In International Council of Women, 1888. Report, pp. 101-3.

Barlow, Florence. "A Business Woman in Kentucky." In World's Congress of Representative Women, Chicago, 1893. Congress of Women, pp. 797-803.

Barnes, Elizabeth Maxwell Carroll Chesnut. "Patriotic Principles of Americanism. Freedom Must Be Earned." Vital Speeches, 27 (June 1, 1916), 496-7.

Barnes, Sandra T. "Political Transition in Urban Africa." Annals, "Africa in Transition," 432 (July, 1977), 26-41.

Barney, Nora Stanton. "Statement." In U. S. Senate. Committee on the Judiciary. Committee on Constitutional Amendments. Equal Rights Amendment (1945), pp. 31-2.

Barney, Susan Hammond. "Police Matrons." In International Council of Women, 1888. Report, pp. 120-3.

Barrett, Kate Harwood Waller. "The Nation's Peril--A Double Standard of Morals." In International Congress of Women, Toronto, 1909. Report, 2, 473-5.

________. "The Need for State Supervision for Both Public and Private Charities." In National Conference of Charities and Correction. Proceedings (1909), pp. 3906.

________. "The Unmarried Mother and Child." In National Conference of Charities and Correction. Proceedings (1910), pp. 96-100.

Barrett, Maude T. "Public Assistance Features of the Social Security Act." In National Conference of Social Work. Proceedings (1942), pp. 326-35.

Barrows, Anna. "New Professions for Women Centering in the Home." In Stanton, E. History of Woman Suffrage, 4, 357-8.

Barrows, Esther G. "The Social Worker and Habit Clinics." In National Conference of Social Work. Proceedings (1924), pp. 397-401.

Barrows, Katharine Isabel Kayes Chapin. "Address: Tribute to Oscar C. McCulloch." In National Conference of Charities and Correction. Proceedings (1892), pp. 230-8.

________. "Manual Training for the Feebleminded." In National Conference of Charities and Correction. Proceedings (1894), pp. 179-87.

________. "What Unitarian Women Are Doing." In International Council of Women, 1888. Report, pp. 83-6.

Barry, Leonora Marie Kearney. "A Report of the General Instructor of Woman's Work, 1889." In Brownlee, W. Women in the American Economy, pp. 209-11.

________. "What the Knights of Labor Are Doing for Women." In International Council of Women, 1888. Report, pp. 153-6.

Barry, Maggie W. "Home Economics." In General Federation of Women's Clubs. Biennial Convention, 16 (1922), 211-4.

Barry, Mary Treadwell. "Statement." In U.S. Congress. Senate. Committee on the Judiciary. Subcommittee on Constitutional Amendments. Abortion, pt. 4, 683-8.

Bartlett, Caroline Julia. "Woman's Call to the Ministry." In World's Congress of Representative Women, Chicago, 1893. A Historical Resume, pp. 229-33.

Bartlett, Harriett M. "Influence of the Medical Setting on Social Case Work Services." In National Conference of Social Work. Proceedings (1940), pp. 258-69.

Barton, Babette B. "Testimony on Features of Federal Income, Estate, and Gift Tax Law Which Have a Disparate Impact on Women." In U.S. Congress. Joint Economic Committee. Economic Problems of Women, pt. 2, 257-62.

Barton, Clara Hawlowe. "Address." In National Conference of Charities and Correction. Proceedings (1891), p. 9.

________. "Address at the National American Woman Suffrage Convention of 1902." In Stanton, E. History of Woman Suffrage, 5, 25-6.

________. "Address by Clara Barton." In Barton, C. The Red Cross, pp. 60-72.

________. "The Red Cross." In International Council of Women, 1888. Report, pp. 103-7.

________. "What Is the Significance of the Red Cross in Its Relation to Philanthropy?" In Barton, C. The Red Cross, pp. 94-103.

Baskett, Janet Davison. "Undifferentiated Case Work the Surest Approach to Rural Social Work: Its Challenge and Its Opportunity: From the School." In National Conference of Social Work. Proceedings (1927), pp. 109-12.

________. "Undifferentiated Case Work Through the Medium of Rural Schools." In National Conference of Social Work. Proceedings (1928), pp. 85-90.

Bass, Charlotta A. "I Accept This Call." In Lerner, G. Black Women in White America, pp. 342-5.

Bass, Rosa Morehead. "Need of Kindergartens." In Conference For the Study of Negro Problems, 2nd, Atlanta, 1897. Social and Physical Conditions of Negroes in Cities, pp. 66-8.

________. "Poverty As a Cause of Mortality." In Conference for the Study of Negro Problems, 1st, Atlanta, 1896. Mortality Among Negroes in Cities, pp. 30-1.

Bass, Zitella Ebert. "Address at a Hearing of the Senate Committee on Woman Suffrage, December 15, 1915." In Stanton, E. History of Woman Suffrage, 5, 464.

Basto, Eloise M. "Statement." In U.S. Congress. Senate. Committee on the Judiciary. Subcommittee on Constitutional Amendments. Women and the "Equal Rights" Amendment, pp. 114-8.

Bates, Josephine White. "Address." In World's Congress of Representative Women, Chicago, 1893. A Historical Resume, pp. 151-3.

Bates, Octavia Williams. "Municipal Suffrage for Women in Michigan." In World's Congress of Representative Women, Chicago, 1893. Congress of Women, pp. 664-7.

________. "The Study of Law for Women." In International Congress of Women, London, 1899, 3, 16-8.

Bauer, Arlene. "Health Activities of Child Caring Agencies: Examinations on Admission." In National Conference of Social Work. Proceedings (1925), pp. 124-5.

Baughman, Ruby. "Elementary Adult Education for Native-and Foreign-Born." In National Conference of Social Work. Proceedings (1921), pp. 471-7.

Bay, Lillian Cantrell. "Nationalism." In World's Congress of Representative Women, Chicago, 1893. Congress of Women, pp. 260-3.

Bayard, Mary Temple. "Women in Journalism." In World's Congress of Representative Women, Chicago, 1893. Congress of Women, pp. 435-7.

Baylor, Edith M.H. "Establishing Foster Parental Relationships." In National Conference of Social Work. Proceedings (1929), pp. 135-41.

________. "When Should the Foster Home Be Prescribed for the Problem Child?" In National Conference of Social Work. Proceedings (1928), pp. 377-83.

Beard, Mary Ritter. "Address at a Hearing of the House Committee on Rules, December 3, 1913." In Stanton, E. History of Woman Suffrage, 5, 388-9.

________. "Address at a Hearing of the House Judiciary Committee, March 3, 1914." In Stanton, E. History of Woman Suffrage, 5, 430-1.

________. "The College and Alumnae in Contemporary Life." In Beard, M. Mary Ritter Beard: A Sourcebook, pp. 152-58.

________. "The Direction of Women's Education." In Beard, M. Mary Ritter Beard: A Sourcebook, pp. 159-67.

________. "Family Health Teaching, Or the Public Health Nurse." In National Conference of Social Work. Proceedings (1917), pp. 224-7.

________. "Report of the Manifesto Committee." In International Congress of Women, Chicago, 1933. Our Common Cause, Civilization, pp. 252-3.

________. "Society's Interest in Human Resources." In National Education Association. Proceedings of the 75th Annual Meeting (1937), pp. 80-91.

________. "Statement to the House Committee on Woman Suffrage." In Beard, M. Mary Ritter Beard: A Sourcebook, pp. 100-7. (Same as "Address At a Hearing of the House Judiciary Committee, March 3, 1914.")

________. Struggling Towards Civilization." In International Congress of Women, Chicago, 1933. Our Common Cause, Civilization, pp. 23-8.

________. "University Discipline For Women--Asset Or Handicap?" In Beard, M. Mary Ritter Beard: A Sourcebook, pp. 147-51. Also Journal of the American Association of University Women, 15 (April, 1932), 129-33.

________. "What Nobody Seems To Know About Woman. Radio Address, 1950." In Beard, M. Mary Ritter Beard: A Sourcebook, pp. 195-9.

________. "Woman--The Pioneer. Radio Address, 1939." In Beard, M. Mary Ritter Beard: A Sourcebook, pp. 193-5.

Beatty, Blanche A. "Negro Child Life in Rural Communities." In National Conference of Social Work. Proceedings (1924), pp. 173-5.

Beck, Mary V. "Captive Nations: Lest We Forget." Vital Speeches, 39 (October 1, 1973), 758-61.

Becker, May Lamberton. "Directed Reading For Children." In New York Herald Tribune. Report of the 2nd Women's Conference on Current Problems, pp. 35-8.

Bedford, Caroline S. "The Effect of an Unemployment Situation in Family Societies." In National Conference of Social Work. Proceedings (1931), pp. 201-10.

________. "Methods of Assembling Material." In National Conference of Social Work. Proceedings (1921), pp. 247-9.

Beecher, Catharine Esther. "The Education of Female Teachers." In Cross, B. The Educated Woman in America, pp. 67-75.

________. "The Evils Suffered by American Women and American Children: The Causes and the Remedy, Presented in an Address by Miss C.E. Beecher, To Meetings of Ladies in Cincinnati, Washington, Baltimore, Philadelphia, New York, and Other Cities." N.Y., Harper, 1846. 16 p.

Bell, Carolyn Shaw. "Alternatives For Social Change: The Future Status of Women." In Epstein, L. Women in the Professions, pp. 123-36.

________. "Testimony on The Treatment of Women Under Social Security and Private Pension Plans." In U.S. Congress. Joint Economic Committee. Economic Problems of Women, pt. 2, 299-302.

________. "Women and Unemployment." Congressional Record, 93rd Cong., 1st sess., 1972, 118, pt. 9, 11314-16.

_______. "Women in Higher Education: An Unsatisfactory Accounting." In Furniss, W. Women in Higher Education, pp. 305-8.

Bell, Dorothy Mays. "Junior College Programs." In Conference on the Present Status and Prospective Trends of Research on the Education of Women, Rye, N. Y., 1957. The Education of Women, pp. 112-5.

Bell, Laura. "A Glimpse of Modern Spain." In World's Congress of Representative Women, Chicago, 1893. Congress of Women, pp. 516-20.

Bellamy, Carol. "Remarks." In Conference on Feminist Perspectives on Housework and Child Care. Feminist Perspectives on Housework and Child Care, p. 8.

_______. "Statement." In U.S. Congress. Senate. Committee on Human Resources. Subcommittee on Labor. Discrimination on the Basis of Pregnancy, pp. 180-6.

Belmont, Alva Erskine Smith Vanderbilt. "Co-ordinating Relief." In New York Herald Tribune. Report of 2nd Women's Conference on Current Problems, pp. 83-7.

Bemis, Annie Louise Sargent. "Human Relations in Public Charity." In National Conference of Social Work. Proceedings (1926), pp. 550-3.

Beneby, Prescola. "Testimony." In U.S. Congress. House. Select Committee on Crime. Drugs in Our Schools, pp. 519-26.

Benedict, Ruth Fulton. "Achievement Award to Ruth Fulton Benedict. Dr. Benedict's Speech of Acceptance." Journal of American Association of University Women (1946), pp. 38-40.

Benjamin, Carrie Shevelson. "Woman's Place in Charitable Work--What It Is And What It Should Be." In Jewish Women's Congress. Papers, pp. 145-56.

Benneson, Cora A. "College Fellowships For Women." In International Council of Women, 1888. Report, pp. 77-80.

Bennett, Marion Tinsley. "Congress in 1943 and 1944. Procedure Must Be Brought Up To Date." Vital Speeches, 10 (February 15, 1944), 280-2.

Benoliel, Jeanne Quint. "Self As Critical Variable in Sensitive Research in Women's Health." In U.S. National Center For Health Services Research. Women and Their Health, pp. 35-9.

Benson, Lucy Wilson. "Security Assistance: Conventional Arms Transfer Policy." Department of State Bulletin, 78 (March, 1978), 42-5.

_______. "Should the President Be Chosen By Direct Popular Vote?"

Congressional Digest, 53 (August-September, 1974), pp. 218-222.

Bentley, Helen Delich. "American Press. A Product of the Time?" Vital Speeches, 35 (March 15, 1970), 329-32.

________. "The Impediments To Rapid Regulatory Action: The Bureaucratic Red Tape." Vital Speeches, 41 (September 1, 1975), 679-82.

________. "Merchant Marine: Stepchild of the Economy." Vital Speeches, 36 (July 1, 1970), 569-72.

________. "Russian Merchant Marine and Naval Supremacy: Awake Before It's Too Late!" Vital Speeches, 42 (November 15, 1975), 72-4.

________. "Shipping: The Conference System." Vital Speeches, 39 (May 15, 1973), 479-80.

Bergman, Maria V. "A Psycholoanalytic Approach to the Genesis of Promiscuity." In Goldman, G. Modern Woman, pp. 211-28.

Bergmann, Barbara R. "Testimony on the Economics of Sex Discrimination in Employment." In U.S. Congress. Joint Economic Committee. Economic Problems of Women, pt. 1, 51-3.

Bernard, Jessie. "Historical and Structural Barriers to Occupational Desegration." In Blaxall, M. Women and the Workplace, pp. 87-94.

________. "The Present Situation in the Academic World of Women Trained in Engineering." In M.I.T. Symposium on American Women in Science and Engineering, 1964. Women and the Scientific Professions, pp. 163-84.

Bernstain, Blanche. "Testimony on Sex Discrimination in Unemployment Insurance, Veterans Programs, and Public Assistance." In U.S. Congress. Joint Economic Committee. Economic Problems of Women, pt. 2, 393-6.

Bernstein, Pearl. "The Danger Line in Public Economy." In International Congress of Women, Chicago, 1933. Our Common Cause, Civilization, pp. 547-55.

Berrien, Laura M. "Statement." In U.S. Congress. Senate. Committee on the Judiciary. Subcommittee on Constitutional Amendments. Equal Rights Amendment (1945), pp. 41-2.

________. "Statement." In U.S. Congress. Senate. Committee on the Judiciary. Subcommittee on Constitutional Amendments. Equal Rights for Men and Women (1938), p. 117.

Berry, Betty. "Public Testimony." In New York (City). Commission on Human Rights. Women's Role in Contemporary Society, pp. 776-8.

Berry, Jane. "University of Kansas City Project for Continuing

Education of Women." In Itasca Conference on the Continuing Education of Women, Itasca State Park, Minnesota, 1962. Education and a Woman's Life, pp. 96-100.

Berry, M. Mabel. "Professional Standards in Social Agencies: The Value to the Agency of Students in Training." In National Conference of Social Work. Proceedings (1925), pp. 687-91.

Berry, Rose V. S. "Address. The Needs of Art To-day." In General Federation of Women's Clubs. Biennial Convention, 16 (1922), 177-82.

________. "The Gift of the Fine Arts Department to the General Federation of Women's Clubs." In General Federation of Women's Clubs. Biennial Convention, 16 (1922), 406-12.

________. "Life and the Literature of To-morrow." In General Federation of Women's Clubs. Biennial Convention, 16 (1922), 249-53.

Betanzos, Amalia V. "Statement." In U.S. Congress. Joint Economic Committee. Economic Problems of Women, pt. 4, 613-6.

Bethune, Mary McLeod. "A Century of Progress of Negro Women." In Lerner, G. Black Women in White America, pp. 579-84.

Beveridge, Edna Annette. "Establishing Policewomen in Maryland in 1912." In National Conference of Charities and Correction. Proceedings (1915), pp. 418-21.

Beveridge, Helen M. "Reformatory and Preventive Work in Illinois." In Conference on Charities and Corrections. Proceedings (1881), pp. 272-8.

Bibb, Grace C. "Art as a Medium of Civilization." In Association for the Advancement of Women. Congress of Women, 3rd. Papers, pp. 105-14.

Bidwell, Annie K. "Address on Presenting a Gift of Land For a Park to Chico, California, 1905." In Harper, I. The Life and Work of Susan B. Anthony, 3, 1367-8.

Biehle, Martha H. "The International Refuges Organization and Social Welfare." In National Conference of Social Work. Proceedings (1948), pp. 58-64.

Biggerstaff, Margaret. "Occupational Therapy." In National Conference of Social Work. Proceedings (1927), pp. 190-1.

Binford, Jessie F. "Community Protective Social Measures." In National Conference of Social Work. Proceedings (1924), pp. 181-7.

________. "Community Responsibility for Recreation Facilities." In International Congress of Women, Chicago, 1933. Our Common Cause, Civilization, pp. 903-7.

________. "Making the Community Safe for the Child." In National Conference of Social Work. Proceedings (1926), pp. 158-64.

Bing, Lucia Johnson. "What the Public Thinks of Social Work." In National Conference of Social Work. Proceedings (1923), pp. 483-7.

Bingham, Anne T. "The Personal Problems of a Group of Workers." In National Conference of Social Work. Proceedings (1920), pp. 346-51.

Bingman, Omi X. "Statement." In U.S. Congress. Senate. Committee on the Judiciary. Subcommittee on Constitutional Amendments. Equal Rights for Men and Women (1938), pp. 38-9.

Bird, Caroline. "On Being Born Female: Integration." Vital Speeches, 35 (November 15, 1968), 88-91.

________. "Statement." In U.S. Congress. Senate. Committee on the Judiciary. Subcommittee on Constitutional Amendments. Women and the "Equal Rights" Amendment, pp. 104-14.

________. "What Do Women Want? An Access to Forums." Vital Speeches, 43 (July 15, 1977), 598-602.

Bird, Diana W. "Should Present Military Assistance Programs of U.S. Foreign Aid Be Substantially Curtailed?" Congressional Digest, 52 (March, 1973), 86-90.

Bird, Ethel. "Social Attitudes Conditioning Immigrant Maladjustments: Twofold Problem of Immigration." In National Conference of Social Work. Proceedings (1923), pp. 303-9.

Birney, Alice Josephine McLellan White. "Address of Welcome." In National Congress of Mothers. Work and Words, pp. 6-10.

Birtwell, Mary L. "Chattel Mortgages." In National Conference of Charities and Correction. Proceedings (1899), pp. 296-305.

Bishop, Frances L. "Committee on Social Hygiene." In General Federation of Women's Clubs. Biennial Convention, 16 (1922), 499-500.

Bissell, Elizabeth. "The Effects of Foster Home Placements." In National Conference of Special Work. Proceedings (1928), pp. 238-45.

Bittenbender, Ada M. "Woman in Law." In International Council of Women, 1888. Report, pp. 173-9.

Bittermann, Helen Robbins. "Statement." In U.S. Congress. Senate. Committee on the Judiciary. Subcommittee on Constitutional Amendments. Equal Rights for Men and Women (1938), pp. 128-35.

Bjorn, Thora Kunigunde. "Vocal Art." In World's Congress of Representative Women, Chicago, 1893. Congress of Women, pp. 710-42.

Black, Agnes Knox. "Women's Influence in Poetry, Fiction, the Drama and History." In International Congress of Women, Toronto, 1909. Report, 1, 3-7.

Black, Shirley Temple. "Responsibility of the Movies." In New York Herald Tribune. Report of the 13th Annual Forum on Current Problems, pp. 78-81.

________. "United States Comments on Work of UNICEF; Statement, December 2, 1969." Department of State Bulletin, 61 (December 29, 1969), 642-3.

________. "United Nations Conference on the Human Environment; Statement, December 15, 1969." Department of State Bulletin, 62 (January 26, 1970), 99-100.

________. "U.S. Discusses Priorities For the 1972 UN Conference on the Human Environment; Statement, September 20, 1971." Department of State Bulletin, 65 (November 8, 1971), 531-4.

________. "Youth-related Activities of the United Nations; Statement, September 30, 1969." Department of State Bulletin, 61 (November 3, 1969), 380-2.

Blackall, Emily Lucas. "Baptist Home Mission Society." In National Council of Women of the U.S., Washington, 1891. Transactions, p. 131.

Blackey, Eileen. "Training the Rural Relief Worker on the Job." In National Conference of Social Work. Proceedings (1935), pp. 635-48.

Blackman, Elinor. "Some Tests for the Evaluation of Case Work Methods." In National Conference of Social Work. Proceedings (1925), pp. 246-51.

Blackwell, Alice Stone. "Address at a Hearing of the House Committee on Rules, December, 1913." In Stanton, E. History of Woman Suffrage, 5, 393-3.

________. "Address to the House Judiciary Committee, February 17, 1892." In Stanton, E. History of Woman Suffrage, 4, 197-8.

________. "The Indifference of Women. Address to the House Judiciary Committee, February 15, 1898." In Stanton, E. History of Woman Suffrage, 4, 320-1. Also in Tanner, L. Voices From Women's Liberation, pp. 88-90.

Blackwell, Antoinette Louisa Brown. "Address." In International Council of Women, 1888. Report, pp. 340-2.

________. "Address at the 7th Annual Meeting of the American Woman Suffrage Association, 1875." In Stanton, E. History of Woman Suffrage, 2, 841-2.

________. "Address at the 10th National Woman's Rights Convention, New York, 1860." In Stanton, E. History of Woman Suffrage, 1, 723-9.

________. "Address at Woman's Rights Convention, Syracuse, New York, September 8, 1852." In Harper, I. The Life and Work of Susan B. Anthony, 1, 74.

________. "Address at the Woman's National Loyal League Convention, May 14, 1863." In Stanton, E. History of Woman Suffrage, 2, 69-73.

________. "Comments at the Syracuse National Convention, September, 1852." In Stanton, E. History of Woman Suffrage, 1, 524-5.

________. "Debate on the Divorce Resolution at the 10th National Woman's Rights Convention, New York, 1860." In Stanton, E. History of Woman Suffrage, 1, 734-5.

________. "Discussion of the Moral Initiative as Related to Women." In World's Congress of Representative Women, Chicago, 1893. A Historical Resume, pp. 321-2.

________. "Heredity." In Association for the Advancement of Women. "Truth, Justice and Honor," pp. 9-17.

________. "Immorality of the Regulation System." In National Purity Congress, 1st, Baltimore, 1895. National Purity Congress, pp. 21-9.

________. "Landmarks." In World's Congress of Representative Women, Chicago, 1893. Congress of Women, pp. 633-6.

________. "On Marriage and Work." In Cott, N. Root of Bitterness, pp. 351-5.

________. "Our Cause is Progressing Triumphantly. Address to the Woman Rights Convention in New York, September, 1853." In Stanton, E. History of Woman Suffrage, 1, 553-4.

________. "The Relation of Woman's Work in the Household to the Work Outside." In Association for the Advancement of Women. Woman's Congress, 1st, Papers, pp. 178-84. Also in Kraditor, A. Up From the Pedestal, pp. 151-9. Also in Scott, A. The American Woman, pp. 135-6. (Same as "On Marriage and Work.")

________. "Remarks on the World's Temperance Convention." In Stanton, E. History of Woman Suffrage, 1, 507.

________. "Report on the World's Temperance Convention at the 4th National Woman's Rights Convention, Cleveland, Ohio, October, 1853." In Stanton, E. History of Woman Suffrage, 1, 152-61.

________. "Resolution and Bible Argument at the Syracuse National Convention, September, 1852." In Stanton, E. History of Woman Suffrage, 1, 535-6.

________. "Response to Address of Welcome." In National Purity Congress, 1st, Baltimore, 1895. National Purity Congress, pp. 17-8.

________. "What Religious Truths Can Be Established by Science and Philosophy." In International Council of Women, 1888. Report, pp. 407-15.

Blackwell, Emily. "The Responsibility of Women in Regard to Questions Concerning Public Morality." In National Purity

Congress, 1st, Baltimore, 1895. National Purity Congress, pp. 72-80.

Blake, Lillie Devereux. "Address to the New York City Suffrage Society, Union League Theatre, April 19, 1876." In Stanton, E. History of Woman Suffrage, 3, 414-5.

________. "The Constitutional Argument. Address to the House Judiciary Committee, 1900." In Stanton, E. History of Woman Suffrage, 4, 374-6.

________. "Discussion of Women as an Actual Force in Politics." In World's Congress of Representative Women, Chicago, 1893. A Historical Resume, pp. 430-2.

________. "Legal Disabilities." In International Council of Women, 1888. Report, pp. 226-9.

________. "Organization Among Women as an Instrument in Promoting the Interests of Political Liberty." In World's Congress of Representative Women, Chicago, 1893. A Historical Resume, pp. 466-7.

________. "Our Forgotten Foremothers." In World's Congress of Representative Women, Chicago, 1893. Congress of Women, pp. 32-5.

________. "Satire on the Rights of Men, Presented to the National Woman Suffrage Association Convention, January, 1887." In Stanton, E. History of Woman Suffrage, 4, 114-5.

________. "Testimony at a Hearing of the House Committee on the Judiciary, January 24, 1880." In Stanton, E. History of Woman Suffrage, 3, 163-66.

________. "Women as Police Matrons." In National Council of Women of the U.S., Washington, 1891. Transactions, pp. 91-4.

Blakeslee, Ruth O. "Law and Administrative Practices as Barriers to Mobility: Remedies in Relation to Human Welfare." In National Conference of Social Work. Proceedings (1939), pp. 232-42.

________. "Regional and State-wide Exchanges." In National Conference of Social Work. Proceedings (1940), pp. 474-84.

Blair, Emily Newell. "Have Women Contributed to the Crisis?" In International Congress of Women, Chicago, 1933. Our Common Cause, Civilization, pp. 71-80.

Blair, Margaret J. "Report of Household Economics Committee." In General Federation of Women's Clubs. Biennial Convention, 9 (1908), 257-63.

Blanchette, Denise. "Testimony." In U.S. Congress. House. Select Committee on Crime. Drugs in Our Schools, pp. 766-9.

Blanchette, Eleanor A.V. "Women Into Management: Vignettes." In Gordon, F. Bringing Women Into Management, pp. 131-4.

Blank, Diane. "Testimony." In U.S. Congress. House. Committee on Education and Labor. Special Subcommittee on Education. Discrimination Against Women, pp. 177-81.

Blatch, Harriet Eaton Stanton. "Address at a Protest Meeting--Headquarters of the National Woman's Party, 1917." In Stevens, D. Jailed for Freedom, pp. 58-9.

________. "Factory Legislation." In International Congress of Women, London, 1899, 6, 50-54.

________. "Manual Training in Primary Schools." In International Congress of Women, London, 1899, 2, 40-44.

________. "Tribute to Susan B. Anthony at Her 80th Birthday Celebration, February 15, 1900." In Harper, I. The Life and Work of Susan B. Anthony, 3, 1186-7.

________. "Voluntary Motherhood." In National Council of Women of the U.S., Washington, 1891. Transactions, pp. 278-85. Also in Kraditor, A. Up From the Pedestal, pp. 167-75.

________. "Woman as an Economic Factor. Address to a Senate Committee, February 15, 1898." In Stanton, E. History of Woman Suffrage, 4, 311.

Blatt, Genevieve. "Speech." In Conference on Women in the War on Poverty, 1967. Proceedings, pp. 3-4, 8-9.

Blau, Francine D. "Sex Segregation of Workers By Enterprise In Clerical Occupations." In Conference on Labor Market Segmentation, Harvard University, 1973. Labor Market Segmentation, pp. 257-75.

Block, Babette. "The Unmarried Mother: Is She Different?" In National Conference of Social Work. Proceedings (1945), pp. 274-83.

Blodgett, Katharine B. "Miracles in Glass." In New York Herald Tribune. Report of the 9th Annual Forum on Current Problems, pp. 127-30.

Bloodworth, Bess. "American Women on the Job." In U.S. Women's Bureau. American Woman--Her Changing Role, pp. 103-4.

Bloomer, Amelia Jenks. "Address at the 2nd Annual Meeting of the Woman's Temperance Society, Utica, N.Y., June 7, 1854." In Bloomer, D. The Life and Writings of Amelia Bloomer, pp. 182-3.

________. "Debate on Divorce Resolution at the New York State Temperance Convention, Rochester, N.Y., 1852." In Bloomer, D. The Life and Writings of Amelia Bloomer, pp. 87-89. Also in Stanton, E. History of Woman Suffrage, 1, 483-4.

________. "Mrs. Bloomer's Speech. At a Temperance Meeting in Metropolitan Hall, New York, February 1853." In Bloomer, D. The Life and Writings of Amelia Bloomer, pp. 103-10.

________. "Mrs. Bloomer's Address. Presentation of Flag to Local Regiment, Council Bluffs, Iowa, 1861." In Bloomer, D. The Life and Writings of Amelia Bloomer, pp. 279-81.

Blount, Anna E. "Address to the Senate Committee, April 19, 1910." In Stanton, E. History of Woman Suffrage, 5, 294-5.

Blumberg, Grace Ganz. "Testimony on Features of Federal Income, Estate and Gift Tax Law Which Have a Disparate Impact on Women." In U.S. Congress. Joint Economic Committee. Economic Problems of Women, pt. 2, 283-8.

Boals, Kay. "The Politics of Cultural Liberation: Male-Female Relations in Algeria." In Carroll, B. Liberating Women's History, pp. 194-211. Also in Jaquette, J. Women in Politics, pp. 322-42.

Boeckel, Florence Brewer. "Civilization Or War?" In International Congress of Women, Chicago, 1933. Our Common Cause, Civilization, pp. 688-94.

Boggs, Grace Lee. "The Black Revolution in America." In Cade, T. The Black Woman, pp. 211-23.

Bogue, Mary F. "Pennsylvania. The Greater Economy of Adequate Grants." In National Conference of Social Work. Proceedings (1919), pp. 303-8.

________. "Problems in the Administration of Mothers' Aid." In National Conference of Social Work. Proceedings (1918), pp. 349-59.

Boie, Maurine. "The Case Worker's Need for Orientation to the Culture of the Client." In National Conference of Social Work. Proceedings (1937), pp. 112-23.

Bolotin, Anita. "Outside Activities of Children's Institutions." In National Conference of Social Work. Proceedings (1928), pp. 116-22.

Bolton, Elizabeth B. "Have It Your Way. Mid-career Women and Their Options." Vital Speeches, 44 (July 1, 1978), 571-3.

Bolton, Frances Payne. "Nature of U.S. Puerto Rican Relations." Department of State Bulletin, 29 (December 7, 1953), 797-8, 802-5.

________. "Presentation of the 1949 Award of the Snow Medal (With Her Reply)." Journal of Social Hygiene, 35 (March, 1949), 115-6.

________. "Treatment of Indians in South Africa." Department of State Bulletin, 29 (November 23, 1953), 728-30.

________. "UN: A Family of Nations." Department of State Bulletin, 29 (November 9, 1953), 628-9.

________. "Wanted: Women to Defend Freedom." In Conference on Women in the Defense Decade, New York, 1951. Women in the Defense Decade, pp. 56-62.

Bond, Elizabeth Powell. "Friends as Promoters of Peace." In

American Peace Congress, 1st, New York, 1907. Proceedings, pp. 267-71.

Bond, Kate. "Organization Among Women as an Instrument in Promoting the Interests of Industry." In World's Congress of Representative Women, Chicago, 1893. A Historical Resume, pp. 605-16.

Bones, Marietta. "Address to the Constitutional Convention of the Dakota Territory, September, 1883." In Stanton, E. History of Woman Suffrage, 3, 665-6.

Bonny, Dorothy Black. "Women's Heritage. Beware of Propaganda." Vital Speeches, 15 (November 15, 1949), 594-7.

Booth, Maud Ballington. "Mothers to the Motherless." In National Congress of Mothers. Work and Words, pp. 93-101.

Borchardt, Selma. "Statement." U.S. Congress. House. Committee on the Judiciary. Equal Rights Amendment to the Constitution (1932), p. 30.

________. "Statement." In U.S. Congress. House. Committee on the Judiciary. Subcommittee No. 1. Equal Rights Amendment (1948), pp. 142-6.

________. "Statement." In U.S. Congress. Senate. Committee on the Judiciary. Subcommittee on Constitutional Amendments. Equal Rights (1931), pp. 47-8.

________. "Statement." In U.S. Congress. Senate. Committee on the Judiciary. Subcommittee on Constitutional Amendments. Equal Rights Amendment (1945), pp. 119-20.

Bosone, Reva Beck. "Statement." In U.S. Congress. House. Committee on Education and Labor. Select Subcommittee on Labor. Equal Pay For Equal Work, pp. 139-41.

Bostanian, Armene E. "Statement." In U.S. Congress. Senate. Committee on the Judiciary. Equal Rights 1970, pp. 391-2.

Bostick, Mary Jane. "Consumerism: A Three-toed Sloth." Congressional Record, 91st Cong., 2nd sess., 1970, 116, pt. 30, 40993-5

Boswell, Helen Varick. "Conditions in the Canal Zone." In General Federation of Women's Clubs. Biennial Convention, 9 (1908), 131-3.

Bosworth, Abigail. "Factors Affecting Decision of Unmarried Mother to Give Up or Keep Her Child, Environmental Factors." Washington, U.S. Children's Bureau, 1945, 8 p.

Bottome, Margaret. "Exhortation." In National Council of Women of the U.S., Washington, 1891. Transactions, pp. 17-9.

Boulding, Elise. "Familial Constraints on Women's Work Roles." In Blaxall, M. Women and the Workplace, pp. 95-117.

Bowen, Georgia M. "Interpretative Publicity as a Function of Social Work: What Part Can the Federation Take in Its Development?" In National Conference of Social Work. Proceedings (1924), pp. 504-9.

Bowen, Janice. "Responsibilities in Placement of Children." In National Conference of Social Work. Proceedings (1947), pp. 301-10.

Bowen, Louise de Koven. "The Delinquent Child of Immigrant Parents." In National Conference of Charities and Correction. Proceedings (1909), pp. 255-60.

_______. "The Need of Recreation." In National Conference of Charities and Correction. Proceedings (1910), pp. 100-5.

_______. "The Treatment of Juvenile Offenders Against the Law." In International Congress of Women, Toronto, 1909. Report, 2, 185-90.

Bowler, Alida C. "Experiments in Preventing Juvenile Delinquency." In National Conference of Social Work. Proceedings (1934), pp. 339-49.

_______. "Recent Statistics on Crime and the Foreign Born." In National Conference of Social Work. Proceedings (1931), pp. 479-94.

Bowles, Ada C. "Women in the Ministry." In International Council of Women, 1888. Report, pp. 180-1.

Bowman, Geline MacDonald. "Chairman's Introduction. Economic Security Through Government." In International Congress of Women, Chicago, 1933. Our Common Cause, Civilization, p. 106.

_______. "The Trained Woman Survives the Depression." In New York Herald Tribune. Report of the 4th Annual Women's Conference on Current Problems, pp. 185-9.

Boyd, Corabel Tarr. "The Young Women's Christian Association: Its Aims and Methods." In World's Congress of Representative Women, Chicago, 1893. A Historical Resume, pp. 847-57.

Boyd, Mary K. "Industrial Training School For Girls." In National Conference of Charities and Correction. Proceedings (1888), pp. 235-6.

Boyd, Neva L. "Chairman's Introduction. Release From Labor--The Problem." In International Congress of Women, Chicago, 1933. Our Common Cause, Civilization, p. 843.

Boyer, Elizabeth. "Statement." In U.S. Congress. House. Committee on Education and Labor. Special Subcommittee on Education. Discrimination Against Women, pp. 17-21.

________. "Statement." In U.S. Congress. Senate. Committee on the Judiciary. Subcommittee on Constitutional Amendments. Women and the 'Equal Rights" Amendment, pp. 126, 128-33.

Boyer, Lyda. "A Case History (Pilot Projects For Continuing Education for Women)." In Itasca Conference on the Continuing Education of Women, Itasca State Park, Minnesota, 1962. Education and a Woman's Life, pp. 92-6.

Boyle, Doris Duffy. "Statement." In U.S. Congress. House. Committee on Education and Labor. Special Subcommittee on Education. Equal Pay for Equal Work. pp. 202-7.

Brackett, Anna C. "Organization as Related to Civilization." In Association for the Advancement of Women, Congress of Women, 3rd. Papers, pp. 73-87.

Bradley, Frances Sage. "Remedial Work for Rural Children." In National Conference of Social Work. Proceedings (1921), pp. 212-5.

________. "Suggestions for the Teaching of Child Hygiene." In National Conference of Charities and Correction. Proceedings (1914), pp. 154-60.

Bradshaw, Lillian M. "Library Response to a Restive World." American Libraries, 1 (July-August, 1970), 688-90.

Brady, Ann. "Public Testimony." In New York (City). Commission on Human Rights. Women's Role in Contemporary Society, pp. 729-30.

Brady, Dorothy S. "The City Worker's Family Budget." In National Conference of Social Work. Proceedings (1948), pp. 310-6.

________. 'Equal Pay, What Are the Facts?" Washington, U.S. Women's Bureau, 1952. 3 p.

Brady, Genevieve Garvan. 'New Importance of Old Youth Movements." In New York Herald Tribune. Report of the 3rd Women's Conference on Current Problems, pp. 61-66.

________. "Scouts and the New Frontier." In New York Herald Tribune. Report of the 4th Annual Women's Conference on Current Problems. pp. 167-9.

Brady, Sue Huffman. "Changing Ideals in Southern Women." In World's Congress of Representative Women, Chicago, 1893. Congress of Women, pp. 306-10.

Bragdon, Helen D. "Comment on Pressures and Opportunities That Face the Educated Woman." In Conference on the Present Status and Prospective Trends of Research on the Education of Women, Rye, N.Y., 1957. The Education of Women, pp. 69-72.

Bragdon, Ida Brownlee. "A Plea For Migrant Children: Lift the Marks From Their Faces." Vital Speeches, 40 (September 1, 1974). 695-9.

Brainerd, Heloise. "Opening Remarks." In Economic Problems of the Caribbean Area, pp. 5-6.

Bram, Susan. "To Have or Have Not: The Social Psychology of the Decision To Have or Not Have Children." In McGuigan, D. New Research on Women at the University of Michigan, pp. 138-9.

Brandon, Dorothy. "Asia's Red Riddle." In New York Herald Tribune. Report of the 18th Annual Forum on Current Problems, pp. 200-2.

Brandt, Lillian. "Statistics of Dependent Families." In National Conference of Charities and Correction. Proceedings (1906), pp. 434-4.

Branham, Lucy. "Speech While Burning President Wilson's Message at Demonstration at Lafayette Monument, September 16, 1918." In Irwin, I. Story of the Woman's Party, pp. 364-5.

Brannick, Catherine. "Schools and Delinquency." In National Conference of Social Work. Proceedings (1918), pp. 162-7.

Braumuller, Luetta E. "Art in Ceramics." In World's Congress of Representative Women, Chicago, 1893. A Historical Resume, pp. 573-5.

Breckinridge, Desha. "Address at a Hearing of the House Committee on Rules, December 3, 1913." In Stanton, E. History of Woman Suffrage, 5, 388.

________. "The Educational Work of the Kentucky Federation of Women's Clubs." In General Federation of Women's Clubs. Biennial Convention, 9 (1908), pp. 290-7.

________. "A New Hope." In National Conference of Charities and Correction. Proceedings (1914), pp. 217-22.

________. "The Story of Irishtown." In National Conference of Charities and Correction. Proceedings (1914), pp. 397-400.

Breckinridge, Sophonisba Preston. "Children and the Depression." In National Conference of Social Work. Proceedings (1932), pp. 126-35.

________. "The Equal Wage." In U.S. Women's Bureau. Proceedings of the Women's Industrial Conference, pp. 85-91.

________. "The Family and the Law." In National Conference of Social Work. Proceedings (1925), pp. 290-7.

________. "The Family in the Community, But Not Yet of the Community." In National Conference of Charities and Correction. Proceedings (1914), pp. 69-75.

________. "Industrial and Economic Problems--Introductory Statement." In National Conference of Social Work. Proceedings (1921), pp. 27-8.

________. "The New Horizons of Professional Education for Social Work." In National Conference of Social Work. *Proceedings* (1936), pp. 119-32.

________. "Promotion of National and State Social Legislation by Social Workers." In National Conference of Social Work. *Proceedings* (1934), pp. 386-94.

________. "Public Charitable Service as a Profession." In National Conference of Social Work. *Proceedings* (1917), pp. 370-1.

________. "Report of the Committee (on Securing and Training Social Workers)." In National Conference of Charities and Correction. *Proceedings* (1911), pp. 365-70.

________. "The Scope and Place of Research in the Program of the Family Society." In National Conference of Social Work. *Proceedings* (1931), pp. 223-31.

________. "What the Schools Are Doing." In National Conference of Social Work. *Proceedings* (1930), pp. 330-40.

________. "What We Have Learned About Emergency Training for Public Relief Administration." In National Conference of Social Work. *Proceedings* (1935), pp. 246-58.

Bremer, Edith Terry. "The Foreign Language Worker in the Fusion Process, An Indispensable Asset to Social Work in America." In National Conference of Social Work. *Proceedings* (1919), pp. 740-6.

________. "Our International Communities and the War." In National Conference of Social Work. *Proceedings* (1918), pp. 442-51.

Brennan, Agnes S. "Training Schools for Nurses--Theory and Practice." In National Conference of Charities and Correction. *Proceedings* (1894), pp. 94-6.

Brenner, Ruth F. "What Facilities Are Essential to the Adequate Care of the Unmarried Mother?" In National Conference of Social Work. *Proceedings* (1942), pp. 426-39.

Brent, Edith S. "Training Schools for Nurses--District Nurses." In National Conference of Charities and Correction. *Proceedings* (1894), pp. 97-100.

Bresette, Linna E. "Statement." In U.S. Congress. Senate. Committee on the Judiciary. Subcommittee on Constitutional Amendments. *Equal Rights Amendment* (1929), pp. 59-60.

________. "Statement." In U.S. Congress. Senate. Committee on the Judiciary. Subcommittee on Constitutional Amendments. *Equal Rights* (1931), pp. 50-1.

________. "Statement." In U.S. Women's Bureau. *Proceedings of the Women's Industrial Conference*, pp. 144-6.

Bridges, Bernice. "The Choice for American Youth." In National Conference of Social Work. *Proceedings* (1948), pp. 217-24.

________. "Teen-Age Centers." In National Conference of Social Work. *Proceedings* (1945), pp. 264-73.

Brink, Carol Ryrie. "Acceptence Paper--Newbery Medal 1936. Caddie Woodlawn." In Miller, B. Newbery Medal Books: 1922-1955, pp. 141-4.

Brisley, Mary Swan. "An Attempt to Articular Processes." In National Conference of Social Work. Proceedings (1924), pp. 292-5.

________. "Family Achievement." In National Conference of Social Work. Proceedings (1928), pp. 262-72.

________. "Parent-Child Relationships in Unmarried Parenthood." In National Conference of Social Work. Proceedings (1939), pp. 435-45.

Bristol, Augusta Cooper. "Enlightened Motherhood." In Association for the Advancement of Women. Congress of Women, 1st. Papers, pp. 10-4.

________. "Labor and Capital." In Association for the Advancement of Women. Truth, Justice and Honor, pp. 43-51.

________. "Woman, The New Factor in Economics." In World's Congress of Representative Women, Chicago, 1893. Congress of Women, pp. 80-6. Also in World's Congress of Representative Women, Chicago, 1893. A Historical Resume, pp. 539-50.

Bronner, Augusta F. "Individual Variations in Mental Equipment." In National Conference of Social Work. Proceedings (1920), pp. 351-9.

Bronson, Laura M. "No Home, and the No Home Influences." In Association for the Advancement of Women. Congress of Women, 1st. Papers, pp. 75-81.

Bronson, Ruth Muskrat. "The Indians' Attitude Toward Cooperation." In National Conference of Social Work. Proceedings (1931), pp. 637-45.

________. "Shall We Repeat Indian History in Alaska." In Moquin, W. Great Documents in American Indian History, pp. 319-25.

Brooks, Mary T. "Remarks at Ceremonies Issuing the 1973 Philatelic-Numismatic Commemorative at Faneuil Hall, Boston, Massachusetts, July 4, 1973." Washington, U.S. Bureau of the Mint, 1973. 2 p.

Brooks, Rozanne M. "Woman's Place Is In The Wrong. The Loyal Opposition." Vital Speeches, 28 (December 15, 1961), 151-4.

Brophy, Frances. "A Combination Heart and Tuberculosis Program." In National Conference of Social Work. Proceedings (1927), pp. 189-90.

Brothers, Joyce. "Meet the MS READ-a-thon: The Written Word." Vital Speeches, 43 (August 1, 1977), 623-6.

Brower, Millicent. "Public Testimony." In New York (City). Commission on Human Rights. Women's Role in Contemporary Society, pp. 789-92.

Brown, Carol A. "New Roles for Women in Health Care Delivery; A U.S. Response to Conditions in the People's Republic of China." In International Conference on Women in Health. Proceedings, pp. 113-5.

Brown, Caroline M. "The Protective Agency for Women and Children." In National Council of Women of the U.S., Washington, 1891. Transactions, pp. 260-3.

Brown, Catherine Wood. "Public Aid for the Feeble-minded." In National Conference of Charities and Correction. Proceedings (1889), pp. 86-8.

Brown, Charlotte B. "A Bureau of Information: The Need of a Post-Graduate School for Nurses." In National Conference of Charities and Correction. Proceedings (1890), pp. 147-54.

Brown, Charlotte Emerson. "The Moral Influence of Women's Associations." In National Council of Women of the U.S., Washington, 1891. Transactions, pp. 303-9.

________. "Organization As a Means of Literary Culture." In World's Congress of Representative Women, Chicago, 1893. A Historical Resume, pp. 147-51. (Read by Julia Pauline Leavens.)

Brown, Charlotte Hawkins. "Speaking Up For the Race at Memphis, Tennessee, October 8, 1920." In Lerner, G. Black Women in White America, pp. 467-72.

Brown, Cora Stanton. "The Policewoman; Discussion." In National Conference of Charities and Correction. Proceedings (1916), pp. 552-4.

Brown, Corinne S. "The Illinois Woman's Alliance." In National Council of Women of the U.S., Washington, 1891. Transactions, pp. 338-41.

Brown, Esther Lucile. "Social Work Against a Background of the Other Professions." In National Conference of Social Work. Proceedings (1932), pp. 520-32.

Brown, Hallie Q. "Discussion of the Organized Efforts of the Colored Women of the South to Improve Their Condition." In World's Congress of Representative Women, Chicago, 1893. A Historical Resume, pp. 724-9.

Brown, Helen Elizabeth. "Statement." In U.S. Congress. Senate. Committee on the Judiciary. Subcommittee on Constitutional Amendments. Equal Rights (1931), pp. 14-5.

________. "What Is the Constitution of the United States Worth to American Women?" Congressional Record, 81st Cong., 2nd sess., 1950, 96, pt. 13, A34-6.

Brown, Josephine C. "Present Relief Situation in the United States." In National Conference of Social Work. Proceedings (1936), pp. 423-3.

________. "Principles, Content, and Objectives of Supervision." In National Conference of Social Work. Proceedings (1938), pp. 528-40.

________. "The Use of Volunteers in Rural Social Work: In Dakota County, Minnesota." In National Conference of Social Work. Proceedings (1922), pp. 267-70.

________. "What We Have Learned About Emergency Training for Public Relief Administration." In National Conference of Social Work. Proceedings (1935), pp. 237-45.

Brown, M. Augusta Gage. "Extracts from Vocal Art." In World's Congress of Representative Women, Chicago, 1893. Congress of Women, pp. 477-83.

Brown, Marcia. "Acceptance Paper (Caldecott Award 1955). Integrity and Intuition." In Miller, B. Caldecott Medal Books: 1938-1957, pp. 267-77.

________. "Caldecott Award Acceptance (1962): Big and Little." In Kingman, L. Newbery and Caldecott Medal Books, 1956-1965, pp. 226-31.

Brown, Martha McLellan. "Institutive Power." In International Council of Women, 1888. Report, pp. 80-2.

Brown, Olympia. "Address to a Hearing of the Congressional Committee on Privileges and Elections, January, 1878." In Stanton, E. History of Woman Suffrage, 3, 95-7.

________. "Debate at the 2nd Annual Meeting of the American Equal Rights Association, May 14, 1868." In Stanton, E. History of Woman Suffrage, 2, 310.

________. "Foreign Rule. Address to the National Woman Suffrage Association Convention of 1889." In Stanton, E. History of Woman Suffrage, 4, 148-9.

________. "Olympia Brown's Attack on Immigrants, Given at the National Woman Suffrage Association's Convention in 1889." In O'Neill, W. The Woman Movement, pp. 122-3. (Same as "Foreign Rule").

Brown, Sara. "Administration of Marriage Laws in Michigan." In National Conference of Social Work. Proceedings (1919), pp. 379-81.

________. "A County Unit for Social Service." In National Conference of Social Work. Proceedings (1917), pp. 645-7.

Brown, Vanessa. "Building Leadership for Peace ..., New Ideas from New Voters: Panel Discussion." In New York Herald Tribune. Report of the 21st Annual Forum on Current Problems, pp. 146-7.

Brownell, Louise. "Co-education in Universities." In International Congress of Women, London, 1899, 2, 167-9.

Browning, Grace. "The Responsibility of the Schools of Social Work for Training for the Public Welfare Services. In National Conference of Social Work. Proceedings (1944), pp. 353-62.

Brownmiller, Susan. "The Status of Women in Communications." In Conference of Professional and Academic Women. Sixteen Reports on the Status of Women in the Professions, 3 p.

______. "Speaking Out on Prostitution, a Victimless Crime." In Lerner, G. The Female Experience, pp. 441-3. Also in Notes from the Third Year: Women's Liberation (New York, 1971), pp. 37-9.

Brungardt, Theresa S. "Fun for the Older Person in the Country." In National Conference of Social Work. Proceedings (1946), pp. 221-7.

Brunswick, Rose. "Statement." In U.S. Congress. Senate. Committee on the Judiciary. Subcommittee on Constitutional Amendments. Equal Rights for Men and Women (1938), p. 32.

Bryan, Anna E. "The Letter Killeth." In National Education Association. Journal of Proceedings and Addresses (1890), pp. 573-81.

Buck, Dorothea D. "The Citizen's Responsibility; A Panel Discussion." In New York Herald Tribune. Report of the 18th Annual Forum on Current Problems, pp. 143-4, 176-7.

Buck, Pearl Sydenstricker. "Acceptance Speech for the Howells Medal." In Harris, T. Pearl S. Buck, pp. 200-201.

______. "Acceptance Speech for the Nobel Prize, December, 1939." In Harris, T. Pearl S. Buck, p. 216-7.

______. "An Address to Graduates." Afraamerican Woman's Journal (Summer and Fall, 1942), pp. 12-7.

______. "Asiatic Problem. The Colored People Are Still Waiting, Still Watchful." Vital Speeches, 8 (March 1, 1942), pp. 303-5.

______. "The Chinese Novel." In Frenz, H. Nobel Lectures, 1901-1967, pp. 361-79.

______. "Commencement Speech on Equality, Delivered at Howard University in Washington, D.C., on June 5, 1942." In Harris, T. Pearl S. Buck, pp. 259-63. (Same as "An Address to Graduates").

______. "Heart of Democracy. Equality for All." Vital Speeches, 8 (April 15, 1942), 395-7.

______. "Like and Unlike in East and West." Vital Speeches, 1 (August 12, 1935), 718-20.

______. "Nobel Acceptance Speech." In Frenz, H. Nobel Lectures, 1901-1967, pp. 359-60.

______. "Nobel Lecture on the Chinese Novel." In Harris, T. Pearl S. Buck, pp. 218-38. (Same as "The Chinese Novel.")

________. "What I See Happening in America." In New York Herald Tribune. Report of the 4th Annual Women's Conference on Current Problems, pp. 86-9.

Bucklin, Loraine Pearce. "Life and Times of Isabella of Castile." In World's Congress of Representative Women, Chicago, 1893. Congress of Women, pp. 450-7.

Buerk, Susan C. "Women's Opportunity ... Starting Your Own Business. Understanding and Overcoming the Obstacles." Vital Speeches, 44 (February 1, 1978), 230-2.

Buffington, Adaline A. "Automobile Migrants." In National Conference of Social Work. Proceedings (1925), pp. 258-64.

________. "Co-ordinating as Done by Charity Organization Societies." In National Conference of Charities and Correction. Proceedings (1916), pp. 483-7.

________. "Seamen with Venereal Disease in the Port of New York." In National Conference of Social Work. Proceedings (1931), pp. 536-40.

Bullock, Electa. "Industrial Women." In World's Congress of Representative Women, Chicago, 1893. Congress of Women, pp. 510-1.

Bullock, Helen Louise Chapel. "Power and Purpose of Women." In World's Congress of Representative Women, Chicago, 1893. Congress of Women, pp. 143-7.

Bullock, Kate. "Developing Community Interest in Foster Homes." In National Conference of Social Work. Proceedings (1942), pp. 396-404.

Bunting, Mary Ingraham. "Adapting the Four-Year College to New Patterns." In Conference on Present Status and Prospective Trends of Research on the Education of Women, Rye, N.Y., 1957. The Education of Women, pp. 102-7.

________. "The Commitment Required of a Woman Entering a Scientific Profession." In M.I.T. Symposium on American Women in Science and Engineering, 1964. Women and the Scientific Professions, pp. 20-4.

________. "Today's Woman Prepares for Tomorrow's World. Introduction to Panel Discussion." In U.S. Women's Bureau. Today's Woman in Tomorrow's World, pp. 9-11.

Burke, Yvonne Watson Brathwaite. "Is the Administration Plan to Terminate the Federal Anti-Poverty Agency Now a Sound National Policy?" Congressional Digest, 52 (August-September, 1973), pp. 219-23.

________. "Statement." In U.S. Congress. House. Committee on Education and Labor. Subcommittee on Equal Opportunities. Equal Opportunity for Displaced Homemakers Act, pp. 4-5, 11-5.

Burkholder, Myrna. "Public Testimony." In New York (City). Commission on Human Rights. Women's Role in Contemporary Society, pp. 420-1.

Burleigh, Celia. "Woman's Right to Be a Woman. Address to the American Woman Suffrage Association Convention, 1870." In Stanton, E. History of Woman Suffrage, 2, 801-2.

Burleigh, Edith N. "Some Principles of Parole for Girls." In National Conference of Social Work. Proceedings (1918), pp. 147-55.

Burlingame, Emeline S. "National Free-Will Baptist Woman's Missionary Society." In National Council of Women of the U.S., Washington, 1891. Transactions, pp. 133-4.

Burnett, Marguerite H. "Adult Immigration Education: In the United States." In National Conference of Social Work. Proceedings (1924), pp. 573-8.

Burnett, Mary Clarke. "Community Councils in Pittsburgh." In National Conference of Social Work. Proceedings (1933), pp. 465-72.

________. "Recruiting of Students by Schools and of Apprentices by Agencies." In National Conference of Social Work. Proceedings (1926), pp. 599-607.

________. "The Role of the Social Worker in Agency-Community Relationships." In National Conference of Social Work. Proceedings (1941), pp. 671-84.

Burnett, Mary Weeks. "National Temperance Hospital." In International Council of Women, 1888. Report, pp. 123-5.

Burns, Eveline M. "Income Security for the Aged." In National Conference of Social Work. Proceedings (1948), pp. 381-94.

________. "The Security Report of the National Resources Planning Board." In National Conference of Social Work. Proceedings (1943), pp. 370-81.

Burns, Lucy. "Speech Summing Up Case for Suffragists Arrested for Picketing the White House, July 4, 1917." In Irwin, I. Story of the Woman's Party, pp. 223-5.

________. "Speech to the National American Woman Suffrage Association Convention, December, 1913." In Stevens, D. Jailed for Freedom, p. 26.

Burris, Carol. "Should Congress Provide for Automatic Adjustments in the Federal Minimum Wage?" Congressional Digest, 56 (May, 1977), pp. 150-2.

Bursch, Ann Dennis. "Electric Power and the Public Welfare. Address to 1926 National Convention of the League of Women Voters." In Beard, M. America Through Women's Eyes, pp. 511-21.

Burt, Mary T. "Address." In National Purity Congress, 1st, Baltimore, 1895. National Purity Congress, pp. 360-3.

Burton, Virginia Lee. "Acceptance Paper (Caldecott Awards 1943). Making Picture Books." In Miller, B. Caldecott Medal Books: 1938-1957, pp. 88-92.

Bush, Loraine B. "How Alabama Organized Her Work for Children." In National Conference of Social Work. Proceedings (1920), pp. 129-33.

Bushnell, Louise. "Integrity: What and How." Vital Speeches, 39 (November 1, 1972), 50-3.

________. "New Lamps for Old? Centralism." Vital Speeches, 31 (December 1, 1964), 112-4.

________. "Pride in America: Let's Start a Renaissance." Vital Speeches, 38 (December 15, 1971), 142-5.

________. "What Is America? Think About Equality." Vital Speeches, 39 (April 1, 1973), 371-3.

________. "What Happened to Eve? The Women's Liberation Movement." Vital Speeches, 36 (October 1, 1970), 749-52.

________. "Would You Believe ... The Secretary of Tomorrow? She Can Reach the Top." Vital Speeches, 38 (June 15, 1972), 537-40.

Bushong, Ruth. "Public Testimony." In New York (City). Commission on Human Rights. Women's Role in Contemporary Society, pp. 525-8.

Butler, Mary Marguerite. "Hrotsvitha of Gandersheim: The Playable Dramas of a Woman Playwright of the Tenth Century." In McGuigan, D. New Research on Women at the University of Michigan, pp. 215-22.

Butler, Sally. "Statement." In U.S. Congress. House. Committee on the Judiciary. Subcommittee No. 1. Equal Rights Amendment (1948), pp. 85-6.

Butler, Selena Sloan. "Need of Day Nurseries." In Conference for the Study of Negro Problems, 2nd, Atlanta, 1897. Social and Physical Conditions of Negroes in Cities, pp. 63-5.

Buxenbaum, Alva. "Public Testimony." In New York (City). Commission on Human Rights. Women's Role in Contemporary Society, pp. 528-31.

Byars, Betsy. "Newbery Award Acceptance--1971." In Kingman, L. Newbery and Caldecott Medal Books: 1966-1975, pp. 68-72.

Byington, Margaret F. "The Confidential Exchange in the Small City." In National Conference of Social Work. Proceedings (1921), pp. 443-6.

________. "Co-ordination of Civil Effort in Small Communities." In National Conference of Charities and Correction. Proceedings (1916), pp. 472-9.

________. "The Future of Home Service." In National Conference of Social Work. Proceedings (1919), pp. 372-4.

________. "Leadership." In National Conference of Charities and Correction. Proceedings (1913), pp. 370-5.

________. "The Possibilities of Centralized Supervision." In National Conference of Social Work. Proceedings (1921), pp. 262-7.

________. "The Scope and Limitations of Family Rehabilitation: Due to Mental Conditions." In National Conference of Charities and Correction. Proceedings (1914), pp. 127-8.

Cabell, Mary Virginia Ellet. "Discussion of Paper on Ethical Influence of Woman in Education." In World's Congress of Representative Women, Chicago, 1893. A Historical Resume, pp. 114-6.

Cabot, Ella Lyman. "The Religious Life of the Child." In National Conference of Social Work. Proceedings (1922), pp. 130-6.

Cade, Toni. "On the Issues of Roles." In Cade, T. The Black Woman, pp. 101-10.

Cahill, Jane E. Furlong. "A Catholic View of the Education of Women." In Conference on the Present Status and Prospective Trends of Research on the Education of Women, Rye, N. Y., 1957. The Education of Women, pp. 87-91.

Cahn, Gladys F. "The Volunteer Gives--And Receives." In National Conference of Social Work. Proceedings (1946), pp. 276-81.

Caldwell, Grace. "Standards of Admission to Day Nurseries." In National Conference of Social Work. Proceedings (1919), pp. 42-5.

Calkins, Adelaide A. "Boarding-out of Dependent Children in Massachusetts." In National Conference of Charities and Correction. Proceedings (1886), pp. 157-61.

Calkins, Mary Whiton. "Address at the College Evening of the 38th Annual Convention of the National American Woman Suffrage Association, February 8, 1906." In Harper I. The Life and Work of Susan B. Anthony, 3, 1391-2.

Calvin, Henrietta W. "What the Club Woman Can Do for Home Economics Education." In General Federation of Women's Clubs. Biennial Convention, 16 (1922), pp. 229-32.

Campbell, Jean E. "Approaches to Correct the Under-representation of Women in the Health Professions: A U.S. Response to a Look at the U.S.S.R. Dentistry as a Career for Women in the United States: A Discussion with Comparisons to the Soviet Union." In International Conference on Women in Health. Proceedings, pp. 33-7.

Campbell, Jean W. "The Nontraditional Student in Academe." In Furniss, W. Women in Higher Education, pp. 192-9.

Campbell, Mary Edith. "The School's Responsibility for the Leisure Time of the Child; In Relation to Its Effect on the Conduct and Efficiency of the Child and His Family." In National Conference of Social Work. Proceedings (1922), pp. 114-6.

_______. "The Strategic Position of the School in Programs of Social Work: From the Point of View of the Social Worker." In National Conference of Social Work. Proceedings (1923), pp. 360-4.

_______. "Vocational Guidance." In National Conference of Social Work. Proceedings (1923), pp. 418-22.

Cannon, Ida M. "Community Relationships Involved in 100 Per Cent Registration in Social Service Exchange: From the Standpoint of Hospital Social Service." In National Conference of Social Work. Proceedings (1932), pp. 180-5.

_______. "How Can We Vitalize the Relationship of Our Public and Private Social Work?" In National Conference of Social Work. Proceedings (1929), pp. 506-13.

_______. "The Relation of Hospital Social Service to Child Health Work." In National Conference of Social Work. Proceedings (1921), pp. 179-82.

_______. "Social Work at Massachusetts General Hospital." In National Conference of Charities and Correction. Proceedings (1908), pp. 153-7.

Cannon, Martha Hughes. "Woman Suffrage in Utah. Address to the House Judiciary Committee, February 15, 1898." In Stanton, E. History of Woman Suffrage, 4, 319-20.

Cannon, Mary Antoinette. "Case Work in the Hospital." In National Conference of Social Work. Proceedings (1924), pp. 311-4.

_______. "Equipment Needed by the Medical Social Worker." In National Conference of Social Work. Proceedings (1925), pp. 672-6.

_______. "Health Problems of the Foreign Born from the Point of View of the Hospital Social Worker." In National Conference of Social Work. Proceedings (1920), pp. 218-23.

_______. "Hospital Work in Relation to Public Health." In National Conference of Social Work. Proceedings (1919), pp. 195-7.

_______. "The Philosophy of Social Work and Its Place in the Professional Curriculum." In National Conference of Social Work. Proceedings (1930), pp. 520-7.

________. "Recent Changes in the Philosophy of Social Workers." In National Conference of Social Work. Proceedings (1933), pp. 597-607.

________. "Underlying Principles and Common Practice in Social Work." In National Conference of Social Work. Proceedings (1928), pp. 564-9.

________. "The Unknown Future." In National Conference of Social Work. Proceedings (1932), pp. 239-45.

Cannon, Mary M. "International Relations, Distaff Side." Washington, U.S. Women's Bureau, 1950, 9 p.

Cantrell, Ellen M. Harrell. "The Moors of Spain." In World's Congress of Representative Women, Chicago, 1893. Congress of Women, pp. 253-9.

Caplan, Sue Roshoff. "Public Testimony." In New York (City). Commission on Human Rights. Women's Role in Contemporary Society, pp. 408-11.

Carner, Lucy P. "Place of Private Group-work Agency in Program of Youth." In National Conference of Social Work. Proceedings (1936), pp. 270-6.

Carpenter, Constance. "Statement." In U.S. Congress. Senate. Committee on the Judiciary. Subcommittee on Constitutional Amendments. Equal Rights Amendment (1929), p. 26.

Carpenter, Elizabeth. "Address." In Conference on Women in the War on Poverty, 1967. Proceedings, pp. 34-5.

Carpenter, Marjorie. "Today's Tensions. Women, the Problem or the Answer." Vital Speeches, 30 (January 1, 1964), 184-6.

Carr, Charlotte E. "Public Relief--Its Relation to Higher Labor Standards and Social Security." In National Conference of Social Work. Proceedings (1937), pp. 163-73.

________. "What One Family Agency Is Doing." In National Conference of Social Work. Proceedings (1930), pp. 325-9.

Carroll, Mollie Ray. "Controlling Labor Reduction." In International Congress of Women, Chicago, 1933. Our Common Cause, Civilization, pp. 349-53.

________. "Report of the Findings Committee." In International Congress of Women, Chicago, 1933. Our Common Cause, Civilization, pp. 248-51.

________. "Social Insurance." In National Conference of Social Work. Proceedings (1934), pp. 251-62.

________. "Unemployment Insurance by Industry: Some Suggestions from Germany." In National Conference of Social Work. Proceedings (1931), pp. 258-63.

Carse, Matilda Bradley. "The Temperance Temple." In National Council of Women of the U.S., Washington, 1891. Transactions, pp. 153-7.

_______. "The Temperance Temple." In International Council of Women, 1888. Report, pp. 125-7.
_______. "Women and Finance." In International Council of Women, 1888. Report, pp. 186-8.

Carson, Rachel Louise. "Acceptance Speech for the Schweitzer Medal of the Animal Welfare Institute, January 7, 1963." In Brooks, P. The House of Life, pp. 315-6.
_______. "Address to a Conference Sponsored by the National Council of Women of the United States, October 11, 1962." In Brooks, P. The House of Life, pp. 301-2.
_______. "National Book Award Acceptance Speech." In Brooks, P. The House of Life, pp. 127-9.
_______. "Rachel Carson Receives Audubon Medal; With Acceptance Address." Audubon Magazine, 66 (March, 1964), 98-9.
_______. "A Statement of Belief: Speech to Theta Sigma Phi, April 21, 1954." In Brooks, P. The House of Life, pp. 324-6.
_______. "Testimony Before a Senate Committee on Environmental Hazards, June 4, 1963." In Brooks, P. The House of Life, pp. 308-9.

Cary, Emma F. "The Elevation of Womanhood Wrought Through the Veneration of the Blessed Virgin." In World's Congress of Representative Women, Chicago, 1893. A Historical Resume, pp. 298-303.

Case, Emma G. "A Day with the Visiting Teacher." In National Conference of Social Work. Proceedings (1923), pp. 428-31.

Casey, Josephine. "Statement." In U.S. Congress. House. Committee on the Judiciary. Equal Rights Amendment to the Constitution (1932), pp. 12-3.

Casey, Lillian S. "Madame Vestris in America." In McGuigan, D. New Research on Women at the University of Michigan, pp. 223-30.

Cass, Rosemary Higgins. "The Career Wife." In Bier, W. Woman in Modern Life, pp. 123-34.

Castendyck, Elsa. "Helping to Prevent Sex Delinquency." In National Conference of Social Work. Proceedings (1943), pp. 140-8.

Catt, Carrie Lane Chapman. "Acceptance Speech on Being Elected President of the National American Woman Suffrage Association, February, 1900." In Harper, I. The Life and Work of Susan B. Anthony, 3, 1172. Also in Stanton, E. History of Woman Suffrage, 4, 388.
_______. "Address at a Hearing of the House Committee on Rules, December 3, 1913." In Stanton, E. History of Woman Suffrage, 5, 389.

________. "Address at a Hearing of the House Judiciary Committee, December 16, 1915." In Stanton, E. History of Woman Suffrage, 5, 469-70.

________. "Address at the Annual Meeting of the Historical and Scientific Society of Berkshire, Massachusetts, July, 1897." In Harper, I. The Life and Work of Susan B. Anthony, 2, 942-3.

________. "Address at the Last or Victory Convention of the National American Woman Suffrage Association, February, 1920." In Catt, C. Woman Suffrage and Politics, pp. 382-3.

________. "Address Before a House Committee, 1904." In Stanton, E. History of Woman Suffrage, 5, 115-6.

________. "Address Delivered at the Banquet, June 4, 1936." In Associated Country Women of the World. Proceedings, pp. 221-3.

________. "Address of Mrs. Carrie Chapman Catt at Senate Hearing, December 15, 1915." In Stanton, E. History of Woman Suffrage, 5, 752-4.

________. "Address to the Executive Council of the National American Woman Suffrage Association, at the 1916 Convention." In Catt, C. Woman Suffrage and Politics, pp. 261-2.

________. "Address to the Kiwanis Club of Nashville, Tennessee, 1920." In Catt, C. Woman Suffrage and Politics, p. 435.

________. "Address to the National American Woman Suffrage Association Convention of 1897." In Stanton, E. History of Woman Suffrage, 4, 274-5.

________. "Address to the 1916 Convention of the National American Woman Suffrage Convention." In Catt, C. Woman Suffrage and Politics, pp. 262-3.

________. "Address to the National American Woman Suffrage Convention of 1920." In Stanton, E. History of Woman Suffrage, 5, 597-9.

________. "American Leadership." In American Peace Congress, 1st, New York, 1907. Proceedings, pp. 281-5.

________. "Carrie Chapman Catt Addresses Congress." In Millstein, B. We, The American Women, pp. 188-90.

________. "Carrie Chapman Catt Describes the Opposition." In Scott, A. One Half the People, pp. 112-3. (Same as "Address of Mrs. Carrie Chapman Catt at Senate Hearing, December 15, 1915").

________. "Danger to Our Government." In Kraditor, A. Up from the Pedestal, pp. 261-2.

________. "Eulogy at Susan B. Anthony's Funeral, March 15, 1906." In Harper, I. The Life and Work of Susan B. Anthony, 3, 1437-9.

________. "For the Sake of Liberty." In Tanner, L. Voices from Women's Liberation, pp. 91-2.

________. "Forward or Backward?" In New York Herald Tribune. Report of the 4th Annual Women's Conference on Current Problems, pp. 236-41.

________. "Only Yesterday." In International Congress of Women, Chicago, 1933. Our Common Cause, Civilization, pp. 235-41.

________. "Practical Points in Patriotism." In National Council of Women of the U.S. Proceedings, 14 (1928), 60-1.

________. "Presentation of Gift to Miss Anthony, at the National American Woman Suffrage Convention of 1900." In Stanton, E. History of Woman Suffrage, 4, 389-90.

________. "President's Annual Address." In Kraditor, A. Up from the Pedestal, pp. 206-11.

________. "Report on Work in Arizona to the National American Woman Suffrage Association Convention of 1899." In Stanton, E. History of Woman Suffrage, 4, 472-3.

________. "Report on Work in Oklahoma at the National American Woman Suffrage Association Convention of 1899." In Stanton, E. History of Woman Suffrage, 4, 888-9.

________. "Report to the National American Woman Suffrage Association Convention of 1916." In Stanton, E. History of Woman Suffrage, 5, 485-6.

________. "Statement by Mrs. Carrie Chapman Catt at Senate Hearing of 1910." In Stanton, E. History of Woman Suffrage, 5, 745-6.

________. "Suffrage Militancy." In Hurwitz, Edith F. "Carrie C. Catt's "Suffrage Militancy." Signs, 3 (Spring, 1978), 739-43.

________. "Why We Ask for the Submission of an Amendment. Address to the National American Woman Suffrage Association Convention of 1900." In Stanton, E. History of Woman Suffrage, 4, 369-72.

________. "The World Movement for Woman Suffrage 1904 to 1911: Is Woman Suffrage Progressing?" In Schneir, M. Feminism, pp. 286-92.

Causey, Ruth. "Testimony." In U.S. Congress. House. Select Committee on Crime. Drugs in Our Schools, pp. 908-9.

Cavanagh, Aileen. "Official Opening of Conference." In International Conference of Women Engineers and Scientists, 1st, New York, 1964. Focus for the Future, pp. I-3-4.

Cavanaugh, Denise E. "Statement." In U.S. Congress. Senate. Select Committee on Small Business. Women and the Small Business Administration, pp. 75-6, 78-81.

Cayvan, Georgia. "The Stage and Its Women." In World's Congress of Representative Women, Chicago, 1893. A Historical Resume, pp. 179-88.

Ceballos, Jacqueline. "Public Testimony." In New York (City). Commission on Human Rights. Women's Role in Contemporary Society, pp. 411-2.

Chace, Elizabeth Buffum. "Relation of Women to Crime and Criminals." In Association for the Advancement of Women, Congress of Women, 3rd. Papers, pp. 127-34.

________. "Report to the American Woman Suffrage Association on the Work of the Rhode Island Association, Philadelphia, 1876." In Stanton, E. History of Woman Suffrage, 3, 343-4.

Chace, Lydia Gardner. "Public School Classes for Mentally Deficient Children." In National Conference of Charities and Correction. Proceedings (1904), pp. 390-401.

Chacon, Estelle. "Statement." In U.S. Congress. House. Committee on Education and Labor. Subcommittee on Equal Opportunity. Equal Opportunity for Displaced Homemakers Act, pp. 62-3.

Chambers, Evelyn. "Youth Plans for a Civilized World: Forum on the College Generation." In International Congress of Women, Chicago, 1933. Our Common Cause, Civilization, pp. 201-2.

Chandler, Lucinda B. "Enlightened Motherhood--How Attainable." In Association for the Advancement of Women. Congress of Women, 1st. Papers, pp. 14-22.

Chaney, Elsa M. "The Mobilization of Women in Allende's Chile." In Jaquette, J. Women in Politics, pp. 267-80.

Chapin, Augusta Jane. "University Extension." In World's Congress of Representative Women, Chicago, 1893. Congress of Women, pp. 393-7.

________. "Woman's Work in the Pulpit and Church." In Association for the Advancement of Women. Congress of Women, 1st. Papers, pp. 99-102.

Chapman, Jane R. "Statement." In U.S. Congress. Senate. Select Committee on Small Business. Women and the Small Business Administration, pp. 117-8.

Chapman, Janet G. "Equal Pay for Equal Work?" In Atkinson, D. Women in Russia, pp. 225-39.

Chapman, Mariana W. "Equal Suffrage as Related to the Purity Movement." In National Purity Congress, 1st, Baltimore, 1895. National Purity Congress, pp. 350-8.

________. "Women as Capitalists and Taxpayers." In Stanton, E. History of Woman Suffrage, 4, 313-4.

Chasan, Evelyn. "Public Testimony." In New York (City). Commission on Human Rights. Women's Role in Contemporary Society, pp. 700-1.

Cheek, Alison M. "Women and Religion." In Hammond, N. Women and Children in Contemporary Society, pp. 3-11.

Chen, Lily Lee. "Statement." In U.S. Congress. House. Committee on Education and Labor. Subcommittee on Equal Opportunities. Equal Opportunity for Displaced Homemakers Act, pp. 25-8.

Chenet, Winifred. "Public Testimony." In New York (City). Commission on Human Rights. Women's Role in Contemporary Society, pp. 522-3.

Cheney, Ednah D. "Address." In International Council of Women, 1888. *Report*, pp. 420-1.

———. "Boston Charities--New England Hospital." In Conference on Charities and Correction. *Proceedings* (1881), pp. 88-90.

———. "Hospitals Managed By and For Women." In International Council of Women, 1888. *Report*, pp. 95-8.

———. "Place of Women in Our Public Schools." In Association for the Advancement of Women. Congress of Women, 3rd. *Papers*, pp. 7-17.

Chickering, Martha A. "Official Recognition and Status of the Social Worker." In National Conference of Social Work. *Proceedings* (1934), pp. 523-31.

———. "The Part Social Workers Have Taken in Promoting Social Legislation in California." In National Conference of Social Work. *Proceedings* (1935), pp. 505-11.

———. "What a Visitor in a Public Agency Should Know." In National Conference of Social Work. *Proceedings* (1938), pp. 541-50.

Chinchilla, Norma S. "Industrialization, Monopoly Capitalism, and Women's Work in Guatemala." In Conference on Women and Development. "Women and National Development: The Complexities of Change." *Signs*, 3 (Autumn, 1977), pp. 38-56.

Chisholm, Shirley Anita St. Hill. "Abortion." *Congressional Record*, 91st Cong., 1st Sess., 1969, 115, pt. 27: 36765-7.

———. "Abortion and Population Control." *Congressional Record*, 91st Cong., 1st Sess., 1969, 115, pt. 28, 38592-4.

———. "Aid to Dependent Children." *Congressional Record*, 93rd Cong., 2nd Sess., 1974, 120, pt. 5, 6304-6.

———. "The Cost of Care." In Chisholm S. *The Good Fight*, pp. 193-9.

———. "Debate on Office of Economic Opportunity." *Congressional Record*, 91st Cong., 1st Sess., 1969, 115, pt. 29, 38842-3.

———. "Economic Justice for Women." In Chisholm, S. *The Good Fight*, pp. 188-92.

———. "Equal Rights Amendment." *Congressional Record*, 91st Cong., 2nd Sess., 1970, 116, pt. 21, 28028-9.

———. "Equal Rights for Women." *Congressional Record*, 91st Cong., 1st Sess., 1969, 115, pt. 10, 13380-1.

———. "Equal Rights Amendment." *Congressional Record*, 92nd Cong., 1st Sess., 1971, pt. 27, 35314-5.

———. "The 51% Minority, 1970." In Lerner, G. *Black Women in White America*, pp. 352-7. Also in Martin, W. *The American Sisterhood*, pp. 144-51.

———. "Is Proposed Conversion of U.S. Armed Forces to an All-Volunteer Basis a Sound National Policy?" *Congressional Digest*, 50 (May, 1971), 154-8.

———. "Pension Legislation for Women." *Congressional Record*, 93rd Cong., 2nd Sess., 1974, 120, pt. 4, 4773-5.

———. "Progress Through Understanding." *Congressional Record*, 91st Cong., 1st Sess., 1969, 115, pt. 12, 15972-3.

________. "Representative Shirley Chisholm Speaks in Support of the Equal Rights Amendment." In Bosmajian, H. This Great Argument, pp. 243-7. (Same as "The 51% Minority").

________. "Should Congress Approve the 'Equal Rights Amendment.'" Congressional Digest, 50 (January 1971), pp. 20-2.

________. "Should Congress Limit the Present Scope of the Federal Food Stamp Program?" Congressional Digest, 54 (May 1975), 151-7.

________. "Statement." In U.S. Congress. House. Committee on Education and Labor. Special Subcommittee on Education. Discrimination Against Women, pp. 189-94. (Same as "The 51% Minority").

________. "Statement." In U.S. Congress. Senate. Committee on the Judiciary. Subcommittee on Constitutional Amendments. Women and the 'Equal Rights" Amendment, pp. 23-5.

Choate, Reba E. "Two Types of Public Welfare Administration." In National Conference of Social Work. Proceedings (1948), pp. 145-52.

Chodorow, Nancy. "Family Structure and Feminine Personality." In Rosaldo, M. Woman, Culture, and Society, pp. 43-66.

Chorpenning, Charlotte. "Contrasting Values of the Drama and Festival in Group Work." In National Conference of Social Work. Proceedings (1939), pp. 352-9.

Christensen, Daphne. "Autos and Mass Transit: Paradox and Confusion." Vital Speeches, 43 (November 15, 1976), 77-81.

Church, Roberta. "Keynote Speech for Workshop Session of Labor and Industry Committee of National Council of Negro Women, Washington, D.C., November 10, 1954." Washington, U.S. Employment Security Bureau, 1954, 6 p.

Churchill, Elizabeth K. "Remarks at the Semi-annual Meeting of the American Woman Suffrage Association, New York, May, 1871." In Stanton, E. History of Woman Suffrage, 2, 812.

Cisler, Lucinda. "Public Testimony." In New York (City). Commission on Human Rights. Women's Role in Contemporary Society, pp. 536-40.

________. "Status of Women in Architecture." In Conference of Professional and Academic Women. Sixteen Reports on the Status of Women in the Professions, 3 p.

Claghorn, Kate Holladay. "The Law's Delay: Lower Court Justice and the Immigrant." In National Conference of Social Work. Proceedings (1923), pp. 178-83.

________. "Some New Developments in Social Statistics." In National Conference of Charities and Correction. Proceedings (1910), pp. 507-15.

________. "The Use and Misuse of Statistics in Social Work. In

National Conference of Charities and Correction. Proceedings (1908), pp. 234-51.

________. "The Work of Voluntary Immigrant Protective Agencies." In National Conference of Social Work. Proceedings (1919), pp. 747-52.

Clapp, Margaret. "Comment on Current Trends in the Education of Women." In Conference on the Present Status and Prospective Trends of Research on the Education of Women, Rye, N.Y., 1957. The Education of Women, pp. 91-2.

Clark, Ann Nolan. "Acceptance Paper--Newbery Medal 1953." In Miller, B. Newbery Medal Books, 1922-1955, pp. 396-404.

Clark, Anna Lewis. "Report of Civil Service Reform Committee." In General Federation of Women's Clubs. Biennial Convention, 9 (1908), pp. 357-61.

Clark, Jane Perry. "American Deportation Procedure: An International Social Problem." In National Conference of Social Work. Proceedings (1927), pp. 559-68.

________. "Detention of Deportees." In National Conference of Social Work. Proceedings (1930), pp. 502-10.

________. "Immigrant Populations." In International Congress of Women, Chicago, 1933. Our Common Cause, Civilization, pp. 665-71.

Clark, Kate Upson. "Women as Publishers." In General Federation of Women's Clubs. Biennial Convention, 9 (1908), pp. 369-72.

Clark, Laura H. "The Faith of Islam." In World's Congress of Representative Women, Chicago, 1893. Congress of Women, pp. 512-5.

Clark, Mary Vida. "The Almshouse." In National Conference of Charities and Correction. Proceedings (1900), pp. 146-58.

Clark, S. Ethel. "Almshouse Property: The Ideal in Amount and Upkeep." In National Conference of Charities and Correction. Proceedings (1912), pp. 445-7.

Clarke, Elizabeth Munro. "A Re-examination of Child-Welfare Functions in Foster-Care Agencies." In National Conference of Social Work. Proceedings (1935), pp. 179-86.

Clarke, Hannah B. "Remarks at the 1st Annual Meeting of the American Woman Suffrage Association, Cleveland, Ohio, November, 1870." In Stanton, E. History of Woman Suffrage, 2, 807-8.

Clarke, Helen I. "Uniform Area Plan for Chicago City-Wide Social Agencies." In National Conference of Social Work. Proceedings (1926), pp. 510-4.

Clay, Laura. "Address of Greeting to the National American Woman Suffrage Association Convention of 1911." In Stanton, E. History of Woman Suffrage, 5, 311-2.

________. "Can Women Be Fighters?" In Tanner, L. Voices from Women's Liberation, pp. 90-1. (Same as "Fitness of Women to Become Citizens from the Standpoint of Physical Development.")

________. "Fitness of Women to Become Citizens from the Standpoint of Physical Development. Address to Senate Committee, February 15, 1898." In Stanton, E. History of Woman Suffrage, 4, 309-10.

Clay, Mary Barr. "Address to the Judiciary Committee of the House, March 8, 1884." In Stanton, E. History of Woman Suffrage, 4, 44-5.

Clayton, Jan. "Statement." In U.S. Congress. Senate. Committee on Labor and Public Welfare. Subcommittee on Alcoholism and Narcotics. Alcohol Abuse Among Women, pp. 14-6.

Cleaves, Margaret Abigail. "The Medical and Moral Care of Female Patients." In Conference of Charities. Proceedings (1879), pp. 73-83.

________. "Women as Hospital Physicians." In Conference of Charities and Correction. Proceedings (1881), pp. 27-30.

Cleland, Virginia S. "Approaches to the Organization of Nurses and Allied Health and Support Personnel. A U.S. Response to the Australian Experience." In International Conference on Women in Health. Proceedings, pp. 79-81.

Clemence, Esther H. "Changing Trends in the Education of Caseworkers." In National Conference of Social Work. Proceedings (1947), pp. 240-50.

Clemens, Lois Gunden. "Members One of Another." In Clemens, L. Woman Liberated, pp. 117-42.

________. "The Problem of Roles." In Clemens, L. Woman Liberated, pp. 35-65.

________. "Using All Gifts Creatively." In Clemens, L. Woman Liberated, pp. 143-51.

________. "Who Is Woman?" In Clemens, L. Woman Liberated, pp. 13-34.

________. "Woman's Natural Strengths." In Clemens, L. Woman Liberated, pp. 66-87.

________. "Women Functioning Under God." In Clemens, L. Woman Liberated, pp. 88-116.

Clement, Fannie F. "The District Nurse in Rural Work." In National Conference of Charities and Correction. Proceedings (1914), pp. 279-88.

Cleveland, Charlotte A. "What Practical Measures Will Promote the Financial Independence of Women." In Association for the Advancement of Women. Congress of Women, 3rd. Papers, pp. 58-9.

Clevenger, Louise M. "How Can We Interpret More Effectively to the Public the Role Played in the Community's Welfare Program by Social Settlement, Recreations Agencies, and National Program Agencies?" In National Conference of Social Work. Proceedings (1932), pp. 382-94.

________. The Influence of Publicity in Developing Community Organization." In National Conference of Social Work. Proceedings (1938), pp. 431-42.

Clifton, Eleanor. "The Role of Personalities in the Treatment of Problem Children in an Institution." In National Conference of Social Work. Proceedings (1926), pp. 442-8.

________. "Some Psychological Effects of the War as Seen by the Social Worker." In National Conference of Social Work. Proceedings (1943), pp. 116-25.

________. "What We Learn from the Child's Own Psychology to Guide Treatment." In National Conference of Social Work. Proceedings (1938), pp. 326-38.

Clifton, Ruth. "The Moline Plan." In New York Herald Tribune. Report of the 14th Annual Forum on Current Problems, pp. 74-7.

Clignet, Remi. "Social Change and Sexual Differentiation in the Cameroun and the Ivory Coast." In Conference on Women and Development. "Women and National Development: The Complexities of Change." Signs, 3 (Autumn, 1977), 224-60.

Close, Mary G. "New Frontiers." In New York Herald Tribune. Report of the 3rd Women's Conference on Current Problems, pp. 67-9.

Clothier, Hannah Hallowell. "The Pure in Heart." In National Purity Congress, 1st, Baltimore, 1895. National Purity Congress, pp. 286-92.

Clow, Lucia B. "The Art of Helping Through the Interview: A Study of Two Interviews." In National Conference of Social Work. Proceedings (1925), pp. 271-6.

Clusen, Ruth Chickering. "Should the Expiring "Special Provision" of the Voting Rights Act Be Further Extended?" Congressional Digest, 54 (June-July, 1975), pp. 178-82.

Clymer, Ella Dietz. "The Light in the East." In World's Congress of Representative Women, Chicago, 1893. A Historical Resume, pp. 289-92.

________. "The National Value of Women's Clubs." In National Council of Women of the U.S., Washington, 1891. Transactions, pp. 296-301.

________. "The Light in the East." In World's Congress of Representative Women, Chicago, 1893. A Historical Resume, pp. 289-92.

________. "The National Value of Women's Clubs." In National Council of Women of the U.S., Washington, 1891. Transactions, pp. 296-301.

Cobb, Mary Emilie Rockwell. "Instructive and Productive Employments. Their Suitability for Industrial Schools and Houses of Refuge." In National Conference of Charities and Correction. Proceedings (1885), pp. 247-57.

________. "Paper on Preventive Work among Children." In National Conference of Charities and Correction. Proceedings (1883), pp. 480-4.

________. "Scholastic and Industrial Education." In National Conference of Charities and Correction. Proceedings (1896), pp. 348-52.

Cochran, Jacqueline. "The Future of Women in the Aviation Industry." In New York Herald Tribune. Report of the 12th Annual Forum on Current Problems, pp. 110-13.

Cockerill, Eleanor. "Casework and the New Emphasis on an Old Concept in Medicine." In National Conference of Social Work. Proceedings (1948), pp. 284-92.

________. "The Use of Current Case-work Concepts Where There Is Physical Illness: From the Experience of the Case Worker in the Medical Agency." In National Conference of Social Work. Proceedings (1939), pp. 304-14.

Coe, Emma R. "Remarks on the Laws of Ohio, at the 4th National Woman's Rights Convention, Cleveland, Ohio, October 1853." In Stanton, E. History of Woman Suffrage, 1, 146-8.

Cohan, Essie. "Statement." In U.S. House. Congress. Committee on Education and Labor. Subcommittee on Equal Opportunity. Equal Opportunity for Displaced Homemakers Act, pp. 35-7.

Cohen, Katherine M. "Life of Artists." In World's Congress of Representative Women, Chicago, 1893. Congress of Women, pp. 428-31.

Cohen, Mary M. "The Influence of the Jewish Religion in the Home." In Jewish Women's Congress. Papers, pp. 115-21.

Cohen, Miriam. "Role of Women in the Organization of the Men's Garment Industry, Chicago, 1910." In McGuigan, D. New Research on Women at the University of Michigan, pp. 77-83.

Cohen, Nina Morais. "Homer and His Poems." In World's Congress of Representative Women, Chicago, 1893. Congress of Women, pp. 113-22.

Cohen, Selma Jeanne. "Woman as Artistic Innovator: The Case of the Choreographer." In McGuigan, D. A Sampler of Women's Studies, pp. 5-16.

Cohn, Fannie M. "A Union Officer Calls for Idealism." In Brownlee, W. Women in the American Economy, pp. 220-4.

Colby, Clara Bewick. "Address to the House Judiciary Committee, February 20, 1886." In Stanton, E. History of Woman Suffrage, 4, 80-1.

________. "Resolutions at the Memorial Services of the National American Woman Suffrage Association Convention of 1898." In Stanton, E. History of Woman Suffrage, 4, 293-6.

________. "Tribute to Susan B. Anthony at Berkshire Historical Society Meeting, July, 1897." In Harper, I. The Life and Work of Susan B. Anthony, 2, 944-5.

________. "Women in Marriage. Address to the National Woman Suffrage Association Convention of 1889." In Stanton, E. History of Woman Suffrage, 4, 151-2.

Colby, Mary Ruth. "Protection of Children in Adoption." In National Conference of Social Work. Proceedings (1938), pp. 146-61.

________. "What Is Happening in County Organization?" In National Conference of Social Work. Proceedings (1932), pp. 439-49.

Colcord, Joanna Carver. "Chairman's Report on What of the Immediate Future of the Family?" In National Conference of Social Work. Proceedings (1919), pp. 315-9.

________. "The Impact of the War upon Community Welfare Organization." In National Conference of Social Work. Proceedings (1943), pp. 241-51.

________. "Necessary Supplement to Unemployment Insurance." In National Conference of Social Work. Proceedings (1937), pp. 463-73.

________. "Relief, Style 1936." In National Conference of Social Work. Proceedings (1936), pp. 291-8.

________. "Report of Committee on Current Relief Program." In National Conference of Social Work. Proceedings (1934), pp. 111-29.

________. "Social Work and the First Federal Relief Programs." In National Conference of Social Work. Proceedings (1943), pp. 382-94.

________. "Strengths of Family Life." In National Conference of Social Work. Proceedings (1930), pp. 180-8.

________. "Training for the Work of Civilian Relief." In National Conference of Social Work. Proceedings (1917), pp. 143-5.

________. "What Has Social Work to Do with the Founding of New Families?" In National Conference of Social Work. Proceedings (1926), pp. 251-9.

Cole, Annette. "Art-isms." In World's Congress of Representative Women, Chicago, 1893. Congress of Women, pp. 600-2.

Cole, Ida B. "Address of Welcome." In General Federation of Women's Clubs. Biennial Convention, 16 (1911), pp. 31-3.

Cole, Margaret Esqueda Montion. "Statement." In U.S. Congress. House. Committee on Education and Labor. Subcommittee on Equal Opportunities. Equal Opportunity for Displaced Homemakers Act, pp. 31-2.

Coleman, Lucy N. "Debate at the Woman's National Loyal League Convention, May 14, 1863." In Stanton, E. History of Woman Suffrage, 2, 62-3.

Coles, Jessie. "Getting What We Want." In International Congress of Women, Chicago, 1933. Our Common Cause, Civilization, pp. 456-60.

Collier, Jane Fishburne. "Women in Politics." In Rosaldo, M. Woman, Culture and Society, pp. 89-96.

Collins, Verla. "1977--The Year of the Nurse. We Are Professionally Competent." Vital Speeches, 43 (July 15, 1977), 590-3.

Colom, Audrey Rowe. "Statement." In U.S. Congress. House. Committee on Government Operations. National Women's Conference, pp. 30-2.

________. "Statement." In U.S. Congress. Senate. Committee on the Judiciary. Subcommittee on Constitutional Amendments. Abortion, pt. 4, 698-701.

Coman, Jean. "What Does the Group Work Process Have to Contribute to a Housing Program?" In National Conference of Social Work. Proceedings (1941), pp. 541-6.

Commander, Lydia Kingsmill. "The Social Value of the Professional Woman." In International Congress of Women, Toronto, 1909. Report, 2, 289-91.

Conine, Martha A. B. "Address to the National American Woman Suffrage Association Convention of 1898 from Colorado." In Stanton, E. History of Woman Suffrage, 4, 302-3.

Conlin, Roxanne Barton. "Government Policy and the Legal Status of Women." In Epstein, L. Women in the Professions, pp. 115-21.

Conner, Leora L. "The Effects on Case Work Services of Social Factors in the Negro's Life: From the Point of View of Socio-Political Factors." In National Conference of Social Work. Proceedings (1942), pp. 460-9.

Conrad, Irene Farnham. "The Need of a Few Fundamental Courses." In National Conference of Social Work. Proceedings (1928), pp. 532-7.

_______. "Professional Standards for Council and Chest Executives." In National Conference of Social Work. Proceedings (1929), pp. 580-6.

Conway, Clara. "Need of a Great College in the South." In World's Congress of Representative Women, Chicago, 1893. Congress of Women, pp. 402-4.

_______. "The Needs of Southern Women." In National Education Association. Journal of Proceedings and Addresses (1884), pp. 169-76.

Cook, Coralie Franklin. "Tribute to Susan B. Anthony, at Her 80th Birthday Celebration, February 15, 1900." In Harper, I. The Life and Work of Susan B. Anthony, 3, 1183. Also in Stanton, E. History of Woman Suffrage, 4, 398-9.

Cook, Edith Valet. "Statement." In U.S. Congress. Senate. Committee on the Judiciary. Subcommittee on Constitutional Amendments. Equal Rights for Men and Women (1938), pp. 73-6.

Cook, Georgiana Hemingway. "The Brahmo Somaj and What It Is Doing for the Women of India." In National Council of Women of the U.S., Washington, 1891. Transactions, pp. 119-29.

Cooley, Clara Aldrich. "Greeting from Honorary Vice-President." In General Federation of Women's Clubs. Biennial Convention, 9 (1908), pp. 44-6.

Cooley, Elizabeth A. "West Palm Beach County, Florida: A Unit for Social Work." In National Conference of Social Work. Proceedings (1926), pp. 467-71.

Cooley, Rossa B. "The Regeneration of the Colored Population in the Rural South." In National Conference of Charities and Correction. Proceedings (1911), pp. 107-10.

Cooney, Barbara. "Caldecott Award Acceptance (1959)." In Kingman, L. Newbery and Caldecott Medal Books: 1966-1975, pp. 199-202.

Cooper, Anna Julia. "The Colored Woman Should Not Be Ignored." In Lerner, G. Black Women in White America, pp. 572-4.

_______. "Discussion of the Intellectual Progress of the Colored Women of the United States since the Emancipation Proclamation." In Loewenberg, B. Black Women in Nineteenth-Century American Life, pp. 329-31. Also in World's Congress of Representative Women, Chicago, 1893. A Historical Resume, pp. 711-5.

Cooper, Janet. "Coming Out." In Conference on the Universities and the Gay Experience. Proceedings, pp. 64-7.

Cooper, Sarah Brown Ingersoll. "Discussion of Woman as a Religious Teacher." In World's Congress of Representative Women, Chicago, 1893. A Historical Resume, pp. 281-3.

________. "The Kindergarten as a Character Builder." In National Conference of Charities and Correction. Proceedings (1885), pp. 222-8. Also in World's Congress of Representative Women, Chicago, 1893. Congress of Women, pp. 296-300.

________. "The Kindergarten as a Child-Saving Work." In National Conference of Charities and Correction. Proceedings (1882), pp. 130-8.

________. "The Kindergarten as an Educational Agency and the Relation of the Kindergarten to Manual Training." In World's Congress of Representative Women, Chicago, 1893. A Historical Resume, pp. 90-8.

________. "Practical Results of Ten Years' Work." In National Conference of Charities and Correction. Proceedings (1889), pp. 186-94.

Cooper, Susan. "Newbery Award Acceptance, 1976." Horn Book Magazine, 52 (August, 1976), 361-6.

Copp, Tracy. "The Need for Women to Enforce Women's Labor Law." In U.S. Women Bureau. Proceedings of the Women's Industrial Conference, pp. 171-4.

________. "Need of State Legislation to Supplement and Follow Up the N.R.A." In National Conference of Social Work. Proceedings (1934), pp. 418-27.

Coppin, Fannie Jackson. "Discussion of the Intellectual Progress of the Colored Women of the United States Since the Emancipation Proclamation." In Loewenberg, B. Black Women in Nineteenth-Century American Life, pp. 315-6. Also in World's Congress of Representative Women, Chicago, 1893. A Historical Resume, pp. 715-7.

Corbally, Marguerite. "From This Mother: The Old Brick Wall Theory." Vital Speeches, 38 (June 15, 1972), 540-1.

Corbett, Lucille K. "The Background of a Family's Religious Life as Social Data." In National Conference of Social Work. Proceedings (1926), pp. 265-9.

Corbin, Caroline Fairfield. "Enlightened Motherhood." In Association for the Advancement of Women. Congress of Women, 1st. Papers, pp. 22-31.

________. "The Higher Womanhood." In World's Congress of Representative Women, Chicago, 1893. Congress of Women, pp. 326-7.

Corbin, Hazel. "An Adequate Local Maternity Program." In National Conference of Social Work. Proceedings (1924), pp. 248-52.

Corin, Leslie. "Public Testimony." In New York (City). Commission on Human Rights. Women's Role in Contemporary Society, pp. 545-7.

Corrigan, Hazel G. "Social Casework in a Social Protection Program." In National Conference of Social Work. Proceedings (1946), pp. 464-7.

Corson, Juliet. "The Evolution of Home." In World's Congress of Representative Women, Chicago, 1893. Congress of Women, pp. 714-8.

Cory, Florence Elizabeth. "The Contribution of Women to the Applied Arts." In World's Congress of Representative Women, Chicago, 1893. A Historical Resume, pp. 565-7.

Coser, Rose Laub. "Why Bother? Is Research on Issues of Women's Health Worthwhile?" In U.S. National Center for Health Services Research. Women and Their Health, pp. 3-9.

Cosgrove, Elizabeth. "Use of Service Ratings in the Evaluation of Performance." In National Conference of Social Work. Proceedings (1940), pp. 616-28.

Costigan, Mabel G. Cory. "Public Control of the Packing Industry, a Factor in Reducing the Cost of Living." In National Conference of Social Work. Proceedings (1921), pp. 316-21.

Cotton, Sallie S. "A National Training School for Women." In National Congress of Mothers. Work and Words, pp. 208-19.

Cottrell, Louise. "The Iowa Plan of Cooperation in County Welfare Work." In National Conference of Social Work. Proceedings (1926), pp. 545-9.

________. "Organization Needed to Support and Free the Local Worker for Undifferentiated Case Work." In National Conference of Social Work. Proceedings (1927), pp. 118-22.

Countryman, Gratia A. "Building for the Future." American Library Association. Bulletin, 28 (July, 1934), 377-88. Also Library Journal, 59 (July, 1934), 541-7.

Couzins, Phoebe Wilson. "Address on the Fifteenth Amendment to a Meeting of the St. Louis Woman Suffrage Association." Revolution, 5 (May 12, 1870), 292-3.

________. "Address to a Convention of the National Woman Suffrage Association, Philadelphia, July, 1876." In Stanton, E. History of Woman Suffrage, 3, 36-8.

________. "Address to the National Woman Suffrage Association Convention, January 1882." In Stanton, E. History of Woman Suffrage, 3, 223-5.

________. "Address to the 3rd Annual Meeting of the American Equal Rights Association, New York, May 1869." In Stanton, E. History of Woman Suffrage, 2, 387-8.

_______. "Testimony at a Hearing of the House Committee on the Judiciary, January 24, 1880." In Stanton, E. History of Woman Suffrage, 3, 170-3.

_______. "Welcoming Address at the National Woman Suffrage Association Convention, St. Louis, Missouri, May 1879." In Stanton, E. History of Woman Suffrage, 3, 142-4.

Cowan, Lillian S. "Environmental Conflicts in the Family and Social Life of the Modern Child." In National Conference of Social Work. Proceedings (1927), pp. 291-4.

Cowles, Betsy M. "Report on Labor." In Woman's Rights Convention, Akron, Ohio, 1851. Proceedings, pp. 14-20.

Cowles, Fleur. "Does the Health of Our Democracy Requirė a Change of Party in November?" In New York Herald Tribune. Report of the 21st Annual Forum on Current Problems, pp. 218-9.

Cox, Luella. "Statement." In U.S. Women's Bureau. Proceedings of the Woman's Industrial Conference, pp. 142-4.

Coyle, Grace Longwell. "The Contribution of Group Experience to the Development of Older Children." In National Conference of Social Work. Proceedings (1941), pp. 387-95.

_______. "Group Work and Social Change (Pugsley Award)." In National Conference of Social Work. Proceedings (1935), pp. 393-405.

_______. "Social Group Work in Recreation." In National Conference of Social Work. Proceedings (1946), pp. 202-8.

_______. "Social Work at the Turn of the Decade." In National Conference of Social Work. Proceedings (1940), pp. 3-26.

Craddock, Carolyn R. "The Return of the Serviceman to His Family and Community: As Seen in Home Service, American National Red Cross." In National Conference of Social Work. Proceedings (1945), pp. 103-8.

Crain, Lucille Cardin. "Dissent in Education." In New York Herald Tribune. Report of the 20th Annual Forum on Current Problems, pp. 135-9.

_______. "What Are Our Schools Teaching about Business? Responsibility Lies with the Taxpayers." Vital Speeches, 16 (August 15, 1950), 657-60.

Cratty, Mabel. "At the Close of a National Convention." In Burton, M. Mabel Cratty, pp. 201-4.

_______. "The Christian Ideal for Woman as Interpreted by the Young Women's Christian Association." In Burton, M. Mabel Cratty, pp. 183-95.

_______. "Giving and Receiving." In Burton, M. Mabel Cratty, pp. 112-3.

_______. "The Goal of Our Calling." In Burton, M. Mabel Cratty, pp. 182-3.

________. "Miss Dodge." In Burton, M. Mabel Cratty, pp. 137-9.

________. "On Being a Builder." In Burton, M. Mabel Cratty, pp. 162-5.

________. "On Being a Christian." In Burton, M. Mabel Cratty, pp. 105-7.

________. "On Being a Leader." In Burton, M. Mabel Cratty, pp. 145-59.

________. "Our Motives and Methods." In Burton, M. Mabel Cratty, pp. 177-82.

________. "Ourselves and Our Religion." In Burton, M. Mabel Cratty, pp. 107-9.

________. "The Qualities of Leadership." In Burton, M. Mabel Cratty, pp. 159-62.

________. "The Qualities of Leadership as Revealed in Miss Dodge." In Burton, M. Mabel Cratty, pp. 126-30.

________. "Some Administrative Problems in the Young Women's Christian Association." In Burton, M. Mabel Cratty, pp. 165-7.

________. "This Day We Sailed West." In Burton, M. Mabel Cratty, pp. 197-201.

________. "Unity with the Creation." In Vurton, M. Mabel Cratty, pp. 110-1.

Crawford, Mary Sinclair. "Statement." In U.S. Congress. Senate. Committee on the Judiciary. Subcommittee on Constitutional Amendments. Equal Rights Amendment (1945), p. 16.

Crawford, Ruth. "Port Problems in Europe and the United States." In National Conference of Social Work. Proceedings (1921), pp. 465-71.

Crocker, Gertrude L. "Statement." In U.S. Congress. House. Committee on the Judiciary. Equal Rights Amendment (1948), pp. 71-2.

Croly, Jane Cunningham. "Women in Journalism." In Association for the Advancement of Women. Congress of Women, 3rd. Papers, pp. 41-51.

________. "Women's Clubs." In International Council of Women, 1888. Report, pp. 217-8.

Cropsey, Nebraska. "The Kindergarten and the Primary School." In World's Congress of Representative Women, Chicago, 1893. A Historical Resume, pp. 103-7.

Crosby, Helen. "Business as an Ally." In National Conference of Social Work. Proceedings (1928), pp. 614-7.

Cross, Kathryn Patricia. "The Woman Student." In Furniss, W. Women in Higher Education, pp. 29-50.

Crutcher, Hester B. "The Problems of a Permanent Child Guidance Clinic." In National Conference of Social Work. Proceedings (1925), pp. 422-5.

Culbert, Jane F. "Health Activities of Child Caring Agencies: The School and Social Problems." In National Conference of Social Work. Proceedings (1925), pp. 130-1.

________. "The Public School as a Little-Used Agency: As a Factor in the Treatment of the Socially Handicapped Child." In National Conference of Social Work. Proceedings (1921), pp. 95-8.

________. "Visiting Teachers and Their Activities." In National Conference of Charities and Correction. Proceedings (1916), pp. 592-8.

Culver, Essie Martha. "A Call to Action." American Library Association Bulletin, 34 (June, 1940), 377-9.

Cummings, Sarah. "Statement." In U.S. Congress. Senate. Committee on the Judiciary. Subcommittee on Constitutional Amendments. Equal Rights for Men and Women (1933), pp. 13-4.

Cummings, Tena. "Testimony." In U.S. Congress. House. Committee on Small Business. Subcommittee on Minority Enterprise and General Oversight. Women in Business, pp. 42-3.

Cunningham, Evelyn. "Statement." In U.S. Congress. Joint Economic Committee. Economic Problems of Women, pt. 4, 585-8, 593-4.

Cunningham, Sarah Jane. "Statement." In U.S. Congress. House. Committee on Education and Labor. Special Subcommittee on Labor. Equal Pay Act, pp. 80-4.

Cummins, Ella Sterling. "The Women Writers of California." In World's Congress of Representative Women, Chicago, 1893. Congress of Women, pp. 184-9.

Curry, H. Ida. "The County as a Unit in Charity Administration--Roundtable." In National Conference of Social Work. Proceedings (1918), pp. 241-4.

________. "Co-Operation or Obstruction in Determining Fields of Activity." In National Conference of Social Work. Proceedings (1937), pp. 495-503.

________. "County Programs of Child Care: What Should a County Program Undertake?" In National Conference of Social Work. Proceedings (1925), pp. 95-9.

________. "Development of County or Town Boards." In National Conference of Social Work. Proceedings (1930), pp. 459-68.

________. "The Extra-Institutional Services of County Institutions." In National Conference of Social Work. Proceedings (1927), pp. 493-8.

________. "A Girl with a Second or Third Illegitimate Child." In National Conference of Charities and Correction. Proceedings (1915), pp. 115-7.

________. "The Status of Social Work in Rural Communities." In National Conference of Social Work. Proceedings (1918), pp. 83-91.

________. "The Use of Committees and Volunteers in Rural Social Work." In National Conference of Social Work. Proceedings (1927), pp. 276-80.

Curtis, Elizabeth Burrill. "Are Women Represented in Our Government? Address to Senate Committee, February 15, 1898." In Stanton, E. History of Woman Suffrage, 4, 314-5.

________. "Universal Suffrage. Address to the National American Woman Suffrage Association Convention of 1896." In Stanton, E. History of Woman Suffrage, 4, 257-8.

Curtis, Florence R. "A Survey of Institution Libraries." In National Conference of Charities and Correction. Proceedings (1916), pp. 355-60.

Curtis, Frances Greely. "Report of the Committee (On Children)." In National Conference of Charities and Correction. Proceedings (1908), pp. 337-8.

________. "What Had the Public a Right to Know About Public and Private Charities and How Shall It Learn About Them." In National Conference of Charities and Correction. Proceedings (1905), pp. 434-5.

Curwen, Mary Thew Wright. "The Wife of Blennerhassett." In World's Congress of Representative Women, Chicago, 1893. Congress of Women, pp. 165-9.

Cutler, Hannah Maria Conant Tracy. "Address to the Convention of the American Woman Suffrage Association, New York, May 1870." In Stanton, E. History of Woman Suffrage, 2, 773-4.

________. "Enlightened Motherhood." In Association for the Advancement of Women. Congress of Women, 1st. Papers, pp. 36-9.

________. "Remarks at the 4th Annual Meeting of the American Woman Suffrage Association, 1872." In Stanton, E. History of Woman Suffrage, 2, 823.

________. "Reply to the Paper of Catherine E. Beecher, at the American Woman Suffrage Association Convention, New York, May 1870." In Stanton, E. History of Woman Suffrage, 2, 788-90.

________. "Speech at the National Convention at Cincinnati, Ohio, October 1855." In Stanton, E. History of Woman Suffrage, 1, 164-5.

Czarnecki, Dorothy. "Statement." In U.S. Congress. House. Committee on Education and Labor. Subcommittee on Employment Opportunities. Legislation to Prohibit Sex Discrimination on the Basis of Pregnancy, pt. 2, 63-66.

________. "Statement." In U.S. Congress. Senate. Committee on the Judiciary. Subcommittee on Constitutional Amendments. Abortion, pt. 2, 312-5.

Dahm, Margaret M. "Testimony on Sex Discrimination in Unemployment Insurance, Veterans Programs, and Public Assistance." In U.S. Congress. Joint Economic Committee. Economic Problems of Women, pt. 2, 341-5.

Daiche, Louise. "Blackwell's Island Hospitals." In National Conference of Charities and Correction. Proceedings (1895), pp. 267-9.

Dall, Caroline Wells Healey. "Address at the New England Convention, May 1859." In Stanton, E. History of Woman Suffrage, 2, 265-70.

________. "Woman's Right to Labor; Or, Low Wages and Hard Work." In Dall, Caroline. Three Lectures Delivered in Boston, November, 1859. (Boston: Walter, Wise and Company, 1860), 184 p.

Danaraj, Shanta. "Son Preference in Taiwan: Verbal Preference and Demographic Behavior." In McGuigan, D. New Research on Women at the University of Michigan, pp. 136-7.

D'Angelo, Antonia. "Statement." In U.S. Congress. Senate. Committee on Labor and Public Welfare. Subcommittee on Alcoholism and Narcotics. Alcohol Abuse Among Women, pp. 9-13.

Daniel, Annie Sturgis. "Testimony on Housing and Tenement Homework." In U.S. Congress. House. Committee on Manufactures on the Sweating System. Report, 52nd Cong., 2nd sess., no. 2309. (January 20, 1893), pp. 181 ff.

Daniels, Katharine A. Holliday. "Consumers' Interests in the National Recovery Act." In International Congress of Women, Chicago, 1933. Our Common Cause, Civilization, pp. 472-5.

D'Arcambal, Agnes L. "How Can We Aid?" In World's Congress of Representation Women, Chicago, 1893. Congress of Women, pp. 148-51.

________. "An Ideal Home for Discharged Prisoners." In National Conference of Charities and Correction. Proceedings (1894), pp. 326-9.

D'Arusmont, Frances Wright see Wright, Frances

Darwin, Mary. "Woman's Right to Serve Her Country." In Noun, L. Strong-Minded Women, pp. 29-31.

D'Aulaire, Ingri. "Acceptance Paper (1940). Working Together on Books for Children." In Miller, B. Caldecott Medal Books: 1938-57, pp. 45-9.

Davidson, Olivia A. "How Shall We Make the Women of Our Race Stronger?" In Washington, B. Papers, 2: 298-305.

Davies, Elspeth. "Learning America's Meaning." In New York Herald Tribune. Report of the 9th Annual Forum on Current Problems, pp. 123-6.

Davies, Margery. "Woman's Place Is at the Typewriter: The Feminization of the Clerical Labor Force." In Conference on Labor Market Segmentation, Harvard University, 1973. Labor Market Segmentation, pp. 279-96.

Davis, Angela Yvonne. "Statement to the Court." In Davis, A. If They Come in the Morning, pp. 209-10.

Davis, Bette Ruth Elizabeth. "Statement." In U.S. Congress. House. Committee on Education and Labor. Subcommittee on Labor. Equal Pay for Equal Work, pt. 2, 238-41.

Davis, D. Elizabeth. "The Return of the Serviceman to His Family and Community: As seen in a Military Hospital at the Point of Discharge." In National Conference of Social Work. Proceedings (1945), pp. 93-103.

Davis, Isabella Charles. "The Kings' Daughters." In National Council of Women of the U.S., Washington, 1891. Transactions, pp. 331-4.

Davis, Katharine Bement. "Civic Efforts of Social Settlements." In National Conference of Charities and Correction. Proceedings (1896), pp. 131-7.

________. "Discussion of Social Research in Public Institutions." In National Conference of Charities and Correction. Proceedings (1916), pp. 386-7.

________. "Equal Moral Standards." In National Council of Woman. Proceedings of the 14th Convention (1928), pp. 62-4.

________. "How the Public May Help." In National Conference of Social Work. Proceedings (1918), pp. 673-4.

________. "Introductory Remarks on Defective Delinquents." In National Conference of Charities and Correction. Proceedings (1916), pp. 508-10.

________. "Outdoor Work for Women Prisoners." In National Conference of Charities and Correction. Proceedings (1909), pp. 289-94.

________. "Report of the Committee (On Law Breakers): The Reformary Method." In National Conference of Charities and Correction. Proceedings (1910), pp. 27-37.

Davis, Mary. "Public Testimony." In New York (City). Commission on Human Rights. Women's Role in Contemporary Society, pp. 298-300.

Davis, Mary Dabney. "Education--New Current." In International Congress of Women, Chicago, 1933. Our Common Cause, Civilization, pp. 717-22.

Davis, Natalie Aemon. "City Women and Religious Change in Sixteenth-Century France." In McGuigan, D. A Sampler of Women's Studies, pp. 17-45.

Davis, Paulina Kellogg Wright. "Appeal from Man's Injustice." In Tanner, L. Voices from Women's Liberation, pp. 56-7.

________. "Comments at the Syracuse National Convention, September 1852." In Stanton, E. History of Woman Suffrage, 1, 533-5.

________. "The History of the Woman's Rights Movement, Read in the Meeting Held in Apollo Hall, New York, October 21, 1870." In Davis, P. A History of the National Woman's Rights Movement, pp. 6-31.

________. "The President's Address." In Papachristou, J. Women Together, pp. 31-2.

________. "President's Address at the 20th Anniversary Convention, New York, October 1870." In Stanton, E. History of Woman Suffrage, 2, 428-36.

________. "President's Address at the Worcester Convention, October 1850." In Stanton, E. History of Woman Suffrage, 1, 222-3. (Same as "President's Address").

Davison, Eloise. "Racing with Science." In New York Herald Tribune. Report of the 6th Annual Forum on Current Problems, pp. 23-5.

Dawley, Almena. "Coordination of Effort in Mental Hygiene in the Community." In National Conference of Social Work. Proceedings (1929), pp. 413-21.

________. "The Essential Similarities in All Fields of Case Work." In National Conference of Social Work. Proceedings (1928), pp. 353-60.

________. "Professional Skills Requisite to a Good Intake Service." In National Conference of Social Work. Proceedings (1937), pp. 255-65.

Day, Florence. "Social Case Work and Social Adjustment." In National Conference of Social Work. Proceedings (1936), pp. 203-11.

Dean, Vera Micheles. "After Victory--What?" In National Conference of Social Work. Proceedings (1942), pp. 66-78.

________. "The Implications of the Peace." In National Conference of Social Work. Proceedings (1945), pp. 17-25.

________. "Implications of the European Situation for the United States." In National Conference of Social Work. Proceedings (1940), pp. 50-60.

________. "The United States and the Communist Threat." In Angeles, P. Challenge to American Youth, pp. 139-44.

Deane, Alice W. 'Women in Banking." In International Congress of Women, Toronto, 1909. Report, 2, 349-50.

De Angeli, Marguerite. "Acceptance Paper--Newbery Medal 1950." In Miller, B. Newbery Medal Books: 1922-1955, pp. 342-52.

Dearborn, Jane B. "The Prevention of Nervous Strain by Home and School Training." In Association for the Advancement of Women. "Truth, Justice and Honor," pp. 92-100.

Deardorff, Neva Ruth. "Areas of Responsibility of Voluntary Social Work During Period of Changing Local and National Governmental Programs." In National Conference of Social Work. Proceedings (1936), pp. 312-23.

________. "Fact Finding and Research as a Basis of Program Making in Social Work." In National Conference of Social Work. Proceedings (1928), pp. 415-24.

________. "Joint Financing of Private Social Work: Enter New York." In National Conference of Social Work. Proceedings (1939), pp. 530-40.

________. "Next Steps in Job Analysis (Pugsley Award)." In National Conference of Social Work. Proceedings (1933), pp. 169-30.

________. "The Objectives of the Professional Organization." In National Conference of Social Work. Proceedings (1925), pp. 636-43.

________. "Philadelphia as a Provider for Dependent Children." In National Conference of Social Work. Proceedings (1925), pp. 525-37.

________. "The School's Responsibility for the Leisure Time of the Child: In Relation to the Services of the School." In National Conference of Social Work. Proceedings (1922), pp. 109-14.

________. "Sociological Research Studies--What Are the Values for the Social Worker of the More Recent Sociological Type of Community Study?" In National Conference of Social Work. Proceedings (1930), pp. 408-19.

Decker, Sarah S. Platt. "Report of the President." In General Federation of Women's Clubs. Biennial Convention, 9 (1908), 66-75.

________. "Response to Addresses of Welcome." General Federation of Women's Clubs. Biennial Convention, 9 (1908), 26-9.

De Crow, Karen. "Address to the 1974 NOW National Conference." Do It Now, 7 (October, 1974), 5.

________. "Keynote Address at 1975 NOW National Conference." Do It Now, 9 (March, 1976), 10-11.

De Fazio, Marjorie. "Public Statement." In New York (City). Commission on Human Rights. Women's Role in Contemporary Society, pp. 726-8.

De Graffenried, Mary Clare. "Testimony on Work as a Labor Department Investigator." In U.S. Industrial Commission on the Relations and Conditions of Capital and Labor. Report (1901), pp. 218-33.

Deinhardt, Barbara. "Mother of Men?" In Furniss, W. Women in Higher Education, pp. 66-9.

De Long, Ethel. "The School as a Community Center." In National Conference of Charities and Correction. Proceedings (1916), pp. 608-14.

Denich, Bette S. "Sex and Power in the Balkans." In Rosaldo, M. Woman, Culture, and Society, pp. 243-62.

Denison, Dimies T.S. "The Long Path." In General Federation of Women's Clubs. Biennial Convention, 9 (1908), 29-35.

________. "Report of Foreign Correspondent." In General Federation of Women's Clubs. Biennial Convention, 16 (1922), 103-5.

Denman, Mary T. "Statement." In U.S. Congress. Senate. Committee on the Judiciary. Subcommittee on Constitutional Amendments. Equal Rights for Men and Women (1938), 114-5.

Dennett, Joann Temple. "Federal Women's Program." Washington, U.S. National Oceanic and Atmospheric Administration, 1973, 27 p.

Dennett, Mary Ware. "Report of the Corresponding Secretary to the National American Woman Suffrage Association Convention of 1913." In Stanton, E. History of Woman Suffrage, 5, 366-8.

Dent, Mary. "Statement." In U.S. Congress. House. Committee on the Judiciary. Equal Rights Amendment to the Constitution (1932), p. 31.

Derian, Patricia M. "Indochinese Refugees." Department of State Bulletin, 78 (March, 1978), pp. 33-5.

DeSarem, Carol. "Statement." In U.S. Congress. Joint Economic Committee. Economic Problems of Women, pt. 4, 619-23.

Detzer, Dorothy. "Vested Interest in War." In International Congress of Women, Chicago, 1933. Our Common Cause, Civilization, pp. 695-700.

Devall, Sarah W. "The Results of the Employment of a Police Matron in the City of Portland, Maine." In Conference of Charities and Correction. Proceedings (1881), pp. 309-17.

DeVore, Ophelia. "Public Testimony." In New York (City). Commission on Human Rights. Women's Role in Contemporary Society, pp. 156-8.

Dewey, Mary H. "The Scope of Day Nursery Work." In National Conference of Charities and Correction. Proceedings (1897), pp. 105-7.

Dexter, Elizabeth H. "Has Case Work a Place in the Administration of Public Relief?" In National Conference of Social Work. Proceedings (1935), pp. 155-65.

_______. "Mental Hygiene in Our Schools: Attitudes of Teachers Toward Problem Behavior." In National Conference of Social Work. Proceedings (1929), pp. 443-51.

_______. "New Concepts and Old People." In National Conference of Social Work. Proceedings (1939), pp. 381-9.

_______. "The Social Case Worker's Attitudes and Problems as They Affect Her Work." In National Conference of Social Work. Proceedings (1926), pp. 436-42.

Deyo, Amanda. "Woman's War for Peace." In World's Congress of Representative Women, Chicago, 1893. A Historical Resume, pp. 733-6.

Diamond, Norma. "Toward an Anthropology of Women." In McGuigan, D. New Research on Women at the University of Michigan, pp. 4-6.

Diaz, Abby Morton. "Address of Mrs. Abby M. Diaz." In Danvers Historical Society, Danvers, Mass. Old Anti-Slavery Days, pp. 42-4.

_______. "Work of Women's Educational and Industrial Union." In International Council of Women, 1888. Report, pp. 198-200.

Dibble, Martha Cleveland. "The Nervous American." In World's Congress of Representative Women, Chicago, 1893. Congress of Women, pp. 704-7.

Dibert, Florence. "Building Junior Membership." In General Federation of Women's Clubs. Biennial Convention, 16 (1922), pp. 15-7.

Di Brazza Savorgnan, Cora Ann Slocomb. "The Italian Woman in the Country." In World's Congress of Representative Women, Chicago, 1893. Congress of Women, pp. 697-703.

Dickason, Gladys. "Gains and Goals of Women Workers." In U.S. Women's Bureau. The American Woman--Her Changing Role, pp. 19-27.

Dickey, Gertrude M. "The Social Service Exchange." In National Conference of Social Work. Proceedings (1918), pp. 319-21.

Dickinson, Anna Elizabeth. "Address to the Chicago Woman Suffrage Convention, 1869." In Stanton, E. History of Woman Suffrage, 3, 567-9.

Dickinson, Lucy Jennings. "The Citizen's Responsibility; A Panel Discussion." In New York Herald Tribune. Report of the 18th Annual Forum on Current Problems, pp. 152-3.

________. "Greetings from the General Federation of Women's Clubs." In New York Herald Tribune. Report of the 8th Annual Forum on Current Problems, pp. 24-5.

________. "Leadership Through Young Minds." In New York Herald Tribune. Report of the 13th Annual Forum on Current Problems, pp. 67-8.

________. "What I Saw in the U.S.S.R." In New York Herald Tribune, Report of the 15th Annual Forum on Current Problems, pp. 70-4.

Dickinson, Mary Lowe. "The King's Daughters." In National Council of Women of the U.S., Washington, 1891. Transactions, pp. 330-1.

________. "The Next Thing in Education." In World's Congress of Representative Women, Chicago, 1893. Congress of Women, pp. 637-42.

________. "Organization among Women as an Instrument in Promoting Religion." In World's Congress of Representative Women, Chicago, 1893. A Historical Resume, pp. 292-7.

________. "Response to Address of Welcome." In National Congress of Mothers. Work and Words, pp. 11-21.

Dietrick, Ellen Battelle. "The Best Methods of Interesting Women in Suffrage. Address to the National American Woman Suffrage Association Convention of 1893." In Stanton, E. History of Woman Suffrage, 4, 208-9.

Dietzel, Laura. "Activity in the Case-Work Relationship." In National Conference of Social Work. Proceedings (1933), pp. 288-90.

Dillaya, Blanche. "Etching." In World's Congress of Representative Women, Chicago, 1893. Congress of Women, pp. 643-4.

Dingman, Helen. "Enriching the Rural Community." In International Congress of Women, Chicago, 1933. Our Common Cause, Civilization, pp. 873-9.

________. "Chairman's Introduction. Security Against Disease." In International Congress of Women, Chicago, 1933. Our Common Cause, Civilization, pp. 587-8.

Dinwiddie, Elizabeth M. "Illustrations from the Annals of the Gulf Division--American Red Cross." In National Conference of Social Work. Proceedings (1920), pp. 288-95.

Dock, Lavinia. "Statement." In U.S. Congress. Senate. Committee on the Judiciary. Subcommittee on Constitutional Amendments. Equal Rights Amendment (1929), p. 27.

Dock, Mira L. "Forestry and Village Improvement." In International Congress of Women, London, 1899, 4, 158-61.

Dodd, Anna A. "Our Spanish-American Neighbors." In World's Congress of Representative Women, Chicago, 1893. Congress of Women, pp. 754-9.

Dodge, Josephine Marshall Jewell. "Neighborhood Work and Day Nurseries." In National Conference of Charities and Correction. Proceedings (1912), pp. 113-8.

Dodson, Martha E. "Publicity." In General Federation of Women's Clubs. Biennial Convention, 16 (1922), 137-9.

Doggett, Kate Newell. "Art for Women." In Association for the Advancement of Women. Congress of Women, 3rd. Papers, pp. 97-104.

Dolan, Elizabeth J. "Statement." In U.S. Congress. Senate. Committee on the Judiciary. Subcommittee on Constitutional Amendments. Equal Rights for Men and Women (1938), p. 37.

Donahoe, Marie L. "Next Steps in State Hospital Social Service." In National Conference of Social Work. Proceedings (1924), pp. 475-9.

Donahue, A. Madorah. "The Case of an Unmarried Mother Who Has Cared for Her Child, and Succeeded." In National Conference of Social Work. Proceedings (1917), pp. 282-4.

________. "A Case of Illegitimacy When Mother and Baby Have Been Dealt with Separately." In National Conference of Charities and Correction. Proceedings (1915), pp. 121-6.

Donlon, Mary H. "Get into Politics up to Your Ears. Women's Political Power Is Not Being Used Effectively." Vital Speeches, 16 (February 15, 1950), 282-4.

________. "Greetings from the Executive Committee." In Conference on Women in the Defense Decade, New York, 1951. Women in the Defense Decade, pp. 9-11.

________. "Law and Government. The Underlying Concept or Philosophy of Our Law." Vital Speeches, 24 (August 1, 1958), 627-30.

________. "The Scope of the Problem." In Conference of the Present Status and Prospective Trends of Research on the Education of Women, Rye, New York, 1957. The Education of Women, pp. 5-14.

Donohue, Mary E. "Preventive Medicine." In World's Congress of Representative Women, Chicago, 1893. Congress of Women, pp. 727-32.

Douglas, Elaine. "Youth Plans for a Civilized World: Forum on the College Generation." In International Congress of Women, Chicago, 1933. Our Common Cause, Civilization, p. 186.

Douglas, Helen Gahagan. "The Campaign Issue." In New York Herald Tribune. Report of the 13th Annual Forum on Current Problems, pp. 210-4.

________. "Freedom Cannot Be Inherited. We Are the Conservative Party." Vital Speeches, 10 (August 1, 1944), 632-4.

Douglass, Jean Loughborough. "The Young Woman of the South." In World's Congress of Representative Women, Chicago, 1893. Congress of Women, pp. 733-6.

Douty, Agnes M. "Address on Job Opportunities in the Labor Market." Washington, U.S. Women's Bureau, 1965.

________. "Conference Summary." In Conference on Woman's Destiny--Choice or Chance? Report, pp. 62-7.

Douvan, Elizabeth M. "Adolescent Girls: Their Attitude Toward Education." In Conference on the Present Status and Prospective Trends of Research on the Education of Women, Rye, N.Y., 1957. The Education of Women, pp. 23-9.

Dowding, Nancy. "Statement." In U.S. Congress. House. Committee on Education and Labor. Special Subcommittee on Education. Discrimination Against Women, pp. 153-8.

Downey, Mary E. "Statement." In U.S. Congress. Senate. Committee on the Judiciary. Subcommittee on Constitutional Amendments. Equal Rights Amendment (1945), p. 34.

Doyle, Ann. "Venereal Disease and Clinics for Civilians Near Military Camps." In National Conference of Social Work. Proceedings (1918), pp. 192-4.

Drake, Julia C. "Youth Plans for a Civilized World: Forum on the College Generation." In International Congress of Women, Chicago, 1933. Our Common Cause, Civilization, pp. 196-7.

Dresden, Marie. "The Case Worker as an Interpreter of Case Work." In National Conference of Social Work. Proceedings (1927), pp. 691-5.

Drinkwater, Barbara. "Maximal Oxygen Uptake of Females." In Harris, D. Women and Sport, pp. 375-86.

DuBois, Mary A. "Thirty Years Experience in Nursery and Child Hospital Work." In National Conference of Charities and Correction. Proceedings (1885), pp. 181-91.

Duffy, Mary. "Address Before State Suffrage Hearing, Albany, N.Y., February 1907." In Blatch, H. Challenging Years, pp. 95-6.

________. "Mary Duffy Speaks Before the Legislature." In Millstein, B. We, The American Women, pp. 187-8. (Same as "Address Before State Suffrage Hearing.")

Dulles, Eleanor Lansing. "The Challenge to the Western Policy for Germany. The Threat to Berlin." Vital Speeches, 15 (March 15, 1959), 324-8.

________. "Education, Communist Style, American Style. The Students of Today Are the Leaders of Tomorrow." Vital Speeches, 23 (July 15, 1957), 590-3.

Du Mars, Miriam Richardson. "No Rocking Chair Age. A Challenge to American Women of Today." Vital Speeches, 17 (March 15, 1951), 341-3.

Dunbar, Sadie Orr. "The Importance of Keeping Informed." In New York Herald Tribune. Report of the 9th Annual Forum on Current Problems, pp. 221-2.

Duncanson, Lillian Davis. "One Phase of Woman's Work for the Municipality." In World's Congress of Representative Women, Chicago, 1893. A Historical Resume, pp. 457-9.

Duniway, Abigail Scott. "Address to the National American Woman Suffrage Association Convention of 1895." In Stanton, E. History of Woman Suffrage, 4, 249.

________. "Address to the State Constitutional Convention, Boise, Idaho, July 16, 1889." In Duniway, A. Path Breaking, pp. 133-41.

________. "Ballots and Bullets." In Duniway, A. Path Breaking, pp. 189-200.

________. "How to Win the Ballot." In Duniway, A. Path Breaking, pp. 156-68.

________. "The Pacific Northwest." In World's Congress of Representative Women, Chicago, 1893. Congress of Women, pp. 90-6.

________. "Success in Sight." In Duniway, A. Path Breaking, pp. 169-78.

________. "Women in Oregon History." In Duniway, A. Path Breaking, pp. 144-53.

Dunlap, Flora. "The Social Result of Legislation Affecting Women Workers." In National Conference of Social Work. Proceedings (1927), pp. 309-12.

Dunlap, Mary J. "Progress in the Care of the Feeble-minded and Epileptics." In National Conference of Charities and Correction. Proceedings (1899), pp. 255-9.

Dunn, Ethel. "Russian Rural Women." In Atkinson, D. Women in Russia, pp. 167-87.

Dunne, Irene. "Freedom Is Responsibility. The Family's Responsibility to the Community." Vital Speeches, 25 (February 15, 1959), 283-5.

Duryea, Florence Spencer. "Near East Relief." In General Federation of Women's Clubs. Biennial Convention, 16 (1922), 158-60.

Dutcher, Elizabeth. "Possibilities of Home Supervision of Moron Women." In National Conference of Social Work. Proceedings (1921), pp. 272-6.

Dworkin, Andrea. "Feminism, Art and My Mother Sylvia." In Dworkin, A. Our Blood, pp. 1-9.

________. "Lesbian Pride." In Dworkin, A. Our Blood, pp. 73-5.

________. "Our Blood: The Slavery of Women in Amerika." In Dworkin, A. Our Blood, pp. 76-95.

________. "The Rape Atrocity and the Boy Next Door." In Dworkin, A. Our Blood, pp. 22-49.

________. "Redefining Nonviolence." In Dworkin, A. Our Blood, pp. 66-72.

________. "Remembering the Witches." In Dworkin, A. Our Blood, pp. 15-21.

________. "Renouncing Sexual Equality." In Dworkin, A. Our Blood, pp. 10-14.

________. "The Root Cause." In Dworkin, A. Our Blood, pp. 96-111.

________. "The Sexual Politics of Fear and Courage." In Dworkin, A. Our Blood, pp. 50-65.

Dwyer, Florence P. "Statement." In U.S. Congress. House. Committee on Education and Labor. Select Subcommittee on Labor. Equal Pay for Equal Work. pp. 132-4.

________. "Statement." In U.S. Congress. Senate. Committee on the Judiciary. Subcommittee on Constitutional Amendments. Women and the "Equal Rights" Amendment, pp. 20-3.

Dye, Nancy Schrom. "Creating a Feminist Alliance: Sisterhood and Class Conflict in the New York Women's Trade Union League, 1903-1914." In Canton, M. Class, Sex, and the Woman Worker, pp. 225-45.

Eagle, Mary Kavanaugh. "Unveiling of the Portrait." In World's Congress of Representative Women, Chicago, 1893. Congress of Women, pp. 816-7.

Earhart, Amelia. "New Wings for Mercury." In New York Herald Tribune. Report of the 4th Annual Women's Conference on Current Problems, pp. 132-5.

Early, Sarah J. "The Organized Efforts of the Colored Women of the South to Improve Their Condition." In World's Congress of Representative Women, Chicago, 1893. A Historical Resume, pp. 718-24.

Easley, Linda. "Community Organizations and Child-care Arrangements." In Hammond, N. Women and Children in Contemporary Society, pp. 90-4.

East, Catherine. "The Current Status of the Employment of Women." In Katzell, M. Women in the Work Force, pp. 7-14.

________. "What Do Women Want?" Congressional Record, 91st Cong., 2nd sess., 1970, 166, pt. 9, 12016-8.

Eastman, Annis Ford Stehley. "The Home and Its Foundations." In World's Congress of Representative Women, Chicago, 1893. Congress of Women, pp. 612-5.

Eastman, Crystal. "Address at a Hearing of the House Judiciary Committee, March 3, 1914." In Stanton, E. History of Woman Suffrage, 5, 429-30.

________. "Statement to the First Feminist Congress, 1919." In Martin, W. The American Sisterhood, pp. 110-13.

________. "Work Accidents and Employer's Liability." In National Conference of Charities and Correction. Proceedings (1910), pp. 414-24.

Eastman, Elizabeth. "Statement." In U.S. Congress. Senate. Committee on the Judiciary. Subcommittee on Constitutional Amendments. Equal Rights for Men and Women (1938), p. 77.

Eastman, Linda Anne. "Presidential Address at Washington Conference." American Library Association Bulletin, 23 (1929), 231-6. Also Libraries, 34 (1929), 247-50.

Eastman, Mary F. "Address on Organizations." In International Council of Women, 1888. Report, pp. 195-8.

________. "Remarks." In National Council of Women of the U.S., Washington, 1891. Transactions, pp. 212-4.

________. "Speech at the 7th Annual Meeting of the American Woman Suffrage Association, 1875." In Stanton, E. History of Woman Suffrage, 2, 845.

________. "Speech at the 9th Annual Meeting of the American Woman Suffrage Association, 1878." In Stanton, E. History of Woman Suffrage, 2, 854.

________. "Woman in Education." In Association for the Advancement of Women. Congress of Women, 3rd. Papers, pp. 18-35.

________. "Woman's Place in Government." In Association for the Advancement of Women. Congress of Women, 1st. Papers, p. 121+.

Eastman, Mehitable. "Address to a Meeting of the Manchester Industrial Reform Association (September 1846)." In Vogel, L. "Hearts to Feel and Tongues to Speak: New England Mill Women in the Early Nineteenth Century." Cantor, M. Class, Sex, and the Woman Worker, pp. 70-1.

Eckstein, Anna B. "A World Petition to the Third Hague Conference." In American Peace Congress, 2nd, Chicago, 1909. Proceedings, pp. 87-91.

Eddy, Mary Baker. "Address Before the Alumni of the Massachusetts Metaphysical College, 1895." In Eddy, M. Miscellaneous Writings, pp. 110-6.

________. "Address Before the Christian Scientist Association of the Massachusetts Metaphysical College in 1893. Subject: Obedience." In Eddy, M. Miscellaneous Writings, pp. 116-20.

________. "Address on the Fourth of July at Pleasant View, Concord, N.H., Before 2,500 Members of the Mother Church, 1897." In Eddy, M. Miscellaneous Writings, pp. 251-3.

________. "Bible Lessons." In Eddy, M. Miscellaneous Writings, pp. 180-202.

________. "Christian Healing; A Sermon Delivered at Boston." In Eddy, M. Retrospection and Introspection, pp. 101-20.

________. "Christian Science in Tremont Temple." In Eddy, M. Miscellaneous Writings, pp. 95-8.

________. "Communion Address, January, 1896." In Eddy, M. Miscellaneous Writings, pp. 120-5.

________. "A Christmas Sermon; Delivered in Chickering Hall, Boston, Mass., On the Sunday Before Christmas, 1888. Subject: The Corporeal and Incorporeal Savior." In Eddy, M. Miscellaneous Writings, pp. 161-8.

________. "Message to the Annual Meeting of the Mother Church, Boston, 1896." In Eddy, M. Miscellaneous Writings, pp. 125-8.

________. "Science and the Senses: Substance of My Address at the National Convention in Chicago, June 13, 1888." In Eddy, M. Miscellaneous Writings, pp. 98-106.

________. "Sunday Services on July Fourth: Extempore Remarks." In Eddy, M. Miscellaneous Writings, pp. 176-7.

Edholm, Mary G. Charlton. "The Traffic in Girls and Florence Crittenton Missions." In National Purity Congress, 1st, Baltimore, 1895. National Purity Congress, pp. 150-7.

Edisen, Adele E. Uskali. "Women in Science." In Conference of Professional and Academic Women. Sixteen Reports on the Status of Women in the Professions, 6 p.

Edison, Mina Miller. "Address of Welcome." In General Federation of Women's Clubs. Biennial Convention, 16 (1922), pp. 29-31.

Edwards, Alice L. "Statement." In U.S. Congress. House. Committee on the Judiciary. Equal Rights Amendment to the Constitution (1932), pp. 34-5.

Edwards, Amanda M. "Agriculture." In World's Congress of Representative Women, Chicago, 1893. Congress of Women, pp. 760-2.

Edwards, India. "The Citizen's Responsibility; A Panel Discussion." In New York Herald Tribune. Report of the 18th Annual Forum on Current Problems, pp. 140-2, 180.

Efron, Edith. "The Free Mind and the Free Market." Vital Speeches, 40 (June 15, 1974), 522-7.

Eggleston, Mary L. "Relation of Case-Work Staffs to Interpretation, Officials, Governing Boards, Volunteers, and the Public." In National Conference of Social Work. Proceedings (1938), pp. 233-41.

Ehrenreich, Barbara. "The Status of Women as Health Care Providers in the United States." In International Conference on Women in Health. Proceedings, pp. 7-13.

Eicher, Lydia S. "Undifferentiated Case Work, the Surest Approach to Rural Social Work: Its Challenge and Its Opportunity: From the Public Department of Welfare." In National Conference of Social Work. Proceedings (1927), pp. 155-8.

Eisenbud, Ruth-Jean. "Female Homosexuality: A Sweet Enfranchisement." In Goldman, G. Modern Women, pp. 247-64.

Eldridge, Ronnie. "Statement." In National League of Cities. Women in Municipal Government, pp. 5-11.

Eliel, Harriet F. "The California Plan for the State Certification of Social Workers." In National Conference of Social Work. Proceedings (1929), pp. 596-604.

Eliot, Martha M. "Health of Our Negro Children." In Washington, U.S. Children's Bureau, 1944. 3 p.

________. "The Work of the Interdepartmental Committee to Coordinate Health and Welfare Activities." In National Conference of Social Work. Proceedings (1939), pp. 101-10.

Ellickson, Katherine. "Statement." In U.S. Congress. Senate. Committee on the Judiciary. Equal Rights 1970, pp. 103-7.

Elliot, Harriet. "Women's Part in Defense Plans." In New York Herald Tribune. Report on the 10th Annual Forum on Current Problems, pp. 19-24.

Elliott, Carolyn M. "Theories of Development: An Assessment." In Conference on Women and Development. 'Women and National Development: The Complexities of Change." Signs, 3 (Autumn 1977), 1-8.

Elliott, Grace Loucks. "Importance of Maturity and a Social Philosophy for Group Leaders and Supervisors." In National Conference of Social Work. Proceedings (1937), pp. 266-75.

Ellis, Mabel B. "How Can Social Information Be Obtained and Made Available for Publicity Purposes?" In National Conference of Social Work. Proceedings (1935), pp. 476-86.

Embry, Marjory. "The Role of the Private Agency: Children's Institutions and Agencies." In National Conference of Social Work. Proceedings (1938), pp. 187-95.

Enderie, Dorothy. "The Milwaukee Recreation System." In National Conference of Social Work. Proceedings (1921), pp. 346-8.

Engel, Dorothy. "Supervision as One Method of Staff Development:

In the Urban Agency." In National Conference of Social Work. Proceedings (1939), pp. 284-94.

Engel, Madeline H. "The Widow." In Bier, W. Woman in Modern Life, pp. 158-82.

Engle, Lavinia. "Unemployment Insurance." In International Congress of Women, Chicago, 1933. Our Common Cause, Civilization, pp. 332-8.

________. "The Voter's Part." In International Congress of Women, Chicago, 1933. Our Common Cause, Civilization, pp. 575-7.

Engle, Randy. "Statement." In U.S. Congress. Senate. Committee on the Judiciary. Subcommittee on Constitutional Amendments. Abortion, pt. 3, 20-1.

Enright, Elizabeth. "Acceptance Paper--Newbery Medal 1939." In Miller, B. Newbery Medal Books, 1922-1955, pp. 172-5.

Epstein, Cynthia Fuchs. "Closing Remarks to the Conference of Professional and Academic Women." In Conference of Professional and Academic Women. Sixteen Reports on the Status of Women in the Professions, 1 p.

________. "Institutional Barriers: What Keeps Women Out of the Executive Suite?" In Gordon, F. Bringing Women into Management, pp. 7-21.

________. "Public Testimony." In New York (City). Commission on Human Rights. Women's Role in Contemporary Society, pp. 424-9.

________. "Success Motivation and Social Structure; Comments on Women and Achievement." In Epstein, L. Women in the Professions, pp. 1-13.

________. "Testimony." In U.S. Congress. Joint Economic Committee. Economic Problems of Women, pt. 4, pp. 592-4.

Estes, Barbara. "The Mental Hospital as a Teaching Center." In National Conference of Social Work. Proceedings (1939), pp. 409-14.

Estes, Eleanor. "Acceptance Paper--Newbery Medal 1952." In Miller, B. Newbery Medal Books, 1922-1955, pp. 379-87.

Estrada, Celia. "Uncontained, Undefined, Unafraid." Do It NOW, 9 (March 1976), 13.

Etheridge, Florence. "Trade Unions in Federal Service." In National Conference of Social Work. Proceedings (1919), pp. 447-52.

Ets, Marie Hall. "Caldecott Award Acceptance--1960." In Kingman, L. Newbery and Caldecott Medal Books, 1966-1975, pp. 209-11.

Evans, Elizabeth Glendower. "Scientific Charity." In National Conference of Charities and Correction. Proceedings (1889), pp. 24-35.

________. "What Do You Know of Children after They Leave Your Institution? Do You Supervise Them?" In National Conference of Charities and Correction. Proceedings (1907), pp. 274-8.

Evans, Shirley. "Public Testimony." In New York (City). Commission on Human Rights. Women's Role in Contemporary Society, pp. 305-9, 523-5.

Everett, Edith M. "Case Work in School Counseling." In National Conference of Social Work. Proceedings (1924), pp. 314-8.

Everett, Gladys. "Civil and Political Rights--Where Are We Now?" In Conference on Woman's Destiny--Choice or Chance? Report, pp. 23-6.

Everett, Martha A. "School Suffrage in Massachusetts." In International Council of Women, 1888. Report, pp. 309-11.

Faatz, Anita J. "Interpretation in the Public Agency." In National Conference of Social Work. Proceedings (1941), pp. 685-95.

Fahy, Ellen T. "Innovations in the Utilization of Nurses, Allied Health and Support Personnel. Innovative Functions of Women Health Workers." In International Conference of Women in Health. Proceedings, pp. 95-7.

Fairbank, Margaret E. "Habits of Thrift." In National Conference of Charities and Correction. Proceedings (1897), pp. 138-9.

________. "Visitation of Children Placed with Families." In National Conference of Charities and Correction. Proceedings (1904), pp. 324-7.

Fairbanks, Caroline Fuller. "Some English Women of the Eighteenth Century." In World's Congress of Representative Women, Chicago, 1893. Congress of Women, pp. 503-7.

Fairbanks, Cornelia Cole. "Address on Convicts." In National Conference of Charities and Correction. Proceedings (1894), pp. 341-2.

Fairchild, Mildred. "Educational Methods in Teaching Workers." In National Conference of Social Work. Proceedings (1935), pp. 323-30.

________. "The Study of Industrial Processes as a Tool for Professional Standards and Education." In National Conference of Social Work. Proceedings (1928), pp. 577-86.

Falconer, Martha Pratt. "The Culture of Family Life Versus Reformatory Treatment." In National Conference of Charities and Correction. Proceedings (1914), pp. 108-10.

________. "Neighborhood Development in Philadelphia." In National Conference of Charities and Correction. Proceedings (1914), pp. 393-5.

________. "Reformatory Treatment of Women." In National Conference of Charities and Correction. Proceedings (1914), pp. 253-6.

________. "Report of the Committee (on Social Hygience)." In National Conference of Charities and Correction. Proceedings (1915), pp. 241-52.

________. "Work of the Girl's Department, Home of Refuge, Philadelphia." In National Conference of Charities and Correction. Proceedings (1908), pp. 391-4.

________. "Work of the Section on Reformatories and Houses of Detention." In National Conference of Social Work. Proceedings (1918), pp. 668-73.

Farians, Elizabeth. "Statement." In U.S. Congress. House. Committee on the Judiciary. Subcommittee No. 4. Equal Rights for Men and Women 1971, pp. 462-9.

________. "Statement." In U.S. Congress. Senate. Committee on the Judiciary. Equal Rights 1970, pp. 373-5.

________. "Statement." In U.S. Congress. Senate. Committee on the Judiciary. Subcommittee on Constitutional Amendments. Women and the "Equal Rights" Amendment, pp. 85-8.

Farnham, Beatrice W. "Interpretation of Social Work in the School Curriculum--How Detroit Lays the Foundation." In National Conference of Social Work. Proceedings (1933), pp. 660-6.

Farnsworth, Beatrice Bordsky. "Bolshevik Alternatives and the Soviet Family: The 1926 Marriage Law Debate." In Atkinson, D. Women in Russia, pp. 139-65.

Farra, Kathryn. "Neighborhood Councils." In National Conference of Social Work. Proceedings (1940), pp. 447-55.

Farrington, Mary Elizabeth. "The Citizen's Responsibility; A Panel Discussion." In New York Herald Tribune. Report of the 18th Annual Forum on Current Problems, pp. 156-7, 173-4.

Fasenmyer, Mary Sarah. "Brainwashed Women." In Conference on Women's Challenge to Management, Arden House, 1971. Corporate Lib, pp. 58-62.

Fasteau, Brenda Feigen. "Public Testimony." In New York (City). Commission on Human Rights. Women's Role in Contemporary Society, pp. 772-3.

________. "Statement." In U.S. Congress. Joint Economic Committee. Economic Problems of Women, pt. 4, pp. 631-4.

________. "Statement." In U.S. Congress. Senate. Committee on the Judiciary. Subcommittee on Constitutional Amendments. Women and the "Equal Rights" Amendment, pp. 41-3.

Faust, Jean. "Public Testimony." In New York (City). Commission on Human Rights. Women's Role in Contemporary Society, pp. 682-700.

________. "Statement." In U.S. Congress. Senate. Committee on the Judiciary. Equal Rights 1970, pp. 383-8.

Feder, Leah. "Changing Emphasis in Professional Education." In National Conference of Social Work. Proceedings (1938), pp. 208-21.

Fee, Elizabeth. "Science and Homosexuality." In Conference on the Universities and the Gay Experience. Proceedings, pp. 35-9.

Felsenthal, Julia I. "The Influence of the Jewish Religion in the Home." In Jewish Women's Congress. Papers, pp. 122-8.

Felton, Katharine C. "Status of Organized Charity in the West." In National Conference of Charities and Correction. Proceedings (1902), pp. 295-302.

________. "The Charities Endorsement Committee." In National Conference of Charities and Correction. Proceedings (1905), pp. 350-8.

Fenske, Virginia. "Supervision and Licensing of Institutions and Homes for Children." In National Conference of Social Work. Proceedings (1947), pp. 324-32.

Ferguson, Adda Lutz. "Statement." In U.S. Congress. House. Committee on the Judiciary. Subcommittee No. 1. Equal Rights Amendment (1948), pp. 32-4.

Fernald, Mabel R. "Practical Applications of Psychology to the Problems of a Clearing House." In National Conference of Charities and Correction. Proceedings (1916), pp. 538-46.

Fescher, Lucy B. "The Visiting Nurse as an Economic Factor." In National Conference of Charities and Correction. Proceedings (1905), pp. 263-72.

Field, Kate. "A Talk." In World's Congress of Representative Women, Chicago, 1893. Congress of Women, pp. 77-9.

Field, Martha R. "Come South, Young Woman." In World's Congress of Representative Women, Chicago, 1893. Congress of Women, pp. 776-81.

________. "Report on Woman's International Press Association." In International Council of Women, 1888. Report, pp. 181-2.

Field, Rachel. "Acceptance Paper--Newbery Medal 1930." In Miller, B. Newbery Medal Books, 1922-1955, pp. 86-8.

Field, Sara Bard. "Speech Representing a Deputation of 300 Women to President Wilson, January 9, 1917." In Irwin, I. The Story of the Woman's Party, pp. 188-9. Also in Stevens, D. Jailed for Freedom, pp. 55-6.

Fields, Annie Adams. "Constitution of a District Conference." In Conference on Charities and Correction. Proceedings (1881), pp. 124-31.

Fields, Daisy B. "Statement." In U.S. Congress. House. Committee on Education and Labor. Special Subcommittee on Education. Discrimination Against Women, pp. 138-46.

________. "Statement." In U.S. Congress. House. Committee on Government Operations. National Women's Conference, pp. 37-8.

________. "Statement." In U.S. Congress. House. Committee on the Judiciary. Subcommittee No. 4. Equal Rights for Men and Women 1971, pp. 438-50.

Fields, Judith. "Academic Freedom: Panel Discussion." In New York Herald Tribune. Report of the 20th Annual Forum on Current Problems, pp. 104-5.

Finegan, Betty. "Statement." In U.S. Congress. Senate. Committee on the Judiciary. Subcommittee on Constitutional Amendments. Women and the "Equal Rights" Amendment, pp. 89-91.

Fisher, Ada Lois Sipvel. "Equal Educational Opportunities." In New York Herald Tribune. Report of the 17th Annual Forum on Current Problems, pp. 82-6.

Fisher, Ella W. "Action Scale to Finer Womanhood. Make a Better Person of Yourself." Vital Speeches, 23 (April 15, 1957), 403-5.

Fisher, Katherine Dummer. "Solving the Conflict." In International Congress of Women, Chicago, 1933. Our Common Cause, Civilization, pp. 774-7.

________. "Speech at Dinner in Honor of Released Prisoners, 1917." In Stevens, D. Jailed for Freedom, p. 156.

Fisse, Elizabeth. "Statement." In U.S. Congress. Senate. Committee on the Judiciary. Subcommittee on Constitutional Amendments. Equal Rights for Men and Women (1938), p. 126.

Fitts, Ada M. "How to Fill the Gap Between the Special Class and the Institution." In National Conference of Charities and Correction. Proceedings (1916), pp. 292-300.

Fitzgerald, Laurine E. "Statement." In U.S. Congress. House.

Committee on Education and Labor. Special Subcommittee on Education. Discrimination Against Women, pp. 158-62.

Fitz-Simons, Louisa. "Undifferentiated Case Work, as Illustrated by the Preliminary Report of the Georgia Study of Negro Child Welfare." In National Conference of Social Work. Proceedings (1928), pp. 90-4.

FitzSimons, Ruth. "Preparation and Direction of Case-Work Personnel: The Washington Training Plan." In National Conference of Social Work. Proceedings (1938), pp. 196-207.

Flannigan, Joan. "Women in the Professions." In New York (City). Commission on Human Rights. Women's Role in Contemporary Society, pp. 358-64.

Fleischauer, Barbara. "Statement." In U.S. Congress. Senate. Committee on Labor and Public Welfare. Subcommittee on Children and Youth. White House Conference on Youth, pp. 41-2.

Fletcher, Alice Cunningham. "Allotment of Land to Indians." In National Conference of Charities and Correction. Proceedings (1887), pp. 172-83.

________. "Legal Conditions of Indian Women." In International Council of Women, 1888. Report, pp. 237-41.

________. "Our Duty to Dependent Races." In National Council of Women of the U.S., Washington, 1891. Transactions, pp. 81-6.

________. "The Preparation of the Indian for Citizenship." In National Conference of Charities and Correction. Proceedings (1892), pp. 59-66.

Fletcher, Shirley. "Testimony." In U.S. Congress. House. Select Committee on Crime. Drugs in Our Schools, pp. 531-40.

Flint, Mary A. "The Value of the Eastern Star as a Factor in Giving Women a Better Understanding of Business Affairs, and Especially Those Relating to Legislative Matters." In World's Congress of Representative Women, Chicago, 1893. A Historical Resume, pp. 500-5.

Flower, Lucy L. "The Merit System in Public Institutions." In National Conference of Charities and Correction. Proceedings (1896), pp. 388-91.

Flowers, Anne. "A Matter of Degree: Education of Women." Vital Speeches, 41 (July 15, 1975), 604-6.

Flynn, Elizabeth Gurley. "Elizabeth Gurley Flynn's Defense." In American Civil Liberties Union. The Trial of Elizabeth Gurley Flynn, 44-48, 97-104.

________. "The Truth about the Paterson Strike." In Kornbluh, J. Rebel Voices, pp. 214-26.

Foley, Alice L. "The Quality Elementary School. Problems Facing Elementary Education." Vital Speeches, 26 (November 15, 1959), 84-6.

Folsom, Marion B. "Pension Drive: Social and Economic Implications." Vital Speeches, 17 (January 1, 1950), 180-4.

Forbes, Carol. "Statement." In U.S. Congress. Senate. Committee on the Judiciary. Equal Rights 1970, pp. 379-81.

Forbes, Esther. "Acceptance Paper--Newbery Medal 1944." In Miller, B. Newbery Medal Books, 1922-1955, pp. 248-54.

Ford, Loretta C. "How to Improve the Utilization of Women in the Health Occupations in Which They Are Well Represented. A U.S. Response to the Swedish Experience." In International Conference on Women in Health. Proceedings, pp. 65-8.

Foreman, Carol Tucker. "Controversy over the Carter Administration Proposals for Welfare Reform." Congressional Digest, 57 (May, 1978), pp. 156-8.

Fosdick, Dorothy. "The World Is Our Framework." In New York Herald Tribune. Report of the 18th Annual Forum on Current Problems, pp. 215-8.

Foster, Abigail Kelley. "Address at Philadelphia Anti-slavery Meeting, 1855." In Stanton, E. History of Woman Suffrage, 1, 336-7.

________. "The Pulpit Has a Bad Influence." In Tanner, L. Voices from Women's Liberation, pp. 74-5.

________. "Remarks at the 1st Annual Meeting of the American Equal Rights Association, May 1867." In Stanton, E. History of Woman Suffrage, 2, 216.

________. "Remarks During Debate at 4th National Woman's Rights Conventions, Cleveland, Ohio, in October 1853." In Stanton, E. History of Woman Suffrage, 1, 134-6.

________. "Speech of Abby Kelley Foster." In American Anti-slavery Society. Proceedings, pp. 70-3.

Foster, Edith. "Constructive Federal-State Relationships: From the Federal Viewpoint." In National Conference of Social Work. Proceedings (1944), pp. 311-8.

________. "Is an Independent Administration of Health and Social Work Desirable?" In National Conference of Social Work. Proceedings (1925), pp. 175-9.

Foster, Judith Ellen Horton. "Non-partisan National Woman's Christian Temperance Union." In National Council of Women of the U.S., Washington, 1891. Transactions, pp. 135-41.

________. "Woman as a Political Leader." In World's Congress of Representative Women, Chicago, 1893. A Historical Resume, pp. 439-45.

_______. "Women in Politics." In International Council of Women, 1888. Report, pp. 304-6.

_______. "Women in Politics." In World's Congress of Representative Women, Chicago, 1893. Congress of Women, pp. 668-9. (Same as "Woman as a Political Leader.")

Foster, Marjorie W. "Legislation, Cooperation, and the Board." In National Conference of Social Work. Proceedings (1946), pp. 304-11.

Foster, Sybil. "Co-ordination of Institution Care of Children with Other Services in the Community." In National Conference of Social Work. Proceedings (1936), pp. 548-61.

_______. "Fees for Adoption Service." In National Conference of Social Work. Proceedings (1947), pp. 344-50.

_______. "Mental-Health Needs in Children's Institutions." In National Conference of Social Work. Proceedings (1937), pp. 549-63.

_______. "Personality Deviations and Their Relation to the Home." In National Conference of Social Work. Proceedings (1925), pp. 431-43.

Fox, Elizabeth G. "The Public Health Nursing Program of the American Red Cross." In National Conference of Social Work. Proceedings (1921), pp. 169-72.

Fox, Paula. "Newbery Award Acceptance--1974." In Kingman, L. Newbery and Caldecott Medal Books, 1966-1975, pp. 116-22.

Foxworth, Jo. "Our Creeping Idiot Savantism: Maturity Can Be Magnificent." Vital Speeches, 32 (July 15, 1966), 596-9.

Frances, Lynn. "Statement." In U.S. Congress. House. Committee on Education and Labor. Subcommittee on Equal Opportunities. Equal Opportunity for Displaced Homemakers Act, p. 32.

Francis, Vida Hunt. "The Delinquent Girl." In National Conference of Charities and Correction. Proceedings (1906), pp. 138-45.

Frank, Henrietta G. "Jewish Women of Modern Days." In Jewish Women's Congress. Papers, pp. 43-51.

Frank, Marjorie H. "Volunteers in Mental Hospitals." In National Conference of Social Work. Proceedings (1948), pp. 240-50.

Franklin, Butler. "Statement." In U.S. Congress. Senate. Committee on the Judiciary. Subcommittee on Constitutional Amendments. Women and the "Equal Rights" Amendment, pp. 136-8.

Frasca, Mary A. "Democracy in Immigrant Neighborhood Life." In National Conference of Social Work. Proceedings (1920), pp. 500-2.

Fraser, Arvonne S. "Statement." In U.S. Congress. House. Select Committee on Aging. Subcommittee on Retirement Income and Employment. Social Security Inequities Against Women, pp. 26-31.

________. "Statement." In U.S. Congress. Senate. Special Committee on Aging. Future Directions in Social Security, pt. 19, 1755-7.

________. "Women: The New Image." Vital Speeches, 37 (July 15, 1971), 599-605.

Frazar, Caroline M. "The Moral Education Society of Boston." In International Council of Women, 1888. Report, p. 272.

Frederick, Pauline. "View from the World Bridge." Vital Speeches, 31 (February 15, 1965), 265-7.

________. "What Are Your Intentions? Peace-making Requires Dedication." Vital Speeches, 28 (September 1, 1962), 689-92.

Freedman, Blanch. "Statement." In U.S. Congress. Senate. Committee on the Judiciary. Subcommittee on Constitutional Amendments. Equal Rights Amendment (1945), pp. 98-102.

Freedom, Virginia Starr. "Statement." In U.S. Congress. House. Committee on the Judiciary. Subcommittee No. 1. Equal Rights Amendment (1948), pp. 37-8.

Freeman, Frankie M. "Something Is Wrong. Civil Rights: A Source of Irritation." Vital Speeches, 36 (April 1, 1970), 364-7.

________. "Statement." In U.S. Congress. House. Committee on Education and Labor. Special Subcommittee on Education. Discrimination Against Women, pp. 222-33.

________. "Testimony." In U.S. Congress. House. Committee on Small Business. Subcommittee on Minority Enterprise and General Oversight. Women in Business, pp. 88-91.

French, Isabelle F. "Spotlight on Engineers and Scientists." In International Conference of Women Engineers and Scientists, 1st, New York, Focus for the Future, pp. I-45-6.

French-Sheldon, May. "Practical Issues of an African Experience." In Congress on Africa, Atlanta, 1895. Africa and the American Negro, pp. 95-101.

________. "Woman as an Explorer." In World's Congress of Representative Women, Chicago, 1893. A Historical Resume, pp. 736-8.

Friday, Lucy. "Work of the Probation Officer in Court." In National Conference of Charities and Corrections. Proceedings (1906), pp. 136-8.

Fried, Edrita. "The Fear of Loving." In Goldman, G. Modern Woman, pp. 43-63.

Fried, Llerena. "This I Remember." In *Essays on American Foreign Policy*. Edited by Margaret F. Morris and Sandra L. Myres. (Austin: University of Texas Press, 1974), pp. 9-21.

Friedan, Betty. "Abortion: A Woman's Civil Right." In Friedan, B. *It Changed My Life*, pp. 123-8.

______. "Address at Founder's Reception--5th Annual Conference, Los Angeles, September 1971." *NOW Acts*, 4 (Fall, 1971), 7-9.

______. "Address at NOW's 6th National Conference." *NOW Acts*, 6 (February 16, 1973), 15.

______. "Beyond the Feminine Mystique--A New Image of Woman." In Conference on Woman's Destiny--Choice or Change? *Report*, pp. 1-10.

______. "The Crisis in Women's Identity." In Friedan, B. *It Changed My Life*, pp. 62-71.

______. "The Crisis of Divorce." In Friedan, B. *It Changed My Life*, pp. 324-8.

______. "The First Year: President's Report to NOW, 1967." In Friedan, B. *It Changed My Life*, pp. 97-103.

______. "Judge Carswell and the 'Sex Plus' Doctrine." In Friedan, B. *It Changed My Life*, pp. 133-36.

______. "The Next Step: Opening Remarks to the Organizing Conference of the National Women's Political Caucus." In Friedan, B. *It Changed My Life*, pp. 170-4.

______. "Our Revolution Is Unique." In Friedan, B. *It Changed My Life*, pp. 111-3.

______. "Statement." In U.S. Congress. Senate. Committee on the Judiciary. Subcommittee on Constitutional Amendments. *Abortion*, pt. 4, 707-10.

______. "Statement." In U.S. Congress. Senate. Committee on the Judiciary. Subcommittee on Constitutional Amendments. *Women and the "Equal Rights" Amendment*, pp. 158-64.

______. "Strike Day, August 26, 1970." In Friedan, B. *It Changed My Life*, pp. 152-4.

______. "Tokenism and the Pseudo-radical Cop-out: Ideological Traps for New Feminists to Avoid." In Friedan, B. *It Changed My Life*, pp. 114-9.

______. "Women's Rights and the Revolution of Rising Expectations." In New York (City). Commission on Human Rights. *Women's Role in Contemporary Society*, pp. 74-82.

Fritz, Angela McCourt. "The Novel Women: Origins of the Feminist Literary Tradition in England and France." In McGuigan, D. *New Research on Women at the University of Michigan*, pp. 20-46.

Frohman, Paula Gail. "Statement." In U.S. Congress. House. Committee on the Judiciary. Subcommittee No. 4. *Equal Rights for Men and Women 1971*, pp. 496-506.

Frost, Winifred. "Exploiting the Employed--Discussion." In International Congress of Women, Chicago, 1933. *Our Common Cause, Civilization*, pp. 306-10.

Fruchter, Rachel. "Public Testimony." In New York (City). Commission on Human Rights. Women's Role in Contemporary Society, pp. 557-60.

Fuller, Ann L. "Liberating the Administrator's Wife." In Furniss, W. Women in Higher Education, pp. 145-52.

Fullerton, Anna M. "The Science of Nursing: A Plea." In National Conference of Charities and Correction. Proceedings (1890), pp. 130-9.

Fulmer, Harriet. "The Housing Problem, and Its Relation to Other Social Problems." In National Conference of Charities and Correction. Proceedings (1908), pp. 145-8.

________. "The Work of the Visiting or District Nurse." In National Conference of Charities and Correction. Proceedings (1902), pp. 200-12.

Funk, Antionette. "Presentation of the Shafroth-Palmer Amendment to the National American Woman Suffrage Convention of 1914." In Stanton, E. History of Woman Suffrage, 5, 416-8.

________. "Report of the Campaign Work to the National American Woman Suffrage Association Convention of 1914." In Stanton, E. History of Woman Suffrage, 5, 419-22.

________. "Report of the Congressional Committee to the National American Woman Suffrage Association Convention of 1915." In Stanton, E. History of Woman Suffrage, 5, 451-2.

Furbush, Edith M. "Summary of Present Legislation on Insanity in Various States, with Program for Meeting the Present Situation." In National Conference of Social Work. Proceedings (1918), pp. 572-83.

Furlong-Cahill, Jane. "Statement." In U.S. Congress. Senate. Committee on the Judiciary. Subcommittee on Constitutional Amendments. Abortion, pt. 3, 197-205.

Furness, Betty. "Betty Furness Speaks for Consumers." Congressional Record, 93rd Cong., 1st sess., 1973, 119, pt. 15, 19100-1.

________. "Statement." In Conference on Women in the War on Poverty, 1967. Proceedings, p. 36.

Fyan, Loleta D. "Presidential Address." ALA Bulletin, 46 (July-August, 1952), 235-7.

________. "Strength, Conviction and Unity." ALA Bulletin, 45 (September, 1951), 275-6.

Gaddess, Mary L. "The Land We Love." In World's Congress of Representative Women, Chicago, 1893. Congress of Women, pp. 221-6.

Gaffney, Fannie Humphreys. "Report of the National Council of the United States." In International Congress of Women, London, 1899, 1, 93-6.

________. "Responsibility of Women as Citizens." In International Congress of Women, London, 1899, 5, 31-7.

________. "Tribute to Susan B. Anthony at Her 80th Birthday Celebration, February 15, 1900." In Harper, I. The Life and Work of Susan B. Anthony, 3, 1181.

Gage, Frances Dana. "Address at the Woman's Rights Convention in New York, September 1853." In Stanton, E. History of Woman Suffrage, 1, 563-4.

________. "Address to the 1st Annual Meeting of the American Equal Rights Association, May 1867." In Stanton, E. History of Woman Suffrage, 2, 197-9, 200.

________. "President's Address." In Stanton, E. History of Woman Suffrage, 1, 111-3. Also in Woman's Rights Convention, Akron, Ohio, 1851. Proceedings, pp. 4-6.

________. "Second Address to the 1st Annual Meeting of the American Equal Rights Association, May 1867." In Stanton, E. History of Woman Suffrage, 2, 211-3.

________. "Speech of Mrs. Frances D. Gage." In American Anti-slavery Society. Proceedings, pp. 84-5.

________. "Third Address to the 1st Annual Meeting of the American Equal Rights Association, May 1867." In Stanton, E. History of Woman Suffrage, 2, 223-4.

Gage, Marie Mott. "Intelligent Treatment of the Body." In World's Congress of Representative Women, Chicago, 1893. Congress of Women, pp. 737-9.

Gage, Matilda Joslyn. "Address." In International Council of Women, 1888. Report, p. 347.

________. "Address at a Convention of the National American Woman Suffrage Association in Washington, D.C., 1884." In Kraditor, A. Up from the Pedestal, pp. 137-40.

________. "Address at a Hearing of the Congressional Committee on Privileges and Elections, January 1878." In Stanton, E. History of Woman Suffrage, 3, 93-5.

________. "Address Report to the 5th Annual National Woman Suffrage Association Convention, Washington, D.C., January 1873." In Stanton, E. History of Woman Suffrage, 2, 522-3.

________. "Address to the 5th Annual National Woman Suffrage Association Convention, Washington, D.C., January 1872." In Stanton, E. History of Woman Suffrage, 2, 523-33.

________. "Address to the National Woman Suffrage Association Convention of 1887." In Stanton, E. History of Woman Suffrage, 4, 118.

________. "Address to the Syracuse National Woman's Rights Convention, September 1852." In Stanton, E. History of Woman Suffrage, 1, 528-30.

________. "Argument for Woman's Suffrage, 1886." In Martin, W. The American Sisterhood, pp. 82-7.

________. "Decade Speech, on the Progress of Education and Industrial Avocations for Women." In Davis, P. A History of the National Woman's Rights Movement, pp. 42-52.
________. "A Plan of Action." In Tanner, L. Voices from Women's Liberation, pp. 68-9.
________. "President's Address at the National Woman Suffrage Association Convention, Washington, D.C., January 1876." In Stanton, E. History of Woman Suffrage, 3, 4.
________. "Remarks on Legal Disabilities at the Women's Rights State Convention, Rochester, N.Y., November 30, 1853." In Stanton, E. History of Woman Suffrage, 1, 579-80.
________. "Remarks on Organization." In International Council of Women, 1888. Report, p. 189.
________. "Review of the Decision in Virginia Minor's Court Case at Convention in Washington, D.C., 1875." In Stanton, E. History of Woman Suffrage, 2, 742-8.
________. "Testimony at a Hearing of the House Judiciary Committee, January 24, 1889." In Stanton, E. History of Woman Suffrage, 3, 167-9.
________. "Woman in the Early Christian Church." In International Council of Women, 1888. Report, pp. 400-7.

Gage, Olive J. "Statement." In U.S. Congress. Senate. Committee on the Judiciary. Subcommittee on Constitutional Amendments. Equal Rights for Men and Women (1938), p. 38.

Gallinger, Eleanor B. "The New Dental Program." In National Conference of Social Work. Proceedings (1927), pp. 204-5.

Galpin, Kate Tupper. "The Ethical Influence of Woman in Education." In World's Congress of Representative Women, Chicago, 1893. A Historical Resume, pp. 107-14.

Gambrell, Mary Latimer. "Old Wine in New Bottles. The Democratic Way of Life." Vital Speeches, 8 (August 15, 1942), 667-71.

Gane, E. Marguerite. "Case Work in Protective Agencies." In National Conference of Social Work. Proceedings (1937), pp. 243-54.
________. "Discussion of the Responsibility of Juvenile Court and Public Agency in Child Welfare." In National Conference of Social Work. Proceedings (1947), pp. 321-3.
________. "A Program for the Protection of Children." In National Conference of Social Work. Proceedings (1946), pp. 379-86.

Gannett, Mary T. Lewis. "Eulogy for Mary B. Anthony's Funeral, February 7, 1907." In Harper, I. The Life and Work of Susan B. Anthony, 3, 1513.

Gano, Eveline. "Address to the Senate Committee, April 19, 1910." In Stanton, E. History of Woman Suffrage, 5, 293-4.

Garcia, Christiane. "Statement." In U.S. Congress. Senate. Committee on Labor and Public Welfare. Subcommittee on Children and Youth. White House Conference on Youth, pp. 35-6.

Garcia, Clotilde. "Statement." In Conference on Women in the War on Poverty, 1967. Proceedings, p. 19.

Gardener, Helen Hamilton. "Heredity and Ethics." In National Purity Congress, 1st, Baltimore, 1895. National Purity Congress, pp. 99-104.

________. "Heredity in Its Relation to a Double Standard of Morals." In World's Congress of Representative Women, Chicago, 1893. A Historical Resume, pp. 374-86.

________. "Historical Facts and Theological Fictions." In Gardener, H. Men, Women, and Gods, and Other Lectures, pp. 79-133.

________. "Men, Women and Gods." In Gardener, H. Men, Women, and Gods, and Other Lectures, pp. 1-46.

________. "The Moral Responsibility of Women in Heredity." In National Council of Women of the U.S., Washington, 1891. Transactions, pp. 130-47.

________. "Sex in Brain." In International Council of Women, 1888. Report, pp. 369-82.

________. "Vicarious Atonement." In Gardener, H. Men, Women, and Gods, and Other Lectures, pp. 47-78.

________. "Woman as an Annex." In World's Congress of Representative Women, Chicago, 1893. A Historical Resume, pp. 488-500.

Gardiner, Elizabeth M. "Health Security for Mother and Child." In International Congress of Women, Chicago, 1933. Our Common Cause, Civilization, pp. 601-5.

________. "A Maternity and Infancy Program for Rural and Semi-rural Communities." In National Conference of Social Work. Proceedings (1926), pp. 396-9.

Gardiner, Evelyn Gail. "Municipal Organization of Social Service in the Proposed New Charter of Grand Rapids." In National Conference of Charities and Correction. Proceedings (1916), pp. 410-5.

Gardner, Jo-Ann Evans. "Breaking Down the Barriers." In Conference of Professional and Academic Women. Sixteen Reports on the Status of Women in the Professions, 2 p.

________. "The Psychology and the Psychological Effects of Discrimination." In New York (City). Commission on Human Rights. Women's Role in Contemporary Society, pp. 90-100.

Garrett, Emma. "Address to the Convention of the American Instructors of the Deaf and Dumb, 1882." In American Instructors of the Deaf and Dumb. Proceedings (1882), p. 65.

Garrett, Mary Smith. "The Next Step in the Education of the Deaf."

In World's Congress of Representative Women, Chicago, 1893. Congress of Women, pp. 443-5.

Garson, Greer. "Education for the Millions Through Pictures." In New York Herald Tribune. Report of the 12th Annual Forum on Current Problems, pp. 32-6.

Gartland, Ruth. "Generic Aspects of Professional Training for Case Work and Group Work: From the Point of View of a Teacher of Case Work." In National Conference of Social Work. Proceedings (1940), pp. 598-606.

Garton, Jean. "Statement." In U.S. Congress. Senate. Committee on the Judiciary. Subcommittee on Constitutional Amendments. Abortion, pt. 1, 319, 327-9.

Gates, Margaret J. "Testimony on Women's Access to Credit and Insurance." In U.S. Congress. Joint Economic Committee. Economic Problems of Women, pt. 1, 202-3.

Gates, Susan Young. "General Conditions of Domestic Service." In International Congress of Women, London, 1899, 6, 92-6.

Gaver, Mary Virginia. "Masters of the Raging Book?" ALA Bulletin, 60 (September, 1966), 794-805.

Gawin, Louise Fry. "Preventive and Public Health Aspects of Rheumatic Fever in Children." Washington, U.S. Children's Bureau, 1945, 4 p.

Gaylord, Gladys. "Restrictions in Regard to Regulation of Birth Imposed by Laws of the Various Civilized Nations." In National Conference of Social Work. Proceedings (1931), pp. 136-42.

Genger, Mina C. "The Financial History of the Newark Bureau of Associated Charities." In National Conference of Charities and Correction. Proceedings (1906), pp. 223-7.

George, Jean Craighead. "Newbery Award Acceptance--1973." In Kingman, L. Newbery and Caldecott Medal Books, 1966-1975, pp. 96-106.

George, Jennie Allen Butt. "Who Are the Builders?" In World's Congress of Representative Women, Chicago, 1893. Congress of Women, pp. 388-92.

George, Zelma. "Speech." In Conference on Women in the War on Poverty, 2nd, 1968. Proceedings, pp. 44-6.

Gerard, Margaret W. "Learning to Know the Child Through the Everyday Contacts of the Case Worker." In National Conference of Social Work. Proceedings (1939), pp. 360-9.

Gestefeld, Ursula N. "Woman as a Religious Teacher." In World's Congress of Representative Women, Chicago, 1893. A Historical Resume, pp. 275-9.

Getman, Lisa. "From Conestoga to Career." In Furniss, W. Women in Higher Education, pp. 63-6.

Gibbons, Mary L. "The Prevention and Treatment of Juvenile Delinquency in Wartime." In National Conference of Social Work. Proceedings (1943), pp. 149-57.

Gibson, Katherine. "County Programs of Child Care: The Relation of Probation to Other County Social Work." In National Conference of Social Work. Proceedings (1925), pp. 103-8.

Giddings, Maria L. "Report on the Common Law." In Woman's Rights Convention, Akron, Ohio, 1851. Proceedings, pp. 11-4.

Gierke, Theola. "Statement." In U.S. Congress. House. Committee on Education and Labor. Select Subcommittee on Labor. Equal Pay for Equal Work, pp. 122-4.

Gilbreth, Lillian Evelyn Moller. "Can the Machine Pull Us Out?" In International Congress of Women, Chicago, 1933. Our Common Cause, Civilization, pp. 39-48.

_______. "A Challenge to Women." In New York Herald Tribune. Report of the 6th Annual Forum on Current Problems, pp. 40-2.

_______. "Closing the Gap." In M.I.T. Symposium on American Women in Science and Engineering, 1964. Women and the Scientific Professions, pp. 217-31.

_______. "Focus on the Future." In International Conference of Women Engineers and Scientists, 1st, New York. Focus for the Future, pp. I-7-8.

_______. "The Home--A Major Industry." In New York Herald Tribune. Report of the 4th Annual Women's Conference on Current Problems, pp. 230-5.

_______. "The Newer Efficiency." In New York Herald Tribune. Report of the 2nd Women's Conference on Current Problems, pp. 11-4.

_______. "Safeguarding Machine Development." In New York Herald Tribune. Report of the 5th Annual Forum on Current Problems, pp. 146-9.

Gildersleeve, Virginia C. "Education for a New Day." In New York Herald Tribune. Report of the 2nd Women's Conference on Current Problems, pp. 133-8.

Gill, Laura Drake. "Co-operation of the National Women's Organizations for Good Schools." In General Federation of Women's Clubs. Biennial Convention, 9 (1908), 286-90.

Gillam, Mabel A. "Some Needed Readjustments in Special Fields of Child Welfare: A New Interpretation of the Task of Day Nurseries. How Large a Part Should They Play in Children's Work?" In National Conference of Social Work. Proceedings (1921), pp. 109-11.

Gillett, Emma Millinda. "Legal Rights of a Married Woman in Her Husband's Property." In International Congress of Women, Toronto, 1909. Report, 2, 223-8.

Gillett, Lucy H. "Basis for Estimating Budgets." In National Conference of Social Work. Proceedings (1936), pp. 192-202.

________. "Education in Food Values as a Preventive of Dietary Deficiencies." In National Conference of Social Work. Proceedings (1919), pp. 231-7.

________. "The Relation of Food Economics to the Nutritive Value of the Diet." In National Conference of Social Work. Proceedings (1917), pp. 227-31.

Gilman, Charlotte Perkins Stetson. "Duty and Honor. Address to the National American Women Suffrage Convention of 1897." In Stanton, E. History of Women Suffrage, 4, 277-8.

________. "Equal Pay for Equal Work." In International Congress of Women, London, 1899, 6, 198-202.

________. "Poverty and Woman." In National Conference of Social Work. Proceedings (1917), pp. 10-5.

Gilson, Mary. "What Women Workers Mean to Industry." In U.S. Women's Bureau. Proceedings of the Women's Industrial Conference, pp. 66-77.

Ginsbury, Ethel L. "The Case Worker in a Veteran Service Center." In National Conference of Social Work. Proceedings (1945), pp. 122-33.

Gittings, Barbara. "Keynote Address." In Conference on the Universities and the Gay Experience. Proceedings, pp. 29-32.

Glenn, Helen. "The Value of Analyzing One's Job." In National Conference of Charities and Correction. Proceedings (1915), pp. 77-9.

Glenn, Mary Willcox. "The Background of a Family's Religious Life as Social Data." In National Conference of Social Work. Proceedings (1926), pp. 259-65.

________. "Case Work Disciplines and Ideals." In National Conference of Charities and Correction. Proceedings (1913), pp. 353-62.

________. "The History of Social Work and Its Place in the Professional Curriculum." In National Conference of Social Work. Proceedings (1930), pp. 511-9.

________. "Personal and Professional Sources of Inspiration for Social Workers: Roots of Courage." In National Conference of Social Work. Proceedings (1931), pp. 72-83.

________. "President's Address: A Prelude to Peace." In National Conference of Charities and Correction. Proceedings (1915), pp. 1-12.

________. "Report of the Committee: The Working Force of Organized Charity." In National Conference of Charities and Correction. Proceedings (1908), pp. 57-69.

________. "Service." In National Conference of Social Work. Proceedings (1928), pp. 13-6.

________. "Some Social Causes of Prostitution." In National Conference of Charities and Correction. Proceedings (1914), pp. 229-36.

Glickman, Rose L. "The Russian Factory Woman, 1880-1904." In Atkinson, D. Women in Russia, pp. 63-83.

Glueck, Eleanor T. "Family, the School, and Crime." Vital Speeches, 1 (May 6, 1935), 516-20.

Godman, Henrietta G. "Argument Against Public Outdoor Relief." National Conference of Charities and Correction. Proceedings (1891), pp. 46-9.

________. "Auxiliary Visitors." In National Conference of Charities and Correction. Proceedings (1904), pp. 126-34.

Goessmann, Helena T. "Discussion of the Trades and Professions Underlying the Home." In World's Congress of Representative Women, Chicago, 1893. A Historical Resume, pp. 589-92.

Goff, Harriet Newell Kneeland. "Temperance." In Association for the Advancement of Women. Congress of Women, 1st. Papers, pp. 147-53.

Gold, Sally. "Women, the Criminal Code, and the Correction System." In New York (City). Commission on Human Rights. Women's Role in Contemporary Society, pp. 512-5.

Goldenberg, Sharon. "Public Testimony." In New York (City). Commission on Human Rights. Women's Role in Contemporary Society, pp. 555-7.

Goldman, Emma. "Address to the International Working Men's Association Congress (Paris, 1937)." In Goldman, E. Red Emma Speaks, pp. 375-85.

________. "Address to the Jury." In Goldman, Emma. Red Emma Speaks, pp. 313-27.

________. "The Child and Its Enemies." In Goldman, E. Red Emma Speaks, pp. 107-15.

________. "The Failure of Christianity." In Goldman, E. Red Emma Speaks, pp. 186-94.

________. "Intellectual Proletarians." In Goldman, E. Red Emma Speaks, pp. 176-85.

________. "Jealousy: Causes and a Possible Cure." In Goldman, E. Red Emma Speaks, pp. 168-75.

________. "Marriage and Love, 1917." In Goldman, E. Red Emma Speaks, pp. 158-67. Also in Martin, W. The American Sisterhood, pp. 224-33.

________. "The Philosophy of Atheism." In Goldman, E. Red Emma Speaks, pp. 195-202.

________. "The Social Importance of the Modern School." In Goldman, E. Red Emma Speaks, pp. 116-25.

________. "The Traffic in Women." In Goldman, E. Red Emma Speaks, pp. 143-57.

________. "The Tragedy of Woman's Emancipation." In Goldman, E. Red Emma Speaks, pp. 133-42. Also in Rossi, A. The Feminist Papers, pp. 508-16.

________. "Victims of Morality." In Goldman, E. Red Emma Speaks, pp. 126-32.

Goldman, Estelle Breman. "The Refugee Alien." In New York Herald Tribune. Report of the 8th Annual Forum on Current Problems, pp. 79-80.

Goldmark, Josephine. "Standard Working Hours." In National Conference of Charities and Correction. Proceedings (1911), pp. 179-86.

Goldsmith, Ethel. "Psychiatry and the Offender in the Community: The Juvenile Offender." In National Conference of Social Work. Proceedings (1925), pp. 543-8.

Goltz, Pat. "Statement." In U.S. Congress. Senate. Committee on the Judiciary. Subcommittee on Constitutional Amendments. Abortion, pt. 3, 107-14.

Gonzalez, Nancie. "Women and the Jural Domain: An Evolutionary Perspective." In McGuigan, D. A Sampler of Women's Studies, pp. 47-57.

Gooding, Mary. "Woman's Need at the Present Day." Revolution, 5 (March 10, 1870), 147.

Goodman, Hilda B. "Relation of the Curative Workshop to the Rehabilitation of Disabled Persons." In National Conference of Social Work. Proceedings (1927), pp. 325-8.

Goodman, Janice. "Public Testimony." In New York (City). Commission on Human Rights. Women's Role in Contemporary Society, pp. 429-33.

________. "Status of Women Students." In Conference of Professional and Academic Women. Sixteen Reports on the Status of Women in the Professions, 2 p.

Goodrich, Annie W. "Community Organization for Health." In International Congress of Women, Chicago, 1933. Our Common Cause, Civilization, pp. 609-19.

Goodwillie, Mary C. "Case Work as a Factor." In National Conference of Charities and Correction. Proceedings (1912), pp. 109-12.

________. "Efficiency in the Use of Volunteers." In National Conference of Charities and Correction. Proceedings (1915), pp. 83-8.

________. "Family Readjustment After the War." In National Conference of Social Work. Proceedings (1919), pp. 383-90.

________. "Volunteers in Family Work." In National Conference of Social Work. Proceedings (1917), pp. 116-8.

Goodwin, Marion Schmadel. "Housekeeper Service in Family Welfare." In National Conference of Social Work. Proceedings (1938), pp. 279-87.

Gordon, Anna Adams. "How to Reach the Children." In International Council of Women, 1888. Report, pp. 118-9.

________. "World Prohibition, World Purity, World Peace; Our International Goal. Address to the Annual Convention of the National Woman's Christian Temperance Union." Philadelphia, 1922.

Gordon, Diana. "The Status of Women in Municipal Government." In Conference of Professional and Academic Women. Sixteen Reports on the Status of Women in the Professions, 2 p.

Gordon, Dorothy. "Youth's Right to Knowledge and Free Speech. The Challenge of Youth Forum Discussions." Vital Speeches, 26 (January 1, 1960), 173-5.

Gordon, Francine, E. "Bringing Women into Management: The Role of the Senior Executive." In Gordon, F. Bringing Women into Management, pp. 113-25.

Gordon, Henrietta L. "Current Trends in Adoption." Washington, U.S. Children's Bureau, 1945, 4 p.

Gordon, Jean M. "Protective Standards for Women Wage Earners." In National Conference of Charities and Correction. Proceedings (1914), pp. 327-32.

________. "Why Are the Children in the Factory." In National Conference of Charities and Correction. Proceedings (1908), pp. 346-51.

Gordon, Kate M. "Report of Committee on Enrolment." (sic) In National American Woman Suffrage Association. Proceedings of the 39th Annual Convention, pp. 31-3.

Gordon, Laura de Force. "Woman's Sphere from a Woman's Standpoint." In World's Congress of Representative Women, Chicago, 1893. Congress of Women, pp. 74-6.

Gottemoller, Ruth. "Implications in the Broader Use of Budgets." In National Conference of Social Work. Proceedings (1947), pp. 294-300.

Gougar, Helen M. Jackson. "Address to the Senate Committee on Woman Suffrage, March 7, 1884." In Stanton, E. History of Woman Suffrage, 4, 37-8.

Gould, Minna Gordon. "Harmonious Adjustment Through Exercise." In World's Congress of Representative Women, Chicago, 1893. Congress of Women, pp. 660-3.

Graber, Phyllis. "Public Testimony." In New York (City). Commission on Human Rights. Women's Role in Contemporary Society, pp. 773-6.

Grace, Lynne S. "Statement." In U.S. Congress. Senate. Committee on the Judiciary. Equal Rights 1970, pp. 352-63.

Graddick, Laura. "Statement." In U.S. Women's Bureau. Proceedings of the Women's Industrial Conference, pp. 152-3.

Grady, Alice H. "A Massachusetts Experiment in Savings Bank Life Insurance." In National Conference of Social Work. Proceedings (1930), pp. 273-8.

Graham, Katharine Meyer. "Press and Its Responsibilities: Finance and Government Security." Vital Speeches, 42 (April 15, 1976), 395-9.

________. "A Vigilant Press: Its Job to Inform." Vital Speeches, 40 (August 15, 1974), 460-2.

Graham, Louise. "Justice in Journalism." In General Federation of Women's Clubs. Biennial Convention, 9 (1908), 399-402.

Granger, Dorothy Shipley. "Statement." In U.S. Congress. Senate. Committee on the Judiciary. Subcommittee on Constitutional Amendments. Equal Rights Amendment (1945), p. 35.

Grannis, Elizabeth Bartlett. "The Christian League for the Promotion of Social Purity." In National Council of Women of the U.S., Washington, 1891. Transactions, pp. 116-9.

________. "Church Union." In National Council of Women of the U.S., Washington, 1891. Transactions, pp. 342-3.

________. "Discussion of Woman as a Religious Teacher." In World's Congress of Representative Women, Chicago, 1893. A Historical Resume, p. 285.

________. "Marriage and Divorce." In International Congress of Women, Toronto, 1909. Report, 2, 237-40.

________. "The National Christian League for the Promotion of Social Purity." In World's Congress of Representative Women, Chicago, 1893. A Historical Resume, pp. 880-6.

________. "Woman as Wife, Mother and Home Builder." In International Congress of Women, Toronto, 1909. Report, 2, 457-62.

Grasso, Ella Tambussi. "Action to Help Older Americans." Congressional Record, 92nd Cong., 2nd sess., 1972, 118, pt. 21, 27183-4.

______. "Aid to North Vietnam." Congressional Record, 93rd Cong., 1st sess., 1973, 119, pt. 16, 20582-3.

______. "The Crown of St. Stephen." Congressional Record, 92nd Cong., 2nd sess., 1972, 118, pt. 3, 3658.

______. "Debate on Constitutional Amendment to Lower Voting Age to 18." Congressional Record, 92nd Cong., 1st sess., 1971, 117, pt. 6, 7551.

______. "The Emergency Employment Bill." Congressional Record, 92nd Cong., 1st sess., 1971, 117, pt. 13, 17378-9.

______. "Emergency Loan Guarantee Act of 1971 to Lockheed Corp." Congressional Record, 92nd Cong., 1st sess., 1971, 117, pt. 21, 28372-3.

______. "Equal Rights Amendment." Congressional Record, 92nd Cong., 1st sess., 1971, 117, pt. 27, 35799.

______. "Food Price Hearing." Congressional Record, 93rd Cong., 1st sess., 1973, 119, pt. 9, 10948-9.

______. "A Full Accounting of All MIA'S." Congressional Record, 93rd Cong., 2nd sess., 1974, 120, pt. 24, 32475.

______. "The Handicapped and Older Americans." Congressional Record, 93rd Cong., 2nd sess., 1974, 120, pt. 9, 11968-9.

______. "House Joint Resolution 191 on School Prayers." Congressional Record, 92nd Cong., 1st sess., 1971, 117, pt. 30, 39941-2.

______. "Imports Continue to Threaten U.S. Ball and Roller Bearing Industries." Congressional Record, 93rd Cong., 1st sess., 1973, 119, pt. 1, 439-40.

______. "A More Realistic and Comprehensive National Policy for Older Americans." Congressional Record, 92nd Cong., 2nd sess., 1971, 117, pt. 34, 44408-9.

______. "Newspersons' Information and Source Protection Act." Congressional Record, 93rd Cong., 1st sess., 1973, 119, pt. 5, 6507-8.

______. "Office of Technology Assessment." Congressional Record, 92nd Cong., 2nd sess., 1972, 118, pt. 3, 3562-3.

______. "Oil Price Statement." Congressional Record, 92nd Cong., 1st sess., 1971, 117, pt. 3, 3384-5.

______. "Price of Meat." Congressional Record, 92nd Cong., 2nd sess., 1972, 118, pt. 8, 9728-9.

______. "Priority Status Needed for Sickle Cell Anemia." Congressional Record, 92nd Cong., 1st sess., 1971, 117, pt. 2, 2296.

______. "Rail Passenger Service." Congressional Record, 92nd Cong., 1st sess., 1971, 117, pt. 34, 43432-3.

______. "Remarks on House Concurrent Resolution 471 on the Status of Soviet Jews." Congressional Record, 92nd Cong., 2nd sess., 1972, 118, pt. 10, 12939-40.

______. "Tax Credit for Parents of Students Attending Nonpublic Elementary and Secondary School." Congressional Record, 92nd Cong., 2nd sess., 1972, 118, pt. 18, 22564-5.

______. "Welfare Reform Needed." Congressional Record, 92nd Cong., 1st sess., 1971, 117, pt. 17, 23155-6.

Graves, Elsa. "Will Women Stay in Industry?" In New York Herald Tribune. Report of the 13th Annual Forum on Current Problems, pp. 134-8.

Graves, Jennie H. "Impact of Taxation on Small Business. Lack of Working Capital Prohibits Expansion." Vital Speeches, 13 (January 15, 1957), 214-6.

Gray, Elizabeth Janet. "Acceptance Paper--Newbery Medal 1943. History Is People." In Miller, B. Newbery Medal Books, 1922-1955, pp. 236-41.

Gray, Virginia. "Female Status: A New Population Policy." In Epstein, L. Women in the Professions, pp. 67-79.

Greathouse, Rebekah. "Statement." In U.S. Congress. House. Committee on the Judiciary. Equal Rights Amendment to the Constitution (1932), pp. 4-5.

________. "Statement." In U.S. Congress. Senate. Committee on the Judiciary. Subcommittee on Constitutional Amendments. Equal Rights for Men and Women (1938), pp. 155-7.

Green, Anna S. "Woman's Awakenment." In World's Congress of Representative Women, Chicago, 1893. Congress of Women, pp. 649-50.

Green, Edith Starrett. "Campus Issues in 1980." PTA Magazine, 62 (April, 1968), 18-20.

________. "Representative Edith Green Speaks in Support of the Equal Rights Amendment." In Bosmajian, H. This Great Argument, pp. 237-42.

________. "The Road Is Paved with Good Intentions: Title IX and What It Is Not." Vital Speeches, 43 (March 1, 1977), 300-3.

________. "School Busing: Are We Hurting the People We Want to Help?" U.S. News & World Report, 67 (August 18, 1969), 72-3.

________. "Should Congress Establish a Major Federal Role in General Financing of U.S. Education?" Congressional Digest, 51 (August-September, 1972), 200-2.

________. "Statement." In U.S. Congress. House. Committee on Education and Labor. Subcommittee on Education. Discrimination Against Women, pp. 3-7.

Green, Elizabeth. "Christmas Gifts." In General Federation of Women's Clubs. Biennial Convention, 9 (1908), 408.

Green, Isabel. "Public Statement." In New York (City). Commission on Human Rights. Women's Role in Contemporary Society, pp. 315-6.

Greenberg, Gloria. "Public Testimony." In New York (City). Commission on Human Rights. Women's Role in Contemporary Society, pp. 412-4.

Greene, Mary Anne. "Legal Condition of Woman in 1492-1892." In World's Congress of Representative Women, Chicago, 1893. Congress of Women, pp. 41-52.

Greenleaf, Jean Brooks. "Address to the House Judiciary Committee, February 17, 1892." In Stanton, E. History of Woman Suffrage, 4, 196-7.

________. "Tribute to Mary S. Anthony, At Her Funeral, February 7, 1907." In Harper, I. The Life and Work of Susan B. Anthony, 3, 1512.

________. "What Woman's New Social Service Owes. Address at Susan B. Anthony's 85th Birthday Celebration." In Harper, I. The Life and Work of Susan B. Anthony, 3, 1348.

Greibel, Helen. "Youth in Industry." In International Congress of Women, Chicago, 1933. Our Common Cause, Civilization, pp. 217-8.

Greitzer, Carol. "Discrimination in Housing, Public Accommodations, and Employment." In New York (City). Commission on Human Rights. Women's Role in Contemporary Society, pp. 143-9.

Greve, Bell. "Opportunities for Developing Better Children's Work Throughout a State: Examples of Activities of State Departments." In National Conference of Social Work. Proceedings (1928), pp. 102-10.

Grew, Mary. "Address." In International Council of Women, 1888. Report, pp. 344-6.

________. "Address to the Semi-Annual Meeting of the American Woman Suffrage Association, New York, May 1871." In Stanton, E. History of Woman Suffrage, 2, 814-5.

________. "Annals of Women's Anti-Slavery Societies." In American Anti-Slavery Society. Proceedings, pp. 124-30.

________. "Closing Address to the 10th National Woman's Rights Convention, New York, May 10-11, 1860." In Stanton, E. History of Woman Suffrage, 1, 735-7.

Griffing, Josephine Sophia White. "Address to the 1st Annual Meeting of the American Equal Rights Association, May 1867." In Stanton, E. History of Woman Suffrage, 2, 221.

________. "Mrs. Griffing's Report of 1871 Work to the National Woman Suffrage Association, May 11, 1871." In Stanton, E. History of Woman Suffrage, 2, 484-9.

Griffiths, Martha Wright. "Can We Still Afford Occupational Segregation? Some Remarks." In Blaxall, M. Women and the Workplace, pp. 7-14.

________. "Equal Rights Amendment." Congressional Record, 93rd Cong., 1st sess., 1972, 118, pt. 5, 6143.

________. "Excerpt from Statement on Pending Health Security Act, April 23, 1974." Congressional Digest, 53 (June, 1974), 174+.

________. "Excerpt from Testimony Before Committee on Finance of the U.S. Senate, September 22, 1967." Congressional Digest, 47 (June, 1968), 180+.

________. "Excerpt from Testimony Before the Subcommittee on Constitutional Amendments, May 5, 1970." Congressional Digest, 50 (January, 1971), 16+.

________. "It Is a National Calamity ... Remarks." In Chmaj, B. American Women and American Studies, pp. 210-2.

________. "Life Without A Newspaper, from an Address to Congress." U.S. News & World Report, 52 (June 11, 1962), 106.

________. "Opening Statement on Features of Federal Income, Estate, and Gift Tax Law Which Have a Disparate Impact on Women." In U.S. Congress. Joint Economic Committee. Economic Problems of Women, pt. 2, 221-3.

________. "Opening Statement on Federal Efforts to End Sex Discrimination in Employment." In U.S. Congress. Joint Economic Committee. Economic Problems of Women, pt. 1, 73-4.

________. "Opening Statement on Sex Discrimination in Unemployment Insurance, Veterans Programs, and Public Assistance." In U.S. Congress. Joint Economic Committee. Economic Problems of Women, pt. 2, 339-41.

________. "Opening Statement on the Economics of Sex Discrimination in Employment." In U.S. Congress. Joint Economic Committee. Economic Problems of Women, pt. 1, 1-3.

________. "Opening Statement on the Treatment of Women Under Social Security and Private Pensions." In U.S. Congress. Joint Economic Committee. Economic Problems of Women, pt. 2, 289-91.

________. "Opening Statement on Women's Access to Credit and Insurance." In U.S. Congress. Joint Economic Committee. Economic Problems of Women, pt. 1, 151-3.

________. "The Rising Tide of Violence. Maintaining Order in a Nation." Vital Speeches, 26 (October 1, 1960), 745-7.

________. "Should Congress Approve the "Equal Rights" Amendment?" Congressional Digest, 50 (January, 1971), 16-20.

________. "Statement." In Conference on Women in the War on Poverty, 1967. Proceedings, p. 35.

________. "Statement." In U.S. Congress. House. Committee on Education and Labor. Special Subcommittee on Education. Discrimination Against Women, pp. 434-9.

________. "Statement." In U.S. Congress. House. Committee on Education and Labor. Select Subcommittee on Labor. Equal Pay for Equal Work, pp. 131-2.

________. "Statement." In U.S. Congress. House. Committee on the Judiciary. Subcommittee no. 4. Equal Rights for Men and Women 1971, pp. 36-42.

________. "Statement." In U.S. Congress. Senate. Committee on the Judiciary. Equal Rights 1970, pp. 222-5.

________. "Statement." In U.S. Congress. Senate. Committee on the Judiciary. Subcommittee on Constitutional Amendments. Women and the "Equal Rights" Amendment, pp. 17-20.

________. "Statement at Senate Hearings on Women and Social Security." In U.S. Congress. Senate. Special Committee on

Aging. Future Directions in Social Security, pt. 18, 1672-4.

________. "Women Are Being Deprived of Legal Rights by the Equal Employment Opportunity Commission." Congressional Record, 89th Cong., 2nd sess., 1966, 112, pt. 10, 13689-94.

Grimke, Angelina. "Address at the Woman's National Loyal League Convention, May 14, 1863." In Stanton, E. History of Woman Suffrage, 2, 54-6, 60-1.

________. "Angelina Grimke's Address." In Stanton, E. History of Woman Suffrage, 2, 334-6.

________. "Angelina Grimke's Speech." In Papachristou, J. Women Together, p. 15.

________. "The Rights of Women and Negroes." In Tanner, L. Voices from Women's Liberation, p. 80.

________. "The Sufferings of the Slaves." In Stanton, E. History of Woman Suffrage, 1, 395-6.

Grinnell, Katherine Van Allen. "Woman in an Ideal Government." In World's Congress of Representative Women, Chicago, 1893. Congress of Women, pp. 628-32.

Groneman, Carol. "She Earns as a Child; She Pays as a Man: Women Workers in a Mid-Nineteenth-Century New York City Community." In Cantor, M. Class, Sex, and the Woman Worker, pp. 83-100.

Gross, Geraldine L. "Statement." In U.S. Congress. Senate. Committee on Labor and Public Welfare. Subcommittee on Labor. Equal Pay Act of 1963, pp. 129, 134-6.

Grover, Eve R. "Statement." In U.S. Congress. Senate. Select Committee on Small Business. Women and the Small Business Administration, pp. 94-5.

Gruber, Ruth. "Alaska--The New Crossroads." In New York Herald Tribune. Report of the 12th Annual Forum on Current Problems, pp. 96-104.

________. "Rediscovery of Alaska. Crossroads of America." Vital Speeches, 10 (January 1, 1944), 181-4.

Gruenberg, Sidonie Matsner. "Health Training of the Preschool Child." In National Conference of Social Work. Proceedings (1925), pp. 221-5.

________. "Where Security Begins." In International Congress of Women, Chicago, 1933. Our Common Cause, Civilization, pp. 723-8.

Guber, Selma. "Sex Role and the Feminine Personality." In Goldman, G. Modern Woman, pp. 75-91.

Guggenheimer, Elinore. "Child Care and Family Services." In New

York (City). Commission on Human Rights. Women's Role in Contemporary Society, pp. 459-69.

Guiney, Mary K. "Planning Services for the Aged in the Local Community." In National Conference of Social Work. Proceedings (1947), pp. 410-7.

Gulick, Alice Gordon. "A Woman's College in Spain." In National Council of Women of the U.S., Washington, 1891. Transactions, pp. 189-92.

Gunderson, Barbara Bates. "Building Leadership for Peace ... New Ideas from New Voters: Panel Discussion." In New York Herald Tribune. Report of the 12th Annual Forum on Current Problems, pp. 148-9, 160.

________. "The Implication of Rivalry." In Farber, S. Man and Civilization: The Potential of Women, pp. 165-87.

Gunn, Barbara A. "And They Came Out of Their Cotton-Batting World: Enjoy, Enjoy." Vital Speeches, 36 (December 1, 1969), 114-5.

________. "Toward a National Policy on Aging: Every Person Counts." Vital Speeches, 37 (July 15, 1971), 597-9.

Gutwillig, Jacqueline G. "Statement." In U.S. Congress. Senate. Committee on the Judiciary. Subcommittee on Constitutional Amendments. Women and the "Equal Rights" Amendment, pp. 118-24.

________. "Testimony on Sex Discrimination in Unemployment Insurance, Veterans Programs, and Public Assistance." In U.S. Congress. Joint Economic Committee. Economic Problems of Women, pt. 2, 373-6, 380-5.

Guyler, Cathryn S. "Social Work Responsibility for the Development of Day Care." In National Conference of Social Work. Proceedings (1942), pp. 440-50.

Guzman, Jessie P. "The Southern Race Problem in Retrospect. South Unable Psychologically to Solve Its Problem Alone." Vital Speeches, 25 (July 1, 1959), 566-8.

Haasis, Bessie Amerman. "War Time Developments in Public Health Nursing." In National Conference of Social Work. Proceedings (1918), pp. 187-9.

Habein, Margaret. "The Liberal Arts Program." In Conference on the Present Status and Prospective Trends of Research on the Education of Women, Rye, N.Y., 1957. The Education of Women, pp. 96-102.

Hackett, Amy. "Feminism and Liberalism in Wilhelmine Germany, 1890-1918." In Carroll, B. Liberating Women's History, pp. 127-36.

Hadley, Lucia Hanna. "Statement." In U.S. Congress. House. Committee on the Judiciary. Subcommittee no. 1. Equal Rights Amendment (1948), p. 40.

Haefner, Ruth. "Family Life in the Rural Community." In National Conference of Social Work. Proceedings (1927), pp. 268-72.

Haener, Dorothy. "Address at the Founder's Reception--5th Annual Meeting of NOW, September, 1971." NOW Acts, 4 (Fall, 1971), 9-11.

________. "Statement." In U.S. Congress. House. Committee on Education and Labor. Special Subcommittee on Labor. Equal Pay Act, pp. 123-30.

________. "Statement." In U.S. Congress. Senate. Committee on Labor and Public Welfare. Subcommittee on Labor. Equal Pay Act of 1963, pp. 151, 154-5.

________. "What Is Labor Doing About Women in the Work Force." In Katzell, M. Women in the Work Force, pp. 43-52.

________. "Women and Employment Benefits: Maternity and Other Fringe Benefits." In New York (City). Commission on Human Rights. Women's Role in Contemporary Society, pp. 364-79.

Hafford, Lida. "Legislative Councils." In General Federation of Women's Clubs. Biennial Convention, 16 (1922), 18-20.

Hagar, Susan. "Statement." In U.S. Congress. Senate. Select Committee on Small Business. Women and the Small Business Administration, pp. 56-61.

Haggart, Mary E. "Address to the House Judiciary Committee, March 8, 1884." In Stanton, E. History of Woman Suffrage, 4, 45-7.

Haggarty, Roni. "Statement." In Conference on Feminist Perspectives on Housework and Child Care. Feminist Perspectives on Housework and Child Care, pp. 9-12.

Hagood, Beatrice S. "Sod Busting for Social Work: Children with Plenty O'Nothin'." In National Conference of Social Work. Proceedings (1939), pp. 480-2.

Hahn, Lorena B. "United National Commission on the Status of Women." In U.S. Women's Bureau. Today's Woman in Tomorrow's World, pp. 89-96.

Hahn, Pauline. "Public Testimony." In New York (City). Commission on Human Rights. Women's Role in Contemporary Society, pp. 767-9.

Hales, Elsie. "Statement." In U. S. Congress. Senate. Committee on the Judiciary. Equal Rights 1970, pp. 381-3.

Haley, Gail E. "Caldecott Award Acceptance--1971." In Kingman, L. Newbery and Caldecott Medal Books, 1966-1975, pp. 223-9.

Hall, Bessie E. "The Social Service Exchange: Is It a Mechanical Overhead, or a Case Work Stimulant?" In National Conference of Social Work. Proceedings (1925), pp. 509-15.

Hall, Emma Amelia. "Reformation of Criminal Girls." In National Conference of Charities and Correction. Proceedings (1883), pp. 188-99.

Hall, Florence Howe. "Message of Julia Ward Howe to the National Arbitration and Peace Congress." In American Peace Congress, 1st, New York, 1907. Proceedings, pp. 117-20.

Hall, Helen. "The Consequences of Social Action for the Group-Work Agency." In National Conference of Social Work. Proceedings (1936), pp. 234-41.

________. "Report of a Survey of the Effects of Unemployment." In National Conference of Social Work. Proceedings (1930), pp. 348-57.

________. "When Leisure Palls." In National Conference of Social Work. Proceedings (1932), pp. 309-14.

________. "When Sickness Strikes." In National Conference of Social Work. Proceedings (1939), pp. 91-100.

Hall, Olive A. "Facilitating Change." In American Home Economics Association. The Adventure of Change, pp. 31-40.

Hall, Sarah C. "Discussion of One Phase of Woman's Work for the Municipality." In World's Congress of Representative Women, Chicago, 1893. A Historical Resume, pp. 462-3.

Hall, Shirley. "Statement." In U. S. Congress. Senate. Committee on the Judiciary. Subcommittee on Constitutional Amendments. Equal Rights Amendment (1945), p. 95.

Hallaren, Mary A. "Military Service--Bridge or Gap? Panel Discussion." In New York Herald Tribune. Report of the 20th Annual Forum on Current Problems, pp. 62-4.

Halliday, Vernon. "Machinery Broker." In General Federation of Women's Clubs. Biennial Convention, 9 (1908), 381-4.

Hamer, Fannie Lou. "The Special Plight and the Role of Black Women." In Lerner, G. Black Women in White America, pp. 609-14.

Hamilton, Alice. "Occupational Diseases." In National Conference of Charities and Correction. Proceedings (1911), pp. 197-207.

_______. "Venereal Diseases in Institutions for Women and Girls." In National Conference of Charities and Correction. Proceedings (1910), pp. 53-6.

_______. "The Work of the Health Committee of the League of Nations." In National Council of Women. Proceedings of the 14th Convention, 1928, pp. 90-1.

Hamilton, Edna L. "Health Programs for Use of Lone Workers in Rural Areas." In National Conference of Social Work. Proceedings (1933), pp. 245-55.

Hamilton, Virginia. "Newbery Award Acceptance--1975." In Kingman, L. Newbery and Caldecott Medal Books, 1966-1975, pp. 129-36.

Hampton, Isabel A. "Training Schools for Nurses." In National Conference of Charities and Correction. Proceedings (1890), pp. 140-6.

Hanaford, Phebe Anne. "Address to Convention of the American Woman Suffrage Association, New York, May 1870." In Stanton, E. History of Woman Suffrage, 2, 790-1.

_______. "Statistics of the Woman Ministry." In Association for the Advancement of Women. Congress of Women, 3rd. Papers, pp. 36-41.

_______. "Woman in the Church and Pulpit." In Association for the Advancement of Women. Congress of Women, 1st. Papers, pp. 102-5.

Hanchette, Helen W. "Family Budget Planning." In National Conference of Social Work. Proceedings (1919), pp. 408-12.

Handley, Virginia B. "The Interpretation to the Community of a Public Agency." In National Conference of Social Work. Proceedings (1925), pp. 137-41.

Handy, Gladys. "Questions for the Future. Research." In U.S. National Center for Health Services Research. Women and Their Health, pp. 86-8.

Hanford, Jeanette. "Family Case Work with Marital Difficulties." In National Conference of Social Work. Proceedings (1937), pp. 226-242.

_______. "Standards of Measurement Used in Staff Evaluations in a Private Agency." In National Conference of Social Work. Proceedings (1942), pp. 531-40.

Hankin, Charlotte A. "Statement." In U.S. Congress. Senate. Committee on the Judiciary. Subcommittee on Constitutional Amendments. Equal Rights for Men and Women (1938), pp. 61-4.

Hanna, Agnes K. "Social Services on the Mexican Border." In National Conference of Social Work. Proceedings (1935), pp. 692-702.

Hanna, Ione Theresa. "Ethics of Social Life." In World's Congress of Representative Women, Chicago, 1893. Congress of Women, pp. 53-7.

Hanna, Rosa Laddon. "Economic Security Under Communism." In International Congress of Women, Chicago, 1933. Our Common Cause, Civilization, pp. 111-21.

________. "Schools and the Rulers of Mankind--Discussion." In International Congress of Women, Chicago, 1933. Our Common Cause, Civilization, pp. 824-7.

Hansen, Nancy. "Even Sea Shells Sing When You Listen. Let Us Not Waste Precious Time Asking Who We Are." Vital Speeches, 41 (June 1, 1975), 550-1.

Hansl, Eva V. "Utilization of Womanpower. An Unnecessary Waste of Human Resources." Vital Speeches, 18 (September 1, 1952), 689-93.

Hanson, Eleanor. "Forty-three Families Treated by Friendly Visiting." In National Conference of Charities and Correction. Proceedings (1907), pp. 315-8.

Harbert, Elizabeth Boynton. "Address on Social Purity." In International Council of Women, 1888. Report, pp. 246-8.

________. "Address to the Committee on Privileges and Elections of the Senate, January 1878." In Stanton, E. History of Woman Suffrage, 3, 76-80.

________. "God Is Love." In International Council of Women, 1888. Report, pp. 415-8.

________. "Higher Education for Women." In Association for the Advancement of Women, Congress for Women, 1st. Papers, pp. 81-3.

Harding, Elizabeth. "How to Improve the Utilization of Nurses, Allied Health, and Support Personnel. A U.S. Response to the Swedish Model." In International Conference on Women in Health. Proceedings, pp. 69-71.

Harding, Eva. "The Place of the Kindergarten in Child-saving." In National Conference of Charities and Correction. Proceedings (1900), pp. 243-6.

Harding, May H. "Individualization of the Child." In National Conference of Social Work. Proceedings (1922), pp. 262-7.

Hardwick, Katherine. "Minimum Educational Requirements Which Should Be Demanded of Those Beginning Family Case Work." In National Conference of Social Work. Proceedings (1922), pp. 245-53.

Haring, Ardyce. "Public Testimony." In New York (City). Commission on Human Rights. Women's Role in Contemporary Society, pp. 398-401.

Harley, Fanny M. "Discussion of Woman as a Religious Teacher." In World's Congress of Representative Women, Chicago, 1893. A Historical Resume, pp. 285-6.

Harmon, Myra Ruth. "Statement." In U.S. Congress. House. Committee on Education and Labor. Special Subcommittee on Education. Discrimination Against Women, pp. 7-12.

________. "Statement." In U.S. Congress. Senate. Committee on the Judiciary. Subcommittee on Constitutional Amendments. Women and the "Equal Rights" Amendment, pp. 11-7.

Harper, Frances Ellen Watkins. "The Afro-American Mother." In National Congress of Mothers. Work and Words, pp. 67-71.

________. "A Black Woman Appeals to White Women for Justice for Her Race." In Lerner, G. The Female Experience, pp. 354-7.

________. "Duty to Dependent Races." In Loewenberg, B. Black Women in Nineteenth-Century American Life, pp. 247-51. Also in National Council of Women of the U.S., Washington, 1891. Transactions, pp. 86-91. (Same as "A Black Woman Appeals to White Women for Justice for Her Race.")

________. "The Neglected Rich." In International Council of Women, 1888. Report, pp. 119-20.

________. "Social Purity: Its Relation to the Dependent Classes." In National Purity Congress, 1st, Baltimore, 1895. National Purity Congress, pp. 328-30.

________. "Woman's Political Future." In Loewenberg, B. Black Women in Nineteenth-Century American Life, pp. 244-7. Also in World's Congress of Representative Women, Chicago, 1893. A Historical Resume, pp. 433-7.

Harper, Grace S. "Some Uses of Social Case Work in Medical Training." In National Conference of Charities and Correction. Proceedings (1915), pp. 49-59.

Harper, Ida A. Husted. "Address at a Hearing of the House Committee on Rules, December 3, 1913." In Stanton, E. History of Woman Suffrage, 5, 386.

________. "Report to the National American Woman Suffrage Convention of 1918-1919." In Stanton, E. History of Woman Suffrage, 5, 571-2.

________. "The Training of Women Journalists." In International Congress of Women, London, 1899, 4, 52-60.

________. "Women in Municipal Government." In World's Congress of Representative Women, Chicago, 1893. A Historical Resume, pp. 451-7.

Harpole, Marinda. "Statement." In U.S. Congress. Senate. Committee on Labor and Public Welfare. Subcommittee on Children and Youth. White House Conference on Youth, pp. 36-7.

Harral, Elizabeth. "The Foster Parent and the Agency in the Adoption Process." In National Conference of Social Work. Proceedings (1941), pp. 411-25.

Harrington, Katherine. "Statement." In U.S. Congress. Senate. Committee on the Judiciary. Subcommittee on Constitutional Amendments. Equal Rights for Men and Women (1933), pp. 10-2.

Harris, Alice Kessler. "Organizing the Unorganizable: Jewish Women and Their Unions." Cantor, M. Class, Sex, and the Woman Worker, pp. 144-65.

Harris, Ann Sutherland. "Patterns of Discrimination and Discouragement in Higher Education." In New York (City). Commission on Human Rights. Women's Role in Contemporary Society, pp. 583-90.

________. "Statement." In U.S. Congress. House. Committee on Education and Labor. Special Subcommittee on Education. Discrimination Against Women, pp. 45-60, 397-414.

Harris, Bertha. "The Lesbian in Literature: Or, Is There Life on Mars?" In Conference on the University and the Gay Experience. Proceedings, pp. 44-52.

Harris, Dorothy V. "Dimensions of Physical Activity." In Harris, D. Women and Sport, pp. 3-15.

________. "Needed Approaches for a Better Understanding of Behavior and Performance." In Harris, D. Women and Sport, pp. 173-82.

________. "Stress Seeking and Sport Involvement." In Harris, D. Women and Sport, pp. 71-89.

Harris, Patricia Roberts. "Problems and Solutions in Achieving Equality for Women." In Furniss, W. Women in Higher Education, pp. 11-26.

________. "Statement Before the Senate Committee on Banking, Housing, and Urban Affairs: April 19, 1977." Washington, U.S. Department of Housing and Urban Development, 1977, 21 p.

________. "U.N. Adopts International Covenants on Human Rights; Statement, December 12, 1966." Department of State Bulletin, 56 (January 16, 1967), 104-7.

________. "View from the Otherside; Address, November 23, 1965." Department of State Bulletin, 54 (January 3, 1966), 16-9.

Hart, Helen. "The Changing Function of the Settlement Under Changing Conditions." In National Conference of Social Work. Proceedings (1931), pp. 289-95.

Hartle, Mary. "Statement." In U.S. Congress. Senate. Committee on the Judiciary. Subcommittee on Constitutional Amendments. Abortion, pt. 2, 327-30.

Hartmann, Heidi. "Capitalism, Patriarchy, and Job Segregation by Sex." In Blaxall, M. Women and the Workplace, pp. 137-69.

Haskell, Mehitable. "Remarks on Women's Wrongs at the 2nd Worcester Convention, October 1851." In Stanton, E. History of Woman Suffrage, 1, 232.

Haskins, Anna C. "Progress in Social Case Work: In Child Welfare." In National Conference of Social Work. Proceedings (1923), pp. 339-41.

Hastings, Constance E. "Peace in the Public Schools." In American Peace Congress, 1st, New York, 1907. Proceedings, pp. 275-80.
________. "Undifferentiated Case Work the Surest Approach to Rural Social Work: Its Challenge and Its Opportunity: From the Private Agency." In National Conference of Social Work. Proceedings (1927), pp. 112-4.

Hatcher, Orie Latham. "Chairman's Introduction. Youth Plans for a Civilized World." In International Congress of Women, Chicago, 1933. Our Common Cause, Civilization, pp. 183-4.

Hatcher, Sherry Lynn. "The Adolescent Experience of Pregnancy and Abortion." In McGuigan, D. New Research on Women at the University of Michigan, pp. 120-5.

Hathaway, Winifred. "Some Needed Readjustments in Special Fields of Child Welfare: The Extension of Non-institutional Care of Children with Seriously Defective Vision." In National Conference of Social Work. Proceedings (1921), pp. 102-5.

Hathway, Marion. "Education for Public Social Services." In National Conference of Social Work. Proceedings (1940), pp. 585-97.
________. "Gaps in Education and Training." In National Conference of Social Work. Proceedings (1948), pp. 465-72.
________. "Social Action and Professional Education." In National Conference of Social Work. Proceedings (1944), pp. 363-73.

Hauser, Consuelo M. "The Essence of Shelter." In International Conference of Women Engineers and Scientists, 1st, New York. Focus for the Future, pp. II-27-36.

Hauser, Elizabeth J. "Headquarters Report for 1906." In National American Woman Suffrage Association. Proceedings of the 39th Annual Convention, pp. 24-9.

Hauser, Rita E. "The Challenge to Women Today." Congressional Record, 91st Cong., 1st sess., 1969, 115, pt. 13, 17911-2.

Havens, Ruth C.D. "The Girl of the Future. Address to the National American Woman Suffrage Association Convention of 1893." In Stanton, E. History of Woman Suffrage, 4, 209-11.

Hawkes, Anna L. Rose. "Factors Affecting College Attendance." In Conference on the Present Status and Prospective Trends of Research on the Education of Women, Rye, N.Y., 1957. The Education of Women, pp. 29-34.

Hawthone, Julia. "Crime: An Address." In National Conference on Charities and Correction. Proceedings (1885), pp. 413-21.

Hay, Mary Garrett. "Address to the National American Woman Suffrage Convention of 1917." In Stanton, E. History of Woman Suffrage, 5, 536-7.

Hayden, Audrey M. "Organization of Social Forces for Prevention of Blindness." In National Conference of Social Work. Proceedings (1938), pp. 656-65.

______. "Organizing the Community for Social Action." In National Conference of Social Work. Proceedings (1942), pp. 584-93.

Hayden, Helen E. "Case Work Possibilities in a Public Assistance Program." In National Conference of Social Work. Proceedings (1945), pp. 326-34.

Hayden, Iola. "Statement." In U.S. Congress. Senate. Select Committee on Small Business. Effects of Government Regulations, pp. 190-2.

Hayes, Ellen. "Woman's Dress from the Standpoint of Sociology." In World's Congress of Representative Women, Chicago, 1893. A Historical Resume, pp. 354-62.

Hayes, Helen. "The American Theatre Comes of Age." In New York Herald Tribune. Report of the 5th Annual Forum on Current Problems, pp. 199-203.

Hayes, Mary H.S. "Job Preparation and Juvenile Guidance on a National Front." In National Conference of Social Work. Proceedings (1939), pp. 146-51.

______. "A Program for Unemployed Youth." In National Conference of Social Work. Proceedings (1935), pp. 374-81.

Hayes, Mary Venette. "Piano Playing Without Piano Practicing." In World's Congress of Representative Women, Chicago, 1893. Congress of Women, pp. 474-6.

Haynes, Lorenza. "The Relation of Young Women to Church Missions." In World's Congress of Representative Women, Chicago, 1893. A Historical Resume, pp. 826-7.

Hazard, Rebecca N. "Speech at the 10th Annual Meeting of the American Woman Suffrage Association, 1879." In Stanton, E. History of Woman Suffrage, 2, 855-6.

Hazel, Rosa H. "Mrs. Rosa H. Hazel at Douglass Memorial Meeting, St. Paul, Minnesota." In Douglass, F. Frederick Douglass on Women's Rights, pp. 171-5.

Hazlett, Adelle. "Address at the Decade Meeting Held at Apollo Hall, October 20, 1870." In Davis, P. A History of the National Woman's Rights Movement, pp. 52-7.

Hearsey, Mildred. "The Control of Syphilis, from the Viewpoint of Medical Social Service." In National Conference of Social Work. Proceedings (1937), pp. 529-35.

Heckler, Margaret Mary O'Shaughnessy. "Should the "District" Method of Electing the President Be Adopted?" Congressional Digest, 49 (January, 1970), 27.
________. "Statement." In U.S. Congress. House. Committee on Government Operations. National Women's Conference, pp. 17-20.
________. "Statement." In U.S. Congress. Senate. Committee on the Judiciary. Subcommittee on Constitutional Amendments. Women and the "Equal Rights" Amendment, pp. 27-32.

Hedger, Caroline. "Medical Inspection in the Schools--Its Technique and Its Results." In National Conference of Social Work. Proceedings (1923), pp. 374-8.
________. "Standards of Hygiene and Equipment of Day Nurseries." In National Conference of Social Work. Proceedings (1919), pp. 45-8.

Hedley, Carolyn. "Public Testimony." In New York (City). Commission on Human Rights. Women's Role in Contemporary Society, pp. 421-4.

Heffelfinger, Elizabeth. "The Citizen's Responsibility; A Panel Discussion." In New York Herald Tribune. Report of the 18th Annual Forum on Current Problems, pp. 145-6, 171-2, 180.

Hefferan, Marie C. Murphy. "What Can the Educator Do?" In International Congress of Women, Chicago, 1933. Our Common Cause, Civilization, pp. 764-9.

Heide, Wilma Scott. "Address to 1974 NOW National Conference." Do It NOW, 7 (October, 1974), 3.
________. "Equal Rights Amendment." In New York (City). Commission on Human Rights. Women's Role in Contemporary Society, pp. 618-23.
________. "Feminism; The Sine Qua Non for a Just Society." Vital Speeches, 38 (April 15, 1972), 403-9.
________. "Revolution: Tomorrow Is NOW!" Vital Speeches, 39 (May 1, 1973), 424-8.
________. "Statement." In U.S. Congress. House. Committee on Education and Labor. Special Subcommittee on Education. Discrimination Against Women, pp. 21-30.

________. "Statement." In U.S. Congress. House. Committee on Education and Labor. Special Subcommittee on Education. Discrimination Against Women, pp. 530-3.

________. "Statement." In U.S. Congress. Senate. Committee on the Judiciary. Equal Rights 1970, pp. 288-95.

________. "Statement." In U.S. Congress. Senate. Committee on the Judiciary. Subcommittee on Constitutional Amendments. Women and the "Equal Rights" Amendment, pp. 191-9.

________. "Women's Liberation Means Putting Sex in Its Place." In Katzell, M. Women in the Work Force, pp. 15-26.

Height, Dorothy. "Address." In Conference on Women in the War on Poverty, 1967. Proceedings, pp. 40-2.

________. "Questions for the Future. Action." In U.S. National Center for Health Services Research. Women and Their Health, pp. 92-4.

________. "Summing Up." In Conference on Women in the War on Poverty, 2nd, 1968. Proceedings, pp. 61-2.

________. "To Be Black and a Woman." In New York (City). Commission on Human Rights. Women's Role in Contemporary Society, pp. 82-5.

Hellinger, Joan. "Statement." In U.S. Congress. Senate. Committee on the Judiciary. Subcommittee on Constitutional Amendments. Equal Rights for Men and Women (1938), pp. 32-4.

Hendricks, Thomasine. "The Learning Process in Agency Settings." In National Conference of Social Work. Proceedings (1944), pp. 343-52.

Hennock, Frieda B. "Women and Future of Broadcasting." Washington, U.S. Federal Communications Commission, 1951, 4 p.

Henrotin, Ellen Martin. "Address." In Jewish Women's Congress. Papers, p. 9.

________. "Address on Woman's Work for Peace." In American Peace Congress, 2nd, Chicago, 1909. Proceedings, pp. 248-50.

________. "The Board of Lady Managers of the Columbian Exposition." In National Council of Women of the U.S., Washington, 1891. Transactions, pp. 320-3.

________. "The Financial Independence of Women." In World's Congress of Representative Women, Chicago, 1893. Congress of Women, pp. 348-53.

________. "The Home and the Economic Waste of War." In American Peace Congress, 1st, New York, 1907. Proceedings, pp. 93-7.

________. "Opening Address." In World's Congress of Representative Women, Chicago, 1893. A Historical Resume, p. 12.

________. "Organization." In National Council of Women of the U.S., Washington, 1891. Transactions, pp. 251-4.

Henry, Edna G. "Bridging the Chasm." In National Conference of Social Work. Proceedings (1920), pp. 212-5.

Henry, Josephine K. "Woman Suffrage in the South. Address to the National American Woman Suffrage Convention of 1895." In Stanton, E. History of Woman Suffrage, 4, 244-5.

Henry, Marguerite. "Acceptance Paper--Newbery Medal 1949." In Miller, B. Newbery Medal Books, 1922-1955, pp. 327-34.

Hepburn, Katharine. "Keeping the Mind of the Nation Young Through Motion Pictures." In New York Herald Tribune. Report of the 8th Annual Forum on Current Problems, pp. 40-1.

Herberg, Dorothy Chave. "Social Research on Women's Professional Careers." In McGuigan, D. New Research on Women at the University of Michigan, pp. 159-62.

de Hericourt, Jeanne. "Address to the 3rd Annual Meeting of the American Equal Rights Association, New York, May 1869." In Stanton, E. History of Woman Suffrage, 2, 394-5.

Herman, Alexis. "Statement." In U.S. Congress. House. Committee on Education and Labor. Subcommittee on Employment Opportunities. Legislation to Prohibit Sex Discrimination on the Basis of Pregnancy, pp. 179-80.

______. "Statement." In U.S. Congress. Senate. Committee on Human Resources. Subcommittee on Labor. Discrimination on the Basis of Pregnancy, pp. 33-5.

Herman, Judith. "Public Testimony." In New York (City). Commission on Human Rights. Women's Role in Contemporary Society, pp. 162-4.

Hernandez, Aileen Clarke. "Address August 26, 1970--Los Angeles Rally." NOW Acts, 3 (September, 1970), 1, 3.

______. "Address to 1974 NOW National Conference." Do It NOW, 7 (October, 1974), 4.

______. "Introduction to Keynote Address." In NOW Acts, 6 (February 16, 1973), 2.

______. "Introductions at Founder's Reception." NOW Acts, 4 (Fall, 1971), 6, 7, 9, 10-1, 11-2.

______. "Revolution: From the Doll's House to the White House!" In NOW Acts, 4 (Fall, 1971), 3-6.

______. "Statement." In U.S. Congress. House. Committee on the Judiciary. Subcommittee No. 4. Equal Rights for Men and Women 1971, pp. 230-42.

______. "Statement." In U.S. Congress. Senate. Committee on the Judiciary. Subcommittee on Constitutional Amendments. Women and the "Equal Rights" Amendment, pp. 38-9.

______. "Testimony on Federal Efforts to End Sex Discrimination in Employment." In U.S. Congress. Joint Economic Committee. Economic Problems of Women, pt. 1, 128-33.

Herrick, Elinore M. "Federal Wage and Hour Regulation." Vital Speeches, 4 (February 1, 1938), 250-1.

________. "Renewing the Battle for Minimum Wage Legislation." Vital Speeches, 3 (January 15, 1937), 223-4.

Herring, Harriet L. "The Southern Industrial Problem as the Social Worker Sees It." In National Conference of Social Work. Proceedings (1930), pp. 309-14.

Hewins, Katharine P. "Shaping the Record to Facilitate Research." In National Conference of Charities and Correction. Proceedings (1916), pp. 460-8.

Hickey, Margaret A. "Bound for the Future. Women's Responsibility for the Future." Vital Speeches, 10 (November 1, 1943), 49-51.

________. "What's Ahead for Woman Who Earns." Washington, U.S. Women's Bureau, 1946, 6 p.

Hicks, Beatrice A. "Welcome and Introduction of Keynote Speaker." In International Conference of Women Engineers and Scientists, 1st, New York. Focus for the Future, pp. I-5-6.

Hicky, Ardelphia. "Statement." In U.S. Congress. House. Committee on Education and Labor. Subcommittee on Equal Opportunities. Equal Opportunity for Displaced Homemakers Act, pp. 29-31.

Hiett, Helen. "Spiritual Contributions to the Strength of Man." In New York Herald Tribune. Report of the 16th Annual Forum on Current Problems, pp. 65-6.

Higgins, Alice L. "Alcohol Problems." In National Conference of Charities and Correction. Proceedings (1911), pp. 140-7.

________. "Comparative Advantages of Municipal and C.O.S. Lodging Houses." In National Conference of Charities and Correction. Proceedings (1904), pp. 148-55.

Higgins, Lois Lundell. "Law Enforcement Responsibility. What Can Police Do?" Vital Speeches, 28 (September 15, 1962), 723-4.

________. "Statement." In U.S. Congress. House. Committee on Education and Labor. Select Subcommittee on Labor. Equal Pay for Equal Work, pt. 2, 263-72.

Higgins, Marguerite. "Report from Korea." In New York Herald Tribune. Report of the 19th Annual Forum on Current Problems, pp. 208-13.

Hiles, Osia Joslyn. "The Mission Indians of California." In National Conference of Charities and Correction. Proceedings (1887), pp. 187-91.

Hilgert, Betty. "Statement." In U.S. Congress. Senate. Committee on the Judiciary. Subcommittee on Constitutional Amendments. Equal Rights Amendment (1929), pp. 50-1.

Hill, Ruth. "Goals for Wanderers." In National Conference of Social Work. Proceedings (1925), pp. 264-71.

_______. "Group Living for the Elderly." In National Conference of Social Work. Proceedings (1948), pp. 4410-8.

_______. "Old and the Needy." Vital Speeches, 1 (February 25, 1935), 38-40.

_______. "Some Community Values in a Social Survey." In National Conference of Social Work. Proceedings (1930), pp. 420-9.

Hilles, Florence Bayard. "Defense Speech at Trial for Picketing White House, 1917." In Stevens, D. Jailed for Freedom, p. 103.

_______. "Statement." In U.S. Congress. Senate. Committee on the Judiciary. Subcommittee on Constitutional Amendments. Equal Rights for Men and Women (1933), p. 2.

Hills, Marilla M. "Report of Free Baptist Missionary Society." In International Council of Women, 1888. Report, p. 200.

Hilton, Alice Mary. "Of Worth and Value: The Human Spirit and the Cybercultural Revolution." Vital Speeches, 32 (March 15, 1966), 335-41.

Hilton, M. Eunice. "Working Women: Their Home Obligations." In U.S. Women's Bureau. American Woman--Her Changing Role, pp. 108-10.

Hilton, Mary N. "Entry and Reentry of Older Women into Labor Market: Older Women in Labor Force." Washington, U.S. Women's Bureau, 1953.

Hinds, Ida K. "Harmonious Culture." In World's Congress of Representative Women, Chicago, 1893. Congress of Women, pp. 438-42.

Hinrichsen, Annie. "The District Almshouse for Illinois." In National Conference of Social Work. Proceedings (1918), pp. 267-70.

Hirshfield, Lillie. "How Can Nations Be Influenced to Protest or Interfere in Cases of Persecution?" In Jewish Women's Congress. Papers, pp. 210-16.

Hitchcock, Emma Louise Bingham. "The Japanese." In World's Congress of Representative Women, Chicago, 1893. Congress of Women, pp. 556-61.

Hitchcock, Jane Elizabeth. "Report of the Sub-committee on Visiting Nursing." In National Conference of Charities and Correction. Proceedings (1905), pp. 257-63.

Hoagland, Merica. "Labor Legislation for Women." In U.S. Women's Bureau. Proceedings of the Women's Industrial Conference, pp. 120-6.

Hobby, Oveta Culp. "Citizen Responsibilities. 'They' Is 'We'." Vital Speeches, 21 (December 15, 1954), 905-8.

________. "The Draft: Education for Citizenship." In New York Herald Tribune. Report of the 17th Annual Forum on Current Problems, pp. 132-6.

Hodder, Jessie D. "Disciplinary Measures in the Management of the Psychopathic Delinquent Women." In National Conference of Social Work. Proceedings (1920), pp. 389-96.

________. "The Next Step in the Treatment of Girls and Women Offenders." In National Conference of Social Work. Proceedings (1918), pp. 117-21.

Hodges, Gertie. "Statement." In U.S. Congress. Joint Economic Committee. Economic Problems of Women, pt. 4, 623-5.

Hodnett, Ida. "Statement." In U.S. Congress. Senate. Committee on the Judiciary. Subcommittee on Constitutional Amendments. Equal Rights for Men and Women (1933), p. 16.

Hoey, Jane M. "Adequate Public Social Services for Migrants." In National Conference of Social Work. Proceedings (1947), pp. 163-75.

________. "The Contribution of Social Work to Government." In National Conference of Social Work. Proceedings (1941), pp. 3-17.

________. "Division on Delinquents and Correction." In National Conference of Social Work. Proceedings (1933), pp. 104-6.

________. "The Federal Government and Desirable Standards of State and Local Government." In National Conference of Social Work. Proceedings (1937), pp. 440-4.

________. "Mass Relocation of Aliens." In National Conference of Social Work. Proceedings (1942), pp. 194-9.

________. "Next Steps in Public Assistance." In National Conference of Social Work. Proceedings (1945), pp. 148-60.

________. "Social Work Concepts and Methods in the Postwar World." In National Conference of Social Work. Proceedings (1944), pp. 35-47.

________. "Understanding the Delinquent: Society in Relation to the Child." In National Conference of Social Work. Proceedings (1931), pp. 87-96.

Hofer, Amalie. "What the Kindergarten Means to Mothers." In National Congress of Mothers. Work and Words, pp. 55-61.

Hoffer, Carol P. "Madam Yoko: Ruler of the Kpa Mende Confederacy." In Rosaldo, M. Woman, Culture, and Society, pp. 173-87.

Hoffman, Clara Cleghorne. "Address." In International Council of Women, 1888. Report, pp. 283-4.

_______. "A Bird's-eye View of the National Woman's Christian Temperance Union." In World's Congress of Representative Women, Chicago, 1893. A Historical Resume, pp. 874-6.

_______. "Organization Among Women Considered with Respect to Philanthropy--Continued." In World's Congress of Representative Women, Chicago, 1893. A Historical Resume, pp. 258-9.

Hoffman, Lois W. "Psychology Looks at the Female." In McGuigan, D. New Research on Women at the University of Michigan, pp. 16-8.

_______. "A Re-examination of the Fear of Success." In McGuigan, D. New Research on Women at the University of Michigan, pp. 105-12.

Hogan, Anna B. "Statement." In U.S. Congress. Senate. Committee on the Judiciary. Subcommittee on Constitutional Amendments. Equal Rights Amendment (1945), pp. 8-9.

Hogan, Louise E. "Dietetics." In National Congress of Mothers. Work and Words, pp. 101-17.

Hogan, Marion G. "Self-employment." In M.I.T. Symposium on American Women in Science and Engineering, 1964. Women and the Scientific Professions, pp. 191-4.

Hogrogian, Nonny. "Caldecott Award Acceptance--1966." In Kingman, L. Newbery and Caldecott Medal Books, 1966-1973, pp. 179-80.

_______. "Caldecott Award Acceptance: How the Caldecott Changed My Life--Twice (1972)." In Kingman, L. Newbery and Caldecott Medal Books, 1966-1975, pp. 237-9.

Hohman, Helen Fisher. "Proposals for Distribution." In International Congress of Women, Chicago, 1933. Our Common Cause, Civilization, pp. 393-9.

Holbrook, Elizabeth L. "A Survey of a Month's Work Made Six Months Afterward." In National Conference of Charities and Correction. Proceedings (1915), pp. 80-3.

Holcomb, Marion. "Youth Plans for a Civilized World: Forum on the College Generation." In International Congress of Women, Chicago, 1933. Our Common Cause, Civilization, pp. 187-8.

Holcombe, Elizabeth J. "Physical Decline of Leisure-class American Women. A Paper Read Before the Woman's Alliance of Syracuse and Other Clubs, and Published by Request." Syracuse, N.Y., Hall & McChesney, 1893. 61 p.

Holder, Evelyn. "Military Service--Bridge or Gap? Panel Discussion." In New York Herald Tribune. Report of the 20th Annual Forum on Current Problems, pp. 78-80.

Hollis, Florence. "Emotional Growth of the Worker Through Supervision." In National Conference of Social Work. Proceedings (1936), pp. 167-78.

_______. "The Impact of the War on Marriage Relationships." In National Conference of Social Work. Proceedings (1943), pp. 104-15.

Hollister, Lillian M. "Fraternal Benefit Associations: Their Origin, Scope and Value." In International Congress of Women, Toronto, 1909. Report, 2, 344-9.

Holloway, Laura C. "Women in Journalism." In International Council of Women, 1888. Report, pp. 167-9.

Holme, Pauline W. "Address to the National Purity Congress, Baltimore Yearly Meeting Committee." In National Purity Congress, 1st, Baltimore, 1895. National Purity Congress, pp. 186-90.

Holt, Charlotte C. "The Woman Who Has Come." In World's Congress of Representative Women, Chicago, 1893. Congress of Women, pp. 190-3.

Holt, Leila M. "Statement." In U.S. Congress. House. Committee on Education and Labor. Select Subcommittee on Labor. Equal Pay for Equal Work, pp. 142-3.

Holt, Marjorie. "Should Manufacture and Sale of Handguns for Private Use Be Prohibited in the United States." Congressional Digest, 54 (December, 1975), 307-9.

Holtzman, Elizabeth. "Should Congress Enact H.R. 10 to Permit Greater Political Activity by Federal Employees?" Congressional Digest, 56 (December, 1977), 299-303.

Homes, Edith M. "The Working Girl's or Working Women's Club in the United States." In International Congress of Women, London, 1899, 7, 102-6.

Honigman, Rhoda. "Women in Engineering." In Conference of Professional and Academic Women. Sixteen Reports on the Status of Women in the Professions, 2 p.

Hood, Laura. "Foreign Organizations and Family Welfare." In National Conference of Social Work. Proceedings (1920), pp. 486-93.

Hooker, Isabella Beecher. "Address." In International Council of Women, 1888. Report, pp. 418-20.

_______. "Address of Mrs. Isabella Beecher Hooker. Address to Judiciary Committee Hearing, 1871." In Stanton, E. History of Woman Suffrage, 2, 458-61.

________. "Address to the Judiciary Committee, U. S. Senate, January 17, 1872." In Stanton, E. *History of Woman Suffrage*, 2, 499-506.

________. "The Constitutional Rights of the Women of the United States." In International Council of Women, 1888. *Report*, pp. 292-304.

________. "Message of Thanks to Members of Congressional Committee Supporting Cause." In Davis, P. *A History of the National Woman's Rights Movement*, pp. 90-1. Also in Stanton, E. *History of Woman Suffrage*, 2, 489-90.

________. "The Queen Isabella Association." In National Council of Women of the U. S., Washington, 1891. *Transactions*, pp. 323-5.

________. "Report of the Year's Work to the National Woman's Suffrage Association Convention, January, 1872." In Stanton, E. *History of Woman Suffrage*, 2, 496-7.

Hooper, Elizabeth M. "The Health of the Child." In International Congress of Women, Toronto, 1909. *Report*, 2, 34-6.

Hopkins, Louisa. "Woman's Work in Education." In National Education Association. *Journal of Proceedings & Addresses* (1884), pp. 157-60.

Hoppock, Anne. "No Time for Panic. We Must Not Lose Our Humanness." *Vital Speeches*, 24 (June 1, 1958), 499-503.

Horrobin, Margaret. "Statement." In U. S. Congress. Senate. Committee on the Judiciary. Subcommittee on Constitutional Amendments. *Abortion*, pt. 2, 291-9.

Horten, Elizabeth. "Instances of After Care of the Insane." In National Conference of Charities and Correction. *Proceedings* (1907), pp. 462-3.

Horton, Mildred McAfee. "Predictions for the Unpredictable Future. Every Big Accomplishment Involves Many Small Ones." *Vital Speeches*, 17 (August 1, 1951), 617-9.

________. "Presidential Address." In *Association of American Colleges Bulletin* (March, 1948), pp. 5-14.

________. "Woman's Responsibility Today. An American Woman's Viewpoint." *Vital Speeches*, 13 (June 1, 1947), 504-6.

Hosch, Florence I. "The Determination of Social Work Salaries." In National Conference of Social Work. *Proceedings* (1946), pp. 297-303.

Hottel, Althea K. "The Citizen's Responsibility: A Panel Discussion." In New York Herald Tribune. *Report of the 18th Annual Forum on Current Problems*, pp. 158-9.

________. "Women's Education: New Needs in Our Time." In Conference on Women in the Defense Decade, New York, 1951. *Women in the Defense Decade*, pp. 70-8.

Houghteling, Leila. "War Time Volunteers in Chicago." In National Conference of Social Work. Proceedings (1918), pp. 678-82.

Houghton, Dorothy Deemer. "Report from Europe." In New York Herald Tribune. Report of the 19th Annual Forum on Current Problems, pp. 55-8.

________. "World Challenges American Educators. The Opportunity to Build New Frontiers of Understanding and Peace." Vital Speeches, 21 (April 15, 1955), 1168-72.

Howard, Amelia Louisa Zacharie. "Moorish Women As I Found Them." In World's Congress of Representative Women, Chicago, 1893. Congress of Women, pp. 463-8.

Howard, Celia. "Statement." In U.S. Congress. Senate. Committee on the Judiciary. Subcommittee on Constitutional Amendments. Equal Rights for Men and Women (1938), pp. 115-6.

Howard, Emma Shafter. "The Women's Agricultural and Horticultural Union." In International Congress of Women, Toronto, 1909. Report, 2, 327-9.

Howard, Katherine G. "What's New in the '52 Campaign?" In New York Herald Tribune. Report of the 21st Annual Forum on Current Problems, pp. 193-7.

Howe, Florence. "Public Testimony." In New York (City). Commission on Human Rights. Women's Role in Contemporary Society, pp. 678-82.

________. "Status of Women in the Academic Profession--Another Perspective." In Conference of Professional and Academic Women. Sixteen Reports on the Status of Women in the Professions, 2 p.

Howe, Julia Ward. "Address at Memorial Service for Lucy Stone During the National American Woman Suffrage Association Convention of 1894." In Stanton, E. History of Woman Suffrage, 4, 225.

________. "Address by the President." In Association for the Advancement of Women. "Truth, Justice and Honor," pp. 7-8.

________. "Address to the American Woman Suffrage Association Convention, New York, May 1870." In Stanton, E. History of Woman Suffrage, 2, 770-1.

________. "Address to the 2nd Session of the American Woman Suffrage Association Convention, New York, May 1870." In Stanton, E. History of Woman Suffrage, 2, 792-5.

________. "Aristophanes." In Howe, J. Is Polite Society Polite?, pp. 133-58.

________. "Benefits of Suffrage for Women." In Association for the Advancement of Women. "Truth, Justice and Honor," pp. 29-42.

________. "Boston, a Little Island of Darkness. Speech at a Suffrage Hearing at the State House in Boston, February 4, 1908." In Howe, J. Julia Ward Howe and the Woman Suffrage Movement, pp. 206-11.

________. "The Chivalry of Reform. Address to the National American Woman Suffrage Association Convention, 1890." In Stanton, E. History of Woman Suffrage, 4, 1970.

________. "Dante and Beatrice." In Howe, J. Is Polite Society Polite?, pp. 181-202.

________. "Extemporaneous Speech Made at a Suffrage Hearing, February, 1884." In Howe, J. Julia Ward Howe and the Woman Suffrage Movement, pp. 198-200.

________. "Greece Revisited." In Howe, J. Is Polite Society Polite?, pp. 77-110.

________. "Greeting to the 9th Biennial Convention of the General Federation of Women's Clubs, June 23, 1908." In General Federation of Women's Clubs. Biennial Convention, 9 (1908), 21-3.

________. "The Halfness of Nature." In Howe, J. Is Polite Society Polite?, pp. 161-78.

________. "Hearing of Massachusetts Legislature, February 1900." In Howe, J. Julia Ward Howe and the Woman Suffrage Movement, pp. 30-1.

________. "How Can Women Best Associate?" In Association for the Advancement of Women. Congress of Women, 1st. Papers, pp. 5-10.

________. "How to Extend the Sympathies of Women." In Howe, J. Julia Ward Howe and the Woman Suffrage Movement, pp. 235-41.

________. "Is Polite Society Polite?" In Howe, J. Is Polite Society Polite?, pp. 3-33.

________. "Let There Be Light." In Howe, J. Julia Ward Howe and the Woman Suffrage Movement, pp. 217-21.

________. "Message of Julia Ward Howe to the National Arbitration and Peace Congress." In American Peace Congress, 1st, New York, 1907. Proceedings, pp. 117-20.

________. "Moral Equality Between the Sexes." In National Purity Congress, 1st, Baltimore, 1895. National Purity Congress, pp. 66-70.

________. "The Moral Initiative as Belonging to Women." In Howe, J. Julia Ward Howe and the Woman Suffrage Movement, pp. 113-35. Also in World's Congress of Representative Women, Chicago, 1893. A Historical Resume, pp. 314-21.

________. "On the Formation of Art Groups." In Association for the Advancement of Women. Congress of Women, 3rd. Papers, pp. 104-5.

________. "Paris." In Howe, J. Is Polite Society Polite?, pp. 37-73.

________. "The Patience of Faith." In Howe, J. Julia Ward Howe and the Woman Suffrage Movement, pp. 230-4.

________. "The Position of Women in Plato's Republic." In Howe, J. Julia Ward Howe and the Woman Suffrage Movement, pp. 48-92.

________. "The Power of Organization." In International Council of Women, 1888. Report, pp. 189-95.

________. "President's Address to the American Woman Suffrage Association, 6th Annual Meeting, October 1874." In Howe, J. Julia Ward Howe and the Woman Suffrage Movement, pp. 15-6. Also in Stanton, E. History of Woman Suffrage, 2, 834-6.

________. "The Relation of the Woman Suffrage Movement to Other Reforms." In National Council of Women of the U.S., Washington, 1891. Transactions, pp. 237-42.

________. "The Salon in America." In Howe, J. Is Polite Society Polite?, pp. 113-29.

________. "Speech at a Suffrage Hearing Before the Massachusetts Legislature." In Howe, J. Julia Ward Howe and the Woman Suffrage Movement, pp. 189-97.

________. "Speech at Legislative Hearing." In Howe, J. Julia Ward Howe and the Woman Suffrage Movement, pp. 202-5.

________. "Speech at Meeting of the American Woman Suffrage Association, Philadelphia, July, 1876." In Stanton, E. History of Woman Suffrage, 2, 847-8.

________. "Speech at the Annual Meeting of an Equal Suffrage Association, 1895." In Howe, J. Julia Ward Howe and the Woman Suffrage Movement, pp. 212-6.

________. "Speech on Equal Rights." In Howe, J. Julia Ward Howe and the Woman Suffrage Movement, pp. 222-9.

________. "Why Are Women the Natural Guardians of Social Morals?" In Howe, J. Julia Ward Howe and the Woman Suffrage Movement, pp. 93-112.

________. "Women in the Greek Drama. Extracts from Julia Ward Howe's Lectures." In World Congress of Representative Women, Chicago, 1893. Congress of Women, pp. 102-3.

Howell, Mary C. "Highlights of the Conference." In International Conference on Women in Health. Proceedings, pp. 169-70.

Howell, Mary Seymour. "The Dawning of the Twentieth Century." In World's Congress of Representative Women, Chicago, 1893. Congress of Women, pp. 679-81.

________. "Gains of the Last Three Years." In National Council of Women of the U.S., Washington, 1891. Transactions, pp. 230-7.

Howes, Ethel Puffer. "Social Progress Within the Home." In National Conference of Social Work. Proceedings (1923), pp. 299-303.

Howlett, Virginia. "Relation of Case-work Staffs to Interpretation, Officials, Governing Boards, Volunteers, and the Public." In National Conference of Social Work. Proceedings (1923), pp. 242-50.

Hoxie, Vinnie Ream. "Lincoln and Farragut." In World's Congress of Representative Women, Chicago, 1893. Congress of Women, pp. 603-8.

________. "Sculpture for Women." In International Congress of Women, Toronto, 1909. Report, 2, 355-6.

Huck, Winnifred Sprague Mason. "Universal Peace Among the Nations of the World." Congressional Record, 67th Cong., 4th sess., 1923, 64, pt. 2, 1827-8.

Huffman, Helen C. "The Importance of Birth Records." In National Conference of Social Work. Proceedings (1947), pp. 351-60.

Hufstedler, Shirley M. "Courtship and Other Legal Arts: The Appellate System." Vital Speeches, 40 (March 15, 1974), 333-7.

________. "In the Name of Justice: The Unending Rush to the Courts." Vital Speeches, 43 (July 1, 1977), 572-6.

Hughes, Sarah T. "Building Leadership for Peace ... New Ideas from New Voters: Panel Discussion." In New York Herald Tribune. Report of the 21st Annual Forum on Current Problems, pp. 156-7, 159.

Hull, Ida L. "The Immigrant as a Factor in Social Case Work; In the Family Welfare Field." In National Conference of Social Work. Proceedings (1925), pp. 589-93.

________. "Special Problems in Italian Families." In National Conference of Social Work. Proceedings (1924), pp. 288-91.

Hull, Joan. "Public Testimony." In New York (City). Commission on Human Rights. Women's Role in Contemporary Society, pp. 320-1.

Hull, Mary Hess. "Woman and Household Labor." In World's Congress of Representative Women, Chicago, 1893. Congress of Women, pp. 609-11.

Hultin, Ida C. "Address on Organization Among Women as an Instrument in Promoting Religion." In World's Congress of Representative Women, Chicago, 1893. A Historical Resume, pp. 297-8.

________. "Extract from Woman and Religion." In World's Congress of Representative Women, Chicago, 1893. Congress of Women, pp. 788-9. (Same as "Address on Organization Among Women as an Instrument in Promoting Religion").

________. "Treatment of the Destitute Classes in the United States." In International Congress of Women, London, 1899, 7, 63-4.

________. "Tribute to Susan B. Anthony at her 80th Birthday Celebration, February 15, 1900." In Harper, I. The Life and Work of Susan B. Anthony, 3, 1183.

Humphrey, Ethel. "The Smallpox Problem in the West." In National Conference of Social Work. Proceedings (1925), pp. 208-10.

Hunt, Harriot Kezia. "Annual Protest on Taxation Read at the Woman's Rights Convention in New York, September 1853." In Stanton, E. History of Woman Suffrage, 1, 565.

________. "Reprint of Remarks by Dr. Hunt in the (New York) Tribune, September 12, 1853." In Stanton, E. History of Woman Suffrage, 1, 576.

Hunt, Irene. "Books and the Learning Process. Newbery Award Acceptance--1967." In Kingman, L. Newbery and Caldecott Medal Books, 1966-1975, pp. 22-8.

Hunt, Mary. "Our Reasons." In International Council of Women, 1888. Report, pp. 127-8.

________. "Statement." In U.S. Congress. Senate. Committee on the Judiciary. Subcommittee on Constitutional Amendments. Abortion, pt. 2, 441-2.

________. "Temperance Education." In World's Congress of Representative Women, Chicago, 1893. A Historical Resume, pp. 388-91.

Hurlbutt, Mary Emerson. "International Aspects of the Migration Problem: Development of International Case Work." In National Conference of Social Work. Proceedings (1922), pp. 487-91.

________. "The Invisible Environment of an Immigrant." In National Conference of Social Work. Proceedings (1923), pp. 309-13.

________. "The Postwar Role of Social Workers." In National Conference of Social Work. Proceedings (1943), pp. 412-21.

________. "The United Nations Relief and Rehabilitation Administration's Task for Displaced Persons." In National Conference of Social Work. Proceedings (1944), pp. 100-8.

Hurst, Fannie. "Are We Coming or Going?" Vital Speeches, 1 (December 3, 1934), 150-60.

________. "Crisis in the History of Women. Let Us Have Action Instead of Lip-Service." Vital Speeches, 9 (May 15, 1943), 479-80.

________. "The Submerged Race." In New York Herald Tribune. Report of 2nd Women's Conference on Current Problems, pp. 39-42.

Huse, Betty. "Care and Treatment of Crippled Children." Washington, U.S. Children's Bureau, 1944, 4 p.

Hutar, Patricia. "Statement Before the Social Committee of the U.N. Economic and Social Council, May 7, 1974 Supporting Holding Conference During International Women's Year." Department of State Bulletin, 70 (June 3, 1974), 612.

________. "Statement of June 20, 1975 to the U.N. World Conference of the International Women's Year Held at Mexico City." Department of State Bulletin, 73 (August 18, 1975), 233-7.

________. "Statement of July 2, 1975 to the U.N. World Conference of the International Women's Year Held at Mexico City." Department of State Bulletin, 73 (August 18, 1975), 237-8.

Hutchinson, Dorothy. "Foster Home Care in Wartime." In National Conference of Social Work. Proceedings (1944), pp. 237-45.

________. "Therapy with Older Children as Seen by the Psychiatrist." In National Conference of Social Work. Proceedings (1940), pp. 344-51.

Hutchinson, Helen. "What Irregular Employment Means to Household and Community." In National Conference of Social Work. Proceedings (1922), pp. 294-9.

Hutchinson, Winnifred. "Citizenship and Domicile Versus Social Considerations in Problems of Migrated Families." In National Conference of Social Work. Proceedings (1935), pp. 679-91.

Iglitzin, Lynne B. "The Making of the Apolitical Woman: Femininity and Sex-Stereotyping in Girls." In Jaquette, J. Women in Politics, pp. 25-36.

Ilma, Viola. "What the Colleges Can Do for Peace." In International Congress of Women, Chicago, 1933. Our Common Cause, Civilization, pp. 205-10.

Indritz, Ruth. "Volunteer Women Speak ORT, The Charity to End Charity, Through Vocational Education." Congressional Record, 91st Cong., 1st sess., 1969, 115, pt. 5, 5768-9.

Ingram, Frances. "A Community Kitchen in a Neighborhood House." In National Conference of Social Work. Proceedings (1918), pp. 459-63.

________. "The Public Dance Hall." In National Conference of Social Work. Proceedings (1919), pp. 507-12.

Ingram, Helene. "The Value of the Fresh Air Movement." In National Conference of Charities and Correction. Proceedings (1907), pp. 286-94.

Insel, Barbara. "Women into Management: Vignettes." In Gordon, F. Bringing Women into Management, pp. 134-6.

Irwin, Helen B. "Conditions in Industry as They Affect Negro Women." In National Conference of Social Work. Proceedings (1919), pp. 521-4.

Isaacs, Marion E. "Christ on the Avenue." In World's Congress of Representative Women, Chicago, 1893. A Historical Resume, pp. 819-33.

Jackson, Jacquelyn Johnson. "New Roles for Women in Health Care Delivery. A U.S. Response to the Cameroonian Experience." In International Conference on Women in Health. Proceedings, pp. 133-5.

Jacobi, Mary Corinna Putnam. "Social Aspects of the Readmission of Women into the Medical Profession." In Association for the Advancement of Women. Congress of Women, 1st. Papers, pp. 168-78.

________. "Women in Science." In World's Congress of Representative Women, Chicago, 1893. A Historical Resume, pp. 195-207. (Read by Julia Holmes Smith.)

Jacobs, Bertha. "The Work of One State." In National Conference of Charities and Correction. Proceedings (1904), pp. 317-20.

Jacobs, Jane. "Downtown Planning. Solving Traffic Problems." Vital Speeches, 25 (January 1, 1959), 190-2.

Jacobs, Pattie Ruffner. "Address at a Hearing of the Senate Committee on Woman Suffrage, December 15, 1915." In Stanton, E. History of Woman Suffrage, 5, 463-4.

Jacobson, Carol. "Public Testimony." In New York (City). Commission on Human Rights. Women's Role in Contemporary Society, pp. 447-8.

Jacobson, Dorothy H. "The War on Hunger: Temptation or Challenge." Vital Speeches, 33 (October 1, 1967), 763-6.

Jacobson, Laura Davis. "How Can Nations Be Influenced to Protest or Interfere in Cases of Persecution?" In Jewish Women's Congress. Papers, pp. 196-209.

Jacoby, Robin Miller. "Feminism and Class Consciousness in the British and American Women's Trade Union Leagues, 1890-1925." In Carroll, B. Liberating Women's History, pp. 137-60. Also in McGuigan, D. New Research on Women at the University of Michigan, pp. 70-6.

________. "The Women's Trade Union League and American Feminism." In Cantor, M. Class, Sex, and the Woman Worker, pp. 203-24.

Jaffray, Julia K. "Committee on Institutional Relations." In General Federation of Women's Clubs. Biennial Convention, 16 (1922), 503-5.

________. "Preventing the First Offender." In New York Herald Tribune. Report of the 4th Annual Woman's Conference on Current Problems, pp. 41-4.

Jahoda, Marie. "Women in Transition, Social Psychologists' Approach, Summary." Washington, U.S. Women's Bureau, 1955, 2 p.

James, Harlean. "Planning the Urban Community." In International Congress of Women, Chicago, 1933. Our Common Cause, Civilization, pp. 866-72.

James, Sara H. "Field Supervision--Unilateral or Integrated?" In National Conference of Social Work. Proceedings (1948), pp. 293-301.

________. "Public Responsibility for the American Indians." In National Conference of Social Work. Proceedings (1947), pp. 176-84.

James, Willie. "Statement." In U.S. Congress. House. Committee on Education and Labor. Subcommittee on Equal Opportunity. Equal Opportunity for Displaced Homemakers Act, p. 53.

Jameson, Elizabeth. "Imperfect Unions: Class and Gender in Cripple Creek, 1894-1904." In Cantor, M. Class, Sex, and the Woman Worker, pp. 166-202.

Janeway, Elizabeth. "Family Life in Transition." In Conference on Women's Challenge to Management, Arden House, 1971. Corporate Lib, pp. 118-24.

Janime, Marie R. "The District Nurse in Co-operative Work." In National Conference of Charities and Correction. Proceedings (1905), pp. 280-4.

Janvier, Carmelite. "The School Program in Case Work with Exceptional Children." In National Conference of Social Work. Proceedings (1942), pp. 451-9.

Jaquette, Jane S. "Women in American Politics." In Jaquette, J. Women in Politics, pp. xiii-xxxvii.

Jarrett, Mary C. "Educational Value to the Community of Mental Hygiene Agencies: Psychiatric Social Work." In National Conference of Social Work. Proceedings (1921), pp. 381-5.

________. "The Mental Hygiene of Industry: Report of Progress on Work Undertaken Under Engineering Foundation." In National Conference of Social Work. Proceedings (1920), pp. 335-42.

________. "The Psychiatric Thread Running Through All Social Case Work." In National Conference of Social Work. Proceedings (1919), pp. 587-93.

________. "War Neuroses (Shell Shock) After the War--Extra-Institutional Preparation." In National Conference of Social Work. Proceedings (1918), pp. 558-64.

Jay, Phyllis C. "The Female Primate." In Farber, S. Man and Civilization: Potential of Woman, pp. 3-12.

Jean, Sally Lucas. "Creating a Demand for Health." In National Conference of Social Work. Proceedings (1920), pp. 12-6.

________. "The Educational Opportunities Presented by the School Luncheon." In National Conference of Social Work. Proceedings (1918), pp. 68-75.

________. "Instruction of School Children in Health Habits and Ideals." In National Conference of Social Work. Proceedings (1923), pp. 378-82.

Jefferson, Mildred. "Statement." In U.S. Congress. Senate. Committee on the Judiciary. Subcommittee on Constitutional Amendments. Abortion, pt. 3, 7-9.

Jelly, Katherine L. "Coeducation: One Student's View." In Furniss, W. Women in Higher Education, pp. 61-3.

Jenkins, Helen Philleo. "Madame de Stael." In World's Congress of Representative Women, Chicago, 1893. Congress of Women, pp. 686-90.

Jenkins, Susan. "Statement." In U.S. Congress. House. Committee on Government Operations. National Women's Conference, pp. 38-9.

Jennings, May M. "The Half of the Nation Outside of the Cities." In General Federation of Women's Clubs. Biennial Convention, 16 (1922), 256-9.

________. "Report of the First Vice President." In General Federation of Women's Clubs. Biennial Convention, 16 (1922), 82-3.

Jennrich, Lorraine. "Some Experiments in Case Work in Motherless Families." In National Conference of Social Work. Proceedings (1936), pp. 158-66.

Jeter, Helen R. "Separation Allowances for Service Men's Families." In National Conference of Social Work. Proceedings (1942), pp. 276-89.

Joachim, Mary Ann. "So Let Your Light Shine. The Role of the Educated Woman in the Modern World." Vital Speeches, 25 (September 15, 1959), 725-8.

Johansson, Sheila Ryan. "Herstory as History: A New Field or Another Fad?" In Carroll, B. Liberating Women's History, pp. 400-30.

Johnesse, Adeline. "Helping the Client to Deal with His Reactions to Restraints Governing Intrafamily Relationships." In National Conference of Social Work. Proceedings (1937), pp. 124-37.

Johns, Laura M. "Municipal Suffrage." In International Council of Women, 1888. Report, pp. 315-8.

________. "Remarks on Women in Industry." In International Council of Women, 1888. Report, pp. 129-31.

Johnson, Adelaide. "Sculpture as a Profession for Women." In International Congress of Women, London, 1899, 3, 75-7.

Johnson, Arlien. "The Administrative Process in Social Work." In National Conference of Social Work. Proceedings (1946), pp. 249-58.

_______. "The County as a Unit for Co-ordinate Planning and Service in Public and Private Social Work (Point of View of Public Officials)." In National Conference of Social Work. Proceedings (1937), pp. 360-8.

_______. "The Obstacle of Limited Participation in Local Social Planning." In National Conference of Social Work. Proceedings (1940), pp. 425-35.

_______. "Science and Social Work." In National Conference of Social Work. Proceedings (1947), pp. 3-18.

Johnson, Eleanor H. "How Mental Hygiene May Help in the Solution of School Problems." In National Conference of Social Work. Proceedings (1921), pp. 395-401.

Johnson, Elizabeth S. "Statement." In U.S. Congress. House. Committee on Education and Labor. Select Subcommittee on Labor. Equal Pay for Equal Work, pp. 143-6.

_______. "Statement." In U.S. Congress. House. Committee on Education and Labor. Special Subcommittee on Labor. Equal Pay Act, pp. 265-8.

Johnson, Ellen C. "The Treatment of Women in Prison." In International Congress of Women, London, 1899, 7, 4-12.

Johnson, Grace. "The Boy and Girl Out on Furlough." In National Conference of Charities and Correction. Proceedings (1898), pp. 384-92.

Johnson, Harriet M. "Mental Hygiene of Younger Children." In National Conference of Social Work. Proceedings (1924), pp. 451-5.

Johnson, Helen Louise. "Cooking as an Art." In World's Congress of Representative Women, Chicago, 1893. Congress of Women, pp. 810-2.

Johnson, Kate Burr. "The Relation of a Board of Public Welfare to the Public." In National Conference of Social Work. Proceedings (1924), pp. 548-51.

_______. "The Work of a Commission of Public Welfare." In National Conference of Social Work. Proceedings (1922), pp. 437-42.

Johnson, Lillian J. "Case Work with Children in Institutions." In National Conference of Social Work. Proceedings (1940), pp. 335-43.

_______. "The Case Worker Looks at Legislative Planning." In National Conference of Social Work. Proceedings (1933), pp. 652-9.

________. "Use of a Small Institution in Treatment of Personality Problems." In National Conference of Social Work. Proceedings (1938), pp. 674-83.

________. "What We Learn from the Child's Own Psychology to Guide Treatment in a Small Institution." In National Conference of Social Work. Proceedings (1938), pp. 313-25.

Johnson, Mariana W. "Memorial to the Constitutional Convention. Adopted by the Woman's Rights Convention, Salem, Ohio, April 19th and 20th, 1850." In Lerner, G. The Female Experience, pp. 343-5.

________. "President's Address at the Westchester (Pennsylvania) Convention, June, 1852." In Stanton, E. History of Woman Suffrage, 1, 351-3.

________. "A Revolution in Human Society." In Tanner, L. Voices of Women's Liberation, pp. 70-1.

Johnston, Lettie L. "Street Trades and Their Regulation." In National Conference of Charities and Correction. Proceedings (1915), pp. 518-26.

Johnston, Rosa. "The Case Worker in Foster Families for Day Care." In National Conference of Social Work. Proceedings (1944), pp. 246-55.

Jones, Amanda Theodosia. "The Woman's Canning and Preserving Company." In National Council of Women of the U.S., Washington, 1891. Transactions, pp. 293-5.

Jones, Edith Kathleen. "Importance of Organized Libraries in Institutions." In National Conference of Charities and Correction. Proceedings (1916), pp. 360-6.

Jones, Elizabeth Orton. "Acceptance Paper--Caldecott Award 1945. Every Child and His Hilltop." In Miller, B. Caldecott Medal Books, 1938-1957, pp. 118-23.

Jones, Faith Jefferson. "The Effects on Case Work Services of Social Factors in the Negro's Life: From the Point of View of Economic Factors." In National Conference of Social Work. Proceedings (1942), pp. 469-80.

Jones, Jane Elizabeth Hitchcock. "Address at the 10th National Woman's Rights Convention, New York, May 10-11, 1860." In Stanton, E. History of Woman Suffrage, 1, 694-9.

________. "Comments at the Syracuse National Convention, September 1, 1852." In Stanton, E. History of Woman Suffrage, 1, 530.

________. "Remarks at the 10th National Woman's Rights Convention, New York, 1860." In Stanton, E. History of Woman Suffrage, 1, 711.

________. "Report of May 16, 1861 to the National Woman's Rights Convention." In Stanton, E. History of Woman Suffrage, 1, 168-70.

_______. "Women of Ohio." In Papachristou, J. Women Together, p. 32.

Jones, Nellie Kedzie. "Then and Now." In Illinois Farmers' Institute, Bloomington, 1943. Addresses, 40th Annual Meeting, pp. 15-8.

Jones, Patricia. "Women in Household Employment." In New York (City). Commission on Human Rights. Women's Role in Contemporary Society, pp. 347-50.

Jones, Susan C. Barber. "Post Office Missions." In World's Congress of Representative Women, Chicago, 1893. A Historical Resume, pp. 821-5.

Jordan, Barbara. "Democratic Convention Keynote Address: Who Then Will Speak for the Common Good?" Vital Speeches, 42 (August 15, 1974), 645-6.

Jordan, Brigitte. "The Cultural Production of Childbirth." In Hammond, N. Woman and Children in Contemporary Society, pp. 33-43.

Jordan, Mary A. "Address at the College Evening of the 38th Annual Convention of the National American Woman Suffrage Association, February 8, 1906." In Harper, I. The Life and Work of Susan B. Anthony, 3, 1391.

Judd, Elizabeth. "Influential Women in Anglo-Saxon England." In McGuigan, D. New Research on Women at the University of Michigan, pp. 50-7.

Kahn, Dorothy C. "Conserving Human Values in Public Welfare Programs." In National Conference of Social Work. Proceedings (1940), pp. 308-19.

_______. "Democratic Principles in Public Assistance." In National Conference of Social Work. Proceedings (1939), pp. 273-83.

_______. "Howard R. Knight and the International Conference of Social Work." In National Conference of Social Work. Proceedings (1948), pp. 13-5.

_______. "The Need for Interpretation of Trends and Accomplishments in Family Social Work." In National Conference of Social Work. Proceedings (1927), pp. 261-7.

_______. "Social Action from the Viewpoint of Professional Organizations." In National Conference of Social Work. Proceedings (1940), pp. 498-507.

_______. "Special Problems in Jewish Families." In National Conference of Social Work. Proceedings (1924), pp. 284-8.

_______. "The Use of Cash, Orders for Goods, or Relief in Kind, in a Mass Program." In National Conference of Social Work. Proceedings (1933), pp. 270-9.

Kaiser, Clara A. "Current Frontiers in Social Group Work." In National Conference of Social Work. Proceedings (1947), pp. 418-28.

________. "Generic Aspects of Professional Training for Case Work and Group Work: From the Point of View of a Teacher of Group Work." In National Conference of Social Work. Proceedings (1940), pp. 606-15.

________. "Has Group Work a Part to Play in the Preservation and Extension of Civil Liberties?" In National Conference of Social Work. Proceedings (1941), pp. 185-97.

Kaiser, Inez. "Testimony." In U.S. Congress. House. Committee on Small Business. Subcommittee on Minority Enterprise and General Oversight. Women in Business, pp. 34-9.

Kamerick, Maureen. "The Woman Artist and the Art Academy: A Case Study in Institutional Prejudice." In McGuigan, D. New Research on Women at the University of Michigan, pp. 249-60.

Kanter, Rosabeth Moss. "The Policy Issues: Presentation VI." In Blaxall, M. Women and the Workplace, pp. 272-91.

Karsner, Rose. "Remarks at a Banquet in Los Angeles Celebrating the Publication of The First Ten Years of American Communism, December 15, 1962." In Cannon, J. Speeches for Socialism, pp. 275-80.

Katz, Kay Jacobs. "Statement." In U.S. Congress. Senate. Committee on the Judiciary. Subcommittee on Constitutional Amendments. Abortion, pt. 2, 318-23.

Katzell, Mildred E. "Opening Remarks." In Katzell, M. Women in the Work Force, pp. 5-6.

Katzenstein, Caroline. "Statement." In U.S. Congress. House. Committee on the Judiciary. Subcommittee No. 1. Equal Rights Amendment (1948), pp. 67-8.

Kauffman, Margaret. "Supervision of Case-work Staffs." In National Conference of Social Work. Proceedings (1938), pp. 222-32.

Kearney, Belle. "Kearney's Speech on the South." In Papachristou, J. Women Together, p. 144.

________. "The South and Woman Suffrage." In Kraditor, A. Up from the Pedestal, pp. 262-5. (Same as "Kearney's Speech on the South.")

Kearnon, Pamela. "Public Testimony." In New York (City). Commission on Human Rights. Women's Role in Contemporary Society, pp. 787-9.

Keeley, Sarah F. "Address." In National Conference of Charities and Correction. Proceedings (1888), pp. 206-9.

________. "Reform Work for Girls." In National Conference of Charities and Correction. Proceedings (1892), pp. 179-82.

Keene, Mary Virginia. "Goethe and Schiller." In World's Congress of Representative Women, Chicago, 1893. Congress of Women, pp. 194-7.

Kefauver, Christine. "Statement." In U. S. Congress. Senate. Committee on the Judiciary. Subcommittee on Constitutional Amendments. Equal Rights for Men and Women (1938), pp. 123-6.

Kellems, Vivien. "Taxes. Is It Not Time That the Women of America Make Themselves Heard?" Vital Speeches, 14 (August 15, 1948), 650-4.

Keller, Helen Adams. "Address of Helen Keller at Mt. Airy (July 8, 1896)." In Keller, H. The Story of My Life, pp. 392-3.

________. "Menace of the Militarist Program. Speech at the Labor Forum, Washington Irving High School, New York City, December 19, 1915." In Keller, H. Helen Keller: Her Socialist Years, pp. 73-4.

________. "A New Light Is Coming. Address at the Sociological Conference, Sagamore Beach, Massachusetts." In Keller, H. Helen Keller: Her Socialist Years, pp. 52-4.

________. "Onward, Comrades! An Address at the Rand School New Year's Eve Ball, December 31, 1920." In Keller, H. Helen Keller: Her Socialist Years, pp. 107-8.

________. "A Plea for Recognition of Soviet Russia. Statement at a Hearing on Russian Free Trade Before the U. S. Senate Foreign Relations Committee." In Keller, H. Helen Keller: Her Socialist Years, pp. 104-6.

________. "Social Causes of Blindness. Speech in Relief of the Massachusetts Association for Promoting the Interests of the Blind, Boston, February 14, 1911." In Keller, H. Helen Keller: Her Socialist Years, pp. 29-30.

________. "Strike Against War. Speech at Carnegie Hall, New York City, January 5, 1916, Under the Auspices of the Women's Peace Party and the Labor Forum." In Keller, H. Helen Keller: Her Socialist Years, pp. 75-81.

________. "What Is the IWW? Speech at the New York City Civic Club, January 1918." In Keller, H. Helen Keller: Her Socialist Years, pp. 91-3.

Keller, Suzanne. "The Future Role of Women." Annals. "The Future Society: Aspects of America in the Year 2000," 408 (July, 1973), 1-12.

Kelley, Florence. "Address of Mrs. Kelley." In Bryn Mawr College. Carola Woerishoffer, Her Life and Work, pp. 59-66.

________. "Address of the Chairman (Committee on Industrial and Economic Problems)." In National Conference of Social Work. Proceedings (1919), pp. 423-5.

________. "Address to the House Judiciary Committee, April 19, 1910." In Stanton, E. History of Woman Suffrage, 5, 306-7.

________. "Child Labor in Illinois." In International Association of Factory Inspectors of North America. Proceedings (1895).

________. "Child Labor Laws." In National Conference of Charities and Correction. Proceedings (1904), pp. 268-73.

________. "Evolution of the Illinois Child Labor Law." In International Association of Factory Inspectors of North America. Proceedings (1897).

________. "Factory Legislation in Illinois." In International Association of Factory Inspectors of North America. Proceedings (1893).

________. "The Family and the Woman's Wage." In National Conference of Charities and Correction. Proceedings (1909), pp. 118-21.

________. "Florence Kelley on Working Girls." In Kraditor, A. Up from the Pedestal, p. 276. (Same as "Kelley on Child Labor and Woman Suffrage.")

________. "Home Work." In U.S. Women's Bureau. Proceedings of the Women's Industrial Conference, pp. 47-52.

________. "How Can Social Agencies Promote the Effectiveness of the Public Schools?" In National Conference of Charities and Correction. Proceedings (1916), pp. 557-59.

________. "Industrial Causes of Juvenile Delinquency." In National Conference of Charities and Correction. Proceedings (1905), pp. 148-9.

________. "Insanitary Conditions Amongst Home Workers." In International Congress of Women, London, 1899, 6, 21-5. (Read by Mrs. F. Nathan.)

________. "Introductory Statement (On Industrial Reorganization After the War)." In National Conference of Social Work. Proceedings (1918), p. 375.

________. "Kelley on Child Labor and Woman Suffrage." In Papachristou, J. Women Together, p. 167.

________. "Minimum Wage Board." In National Conference of Charities and Correction. Proceedings (1912), pp. 395-403.

________. "The Moral Dangers of Premature Employment." In National Conference of Charities and Correction. Proceedings (1906), pp. 157-64.

________. "The Need of Uniformity in Labor Legislation." In International Association of Factory Inspectors of North America. Proceedings (1894).

________. "The Present Status of Minimum Wage Legislation." In National Conference of Charities and Correction. Proceedings (1913), pp. 229-34.

________. "Prison Labor." In National Conference of Charities and Correction. Proceedings (1912), pp. 219-20.

________. "Report of the Committee (on Standards of Living and Labor): Minimum Wage Boards." In National Conference of Charities and Correction. Proceedings (1911), pp. 148-56.

________. "The Right to Know the Truth." In National Conference of Social Work. Proceedings (1920), pp. 57-9.

________. "Social Standards in Industry: Progress of Labor Legislation for Women." In National Conference of Social Work. Proceedings (1923), pp. 112-6.

________. "Statement." In U.S. Congress. Senate. Committee on the Judiciary. Subcommittee on Constitutional Amendments. Equal Rights Amendment (1929), pp. 55-7.

________. "The Sweating System." In International Association of Factory Inspectors of North America. Proceedings (1896).

________. "Use and Abuse of Factory Inspection." In National Conference of Charities and Correction. Proceedings (1903), pp. 135-8.

________. "Voluntary Agencies." In National Conference of Charities and Correction. Proceedings (1914), pp. 365-6.

________. "What Our Official Statistics Do Not Tell Us." In National Conference of Charities and Correction. Proceedings (1910), pp. 502-7.

________. "The Working Child." In National Conference of Charities and Correction. Proceedings (1896), pp. 161-5.

________. "Working Woman's Need of the Ballot." In Kraditor, A. Up from the Pedestal, pp. 273-6. Also in Stanton, E. History of Woman Suffrage, 4, 311-3. Also in Tanner, L. Voices of Women's Liberation, pp. 97-8.

________. "The Young Breadwinners' Need of Women's Enfranchisement." In Kraditor, A. Up from the Pedestal, pp. 276-7.

Kellogg, Angie L. "What Educational Psychology Can Contribute to Case Work with the Normal Family." In National Conference of Social Work. Proceedings (1918), pp. 329-34.

Kellogg, Ella E. Eaton. "Purity and Parental Responsibility." In National Purity Congress, 1st, Baltimore, 1895. National Purity Congress, pp. 214-23.

Kelly, Alice. "Youth Plans for a Civilized World: Forum on the College Generation." In International Congress of Women, Chicago, 1933. Our Common Cause, Civilization, pp. 192-3.

Kelly, Edna Flannery. "Principles of International Law Concerning Friendly Relations Among States: Sovereign Equality of States." Department of State Bulletin, 50 (February 11, 1964), 264-7.

________. "Principles of International Law Concerning Friendly Relations and Cooperation Among States: Peaceful Settlement of Disputes." Department of State Bulletin, 50 (January 13, 1964), 57-66.

________. "Statement." In U.S. Congress. House. Committee on Education and Labor. Select Subcommittee on Labor. Equal Pay for Equal Work, pp. 179-80.

Kelly, Joan. "Housewife-Mother: The Institution and the Experience." In Conference on Feminist Perspectives on Housework and Child Care. Feminist Perspectives on Housework and Child Care, pp. 35-48.

Kempshall, Anna. "Tentative Observations on Basic Training." In National Conference of Social Work. Proceedings (1925), pp. 677-81.

Kennard, Beulah E. "Emotional Life of Girls." In National Conference of Charities and Correction. Proceedings (1912), pp. 146-8.

Kennedy, Florynce. "To Be Black and a Woman." In New York (City). Commission on Human Rights. Women's Role in Contemporary Society, pp. 85-9.

Kennedy, Mary. "Statement." In U.S. Congress. Senate. Committee on the Judiciary. Subcommittee on Constitutional Amendments. Equal Rights Amendment (1945), pp. 35-7.

Kennicke, Lee. "Masks of Identity." In Harris, D. Women and Sport, pp. 157-68.

Kenny, Mary E. "Organization of Working Women." In World's Congress of Representative Women, Chicago, 1893. A Historical Resume, pp. 871-4.

Kenyon, Dorothy. "Public Testimony." In New York (City). Commission on Human Rights. Women's Role in Contemporary Society, pp. 540-5.

________. "Statement." In U.S. Congress. House. Committee on Education and Labor. Select Subcommittee on Labor. Equal Pay for Equal Work, pt. 2, 231-8.

________. "Statement." In U.S. Congress. Senate. Committee on the Judiciary. Subcommittee on Constitutional Amendments. Equal Rights Amendment (1929), p. 40.

________. "Technique of Utilizing American Political Machinery to Secure Social Action." In National Conference of Social Work. Proceedings (1936), pp. 412-20.

Kerby-Miller, Wilma A. "Academic Employment." In M.I.T. Symposium on American Women in Science and Engineering, 1964. Women and the Scientific Professions, pp. 185-90.

Kessler-Harris, Alice. "Statement." In Conference on Feminist Perspectives on Housework and Child Care. Feminist Perspectives on Housework and Child Care, pp. 15-9.

________. "Stratifying by Sex: Understanding the History of Working Women." In Conference on Labor Market Segmentation, Harvard University, 1973. Labor Market Segmentation, pp. 217-42.

________. "Women, Work and the Social Order." In Carroll, B. Liberating Women's History, pp. 330-43. (Same as "Stratifying by Sex").

Ketcham, Emily Burton. "Are Women Citizens and People?" In World's Congress of Representative Women, Chicago, 1893. Congress of Women, pp. 361-4.

Keys, Martha. "Statement." In International Conference on Women in Health. Proceedings, pp. 167-8.

Keyser, Harriette A. "Organizing Among Women as an Instrument in Promoting the Interests of Industry." In World's Congress of Representative Women, Chicago, 1893. A Historical Resume, pp. 617-22.

Keyserling, Mary Dublin. "Address." In Conference on Women in the War on Poverty, 1967. Proceedings, pp. 15-6.

________. "American Women at Work, New Challenges and New Responsibilities." Washington, U.S. Women's Bureau, 1966, 15 p.

________. "Challenges Ahead." Washington, U.S. Women's Bureau, 1965, 11 p.

________. "Employment Opportunities for Women." Washington, U.S. Women's Bureau, 1965, 13 p.

________. "Facing Facts About Women's Lives Today." Washington, U.S. Women's Bureau, 1965, 14 p.

________. "International Cooperation and Economic Advance of Women." Washington, U.S. Women's Bureau, 1965, 4 p.

________. "Negro Women in United States, New Roles, New Challenges." Washington, U.S. Women's Bureau, 1966, 18 p.

________. "New Horizons for Women, Talk." Washington, U.S. Women's Bureau, 1964, 15 p.

________. "New Opportunities and Responsibilities of Women, Convocation Address." Washington, U.S. Women's Bureau, 1964, 16 p.

________. "Recent Federal Employment Policy Developments, New Progress for Women." Washington, U.S. Women's Bureau, 1966, 15 p.

________. "Remarks on Labor Standard Improvement and Greater Employment Opportunity." Washington, U.S. Women's Bureau, 1966, 6 p.

________. "Research and Your Job." Washington, U.S. Women's Bureau, 1964, 16 p.

________. "Should Congress Approve the "Equal Rights" Amendment?" Congressional Digest, 50 (January, 1971), 27-31.

________. "The Socioeconomic Waste: Underutilization of Women." In New York (City). Commission on Human Rights. Women's Role in Contemporary Society, pp. 67-73.

________. "Statement." In U.S. Congress. House. Committee on the Judiciary. Subcommittee no. 4. Equal Rights for Men and Women 1971, pp. 471-86.

________. "Statement." In U.S. Congress. Senate. Committee on the Judiciary. Equal Rights 1970, pp. 149-56.

________. "Summary of Speech on Guidance Counselors Needed for Career and Employment Decisions." Washington, U.S. Women's Bureau, 1965, 4 p.

________. "Womanpower Needed." Washington, U.S. Women's Bureau, 1966, 7 p.

________. "Women Wage Earners, New Challenges and Opportunities." Washington, U.S. Women's Bureau, 1965, 7 p.

________. "Your Talents, Let's Not Waste Them." Washington, U.S. Women's Bureau, 1967, 8 p.

Kilgore, Carrie Burnham. "The Address ... Before the Legislature of Pennsylvania Delivered in the Hall of the House of Representatives, at Harrisburg, March 23rd, 1881." Philadelphia, Allen, Lane & Scott's Printing House, 1881, 31 p.

Kimball, Norma M. "Participants and Policy Making." In National Conference of Social Work. Proceedings (1939), pp. 348-51.

Kimber, Diana C. "District Nursing in London." In National Conference of Charities and Correction. Proceedings (1895), pp. 273-5.

King, Anna. "The Present Opportunity of the City Home Service Section." In National Conference of Social Work. Proceedings (1919), pp. 374-8.

King, Coretta Scott. "Speech at Memphis City Hall." In King, C. My Life with Martin Luther King, Jr., pp. 344-7.

King, Edith Shatto. "Relations and Duties of Public Health Nurses and Social Workers in the Diagnosis, Treatment, and Control of Syphilis." In National Conference of Social Work. Proceedings (1922), pp. 218-22.

King, Elizabeth T. "The Admission of Women to the Medical School of the Johns Hopkins University." In National Council of Women of the U.S., Washington, 1891. Transactions, pp. 199-203.

King, Ellen Eva. "Tell Us the Truth!" In New York Herald Tribune. Report of the 8th Annual Forum on Current Problems, pp. 32-3.

King, Georgia Swift. "Intemperance as a Cause of Mortality." In Conference of the Study of Negro Problems, 1st Atlanta, 1896. Mortality Among Negroes in Cities, pp. 26-9.

________. "Mothers Meetings." In Conference for the Study of Negro Problems, 2nd, Atlanta, 1897. Social and Physical Condition of Negroes in Cities, pp. 61-2.

King, Julia. "Physical Culture." In National Congress of Mothers. Work and Words, pp. 193-9.

King, Mary E. "Statement." In U.S. Congress. Senate. Committee on Human Resources. Nomination Hearing on Mary E. King, pp. 14-5, 18-9.

Kingsbury, Susan M. "Statement." In U.S. Congress. Senate. Committee on the Judiciary. Subcommittee on Constitutional Amendments. Equal Rights for Men and Women (1938), pp. 78-82.

________. "The Study of Industrial Processes as a Tool for Professional Standards and Education." In National Conference of Social Work. Proceedings (1928), p. 577.

Kinney, Alice. "Women as Farmers." In General Federation of Women's Clubs. Biennial Convention, 9 (1908), 376-9.

Kinsella, Nina. "The Arrested Offender." In National Conference of Social Work. Proceedings (1937), pp. 582-90.

________. "County Jails." In National Conference of Social Work. Proceedings (1932), pp. 136-44.

Kirchway, Freda. "Ninety Years Young; Excerpt from Address, June 19, 1955." Nation, 181 (July 9, 1955), 43-4.

Kirkwood, Louise J. "Methods of Industrial Training for Girls." In National Conference of Charities and Corrections. Proceedings (1885), pp. 210-9.

Kirschbaum, Kathryn. "Statement." In National League of Cities. Women in Municipal Government, pp. 1-4.

Kirwan, Katharine T. "Rural Case Work--Progress of Undifferentiated Case Work Made in the Children's Aid Society of Baltimore County." In National Conference of Social Work. Proceedings (1928), pp. 81-5.

Kitchelft, Florence L. C. "Is the Equal-Rights Amendment Equitable to Women." Congressional Record, 79th Cong., 2d sess., 1946, 92, pt. 12, A4782.

Kleinberg, Susan J. "The Systematic Study of Urban Women." In Cantor, M. Class, Sex, and the Woman Worker, pp. 20-42. Also Historical Methods Newsletter, 9 (December, 1975), 14-25.

Klotzburger, Katherine M. "Advisory Committee Role in Constructing Affirmative Action Programs." In Furniss, W. Women in Higher Education, pp. 229-33.

________. "The Position of Women in Their Professional Associations." In Conference of Professional and Academic Women. Sixteen Reports on the Status of Women in the Professions, 4 p.

________. "Public Testimony." In New York (City). Commission on Human Rights. Women's Role in Contemporary Society, pp. 719-25.

Kluckhohn, Florence Rockwood. "Horizons for Women, American Woman's Role." Washington, U.S. Women's Bureau, 1955, 9 p.

Knapp, Pauline Park Wilson. "Comment on Background and Purpose of the Conference on the Present Status and Prospective Trends of Research on the Education of Women." In Conference on the Present Status and Prospective Trends of Research on the Education of Women, Rye, N.Y., 1957. Education of Women, pp. 17-8.

Knapp, Pauline Park Wilson 174

________. "Research in Progress at the Merrill-Palmer School." In Michigan State University, East Lansing, School of Home Economics. Potentialities of Women in the Middle Years, pp. 31-3.

Knauer, Virginia Harrington Wright. "Price Controls and Revenues: Federal Regulations." Vital Speeches, 41 (February 15, 1975), 275-8.

Knaust, Elisabeth. "Nazi Propaganda in the United States." In New York Herald Tribune. Report of the 9th Annual Forum on Current Problems, pp. 17-20.

Koch, Adrienne. "Two Cheers for Equality." In Farber, S. Man and Civilization: The Potential of Woman, pp. 199-215.

Koester, Matilda F. "Statement." In U. S. Women's Bureau. Proceedings of the Women's Industrial Conference, pp. 140-2.

Kohut, Rebekah. "Mission-work Among the Unenlightened Jews." In Jewish Women's Congress. Papers, pp. 187-95.

________. "Parental Reverence as Taught in the Hebrew Home." In National Congress of Mothers. Work and Words, pp. 61-7.

Kollock, Florence E. "Women in the Pulpit." In World's Congress of Representative Women, Chicago, 1893. A Historical Resume, pp. 221-8.

Komarovsky, Mirra. "Cultural and Psychohistorical Background of Women's Status in America." In New York (City). Commission on Human Rights. Women's Role in Contemporary Society, pp. 63-7.

________. "Presidential Address: Some Problems in Role Analysis." American Sociological Review, 38 (December, 1973), 649-62.

Komisar, Lucy. "Public Testimony." In New York (City). Commission on Human Rights. Women's Role in Contemporary Society, pp. 293-8.

________. "Statement." In U. S. Congress. House. Committee on Education and Labor. Special Subcommittee on Education. Discrimination Against Women, pp. 105-17.

________. "Women in the Media; In Honor of Margaret Fuller, America's First Woman Journalist. Who Would Not Think We Have Come Very Far (Baby)." In Conference of Professional and Academic Women. Sixteen Reports on the Status of Women in the Professions, 7 p.

Konigsburg, Elaine Lobl. "Newbery Award Acceptance--1968." In Kingman, L. Newbery and Caldecott Medal Books, 1966-1975, pp. 36-41.

Konopka, Gisela. "Therapy Through Social Group Work." In National Conference of Social Work. Proceedings (1946), pp. 228-36.

Koontz, Elizabeth Duncan. "American Women at Crossroads." Washington, U.S. Women's Bureau, 1970, 16 p.

________. "Household Employment, Quiet Revolution." Washington, U.S. Women's Bureau, 1969, 8 p.

________. "Speech at Windham College." New York Times, June 9, 1970, p. 24, col. 5.

________. "Statement." In U.S. Congress. House. Committee on Education and Labor. Special Subcommittee on Education. Discrimination Against Women, pp. 249-61.

________. "Testimony on Federal Efforts to End Sex Discrimination in Employment." In U.S. Congress. Joint Economic Committee. Economic Problems of Women, pt. 1, 112-8.

________. "Women in the Labor Force." In New York (City). Commission on Human Rights. Women's Role in Contemporary Society, pp. 184-90.

Kopelov, Connie. "Statement." In U.S. Congress. House. Committee on Education and Labor. Select Subcommittee on Labor. Equal Pay for Equal Work, pt. 2, 241-5.

Kovner, Sarah. "Women's Share in Political and Governmental Decision-making." In New York (City). Commission on Human Rights. Women's Role in Contemporary Society, pp. 639-42.

Kraus, Hertha. "Contribution of Case Work to the Administration of Social Insurance--A Critical Analysis of European Experience." In National Conference of Social Work. Proceedings (1936), pp. 146-57.

________. "Lay Participation in Social Work as It Affects the Public Agency." In National Conference of Social Work. Proceedings (1934), pp. 223-9.

________. "The Plight of Refugees in a Preoccupied World." In National Conference of Social Work. Proceedings (1940), pp. 150-7.

Kraus-Boelte, Maria. "The Kindergarten and the Mission of Woman." In National Education Association. Addresses and Proceedings (1877), pp. 207-16.

Kravits, Joanna. "Sex Differences in Health Care: Social Survey Research Methods." In U.S. National Center for Health Services Research. Women and Their Health, pp. 75-9.

Krecker, Elizabeth. "Discussion of the Ethics of Dress." In World's Congress of Representative Women, Chicago, 1893. A Historical Resume, pp. 350-1.

Kreps, Juanita Morris. "Address Before the National League of Cities' Congressional City Conference, Washington Hilton Hotel, Washington, D.C., March 6, 1977." Washington, U.S. Department of Commerce, Office of the Secretary, 1977, 10 p.

________. "Remarks at the U.S. Conference of Mayors, Tucson, Arizona, June 14, 1977." Washington, U.S. Department of Commerce, Office of the Secretary, 1977, 10 p.

________. "Remarks Before the Opportunities Industrialization Centers of America, Detroit, Michigan, June 8, 1977." Washington, U.S. Department of Commerce, Office of the Secretary, 1977, 10 p.

________. "Six Cliches in Search of a Woman; Happily Ever After." Vital Speeches, 31 (December 15, 1964), 147-9.

________. "The Sources of Inequality." In Conference on Women's Challenge to Management, Arden House, 1971. Corporate Lib, pp. 85-96.

________. "The Status of Women. The Economic Change." Vital Speeches, 28 (September 1, 1962), 698-701.

________. "Testimony." In U.S. Congress. House. Committee on Small Business. Subcommittee on Minority Enterprise and General Oversight. Women in Business, pp. 99-102.

________. "Thoughts About Government and Business: Changing Public Habits and Attitudes." Vital Speeches, 43 (August 1, 1977), 610-2.

________. "Who Is Responsible for the Quality of Life? The Business Systems and Government." Vital Speeches, 41 (May 15, 1975) 453-8.

________. "Women in Academia: Today Is Different." In Epstein, L. Women in the Professions, pp. 15-23.

________. "The Women Professional in Higher Education." In Furniss, W. Women in Higher Education, pp. 75-90.

Krupsak, Mary Ann. "Remarks." In Conference on Feminist Perspectives on Housework and Child Care. Feminist Perspectives on Housework and Child Care, p. 7.

________. "Women and the New York Labor Laws." In New York (City). Commission on Human Rights. Women's Role in Contemporary Society, pp. 328-37.

Kuhn, Maggie. "Controversey over the Carter Administration Proposals for Welfare Reform." Congressional Digest, 57 (May, 1978), 147-51.

Kyle, Constance. "Case Work in Unions." In National Conference of Social Work. Proceedings (1944), pp. 228-36.

Kyrk, Hazel. "The Economic Role of Women Forty-five to Sixty-five." In Michigan State University, East Lansing, School of Home Economics. Potentialities of Women in the Middle Years, pp. 127-41.

________. "Family Responsibilities of Earning Women." In U.S. Women's Bureau. American Woman--Her Changing Role, pp. 59-68.

________. "Who Gets It? Who Spends It?" In International Congress of Women, Chicago, 1933. Our Common Cause, Civilization, pp. 385-92.

Labaree, Mary S. "The Purpose of Statewide Statistics in Building the Foundation for the Prevention of Delinquency." In National Conference of Social Work. Proceedings (1927), pp. 498-502.

________. "Unmarried Parenthood Under the Social Security Act." In National Conference of Social Work. Proceedings (1939), pp. 446-57.

La Barraque, Christine. "What the Seeing Woman Can Do for the Blind Woman in a Business-like Way." General Federation of Women's Clubs. Biennial Convention, 9 (1908), 379-81.

LaDu, Blanche L. "Co-ordination of State and Local Units for Welfare Administration." In National Conference of Social Work. Proceedings (1933), pp. 494-505.

________. "What Minnesota Is Doing for the Indians." In National Conference of Social Work. Proceedings (1931), pp. 626-36.

La Follette, Isabel B. "Employment Opportunities in the Woman's Service Exchange Program of Madison, Wisconsin." In Michigan State University, East Lansing, School of Home Economics. Potentialities of Women in the Middle Years, pp. 159-67.

Laich, Katherine. "Our Highest Common Denominator." American Libraries, 3 (October, 1972), 1006-10.

Lake, Harriet. "Report of Outlook Committee." In General Federation of Women's Clubs. Biennial Convention, 9 (1908), 328-30.

Lake, Isabel Wing. "Graded Homes." In National Purity Congress, 1st, Baltimore, 1895. National Purity Congress, pp. 300-4.

________. "The Tempted Woman." In World's Congress of Representative Women, Chicago, 1893. Congress of Women, pp. 574-5.

Lake, Leonara Marie. "Is Labor Dignified?" In World's Congress of Representative Women, Chicago, 1893. Congress of Women, pp. 508-9.

Lally, Dorothy. "The Interrelationships of Merit Systems and the Quality of Public Welfare Personnel." In National Conference of Social Work. Proceedings (1942), pp. 553-62.

Lamb, Marjorie. "Cold War Thaw. An Asset or a Liability." Vital Speeches, 22 (November 1, 1955), 50-3.

________. "The Communist Apparatus in Canada Today: Respectability and Acceptance." Vital Speeches, 30 (December 15, 1963), 141-4.

Lamphere, Louise. "Strategies, Cooperation, and Conflict Among Women in Domestic Groups." In Rosaldo, M. Woman, Culture, and Society, pp. 97-112.

Lancione, Ida. "Statement." In U.S. Congress. Senate. Committee on the Judiciary. Subcommittee on Constitutional Amendments. Abortion, pt. 4, 667-73.

Lane, Ann J. "Women in Society: A Critique of Frederick Engels." In Carroll, B. Liberating Women's History, pp. 4-25.

Laney, Lucy Craft. "Address Before the Women's Meeting." In Conference for the Study of Negro Problems 2nd Atlanta, 1897. Social and Physical Conditions of Negroes in Cities, pp. 55-7.

________. "The Burden of the Educated Colored Woman." In Loewenberg, B. Black Women in Nineteenth-Century American Life, pp. 297-301.

________. "General Conditions of Mortality." In Conference for the Study of Negro Problems, 1st, Atlanta, 1896. Mortality Among Negroes in Cities, pp. 35-7.

Langhorne, Orra. "Testimony to the Senate." In Scott, A. One Half the People, p. 104.

Lankton, Freeda M. "The Medical Profession for Woman." In World's Congress of Representative Women, Chicago, 1893. Congress of Women, pp. 268-72.

Lansburg, Therese. "Statement." In U.S. Congress. Senate. Committee on Labor and Public Welfare. Subcommittee on Children and Youth. White Conference on Children, pp. 77-91.

Lansing, Marjorie. "The American Woman: Voter and Activist." In Jacquette, J. Women in Politics, pp. 5-24.

________. "Women: The New Political Class." In McGuigan, D. A Sampler of Women's Studies at the University of Michigan, pp. 59-75.

Lape, Esther Everett. "Report on Research Among 5,000 Doctors." In New York Herald Tribune. Report of the 8th Annual Forum on Current Problems, pp. 71-4.

Lapidus, Gail Warshofsky. "Modernization Theory and Sex Roles in Critical Perspective: The Case of the Soviet Union." In Jaquette, J. Women in Politics, pp. 243-56.

________. "Occupational Segregation and Public Policy: A Comparative Analysis of American and Soviet Patterns." In Blaxall, M. Women and the Workplace, pp. 119-36.

________. "Sexual Equality in Soviet Policy: A Developmental Perspective." In Atkinson, D. Women in Russia, pp. 155-38.

Larned, Ruth. "The Tangled Threads of Migrant Family Problems." In National Conference of Social Work. Proceedings (1930), pp. 469-77.

Lash, Trudi. "Child Care and Family Services." In New York (City). Commission on Human Rights. Women's Role in Contemporary Society, pp. 453-8.

Latham, Jean Lee. "Newbery Acceptance Speech--1956." In Kingman, L. Newbery and Caldecott Medal Books, 1956-1965, pp. 16-24.

Lathrap, Mary T. "The National Woman's Christian Temperance Union." In National Council of Women of the U. S., Washington, 1891. Transactions, pp. 141-52.

________. "Women in the Methodist Church." In National Council of Women of the U. S., Washington, 1891. Transactions, pp. 107-12.

Lathrop, Dorothy P. "Acceptance Paper--Caldecott Award 1938." In Miller, B. Caldecott Medal Books, 1938-1975, pp. 7-15.

Lathrop, Julia Clifford. "Child Welfare Standards a Test of Democracy." In National Conference of Social Work. Proceedings (1919), pp. 5-9.

________. "The Children's Bureau." In National Conference of Charities and Correction. Proceedings (1912), pp. 30-3.

________. "The Imperatives of International Relations: Social Implications." In National Conference of Social Work. Proceedings (1928), pp. 72-7.

________. "Institutional Records and Industrial Causes of Dependency." In National Conference of Charities and Correction. Proceedings (1910), pp. 515-23.

________. "Introductory Statement (On Public Schools and Social Service)." In National Conference of Charities and Correction. Proceedings (1916), pp. 555-6.

________. "Our Nation's Obligation to Her Children." In National Conference of Social Work. Proceedings (1921), pp. 68-71.

________. "Participation in International Child Welfare Work." In National Conference of Social Work. Proceedings (1926), pp. 126-31.

________. "Report of the Committee on State Supervision and Administration." In National Conference of Charities and Correction. Proceedings (1905), pp. 420-33.

________. "State Care for Mothers and Infants." In National Conference of Social Work. Proceedings (1918), pp. 389-92.

________. "Training Schools for Nurses--District Nurses." In National Conference of Charities and Correction. Proceedings (1894), pp. 340-1.

________. "The Transition from Charities and Correction to Social Work--1873 to 1923-- Then?" In National Conference of Social Work. Proceedings (1923), pp. 199-203.

________. "Uniform Legislation." In National Conference of Charities and Correction. Proceedings (1915), pp. 111-4.

________. "Village Care for the Insane." In National Conference of Charities and Correction. Proceedings (1902), pp. 185-99.

________. "What the Indian Service Needs." In National Conference of Social Work. Proceedings (1930), pp. 641-50.

________. "What the Settlement Work Stands For." In National Conference of Charities and Correction. Proceedings (1896), pp. 106-10.

Latimer, Edna S. "Address at the Columbia Theatre in Washington, November 15, 1914." In Irwin, I. The Story of the Woman's Party, pp. 81-3.

Lattimore, Florence. "Children's Institutions and the Accident Problem." In National Conference of Charities and Correction. Proceedings (1910), pp. 425-33.

Lauder, A. Estelle. "Statement." In U. S. Congress. House. Committee on the Judiciary. Equal Rights Amendment to the Constitution (1932), pp. 27-30.

Laughlin, Gail. "Address at a Procession of Suffragists, at the Panama-Pacific Exposition of 1915." In Irwin, I. The Story of the Woman's Party, pp. 103-4.

________. "Conditions of Wage-earning Women." In Tanner, L. Voices from Women's Liberation, pp. 93-4.

Lavine, Thelma Z. "The Motive to Achieve Limited Success: The New Woman Law School Applicant." In Furniss, W. Women in Higher Education, pp. 187-91.

Laws, Gertrude. "Can Parental Education Be Applied?" In National Conference of Social Work. Proceedings (1929), pp. 147-52.

Laws, Judith Long. "Statement." In U. S. Congress. House. Committee on the Judiciary. Subcommittee No. 4. Equal Rights for Men and Women 1971, pp. 414-25.

________. "Work Aspiration of Women: False Leads and New Starts." In Blaxall, M. Women and the Workplace, pp. 33-49.

Layzer, Judith. "Public Testimony." In New York (City). Commission on Human Rights. Women's Role in Contemporary Society, pp. 401-5.

Lazarus, Esther. "Integration of Supervision with the Total Program of the Agency." In National Conference of Social Work. Proceedings (1947), pp. 251-60.

Leach, Ruth M. "Training on the Job After College." In Institute of Women's Professional Relations. War and Post-War Employment and Its Demands for Educational Adjustments, pp. 199-204.

________. "Women and the Top Jobs." In National Association of Manufacturers. War Congress of American Industry, 2nd, New York, 1943, pp. 3-10.

Learned, Lucilia W. "Results of Club Life Among Women upon the Home." In World's Congress of Representative Women, Chicago, 1893. A Historical Resume, pp. 796-9.

Lease, Mary Elizabeth. "Synopsis of Peace." In World's Congress of Representative Women, Chicago, 1893. Congress of Women, pp. 412-3.

________. "Women in the Farmers' Alliance." In National Council of Women of the U.S., Washington, 1891. Transactions, pp. 157-9, 214-6.

Leavitt, Henrietta D. "The Work of Women in Modern Astronomy." In International Congress of Women, Toronto, 1909. Report, 1, 444-50.

Leavitt, Mary Clement. "Temperance and Purity." In National Purity Congress, 1st, Baltimore, 1895. National Purity Congress, pp. 166-72.

LeBaron, Helen R. "An Evaluation of Home Economics Training." In Conference on the Present Status and Prospective Trends of Research on the Education of Women, Rye, N.Y., 1957. The Education of Women, pp. 108-12.

Ledbetter, Eleanor E. "Recent Development in Library Work with Immigrants." In National Conference of Social Work. Proceedings (1924), pp. 587-93.

Lee, Dorothy McCullough. "Local Government and World Affairs." In New York Herald Tribune. Report of the 17th Annual Forum on Current Problems, pp. 191-4.

Lee, Elizabeth A. "Court Procedure in Securing Support for a Child of Illegitimate Birth." In National Conference of Social Work. Proceedings (1922), pp. 127-30.

Lefkowitz, Mary. "Classical Mythology and the Role of Women in Modern Literature." In McGuigan, D. A Sampler of Women's Studies, pp. 77-84.

Leis, Nancy B. "Women in Groups: Ijaw Women's Associations." In Rosaldo, M. Women, Culture, and Society, pp. 223-41.

Leiter, Frances W. "Physical Education for Women." In World's Congress of Representative Women, Chicago, 1893. A Historical Resume, pp. 877-9.

Leith, Suzette. "Chinese Women in the Early Communist Movement." In McGuigan, D. New Research on Women at the University of Michigan, pp. 165-87.

L'Engle, Madeleine. "Newbery Award Acceptance. The Expanding Universe." In Kingman, L. Newbery and Caldecott Medal Books, 1956-1965, pp. 119-23.

Lenroot, Katharine F. "American Childhood Challenges American Democracy." In National Conference of Social Work. Proceedings (1940), pp. 27-37.

________. "Current National Developments and Problems in Public Welfare, Children's Services." Washington, U.S. Children's Bureau, 1945, 6 p.

________. "The Federal Government and Desirable Standards of State and Local Administration." In National Conference of Social Work. Proceedings (1937), pp. 432-9.

________. "Government Provision for Social Work Statistics on a National Scale from the Point of View of the Registration of Social Statistics." In National Conference of Social Work. Proceedings (1931), pp. 414-20.

________. "Progressive Methods of Care for Children Pending Juvenile Court Hearing." In National Conference of Social Work. Proceedings (1926), pp. 135-41.

________. "Remarks at Jane Addams Memorial Service." In National Conference of Social Work. Proceedings (1935), pp. 1-3.

________. "Social Work and the Social Order (Presidential Address)." In National Conference of Social Work. Proceedings (1935), pp. 25-37.

________. "Statement at Public Hearings on Juvenile Delinquency Before Subcommittee on Wartime Health and Education of Committee on Education and Labor, Senate, November 30, 1943." Washington, U.S. Children's Bureau, 1944, 25 p.

________. "Trends in Public Services for Children." Washington, U.S. Children's Bureau, 1944, 7 p.

________. "The United States Program for the Care of Refugee Children." In National Conference of Social Work. Proceedings (1941), pp. 198-207.

Lenski, Lois. "Acceptance Paper--Newbery Medal 1946. Seeing Others as Ourselves." In Miller, B. Newbery Medal Books, 1922-1955, 278-87.

Lent, Mary E. "Public Health Nursing and the War." In National Conference of Social Work. Proceedings (1917), pp. 214-8.

________. "Sanitary Conditions About Military Camps, and Parts Played by the Public Health Nursing." In National Conference of Social Work. Proceedings (1918), pp. 189-92.

Leonard, Anna Byford. "Discussion of Paper on the Ethical Influence of Woman in Education." In World's Congress of Representative Women, Chicago, 1893. A Historical Resume, pp. 116-7.

Leonard, Clara T. "Family Homes for Pauper and Dependent Children." In Conference on Charities. Proceedings (1879), pp. 170-8.

Leonard, Margery C. "Should Congress Approve the "Equal Rights" Amendment?" Congressional Digest, 50 (January, 1971), 22-4.

________. "Statement." In U.S. Congress. Senate. Committee on the Judiciary. Subcommittee on Constitutional Amendments. Women and the "Equal Rights" Amendment, pp. 133-6.

Leopold, Alice K. "The Challenge of Tomorrow. Womanpower." Vital Speeches, 24 (May 15, 1958), 478-80.

________. "Civil Defense Begins at Home." Washington, U.S. Women's Bureau, 1958, 7 p.

________. "Role of Mature Woman in Economy." Washington, U. S. Women's Bureau, 1957, 8 p.

________. "Search for Skills." Washington, U. S. Women's Bureau, 1956, 23 p.

________. "Speech Before Girl's Nation, August 3, 1954." Washington, U. S. Women's Bureau, 1954, 4 p.

________. "Welcome." In U. S. Women's Bureau. Today's Woman in Tomorrow's World, pp. 1-2.

________. "Welcome Address at Conference on Effective Use of Womanpower, March 10-11, 1955." Washington, U. S. Women's Bureau, 1955, 5 p.

________. "What It Takes to Be Tops as Woman Executive, Outline of Address." Washington, U. S. Women's Bureau, 1959, 7 p.

________. "Womanpower in Changing World." Washington, U. S. Women's Bureau, 1959, 12 p.

________. "Women's New Role on International Scene." Washington, U. S. Women's Bureau, 1957, 17 p.

Leopold, Sadie G. "Women Wage-Workers: With Reference of Directing Immigrants." In Jewish Women's Congress. Papers, pp. 108-14.

Lepper, Mary M. "A Study of Career Structures of Federal Executives: A Focus on Women." In Jaquette, J. Women in Politics, pp. 109-30.

Lerner, Gerda. "The American Housewife: A Historical Perspective." In Conference on Feminist Perspectives on Housework and Child Care. Feminist Perspectives on Housework and Child Care, pp. 22-34.

________. "Placing Women in History: A 1975 Perspective." In Carroll, B. Liberating Women's History, pp. 357-67. Also Feminist Studies, 3 (1975), 5-15.

Lerrigo, Edith. "Address." In Conference on Women in the War on Poverty, 1967. Proceedings, pp. 48-50.

Lervold, Linda. "Public Testimony." In New York (City). Commission on Human Rights. Women's Role in Contemporary Society, pp. 414-7.

Lesley, Susan Inches. "Foundlings and Deserted Children." In Conference on Charities and Correction. Proceedings (1881), pp. 282-6.

Levinson, Frances T. "Counseling in the Family Agency." In National Conference of Social Work. Proceedings (1947), pp. 270-8.

Lewelling, Angie Cook. "Report of Iowa." In National Conference of Charities and Correction. Proceedings (1882), pp. 172-4.

Lewis, Elizabeth Foreman. "Acceptance Paper--Newbery Medal 1933." In Miller, B. Newbery Medal Books, 1922-1955, pp. 111-3.

Lewis, Grace Anna. "Science for Women." In Association for the Advancement of Women. Congress of Women, 3rd. Papers, pp. 63-73.

Lewis, Hazel M. "Vocational and Employment Guidance of Older Children." In National Conference of Social Work. Proceedings (1940), pp. 99-108.

Lewis, Helen M. "Should the Federal Government Assume a Direct Role in the Regulation of Surface Mining of Coal in the States?" Congressional Digest, 53 (May, 1974), 156-8.

Lewis, Helen Morris. "Testimony to the Senate." In Scott, A. One Half the People, pp. 102-4. Also in U.S. Congress. Senate. Committee on Woman Suffrage. Report of the Hearing Before the Committee on Woman Suffrage, 54th Cong., 1st sess., 1896, Dec. 157, pp. 3-23.

Lewis, Mary Ann. "New Roles for Women in Health Care Delivery. A U.S. Response to the Cameroon Experience." In International Conference on Women in Health. Proceedings, pp. 129-31.

Lewis, Ora Mabelle. "Medical Social Service as a Factor in Protective Work." In National Conference of Social Work. Proceedings (1920), pp. 148-51.

Libbey, Betsey. "The Art of Helping by Changing Habit." In National Conference of Social Work. Proceedings (1925), pp. 276-84.

________. "Case Work in a Family Agency." In National Conference of Social Work. Proceedings (1924), pp. 321-4.

________. "The Philadelphia Experiment." In National Conference of Social Work. Proceedings (1919), pp. 332-6.

Lichtman, Sina. "Motifs for Living." In International Congress of Women, Chicago, 1933. Our Common Cause, Civilization, pp. 755-9.

Liggett, Claire. "Statement." In U.S. Congress. Senate. Committee on the Judiciary. Subcommittee on Constitutional Amendments. Equal Rights for Men and Women (1938), pp. 127-8.

Lincoln, Alice N. "The Almshouse Hospital." In National Conference of Charities and Correction. Proceedings (1902), pp. 212-7.

________. "Classification of Paupers. Is It Practicable in the U.S. to Classify Almshouse Inmates According to Character & Conduct?" In National Conference of Charities and Correction. Proceedings (1898), pp. 184-91.

________. "The Fixvale-Union Cottage Homes, and Classification of Public Dependents." In National Conference of Charities and Correction. *Proceedings* (1905), pp. 403-10.

________. "Housing Reform in Boston." In National Conference of Charities and Correction. *Proceedings* (1902), pp. 355-8.

Lincoln, Leontine. "Report of the Standing Committee--State Boards and Commission." In National Conference of Charities and Correction. *Proceedings* (1900), pp. 167-72.

Lincoln, Martha D. "The Press--Its Powers and Possibilities." In National Council of Women of the U.S., Washington, 1891. *Transactions*, pp. 344-7.

Lincoln, Mary J. Bailey. "Cookery." In World's Congress of Representative Women, Chicago, 1893. *Congress of Women*, pp. 138-42.

Linderholm, Natalie W. "The Social Worker's Responsibility for the Reputation of the Profession." In National Conference of Social Work. *Proceedings* (1945), pp. 212-9.

Lindsey, Matilda. "Statement." In U.S. Congress. House. Committee on the Judiciary. *Equal Rights Amendment to the Constitution* (1932), pp. 33-4.

Lipman-Blumen, Jean. "Overview: Demographic Trends and Issues in Women's Health." In U.S. National Center for Health Services Research. *Women and Their Health*, pp. 11-22.

________. "Toward a Homosocial Theory of Sex Roles: An Explanation of the Sex Segregation of Social Institutions." In Blaxall, M. *Women and the Workplace*, pp. 15-31.

Lippincott, Sara Jane. (Grace Greenwood) "A Statement of Facts." In World's Congress of Representative Women, Chicago, 1893. *A Historical Resume*, pp. 891-4.

________. "Tribute to Pioneers of Suffrage Movement." In International Council of Women, 1888. *Report*, pp. 353-5.

Lipscomb, Mary A. Rutherford. "Woman as a Financier." In World's Congress of Representative Women, Chicago, 1893. *Congress of Women*, pp. 469-70.

Lipton, Marge. "Public Testimony." In New York (City). Commission on Human Rights. *Women's Role in Contemporary Society*, pp. 718-9.

Littleton, Betty. "Women's Education: To Discover Ourselves as Women." *Vital Speeches*, 41 (August 15, 1975), 658-61.

Liveright, Alice F. "The Growing Importance of State Welfare Work--In Financial Support for Local Welfare Services." In National Conference of Social Work. *Proceedings* (1932), pp. 416-26.

_______. "Possibilities of Volunteer Service in Public Agencies." In National Conference of Social Work. Proceedings (1933), pp. 439-46.

Livermore, Mary Ashton Rice. "Address." In National Purity Congress, 1st, Baltimore, 1895. National Purity Congress, pp. 378-83.

_______. "Address to the Convention of the American Woman Suffrage Association, New York, May 1870." In Stanton, E. History of Woman Suffrage, 2, 777-80.

_______. "Debate at the 3rd Annual Meeting of the American Equal Rights Association, New York, May 1869." In Stanton, E. History of Woman Suffrage, 2, 397-8.

_______. "Industrial Gains of Women During the Last Half-Century." In International Council of Women, 1888. Report, pp. 131-7.

_______. "Superfluous Women." In Association for the Advancement of Women. Congress of Women, 3rd. Papers, pp. 87-93.

Livingston, Lida. "Communecology: A Concept for More Effective Communication." Vital Speeches, 35 (October 1, 1969), 765-8.

Lloyd, Ruth. "Psychiatric Social Work in Relation to a State Mental Hygiene Program." In National Conference of Social Work. Proceedings (1925), pp. 411-4.

Lloyd-Jones, Esther. "Progress Report of Pertinent Research." In Michigan State University, East Lansing, School of Home Economics. Potentialities of Women in the Middle Years, pp. 19-29.

Locke, Josephine C. "Concludes Discussion of the Moral Initiative as Related to Woman." In World's Congress of Representative Women, Chicago, 1893. A Historical Resume, pp. 324-7.

Lockett, Betty A. "Opening Remarks." In International Conference on Women in Health. Proceedings, pp. 1-2.

Lockwood, Belva A. "Annual Report to the 8th Annual Convention of the National Woman Suffrage Association, Washington, D.C., January 1876." In Stanton, E. History of Woman Suffrage, 3, 5-7.

_______. "Remarks at the Conference of Delegates." In American Peace Congress, 1st New York, 1907. Proceedings, pp. 309-10.

_______. "What Are the Activities, the Object and Aims of the National Arbitration Society." In American Peace Congress, 3rd, Baltimore, 1911. Proceedings, pp. 190-5.

Lockwood, Mary S. "The Evolution of Women in Literature." In National Council of Women of the U.S., Washington, 1891. Transactions, pp. 253-6.

________. "Presentation of Portrait." In World's Congress of Representative Women, Chicago, 1893. Congress of Women, p. 816.

Logan, Adella Hunt. "Prenatal and Hereditary Influences." In Conference for the Study of Negro Problems, 2nd Atlanta, 1897. Social and Physical Condition of Negroes in Cities, pp. 37-40.

Logan, Olive. "Address to the 3rd Annual Meeting of the American Equal Rights Association, New York, May 1869." In Stanton, E. History of Woman Suffrage, 2, 385-6.

Long, Elizabeth. "Old Age Assistance Administration: Varieties of Practice in the United States." In National Conference of Social Work. Proceedings (1937), pp. 507-16.

Long, Nira. "The Policy Issues: Presentation II." In Blaxall, M. Women and the Workplace, pp. 259-64.

Longley, Margaret V. "Remarks at the 4th Annual Meeting of the American Woman Suffrage Association, 1872." In Stanton, E. History of Woman Suffrage, 2, 822-3.

Loomis, Alice M. "Some Experiments in Research in Social Behavior." In National Conference of Social Work. Proceedings (1935), pp. 353-63.

Lord, Eleanor Louisa. "Educated Women as Factors in Industrial Competition. A Paper Presented to the Association of Collegiate Alumnae, October 24, 1891." (n. p.) 1891, 11 p.

________. "International Arbitration." In World's Congress of Representative Women, Chicago, 1893. Congress of Women, pp. 281-5.

________. "War from the Standpoint of Eugenics." In American Peace Congress, 3rd, Baltimore, 1911. Proceedings, pp. 59-77.

Lord, Mary Pillsbury. "Building Leadership for Peace ... New Ideas from New Voters: Panel Discussion." In New York Herald Tribune. Report of the 21st Annual Forum on Current Problems, pp. 158-9.

________. "The Citizen's Responsibility; A Panel Discussion." In New York Herald Tribune. Report of the 18th Annual Forum on Current Problems, pp. 174-6.

________. "Forced Labor. The Wholesale Suppression of Human Rights by Government." Vital Speeches, 20 (December 15, 1953), 139-43.

________. "Non-partisan Appeal for a Full Vote." In New York Herald Tribune. Report of the 13th Annual Forum on Current Problems, pp. 172-3.

Loring, Rosalind. "Expanding Opportunities Through Continuing Education." In Furniss, W. Women in Higher Education, pp. 199-204.

Lothrop, Alice Louise Higgins. "Helping Widows to Bring up Citizens." In National Conference of Charities and Correction. Proceedings (1910), pp. 138-44.

________. "The Responsibility of Medical Social Workers." In National Conference of Charities and Correction. Proceedings (1916), pp. 502-7.

Louchheim, Katie. "Citizen in a Changing World: Women of Today." Vital Speeches, 30 (November 15, 1963), 93-6.

Loud, Huldah B. "Women in the Knights of Labor." In International Council of Women, 1888. Report, pp. 143-6, 163.

Louis, Minnie D. "Mission-work Among the Unenlightened Jews." In Jewish Women's Congress. Papers, pp. 170-86.

________. "Woman--The Inciter to Reform." In World's Congress of Representative Women, Chicago, 1893. Congress of Women, pp. 539-43.

________. "Woman's Place in Hebrew Thought." In World's Congress of Representative Women, Chicago, 1893. A Historical Resume, pp. 267-74.

Lourie, Margaret. "Literary Women and the Masculated Sensibility." In McGuigan, D. New Research on Women at the University of Michigan, pp. 11-5.

Love, Nancy Harkness. "Women in Aviation." In New York Herald Tribune. Report of the 11th Annual Forum on Current Problems, pp. 164-7.

Lovell, Mary F. "Preventive Work as Carried on in the Public School of America." In International Congress of Women, London, 1899, 7, 34-9.

Lovering, Elizabeth C. "Enlightened Motherhood." In Association for the Advancement of Women. Congress of Women, 1st. Papers, pp. 31-6.

Low, Minnie F. "Co-operation Between Courts and Voluntary Public Agencies." In National Conference of Charities and Correction. Proceedings (1912), pp. 465-6.

________. "The Wider Use of Registration." In National Conference of Social Work. Proceedings (1920), pp. 455-61.

Low, Ruth Hull. "Statement." In U.S. Congress. Senate. Committee on the Judiciary. Subcommittee on Constitutional Amendments. Equal Rights Amendment (1945), pp. 95-6.

Lowe, Caroline A. "Address to a Joint Hearing of the Senate Judiciary Committee and the Senate Committee on Woman Suffrage, March 13, 1912." In Stanton, E. History of Woman Suffrage, 5, 350-1.

________. "On Behalf of 7,000,000 Wage-earning Women...." In Scott, A. One Half the People, pp. 122-6. (Same as "Address to a Joint Hearing....")

Lowell, Josephine Shaw. "A Better System of Public Charities and Correction for Cities." In Conference on Charities and Correction. Proceedings (1881), pp. 168-85.

________. "Civil Service Reform." In National Conference of Charities and Correction. Proceedings (1898), pp. 256-61.

________. "The Economic and Moral Effects of Public Outdoor Relief." In National Conference of Charities and Correction. Proceedings (1890), pp. 81-91.

________. "How to Adapt Charity Organization Methods to Small Communities." In National Conference of Charities and Correction. Proceedings (1887), pp. 135-43.

________. "One Means of Preventing Pauperism." In Conference on Charities. Proceedings (1879), pp. 189-200.

________. "Poverty and Its Relief: Methods Possible in the City of New York." In National Conference of Charities and Correction. Proceedings (1895), pp. 44-54.

________. "Scientific Charity." In Association for the Advancement of Women. "Truth, Justice and Honor," pp. 72-80.

Lowrie, Jean E. "Inaugural Address--What Is Librarianship?" American Libraries, 4 (October, 1973), 552-66.

Lowry, Fern. "A Philosophy of Supervision in Social Case Work." In National Conference of Social Work. Proceedings (1936), pp. 108-18.

Lowry, Pamela Lee. "Statement." In U.S. Congress. Senate. Committee on the Judiciary. Subcommittee on Constitutional Amendments. Abortion, pt. 3, 169-76.

Lowther, Dollie. "Summary of February 17, Evening Session." In U.S. Women's Bureau. American Woman--Her Changing Role, pp. 105-7.

Lozier, Jennie. "Educational Training in Its Bearing Upon the Promotion of Social Purity." In World's Congress of Representative Women, Chicago, 1893. A Historical Resume, pp. 127-31.

Lubic, Ruth Watson. "Innovations in the Utilization of Nurses, Allied Health and Support Personnel. A U.S. Response to a Look at Colombia." In International Conference on Women in Health. Proceedings, pp. 99-101.

Luce, Clare Boothe. "America and World Communism. Shall It Be One World?" Vital Speeches, 11 (August 15, 1945), 647-9.

________. "America in the Post-war Air World. Be Practical--Ration Globaloney." Vital Speeches, 9 (March 15, 1943), 331-6.

________. "American Morality and Nuclear Diplomacy. The Force of Our Free Spirits." Vital Speeches, 28 (February 15, 1962), 262-7.

________. "Chamber of Commerce and Communism. The Devil's Cleverist Trick." Vital Speeches, 13 (May 15, 1947), 465-7.

________. "China's Government. Federal Union Offers Real Solution." Vital Speeches, 12 (November 15, 1945), 94-6.

________. "Crisis in Soviet-Chinese Relations: The Two Red Giants." Vital Speeches, 30 (July 15, 1964), 591-4.

________. "Crisis in the United Nations: American Public Opinion." Vital Speeches, 31 (February 1, 1965), 236-41.

________. "Greater and Freer America. G. I. Joe's Future." Vital Speeches, 10 (July 15, 1944), 586-8.

________. "Italy in 1955. Problems Which Italy Confronts Today." Vital Speeches 21 (March 1, 1955), 1070-3.

________. "Newsblackout of the Fifth Army. Fixed Tour of Duty for Infantry." Vital Speeches, 11 (March 1, 1945), 305-7.

________. "Permanent Revolution. The Concept of Liberty Under Law Is Universal." Vital Speeches, 21 (August 15, 1955), 1415-7.

________. "Racial Cooperation." In New York Herald Tribune. Report of the 11th Annual Forum on Current Problems, pp. 178-82.

________. "Saintly Scientist. George Washington Carver." Vital Speeches, 13 (February 1, 1947), 241-5.

________. "Search for an American Foreign Policy. Yardsticks to Measure Our Objectives." Vital Speeches, 10 (July 1, 1944), 550-4.

________. "The Seventeen Year Trend to Castro: The Art of Economic Brinkmanship." Vital Speeches, 19 (March 1, 1963), 295-9.

________. "U. S. Foreign Policy and Italy: The Communist and Detente." Vital Speeches, 42 (June 1, 1976), 482-4.

________. "U. S. Foreign Policy and World Communism. The Jungle World of Sovereign States." Vital Speeches, 44 (August 15, 1978), 645-7.

________. "Unpreparedness of the Individual." In New York Herald Tribune. Report of the 10th Annual Forum on Current Problems, pp. 30-3.

________. "Waging the Peace." In New York Herald Tribune. Report of the 13th Annual Forum on Current Problems, pp. 215-9.

________. "Waging the Peace. Blueprints of Past Lacked Courage and Loyalty." Vital Speeches, 11 (November 1, 1944), 43-4.

________. "What's Wrong with the American Press? The Debasement of Popular Taste." Vital Speeches, 26 (July 1, 1960), 538-41.

Ludington, Flora Belle. "Report to Council, June 25, 1954, Minneapolis." ALA Bulletin, 48 (September, 1954), 439-41.

________. "Taproot, Trunk and Branches." ALA Bulletin, 47 (September, 1953), 345.

Ludington, Katharine. "Address Before Annual Convention. (Connecticut Woman Suffrage Convention)." Suffrage News Bulletin, 5 (December, 1918), 1-2.

_______. "Address for a Deputation of Connecticut Women to the Chairman of the Republican Party, Will Hays, August, 1920." In Catt, C. Woman Suffrage and Politics, pp. 403-4.

Luers, Margaret. "Statement." In U.S. Congress. House. Committee on the Judiciary. Equal Rights Amendment to the Constitution (1932), p. 17.

Lummis, Jessie D. "The Responsibility of State and Municipal Authorities to the Migrant Consumptive." In National Conference of Social Work. Proceedings (1925), pp. 194-200.

Lumsden, May. "Health and the New Housing." In National Conference of Social Work. Proceedings (1936), pp. 562-8.

Lund, Henrietta J. "Case Work as Applied to Rural Communities." In National Conference of Social Work. Proceedings (1920), pp. 295-7.

_______. "Progress in Social Case Work: Among the Indians." In National Conference of Social Work. Proceedings (1923), p. 341.

Lundberg, Emma O. "The Child-Mother as a Delinquency Problem." In National Conference of Social Work. Proceedings (1920), pp. 167-8.

_______. "Illegitimacy in Europe as Affected by the War." In National Conference of Social Work. Proceedings (1917), pp. 299-304.

_______. "Interpretation and Support of Public Welfare Work: Publications and Uniform Social Data." In National Conference of Social Work. Proceedings (1925), pp. 650-5.

_______. "The Juvenile Court as a Constructive Social Agency." In National Conference of Social Work. Proceedings (1922), pp. 155-60.

_______. "The Present Status of Mothers' Pensions Administration." In National Conference of Social Work. Proceedings (1921), pp. 237-40.

_______. "Progress in Legal Protection for Children Born Out of Wedlock." In National Conference of Social Work. Proceedings (1922), pp. 124-7.

_______. "Progress Toward Better Laws for the Protection of Children Born Out of Wedlock." In National Conference of Social Work. Proceedings (1920), pp. 111-15.

Lunde, Laura Hughes. "Children at Work." In International Congress of Women, Chicago, 1933. Our Common Cause, Civilization, pp. 316-20.

Lyday, June F. "The Place of the Mobile Clinic in a Rural Community." In National Conference of Social Work. Proceedings (1927), pp. 408-17.

Lyells, Ruby B. Stutts. "Accent on Youth. Tomorrow's Hope; Or Despair." Vital Speeches, 12 (December 15, 1945), 156-8.

________. "A Look Ahead. What the Negro Wants." Vital Speeches, 15 (August 15, 1949), 659-62.

________. "New Emancipation. Responsibilities of the Negro." Vital Speeches, 10 (March 15, 1944), 349-52.

________. "Woman-power for a Better World. Civilizing Influence in a Man's World." Vital Speeches, 14 (January 15, 1948), 217-20.

Lynde, Mary Elizabeth Blanchard. "Prevention in Some of Its Aspects and Woman's Part in It." In Conference on Charities. Proceedings (1879), pp. 162-70.

________. "The Treatment of Criminal and Erring Women." In Conference on Charities and Correction. Proceedings (1880), pp. 249-51.

Lyon, Phyllis. "Keynote Address at the 1974 NOW National Conference." Do It NOW, 7 (October, 1974), 6.

Lyons, Suzie L. "The Training of Social Service Workers in Psychiatric Field Work." In National Conference of Social Work. Proceedings (1920), pp. 396-8.

McAnarney, Elizabeth R. "The Impact of Medical Women in United States Medical Schools." In Spieler, C. Women in Medicine--1976, pp. 9-58.

McCabe, Rita. "Panel Discussion on Women and the Scientific Professions at M. I. T. --Statement." In M. I. T. Symposium on American Women in Science and Engineering, 1964. Women and the Scientific Professions, pp. 24-8.

McCaffrey, Carlyn. "Statement." In U. S. Congress. Joint Economic Committee. Economic Problems of Women, pt. 4, 604-9.

McCall, Bertha. "Migration Problems and the Federal Government." In National Conference of Social Work. Proceedings (1940), pp. 130-9.

McCamman, Dorothy. "Statement at Senate Hearings on Women and Social Security." In U. S. Congress. Senate. Special Committee on Aging. Future Directions in Social Security, pt. 18, 1667.

McClenahan, Bessie A. "County Organization of Welfare Agencies." In National Conference of Social Work. Proceedings (1918), pp. 595-604.

Maccoby, Eleanor E. "Women's Intellect." In Farber, S. Man and Civilization: The Potential of Woman, pp. 24-39.

McConnell, Beatrice. "The Employment of Minors in Wartime." In National Conference of Social Work. Proceedings (1943), pp. 158-69.

McCord, Elizabeth. "Child Guidance Clinics and Child Caring Agencies: The Value of the Psychiatric Approach for All Children's Case Workers." In National Conference of Social Work. Proceedings (1928), pp. 110-6.

________. "A Cooperative Experiment Between Public and Private Agencies." In National Conference of Social Work. Proceedings (1932), pp. 166-74.

McCormick, Anne O'Hare. "United States as World Leader. Don't Limit Our Aims." Vital Speeches, 13 (May 1, 1947), 432-5.

McCormick, Ruth Hanna. "Report of Special Campaign Committee to the National American Woman Suffrage Association Convention of 1914." In Stanton, E. History of Woman Suffrage, 5, 418-9.

________. "Report of the Campaign Committee to the National American Woman Suffrage Association Convention of 1914." In Stanton, E. History of Woman Suffrage, 5, 412-3, 414-6.

________. "Welfare Work." In General Federation of Women's Clubs. Biennial Convention, 9 (1908), 313-4.

McCowen, Jennie. "The Prevention of Insanity." In National Conference of Charities and Correction. Proceedings (1882), pp. 36-43.

________. "Report from Iowa." In National Conference of Charities and Correction. Proceedings (1882), pp. 169-72.

McCoy, Helen I. "The Philadelphia Plan of a Central Bureau of Inquiry and Specialized Care." In National Conference of Social Work. Proceedings (1922), pp. 145-50.

McCulloch, Catharine Waugh. "The Protective Power of the Ballot. Address to the House Judiciary Committee, 1900." In Stanton, E. History of Woman Suffrage, 4, 378-80.

McDiarmid, Clara A. "Our Neighbors, the Alaskan Women." In World's Congress of Representative Women, Chicago, 1893. Congress of Women, pp. 723-6.

McDoal, Margaret. "Statement." In U. S. Congress. Senate. Committee on the Judiciary. Subcommittee on Constitutional Amendments. Equal Rights for Men and Women (1938), p. 127.

McDonald, Cora Martin. "Literature for Young People." In World's Congress of Representative Women, Chicago, 1893. Congress of Women, pp. 264-7.

MacDonald, Flora. "Interior Decorator." In General Federation of Women's Clubs. Biennial Convention, 9 (1908), 392-6.

MacDonald, Lybbi. "Testimony." In U.S. Congress. House. Select Committee on Crime. Drugs in Our Schools, pp. 620-5.

MacDonald, Ruth. "Human Values and Energy Conservation: Our Common Concern." Vital Speeches, 41 (September 1, 1975), 699-702.

MacDonald, V. May. "Function of the Social Worker in Relation to the Community." In National Conference of Social Work. Proceedings (1919), pp. 637-43.

________. "Social Work and the National Committee for Mental Hygiene." In National Conference of Social Work. Proceedings (1920), pp. 398-400.

MacDougal, Sarah. "Two Powers--Women and the Press." In General Federation of Women's Clubs. Biennial Convention, 16 (1922), 132-3.

MacDougald, Elise Johnson. "The School and Its Relation to the Vocational Life of the Negro." In National Conference of Social Work. Proceedings (1923), pp. 415-8.

McDowell, Mary E. "Friendly Visiting." In National Conference of Charities and Correction. Proceedings (1896), pp. 253-6.

________. "How Casual Work Undermines Family and Neighborhood Life." In National Conference of Charities and Correction. Proceedings (1909), pp. 150-6.

________. "The Need for Women to Enforce Women's Labor Laws." U.S. Women's Bureau. Proceedings of the Women's Industrial Conference, pp. 184-8.

________. "The Quota Law and the Family." In National Conference of Social Work. Proceedings (1930), pp. 478-85.

________. "The Relation of Community Work to Family Life." In National Conference of Social Work. Proceedings (1926), pp. 379-83.

________. "The Settlement and Organized Charity." In National Conference of Charities and Correction. Proceedings (1896), pp. 123-7.

________. "The Significance to the City of Its Local Community Life." In National Conference of Social Work. Proceedings (1917), pp. 458-62.

________. "Woman's Industrial and International Interests." In American Peace Congress, 2nd, Chicago, 1909. Proceedings, pp. 263-6.

________. "Work for Normal Young Working Women." In National Conference of Charities and Correction. Proceedings (1907), pp. 319-26.

McFarland, Carmen. "How Lay Citizens Can Influence the Local Administration of Health." In National Conference of Social Work. Proceedings (1940), pp. 508-16.

McFarlane, Catharine. "Physiological Changes and Adjustments: From the Standpoint of a Physician." In Michigan State University, East Lansing, School of Home Economics. Potentialities of Women in the Middle Years, pp. 49-58.

McGee, Lucy Castina. "The Home of the Future." In World's Congress of Representative Women, Chicago, 1893. Congress of Women, pp. 249-52.

McGerr, Helen. "Statement." In U.S. Congress. Senate. Committee on the Judiciary. Subcommittee on Constitutional Amendments. Equal Rights (1931), p. 15.

McGowan, Carolyn L. "Counseling in Industry." In National Conference of Social Work. Proceedings (1943), pp. 227-30.

McGuire, Louise. "Social-work Basis for Prevention and Treatment of Delinquency and Crime: Community Factors." In National Conference of Social Work. Proceedings (1936), pp. 579-89.

McHugh, Rose J. "The Background of a Family's Religious Life as Social Data." In National Conference of Social Work. Proceedings (1926), pp. 270-2.

________. "A Constructive Program for the Aged." In National Conference of Social Work. Proceedings (1947), pp. 391-401.

________. "The Organization of Social Service in Connection with State Institutions." In National Conference of Social Work. Proceedings (1935), pp. 598-607.

________. "Some Conclusions from a Series of Studies by the National Catholic Welfare Conference." In National Conference of Social Work. Proceedings (1929), pp. 125-34.

McIntosh, Margaret Millicent Cary. "Can the Intellect Survive? Meeting the Circumstances of Living." Vital Speeches, 15 (July 1, 1949), 559-60.

________. "Education for What? A Challenge to Teaching." In New York Herald Tribune. Report of the 17th Annual Forum on Current Problems, pp. 54-7.

________. "Goals of Progressive Education Not Sufficient Today. Educators Must Provide Moral Synthesis." Vital Speeches, 15 (November 15, 1948), 90-1.

________. "New Horizons for Women. The Modern Home Is a Cooperative Venture." Vital Speeches, 19 (March 1, 1953), 311-2.

Mackenzie, Constance. "Free Kindergartens." In National Conference of Charities and Corrections. Proceedings (1886), pp. 48-53.

________. "Playgrounds in Cities." In National Congress of Mothers, Work and Words, pp. 155-64.

McLaughlin, Mary Louise. "Pottery in the Household." In World's Congress of Representative Women, Chicago, 1893. A Historical Resume, pp. 575-8.

MacLean, Annie Marion. "Abstract of an Address on Industrial Conditions for Women." In International Congress of Women, Toronto, 1909. Report, 1, 8-9.

McLean, Elizabeth J. "Urbanization for the Future." In International Conference of Women Engineers and Scientists, 1st, New York. Focus for the Future, pp. IV-1-13.

McLemore, Ethel Ward. "Restoring Stability to the Family. Emotional Disturbances Brought on by the Demands of Business." Vital Speeches, 21 (July 1, 1955), 1330-4.

McLennan, Helen. "Sod Busting for Social Work in Rural Michigan." In National Conference of Social Work. Proceedings (1939), pp. 477-80.

MacMurchy, Helen. "The Relation of Feeble-Mindedness to Other Social Problems." In National Conference of Charities and Correction. Proceedings (1916), pp. 229-35.

McMurray, Georgia L. "Social Work." In Conference of Professional and Academic Women. Sixteen Reports on the Status of Women in the Professions, 3 p.

McNally, Gertrude. "Statement." In U. S. Congress. Senate. Committee on the Judiciary. Subcommittee on Constitutional Amendments. Equal Rights Amendment (1929), pp. 44-5.

McNary, Jean. "Youth Plans for a Civilized World: Forum on the College Generation." In International Congress of Women, Chicago, 1933. Our Common Cause, Civilization, pp. 197-8.

McNeel, Barbara. "Statement." In U. S. Congress. Senate. Committee on the Judiciary. Subcommittee on Constitutional Amendments. Abortion, pt. 1, 259-61.

McNeier, Laura. "Ladies of the Grand Army of the Republic." In International Council of Women, 1888. Report, pp. 88-9.

MacQuillin, Lillian G. "Club House Manager." In General Federation of Women's Clubs. Biennial Convention, 9 (1908), 385-92.

McRae, Emma Mont. "Testimony at a Hearing of the House Committee on the Judiciary, January 24, 1880." In Stanton, E. History of Woman Suffrage, 3, 161.

McWilliam, Nancy. "Contemporary Feminism, Consciousness-raising, and Changing Views of the Political." In Jaquette, J. Women in Politics, pp. 157-70.

McWilliams, Marie. "Testimony of American Broadcasting Company." In U. S. Equal Employment Opportunity Commission. Hearings on Discrimination in White Collar Employment, pp. 369-72.

Macy, Henrietta. "Youth in Industry." In International Congress of Women, Chicago, 1933. Our Common Cause, Civilization, pp. 211-3.

Madar, Olga M. "Statement." In U.S. Congress. House. Committee on the Judiciary. Subcommittee No. 4. Equal Rights for Men and Women 1971, pp. 384-92.

_______. "Statement." In U.S. Congress. Senate. Committee on the Judiciary. Subcommittee on Constitutional Amendments. Women and the "Equal Rights" Amendment, pp. 207-13.

Madison, Bernice. "Social Services for Women: Problems and Priorities." In Atkinson, D. Women in Russia, pp. 307-32.

Magee, Elizabeth S. "Opportunities for Social Workers to Participate in Social Legislation." In National Conference of Social Work. Proceedings (1935), pp. 487-96.

_______. "Role of Women's Legislation in Meeting Basic Problems of Working Conditions." Washington, U.S. Women's Bureau, 1948, 5 p. Also in U.S. Women's Bureau. American Woman--Her Changing Role, pp. 28-32.

_______. "Statement." In U.S. Congress. Senate. Committee on the Judiciary. Subcommittee on Constitutional Amendments. Equal Rights Amendment (1945), pp. 143-4.

_______. "Unemployment Insurance: Ohio Takes Stock." In National Conference of Social Work. Proceedings (1932), pp. 285-93.

Maguire, Margaret. "Public Testimony." In New York (City). Commission on Human Rights. Women's Role in Contemporary Society, pp. 314-5.

Maher, Mary A. B. "The Catholic Woman as an Educator." In World's Congress of Representative Women, Chicago, 1893. A Historical Resume, pp. 134-7.

Main, Charlotte Emerson. "Patriotism in Civil Service Reform." In General Federation of Women's Clubs. Biennial Convention, 9 (1908), 361-3.

Mallory, Claude Houze Melvin. "Psychiatry, Social Service, and Society." In National Conference of Social Work. Proceedings (1925), pp. 404-7.

Maloney, Mollie. "Statement." In U.S. Congress. Senate. Committee on the Judiciary. Subcommittee on Constitutional Amendments. Equal Rights for Men and Women (1938), pp. 108-10.

Maltese, Francesca. "Notes for a Study of the Automobile Industry." In Conference on Labor Market Segmentation, Harvard University, 1973. Labor Market Segmentation, pp. 85-93.

Manis, Jean Denby. "Fertility Motivations and Career Conflicts in Educated Women." In McGuigan, D. New Research on Women at the University of Michigan, pp. 126-31.

Mann, Marty. "What Shall We Do About Alcoholism? Alcoholics Anonymous." Vital Speeches, 13 (February 1, 1947), 253-6.

Mannes, Marya. "The Exercise of Conscience. "Is It Good?" Not "Will It Sell?" Should Be the Criterion." Vital Speeches, 27 (May 1, 1961), 441-3.

________. "The Problems of Creative Women." In Farber, S. Man and Civilization: The Potential of Woman, pp. 116-30.

________. "Problems of Creative Woman." In Scott, A. The American Woman, pp. 175-7.

Mannheimer, Louise. "Jewish Women of Biblical and of Mediaeval Times." In Jewish Women's Congress. Papers, pp. 15-25.

Manning, Agnes M. "Complete Freedom for Women." In World's Congress of Representative Women, Chicago, 1893. Congress of Women, pp. 107-12.

Manning, Caroline. "The Industrial Woman Looks at the Problems." In National Conference of Social Work. Proceedings (1930), pp. 290-4.

Manor, Stella P. "Planning Training for Future Womanpower." Washington, U.S. Women's Bureau, 1958, 10 p.

Manus, Rosa. "Excessive Nationalism--Discussion." In International Congress of Women, Chicago, 1933. Our Common Cause, Civilization, pp. 684-6.

Marble, Ellen M.S. "Address." In International Council of Women, 1888. Report, pp. 318-9.

Marcus, Grace F. "Application of Psychology to Case Work." In National Conference of Social Work. Proceedings (1932), pp. 226-33.

________. "The Case Worker's Problem in Interpretation." In National Conference of Social Work. Proceedings (1936), pp. 133-45.

________. "Changes in the Theory of Relief Giving." In National Conference of Social Work. Proceedings (1941), pp. 267-79.

________. "Community Organization for Child Guidance Clinic Work." In National Conference of Social Work. Proceedings (1925), pp. 415-8.

________. "The Effects of Financial Dependency and Relief Giving Upon Social Attitudes." In National Conference of Social Work. Proceedings (1928), pp. 218-25.

________. "Helping the Client to Use His Capacities and Resources." In National Conference of Social Work. Proceedings (1948), pp. 251-9.

_______. "How Case Work Training May Be Adapted to Meet the Worker's Personal Problems." In National Conference of Social Work. Proceedings (1927), pp. 385-92.

_______. "The Responsibility of the Case Worker in the Conflict Between the Interests of the Individual and the Interests of Society." In National Conference of Social Work. Proceedings (1940), pp. 574-84.

_______. "The Responsibility of the Psychiatric Social Worker: A Further Consideration of Psychiatric Social Work." In National Conference of Social Work. Proceedings (1946), pp. 336-41.

_______. "The Status of Social Case Work Today." In National Conference of Social Work. Proceedings (1925), pp. 125-40.

_______. "Worker and Client Relationships." In National Conference of Social Work. Proceedings (1946), pp. 342-52.

Margolin, Olya. "Working Women: Their Citizenship Responsibilities." In U.S. Women's Bureau. American Woman--Her Changing Role, pp. 111-13.

Marieskind, Helen I. "New Roles for Women in Health Care Delivery: A U.S. Response to Conditions in China. The Women's Health Movement: Political, Social and Working Roles for Women in Health Care Delivery." In International Conference on Women in Health. Proceedings, pp. 117-21.

Mark, Mary Louise. "The Needs in Human Relationships." In National Conference of Social Work. Proceedings (1932), pp. 617-26.

Markajani, Mary. "Statement." In U.S. Congress. House. Committee on the Judiciary. Subcommittee No. 1. Equal Rights Amendment (1948), pp. 30-2.

Marlowe, Julia. "Woman's Work upon the Stage." In World's Congress of Representative Women, Chicago, 1893. A Historical Resume, pp. 188-92.

Marot, Helen. "Address of Miss Marot." In Bryn Mawr College. Carola Woerishoffer, Her Life and Work, pp. 66-76.

Marriner, Jessie L. "The Co-ordination of Public and Private Agencies in a State Program of Public Health Nursing." In National Conference of Social Work. Proceedings (1920), pp. 204-8.

Marsh, Marguerite. "Common Attitudes Toward the Unmarried Father." In National Conference of Social Work. Proceedings (1940), pp. 377-88.

Marshall, Sarah E. "Bringing People and Services Together." In National Conference of Social Work. Proceedings (1946), pp. 165-71.

Marston, Helen M. "Rutgers--The State University, Ford Foundation Program for the Retraining in Mathematics of College Graduate Women." In Itasca Conference on the Continuing Education of Women, Itasca State Park, Minnesota, 1962. Education and a Woman's Life, pp. 101-5.

Martens, Elsie. "Case Work Treatment of Emotional Maladjustment in Marriage." In National Conference of Social Work. Proceedings (1944), pp. 256-67.

Martin, Edna. "Statement Concerning Her Abduction Before the Senate Committee on Labor and Public Welfare, November 17, 1947." In Baxandall, R. America's Working Women, pp. 320-5.

Martinez, Sally. "Statement." In U.S. Congress. House. Committee on Education and Labor. Subcommittee on Equal Opportunities. Equal Opportunity for Displaced Homemakers Act, pp. 21-3.

Marwedel, Emma. "Practical Culture." In Association for the Advancement of Women. Congress of Women, 1st. Papers, pp. 142-6.

Mason, Frances. "Address: Art and the Next Generation." In General Federation of Women's Clubs. Biennial Convention, 16 (1922), 185-8.

Mason, Lucy Randolph. "Government Lends a Hand." In International Congress of Women, Chicago, 1933. Our Common Cause, Civilization, pp. 467-71.

________. "Progress and Administration of Minimum Wage Laws in 1933." In National Conference of Social Work. Proceedings (1933), pp. 378-86.

Matisoff, Nancy. "Should the Federal Government Assume a Direct Role in the Regulation of Surface Mining of Coal in the States?" Congressional Digest, 53 (May, 1974), 144-8.

Mattfeld, Jaquelyn A. "Many Are Called, but Few Are Chosen." In Furniss, W. Women in Higher Education, pp. 121-7.

Matthews, Burnita Shelton. "Statement." In U.S. Congress. House. Committee on the Judiciary. Subcommittee No. 1. Equal Rights Amendment (1948), pp. 15-20, 186-91.

________. "Statement." In U.S. Congress. House. Committee on the Judiciary. Equal Rights Amendment to the Constitution (1932), pp. 51-4.

________. "Statement." In U.S. Congress. Senate. Committee on the Judiciary. Subcommittee on Constitutional Amendments. Equal Rights Amendment (1929), p. 2.

________. "Statement." In U.S. Congress. Senate. Committee on the Judiciary. Subcommittee on Constitutional Amendments. Equal Rights for Men and Women (1933), pp. 5-10.

________. "Statement." In U.S. Congress. Senate. Committee on the Judiciary. Subcommittee on Constitutional Amendments. Equal Rights for Men and Women (1938), pp. 140-8.

________. "Statement Before the Senate Hearing on the Equal-Rights Amendment, 1931." In Kraditor, A. Up from the Pedestal, pp. 293-5, 301. Also in U.S. Congress. Senate. Committee on the Judiciary. Subcommittee on Constitutional Amendments. Equal Rights (1931), pp. 5-14, 66-7.

Matthews, Ellen Nathalie. "Work Opportunities and School Training for Coal-Miners' Children." In National Conference of Social Work. Proceedings (1921), pp. 287-92.

Matthews, Esther. "Employment Implications of Psychological Characteristics of Men and Women." In Katzell, M. Women in the Work Force, pp. 27-41.

May, Catherine. "The American Farmer: The Consumers' Real Protector." Vital Speeches, 36 (August 1, 1970), 625-8.

________. "Every Man Should Have His Say: Free Discussion." Vital Speeches, 31 (August 1, 1965), 622-4.

Mayer, Maria Goeppert. "Shell Model; Address, December 12, 1963." Science, 145 (September 4, 1964), 99-106.

Mayer, Shirley. "Public Testimony." In New York (City). Commission on Human Rights. Women's Role in Contemporary Society, pp. 531-6.

Maymi, Carmen R. "Explanation of Vote on Draft Resolution on World Conference of the International Women's Year." Department of State Bulletin, 74 (January 26, 1976), 114-5.

________. "Statement." In National League of Cities. Women in Municipal Government, pp. 13-23.

________. "Statement of December 3, 1976 on the Fulfillment of Goals of International Women's Year in the U.N." Department of State Bulletin, 74 (January 26, 1976), 110-4.

Meacham, Colquitt L. "The Law: Where It Is and Where It's Going." In Gordon, F. Bringing Women into Management, pp. 59-76.

Mead, Lucia Ames. "America's Danger and Opportunity." In American Peace Congress, 5th, San Francisco, 1915. Proceedings, pp. 124-33.

________. "History of the Peace Movement." In American Peace Congress, 1st, New York, 1907. Proceedings, pp. 88-92.

________. "Remarks at the Conference of Delegates." In American Peace Congress, 1st, New York, 1907. Proceedings, pp. 314-6.

________. "Report of Committee on Peace and Arbitration." In National American Woman Suffrage Association. Proceedings of the 39th Annual Convention, pp. 41-3.

________. "Some Common Fallacies." In American Peace Congress, 2nd, Chicago, 1909. *Proceedings*, pp. 254-60.

Mead, Margaret. "Aging Differently in the Space Age; Excerpts from Address." *Recreation*, 57 (May, 1964), 219+.

________. "Changing World of Living; Address." *Science Digest*, 62 (September, 1967), 38-43.

________. "Crisis of Self: America's Secret War; Remarks at the 1973 Congress for Recreation and Parks." *Parks & Recreation*, 9 (March 1974), 24-8+.

________. "A Cultural Dilemma." In Fremon, S. *Women and Men*, pp. 47-57.

________. "Future Family; Adaptation of Address. February 12, 1970." *Trans-Action*, 8 (September, 1971), 50-3.

________. "Generation Gap; Adaptation of Address." *Science*, 164 (April 11, 1964), 135.

________. "How Fares the American Family? Address." *National Parent-Teacher*, 49 (February, 1955), 22-5.

________. "Mental Health in Our Changing Culture; Excerpts from Address." *MH*, 56 (Summer, 1972), 6-8.

________. "Public Policy and Behavior Science; Excerpts from Testimony Before the U. S. Senate Foreign Relations Committee, June 20, 1969." *Bulletin of the Atomic Scientists*, 25 (December, 1969), 8-10.

________. "Revise Role of Teacher; Summary of Address." *Science News-Letter*, 73 (April 2, 1958), 229.

________. "Symposium on Knowledge and Problems of Race: Introductory Remarks; Excerpts from Science and the Concept of Race." *School and Society*, 96 (Summer, 1968), 311-4.

________. "Towards a Human Science; Adaptation of Address." *Science*, 191 (March 5, 1976), 903-9.

________. "Wanted: Young Scientists: Summary of Address." *Science Newsletter*, 76 (August 8, 1959), 82.

________. "What Is Happening to the American Family?" In National Conference of Social Work. *Proceedings* (1947), pp. 61-74.

________. "What Kind of World Do We Want? Contributions by Social Science and by Women." *Vital Speeches*, 9, (June 1, 1943), 510-1.

________. "Women's Rights: A Cultural Dilemma." In New York (City). Commission on Human Rights. *Women's Role in Contemporary Society*, pp. 175-84. (Same as "A Cultural Dilemma").

Meade, Mabel. "Playgrounds." In National Conference of Charities and Correction. *Proceedings* (1906), pp. 396-400.

Meanes, Lenna L. "Co-operation with the Women's Foundation for Health." In General Federation of Women's Clubs. *Biennial Convention*, 16 (1922), 362-66.

Mears, Judith. "Statement." In U. S. Congress. Senate. Committee on the Judiciary. Subcommittee on Constitutional Amendments. *Abortion*, pt. 4, 280-97.

Mecklenburg, Marjory. "Statement." In U.S. Congress. Senate. Committee on the Judiciary. Subcommittee on Constitutional Amendments. Abortion, pt. 4, 643-53.

Meigs, Cornelia. "Acceptance Paper--Newbery Medal 1934." In Miller, B. Newbery Medal Books, 1922-1955, pp. 122-4.

Meigs, Grace L. "Infant Welfare Work in War Time." In National Conference of Social Work. Proceedings (1917), pp. 192-206.

Meloney, Marie Mattingley. "The New World Power--Mass Opinion." In New York Herald Tribune. Report of the 8th Annual Forum on Current Problems, pp. 42-4.

________. "Twenty Years of Pioneering." In New York Herald Tribune. Report of the 6th Annual Forum on Current Problems, pp. 22-3.

________. "What Man Cannot Destroy." In New York Herald Tribune. Report of the 9th Annual Forum on Current Problems, pp. 49-51.

________. "You Have Been Warned." In New York Herald Tribune. Report of the 10th Annual Forum on Current Problems, pp. 246-50.

Mendum, Gladys. "Child Welfare Work in a Rural Community." In National Conference of Social Work. Proceedings (1919), pp. 20-6.

________. "Conditions Breeding Delinquency in Rural Communities." In National Conference of Social Work. Proceedings (1927), pp. 143-52.

Meredith, Virginia C. "The Columbian Exposition." In National Council of Women of the U.S., Washington, 1891. Transactions, pp. 318-20.

________. "Stock Breeding." In International Congress of Women, London, 1899, 4, 132-4.

Meriwether, Lide A. "Address to the House Judiciary Committee, February 17, 1892." In Stanton, E. History of Woman Suffrage, 4, 195-6.

________. "Organized Motherhood." In World's Congress of Representative Women, Chicago, 1893. Congress of Women, pp. 747-51.

Merrill, Estelle M. H. "The New England Woman's Press Association." In National Council of Women of the U.S., Washington, 1891. Transactions, pp. 285-6.

Merrill, Marjorie Anne. "Lessons Learned in Personnel Selection and Management in Emergency Relief Administration." In National Conference of Social Work. Proceedings (1936), pp. 538-47.

Meyer, Agnes Elizabeth Ernst. "British Home Front Compared with Ours. If Democracy Is Worth Fighting For, It Is Worth Fighting With." Vital Speeches, 9 (May 15, 1943), 459-64.

________. "Federal Aid to Education." In New York Herald Tribune. Report of the 17th Annual Forum on Current Problems, pp. 91-6.

________. "Freedom of the Mind." In Loveman, Amy, ed. Varied Harvest (N. Y.: Putnam, 1953), pp. 31-7.

________. "The Middle-Aged Woman in Contemporary Society." In Michigan State University, East Lansing, School of Home Economics. Potentialities of Women in the Middle Years, pp. 145-58.

Meyer, Annie Nathan. "Do We Need Emerson Today? New Theories of Living Are Being Forced upon Us." Vital Speeches, 5 (February 15, 1939), 261-4.

________. "A New Phase of Women's Education in America." In National Council of Women of the U. S., Washington, 1891. Transactions, pp. 178-88.

________. "Woman's Place in Letters." In World's Congress of Representative Women, Chicago, 1893. Congress of Women, pp. 135-7.

________. "Woman's Place in the Republic of Letters." In World's Congress of Representative Women, Chicago, 1893. A Historical Resume, pp. 140-4. (Same as "Woman's Place in Letters").

Meyering, Anne C. "Women in Families and History." In Hammond, N. Women and Children in Contemporary Society, pp. 95-102.

Meyers, Sister Bertrande, D. C. "Raise Your Voice: Cast Your Vote." Vital Speeches, 33 (August 15, 1967), 661-4.

Michaels, Rena A. "Co-education." In International Council of Women, 1888. Report, pp. 75-7.

________. "Women as Educators." In International Council of Women, 1888. Report, pp. 165-7.

Miles, Minnie C. "Statement." In U. S. Congress. Senate. Committee on Labor and Public Welfare. Subcommittee on Labor. Equal Pay Act of 1963, pp. 89-94.

Milhous, Katherine. "Acceptance Paper--Caldecott Award 1951. The Egg Tree and How It Grew." In Miller, B. Caldecott Medal Books, 1938-1957, pp. 213-21.

Millar, Margaret. "Modern Use of Older Treatment Methods." In National Conference of Social Work. Proceedings (1937), pp. 205-15.

Millay, Edna St. Vincent. "Termites in America." In New York Herald Tribune. Report of the 9th Annual Forum on Current Problems, pp. 10-11.

Milledge, Luetta C. "To Speak of Eagles. Education: The Expression of the Individual." Vital Speeches, 40 (November 1, 1973), 49-51.

Miller, Annie Jenness. "Dress Improvement." In World's Congress of Representative Women, Chicago, 1893. Congress of Women, pp. 695-6.

_______. "Science in the Kitchen." In Association for the Advancement of Women. Congress of Women, 3rd. Papers, pp. 114-7.

Miller, Emma Guffey. "The Equal Rights Amendment." Congressional Record, 79th Cong., 1st sess., 1945, 91, pt. 10, A994-7.

_______. "Statement." In U.S. Congress. House. Committee on Education and Labor. Select Subcommittee on Labor. Equal Pay for Equal Work, pp. 141-2.

_______. "Statement." In U.S. Congress. House. Committee on the Judiciary. Subcommittee No. 1. Equal Rights Amendment (1948), pp. 10-3.

_______. "Statement." In U.S. Congress. Senate. Committee on the Judiciary. Subcommittee on Constitutional Amendments. Equal Rights for Men and Women (1938), pp. 94-9.

_______. "Statement." In U.S. Congress. Senate. Committee on the Judiciary. Subcommittee on Constitutional Amendments. Equal Rights Amendment (1945), pp. 3-6, 50-1, 149-50.

_______. "Statement." In U.S. Congress. Senate. Committee on the Judiciary. Subcommittee on Constitutional Amendments. Equal Rights (1956), pp. 18-21.

Miller, Frieda S. "Government Regulation of Wages and Hours: The States and Their Opportunity." In National Conference of Social Work. Proceedings (1939), pp. 199-208.

_______. "Older Women Workers, Statement at Public Hearing of New York State Joint Legislative Committee on Problems of the Aging, December 14, 1950, in New York City." Washington, U.S. Women's Bureau, 1951, 6 p.

_______. "Patterns of Women in Industry." Washington, U.S. Women's Bureau, 1945, 9 p.

_______. "Report Before Conference of Women's Organizations, March 14, 1946 on United Nations Sessions in London." Washington, U.S. Women's Bureau, 1946, 12 p.

_______. "Role of Women in National Economy." Washington, U.S. Women's Bureau, 1949, 9 p.

_______. "Statement." In U.S. Congress. House. Committee on the Judiciary. Subcommittee No. 1. Equal Rights Amendment (1948), pp. 100-6.

_______. "Statement." In U.S. Congress. Senate. Committee on the Judiciary. Subcommittee on Constitutional Amendments. Equal Rights Amendment (1945), pp. 145-6.

_______. "Statement Against the Equal-Rights Amendment at the Senate Committee Hearings, 1931." In Kraditor, A. Up from the Pedestal, pp. 299-300. Also in U.S. Congress. Senate. Committee on the Judiciary. Subcommittee on Constitutional Amendments. Equal Rights (1931), pp. 36-40.

________. "War and Postwar Adjustments of Women Workers." Washington, U.S. Women's Bureau, 1945, 7 p.

________. "Where Do We Stand on Minimum Wage." Washington, U.S. Women's Bureau, 1947, 9 p.

________. "Who Works, Where and Why." Washington, U.S. Women's Bureau, 1948, 9 p. Also in U.S. Women's Bureau. The American Woman--Her Changing Role, pp. 10-8.

Miller, Kate Oldham. "An Ideal Home for Children." In World's Congress of Representative Women, Chicago, 1893. Congress of Women, pp. 782-6.

Miller, Margaret. "Statement." In U.S. Congress. House. Committee on Education and Labor. Subcommittee on Equal Opportunity. Equal Opportunity for Displaced Homemakers Act, pp. 51-3.

Miller, Pauline. "The Confidential Relationship in Social Work Administration." In National Conference of Social Work. Proceedings (1942), pp. 574-83.

Miller, Phyllis. "Testimony." In U.S. Congress. House. Select Committee on Crime. Drugs in Our Schools, pp. 561-5, 817-22.

Miller, Ruth. "Statement." In U.S. Congress. House. Committee on the Judiciary. Subcommittee No. 4. Equal Rights for Men and Women 1971, pp. 252-63.

________. "Statement." In U.S. Congress. Senate. Committee on the Judiciary. Equal Rights 1970, pp. 229-33.

Millett, Kate. "The Image of Women in Arts and Letters." In New York (City). Commission on Human Rights. Women's Role in Contemporary Society, pp. 608-12.

________. "The Status of Women in the Academic Profession." In Conference of Professional and Academic Women. Sixteen Reports on the Status of Women in the Professions, 4 p.

Mills, Elizabeth Tabor. "Co-operative Case-work Services to Sick People in Rural Areas." In National Conference of Social Work. Proceedings (1938), pp. 177-86.

Mills, Harriet May. "The Winning of Educational Freedom. Address to the National American Woman Suffrage Association Convention of 1900." In Stanton, E. History of Woman Suffrage, 4, 354-6. Also in Tanner, L. Voices from Women's Liberation, pp. 95-6.

Mills, Thelma. "Summary of February 17, Morning Session." In U.S. Women's Bureau. American Woman--Her Changing Role, pp. 99-102.

Millstein, Sally. "Public Testimony." In New York (City). Commission on Human Rights. Women's Role in Contemporary Society, pp. 435-41.

Milner, Esther. "The Mother's Role." In Milner, E. Dialogue on Women, pp. 73-81.

________. "Public Testimony." In New York (City). Commission on Human Rights. Women's Role in Contemporary Society, pp. 709-18.

Miner, Maude E. "A Community Program for Protective Work." In National Conference of Social Work. Proceedings (1920), pp. 140-8.

________. "The Girls' Protective League." In National Conference of Charities and Correction. Proceedings (1915), pp. 260-7.

________. "The Policewoman and the Girl Problem." In National Conference of Social Work. Proceedings (1919), pp. 134-9.

________. "Protective Work for Girls in War Time." In National Conference of Social Work. Proceedings (1918), pp. 656-65.

________. "Report of the Committee (on Social Hygiene)." In National Conference of Charities and Correction. Proceedings (1914), pp. 197-205.

________. "Treatment of Women Offenders." In National Conference of Charities and Correction. Proceedings (1912), pp. 230-3.

Minick, Clara Babst. "The Naturalization Law and Its Administration." In National Conference of Social Work. Proceedings (1926), pp. 576-82.

Mink, Patsy Takemoto. "Oceans: Antarctic Resource and Environmental Concerns." Department of State Bulletin, 78 (April, 1978), 51-4.

________. "Science and Its Interrelationship with Foreign Policy: Speech." Washington, U.S. Department of State, Bureau of Public Affairs, Office of Media Services, 1977, 6 p.

________. "Should Congress Adopt the Nixon Administration's Program for 'Revenue Sharing'?" Congressional Digest, 50 (April, 1971), 119-21.

________. "Statement." In Conference on Women in the War on Poverty, 1967. Proceedings, p. 35.

________. "Statement." In U.S. Congress. House. Committee on Government Operations. National Women's Conference, pp. 10-2.

________. "Visions of the Future." Department of State Bulletin, 78 (February, 1978), 42-5.

Minor, Virginia Louisa. "Opening Address to the Convention of the Woman Suffrage Association of Missouri, St. Louis, October, 1869." In Lerner, G. The Female Experience, pp. 350-1. Also in Stanton, E. History of Woman Suffrage, 2, 409-10.

Minton, Eunice. "Changing the Program of a Public Welfare Agency." In National Conference of Social Work. Proceedings (1941), pp. 662-70.

Missakian, Elizabeth. "Public Testimony." In New York (City). Commission on Human Rights. Women's Role in Contemporary Society, pp. 417-20.

Mitchell, Edith J. "Certification and Reclassification in the Civil Service." In National Conference of Social Service. Proceedings (1931), pp. 563-70.

Mitchell, Lily E. "The Place of Mothers' Aid in a State Program of Child Welfare." In National Conference of Social Work. Proceedings (1928), pp. 478-91.

Mitchell, Louise. "An Address Delivered by Louise Mitchell, United Tailoresses Society." In Janiewski, Dolores. "Making Common Cause: The Needlewomen of New York, 1831-69." Signs, 1 (Spring, 1976), 779-81.

Mitchell, Maria. "Address of the President." In Association for the Advancement of Women. Congress of Women, 3rd. Papers, pp. 1-7.

________. "The Higher Education of Woman." In Association for the Advancement of Women. Congress of Women, 1st. Papers, pp. 89-93.

Mitchell, Ruth Crawford. "The New Quota Law in the United States." In National Conference of Social Work. Proceedings (1924), pp. 594-8.

Mock, June. "Testimony." In U.S. Congress. House. Select Committee on Crime. Drugs in Our Schools, pp. 526-30.

Mohl, Aurelia H. "An Idea and Its Results." In International Council of Women, 1888. Report, pp. 184-6.

Mohr, Jennie. "Educating Women for Safety and Health." Washington, U.S. Women's Bureau, 1944, 7 p.

Molamphy, Teresa M. "Statement." In U.S. Women's Bureau. Proceedings of the Women's Industrial Conference, pp. 158-9.

Moloney, Elizabeth F. "Massachusetts. The Family Budget and the Adequacy of Relief." In National Conference of Social Work. Proceedings (1919), pp. 299-303.

Molz, Redmond Kathleen. "Libraries and the Development and Future of Tax Support." In Libraries and the Life of the Mind in America, pp. 41-63.

Monahan, Florence. "Community Responsibility for Recreation Facilities--Discussion." In International Congress of Women, Chicago, 1933. Our Common Cause, Civilization, pp. 908-11.

Moncure, Dorothy Ashby. "Statement." In U. S. Congress. Senate. Committee on the Judiciary. Subcommittee on Constitutional Amendments. Equal Rights for Men and Women (1938), pp. 117-23.

Monroe, Harriet Earhart. "Synopsis of the Making of Citizens." In World's Congress of Representative Women, Chicago, 1893. Congress of Women, pp. 311-5.

Montgomery, Alice B. "The Child of the Juvenile Court." In National Conference of Charities and Correction. Proceedings (1905), pp. 167-72.

________. "The Reaction of Children's Case Work in the Development of the Constructive and Preventive Work of a Community: In the Removal of Degrading Causes." In National Conference of Charities and Correction. Proceedings (1915), pp. 138-45.

Montgomery, Helen Barrett. "Eulogy at Mary S. Anthony's Funeral, February 7, 1907." In Harper, I. The Life and Work of Susan B. Anthony, 3, 1512-3.

Montgomery, Sarah L. "Discipline and Training of Girls in Industrial Schools." In National Conference of Charities and Correction. Proceedings (1908), pp. 198-201.

Moody, Helen Wills. "Maintaining the Balance Between Life and Play." In New York Herald Tribune. Report of the 8th Annual Forum on Current Problems, pp. 17-8.

Moon, Mary Gillette. "The Unattached Woman." In National Conference of Social Work. Proceedings (1934), pp. 195-203.

Moore, Dorothea. "The Saving of Telegraph Hill." In National Conference of Charities and Correction. Proceedings (1905), pp. 375-83.

Moore, Eva Perry. "Address at the College Evening of the 38th Annual Convention of the National American Woman Suffrage Association, February 8, 1906." In Harper, I. The Life and Work of Susan B. Anthony, 3, 1392-3.

________. "Address to Peace Congress." In American Peace Congress, 2nd, Chicago, 1909. Proceedings, pp. 260-2.

Moore, Gwen. "Statement." In U. S. Congress. House. Committee on Education and Labor. Subcommittee on Equal Opportunity. Equal Opportunity for Displaced Homemakers Act, pp. 55-7.

Moore, Katherine. "The Evolution of Psychiatric Social Work (Shown by Use of a Case Presentation)." In National Conference of Social Work. Proceedings (1930), pp. 378-86.

Moore, Madeline U. "Case Work and Credit System Problems." In National Conference of Social Work. Proceedings (1942), pp. 518-30.

________. "Research in the Child Welfare Field: A Study of Intake in Westchester County." In National Conference of Social Work. Proceedings (1927), pp. 132-7.

Moore, Sarah W. "Labor Camp Schools." In National Conference of Charities and Correction. Proceedings (1909), pp. 236-8.

Moque, Alice Lee. "Reproduction and Natural Law." In National Council of Women of the U. S., Washington, 1891. Transactions, pp. 123-30.

Moreland, Mary L. "Discussion on Woman's Call to the Ministry." In World's Congress of Representative Women, Chicago, 1893. A Historical Resume, pp. 234-5.

Morey, Anna R. "Fine Arts Slides." In General Federation of Women's Clubs. Biennial Convention, 16 (1922), 184.

Morgan, Anna. "The Art of Elocution." In World's Congress of Representative Women, Chicago, 1893. Congress of Women, pp. 597-9.

Morgan, Laura Puffer. "Statement." In U. S. Congress. Senate. Committee on the Judiciary. Subcommittee on Constitutional Amendments. Equal Rights (1931), pp. 48-9.

Morgan, Robin. "What Robin Morgan Said at Denver." Journal of Home Economics, 65 (January, 1973), 13.

Morganthau, Ruth S. "From European Colonies to the Third World--The Developing States of Africa." Annals, "Africa in Transition," 432 (July, 1977), 80-95.

Morlock, Maud. "Establishment of Paternity." In National Conference of Social Work. Proceedings (1940), pp. 363-76.

Morris, Clara. "Woman in the Emotional Drama." In World's Congress of Representative Women, Chicago, 1893. A Historical Resume, pp. 175-9.

Morris, Harriet N. "Missionary Work." In International Council of Women, 1888. Report, pp. 98-9.

Morrisey, Elizabeth. "Status of Women. To Be Equal Does Not Mean to Be Identical." Vital Speeches, 25 (November 1, 1948), 55-60.

Morrison, Jane. "Youth Plans for a Civilized World: Forum on the College Generation." In International Congress of Women, Chicago, 1933. Our Common Cause, Civilization, pp. 195-6.

Morrow, Elizabeth Reeve Cutter. "College Women and the New Leisure." Vital Speeches, 1 (November 19, 1934), 122-3.

________. "Lasting Effects of Women's War Activities." In New York Herald Tribune. Report of the 11th Annual Forum on Current Problems, pp. 138-42.

Morsch, Lucille M. "Promoting Library Interests Throughout the World." ALA Bulletin, 51 (September, 1957), 579-84.

Morse, Fannie French. "The Methods Most Helpful to Girls." In National Conference of Charities and Correction. Proceedings (1904), pp. 306-11.

Morse, Frances R. "How Can We Further the Organization of Charities?" In National Conference of Charities and Correction. Proceedings (1897), pp. 177-81.

Mortenson, Clara E. "The Minimum Wage at Work in the District of Columbia." In National Conference of Social Work. Proceedings (1920), pp. 298-304.

Morton, Florrinell F. "United by Common Interests and Common Purposes." ALA Bulletin, 55 (September, 1961), 712-6.

Moses, Yolanda T. "Female Status, the Family, and Male Dominance in a West Indian Community." In Conference on Women and Development. "Women and National Development: The Complexities of Change." Signs, 3 (Autumn, 1977), 142-53.

Mosher, Frances Stewart. "Discussion of Paper on the Ethical Influence of Woman in Education." In World's Congress of Representative Women, Chicago, 1893. A Historical Resume, pp. 117-9.

Moskowitz, Belle Linder Israels. "The Dance Problem." In National Conference of Charities and Correction. Proceedings (1912), pp. 140-6.

________. "How Far Have Social Welfare Considerations Entered into State, National and Local Elections." In National Conference of Social Work. Proceedings (1923), pp. 465-9.

________. "Recreation in Rural Communities." In National Conference of Charities and Correction. Proceedings (1911), pp. 103-7.

Mott, Alice J. "The Education and Custody of the Imbecile." In National Conference of Charities and Correction. Proceedings (1894), pp. 168-79.

Mott, Emma Pratt. "Katharina in the Taming of the Shrew." In World's Congress of Representative Women, Chicago, 1893. Congress of Women, pp. 544-54.

Mott, Lucretia Coffin. "Address to the 1st Annual Meeting of the American Equal Rights Association, May 1867." In Stanton, E. History of Woman Suffrage, 2, 199-200.

________. "Comments at the Syracuse National Convention, September, 1852." In Stanton, E. History of Woman Suffrage, 1, 527-8.

________. "Comments on Women's Property Rights at Westchester (Penn.) Convention, June 1852." In Stanton, E. History of Woman Suffrage, 1, 359-60.

________. "Debate During the 4th National Convention, Cleveland, Ohio, October 1853." In Stanton, E. History of Woman Suffrage, 1, 143.

________. "A Demand for the Political Rights of Women." In Tanner, L. Voices from Women's Liberation, pp. 50-2.

________. "Discourse at Friends' Meeting, Fifteenth Street, New York. Delivered Eleventh Month 11th, 1866." In Hallowell, A. Life and Letters of James and Lucretia Mott, pp. 529-39.

________. "Discourse in the Assembly Buildings in Philadelphia on Woman and the Bible, and Women's Rights." In Stanton, E. History of Woman Suffrage, 1, 368-75.

________. "Discourse on Women, 1849." In Hallowell, A. Life and Letters of James and Lucretia Mott, pp. 487-506. Also in Martin, W. The American Sisterhood, pp. 53-60.

________. "Extract from Address by Lucretia Mott at the Anti-Sabbath Convention, Held in Boston, Mass., March 23rd and 24th, 1848." In Hallowell, A. Life and Letters of James and Lucretia Mott, pp. 479-87.

________. "Extracts from Reports of Lucretia Mott's Addresses at the Annual Meetings of the Free Religious Association, in Boston." In Hallowell, A. Life and Letters of James and Lucretia Mott, pp. 550-7.

________. "Not Christianity, but Priestcraft." In Schnier, M. Feminism, pp. 99-102. Also in Stanton, E. History of Woman Suffrage, 1, 380-1.

________. "Remarks at the 1st Annual Meeting of the American Equal Rights Association, May 1867." In Stanton, E. History of Woman Suffrage, 2, 184-5.

________. "Remarks on a Public Disturbance at the Women's Rights Convention in New York, September, 1853." In Stanton, E. History of Woman Suffrage, 1, 557-8.

________. "Sermon Delivered at Bristol, Pa., 6th Mo. 6th, 1860." In Hallowell, A. Life and Letters of James and Lucretia Mott, pp. 522-8.

________. "A Sermon Delivered at Yardleyville, Bucks Co., Pa., Ninth Mo. 26th, 1858." In Hallowell, A. Life and Letters of James and Lucretia Mott, pp. 506-21. Also Liberator, 28 (October 29, 1858), 176.

________. "Sermon on the Religious Aspect of the Age. Delivered at Friends' Meeting, Race Street, Philadelphia, First Month 3rd, 1869, on Her 76th Birthday." In Hallowell, A. Life and Letters of James and Lucretia Mott, pp. 539-49.

________. "Speech of Lucretia Mott." In American Anti-Slavery Society. Proceedings, pp. 64-7.

Moynahan, Rosalie M. "Statement." In U. S. Congress. House. Committee on the Judiciary. Subcommittee No. 1. Equal Rights Amendment (1948), pp. 20-3.

Mudgett, Mildred D. "The Development of Greater Sympathy and Understanding Between Parents and Children." In National Conference of Social Work. Proceedings (1924), pp. 280-4.

_______. "The Place of Field Work in Training for Social Work: Its Educational Content." In National Conference of Social Work. Proceedings (1930), pp. 562-8.

_______. "Research as a Method of Training for Social Work." In National Conference of Social Work. Proceedings (1928), pp. 549-55.

_______. "When People Apply at a Marriage License Bureau." In National Conference of Social Work. Proceedings (1925), pp. 284-90.

Mueller, Kate Hevner. "The Cultural Pressures on Women." In Conference on the Present Status and Prospective Trends of Research on the Education of Women, Rye, N. Y., 1957. The Education of Women, pp. 49-56.

Mueller, Martha. "Women and Men, Power and Powerlessness in Lesotho." In Conference on Women and Development. "Women and National Development: The Complexities of Change." Signs, 3 (Autumn, 1977), 154-66.

Muller, Charlotte F. "Methodological Issues in Health Economics Research Relevant to Women." In U. S. National Center for Health Services Research. Women and Their Health, pp. 44-51.

Mulligan, Joan E. "Public Policy and Childbearing." In Hammond, N. Women and Children in Contemporary Society, pp. 44-52.

Murphy, Anna. "Statement." In U. S. Congress. Senate. Committee on the Judiciary. Subcommittee on Constitutional Amendments. Equal Rights Amendment (1945), p. 94.

Murphy, Emily F. "The Administration of Criminal Justice in Canada." In National Conference of Social Work. Proceedings (1924), pp. 176-80.

Murphy, Irene E. "Detroit's Experience with the Wartime Care of Children." In National Conference of Social Work. Proceedings (1943), pp. 133-9.

Murphy, Mary E. "Health Activities of Child Caring Agencies: Continuous Health Supervision." In National Conference of Social Work. Proceedings (1925), pp. 125-7.

Murray, Agnes L. "Case Work Above the Poverty Line." In National Conference of Social Work. Proceedings (1918), pp. 340-3.

Murray, Mae. "International Kindergarten Union." In General Federation of Women's Clubs. Biennial Convention, 16 (1922), 93-4.

Murray, Mary A. "Statement." In U. S. Congress. House. Committee on the Judiciary. Subcommittee No. 1. Equal Rights Amendment (1948), pp. 44-6.

________. "Statement." In U. S. Congress. Senate. Committee on the Judiciary. Subcommittee on Constitutional Amendments. Equal Rights Amendment (1929), pp. 18-21.

________. "Statement." In U. S. Congress. Senate. Committee on the Judiciary. Subcommittee on Constitutional Amendments. Equal Rights for Men and Women (1938), pp. 111-3.

Murray, Pauline. "Equal Rights Amendment." In New York (City). Commission on Human Rights. Women's Role in Contemporary Society, pp. 612-8.

________. "Statement." In U. S. Congress. House. Committee on Education and Labor. Special Subcommittee on Education. Discrimination Against Women, pp. 67-86.

Murray, Virginia M. "The Runaway and the Stranded Girl." In National Conference of Social Work. Proceedings (1920), pp. 175-80.

________. "Training for Successful Work with Immigrants: Training and Use of Nationality Workers." In National Conference of Social Work. Proceedings (1922), pp. 484-7.

Mussey, Ellen Spencer. "The Woman Attorney and Counsellor." In International Congress of Women, Toronto, 1909. Report, 2, 332-4.

Myers, Harriet W. "Birds and Flowers." In General Federation of Women's Clubs. Biennial Convention, 16 (1922), 553-5.

Myerson, Bess. "Women and the Employment Agencies." In New York (City). Commission on Human Rights. Women's Role in Contemporary Society, pp. 325-8.

Nachimias, Vivianne T. "Panelist Statement." In M. I. T. Symposium on American Women in Science and Engineering, 1964. Women and the Scientific Professions, pp. 29-34.

Nairne, Lillie H. "Private Living Arrangements for Elderly People." In National Conference of Social Work. Proceedings (1946), pp. 483-90.

Nathan, Cynthia R. "Needs for Social Case Work as Revealed in Groups." In National Conference of Social Work. Proceedings (1944), pp. 208-18.

Nathan, Maud. "The Ethics of Spending." In International Congress of Women, London, 1899, 6, 215-9.

______. "Industry and Its Relation to Peace." In American Peace Congress, 1st, New York, 1907. Proceedings, pp. 101-6.

Navarro, Marysa. "The Case of Eva Peron." In Conference on Women and Development. "Women and National Development: The Complexities of Change." Signs, 3 (Autumn, 1977), 229-40.

Neal, Juana A. "New Avenue of Employment and Investment for Business Women." In World's Congress of Representative Women, Chicago, 1893. A Historical Resume, pp. 559-61.

Neil, Jane A. "Public School Classes for Crippled Children." In National Conference of Social Work. Proceedings (1923), pp. 382-7.

Neill, Esther W. "Statement." In U. S. Congress. Senate. Committee on the Judiciary. Subcommittee on Constitutional Amendments. Equal Rights for Men and Women (1938), p. 37.

Nelson, Amanda. "Youth and the Industrial Slack." In International Congress of Women, Chicago, 1933. Our Common Cause, Civilization, pp. 297-300.

Nelson, Cynthia. "New Way of Viewing Key Questions for Investigation. Cultural: Reconceptualizing Health Care." In U. S. National Center for Health Services Research. Women and Their Health, pp. 58-62.

Nelson, Julia B. "Address to the House Judiciary Committee, February 10, 1886." In Stanton, E. History of Woman Suffrage, 4, 79.

Nelson, Leah. "Public Testimony." In New York (City). Commission on Human Rights. Women's Role in Contemporary Society, pp. 785-6.

Nesbitt, Florence. "The Family Budget and Its Supervision." In National Conference of Social Work. Proceedings (1918), pp. 359-65.

______. "The Significance of the Rise in Relief-giving During the Past Five Years: Its Relation to Standard of Case Work." In National Conference of Social Work. Proceedings (1922), pp. 236-41.

Ness, Evaline. "Caldecott Acceptance Speech--1967." Kingman, L. Newbery and Caldecott Medal Books, 1966-1975, pp. 186-91.

Nestor, Agnes. "Exploiting the Employed." In International Congress of Women, Chicago, 1933. Our Common Cause, Civilization, pp. 303-5.

________. "The Need for Women to Enforce Women's Labor Laws." In U. S. Women's Bureau. Proceedings of the Women's Industrial Conference, pp. 178-84.

________. "Statement." In U. S. Women's Bureau. Proceedings of the Women's Industrial Conference, pp. 146-8.

________. "What Labor Is Doing." In National Conference of Social Work. Proceedings (1930), pp. 315-9.

________. "Workers' Education for Women in Industry." In National Conference of Social Work. Proceedings (1924), pp. 345-8.

Neuberger, Maurine Brown. "Statement." In U. S. Congress. Senate. Committee on Labor and Public Welfare. Subcommittee on Labor. Equal Pay Act of 1963, pp. 13-4.

Neufeld, Elizabeth B. "The Development of Existing Neighborhood Activities." In National Conference of Charities and Correction. Proceedings (1914), pp. 407-10.

Neugarten, Bernice L. "Kansas City Study of Adult Life." In Michigan State University, East Lansing, School of Home Economics. Potentialities of Women in the Middle Years, pp. 35-45.

Neumann, Frederika. "The Use of Psychiatric Consultation by a Case Work Agency." In National Conference of Social Work. Proceedings (1945), pp. 242-50.

Neustaedter, Eleanor. "The Case Worker's Role in Treatment." In National Conference of Social Work. Proceedings (1932), pp. 204-14.

________. "The Integration of Economic and Psychological Factors in Family Case Work." In National Conference of Social Work. Proceedings (1930), pp. 198-216.

Neville, Emily. "Newbery Award Acceptance--1964. Out Where the Real People Are." In Kingman, L. Newbery and Caldecott Medal Books, 1956-1965, pp. 131-6.

Newbold, Florence L. "A Community-wide Volunteer Placement Bureau." In National Conference of Social Work. Proceedings (1935), pp. 466-75.

Newcomer, Mabel. "Economics of Disarmament. Expansion in Civilian Markets at Home and Abroad." Vital Speeches, 13 (February 1, 1957), 230-4.

________. "How Are We Going to Pay for Defense? There Is a Possibility of Marked Inflation." Vital Speeches, 7 (March 15, 1941), 343-5.

Newman, Angie F. "Report on Jail Work of the W. C. T. U. in Nebraska." In National Conference of Charities and Correction. Proceedings (1883), pp. 460-3.

Newman, Pauline. "Statement." In U.S. Congress. Senate. Committee on the Judiciary. Subcommittee on Constitutional Amendments. *Equal Rights for Men and Women* (1938), pp. 21-8.

________. "We Have Kept the Faith." In Stein, Leon. *Out of the Sweatshop*, pp. 341-2.

Newmann, Frederika. "The Effects on the Child of an Unstable House Situation." In National Conference of Social Work. *Proceedings* (1928), pp. 346-53.

Newton, Frances. "The Mother's Greatest Needs." In National Congress of Mothers. *Work and Words*, pp. 148-54.

Neymann, Clara. "German and American Independence Contrasted. Address to the National Woman Suffrage Association Convention of February, 1886." In Stanton, E. *History of Woman Suffrage*, 4, 73-4.

________. "Sentimentalism in Politics." In International Council of Women, 1888. *Report*, pp. 398-9.

Nichols, Clarina Howard. "Address on Divorce at Woman's Rights Convention, Syracuse, N.Y., September 8, 1852." In Harper, I. *The Life and Work of Susan B. Anthony*, 1, 74. Also in Stanton, E. *History of Woman Suffrage*, 1, 525-6.

________. "Comments on the Declaration of Sentiments Adopted at the Westchester Convention at the Syracuse National Convention, September 1852." In Stanton, E. *History of Woman Suffrage*, 1, 522.

________. "Remarks at the Woman's Rights Convention in New York, September 1853." In Stanton, E. *History of Woman Suffrage*, 1, 561, 562-3.

Nicholson, Edna. "Private Living Arrangements for Elderly People." In National Conference of Social Work. *Proceedings* (1946), pp. 477-83.

Nickel, Lucille F. "The Role and Aims of the Social Worker in Treatment." In National Conference of Social Work. *Proceedings* (1929), pp. 432-42.

Nolan, Mary I. "Statement on Release from Prison." In Stevens, D. *Jailed for Freedom*, pp. 196-9.

Nolan-Haley, Jacqueline M. "Statement." In U.S. Congress. Senate. Committee on Human Resources. Subcommittee on Labor. *Discrimination on the Basis of Pregnancy, 1977*, pp. 432-4.

Norrell, Catherine D. "Roads to International Understanding. Address, January 15, 1963." *Department of State Bulletin*, 48 (February 11, 1963), 214-7.

Norris, Frances S. "Statement." In U.S. Congress. House. Committee on Education and Labor. Special Subcommittee on Education. Discrimination Against Women, pp. 162-76.

Norris, Mary E. Cherry. "An Appeal of Art to the Lovers of Art." In World's Congress of Representative Women, Chicago, 1893. Congress of Women, pp. 674-8.

Norton, Eleanor Holmes. "The Challenge to Women--Organizing Around an Issue." In Conference of Professional and Academic Women. Sixteen Reports on the Status of Women in the Professions, 3 p.

________. "Statement." In U.S. Congress. Joint Economic Committee. Economic Problems of Women, pt. 4, 505-9.

________. "Statement." In U.S. Congress. Senate. Committee on Human Resources. Nomination Hearing on Eleanor Holmes Norton, pp. 7-10, 17-8, 19-20, 25-6, 37-8.

________. "A Strategy for Change." In New York (City). Commission on Human Rights. Women's Role in Contemporary Society, pp. 54-63.

Norton, Mary T. "Wage and Hour Legislation, the Object of the Law." Vital Speeches, 4 (June 1, 1938), 485-6.

Norwood, Janet L. "The Policy Issues: Presentation V." In Blaxall, M. Women and the Workplace, pp. 278-81.

Nutt, Alice Scott. "The Future of the Juvenile Court as a Casework Agency." In National Conference of Social Work. Proceedings (1939), pp. 370-80.

________. "The Responsibility of Juvenile Court and Public Agency in Child Welfare." In National Conference of Social Work. Proceedings (1947), pp. 311-21.

Nutting, Mary Adelaide. "Address of the President." In American Society of Superintendent of Training Schools for Nurses. Annual Report (1897), p. 5.

________. "Address of the President." In American Society of Superintendents of Training Schools for Nurses. Annual Report (1910), p. 16.

________. "Address of the President." In American Society of Superintendents of Training Schools for Nurses. Annual Report (1911), p. 18.

________. "Graduating Address." Johns Hopkins Nurses Alumnae Magazine (August, 1906), pp. 121-9.

Oakley, Imogen B. "Report--Civil Service Conference." In General Federation of Women's Clubs. Biennial Convention, 16 (1922), 612-3.

Oatman, Miriam E. "Statement." In U.S. Congress. Senate.

Committee on the Judiciary. Subcommittee on Constitutional Amendments. Equal Rights for Men and Women (1938), pp. 153-4.

O'Bannon, Dona. "Testimony." In U.S. Congress. House. Committee on Small Business. Subcommittee on Minority Enterprise and General Oversight. Women in Business, pp. 15-8.

Oberholtzer, Sara Louise Vickers. "The Popular Inculcation of Economy." In World's Congress of Representative Women, Chicago, 1893. A Historical Resume, pp. 119-27.

________. "School Savings-Banks." In National Council of Women of the U.S., Washington, 1891. Transactions, pp. 209-12.

Oberndorfer, Mary. "Introductory Remarks--Music in Your Community." In General Federation of Women's Clubs. Biennial Convention, 16 (1922), 343-6.

O'Connor, Alice W. "Citizenship and Domicile Versus Social Considerations in Problems of Migrated Families." In National Conference of Social Work. Proceedings (1935), pp. 667-78.

O'Connor, Lillian. "Let's Keep One Stake in Tomorrow: Women of Today." Vital Speeches, 34 (January 15, 1968), 214-7.

________. "Progress of Humanity. What You Can Contribute to Man's Progress." Vital Speeches, 20 (September 15, 1954), 729-31.

O'Day, Caroline Goodwin. "Congresswoman." Vital Speeches, 1 (March 11, 1935), 381-3.

Odencrantz, Louise C. "Social Case Work in Industry: Personnel Work in Factories." In National Conference of Social Work. Proceedings (1923), pp. 116-21.

________. "Social Work Jobs Analyzed." In National Conference of Social Work. Proceedings (1927), pp. 597-605.

________. "Statement." In U.S. Women's Bureau. Proceedings of the Women's Industrial Conference, pp. 159-60.

O'Donnell, Gladys. "Statement." In U.S. Congress. Senate. Committee on the Judiciary. Equal Rights 1970, pp. 344-8.

Ogle, Dora. "Statement." In U.S. Congress. Senate. Committee on the Judiciary. Subcommittee on Constitutional Amendments. Equal Rights Amendment (1929), p. 22.

O'Laughlin, Bridget. "Mediation of Contradiction: Why Mbum Women Do Not Eat Chicken." In Rosaldo, M. Woman, Culture, and Society, pp. 301-18.

O'Leary, Helen B. "The Ladies' Physiological Institute of Boston." In National Council of Women of the U.S., Washington, 1891. Transactions, pp. 341-2.

Olmstead, Cleta. "Youth Plans for a Civilized World: Forum on the College Generation." In International Congress of Women, Chicago, 1933. Our Common Cause, Civilization, pp. 190-2.

Onahan, Mary Josephine. "Catholic Women's Part in Philanthropy." In World's Congress of Representative Women, Chicago, 1893. A Historical Resume, pp. 818-20.

Oppenheimer, Valerie K. "A Sociologist's Skepticism." In Conference on Women's Challenge to Management, Arden House, 1971. Corporate Lib, pp. 30-8.

O'Reilly, Leonora. "The Cry of Humanity." In American Peace Congress, 1st, New York, 1907. Proceedings, pp. 232-8.
________. "Testimony to the Senate." In Scott, A. One Half the People, pp. 126-8.

O'Reilly, Mary Boyle. "The Problem of Truancy." In National Conference of Charities and Correction. Proceedings (1909), pp. 53-4.

Ormsbee, Frances Wadhams Davenport. "Samoa--Its People and Their Customs." In World's Congress of Representative Women, Chicago, 1893. Congress of Women, pp. 590-6.

Ormsby, Mary Frost. "Discussion of Woman as a Political Leader." In World's Congress of Representative Women, Chicago, 1893. A Historical Resume, pp. 446-8.

Orshansky, Mollie. "Speech." In Conference on Women in the War on Poverty, 1967. Proceedings, pp. 9-15.

Ortner, Sherry B. "Is Female to Male as Nature Is to Culture?" In Rosaldo, M. Women, Culture, and Society, pp. 67-87.

Osborn, Hazel. "Problems in Teen-age Hangouts." In National Conference of Social Work. Proceedings (1944), pp. 148-59.

Oslund, Genevieve H. "Statement." In U.S. Congress. Senate. Committee on the Judiciary. Subcommittee on Constitutional Amendments. Equal Rights (1956), pp. 28-9.

Ostazeski, Aileen. "The Childless Married Woman." In Bier, W. Woman in Modern Life, pp. 135-43.

O'Steen, Sherrie. "Statement." In U.S. Congress. House. Committee on Education and Labor. Subcommittee on Employment Opportunities. Legislation to Prohibit Sex Discrimination on the Basis of Pregnancy, pp. 50-1.

Overholser, Winfred. "The Problems of Mental Disease in an Aging Population." In National Conference of Social Work. Proceedings (1941), pp. 455-63.

Ovitz, Delia G. "The Library's Relation to Neighborhood and Community Work." In National Conference of Social Work. Proceedings (1941), pp. 455-63.

Owen, Ruth Bryan. "Place of Women in the Present Crisis." In New York Herald Tribune. Report of the 3rd Women's Conference on Current Problems, pp. 20-3.

Owings, Chloe. "The Trail of Social Hygiene in Social Work: Prevention Versus Salvage." In National Conference of Social Work. Proceedings (1927), pp. 231-5.

Ozbirn, Catherine Freeman. "From Where I Stand. Responsible, Responsive Citizenship Program." Vital Speeches, 26 (September 15, 1960), 718-20.

Pace, Sally. "Testimony." In U. S. Congress. House. Select Committee on Crime. Drugs in Our Schools, pp. 631-9.

Paddock, Sarah Sands. "Industrial and Technological Training." In National Conference of Charities and Correction. Proceedings (1884), pp. 207-21.

Pagan de Colon, Petroamerica. "The Status of the Migrant. People with the Same Aspirations." Vital Speeches, 28 (May 1, 1962), 445-8.

Paige, Clara Paul. "Case-work Objectives--Achieved in Volume." In National Conference of Social Work. Proceedings (1934), pp. 399-407.

Palffy, Eleanor. "Art of Living for Woman Today. Be Stingy with Time." Vital Speeches, 8 (January 15, 1942), 224.

Palmer, Alice Freeman. "Three Types of Women's Colleges." In Palmer, G. The Teacher, pp. 313-36.

________. "Why Go to College." In Palmer, G. The Teacher, pp. 364-95.

________. "Women's Education at the World's Fair." In Palmer, G. The Teacher, pp. 351-63.

________. "Women's Education in the Nineteenth Century." In Palmer, G. The Teacher, pp. 337-50.

Palmer, Alison. "Prophets, Old and New." Women Speaking, 4 (January-March, 1978), 16-7.

Palmer, Bertha M. Honore. "Address Delivered by Mrs. Potter Palmer, President of the Board of Lady Managers, on the Occasion of the Opening of the Woman's Building, May 1st, 1893." In World's Congress of Representative Women, Chicago, 1893. Congress of Women, pp. 25-9.

________. "The Board of Lady Managers of the Columbian Exposition." In National Council of Women of the U. S., Washington, 1891. Transactions, pp. 315-8.

________. "Closing Address." In World's Congress of Representative Women, Chicago, 1893. Congress of Women, pp. 820-4.

________. "Welcoming Address." In World's Congress of Representative Women, Chicago, 1893. A Historical Resume, pp. 11-2. (Same as "Address Delivered by Mrs. Potter Palmer.")

Palmer, Sarah Eddy. "Is Woman the Weaker Vessel?" In World's Congress of Representative Women, Chicago, 1893. Congress of Women, pp. 432-4.

Palmer, Sophia F. "The Trained Nurse." In National Conference of Charities and Corrections. Proceedings (1895), pp. 259-64.

Pannell, Anne G. "A Nation's Strength Begins in the Home. Parents Are the Real Molders of Character." Vital Speeches, 18 (December 15, 1951), 145-7.

Papanek, Hanna. "Development Planning for Women." In Conference on Women and Development. "Women and National Development: The Complexities of Change." Signs, 3 (Autumn, 1977), 14-21.

Paradise, Viola I. "Creative Writing for Social Work." In National Conference of Social Work. Proceedings (1932), pp. 575-88.

________. "Industry and the Home: Behind the Statistic." In National Conference of Social Work. Proceedings (1923), pp. 314-21.

Parisi, Angela R. "Building Leadership for Peace ... New Ideas from New Voters. Panel Discussion." In New York Herald Tribune. Report of the 21st Annual Forum on Current Problems, pp. 144-5.

Park, Maud May Wood. "Address at the College Evening of the 38th Annual Convention of the National American Woman Suffrage Association, February 8, 1906." In Harper, I. The Life and Work of Susan B. Anthony, 3, 1393.

________. "Address of the President." In League of Women Voters. Fourth Annual Convention, pp. 3-16, 56-64.

________. "Greetings from National League of Women Voters." In General Federation of Women's Clubs. Biennial Convention, 16 (1922), 109-12.

________. "Mrs. Park's Greetings for the National League of Women Voters to the Pan-American Conference of Women." In League of Women Voters. 3rd Annual Convention and Proceedings of the Pan-American Conference of Women, pp. 187-8.

________. "President's Address." In League of Women Voters. 2nd Annual Convention, pp. 69-81.

________. "President's Address." In League of Women Voters. 3rd Annual Convention, pp. 89-98.

________. "Report of the Congressional Committee to the National American Woman Suffrage Association Convention of 1917." In Stanton, E. History of Woman Suffrage, 5, 523-6.

________. "Statement." In U.S. Congress. Senate. Committee on the Judiciary. Subcommittee on Constitutional Amendments. Equal Rights Amendment (1929), pp. 38-9.

Park, Rosemary. "Like Their Fathers Instead." In Conference on Women's Challenge to Management, Arden House, 1971. Corporate Lib, pp. 39-57.

Parker, Ida R. "The Study of Agency Interrelationships." In National Conference of Social Work. Proceedings (1931), pp. 526-35.

Parker, Janet Marsh. "The Duty of the American White Woman to the American Black Woman." In Association for the Advancement of Women. "Truth, Justice and Honor," pp. 101-8.

Parker, Laura Hiller. "Migratory Children." In National Conference of Social Work. Proceedings (1927), pp. 302-9.

Parker, Valeria H. "The Family Keystone." In International Congress of Women, Chicago, 1933. Our Common Cause, Civilization, pp. 729-42.

________. "Hidden Problems in Hard Times." In National Conference of Social Work. Proceedings (1932), pp. 156-66.

________. "The Social Worker in a Sound Social Hygiene Program." In National Conference of Social Work. Proceedings (1921), pp. 120-3.

________. "The Yesterday, Today and Tomorrow of the National Council of Women." In National Council of Women of the United States. Proceedings of the 14th Convention (1928), pp. 17-27.

Parmenter, Laura S. "The Case of an Unmarried Mother Who Has Cared for Her Child, and Failed." In National Conference of Social Work. Proceedings (1917), pp. 285-7.

Parr, Mary E. "The Personalising Process: Union Differentiates." Vital Speeches, 32 (March 15, 1966), 341-4.

________. "World Harvest: Woman's Talent, Woman's Role in the Changing World." Vital Speeches, 26 (December 1, 1959), 121-4.

Parson, Mary Jean. "Idealism: What's Wrong with It? A Declaration of Independence for Broadcasters." Vital Speeches, 42 (November 1, 1975), 56-9.

Paterson, Katherine. "Newbery Award Acceptance--1978." Hornbook, 54 (August, 1978), 361-7.

Patraka, Vivian M. "Lillian Hellman: Dramatist of the Second Sex." In McGuigan, D. New Research on Women at the University of Michigan, pp. 231-5.

Patridge, Lelia. "Speech at the 9th Annual Meeting of the American Woman Suffrage Association, 1878." In Stanton, E. History of Woman Suffrage, 2, 852-3.

Patten, Marjorie. "Social Work Under Church Auspices, and Social Work Under Community Auspices: From the Standpoint of the Rural Community." In National Conference of Social Work. Proceedings (1923), pp. 262-6.

Paul, Alice. "Address at a Meeting of the Advisory Council of the Congressional Union in New York City on March 31, 1915." In Irwin, I. Story of the Woman's Party, pp. 99-100.

________. "Address at the Organizational Convention of the National Woman's Party, March 2, 1917." In Irwin, I. Story of the Woman's Party, pp. 200-1.

________. "Address Before the Advisory Council of the Congressional Union Conference, August 29 and 30, 1914." In Irwin, I. Story of the Woman's Party, pp. 75-7. Also in Stevens, D. Jailed for Freedom, pp. 33-4.

________. "Comment After Defeat in House Judiciary Committee, March, 1916." In Irwin, I. Story of the Woman's Party, pp. 142-3.

________. "Speech at a Suffrage Hearing Before the House Judiciary Committee, December 16, 1915." In Irwin, I. Story of the Woman's Party, pp. 119-22.

________. "Speech Before the 3rd Conference of the Congressional Union's Advisory Council, April 8, 1916." In Irwin, I. Story of the Woman's Party, pp. 149-51.

________. "Statement on Leaving Prison." In Stevens, D. Jailed for Freedom, p. 241.

Paul, Helen. "Regional Coordination." American Library Association. Bulletin, 28 (July, 1934), 389-93.

Paul, Lois. "The Mastery of Work and the Mystery of Sex in a Guatemalan Village." In Rosaldo, M. Woman, Culture, and Society, pp. 281-99.

Paul, Nanette B. "Costumes and Customs from the Holy Land." In General Federation of Women's Clubs. Biennial Convention, 16 (1922), 284-8.

Peabody, Mary H. "A Study in Goethe's Faust." In World's Congress of Representative Women, Chicago, 1893. Congress of Women, pp. 205-10.

Pearson, Lucy H. "Student Fellowship." In General Federation of Women's Clubs. Biennial Convention, 16 (1922), 167-8.

Peaslie, Abbie A. C. "The Relation of Woman to Our Present Political Problems." In World's Congress of Representative Women, Chicago, 1893. A Historical Resume, pp. 505-10.

Peck, Maria Purdy. "Education as a Preparation for Life." In International Congress of Women, London, 1899, 2, 13-7.

_______. "Law and Women." In World's Congress of Representative Women, Chicago, 1893. Congress of Women, 623-7.

Peden, Katherine. "Statement." In U.S. Congress. House. Committee on Education and Labor. Select Subcommittee on Labor. Equal Pay for Equal Work, pp. 197-201.

Peipho, Irma. "Statement." In U.S. Congress. Senate. Committee on the Judiciary. Subcommittee on Constitutional Amendments. Equal Rights Amendment (1945), pp. 113-4.

Pell, Sarah Gibbs Thompson. "Statement." In U.S. Congress. Senate. Committee on the Judiciary. Subcommittee on Constitutional Amendments. Equal Rights for Men and Women (1938), pp. 138-40.

Pelton, Garnet Isabel. "The History and Status of Hospital Social Work." In National Conference of Charities and Correction. Proceedings (1910), pp. 332-41.

Pena, Ada. "Statement." In U.S. Congress. House. Committee on Government Operations. National Women's Conference, pp. 43-5.

Penfield, Jean Nelson. "Address at a Joint Hearing of the Senate Judiciary Committee and the Senate Committee on Woman Suffrage, March 13, 1912." In Stanton, E. History of Woman Suffrage, 5, 352-3.

Penna, Zolia. "Public Testimony." In New York (City). Commission on Human Rights. Women's Role in Contemporary Society, pp. 302-3.

Peratis, Kathleen. "Statement." In U.S. Congress. Joint Economic Committee. Economic Problems of Women, pt. 4, pp. 599-601.

Perkins, Frances. "Address at a Meeting of the Board of Trustees of Mount Holyoke, May 1944." In Martin, G. Madam Secretary, p. 376.

_______. "Address at 21st Annual Convention of International Association of Governmental Labor Officials." In Washington, U.S. Bureau of Labor Statistics. Bulletins, 619 (1936), 38-43.

_______. "Address Before New York Board of Trade." New York Times, December 13, 1934, p. 3.

_______. "Address Before the Annual Convention of the American Federation of Labor, October 8, 1941." Congressional Digest, 20 (November, 1941), 287-8.

_______. "Address to a Group of Government Personnel Workers." Christian Science Monitor, October 31, 1946, p. 8.

________. "Address to Annual Convention of American Federation of Labor, New Orleans, La., November 20, 1944." Washington, U.S. Labor Department, 1944, 17 p.

________. "After-care for Industrial Compensation Cases." In National Conference of Social Work. Proceedings (1921), pp. 58-63.

________. "Comments to Judiciary Committee of House of Representatives on Equal Rights Amendments, 1945." Washington, U.S. Women's Bureau, 1949, 21 p.

________. "Eulogy for Florence Kelley, March, 1932." In Martin, G. Madam Secretary, p. 230.

________. "Federal Unemployment Insurance." In New York Herald Tribune. Report of the 4th Annual Women's Conference on Current Problems, pp. 49-55.

________. "The Future of the Woman Who Works for Wages." Better Times, 14 (June 5, 1933), 6-7.

________. "Governments' Share in the Solution of Modern Work Problems." Personnel Journal, 8 (February, 1930), 341-7.

________. "Improving Working Conditions in Industry." In New York Herald Tribune. Report of the 3rd Women's Conference on Current Problems, pp. 24-6.

________. "Labor Day Address over Columbia Broadcasting System Network, September 6, 1943." Washington, U.S. Department of Labor, 1943, 6 p.

________. "Labor Day Address over Columbia Broadcasting System Network, September 4, 1944." Washington, U.S. Labor Department, 1944, 4 p.

________. "The Labor Question." In New York Herald Tribune. Report of the 6th Annual Forum on Current Problems, pp. 146-52.

________. "Miss Perkins Asks Child Labor Ban. Abandon's Prepared Address to Urge Professional Women to Support Amendment." New York Times, February 27, 1937, p. 3, col. 6.

________. "Miss Perkins Asks Social Insurance." New York Times, August 14, 1934, p. 3.

________. "My Job." American Labor Legislation Review, 19 (June, 1929), 164-70. Also Survey, 61 (March 15, 1929), 773-5.

________. "The Nation's Workers." In National Conference of Catholic Charities. Proceedings (1933), pp. 57-65.

________. "Not in Vain." In Stein, L. Out of the Sweatshop, pp. 200-1.

________. "The Outlook for Economic and Social Security in America." In National Conference of Social Work. Proceedings (1935), pp. 54-63.

________. "The Outlook in Unemployment Relief." In National Conference of Catholic Charities. Proceedings (1931), pp. 35-6.

________. "Remarks at Jane Addams Memorial Service." In National Conference of Social Work. Proceedings (1935), pp. 16-9.

________. "Remarks on Maternity Care for Foreign-born Women." In American Association for Study and Prevention of Infant Mortality. Transactions (1918), pp. 236-40.

________. "The Significance of Social Security." In Leuchtenburg, W. The New Deal, pp. 81-6.

________. "The Social Security Act." Vital Speeches, 1 (September 9, 1935), 792-4. (Same as "The Significance of Social Security.")

________. "Social Seer." The Family, 9 (February, 1929), 338-9.

________. "Testimony Before Factory Investigating Commission, December, 1912." In Martin, G. Madam Secretary, pp. 114-6. Also in New York (State). Factory Investigating Commission. Second Report (1913), 14, 1576-82.

________. "Testimony Before the Factory Investigating Commission." In Martin, G. Madam Secretary, p. 107. Also in New York (State). Factory Investigating Commission. Third Report (1914), 3, 546, 564; 4, 1463.

________. "Testimony on Cellar Bakeries in New York." In Martin, G. Madam Secretary, p. 107. Also in New York (State). Factory Investigating Commission. Preliminary Report (1912), 1, 310-35.

________. "Tribute to Eleanor Roosevelt at Breakfast Rally for Women Delegates to the 1936 Democratic Convention." In Martin, G. Madam Secretary, p. 364-5.

________. "What Is Worth Working for in America?" In National Conference of Social Work. Proceedings (1941), pp. 32-40.

________. "Women Workers." American Federationist, 36 (September, 1929), 1073-9.

________. "Worker's Stake in Safety." Washington, U.S. Department of Labor, 1940, 10 p.

Perkins, Sarah Marie C. Linton. "The Higher Education of Women." In Association for the Advancement of Women. Congress of Women, 1st. Papers, pp. 83-9.

________. "Uses of Money." In Association for the Advancement of Women. Congress of Women, 3rd. Papers, pp. 51-7.

Perlman, Helen Harris. "Casework Services in Public Welfare." In National Conference of Social Work. Proceedings (1947), pp. 261-9.

Perry, Martha. "Values and Limitations of the Evaluation Process as Seen by the Worker." In National Conference of Social Work. Proceedings (1940), pp. 638-47.

Perry, Mary E. "Minority Report of the Report of Committee on Colonies for Segregation of Defectives." In National Conference of Charities and Correction. Proceedings (1903), pp. 253-4.

Persing, Bobbye. "Statement." In U.S. Congress. Senate. Select Committee on Small Business. Effects of Government Regulations, pp. 166-8.

Petersen, Anna M. "The Administrative Problems of a Woman's Reformatory." In National Conference of Social Work. Proceedings (1922), pp. 164-8.

Petersham, Maud. "Acceptance Paper--Caldecott Award 1946. A Short Tale of the Depressions and the Peaks That Occur in the Making of the Little Pretty Picture Book." In Miller, B. Caldecott Medal Books, 1938-1957, pp. 134-7.

Peterson, Esther. "Address on Equality Through Opportunities Training, Employment, Education, Etc." Washington, U. S. Women's Bureau, 1961, 18 p.

________. "Address on Modern American Woman, Status and Opportunity." Washington, U. S. Labor Department, 1963, 20 p.

________. "Address on Women & Their Accomplishments Through National and International Women's Organizations." Washington, U. S. Women's Bureau, 1962, 11 p.

________. "Address on Woman's Status in Industry, Business, Society, Etc." Washington, U. S. Department of Labor, 1968, 14 p.

________. "Address on Work Opportunities Through Education." Washington, U. S. Department of Labor, 1963, 10 p.

________. "The Contribution of American Women to National and International Affairs. Achievements and Goals of American Women." In U. S. Women's Bureau. Today's Woman in Tomorrow's World, pp. 67-74.

________. "The Impact of Education." In Barber, S. Man and Civilization: The Potential of Women, pp. 88-98.

________. "Importance of the Home-maker." Vital Speeches, 28 (August 15, 1962), 662-5.

________. "Let's Look Ahead." Washington, U. S. Women's Bureau, 1965, 18 p.

________. "The Need for Educated Womanpower." In Conference on Woman's Destiny--Choice or Chance? Report, pp. 11-7.

________. "Needs and Opportunities in Our Society for the Educated Woman." In Itasca Conference on the Continuing Education of Women, Itasca State Park, Minnesota, 1962. Education and a Woman's Life, pp. 51-71.

________. "Opportunities and Trends in Employment of Women in Business, Summary of Address." Washington, U. S. Department of Labor, 1963, 3 p.

________. "Should the Congress Approve the Proposed "Fair Packaging and Labeling Act"?" Congressional Digest, 45 (June-July, 1966), 180-4.

________. "Statement." In U. S. Congress. House. Committee on Education and Labor. Special Subcommittee on Labor. Equal Pay Act, pp. 10-3, 30-3, 35-8, 58.

________. "Statement." In U. S. Congress. House. Committee on Education and Labor. Select Subcommittee on Labor. Equal Pay for Equal Work, pp. 24-35, 77-86.

________. "Statement." In U. S. Congress. Senate. Committee on Labor and Public Welfare. Subcommittee on Labor. Equal Pay Act of 1963, pp. 66-8.

________. "The War on Poverty--What Is the Federal Government Doing?" In Conference on Women in the War on Poverty, 2nd, 1968. Proceedings, pp. 16-7.

Peterson, Martha E. "Women, Autonomy, and Accountability in Higher Education." In Furniss, W. Women in Higher Education, pp. 3-10.

Pettigrew, L. Eudora. "Education and Socialization." In Hammond, N. Women and Children in Contemporary Society, pp. 17-23.

Phelps, Ethel L. "The Clothing Program for Federated Clubs." In General Federation of Women's Clubs. Biennial Convention, 16 (1922), 560-2.

Philbrook, Mary. "Legal Aid." In National Conference of Charities and Correction. Proceedings (1903), pp. 283-5.

________. "Statement." In U. S. Congress. Senate. Committee on the Judiciary. Subcommittee on Constitutional Amendments. Equal Rights Amendment (1945), pp. 40-1.

Phillips, Elsie Cole. "Address to a Joint Hearing of the Senate Judiciary Committee and Senate Committee on Woman Suffrage, March 13, 1912." In Stanton, E. History of Woman Suffrage, 5, 348-9.

Phillips, Lena Madesin. "Chairman's Introduction." In International Congress of Women, Chicago, 1933. Our Common Cause, Civilization, p. 3.

________. "Chairman's Introduction, Working Session." In International Congress of Women, Chicago, 1933. Our Common Cause, Civilization, p. 244.

________. "Shall It Be Progress?" In International Congress of Women, Chicago, 1933. Our Common Cause, Civilization, pp. 14-9.

________. "Why Call It Peace?" In New York Herald Tribune. Report of the 8th Annual Forum on Current Problems, pp. 145-8.

________. "Will the Professional Woman Progress or Perish?" In New York Herald Tribune. Report of the 4th Annual Women's Conference on Current Problems, pp. 225-9.

Phillips, Madge. "Sociological Considerations of the Female Participant." In Harris, D. Women and Sport, pp. 185-202.

Phillips, Mary. "Public Testimony." In New York (City). Commission on Human Rights. Women's Role in Contemporary Society, pp. 407-8.

Piepho, Irma. "Statement." In U. S. Congress. House. Committee on the Judiciary. Subcommittee No. 1. Equal Rights Amendment (1948), pp. 147-8.

Pierce, Bessie. "Schools and the Rulers of Mankind--Discussion." In International Congress of Women, Chicago, 1933. Our Common Cause, Civilization, pp. 828-30.

Pierson, Mary J. "Peace Work in the Schools." In American Peace Congress, 2nd, Chicago, 1909. Proceedings, pp. 51-5.

________. "The Young People's International Federation League." In American Peace Congress, 2nd, Chicago, 1909. Proceedings, pp. 389-96.

Pilpel, Harriet Fleischl. "Libraries and the First Amendment." In Libraries and the Life of the Mind in America, pp. 86-106.

________. "Statement." In U.S. Congress. Senate. Committee on the Judiciary. Subcommittee on Constitutional Amendments. Abortion, pt. 4, pp. 229-31.

Pinchot, Cornelia Bryce. "Statement." In U.S. Congress. Senate. Committee on the Judiciary. Subcommittee on Constitutional Amendments. Equal Rights for Men and Women (1938), pp. 56-60.

Pincus, Jane. "Address at the Columbia Theatre in Washington, November 15, 1914." In Irwin, I. The Story of the Woman's Party, pp. 83-4.

Platt, Marguerite. "Statement." In U.S. Congress. Joint Economic Committee. Economic Problems of Women, pt. 4, pp. 603-4.

Plebanek, Tillie. "Youth in Industry." In International Congress of Women, Chicago, 1933. Our Common Cause, Civilization, pp. 214-6.

Plummer, Mary A. "Report of Corresponding Secretary." General Federation of Women's Clubs. Biennial Convention, 16 (1922), 52-4.

Plummer, Mary Wright. "The Seven Joys of Reading." Sewanee Review, 18 (October, 1910), 454-65.

________. "Training for Librarianship and the Work of Children's Libraries." In International Congress of Women, Toronto, 1909. Report, 1, 372-9.

________. "The Training of Women as Librarians." In International Congress of Women, London, 1899, 4, 211-6.

Pogrebin, Letty Cottin. "Rethinking Housework." In Conference on Feminist Perspectives on Housework and Child Care. Feminist Perspectives on Housework and Child Care, pp. 49-59.

Poletti, Jean Ellis. "The Woman Voter." In New York Herald Tribune. Report of the 10th Annual Forum on Current Problems, pp. 158-62.

Pollard, Marie Antionette Nathalie. "Foot Free in God's Country." In World's Congress of Representative Women, Chicago, 1893. Congress of Women, pp. 293-5.

Pollitzer, Anita. "Statement." In U.S. Congress. House. Committee on Education and Labor. Select Subcommittee on Labor. Equal Pay for Equal Work, pt. 2, 327-9.

_______. "Statement." In U. S. Congress. House. Committee on the Judiciary. Subcommittee No. 1. Equal Rights Amendment (1948), pp. 40-3, 191-2.

_______. "Statement." In U. S. Congress. Senate. Committee on the Judiciary. Subcommittee on Constitutional Amendments. Equal Rights (1931), pp. 16-7, 67.

_______. "Statement." In U. S. Congress. Senate. Committee on the Judiciary. Subcommittee on Constitutional Amendments. Equal Rights for Men and Women (1938), pp. 161-5.

_______. 'Statement." In U. S. Congress. Senate. Committee on the Judiciary. Subcommittee on Constitutional Amendments. Equal Rights Amendment (1945), pp. 39-40.

_______. "Statement Before the Senate Committee on the Equal-Rights Amendment, 1931." In Kraditor, A. Up from the Pedestal, pp. 295-6.

Polowy, Carol. "Sex Discrimination: The Legal Obligations of Educational Institutions." Vital Speeches, 41 (February 1, 1975), 237-41.

Pomeroy, Sarah B. "A Classical Scholar's Perspective on Matriarchy." In Carroll, B. Liberating Women's History, pp. 217-23.

Poole, Grace Morrison. "Chairman's Introduction. The World as It Could Be." In International Congress of Women, Chicago, 1933. Our Common Cause, Civilization, p. 50.

_______. "Propaganda and Organized Women." In New York Herald Tribune. Report of the 5th Annual Forum on Changing Problems, pp. 239-40.

Poole, Hester M. "Difficulties and Delights of Women's Clubs." In National Council of Women of U. S., Washington, 1891. Transactions, pp. 301-3.

Pope, Jacke. "Hunger in the United States: Women and Children First." In Hammond, N. Women and Children in Contemporary Society, pp. 24-8.

Poppenheim, Mary B. "Report of Literature Committee." In General Federation of Women's Clubs. Biennial Convention, 9 (1908), 108-17.

Porter, Florence Collins. "The Power of Womanliness in Dealing with Stern Problems." In World's Congress of Representative Women, Chicago, 1893. A Historical Resume, pp. 391-4.

Porter, Rose. "The Cost of Maintaining Good Case Work in a Public Agency." In National Conference of Social Work. Proceedings (1925), pp. 242-6.

Porter, Sylvia Field Feldman. "Are We a Nation of Economic Illiterates? Make Peace Synonymous with Prosperity." Vital Speeches, 26 (April 1, 1960), 366-70.

________. "Charter of Economic Human Rights. Economic and Human Rights Tied into One Package." Vital Speeches, 23 (September 1, 1957), 678-81.

Portz, Eileen. "Influence of Birth Order and Sibling Sex on Sports Participation." In Harris, D. Women and Sport, pp. 225-34.

Post, Katharine F. "The Use of Available Resources." In National Conference of Social Work. Proceedings (1946), pp. 539-46.

Poston, Ersa. "Women in Government Employment." In New York (City). Commission on Human Rights. Women's Role in Contemporary Society, pp. 341-5.

Potter, Ellen C. "Coordination and Development of Welfare Service in the County." In National Conference of Social Work. Proceedings (1932), pp. 450-8.

________. "Co-ordination of State and Local Units for Welfare Administration." In National Conference of Social Work. Proceedings (1933), pp. 481-93.

________. "The Future Development of the Almshouse." In National Conference of Social Work. Proceedings (1926), pp. 527-32.

________. "How to Secure a Continuing and Progressive Policy in Public Social Work and Institutions." In National Conference of Social Work. Proceedings (1925), pp. 578-83.

________. "An Institutional Program in the Field of Corrections." In National Conference of Social Work. Proceedings (1924), pp. 212-20.

________. "Personnel in the Public Service from the Administrator's Point of View." In National Conference of Social Work. Proceedings (1935), pp. 608-17.

________. "Recent Developments in the Organization and Operation of Public Welfare Departments: The Bureau System." In National Conference of Social Work. Proceedings (1924), pp. 563-5.

________. "Resources for Care of the Chronically Ill: Maintenance." In National Conference of Social Work. Proceedings (1946), pp. 514-22.

________. "The Year of Decision for Social Work." In National Conference of Social Work. Proceedings (1945), pp. 1-16.

Potter, Frances Squire. "In Non-essentials, Liberty." In General Federation of Women's Clubs. Biennial Convention, 9 (1908), 414-7.

Potter, Helen L. D. "Woman in the Industrial Arts." In Association for the Advancement of Women. Congress of Women, 1st. Papers, pp. 105-9.

Potter, Jennie O'Neil. "The Monologue as an Entertainment." In World's Congress of Representative Women, Chicago, 1893. Congress of Women, pp. 682-5.

Potts, Eugenia Dunlap. "Woman's Work in Kentucky." In World's Congress of Representative Women, Chicago, 1893. Congress of Women, pp. 562-8.

Powell, Anna Rice. "The American Purity Alliance and Its Work." In National Purity Congress, 1st, Baltimore, 1895. National Purity Congress, pp. 130-7.

________. "The International Federation for the Abolition of State Regulation of Vice." In International Council of Women, 1888. Report, pp. 252-7.

Powell, Susie V. "A Plan of County Co-operation." In General Federation of Women's Clubs. Biennial Convention, 16 (1922), 562-8.

Powers, Edith E. "Rural Conditions in Pennsylvania." In National Conference of Charities and Correction. Proceedings (1911), pp. 421-3.

Powers, Margaret J. "The Industrial Cost of the Psychopathic Employee." In National Conference of Social Work. Proceedings (1920), pp. 342-6.

Pratt, Anna B. "Courses of Training for Visiting Teachers." In National Conference of Social Work. Proceedings (1923), pp. 425-8.

Pratt, Lucille M. "The Philosophy and Use of Budget Standards." In National Conference of Social Work. Proceedings (1947), pp. 288-93.

Prescott, Lydia A. "The Economic Independence of Women." In World's Congress of Representative Women, Chicago, 1893. Congress of Women, pp. 526-30.

Pressman, Sonia. "Job Equality for Women." In U.S. Congress. House. Committee on Education and Labor. Special Subcommittee on Education. Discrimination Against Women, pp. 533-7.

________. "Statement." In U.S. Congress. House. Committee on Education and Labor. Special Subcommittee on Labor. Equal Pay Act, pp. 211-4.

________. "Statement." In U.S. Congress. Senate. Committee on Labor and Public Welfare. Subcommittee on Labor. Equal Pay Act of 1963, pp. 169-71.

________. "The Status of Women in the Federal Government." In Conference of Professional and Academic Women. Sixteen Reports on the Status of Women in the Professions, 4 p.

Prestage, Jewel. "Black Women Officeholders: The Case of State Legislators." In Epstein, L. Women in the Professions, pp. 81-96.

Preston, Ann. "Ann Preston's Address--Westchester, Penn. Convention, June, 1852." In Stanton, E. History of Woman Suffrage, 1, 360-4.

________. "What Does Woman Want?" In Tanner, L. Voices from Women's Liberation, pp. 71-3.

Preston, Emily. "Artistic Book Binding." In General Federation of Women's Clubs. Biennial Convention, 9 (1908), 372-6.

Preston, Josephine Corliss. "Report of Community Service Division." In General Federation of Women's Clubs. Biennial Convention, 16 (1922), 237-40.

Prewett, Virginia. "World Population and Food Problems: The Need for Awareness." Vital Speeches, 34 (April 15, 1968), 404-7.

Prewitt, Audra L. "Bar vs. Bench: New Fears in an Old Relationship." In Essays on the Gilded Age. Edited by Margaret F. Morris. (Austin, Texas: University of Texas at Austin, 1973), pp. 11-21.

Prewitt, Lena B. "The Employment Rights of the Female: The Present Challenge." Vital Speeches, 40 (December 15, 1973), 137-41.

________. "The Need for Quality Instruction: To the Teacher." Vital Speeches, 33 (November 1, 1966), 49-50.

Price, Abby. "Comments at the Syracuse National Convention, September 1852." In Stanton, E. History of Woman Suffrage, 1, 532-3.

Price, Minnie Wright. "Friendly Visiting." In Conference for the Study of Negro Problems, 2nd, Atlanta, 1897. Social and Physical Condition of Negroes in Cities, pp. 58-60.

Prier, Maud. "Charity Organization in the Smaller Cities." In National Conference of Charities and Correction. Proceedings (1907), pp. 379-83.

Prosser, Lucienne. "Universal Service for America." In New York Herald Tribune. Report of the 10th Annual Report on Current Problems, pp. 16-8.

Putnam, Elizabeth C. "Auxiliary Visitors. Volunteer Visiting of State Wards in Connection with Official Work." In National Conference of Charities and Correction. Proceedings (1884), pp. 123-31.

________. "Dependent and Delinquent Children in This Country and Abroad." In National Conference of Charities and Correction. Proceedings (1890), pp. 190-202.

________. "Paper on the System of Visiting the Girls and Small Boys Who Are Wards of the State in Massachusetts." In National Conference of Charities and Correction. Proceedings (1883), pp. 477-80.

_______. "Pre-natal Care." In National Conference of Charities and Correction. Proceedings (1911), pp. 349-54.

_______. "The Work of the Auxiliary Visitors Appointed to Assist the Department of the Massachusetts State Board in Charge of the Visitation of Dependent and Delinquent Children." In Conference of Charities and Correction. Proceedings (1881), pp. 287-301.

Putnam, Marian C. "Friendly Visiting." In National Conference of Charities and Correction. Proceedings (1887), pp. 149-55.

Putnam, Patricia K. "Statement." In U.S. Congress. Senate. Committee on Human Resources. Subcommittee on Labor. Discrimination on the Basis of Pregnancy, pp. 366-71.

Quaife, Frances. "District Nursing." In National Conference of Charities and Correction. Proceedings (Special Meeting, 1897), 100-2.

Quinn, Lillian A. "How to Establish a Community Service." In National Conference of Social Work. Proceedings (1946), pp. 186-94.

Quinton, Amelia S. "Discussion of Woman as a Minister of Religion." In World's Congress of Representative Women, Chicago, 1893. A Historical Resume, pp. 240-1.

_______. "The Woman's National Indian Association." In World's Congress of Representative Women, Chicago, 1893. Congress of Women, pp. 71-3.

_______. "The Work and Objects of the Woman's National Indian Association." In International Council of Women, 1888. Report, pp. 100-1.

Radcliff, Dolores. "Statement." In U.S. Congress. Joint Economic Committee. Economic Problems of Women, pt. 4, pp. 626-31.

Radebaugh, Kathryn M. "Rehabilitation Work." In National Conference of Social Work. Proceedings (1927), pp. 194-6.

Ramey, Estelle. "Approaches to Correct the Underrepresentation of Women in the Health Professions. A U.S. Response to the Scandinavia Experience." In International Conference on Women in Health. Proceedings, pp. 51-2.

Ramey, Margaret. "Statement." In U.S. Congress. House. Committee on the Judiciary. Subcommittee No. 4. Equal Rights for Men and Women 1971, pp. 243-5.

Ramsey, Annie. "Work of the Probation Officer Preliminary to the Trial." In National Conference of Charities and Correction. Proceedings (1906), pp. 132-6.

Rand, Ayn. "Faith and Force, the Destroyers of the Modern World. The Age of Guilt." Vital Speeches, 26 (August 1, 1960), 630-6.

Randall, Emily B. "Admissions and Records in an Almshouse." In National Conference of Social Work. Proceedings (1926), pp. 523-6.

Rankin, Jeannette. "Address on Raker Resolution to Establish a House Committee on Woman Suffrage, September 24, 1917." In Josephson, H. Jeannette Rankin, pp. 93-4.

________. "Debate on Resolution Authorizing the President to Requisition the Copper Mines of Montana During Labor Unrest." In Josephson, H. Jeannette Rankin, pp. 90-1.

________. "First Speech in Congress to Offer an Amendment to the Lever Bill, May 28, 1917." In Josephson, H. Jeannette Rankin, p. 85.

________. "Speech at Joint Session of Congress to Declare War Against Austria-Hungary, December, 1917." In Josephson, H. Jeannette Rankin, pp. 84-5.

________. "Testimony on Neutrality Act Before House Foreign Affairs, Committee, February 16, 1937." In Josephson, H. Jeannette Rankin, p. 146.

Rappaport, Mazie F. "Casework in Social Protection." In National Conference of Social Work. Proceedings (1946), pp. 452-63.

Rathbone, Josephine Adams. "Creative Librarianship." In American Library Association. Bulletin, 26 (1932), 305-11.

Rattley, Jessie. "Statement." In National League of Cities. Women in Municipal Government, pp. 25-8.

Raushenbush, Esther. "Sarah Lawrence College, the Center for Continuing Education." In Itasca Conference on the Continuing Education of Women, Itasca State Park, Minnesota, 1962. Education and a Woman's Life, pp. 105-10.

Ravenhill, Margaret. "The Woman's Health Protective Association." In National Council of Women of the U.S., Washington, 1891. Transactions, pp. 347-51.

Ravner, Pearl C. "Entry and Reentry of Older Women into Labor Market: Psychological Barriers to Employment of Mature Women." Washington, U.S. Women's Bureau, 1953.

Rawalt, Marguerite. "Statement." In U. S. Congress. House. Committee on Education and Labor. Special Subcommittee on Education. Discrimination Against Women, pp. 390-6.

________. "Statement." In U. S. Congress. House. Committee on the Judiciary. Subcommittee No. 4. Equal Rights for Men and Women 1971, pp. 194-208.

________. "Statement." In U. S. Congress. Senate. Committee on the Judiciary. Subcommittee on Constitutional Amendments. Women and the "Equal Rights" Amendment, pp. 74-84.

Ray, Alice Kunz. "A Good Adoption Program: Can Standards Be Maintained Without Sacrificing Flexibility?" In National Conference of Social Work. Proceedings (1945), pp. 294-304.

Ray, Dixie Lee. "Biologist Looks at the Energy Crisis; Address June 17, 1974." Bioscience, 24 (September, 1974), 495-7.

________. "General Conference of the International Atomic Energy Agency Holds 17th Session at Vienna; Statement, September 18, 1973." Department of State Bulletin, 69 (October 22, 1973), 513-7.

________. "General Conference of the International Atomic Energy Agency Holds 18th Session at Vienna; Statement, September 17, 1974." Department of State Bulletin, 71 (October 21, 1974), 552-7.

________. "Miracle of Water: Excerpts from Address, April, 1968." American Forests, 74 (November, 1978), 8+.

Razovsky, Cecilia. "Humanitarian Effects of the Immigration Law." In National Conference of Social Work. Proceedings (1927), pp. 518-30.

________. "The Quota Law and the Effect of Its Administration in Contiguous Territory." In National Conference of Social Work. Proceedings (1924), pp. 613-7.

________. "The Visa and Quota Law as They Affect the Clients of Social Agencies." In National Conference of Social Work. Proceedings (1925), pp. 599-606.

Read, Leslie Stringfellow. "Report--Mrs. Leslie Stringfellow Read, Chairman Publicity." In General Federation of Women's Clubs. Biennial Convention, 16 (1922), pp. 140-8.

Reed, Anna Y. "Is Guidance a Racket? The Ultimate of Confusion." Vital Speeches, 4 (August 1, 1938), 636-8.

________. "Public Charities in Washington." In National Conference of Charities and Correction. Proceedings (1913), pp. 194-204.

Reed, Caroline Gallup. "Historic Women of Egypt." In World's Congress of Representative Women, Chicago, 1893. Congress of Women, pp. 240-2.

Reed, Carolyn. "Statement." In Conference on Feminist Perspectives on Housework and Child Care. Feminist Perspectives on Housework and Child Care, pp. 12-4.

Reed, Elizabeth Armstrong. "Assyrian Mythology." In World's Congress of Representative Women, Chicago, 1893. Congress of Women, pp. 719-22.

Reel, Estelle. "Address to the National American Woman Suffrage Association Convention of 1898." In Stanton, E. History of Woman Suffrage, 4, 301-2.

Rees, Mina. "The Graduate Education of Women." In Furniss, W. Women in Higher Education, pp. 178-87.

________. "Panelist Statement." In M. I. T. Symposium on American Women in Science and Engineering, 1964. Women and the Scientific Professions, pp. 34-40.

Reese, Cara. "We, the Women." In World's Congress of Representative Women, Chicago, 1893. Congress of Women, pp. 328-31.

Reeves, Margaret. "Community Planning in Rural Communities." In National Conference of Social Work. Proceedings (1935), pp. 435-45.

Regan, Agnes Gertrude. "Statement." In U. S. Congress. House. Committee on the Judiciary. Equal Rights Amendment to the Constitution (1932), pp. 32-3.

________. "Statement." In U. S. Congress. Senate. Committee on the Judiciary. Subcommittee on Constitutional Amendments. Equal Rights for Men and Women (1933), p. 27.

________. "Statement." In U. S. Congress. Senate. Committee on the Judiciary. Subcommittee on Constitutional Amendments. Equal Rights for Men and Women (1938), pp. 35-7.

Regensburg, Jeanette. "The Place of the Home in Treatment." In National Conference of Social Work. Proceedings (1927), pp. 380-4.

Reid, Helen Rogers. "An American Newspaper and the United Nations." In New York Herald Tribune. Report of the 21st Annual Forum on Current Problems, pp. 6-7.

________. "Introduction to the Forum." In New York Herald Tribune. Report of the 8th Annual Forum on Current Problems, p. 2.

________. "Introduction to the Forum." In New York Herald Tribune. Report of the 9th Annual Forum on Current Problems, pp. 2-3.

________. "Opening the Forum." In New York Herald Tribune. Report of the 14th Annual Forum on Current Problems, pp. 3-4.

________. "Opening the Forum." In New York Herald Tribune. Report of the 15th Annual Forum on Current Problems, pp. 3-4.

________. "Opening the Forum." In New York Herald Tribune. Report of the 16th Annual Forum on Current Problems, p. 3.

________. "Welcome to the Delegates." In New York Herald Tribune. Report of the 5th Annual Forum on Current Problems, pp. 2-4.

________. "Welcome to the Delegates." In New York Herald Tribune. Report of the 10th Annual Forum on Current Problems, pp. 1-2.

Reinhardt, Aurelia Henry. "Women in the American University of the Future." In Stanford University. University & the Future of America, (Stanford, California: Stanford University Press, 1941), pp. 70-88.

Relich, Marijana. "Statement." In U.S. Congress. Senate. Committee on the Judiciary. Equal Rights, 1970, pp. 122-33.

Remond, Sarah Parker. "Miss Remond's First Lecture in Dublin." In Loewenberg, B. Black Women in Nineteenth-century American Life, pp. 225-33.

________. "The Negroes in the United States of America." Journal of Negro History, 27 (April, 1942), 216-8.

Renard, Blanche. "Making Human Geography Talk." In National Conference of Social Work. Proceedings (1928), pp. 624-6.

________. "Uniform Districting in a Large City for Social and Civic Purposes." In National Conference of Social Work. Proceedings (1926), pp. 500-4.

Renner, Allie. "Public Testimony." In New York (City). Commission on Human Rights. Women's Role in Contemporary Society, pp. 797-9.

Reynolds, Bertha C. "Environmental Handicaps of Four Hundred Habit Clinic Children." In National Conference of Social Work. Proceedings (1925), pp. 453-9.

________. "The Mental Hygiene of Young Children: From the Point of View of a Psychiatric Social Worker in a Habit Clinic." In National Conference of Social Work. Proceedings (1924), pp. 447-51.

________. "The Status of Social Case Work Today." In National Conference of Social Work. Proceedings (1935), pp. 141-5.

________. "Treatment Processes as Developed by the Social Worker." In National Conference of Social Work. Proceedings (1926), pp. 400-7.

Reynolds, Minnie J. "Address to the Senate Committee, April 19, 1910." In Stanton, E. History of Woman Suffrage, 5, 296-7.

Reynolds, Rosemary. "Need of Case Work in a Public Relief Agency." In National Conference of Social Work. Proceedings (1938), pp. 162-76.

Rice, Florence. "Testimony Concerning Discrimination in the ILGWU at Hearings Held in 1962 by the House Committee on Labor, Education and Welfare." In Lerner, G. Black Women in White America, pp. 282-3.

Rich, Ellen Moore. "The Art of Living." In World's Congress of Representative Women, Chicago, 1893. Congress of Women, pp. 365-70.

Rich, Margaret E. "The Effect of Joint Administration on Case Work Practices." In National Conference of Social Work. Proceedings (1940), pp. 517-27.

________. "Professional Training from the Point of View of the Family Field." In National Conference of Social Work. Proceedings (1929), pp. 286-97.

Richards, Ellen Henrietta Swallow. "Clean Food." In General Federation of Women's Clubs. Biennial Convention, 9 (1908), 152-5.

________. "Food for Students." In World's Congress of Representative Women, Chicago, 1893. Congress of Women, p. 713.

________. "How Can the Increased Cost of Living Be Regulated to Meet the Decrease in the Salaries of Clerks and Professional Men?" In General Federation of Women's Clubs. Biennial Convention, 9 (1908), pp. 263-5.

Richards, Emily S. "The Legal and Political Status of Woman in Utah." In World's Congress of Representative Women, Chicago, 1893. A Historical Resume, pp. 913-5.

________. "Women's Relief Associations." In International Council of Women, 1888. Report, pp. 107-9.

Richards, Esther Loring. "The Elementary School and the Individual Child." In National Conference of Social Work. Proceedings (1921), pp. 351-5.

________. "Formulating the Problem in Social Case Work with Children." In National Conference of Social Work. Proceedings (1927), pp. 371-9.

Richards, Florence H. "Methods of Instruction in Sex Education." In National Conference of Social Work. Proceedings (1923), pp. 438-40.

Richards, Jane. "The National Woman's Relief Society." In National Council of Women of the U. S., Washington, 1891. Transactions, p. 258.

Richards, Linda. "The Moral Influence of Trained Nurses in Hospitals." In National Conference of Charities and Correction. Proceedings (1895), pp. 256-9.

________. "Training Schools for Nurses--Mission Training Schools." In National Conference of Charities and Correction. Proceedings (1894), pp. 100-2.

Richardson, Anne B. "The Cooperation of Women in Philanthropy." In National Conference of Charities and Correction. Proceedings (1892), pp. 216-22.

________. "Massachusetts Institutions: Supplementary Work in the Care of Dependent and Delinquent Children." In National Conference of Charities and Correction. Proceedings (1886), pp. 131-8.

________. "The Massachusetts System of Placing and Visiting Children." In Conference on Charities and Correction. Proceedings (1880), pp. 186-200.

Richardson, Ellen A. "Character Building in Education." In National Council of Mothers. Work & Words, pp. 200-7.

Richardson, Henrietta F. "Ambulances of the Air." In New York Herald Tribune. Report of the 12th Annual Forum on Current Problems, pp. 181-3.

Richardson, Victoria M. "Report of Western Women's Unitarian Conference." In International Council of Women, 1888. Report, p. 88.

Richman, Julia. "Special Classes and Special Schools for Delinquent and Backward Children." In National Conference of Charities and Correction. Proceedings (1907), pp. 230-43.

________. "Women Wage-workers: With Reference to Directing Immigrants." In Jewish Women's Congress. Papers, pp. 91-107.

Richmond, Mary E. "The Art of Beginning in Social Work." In National Conference of Charities and Correction. Proceedings (1911), pp. 373-80.

________. "Charitable Co-operation." In National Conference of Charities and Correction. Proceedings (1901), pp. 298-313.

________. "The Family and the Social Worker." In National Conference of Charities and Correction. Proceedings (1908), pp. 76-81.

________. "Friendly Visiting." In National Conference of Charities and Correction. Proceedings (1907), pp. 307-15.

________. "How Social Workers Can Aid Housing Reform." In National Conference of Charities and Correction. Proceedings (1911), pp. 326-30.

________. "Medical and Social Co-operation." In National Conference of Charities and Correction. Proceedings (1912), pp. 359-63.

________. "The Message of the Associated Charities." In National Conference of Charities and Correction. Proceedings (1901), pp. 327-9.

________. "The Need of a Training-school in Applied Philanthropy." In National Conference of Charities and Correction. Proceedings (1897), pp. 181-6.

________. "Organization Among Women Considered with Respect to Philanthropy." In World's Congress of Representative Women, Chicago, 1893. A Historical Resume, pp. 254-8. (Read by Harriet Taylor Upton)

________. "Report of the Committee (on Families and Neighborhoods): The Interrelation of Social Movements." In National Conference of Charities and Correction. _Proceedings_ (1910), pp. 212-8.

________. "The Social Case Worker in a Changing World." In National Conference of Charities and Correction. _Proceedings_ (1915), pp. 43-9.

________. "The Social Case Worker's Task." In National Conference of Social Work. _Proceedings_ (1917), pp. 112-5.

________. "Some Next Steps in Social Treatment." In National Conference of Social Work. _Proceedings_ (1920), pp. 254-8.

________. "War and Family Solidarity." In National Conference of Social Work. _Proceedings_ (1918), pp. 287-97.

Richter, Melissa. "Patterns of Discrimination and Discouragement in Higher Education." In New York (City). Commission on Human Rights. _Women's Role in Contemporary Society_, pp. 602-8.

Riger, Stephanie. "The Effects of Participation in Women's Consciousness-Raising Groups." In McGuigan, D. _New Research on Women at the University of Michigan_, pp. 113-5.

Riggs, Anna Rankin. "God's Thought of Women." In World's Congress of Representative Women, Chicago, 1893. _Congress of Women_, pp. 813-5.

Ripley, Mary A. "Employment of Married Women in the Public Schools." In National Council of Women of the U.S., Washington, 1891. _Transactions_, pp. 204-9.

Rippin, Jane Deeter. "The Co-ordination of the Juvenile Court with Other Courts." In National Conference of Social Work. _Proceedings_ (1917), pp. 276-8.

________. "Municipal Detention for Women." In National Conference of Social Work. _Proceedings_ (1918), pp. 132-9.

________. "Specific Problems in Camp Communities." In National Conference of Social Work. _Proceedings_ (1918), pp. 666-7.

Rittenhouse, Irma. "Commentary on the Role of Women's Legislation in Meeting Basic Problems of Working Conditions." In U.S. Women's Bureau. _American Woman--Her Changing Role_, pp. 33-6.

Rivers, Dorothy. "Statement." In U.S. Congress. Senate. Select Committee on Small Business. _Women and Small Business Administration_, pp. 101-4.

Robb, Christine C. "The Problem of Meeting the Needs of the Social Worker Who Refers Cases to a Psychiatric Clinic." In National Conference of Social Work. _Proceedings_ (1927), pp. 399-408.

Robb, Isabel Adams Hampton. "The Organization of Trained Nurses' Alumnae Associations." In International Congress of Women, London, 1899, 4, 28-33. (Read by Lucy Walker)

Robbins, Jane E. "Bureau and Political Influences in Neighborhood Civic Problems." In National Conference of Social Work. Proceedings (1925), pp. 391-5.

Roberts, Abby. "National Organization for Public Health Nursing." In General Federation of Women's Clubs. Biennial Convention, 16 (1922), 115-7.

________. "Nursing Education and Opportunities for the Colored Nurse." In National Conference of Social Work. Proceedings (1928), pp. 183-8.

Roberts, Eunice C. "Comment on Patterns of Higher Education for Women." In Conference on the Present Status and Prospective Trends of Research on the Education of Women, Rye, N. Y., 1957. The Education of Women, pp. 115-8.

Roberts, Janice Sue. "Statement." In U. S. Congress. Senate. Select Committee on Small Business. Effects of Government Regulations, pp. 162-3.

Roberts, Joan I. "Women's Right to Choose, or Men's Right to Dominate." In Furniss, W. Women in Higher Education, pp. 50-5.

Roberts, Lillian. "Union and Blue-collar Women." In New York (City). Commission on Human Rights. Women's Role in Contemporary Society, pp. 345-6.

Roberts, Sylvia. "Statement." In U. S. Congress. House. Committee on Education and Labor. Special Subcommittee on Education. Discrimination Against Women, pp. 87-104.

Robertson, Alice. "Remarks." In U. S. Women's Bureau. Proceedings of the Women's Industrial Conference, pp. 41-3.

Robey, Gertrude James. "Statement." In U. S. Congress. Senate. Committee on the Judiciary. Subcommittee on Constitutional Amendments. Equal Rights Amendment (1929), p. 23.

Robins, Mary Drier. "The Social Perils of Lawlessness." In Smith, F. Law vs. Lawlessness, pp. 46-53.

________. "Standard of Payment for Women for Girls." In National Conference of Charities and Correction. Proceedings (1911), pp. 177-9.

________. "The Value of Unions." In Brownlee, W. Women in the American Economy, pp. 218-20.

________. "What Industry Means to Women Workers." In U. S. Women's Bureau. Proceedings of the Women's Industrial Conference, pp. 34-41.

Robinson, Alice C. "Address of Welcome." In National Purity Congress, 1st, Baltimore, 1895. National Purity Congress, pp. 10-2.

Robinson, Cornelia S. "Trade Unions and the Labour Problem." In International Congress of Women, London, 1899, 6, 164-7.

Robinson, Daisy E. O. "Social Hygiene. The Responsibility of Women's Organizations in the Social Hygiene Movement." In General Federation of Women's Clubs. Biennial Convention, 16 (1922), 368-71.

Robinson, Emily. "Report on Education." In Woman's Rights Convention, Akron, Ohio, 1851. Proceedings, pp. 20-5.

Robinson, Harriet H. "Political Parties and Woman Suffrage." In International Council of Women, 1888. Report, pp. 306-9.

Robinson, Jane Bancroft. "The Modern Deaconess Movement." In World's Congress of Representative Women, Chicago, 1893. A Historical Resume, pp. 244-54.

Robinson, Maria S. "A Floating Hospital." In National Conference of Charities and Correction. Proceedings (1895), pp. 269-72.

Robinson, Mary. "Peculiar Insecurities of Women as Workers." In International Congress of Women, Chicago, 1933. Our Common Cause, Civilization, pp. 321-31.

Robinson, Virginia P. "Analysis of Processes in the Records of Family Case Working Agencies." In National Conference of Social Work. Proceedings (1921), pp. 253-6.

________. "Psychoanalytic Contributions to Social Case Work Treatment." In National Conference of Social Work. Proceedings (1931), pp. 329-46.

Robison, Louise Y. "Chairman's Introduction. Women in a Changing World." In International Congress of Women, Chicago, 1933. Our Common Cause, Civilization, pp. 69-70.

Robnett, Florence Schee. "A Look at the Problem." In International Congress of Women, Chicago, 1933. Our Common Cause, Civilization, pp. 891-3.

Roche, Josephine. "The Effect of the Cable Law on the Citizenship Status of Foreign Women." In National Conference of Social Work. Proceedings (1925), pp. 611-6.

________. "Health Ahead." In National Conference of Social Work. Proceedings (1939), pp. 77-8.

________. "The Place of the Foreign Language Press in an Educational Program." In National Conference of Social Work. Proceedings (1921), pp. 481-5.

________. "Report on the Washington Health Conference." In New York Herald Tribune. Report of the 8th Annual Forum on Changing Problems, pp. 56-8.

________. "Youth Opportunities Today and Social Security Safeguards." In New York Herald Tribune. Report of the 5th Annual Forum on Changing Problems, pp. 92-7.

Rochester, Anna. "Infant Mortality as an Economic Problem." In National Conference of Social Work. Proceedings (1919), pp. 197-202.

Rockwood, Edith. "Organizing the Community for Legislative Reform." In National Conference of Social Work. Proceedings (1928), pp. 411-5.

Rodgers-Rose, La Frances. "New Ways of Viewing Key Questions for Investigation. Social Psychological: Relations Between Black Males and Females--Toward a Definition." In U.S. National Center for Health Services Research. Women and Their Health, pp. 62-72.

Rodriguez, Grisel. "Coeds View an Undergraduate Campus." In Furniss, W. Women in Higher Education, pp. 69-71.

Rodriguez-Trios, Helen. "Analysis of the Role of Women in Health Care Decisionmaking. A U.S. Response to a Look at the Philippines." In International Conference on Women in Health. Proceedings, pp. 163-5.

Roebling, Mary Gindhart. "Power and Influence of Women: Dedication to Family and Nation." Vital Speeches, 31 (September 1, 1965), 689-91.

Roemer, Ruth. "Innovations in the Utilization of Nurses, Allied Health and Support Personnel. A U.S. Response to a Look at Colombia." In International Conference on Women in Health. Proceedings, pp. 91-3.

Roessing, Jeanie Bradley. "Report of the National Congressional Committee to the National American Woman Suffrage Association Convention of 1916." In Stanton, E. History of Woman Suffrage, 5, 503-11.

Rogers, Agnes. "Elegance Is Not Undemocratic. Stop the Search for the Lowest Common Denominator." Vital Speeches, 16 (December 1, 1949), 126-8.

Rogers, Caroline Gilkey. "Address to the Senate Committee on Woman Suffrage, March 7, 1884." In Stanton, E. History of Woman Suffrage, 4, 38-9.

Rogers, Edith Nourse. "Tragedy of the Highways." Vital Speeches, 2 (April 6, 1936), 439-40.

Rogers, Helen W. "The Probation System of the Juvenile Court of Indianapolis." In National Conference of Charities and Correction. Proceedings (1904), pp. 369-79.

Rogers, Lina B. "The Physician and the Nurse in the Public School." In National Conference of Charities and Correction. Proceedings (1905), pp. 273-80.

Rogers, Martha P. "The Role of the Equal Employment Opportunity Commission." In Furniss, W. Women in Higher Education, pp. 219-23.

Rogers, May. "The Novel as the Educator of the Imagination." In World's Congress of Representative Women, Chicago, 1893. Congress of Women, pp. 586-9.

Rollins, Alice Wellington. "Woman in the Republic of Letters." In World's Congress of Representative Women, Chicago, 1893. A Historical Resume, pp. 144-6. (Read by Mary Lowe Dickinson.)

Rollins, Marion Benedict. "The Place of Religion in a Liberal Arts Curriculum. The Academic Study of Religion." Vital Speeches, 25 (December 15, 1958), 143-6.

Rom, Gundrun. "Family Problems Resulting from the Present Deportation System." In National Conference of Social Work. Proceedings (1927), pp. 568-72.

Roman, Sallie Rhett. "Extracts from Possibilities of the Southern States." In World's Congress of Representative Women, Chicago, 1893. Congress of Women, pp. 579-85.

Rooney, Miriam Therese. "Kinds of Government and the Growth of Isms. Property and Force vs. Personality and Reason." Vital Speeches, 15 (December 1, 1948), 107-9.

Roosevelt, Anna Eleanor. "The American Woman's Place in the World Today." In New York Herald Tribune. Report of the 5th Annual Forum on Current Problems, pp. 9-12.

________. "At Unity House." In Stein, L. Out of the Sweatshop, pp. 254-5.

________. "The Backlog of Preparedness." In New York Herald Tribune. Report of the 10th Annual Forum on Current Problems, pp. 7-10.

________. "Better Housing." In New York Herald Tribune. Report of the 5th Annual Forum on Current Problems, pp. 59-63.

________. "Greeting Delivered at Constitution Hall, June 1, 1936." In Associated Country Women of the World. Proceedings, p. 211.

________. "Humanistic Democracy--The American Ideal." In New York Herald Tribune. Report of the 9th Annual Forum on Current Problems, pp. 38-40.

________. "Opening Address." In New York Herald Tribune. Report of the 4th Annual Women's Conference on Current Problems, pp. 15-7.

________. "Responsibilities to Our Men and Women in the Services." In New York Herald Tribune. Report of the 12th Annual Forum on Current Problems, pp. 65-8.

________. "Statement." In U. S. Congress. House. Committee on Education and Labor. Select Subcommittee on Labor. Equal Pay for Equal Work, pt. 2, 224-6.

________. "United Nations and You. Language Difficulties Are Barriers to Confidence." Vital Speeches, 12 (May 1, 1946), 444-5.

________. "Young America." In New York Herald Tribune. Report of the 3rd Women's Conference on Current Problems, pp. 102-5.

________. "Youth's Contribution." In New York Herald Tribune. Report of the 8th Annual Forum on Current Problems, pp. 5-7.

Roosevelt, Edith Kermit. "American Education and the Child. Philosophical Ideas Old and New." Vital Speeches, 26 (March 15, 1960), 334-7.

Roosevelt, Eleanor Butler Alexander. "Sino-Japanese Dossier. Eye-witness." Vital Speeches, 3 (September 1, 1937), 697-8.

Rosaldo, Michelle Zimbalist. "Woman, Culture, and Society: A Theoretical Overview." In Rosaldo, M. Woman, Culture and Society, pp. 17-42.

Rose, Dorothy. "Statement." In U. S. Congress. Senate. Committee on the Judiciary. Subcommittee on Constitutional Amendments. Equal Rights for Men and Women (1938), pp. 40-2.

Rose, Ernestine Louise Siismondi Potowski. "Address at the 2nd National Convention at Worcester, October 1851." In Stanton, E. History of Woman Suffrage, 1, 237-42.

________. "Address at the 10th National Woman's Rights Convention, New York, May 10-11, 1860." In Stanton, E. History of Woman Suffrage, 1, 692-4.

________. "Address at the Woman's National Loyal League Convention, May 14, 1863." In Stanton, E. History of Woman Suffrage, 2, 73-8.

________. "Address Before a House Committee of the New York State Legislature, February 1854." In Stanton, E. History of Woman Suffrage, 1, 607-8.

________. "Address to the 1st Annual Meeting of the American Equal Rights Association, May 1867." In Stanton, E. History of Woman Suffrage, 2, 208-10.

________. "Address to the Woman's Rights State Convention, Rochester, N. Y., November 30, and December 1, 1853." In Stanton, E. History of Woman Suffrage, 2, 579.

________. "Comments on the Bible Issue at the Syracuse National Convention, September 1852." In Stanton, E. History of Woman Suffrage, 1, 536-9.

________. "Debate at the 3rd Annual Meeting of the American Equal Rights Association, New York, May 1869." In Stanton, E. History of Woman Suffrage, 2, 389.

________. "Debate at the Woman's National Loyal League Convention, May 14, 1863." In Stanton, E. History of Woman Suffrage, 2, 60, 64.

________. "Debate on the Divorce Resolutions at the 10th National Woman's Rights Convention, New York, May 10-11, 1860." In Stanton, E. History of Woman Suffrage, 1, 729-32.

________. "Equal Rights for Women; Speeches by Ernestine L. Rose at the Third National Woman's Rights Convention, Syracuse, N.Y., September 8-10, 1852." In Schappes, M. A Documentary History of the Jews in the United States: 1654-1875, pp. 324-32.

________. "Ernestine Rose at Worcester." In Papachristou, J. Women Together, pp. 34-5. (Same as "Address at the 2nd National Convention at Worcester, October 1851").

________. "Mrs. Rose Moves Change of Name from Equal Rights Association to Woman's Suffrage Association, at the 3rd Annual Meeting of the American Equal Rights Association, New York, May 1869." In Stanton, E. History of Woman Suffrage 2, 396-7.

________. "On Legal Discrimination." In Kraditor, A. Up from the Pedestal, pp. 222-8. (Same as "Address at the 2nd National Convention at Worcester, October 1851.")

________. "Petitions Were Circulated." In Schneir, M. Feminism, pp. 125-7. (Same as "Address at the 10th National Woman's Rights Convention, New York, May 10-11, 1860.")

________. "President's Address at the 5th National Convention in Philadelphia, October 1854." In Stanton, E. History of Woman Suffrage, 1, 376-7.

________. "Remarks at the 7th National Convention, New York, November 25, 1856." In Stanton, E. History of Woman Suffrage, 1, 641.

________. "Remarks at the 10th National Woman's Rights Convention, New York, May 10-11, 1860." In Stanton, E. History of Woman Suffrage, 1, 710-11.

________. "Remarks at Woman's Rights Convention, Syracuse, New York, September 8, 1852." In Harper, I. The Life and Work of Susan B. Anthony, 1, 77.

________. "Remarks at the Woman's Rights Convention in New York, September 1853." In Stanton, E. History of Woman Suffrage, 1, 561-2.

________. "Remarks During Debate at the 4th National Convention, October 1853 in Cleveland, Ohio." In Stanton, E. History of Woman Suffrage, 1, 133-4, 139.

________. "Remarks on Wills at the Woman's Rights Convention, in New York, September 1853." In Stanton, E. History of Woman Suffrage, 1, 564.

________. "Remarks on Women's Condition at the 7th National Convention, New York, November 25, 1856." In Stanton, E. *History of Woman Suffrage*, 1, 661-5.

________. "Remove the Legal Shackles from Women." In Tanner, L. *Voices from Women's Liberation*, pp. 64-5.

________. "Reprint of Remarks by Mrs. Rose in the *Tribune*, September 12, 1853." In Stanton, E. *History of Woman Suffrage*, 1, 575-6.

________. "Speech of Ernestine L. Rose at the Infidel Convention, New York, May 4, 1845." In Suhl, Y. *Ernestine L. Rose and the Battle for Human Rights*, pp. 279-80.

________. "Speech of Ernestine L. Rose at the Second National Woman's Rights Convention, Worcester, Massachusetts, October 15, 1851." In Suhl, Y. *Ernestine L. Rose and the Battle for Human Rights*, pp. 281-4.

________. "Speech of Ernestine L. Rose at the Thomas Paine Anniversary Celebration, New York, January 29, 1850." In Suhl, Y. *Ernestine L. Rose and the Battle for Human Rights*, pp. 280-1.

________. "Speech of Ernestine L. Rose at the Thomas Paine Anniversary Celebration, New York, January 29, 1852." In Suhl, Y. *Ernestine L. Rose and the Battle for Human Rights*, p. 284.

Rose, Flora. "Maintaining Standards of Living in the New Day." In New York Herald Tribune. *Report of the 2nd Women's Conference on Current Problems*, pp. 25-8.

Rosenberg, Anna M. "Mobilization in Action." In New York Herald Tribune. *Report of the 19th Annual Forum on Current Problems*, pp. 170-3.

________. "What the Community Can Do." In New York Herald Tribune. *Report of the 13th Annual Forum on Current Problems*, pp. 35-9.

Rosenberg, Pauline Hanauer. "Influence of the Discovery of America on the Jews." In Jewish Women's Congress. *Papers*, pp. 66-73.

Rosenhan, Mollie Schwartz. "Images of Male and Female in Children's Readers." In Atkinson, D. *Women in Russia*, pp. 293-305.

Ross, Dorothy. "A Modest Beginning and a Modest Proposal." In Furniss, W. *Women in Higher Education*, pp. 99-104.

Ross, Elizabeth H. "Social Work's Responsibilities for Veterans." In National Conference of Social Work. *Proceedings* (1946), pp. 360-70.

Ross, Jean. "Statement." In U.S. Congress. House. Committee on Education and Labor. Special Subcommittee on Education. *Discrimination Against Women*, pp. 13-6.

Ross, Susan Deller. "Statement." In U. S. Congress. House. Committee on Education and Labor. Special Subcommittee on Education. Discrimination Against Women, pp. 181-5, 186-8.

________. "Statement." In U. S. Congress. House. Committee on Education and Labor. Subcommittee on Employment Opportunities. Legislation to Prohibit Sex Discrimination on the Basis of Pregnancy, pp. 47-50.

________. "Statement." In U. S. Congress. Senate. Committee on Human Resources. Subcommittee on Labor. Discrimination on the Basis of Pregnancy, pp. 117-21.

Rossi, Alice Schaerr. "Barriers to the Career Choice of Engineering, Medicine, or Science Among American Women." In M. I. T. Symposium on American Women in Science and Engineering, 1964. Women and the Scientific Professions, pp. 51-127.

________. "Feminist History in Perspective: Sociological Contributions to Biographic Analysis." In McGuigan, D. A Sampler of Women's Studies, pp. 85-108.

________. "Women in the Seventies: Problems and Possibilities." In U. S. Congress. House. Committee on Education and Labor. Special Subcommittee on Education. Discrimination Against Women, pp. 314-29.

Rothman, Ellen. "Public Testimony." In New York (City). Commission on Human Rights. Women's Role in Contemporary Society, pp. 563-4.

Rothrock, Mary U. "Libraries in a New Era." ALA Bulletin, 40 (July, 1946), 227-9.

Rothstein, Adrienne. "Public Testimony." In New York (City). Commission on Human Rights. Women's Role in Contemporary Society, pp. 560-1.

Roudebush, Dorothy. "Statement." In U. S. Congress. Senate. Committee on the Judiciary. Subcommittee on Constitutional Amendments. Abortion, pt. 3, pp. 176-81.

Roundtree, Martha. "Crusade for Morality: Women Power." Vital Speeches, 36 (July 15, 1970), 597-602.

Routzahn, Mary Swain. "Available Channels of Publicity." In National Conference of Social Work. Proceedings (1926), pp. 643-5.

________. "Interpreting the Social Worker to the Public." In National Conference of Social Work. Proceedings (1931), pp. 541-50.

Rowe, Bess M. "The Farm Family and Buying Power." In International Congress of Women, Chicago, 1933. Our Common Cause, Civilization, pp. 410-6.

Rowe, Clara Louise. "Interpreting Professional Standards of Social Work to the Public: From the Viewpoint of a National Agency." In National Conference of Social Work. Proceedings (1926), pp. 679-82.

Rowe, Louise Osborne. "Municipalization of Charitable and Correctional Work in Chicago." In National Conference of Charities and Correction. Proceedings (1916), pp. 396-400.

Rubin, Ethel. "Statement." In U.S. Congress. House. Committee on Education and Labor. Special Subcommittee on Education. Discrimination on the Basis of Pregnancy, pp. 442-5.

Ruckelshaus, Jill. "Statement." In U.S. Congress. House. Committee on Government Operations. National Women's Conference, pp. 23-6.

Rude, Anna E. "The Federal Children's Bureau." In National Conference of Social Work. Proceedings (1921), pp. 188-91.

Ruffin, Josephine St. Pierre. "The Beginnings of the National Club Movement." In Lerner, G. Black Women in White America, pp. 440-3.

________. "From Josephine St. Pierre Ruffin's Speech." In Papachristou, J. Women Together, pp. 120-1. (Same as "The Beginnings of the National Club Movement.").

Ruffra, Jean. "Should Congress Curtail the Use of "Busing" for School Desegregation?" Congressional Digest, 53 (April, 1974), 122-6.

Rugek, Sheryl K. "Emergent Modes of Utilization: Gynecological Self Help." In U.S. National Center for Health Services Research. Women and Their Health, pp. 80-4.

Ruhl, Julia A. "Report of Mrs. Julia A. Ruhl, Chairman Membership Committee." In General Federation of Women's Clubs. Biennial Convention, 16 (1922), 89-91.

Rumbarger, Margaret L. "The Great Quota Debate and Other Issues in Affirmative Action." In Furniss, W. Women in Higher Education, pp. 207-14.

Russell, Liane B. "Should the Federal Government Assume a Direct Role in the Regulation of Surface Mining of Coal in the States?" Congressional Digest, 53 (May, 1974), 150-6.

Russell, Patricia. "Statement." In National League of Cities. Women in Municipal Government, pp. 29-35.

Ryther, Margherita. "Place and Scope of Psychiatric Social Work in Mental Hygiene." In National Conference of Social Work. Proceedings (1919), pp. 575-82.

Sachs, Bernice. "Discussion of the Psychological and Physiological Aspects of Woman and the Role They Play in Her Destiny." In Conference on Woman's Destiny--Choice or Chance? Report, pp. 19-21.

Sacks, Karen. "Engels Revisited: Women, the Organization of Production, and Private Property." In Rosaldo, M. Woman, Culture, and Society, pp. 207-22.

Safford, Mary A. "Woman as a Minister of Religion." In World's Congress of Representative Women, Chicago, 1893. A Historical Resume, pp. 236-40.

St. Denis, Ruth. "Creative Uses of the Arts--The Dance." In International Congress of Women, Chicago, 1933. Our Common Cause, Civilization, pp. 922-6.

________. "Winging One's Own Way." In International Congress of Women, Chicago, 1933. Our Common Cause, Civilization, pp. 173-7.

St. George, Katharine. "The Equal Rights Amendment." Congressional Record, 86th Cong., 1st sess., 1959, 105, pt. 11, 19329.

________. "Statement." In U.S. Congress. House. Committee on the Judiciary. Subcommittee No. 2. Equal Rights Amendment (1948), pp. 6-8.

________. "Statement." In U.S. Congress. Senate. Committee on the Judiciary. Subcommittee on Constitutional Amendments. Equal Rights (1956), pp. 15-8.

St. John, Eugenia. "Discussion on Woman's Call to the Ministry." In World's Congress of Representative Women, Chicago, 1893. A Historical Resume, pp. 233-4.

St. John, Jacqueline D. "Reflections and Perspectives on the Women's Movement in 1976: The Equal Rights Amendment." Vital Speeches, 43 (November 15, 1976), 4-7.

________. "Women's Legislative Issues: Today and Tomorrow." Vital Speeches, 38 (June 15, 1972), 528-32.

Salazar, Grace. "Statement." In U.S. Congress. Senate. Select Committee on Small Business. Effects of Government Regulation, pp. 163-5.

Salmon, Lucy M. "Address at the College Evening of the 38th Annual Convention of the National American Woman Suffrage Association, February 8, 1906." In Harper, I. The Life and Work of Susan B. Anthony, 3, 1390-1.

Saloman, Alice. "The Relation of the Church to Social Work." In National Conference of Social Work. Proceedings (1923), pp. 228-31.

Sampson, Edith Spurlock. "Choose One of Five: Its Your Life." Vital Speeches, 31 (August 15, 1965), 661-3.

________. "Equal Opportunity & Equal Responsibility. These Are Two Sides of the Same Single Coin." Vital Speeches, 23 (June 15, 1957), 519-52.

________. "How Can We Go Forward? Panel Discussion." In New York Herald Tribune. Report of the 19th Annual Forum on Current Problems, pp. 114-8.

________. "Show the East How the Freedom Revolution Works. Industrial Civilizations Are Built from the Bottom Up." Vital Speeches, 17 (February 15, 1951), 272-5.

Samuels, Louise. "Statement." In U.S. Congress. Senate. Committee on the Judiciary. Subcommittee on Constitutional Amendments. Equal Rights for Men and Women (1938), p. 83.

Sanday, Peggy R. "Female Status in the Public Domain." In Rosaldo, M. Woman, Culture, and Society, pp. 189-206.

Sanders, Beulah. "Multiple Jeopardies of the Welfare Mother." In New York (City). Commission on Human Rights. Women's Role in Contemporary Society, pp. 475-83.

Sanders, Catherine. "The Relationship Between Children and Family Case Working Agencies: Relationships in Technique." In National Conference of Social Work. Proceedings (1922), pp. 241-5.

Sanders, Inez. "Statement." In U.S. Congress. House. Committee on Education and Labor. Subcommittee on Equal Opportunity. Equal Opportunity for Displaced Homemakers Act, p. 61.

Sandler, Bernice. "Academic Women Attack Institutional Discrimination." In Lerner, G. The Female Experience, pp. 251-6.

________. "Affirmative Action on the Campus: Like It or Not, Uncle Sam Is Here to Stay." In Furniss, W. Women in Higher Education, pp. 324-7.

________. "Patterns of Discrimination and Discouragement in Higher Education." In New York (City). Commission on Human Rights. Women's Role in Contemporary Society, pp. 567-82.

________. "The Policy Issues: Presentation IV." In Blaxall, M. Women and the Workplace, pp. 273-7.

________. "Statement." In U.S. Congress. House. Committee on Education and Labor. Special Subcommittee on Education. Discrimination Against Women, pp. 60-7, 414-34. (Same as "Academic Women Attack Institutional Discrimination.")

________. "Statement." In U.S. Congress. House. Committee on the Judiciary. Subcommittee No. 4. Equal Rights for Men and Women 1971, pp. 263-90.

________. "Statement." In U.S. Congress. Senate. Committee on the Judiciary. Subcommittee on Constitutional Amendments. Women and the "Equal Rights" Amendment, pp. 124-8.

________. "Testimony on Federal Efforts to End Sex Discrimination in Employment." In U.S. Congress. Joint Economic Committee. Economic Problems of Women, pt. 1, 118-21.

________. "Women in Higher Education: What Constitutes Equality?" Vital Speeches, 38 (June 15, 1972), 532-7.

Sandmann, Ruth. "Youth of All Nations." In New York Herald Tribune. Report of the 13th Annual Forum on Current Problems, pp. 82-4.

Sands, Susan. "Public Testimony." In New York (City). Commission on Human Rights. Women's Role in Contemporary Society, pp. 405-7.

Sanger, Margaret Higgins. "Speech at Dinner Given in Her Honor, January 23, 1916." In Sanger, M. My Fight for Birth Control, pp. 132-4.

________. "Speech at 6th International Neo-Mathusian and Birth Control Conference, March 1925." In Sanger, M. My Fight for Birth Control, pp. 289-91.

________. "Speech Before Senate Sub-committee, February 13, 1931." In Sanger, M. My Fight for Birth Control, pp. 353-5.

Sangster, Margaret Elizabeth. "Reading Courses for Mothers." In National Congress of Mothers. Work & Words, pp. 171-6.

Saporta, Sarah. "The Status of Women in Art." In Conference of Professional and Academic Women. Sixteen Reports on the Status of Women in the Professions, 4 p.

Sartain, Emily. "Art in Its Various Branches as a Profession for Women." In International Congress of Women, London, 1899, 3, 64-74.

________. "Discussion of the Contribution of Women to the Applied Arts." In World's Congress of Representative Women, Chicago, 1893. A Historical Resume, pp. 567-70.

Sassower, Doris L. "Women in Law." In Conference of Professional and Academic Women. Sixteen Reports on the Status of Women in the Professions, 4 p.

________. "Women in the Professions." In Conference of Professional and Academic Women. Sixteen Reports on the Status of Women in the Professions, 6 p.

________. "Women in the Professions." In New York (City). Commission on Human Rights. Women's Role in Contemporary Society, pp. 350-7.

Satterthwaite, Laura H. "The Great Need of the Moral Crusade." In National Purity Congress, 1st, Baltimore, 1895. National Purity Congress, pp. 58-64.

Sawhill, Isabel. "Discrimination and Poverty Among Women Who Head Families." In Blaxall, M. Women and the Workplace, pp. 201-11.

Sawyer, Ruth. "Acceptance Paper--Newbery Medal 1937." In Miller, B. Newbery Medal Books, 1922-1955, pp. 152-6.

Sawyer, Winona Branch. "The Legal Profession for Women." In World's Congress of Representative Women, Chicago, 1893. Congress of Women, pp. 273-6.

Saxon, Elizabeth Lisle. "Testimony at a Hearing of the U.S. Senate, Committee on the Judiciary, January 23, 1880." In Stanton, E. History of Woman Suffrage, 3, 157-8.

______. "The Truth Shall Make You Free." In International Council of Women, 1888. Report, pp. 248-52.

Sayles, Lita Barney. "Co-operation, the Law of the New Civilization." In International Council of Women, 1888. Report, pp. 152-3.

Schaefer, Leah Cahan. "Frigidity." In Goldman, G. Modern Woman, pp. 165-77.

Schepps, Mollie. "Senators vs. Working Women." In Baxandall, R. America's Working Women, pp. 216-8.

Schiff, Dorothy. "Does the Health of Our Democracy Require a Change of Party in November: Panel Discussion." In New York Herald Tribune. Report of the 21st Annual Forum on Current Problems, pp. 220-4.

Schiffer, Lois. "Statement." In U.S. Congress. Senate. Committee on the Judiciary. Subcommittee on Constitutional Amendments. Abortion, pt. 4, 701-5.

Schiller, Anita R. "Sex and Library Careers." In Myers, M. Women in Librarianship, pp. 11-20.

Schiller, Lee Chambers. "Feminist Culture from 1790 to 1850: A Trans-Atlantic Community." In McGuigan, D. New Research on Women at the University of Michigan, pp. 58-69.

Schindler, Annemarie. "Professional and In-Service Training for Group Work." In National Conference of Social Work. Proceedings (1945), pp. 251-63.

Schisby, Marion. "Emigration Conditions in European Ports of Embarkation." In National Conference of Social Work. Proceedings (1926), pp. 571-6.

______. "Hindus and American Citizenship." In National Conference of Social Work. Proceedings (1927), pp. 579-81.

________. "Pending Immigration Legislation." In National Conference of Social Work. Proceedings (1928), pp. 459-9.

Schleman, Helen B. "Student Government: Human Trust." Vital Speeches, 34 (June 15, 1968), 527-9.

________. "Women Might Have Helped: Some Problems Ahead." Vital Speeches, 35 (August 15, 1969), 663-8.

Schletzer, Vera. "University of Minnesota, The Minnesota Plan." In Itasca Conference on the Continuing Education of Women, Itasca State Park, Minnesota, 1962. Education and a Woman's Life, pp. 120-3.

Schmalzreid, Beverly. "Day Care Services for Children of Campus Employees." In Furniss, W. Women in Higher Education, pp. 140-4.

Schmidt, Dolores Barracano. "The Great American Bitch." In Chmaj, B. American Women and American Studies, pp. 254-8.

Schmidt, Frances. "Values and Limitations of the Evaluation Process: As Seen by the Supervisor." In National Conference of Social Work. Proceedings (1940), pp. 629-38.

Schneiderman, Rose. "Remarks." In U. S. Women's Bureau. Proceedings of Women's Industrial Conference, pp. 138-40.

________. "Statement." In U. S. Congress. Senate. Committee on the Judiciary. Subcommittee on Constitutional Amendments. Equal Rights Amendment (1929), pp. 45-7.

________. "Statement." In U. S. Congress. Senate. Committee on the Judiciary. Subcommittee on Constitutional Amendments. Equal Rights (1931), pp. 32-6.

________. "Statement Against the Equal-Rights Amendment at the Senate Committee Hearings, 1931." In Kraditor, A. Up from the Pedestal, pp. 296-9.

________. "Triangle Fire Speech." In Martin, G. Madam Secretary, pp. 87-8. Also in Schneiderman, R. All For One, pp. 100-2.

________. "Triangle Memorial Speech." In Baxandall, R. America's Working Women, pp. 203-4. (Same as "Triangle Fire Speech").

________. "We Have Found You Wanting." In Stein, L. Out of the Sweatshop, pp. 196-7. (Same as "Triangle Fire Speech").

Schofield, Martha. "Slavery's Legacy of Impurity." In National Purity Congress, 1st, Baltimore, 1895. National Purity Congress, pp. 174-8.

Schoonmaker, Nancy. "The New Woman in the New Europe." In General Federation of Women's Clubs. Biennial Convention, 16 (1922), 240-1.

Schoonover, Jean Way. "Why Corporate America Fears Women: Business and the New Woman." Vital Speeches, 40 (April 15, 1974), 414-6.

Schorr, Lee. "Address." In Conference on Women in the War on Poverty, 1967. Proceedings, pp. 27-9.

Schpritzer, Felicia. "Public Testimony." In New York (City). Commission on Human Rights. Women's Role in Contemporary Society, pp. 168-72.

Schroeder, Patricia. "You Can Do It." In Tolchin, S. Clout, pp. 259-61.

Schryver, Anna A. "Nature Studies in the Home." In National Congress of Mothers. Work & Words, pp. 220-9.

Schuck, Victoria. "Statement." In U. S. Congress. House. Committee on Education and Labor. Special Subcommittee on Education. Discrimination Against Women, pp. 147-52.

Schulze, Susanne. "Group Living and the Dependent Child." In National Conference of Social Work. Proceedings (1946), pp. 387-97.

Schurr, Cathleen. "Statement." In U. S. Congress. House. Committee on the Judiciary. Subcommittee No. 4. Equal Rights for Men and Women 1971, pp. 450-62.

Schweitzer, Ada E. "What State Divisions of Child Hygiene Are Doing to Promote Child Health." In National Conference of Social Work. Proceedings (1921), pp. 175-9.

Sclair, Violet. "Leadership Through Young Minds." In New York Herald Tribune. Report of the 13th Annual Forum on Current Problems, pp. 65-6.

Scott, Ann. "Public Testimony." In New York (City). Commission on Human Rights. Women's Role in Contemporary Society, pp. 703-8.

________. "Statement." In U. S. Congress. House. Committee on Education and Labor. Special Subcommittee on Education. Discrimination Against Women, pp. 30-43.

Scott, K. Frances. "The Citizen's Responsibility; A Panel Discussion." In New York Herald Tribune. Report of the 18th Annual Forum on Current Problems, pp. 154, 177-8.

Scott, Masha. "Russian-American Wife." In New York Herald Tribune. Report of the 14th Annual Forum on Current Problems, pp. 74-7.

Scott, Melinda. "Address at Mass Meeting Before Calling on President Wilson, February, 1914." In Irwin, I. Story of the Woman's Party, pp. 57-8.

________. "Labor Legislation for Women." In U.S. Women's Bureau. Proceedings of the Women's Industrial Conference, pp. 110-20.

Scott, Nell. "Social Workers and Labor Unions: Social Work Touches an Organized Industry." In National Conference of Social Work. Proceedings (1929), pp. 354-64.

________. "Some New Problems for the Family Agency Arising Out of Industry." In National Conference of Social Work. Proceedings (1929), pp. 309-16.

Scott, Teresa. "Statement." In U.S. Congress. Senate. Committee on Human Resources. Subcommittee on Labor. Discrimination on the Basis of Pregnancy, pp. 294-8.

Scribner, Anne Townsend. "The Savings Society." In National Conference of Charities and Corrections. Proceedings (1887), pp. 143-9.

Scudder, Alice May. "Discussion of Woman as a Religious Teacher." In World's Congress of Representative Women, Chicago, 1893. A Historical Resume, pp. 279-81.

________. "Woman's Work in the Society of Christian Endeavor." In World's Congress of Representative Women, Chicago, 1893. A Historical Resume, pp. 840-3.

Scull, Sarah Amelia. "Study of Greek Art." In World's Congress of Representative Women, Chicago, 1893. Congress of Women, pp. 423-7.

Sears, Aimee. "Training for Successful Work with Immigrants: Training of American Workers." In National Conference of Social Work. Proceedings (1922), pp. 482-4.

Sears, Amelia. "Introductory Statement by the Chairman (On the Role of the Volunteer in Social Work.)" In National Conference of Social Work. Proceedings (1918), p. 677.

________. "Outline of the First Interview." In National Conference of Social Work. Proceedings (1921), pp. 249-52.

________. "The Psychology of Co-operation." In National Conference of Charities and Correction. Proceedings (1915), pp. 57-62.

Sechrest, Lee. "Ethnical Problems in Medical Experimentation Involving Women." In U.S. National Center for Health Services Research. Women and Their Health, pp. 40-4.

Segal, Tess. "Public Testimony." In New York (City). Commission on Human Rights. Women's Role in Contemporary Society, pp. 793-6.

Seidenberg, Faith. "Family Property, and Domicile Law in the State of New York." In New York (City). Commission on Human Rights. Women's Role in Contemporary Society, pp. 623-8.

Seifer, Nancy. "Statement." In U.S. Congress. Joint Economic Committee. Economic Problems of Women, pt. 4, 601-3.

Sellers, Georgianna. "Statement." In U.S. Congress. Senate. Committee on the Judiciary. Equal Rights 1970, pp. 285-7.

________. "Statement." In U.S. Congress. Senate. Committee on the Judiciary. Subcommittee on Constitutional Amendments. Women and the "Equal Rights" Amendment, pp. 201-7.

________. "Statement Before the Senate Judiciary Committee Hearings on the Equal-Rights Amendment (May 6, 1970)." In Baxandall, R. America's Working Women, pp. 379-81.

Sells, Dorothy. "Minimum Wage: Home Worker and Union Worker." In National Conference of Social Work. Proceedings (1936), pp. 365-74.

Seredy, Kate. "Acceptance Paper--Newbery Medal 1938." In Miller, B. Newbery Medal Books, 1922-1955, pp. 163-5.

Sergio, Lisa. "The Idea Takes Root." In U.S. Women's Bureau. American Woman--Her Changing Role, pp. 52-7.

Servis, Martha R. "Statement." In U.S. Congress. Senate. Committee on the Judiciary. Subcommittee on Constitutional Amendments. Equal Rights for Men and Women (1938), pp. 149-51.

Seton, Grace Thompson. "Report of the International Women Writers' Concave." In International Congress of Women, Chicago, 1933. Our Common Cause, Civilization, pp. 254-6.

Severance, Caroline Maria Seymour. "Argument and Appeal at the Women's Rights Convention in New York, September 1853." In Stanton, E. History of Woman Suffrage, 1, 569.

________. "Discussion of Paper on Kindergarten." In World's Congress of Representative Women, Chicago, 1893. A Historical Resume, p. 99.

________. "President's Address at the New England Convention of 1859." In Stanton, E. History of Woman Suffrage, 1, 262-3.

Sewall, May Wright. "Address at the Conference for Peace Workers." In American Peace Congress, 1st, New York, 1907. Proceedings, pp. 292-3.

________. "Address on Organization." In International Council of Women, 1888. Report, pp. 220-2.

________. "Address to the Senate Committee on Woman Suffrage, March 7, 1884." In Stanton, E. History of Woman Suffrage, 4, 36-7.

________. "Culture--Its Fruit and Its Price." In World's Congress of Representative Women, Chicago, 1893. Congress of Women, pp. 771-5.

________. "The Economy of Woman's Forces Through Organization." In World's Congress of Representative Women, Chicago, 1893. A Historical Resume, pp. 37-44.

________. "Fitness of Women to Become Citizens from the Standpoint of Education and Mental Development. Address to Senate Committee, February 15, 1898." In Stanton, E. History of Woman Suffrage, 4, 307-8.

________. "Higher Education for Women in the United States." In International Council of Women, 1888. Report, pp. 51-63.

________. "The International Council of Women." In American Peace Congress, 1st, New York, 1907. Proceedings, pp. 120-3.

________. "Opening Address." In World's Congress of Representative Women, Chicago, 1893. A Historical Resume, pp. 13-8.

________. "Remarks on Interest in Political Questions." In International Congress of Women, London, 1899, 5, 42-4.

________. "Tribute to Susan B. Anthony at Berkshire Historical Society Meeting, July, 1897." In Harper, I. The Life and Work of Susan B. Anthony, 2, 944.

________. "Tribute to Susan B. Anthony at Her 80th Birthday Celebration, February 15, 1900." In Harper, I. The Life and Work of Susan B. Anthony, 3, 1181-2.

________. "Woman's Part in the Promotion of Internationalism." In American Peace Congress, 3rd, Baltimore, 1911. Proceedings, pp. 417-21.

________. "Woman's Work in Education." In National Education Association. Journal of Proceedings & Addresses (1884), pp. 153-6.

Sexton, Virginia Staudt. "Psychological Fulfillment for the Woman." In Bier, W. Woman in Modern Life, pp. 249-62.

Seymour, Gertrude. "The Relation of Health Officers and Social Work." In National Conference of Social Work. Proceedings (1917), pp. 246-51.

Seymour, Mary F. "Occupations of Women to Date." In National Council of Women of the U. S., Washington, 1891. Transactions, pp. 250-2.

Shack, Barbara. "Statement." In U. S. Congress. Joint Economic Committee. Economic Problems of Women, pt. 4, 616-9.

________. "Testimony on Women's Access to Credit and Insurance." In U. S. Congress. Joint Economic Committee. Economic Problems of Women, pt. 1, 168-73.

Shaeffer, Ruth G. "The Policy Issues: Presentation I." In Blaxall, M. Women and the Workplace, pp. 253-8.

Shafer, Ruth I. "Welcome and Opening Message." In International Conference of Women Engineers and Scientists, 1st, New York. Focus for the Future, p. I-1.

Shainess, Natalie. "A Psychiatrist's View: Images of Woman--Past and Present, Overt and Obscured." In Morgan, R. Sisterhood Is Powerful, pp. 230-45.

Shambaugh, Jeannette. "Youth Plans for a Civilized World: Forum on the College Generation." In International Congress of Women, Chicago, 1933. Our Common Cause, Civilization, pp. 198-9.

Shannon, Monica. "Acceptance Paper--Newbery Medal 1935. Bewitched Mountains." In Miller, B. Newbery Medal Books, 1922-1955, pp. 131-4.

Shattuck, Harriette Robinson. "Address, Social Purity." In International Council of Women, 1888. Report, pp. 276-8.

________. "Remarks on Philanthropy." In International Council of Women, 1888. Report, p. 83.

Shaw, Anna Howard. "Address at a Hearing of the Senate Committee on Woman Suffrage, December 15, 1915." In Stanton, E. History of Woman Suffrage, 5, 462-3.

________. "Address at a Reception by President Wilson of a Delegation from the National American Woman Suffrage Association, December 8, 1913." In Stanton, E. History of Woman Suffrage, 5, 375.

________. "Address to the House Judiciary Committee, February 17, 1892." In Stanton, E. History of Woman Suffrage, 4, 199-200.

________. "Address to the House Judiciary Committee, 1900." In Stanton, E. History of Woman Suffrage, 4, 380-1.

________. "Address to the National American Woman Suffrage Convention of 1913." In Stanton, E. History of Woman Suffrage, 5, 371.

________. "Address to the National American Woman Suffrage Association Convention of 1917." In Stanton, E. History of Woman Suffrage, 5, 534-6.

________. "Anecdote About Miss Anthony at the National American Woman Suffrage Association Convention of 1900." In Harper, I. The Life and Work of Susan B. Anthony, 3, 1166. Also in Stanton, E. History of Woman Suffrage, 4, 351-2.

________. "Discussion of the Effects of Modern Changes in Industrial and Social Life on Woman's Marriage Prospects." In World's Congress of Representative Women, Chicago, 1893. A Historical Resume, pp. 599-602.

________. "Eulogy for Mary S. Anthony, at Her Funeral, February 7, 1906." In Harper, I. The Life and Work of Susan B. Anthony, 3, 1513.

________. "The Fate to Republics." In World's Congress of Representative Women, Chicago, 1893. Congress of Women, pp. 152-6.

________. "Final Tribute at Susan B. Anthony's Funeral, March 15, 1906." In Harper, I. The Life and Work of Susan B. Anthony, 3, 1440-3.

________. "From Address of Dr. Anna Howard Shaw When Resigning the Presidency of the National American Woman Suffrage Association, December 15, 1915." In Stanton, E. History of Woman Suffrage, 5, 750-2.

________. "God's Women." In National Council of Women of the U.S., Washington, 1891. Transactions, pp. 242-9.

________. "The Heavenly Vision. Sermon Preached March 24, 1888, at International Council of Women, Washington, D.C." In Stanton, E. History of Woman Suffrage, 4, 128-33.

________. "Let No Man Take Thy Crown. Sermon in Metzerott's Music Hall During the National American Woman Suffrage Association Convention of 1894." In Stanton, E. History of Woman Suffrage, 4, 229-31.

________. "Memorial Tributes to Mrs. Ralph Waldo Emerson and Anna Oliver at the National American Woman Suffrage Association Convention, 1893." In Stanton, E. History of Woman Suffrage, 4, 206-7.

________. "Opening Address at the National American Woman Suffrage Association Convention of 1914." In Stanton, E. History of Woman Suffrage, 5, 399.

________. "Opening Remarks." In National Council of Women of the U.S., Washington, 1891. Transactions, p. 20.

________. "President's Address at the National American Woman Suffrage Association Convention of 1905." In Stanton, E. History of Woman Suffrage, 5, 124-6.

________. "President's Address at the National American Woman Suffrage Association Convention of 1906." In Harper, I. The Life and Work of Susan B. Anthony, 3, 1387-8. Also in Stanton, E. History of Woman Suffrage, 5, 156-61.

________. "President's Address at the National American Woman Suffrage Association Convention of 1915." In Stanton, E. History of Woman Suffrage, 5, 445-6.

________. "Remarks on Emotionalism in Politics Given at the National American Woman Suffrage Association Convention in 1913." In O'Neill, W. The Woman Movement, pp. 183-4.

________. "Report of the Vice-President-At-Large to the National American Woman Suffrage Association Convention of 1896." In Stanton, E. History of Woman Suffrage, 4, 253-4.

________. "School Suffrage." In International Council of Women, 1888. Report, pp. 311-3.

________. "Sermon Preached in the Hall of Washington, on Sunday Morning, May 21st, 1893." In World Congress of Representative Women, Chicago, 1893. A Historical Resume, pp. 857-69.

________. "Sermon, the Heavenly Vision." In International Council of Women, 1888. Report, pp. 24-9. (Same as "The Heavenly Vision.")

________. "The Temperance Problem." In International Congress of Women, London, 1899, 7, 160-3.

________. "Tribute to Susan B. Anthony at Berkshire Historical Society Meeting, July, 1897." In Harper, I. The Life and Work of Susan B. Anthony, 2, 945-6.

________. "Tribute to Susan B. Anthony, at Her 80th Birthday Celebration, February 15, 1900." In Harper, I. The Life & Work of Susan B. Anthony, 3, 1187. Also in Stanton, E. History of Woman Suffrage, 4, 402-3.

________. "What is Americanism? Address at the National American Woman Suffrage Association Convention of 1916." In Stanton, E. History of Woman Suffrage, 5, 511-2.

________. "Women's Responsibility in the Peace Movement." In American Peace Congress, 1st, New York, 1907. Proceedings, pp. 285-7.

Shaw, Daisy K. "Statement." In U.S. Congress. House. Committee on Education and Labor. Special Subcommittee on Education. Discrimination Against Women, pp. 119-29.

Shaw, Thelma. "Community Representation and Participation in Community Organization." In National Conference of Social Work. Proceedings (1948), pp. 232-9.

Sheenan, Patricia Queenan. "Remarks." In Conference on Women in the War on Poverty, 2nd, 1968. Proceedings, pp. 46-9.

Sheffield, Ada Eliot. "Identifying Clue-Aspects in Social Case Work." In National Conference of Social Work. Proceedings (1921), pp. 242-7.

________. "Introductory Remarks (On Co-operative Credit)." In National Conference of Charities and Correction. Proceedings (1916), pp. 419-20.

________. "The Nature of the Stigma upon the Unmarried Mother and Her Child." In National Conference of Social Work. Proceedings (1920), pp. 119-22.

________. "Program of the Committee on Illegitimacy--Committee Report." In National Conference of Social Work. Proceedings (1919), pp. 74-81.

________. "Public Agencies as Public Carriers of Ideas." In National Conference of Social Work. Proceedings (1922), pp. 82-9.

________. "Public Relief Officials." In National Conference of Social Work. Proceedings (1924), pp. 539-44.

Sheibley, Evangeline. "Professional Education in the Agency Setting." In National Conference of Social Work. Proceedings (1947), pp. 448-60.

Sheldon, Elizabeth B. "The Educational Value of Applied Arts." In World's Congress of Representative Women, Chicago, 1893. Congress of Women, pp. 790-2.

Sheldon, May French. "An African Expedition." In World's Congress of Representative Women, Chicago, 1893. Congress of Women, pp. 131-4.

Shepperd, Juniata. "How Shall We Teach the Mother to Recognize the Necessity of a Sanitary Home?" In General Federation of Women's Clubs. Biennial Convention, 9 (1908), 271-3.

Sherif, Carolyn W. "Dreams and Dilemmas of Being a Woman Today." In Myers, M. Women in Librarianship, pp. 23-45.

________. "Females in the Competitive Process." In Harris, D. Women and Sport, pp. 115-39.

Sherman, Caroline B. "Which Way Agriculture?" In International Congress of Women, Chicago, 1933. Our Common Cause, Civilization, pp. 417-20.

Sherman, Caroline K. "Characteristics of the Modern Woman." In World's Congress of Representative Women, Chicago, 1893. Congress of Women, pp. 764-70.

Sherman, Julia Edwards. "New Field for Women." In World's Congress of Representative Women, Chicago, 1893. Congress of Women, pp. 670-3.

Sherwin, Belle. "Address of the President. The Way of the League." In League of Women Voters. Proceedings of the 7th Annual Convention, pp. 40-5.

________. "Among the Pillars of Society." In League of Women Voters. Meeting of the General Council, Washington, D. C., April 14, 1931, pp. 3-11.

________. "Facing the Future." In League of Women Voters. Biennial Convention, 3 (1932), 3-14.

________. "Pointing the Way in 1933. Address of the President." In League of Women Voters. Meeting of the General Council, Washington, D. C., April 25, 1933, pp. 3-8.

________. "The President's Address. Taking Part in Government." In League of Women Voters. Proceedings of the 8th National Convention, pp. 37-44.

________. "Ten Years of Growth." In League of Women Voters. Proceedings of the Tenth Anniversary Convention, Louisville, Kentucky, April 28-May 3, 1930, pp. 3-18.

Sherwin, Ella. "Statement." In U. S. Congress. Senate. Committee on the Judiciary. Subcommittee on Constitutional Amendments. Equal Rights Amendment (1945), p. 15.

Sherwood, Emily S. "Modern Charities and Church Work." In National Council of Women of the U. S., Washington, 1891. Transactions, pp. 112-6.

Sherwood, Kate Brownlee. "Insurance Against Piracy of Brains." In World's Congress of Representative Women, Chicago, 1893. A Historical Resume, pp. 158-61.

________. "The Past, Present, and Future of the Woman's Relief Corps." In World's Congress of Representative Women, Chicago, 1893. A Historical Resume, pp. 917-20.

________. "Woman's Relief Corps." In National Council of Women of the U. S., Washington, 1891. Transactions, pp. 94-7.

Shields, Laurie. "Statement." In U. S. Congress. House. Committee on Education and Labor. Subcommittee on Equal Opportunity. Equal Opportunity for Displaced Homemakers Act, pp. 42-5.

Shields, Louise F. "Migratory Workers in Agriculture." In National Conference of Social Work. Proceedings (1925), pp. 347-53.

Shontz, Eva Marshall. "A Call of Old Glory for Heroism." In American Peace Congress, 5th, San Francisco, 1915. Proceedings, pp. 117-23.

Shoup, Jane R. "Statement." In U. S. Congress. Senate. Committee on the Judiciary. Subcommittee on Constitutional Amendments. Abortion, pt. 3, pp. 186-90.

Shriver, Lucille H. "Statement." In U. S. Congress. House. Committee on the Judiciary. Subcommittee No. 4. Equal Rights for Men and Women 1971, pp. 140-8.

________. "Statement." In U. S. Congress. Senate. Committee on the Judiciary. Equal Rights 1970, pp. 329-35.

Shuler, Nettie Rogers. "Report of Campaigns and Surveys Committee to the National American Woman Suffrage Association Convention of 1918-1919." In Stanton, E. History of Woman Suffrage, 5, 554-8.

________. "Report of the Corresponding Secretary to the National American Woman Suffrage Association Convention of 1920." In Stanton, E. History of Woman Suffrage, 5, 601-8.

Shulman, Colette. "The Individual and the Collective." In Atkinson, D. Women in Russia, pp. 375-84.

Shuman, Cora V. "The Girl with a First Baby, Who Is Not Feeble-minded." In National Conference of Charities and Correction. Proceedings (1915), pp. 114-5.

Sibley, Agnes. "Paradox and Poetic Truth: The Beauty of Life." Vital Speeches, 32 (March 15, 1966), 344-51.

Sicherman, Barbara. "The Invisible Woman: The Case for Women's Studies." In Furniss, W. Women in Higher Education, pp. 155-73.

Sickels, Lucy M. "Industrial Training in Girls' Schools." In National Conference of Charities and Correction. Proceedings (1897), pp. 127-31.

________. "Woman's Influence in Juvenile Reformatories." In National Conference of Charities and Correction. Proceedings (1894), pp. 164-7.

Sidel, Ruth. "New Roles for Women in Health Care Delivery. Conditions in the People's Republic of China." In International Conference on Women in Health. Proceedings, pp. 103-11.

Siegel, Marian. "Testimony." In U.S. Congress. House. Select Committee to Crime. Drugs in Our Schools, pp. 757-62.

Sigworth, Heather. "Issues in Nepotism Rules." In Furniss, W. Women in Higher Education, pp. 110-20.

Silva, Vilma. "Public Testimony." In New York (City). Commission on Human Rights. Women's Role in Contemporary Society, p. 319.

Silver, Clara. "Address Before State Suffrage Hearing, Albany, New York, February, 1907." In Blatch, H. Challenging Years, p. 97.

Simkhovitch, Mary Melinda Kingsbury. "Address of Mrs. Simkhovitch." In Bryn Mawr College. Carola Woerishoffer, Her Life and Work, pp. 83-92.

________. "The Case Work Plane." In National Conference of Charities and Correction. Proceedings (1909), pp. 137-49.

________. "The Enlarged Function of the Public School." In National Conference of Charities and Correction. Proceedings (1904), pp. 471-86.

________. "The Place of Recreation in the Settlement Program." In National Conference of Social Work. Proceedings (1930), pp. 372-7.

________. "Remarks at Jane Addams Memorial Service." In National Conference of Social Work. Proceedings (1935), pp. 5-8.

________. "Standards and Tests of Efficiency in Settlement Work." In National Conference of Charities and Correction. Proceedings (1911), pp. 299-305.

Simmons, Adele. "Education and Ideology in Nineteenth-century America: The Response of Educational Institutions to the Changing Role of Women." In Carroll, B. Liberating Women's History, pp. 115-26.

Simmons, Lorri D. "Testimony." In U.S. Congress. House. Committee on Small Business. Subcommittee on Minority Enterprise and General Oversight. Women in Business, pp. 50-4.

Simon, Dorothy M. "Panelist Statement." In M.I.T. Symposium on American Women in Science and Engineering, 1964. Women and the Scientific Professions, pp. 41-4.

Sindona, Michele. "From Multi-nationals to Cosmo-corporations: The World Economic Welfare." Vital Speeches, 41 (September 1, 1957), 689-94.

________. "The Phantom Petrodollar: A Deposit Withdrawal Program." Vital Speeches, 41 (June 15, 1975), 528-31.

Skelsey, Alice. "Mrs. Homemaker--Mrs. Wonderful: The Myths from Women's Lib." Vital Speeches, 39 (February 15, 1973), 286-8.

Skiles, Jacqueline. "Public Testimony." In New York (City). Commission on Human Rights. Women's Role in Contemporary Society, pp. 766-7.

Skinner, Cornelia Otis. "Life Is Simple. Find the Courage to Maximize Your Lives." Vital Speeches, 16 (August 15, 1950), 661-3.

Sklar, Kathryn K. "Four Levels of Women's History." In McGuigan, D. New Research on Women at the University of Michigan, pp. 7-10.

Slagle, Eleanor Clark. "Occupational Therapy." In General Federation of Women's Clubs. Biennial Convention, 16 (1922), 366-8.

Slaughter-Morton, Rosalie. "A Higher Standard of Morality." In International Congress of Women, Toronto, 1909. Report, 1, 69-87.

Sloane, Madeleine Edison. "Health Security for Mother and Child--Discussion." In International Congress of Women, Chicago, 1933. Our Common Cause, Civilization, pp. 606-8.

Slocum, Flora. "Life Insurance in Dependent Families." In National Conference of Social Work. Proceedings (1929), pp. 282-5.

Smalley, Ruth. "The School Social Worker and the Social Development of the Child." In National Conference of Social Work. Proceedings (1945), pp. 284-93.

Smith, Abby Hadassah. "Abby H. Smith's Speech Before the Rhode Island Suffrage Society at Its Annual Meeting." In Smith, J. Abby Smith and Her Cows, pp. 48-9.

________. "Abby Smith's Appeal to Her Townsmen." In Smith, J. Abby Smith and Her Cows, pp. 32-3.

________. "Address at the Dayville (Killingly) Fair and Festival, August 27, 1875." In Smith, J. Abby Smith and Her Cows, pp. 60-1.

________. "Address at the Melrose Convention." In Smith, J. Abby Smith and Her Cows, pp. 52-3.

________. "Miss Abby Smith's Address at Hearing Before the Committee on Woman Suffrage, Hartford, Connecticut." In Smith, J. Abby Smith and Her Cows, pp. 41-2.

________. "Speech of Abby Smith, July 11, 1874." In Smith, J. Abby Smith and Her Cows, p. 44.

________. "Speech of Miss Abby H. Smith, of Glastonbury, Before the Town Meeting of That Place November 5th 1873." In Smith, J. Abby Smith and Her Cows, pp. 9-11.

Smith, Anne. "Group Play in a Hospital Environment." In National Conference of Social Work. Proceedings (1935), pp. 346-52.

Smith, Carrie Weaver. "Can the Institution Equip the Girl for Normal Social Relationships?" In National Conference of Social Work. Proceedings (1925), pp. 108-16.

________. "The Elimination of the Reformatory." In National Conference of Social Work. Proceedings (1921), pp. 127-32.

________. "The Unadjusted Girl." In National Conference of Social Work. Proceedings (1920), pp. 180-3.

________. "Venereal Disease Problems in Institutions." In National Conference of Social Work. Proceedings (1928), pp. 432-42.

Smith, Clara Holbrook. "Home Side of Progress." In World's Congress of Representative Women, Chicago, 1893. Congress of Women, pp. 332-6.

Smith, Constance. "Radcliffe Institute for Independent Study." In Itasca Conference on the Continuing Education of Women, Itasca State Park, Minnesota, 1962. Education and a Woman's Life, pp. 111-6.

Smith, Elizabeth Oakes. "Comments at the Syracuse National Convention, September, 1852." In Stanton, E. History of Woman Suffrage, 1, 522-4.

________. "A Dissolution of the Existing Social Compact." In Tanner, L. Voices from Women's Liberation, p. 67.

Smith, Esther. "Public Testimony." In New York (City). Commission on Human Rights. Women's Role in Contemporary Society, pp. 547-9.

Smith, Ethel M. "Report of the Congressional Committee to the National American Woman Suffrage Association Convention of 1915." In Stanton, E. History of Woman Suffrage, 5, 448-50.

Smith, Eva Munson. "Woman in Sacred Song." In World's Congress of Representative Women, Chicago, 1893. Congress of Women, pp. 416-22.

Smith, Frances A. "Continued Care of Families." In National Conference of Charities and Correction. Proceedings (1895), pp. 87-93.

Smith, Gertrude A. "What Are the Case-work Needs of the Aged?" In National Conference of Social Work. Proceedings (1938), pp. 587-95.

Smith, Hannah Whitall. "Address at a Meeting of the National Woman Suffrage Association, Philadelphia, 1882." In Stanton, E. History of Woman Suffrage, 3, 230.

________. "World's Woman's Temperance Union." In International Council of Women, 1888. Report, pp. 114-6.

Smith, Ida B. Wise. "Chairman's Introduction. Joy in Living." In International Congress of Women, Chicago, 1933. Our Common Cause, Civilization, pp. 171-2.

Smith, Jane Norman. "Statement." In U.S. Congress. House. Committee on the Judiciary. Equal Rights Amendment to the Constitution (1932), pp. 6-9.

________. "Statement." In U.S. Congress. Senate. Committee on the Judiciary. Subcommittee on Constitutional Amendments. Equal Rights for Men and Women (1938), pp. 151-3.

Smith, Julia Eveling. "Address at the Melrose Convention." In Smith, J. Abby Smith and Her Cows, pp. 53-4.

________. "Address to Congressional Committee on Privileges and Elections, January, 1878." In Stanton, E. History of Woman Suffrage, 3, 76.

________. "Address--Worchester Convention, February 20, 1874." In Smith, J. Abby Smith and Her Cows, p. 30.

________. "Taxation Without Representation." In Smith, J. Abby Smith and Her Cows, p. 49.

________. "Testimony at a Hearing of the U.S. Senate, Committee on the Judiciary, January 3, 1880." In Stanton, E. History of Woman Suffrage, 3, 156-7.

Smith, Julia Holmes. "The Mourning Garb." In Association for the Advancement of Women. "Truth, Justice, and Honor," pp. 18-28.

Smith, Lillian Eugenia. "The Race Question: A Problem Above Politics." In New York Herald Tribune. Report of the 13th Annual Forum on Current Problems, pp. 193-7.

________. "Ten Years from Today. We Are Changing Rapidly, Without Violence." Vital Speeches, 17 (August 15, 1951), 669-72.

Smith, Madeline. "Public Testimony." In New York (City). Commission on Human Rights. Women's Role in Contemporary Society, pp. 158-60, 549-52.

Smith, Margaret Chase. "Address on Nuclear Credibility to Senate and President, September 21, 1961." In Smith, M. Declaration of Conscience, pp. 261-72.

________. "Campaign Speech on U.S. Air Force, September 12, 1954." In Smith, M. Declaration of Conscience, pp. 153-62.

________. "Closure of Kittery-Portsmouth Naval Shipyard." In Smith, M. Declaration of Conscience, pp. 499-501.

________. "A Declaration of Conscience: June 1, 1950." In Smith, M. Declaration of Conscience, pp. 12-7.

________. "Election Eve Campaign Speech, 1st Senate Campaign, November 1948." In Smith, M. Declaration of Conscience, pp. 113-7.

________. "Final Statement at End of Television Debate with Eleanor Roosevelt, November 4, 1956." In Smith, M. Declaration of Conscience, pp. 209-10.

________. "Growing Confusion. Need for Patriotic Thinking." Vital Speeches, 16 (June 1, 1950), 552-4.

________. "How Much Should Government Do--On Health, Education and Housing? Panel Discussion." In New York Herald Tribune. Report of the 18th Annual Forum on Changing Problems, pp. 114-6.

________. "Impatience and Generosity. Comments on European and Asian Trips." Vital Speeches, 21 (May 15, 1955), 1230-3.

________. "In Pursuit of the Golden Age for Women." In Smith, M. Declaration of Conscience, pp. 98-101.

________. "The Kennedy Twist." In Smith, M. Declaration of Conscience, pp. 293-306.

________. "Margaret Smith's Answer to a Smear." In Smith, M. Declaration of Conscience, pp. 451-7.

________. "Nuclear Credibility." In Smith, M. Declaration of Conscience, pp. 476-7.

________. "Opening and Closing Statements at a Debate with Lucia Cormier, WCSH-TV, Portland, Maine, November 6, 1960." In Smith, M. Declaration of Conscience, pp. 252-3.

________. "Presidential Candidacy Announcement." In Smith, M. Declaration of Conscience, pp. 346-72.

________. "2nd Address on Nuclear Credibility, Senate, September 21, 1962." In Smith, M. Declaration of Conscience, pp. 275-84.

________. "Second Declaration of Conscience." In Smith, M. Declaration of Conscience, pp. 431-5.

________. "Senate Speech on Ratification of the Nuclear Test Ban Treaty." In Smith, M. Declaration of Conscience, pp. 322-6.

________. "Senate Speech on Safeguard ABM System." In Smith, M. Declaration of Conscience, pp. 399-404.

________. "Senate Speech on Support for Medical Research, January 12, 1956." In Smith, M. Declaration of Conscience, pp. 173-93.

________. "Speech on Closure of Kittery-Portsmouth Naval Shipyard." In Smith, M. Declaration of Conscience, pp. 342-5.

________. "Speech on the Nuclear Test Ban Treaty." In Smith, M. Declaration of Conscience, pp. 315-8.

________. "The Square." In Smith, M. Declaration of Conscience, pp. 422-4.

________. "Statement at the Senate Armed Forces Hearings on the Promotion of Jimmy Stewart to Brigadier General, May 2, 1957." In Smith, M. Declaration of Conscience, pp. 226-7.

________. "This I Believe." In Smith, M. Declaration of Conscience, pp. 446-8.

________. "U.S. Faces Choice Between Anarchy and Repression." *U.S. News & World Report*, 68 (June 15, 1970), 45-6. (Same as "Second Declaration of Conscience.")

________. "Woman, the Key Individual of Our Democracy. Think Well, Then Speak Your Mind." *Vital Speeches*, 19 (August 15, 1953), 657-9.

Smith, Marion E. "Training Schools for Nurses--Trained Nurses in Hospitals for the Insane." In National Conference of Charities and Correction. *Proceedings* (1894), pp. 102-5.

Smith, Marjorie J. "Social Case Work in Public Assistance." In National Conference of Social Work. *Proceedings* (1944), pp. 319-25.

Smith, Mary Stuart. "The Virginia Woman of Today." In World's Congress of Representative Women, Chicago, 1893. *Congress of Women*, pp. 408-11.

Smith, May Riley. "The Voice of the Forest." In General Federation of Women's Clubs. *Biennial Convention*, 9 (1908), 242-52.

Smith, Virginia Thrall. "The Co-operation of Women in Philanthropic and Reformatory Work." In National Conference of Charities and Correction. *Proceedings* (1891), pp. 230-41.

________. "The Economy of the State in the Care of Dependent and Neglected Children." In National Conference of Charities and Correction. *Proceedings* (1887), pp. 238-42.

________. "The Kindergarten." In World's Congress of Representative Women, Chicago, 1893. *Congress of Women*, pp. 178-80.

________. "Report of the Committee on Preventive Work Among Children." In National Conference of Charities and Correction. *Proceedings* (1886), pp. 124-31.

________. "The Work of Temporary Homes and of Finding Homes for Children in Connecticut." In National Conference of Charities and Correction. *Proceedings* (1885), pp. 210-9.

Smith, Zilpha Drew. "The Education of the Friendly Visitor." In National Conference of Charities and Correction. *Proceedings* (1892), pp. 445-9.

________. "Field Work." In National Conference of Charities and Correction. *Proceedings* (1915), pp. 622-6.

________. "How to Get and Keep Visitors." In National Conference of Charities and Correction. *Proceedings* (1887), pp. 156-62.

________. "Introduction to Discussion on Needy Families in Their Homes." In National Conference of Charities and Correction. *Proceedings* (1901), pp. 284-9.

________. "Possibilities of the Social Workers' Club." In National Conference of Charities and Correction. *Proceedings* (1911), pp. 388-9.

________. "Report of the Committee on the Organization of Charity." In National Conference of Charities and Correction. *Proceedings* (1888), pp. 120-30.

________. "Volunteer Visiting." In National Conference of Charities and Correction. Proceedings (1884), pp. 69-72.

Smith-Rosenberg, Carroll. "New Way of Viewing Key Questions for Investigation. Historical: Women, History and New Insights." In U.S. National Center for Health Services Research. Women and Their Health, pp. 53-8.

Smythe, Mabel M. "Feminism and Black Liberation." In Furniss, W. Women in Higher Education, pp. 279-81.

Snedden, Mary C. "The Eastern Star, Its Origin, Progress, and Development." In World's Congress of Representative Women, Chicago, 1893. A Historical Resume, pp. 920-4.

Solenberger, Edith Reeves. "Some Needed Readjustments in Special Fields of Child Welfare: The Extension of Non-Institutional Care for Crippled Children." In National Conference of Social Work. Proceedings (1921), pp. 105-8.

Sollars, Sarah V. "Statement." In U.S. Congress. House. Committee on the Judiciary. Subcommittee No. 1. Equal Rights Amendment (1948), pp. 149-51.

Solomon, Hannah Greenebaum. "Address." In Jewish Women's Congress. Papers, pp. 10-2, 166-7.

Sommer, Anita. "Testimony." In U.S. Congress. House. Select Committee on Crime. Drugs in Our Schools, pp. 590-1.

Sommer, Tish. "Statement." In U.S. Congress. House. Committee on Education and Labor. Subcommittee on Equal Opportunity. Equal Opportunity for Displaced Homemakers Act, pp. 48-51.

________. "Statement." In U.S. Congress. House. Select Committee on Aging. Subcommittee on Retirement Income and Employment. Social Security Inequities Against Women, pp. 1-13, 17-20.

________. "Statement." In U.S. Congress. Senate. Special Committee on Aging. Future Directions in Social Security, pt. 18, 1679-82.

Sorensen, Virginia. "Newbery Award Acceptance--1957." In Kingman, L. Newbery and Caldecott Medal Books, 1956-1965, pp. 34-42.

Soule, Caroline A. "A Collegiate Education for Women, and the Necessity of a Woman-Professor in the Mixed College." In Association for the Advancement of Women. Congress of Women, 1st. Papers, pp. 61-7.

Spain, Frances Lander. "Upon the Shining Mountains." ALA Bulletin, 34 (July-August, 1960), 599-602.

Spain, Jayne Baker. "Job Stereotyping: A Time for Change." Vital Speeches, 39 (July 1, 1973), 549-51.

________. "A Woman Could Be President: It's Getting More Reasonable." Vital Speeches, 37 (April 1, 1977), 357-9.

Spaulding, Edith R. "Mental and Physical Factors in Prostitution." In National Conference of Charities and Correction. Proceedings (1914), pp. 222-9.

________. "The Short-Term Offender." In National Conference of Charities and Correction. Proceedings (1914), pp. 52-3.

________. "The Training School of Psychiatric Social Work at Smith College." In National Conference of Social Work. Proceedings (1919), pp. 606-10.

Speare, Elizabeth George. "Newbery Award Acceptance--1959." In Kingman, L. Newbery and Caldecott Medal Books, 1956-1965, pp. 72-7.

________. "Newbery Award Acceptance--1962: Report of a Journey." In Kingman, L. Newbery and Caldecott Medal Books, 1956-1965, pp. 111-5.

Spelman, Judith Ann. "Analysis of the Role of Women in Health Care Decisionmaking. A U.S. Response to a Look at Poland. The Class Nature of Decisionmaking Among Women." In International Conference on Women in Health. Proceedings, pp. 151-3.

Spencer, Anna Carpenter Garlin. "Advantages and Dangers of Organization." In World's Congress of Representative Women, Chicago, 1893. Congress of Women, pp. 170-7.

________. "Duty to the Women of Our New Possessions." In Kraditor, A. Up from the Pedestal, pp. 266-73.

________. "Fitness of Women to Become Citizens from the Standpoint of Moral Development. Address to Senate Committee, February 15, 1898." In Stanton, E. History of Woman Suffrage, 4, 308-9.

________. "Our Duty to the Women of Our New Possessions. Address to the National American Woman Suffrage Association Convention of 1899." In Stanton, E. History of Woman Suffrage, 4, 328-31. (Same as "Duty to the Women of Our New Possessions.")

________. "Remarks at the Conference of Delegates." In American Peace Congress, 1st, New York, 1907. Proceedings, pp. 318.

________. "Social Work Under Church Auspices, and Social Work Under Community Auspices: From the Standpoint of the Urban Community." In National Conference of Social Work. Proceedings (1923), pp. 258-9.

________. "The Sociological and Practical Value of Our Accumulated Knowledge." In National Conference of Charities and Correction. Proceedings (1904), pp. 223-33.

________. "State Control and Social Care of the Vicious and Dependent Classes: Woman's Share in the Work." In National Council of Women of the U.S., Washington, 1891. Transactions, pp. 56-69.

________. "What Machine Dominated Industry Means in Relation to Women's Work: The Need of New Training and Apprenticeship for Girls." In National Conference of Charities and Correction. Proceedings (1910), pp. 201-11.

________. "Women of Our New Possessions. Speech Delivered in 1898." In Beard, M. America Through Women's Eyes, pp. 280-2. (Same as "Duty to the Women of Our New Possessions.")

Spencer, Sara A. "Report from the District of Columbia." In Conference on Charities and Correction. Proceedings (1881), p. 55.

________. "Report of District of Columbia." In National Conference of Charities and Correction. Proceedings (1882), pp. 164-9.

Spencer, Sara J. "Co-education of the Sexes, Based upon the Law of Sex." In Association for the Advancement of Women. Congress of Women, 1st. Papers, pp. 52-5.

Spencer, Sue. "Major Issues in Social Work Education." In National Conference of Social Work. Proceedings (1947), pp. 435-47.

Spiegel, Marjorie M. "Youth Plans for a Civilized World: Forum on the College Generation." In International Congress of Women, Chicago, 1933. Our Common Cause, Civilization, pp. 199-200.

Spiegel, Rose. "Depressions and the Feminine Situation." In Goldman, G. Modern Woman, pp. 189-204.

Spink, Mary A. "Psychopathic Hospitals." In National Conference of Charities and Correction. Proceedings (1903), pp. 428-34.

Spinks, Dorothy Matthews. "Statement." In U.S. Congress. House. Committee on the Judiciary. Subcommittee No. 1. Equal Rights Amendment (1948), pp. 68-9.

Spohn, Adelaide. "To What Shall We Hold Fast in Nutrition During Periods of Lower Income?" In National Conference of Social Work. Proceedings (1932), pp. 167-79.

Spohn, Roberta. "Public Testimony." In New York (City). Commission on Human Rights. Women's Role in Contemporary Society, pp. 516-21.

Sporborg, Constance A. "How Can Women Fight Marijuana?" In New York Herald Tribune. Report of the 8th Annual Forum on Current Problems, pp. 34-6.

________. "Public Forums and Public Opinion." In New York Herald Tribune. Report of the 5th Annual Forum on Current Problems, pp. 246-8.

________. "The Struggle for Security." In New York Herald Tribune. Report of the 4th Annual Women's Conference on Current Problems, pp. 242-4.

Springen, Phyllis Jones. "The Dimensions of the Oppression of Women: Unequal Pay for Equal Work." Vital Speeches, 37 (February 15, 1971), 265-7.

Springer, Adele I. "Woman's Role in the Machinery of Government. Past, Present and Future." Vital Speeches, 23 (April 1, 1957), 373-6.

Springer, Gertrude. "The Responsibility of the Social Worker in a Democracy." In National Conference of Social Work. Proceedings (1942), pp. 57-65.

Springer, Maida. "Statement." In U.S. Congress. Senate. Committee on the Judiciary. Subcommittee on Constitutional Amendments. Equal Rights Amendment (1945), p. 122.

Stabler, Dorothy. "The Effect of Staff Turnover on Families Under Care, as Demonstrated in Changes of Plan and Treatment and General Tempo of Work." In National Conference of Social Work. Proceedings (1927), pp. 257-61.

Stack, Carol B. "Sex Roles and Survival Strategies in an Urban Black Community." In Rosaldo, M. Woman, Culture, and Society, pp. 113-28.

Staley, Sara G. "Address of the Ladies' Anti-slavery Society of Delaware, Ohio to the Convention of Disfranchised Citizens of Ohio." In Aptheker, H. A Documentary History of the Negro People in the U.S. from Colonial Times Through the Civil War, pp. 380-3.

Stanley, Julia P. "Coming Out." In Conference on the University and the Gay Experience. Proceedings, pp. 81-7.

Stanton, Elizabeth Cady. "Address." In International Council of Women, 1888. Report, pp. 322-5.

________. "Address at a Hearing of the Joint Committee of Congress of the District of Columbia, January 22, 1870." Revolution, 5 (January 27, 1870), 58-60.

________. "Address at Hearings by the Congressional Committee on Privileges and Elections, January 1878." In Stanton, E. History of Woman Suffrage, 3, 80-93.

________. "Address at the Decade Meeting, on Marriage and Divorce." In Davis, P. A History of the National Woman's Rights Movement, pp. 60-83.

________. "Address at the 1st Annual Meeting of the Woman's State Temperance Society, Rochester, N.Y., June 1, 1853." In Harper, I. The Life and Work of Susan B. Anthony, 1, 92.

________. "Address at the 1st Meeting of the American Equal Rights Association, May 10, 1866." In Stanton, E. History of Woman Suffrage, 2, 1974.

________. "Address at the First Suffrage Convention Held in Washington, D. C., 1869." In Catt, C. Woman Suffrage and Politics, pp. 68-9.

________. "Address at the 10th National Woman's Rights Convention in Cooper Institute, New York, May 10, 1860." In Lutz, Alma. Created Equal, pp. 114-5. (Same as "Address at the Decade Meeting.")

________. "Address Before the New York State Legislature, February 1854." In Lutz, Alma. Created Equal, pp. 92-3.

________. "Address on Divorce Resolutions at the 10th National Woman's Rights Convention, New York, May 10-11, 1860." In Harper, I. Life and Work of Susan B. Anthony, 1, 193. Also in Stanton, E. History of Woman Suffrage, 1, 716-22. (Same as "Address at the Decade Meeting, On Marriage and Divorce.")

________. "Address to the National Woman's Rights Convention, Held in Washington, D. C., January 1869." In Stanton, E. History of Woman Suffrage, 2, 348-55. (Same as "Address at the First Suffrage Convention Held in Washington, D. C., 1869.")

________. "Address to the New York State Legislature, 1854." In Schneir, Miriam. Feminism, pp. 110-6. (Same as "Address Before the New York State Legislature, February 1854.")

________. "Address to the New York State Legislature, 1860." In Schneir, M. Feminism, pp. 117-21. (Same as "Excerpt from 2nd Address to the New York Legislature, March 19, 1860.")

________. "Address to the New York State Legislature, January 23, 1867." In Stanton, E. History of Woman Suffrage, 2, 271-82.

________. "Address to the Senate Committee on Woman Suffrage, April 2, 1888." In Stanton, E. History of Woman Suffrage, 4, 138-9.

________. "Address to the Senate Judiciary Committee, January 17, 1872." In Stanton, E. History of Woman Suffrage, 2, 506-13.

________. "Address to the Senate Select Committee on Woman Suffrage, February 8, 1890." In Stanton, E. History of Woman Suffrage, 4, 158-61.

________. "The Civil and Social Evolution of Woman." In World's Congress of Representative Women, Chicago, 1893. A Historical Resume, pp. 327-9. (Read by Susan B. Anthony).

________. "Closing Address." In International Council of Women, 1888. Report, pp. 431-8.

________. "The Co-education of the Sexes." In Association for the Advancement of Women. Congress of Women, 1st. Papers, pp. 39-52.

________. "Concluding Remarks at the Anniversary Meeting of the Woman's National Loyal League, May 12, 1864." In Stanton, E. History of Woman Suffrage, 2, 87.

________. "The Degradation of Disfranchisement. Read to the National American Woman Suffrage Association by Susan B. Anthony, February 26, 1891." In Stanton, E. History of Woman Suffrage, 4, 176-8.

_______. "The Demand for the Vote." In Scott, A. The American Woman, pp. 90-4.

_______. "Elizabeth Cady Stanton on the Politics of Woman Suffrage." In Scott, A. One Half the People, pp. 60-7. (Same as "Address to the National Woman's Rights Convention ...").

_______. "The Ethics of Suffrage." In World's Congress of Representative Women, Chicago, 1893. A Historical Resume, pp. 482-8.

_______. "Eulogy for Lucretia Mott--Memorial Service in 1881." In Beard, M. America Through Women's Eyes, pp. 182-3.

_______. "Excerpt from Second Address to the New York Legislature, March 19, 1860." In Lutz, Alma. Created Equal, p. 110.

_______. "The Friendships of Women." In Harper, I. The Life and Work of Susan B. Anthony, 2, 667.

_______. "Lucretia Mott: Eulogy at the Memorial Services Held in Washington by the National Woman Suffrage Association, January 19, 1881." In Stanton, E. History of Woman Suffrage, 1, 407-31. (Same as "Eulogy for Lucretia Mott.")

_______. "The Matriarchate, or Mother-age." In National Council of Women of the U.S., Washington, 1891. Transactions, pp. 218-27.

_______. "Mrs. Stanton's Address (at the 1st Annual Meeting of the Woman's State Temperance Society, Rochester, 1853)." In Stanton, E. History of Woman Suffrage, 1, 493-7. (Same as "Address at the 1st Annual Meeting of the Woman's State Temperance Society.")

_______. "Mrs. Stanton's Address to the Legislature of the State of New York Read at the Albany, N.Y., Convention, February 1854." In Stanton, E. History of Woman Suffrage, 1, 595-605. (Same as "Address Before the New York State Legislature, February 1854.")

_______. "On Labor." In DuBois, Ellen. "On Labor and Free Love: Two Unpublished Speeches of Elizabeth Cady Stanton." Signs, 1 (Autumn, 1975), 260-3.

_______. "On Marriage and Divorce." In DuBois, Ellen. "On Labor and Free Love: Two Unpublished Speeches of Elizabeth Cady Stanton." Signs, 1 (Autumn, 1975), 265-8.

_______. "Opening Address to the National American Woman Suffrage Association Convention, February 18, 1890." In Stanton, E. History of Woman Suffrage, 4, 165-6.

_______. "Our Young Girls." In Papachristou, J. Women Together, p. 112.

_______. "President's Address at New York State Temperance Convention, Rochester, New York, April 20, 1852." In Stanton, E. History of Woman Suffrage, 1, 481-3.

_______. "President's Address at the Eleventh National Woman's Rights Convention, May 10, 1866." In Stanton, E. History of Woman Suffrage, 2, 153-4.

_______. "President's Address to the National Woman Suffrage Association Convention, May 10, 1870." Revolution, 5 (May 19, 1870), 305-7.

________. "Remarks on Religion at the National Woman Suffrage Association Convention, January 1885." In Stanton, E. History of Woman Suffrage, 4, 60-1.

________. "Second Address to the New York State Legislature, Judiciary Committee, February 18, 1860." In Stanton, E. History of Woman Suffrage, 1, 679-85. (Same as "Address to the New York State Legislature, 1860.")

________. "The Solitude of Self. Address to the Senate Committee on Woman Suffrage, February 10, 1892." In Lerner, G. The Female Experience, pp. 490-3. Also in Schneir, M. Feminism, pp. 157-9. Also in Stanton, E. History of Woman Suffrage, 4, 189-91.

________. "Speech at the National Woman Suffrage Association Convention May 1872." In Lutz, A. Created Equal, pp. 219-20.

________. "Speech Before Congressional Committee on the District of Columbia, 1870." In Stanton, E. History of Woman Suffrage, 2, 411-4. (Same as "Address at a Hearing of the Joint Committee of Congress of the District of Columbia, January 22, 1870.")

________. "Speech Before the Legislature, 1860." In Martin, W. The American Sisterhood, pp. 69-78. (Same as "Address to the New York State Legislature, 1860.")

________. "Stanton, Defends Woodhull." In Papachristou, J. Women Together, p. 76.

________. "Stanton's Address." In Papachristou, J. Women Together, p. 21. (Same as "Mrs. Stanton's Address (at the 1st Annual Meeting of the Woman's State Temperance Society, Rochester, 1853).")

________. "Statement at the 1st Woman's State Temperance Convention in Corinthian Hall, Rochester, on April 20, 1852." In Lutz, A. Created Equal, pp. 77-8. (Same as "Address at the 1st Annual Meeting of the Woman's State Temperance Society.")

________. "This is the Negro's Hour." In Tanner, L. Voices from Women's Liberation, pp. 81-2. (Same as "Address at the 1st Meeting of the American Equal Rights Association, May 10, 1866.")

________. "Toast to the Women of Nebraska, at Celebration in Lincoln, Nebraska, 1875." In Lutz, A. Created Equal, p. 198.

________. "Welcoming Address at the International Council of Women, March 25, 1888." In International Council of Women, 1888. Report, pp. 31-9. Also in Stanton, E. History of Woman Suffrage, 4, 133-5.

________. "Womanliness." In Schneir, M. Feminism, pp. 155-6.

Stanton, Helen A. "Public Testimony." In New York (City). Commission on Human Rights. Women's Role in Contemporary Society, pp. 300-2.

Starkweather, Louise A. "Sod Busting for Social Work in White Pine County, Nevada." In National Conference of Social Work. Proceedings (1939), pp. 482-4.

________. "Woman as an Investor." In World's Congress of Representative Women, Chicago, 1893. Congress of Women, pp. 62-6.

Stead, Bette Ann. "Why Help Women into Careers? A Look at Today's Reality." Vital Speeches, 44 (December 15, 1977), 157-60.

________. "Women in Management: Gaining Acceptance on an Equal Basis." Vital Speeches, 41 (July 15, 1975), 589-91.

Stearns, Nancy. "Access to Abortion and Family Planning." In New York (City). Commission on Human Rights. Women's Role in Contemporary Society, pp. 499-504.

Stebbins, Catharine A. "Testimony at a Hearing of the House Committee on the Judiciary, January 24, 1880." In Stanton, E. History of Woman Suffrage, 3, 162-3.

Stecker, H. Dora. "Some Desirable Goals for Motion Pictures." In National Conference of Social Work. Proceedings (1927), pp. 360-70.

Steinbrecher, Ann. "Youth Plans for a Civilized World: Forum on the College Generation." In International Congress of Women, Chicago, 1933. Our Common Cause, Civilization, pp. 202-3.

Steinem, Gloria. "Statement." In U.S. Congress. Senate. Committee on the Judiciary. Subcommittee on Constitutional Amendments. Women and the "Equal Rights" Amendment, pp. 102-6, 111-4.

________. "Woman and Attitudes Toward War, National Priorities, and Values." In New York (City). Commission on Human Rights. Women's Role in Contemporary Society, pp. 642-7.

Steinmann, Anne. "Public Testimony." In New York (City). Commission on Human Rights. Women's Role in Contemporary Society, pp. 153-6.

Stephenson, Marion. "Blind People Do Not Fear Snakes. Advertising: Is It Legal, Moral & Ethical?" Vital Speeches, 37 (July 15, 1971), 583-6.

Sterling, Toni. "Statement." In U.S. Congress. Senate. Committee on Human Resources. Subcommittee on Labor. Discrimination on the Basis of Pregnancy, p. 292.

Stern, Bernice F. Friedman. "Tribute to the Important Contribution of the Woman Volunteer in a Democratic Society." In Conference on Woman's Destiny--Choice or Chance? Report, pp. 21-2.

Stern, Eva L. "Charity as Taught by the Mosaic Law." In Jewish Women's Congress. Papers, pp. 133-44.

Sternberger, Estelle M. "Report of the Committee on Plan of Action." In International Congress of Women, Chicago, 1933. Our Common Cause, Civilization, pp. 270-2.

Stevens, Doris. "Nationality Rights." In New York Herald Tribune. Report of the 4th Annual Women's Conference on Current Problems, pp. 220-4.

________. "Statement." In U. S. Congress. Senate. Committee on the Judiciary. Subcommittee on Constitutional Amendments. Equal Rights Amendment (1945), pp. 32-3.

________. "Summing Up for the Defense of Arrested Pickets." In Stevens, D. Jailed for Freedom, pp. 104-5.

Stevens, Myra. "Necessary Modifications of Child Welfare Services to Meet the Needs of Dependent Negro Children." In National Conference of Social Work. Proceedings (1945), pp. 305-13.

Stevens, Victoria. "Public Testimony." In New York (City). Commission on Human Rights. Women's Role in Contemporary Society, pp. 166-8.

Stevenson, Letitia Green. "Response to an Address of Welcome." In World's Congress of Representative Women, Chicago, 1893. A Historical Resume, pp. 915-7.

Stevenson, Marietta. "The Expanding Role of Government--Discussion." In International Congress of Women, Chicago, 1933. Our Common Cause, Civilization, pp. 493-5.

________. "The States and a Federal Department of Welfare." In National Conference of Social Work. Proceedings (1946), pp. 110-21.

Stevenson, Mary. "Women's Wages and Job Segregation." In Conference on Labor Market Segmentation, Harvard University, 1973. Labor Market Segmentation, pp. 243-53.

Stevenson, Mary L. "We, the Public. Our Responsibility in Politics." Vital Speeches, 25 (August 15, 1959), 664-6.

Stevenson, Matilda Coxe Evans. "From the Zuni Scalp Ceremonial." In World's Congress of Representative Women, Chicago, 1893. Congress of Women, pp. 484-7.

Stevenson, Sarah Hackett. "Chicago Women." In World's Congress of Representative Women, Chicago, 1893. Congress of Women, pp. 708-12.

________. "The Training and Qualification of Women Doctors." In International Congress of Women, London, 1899, 3, 47-53.

________. "Women in Medicine." In International Council of Women, 1888. Report, pp. 169-73.

Stewart, Alice E. "Public Health Nursing and Tuberculosis." In National Conference of Social Work. Proceedings (1917), pp. 218-24.

Stewart, Helena R. "Co-ordinating as Done by the Public Health Nurse." In National Conference of Charities and Correction. Proceedings (1916), pp. 480-3.

Stewart, Jane A. "National Women's Trade Union League." Chautauquan, 59 (1910), 116-20.

Stewart, Jennie E. Douglas. "The Needlework Guild of America." In World's Congress of Representative Women, Chicago, 1893. A Historical Resume, pp. 895-903.

Stewart, Maria W. Miller. "An Address, Delivered at the African Masonic Hall, Boston, 27 February 1833." In Loewenberg, B. Black Women in Nineteenth-Century American Life, pp. 195-7.

________. "Lecture, Delivered at the Franklin Hall, Boston, 21 September 1832." In Loewenberg, B. Black Women in the Nineteenth-Century American Life, pp. 192-5.

________. "Mrs. Stewart's Farewell Address to Her Friends in the City of Boston, 21 September 1833." In Loewenberg, B. Black Women in Nineteenth-Century American Life, pp. 197-200.

________. "Sufferings During the War." In Lerner, G. Black Women in White America, pp. 83-5.

________. "Throw Off Your Fearfulness and Come Forth!" In Lerner, G. Black Women in White America, pp. 526-50. (Same as "An Address, Delivered at the African Masonic Hall, Boston, 27 February 1833").

________. "What if I Am a Woman?" In Lerner, G. Black Women in White America, pp. 563-6. (Same as "Mrs. Stewart's Farewell Address to Her Friends in the City of Boston, 21 September 1833").

Stewart, Mary. "Junior Employment Problems." In National Conference of Social Work. Proceedings (1921), pp. 297-300.

Stewart, Mary A. "Testimony at a Hearing of the U.S. Senate, Committee on the Judiciary, January 23, 1880." In Stanton, E. History of Woman Suffrage, 3, 158-9.

Stewart, Sarah A. "The International Kindergarten Union." In World's Congress of Representative Women, Chicago, 1893. A Historical Resume, pp. 779-84.

Stimpson, Catharine R. "Conflict, Probable; Coalition, Possible; Feminism and the Black Movement." In Furniss, W. Women in Higher Education, pp. 261-78.

Stitt, Jane. "Statement." In U.S. Congress. Senate. Committee on the Judiciary. Subcommittee on Constitutional Amendments. Abortion, pt. 1, 264-6.

Stitt, Louise. "Government Regulation of Wages and Hours: Progress Under the Federal Fair Labor Standards Act." In National Conference of Social Work. Proceedings (1939), pp. 191-9.

________. "Statement." In U.S. Congress. Senate. Committee on the Judiciary. Subcommittee on Constitutional Amendments. Equal Rights (1956), pp. 42-8.

Stoler, Ann. "Class Structure and Female Autonomy in Rural Java." In Conference on Women and Development. "Women and National Development: The Complexities of Change." Signs, 3 (Autumn, 1977), 74-99.

Stone, Hannah M. "Family Limitation and Family Health." In National Conference of Social Work. Proceedings (1928), pp. 199-203.

Stone, Katherine. "The Origins of Job Structures in the Steel Industry." In Conference on Labor Market Segmentation, Harvard University, 1973. Labor Market Segmentation, pp. 27-84.

Stone, Kathryn H. "Statement." In U.S. Congress. House. Committee on the Judiciary. Subcommittee No. 1. Equal Rights Amendment (1948), pp. 170-4.

Stone, Lucinda Hinsdale. "A Demand for Women in the Faculties of Co-educational Colleges and Universities." In National Council of Women of the U.S., Washington, 1891. Transactions, pp. 169-78.

________. "Higher Lessons of the World's Fair." In World's Congress of Representative Women, Chicago, 1893. Congress of Women, pp. 446-9.

Stone, Lucy. "Address." In International Council of Women, 1888. Report, pp. 241-5, 331-5.

________. "Address at the Woman's Rights Convention, in New York, September, 1853." In Stanton, E. History of Woman Suffrage, 1, 554-5.

________. "Address at Women's Rights Convention, Syracuse, N.Y., September 8, 1852." In Harper, I. The Life and Work of Susan B. Anthony, 1, 73-4.

________. "Address of Mrs. Lucy Stone." In Danvers Historical Society, Danvers, Massachusetts. Old Anti-slavery Days, pp. 38-41.

________. "Address on Women and Religion at the 7th National Convention, New York, November 15, 1856." In Stanton, E. History of Woman Suffrage, 1, 650-3.

________. "Address to the Semi-annual Meeting of the American Woman Suffrage Association, New York, May, 1871." In Stanton, E. History of Woman Suffrage, 2, 811.

________. "Address to the Senate Committee on Women Suffrage, February 20, 1892." In Stanton, E. History of Woman Suffrage, 4, 191-3.

________. "Annual Report of the Chairman of the Executive Committee of the American Woman Suffrage Association, at the 1st Annual Meeting, Cleveland, Ohio, November, 1870." In Stanton, E. History of Woman Suffrage, 2, 803-4.

_______. "Closing Address of the Annual Meeting of the American Woman Suffrage Association, 1885." In Stanton, E. History of Woman Suffrage, 4, 415-6.

_______. "Comments at the Syracuse National Convention, September, 1852." In Stanton, E. History of Woman Suffrage, 1, 524, 531-2. (Same as "Address at Women's Rights Convention, Syracuse, N. Y.")

_______. "Concluding Remarks at the Woman's National Loyal League Convention, May 14, 1863." In Stanton, E. History of Woman Suffrage, 2, 78.

_______. "Debate at the 3rd Annual Meeting of the American Equal Rights Association, New York, May 1869." In Stanton, E. History of Woman Suffrage, 2, 383-4, 389.

_______. "Debate at the 4th National Convention, Cleveland, Ohio, October, 1853." In Stanton, E. History of Woman Suffrage, 1, 163.

_______. "Debate at the Women's National Loyal League Convention, May 14, 1863." In Stanton, E. History of Woman Suffrage, 2, 64-5.

_______. "Debate on the Elevation of Women at the 2nd Worcester Convention, October, 1851." In Stanton, E. History of Woman Suffrage, 1, 233.

_______. "Disappointment Is the Lot of Woman." In Tanner, L. Voices from Women's Liberation, pp. 75-7.

_______. "Extemporaneous Speech at a National Women's Rights Convention in Cincinnati in October 1855." In Kraditor, A. Up from the Pedestal, pp. 71-3. (Same as "Disappointment Is the Lot of Woman.")

_______. "I Have Been a Disappointed Woman." In Stanton, E. History of Woman Suffrage, 1, 165-7. (Same as "Disappointment Is the Lot of Woman.")

_______. "Lucy Stone's Speech." In Papachristou, J. Women Together, pp. 33-4. (Same as "Disappointment Is the Lot of Woman.")

_______. "President's Address at the 7th National Convention, New York, November 25 & 26, 1856." In Stanton, E. History of Woman Suffrage, 1, 632-3.

_______. "President's Closing Remarks at the 7th National Convention, New York, November 25 & 27, 1853." In Stanton, E. History of Woman Suffrage, 1, 665-6.

_______. "The Progress of Fifty Years." In World's Congress of Representative Women, Chicago, 1893. Congress of Women, pp. 58-61.

_______. "Remarks on the Case of Mrs. Norton at the Woman's Rights Convention in New York, September 1853." In Stanton, E. History of Woman Suffrage, 1, 565-6.

_______. "Reprint of Remarks in the (New York) Tribune, September 12, 1853." In Stanton, E. History of Woman Suffrage, 1, 576.

_______. "Speech at the Concord Convention of the Massachusetts Suffrage Association, May 1875." In Stanton, E. History of Woman Suffrage, 3, 271.

_______. "Speech Before the National Women's Rights Convention of 1855." In Martin, W. The American Sisterhood, pp. 47-50. (Same as "Disappointment Is the Lot of Woman.")

________. "Speech of Lucy Stone." In American Anti-slavery Society. Proceedings, pp. 82-4.

Stone, Margaret F. "Statement." In U. S. Congress. House. Committee on the Judiciary. Subcommittee No. 1. Equal Rights Amendment (1948), pp. 111-4.

Stooms, Lillian B. "Opportunities for Women in the Food Industries." In New York Herald Tribune. Report of the 4th Annual Women's Conference on Current Problems, pp. 215-9.

Stowell, Louisa Reed. "Retrospection." In International Council of Women, 1888. Report, pp. 72-5.

Strati, Joan. "Body Image and Performance." In Harris, D. Women and Sport, pp. 61-70.

Straus, Dorothy. "Statement." In U. S. Congress. Senate. Committee on the Judiciary. Subcommittee on Constitutional Amendments. Equal Rights for Men and Women (1938), pp. 206, 34-5, 39-40, 92.

Strauss, Anna Lord. "The Citizen's Responsibility; A Panel Discussion." In New York Herald Tribune. Report of the 18th Annual Forum on Current Problems, pp. 146-8, 178.

________. "Statement." In U. S. Congress. Senate. Committee on the Judiciary. Subcommittee on Constitutional Amendments. Equal Rights Amendment (1945), pp. 120-2.

Street, Ida M. "George Eliot." In World's Congress of Representative Women, Chicago, 1893. Congress of Women, pp. 286-92.

Streeter, Lilian Carpenter. "The Relation of Mental Defect to the Neglected, Dependent and Delinquent Children of New Hampshire." In National Conference of Charities and Correction. Proceedings (1915), pp. 340-52.

Stricker, Margery. "The Intellectual. His Journey and His Home." Vital Speeches, 24 (September 1, 1958), 701-3.

Strickland, Martha. "Woman's Position and Influence in the Civil Law." In World's Congress of Representative Women, Chicago, 1893. A Historical Resume, pp. 467-82.

Strober, Myra H. "Bringing Women into Management: Basic Strategies." In Gordon, F. Bringing Women into Management, pp. 77-96.

________. "Toward Dimorphics: A Summary Statement to the Conference on Occupational Segregation." In Blaxall, M. Women and the Workplace, pp. 293-302.

Strohm, Edna. "The Voter's Part." In International Congress of Women, Chicago, 1933. Our Common Cause, Civilization, pp. 578-80.

Strommen, Ellen A. "Learning Not To: It Takes a Long Time." In Hammond, N. Women and Children in Contemporary Society, pp. 55-61.

Strong, Anna Louise. "The Child Welfare Exhibit as a Means of Child Helping." In National Conference of Charities and Correction. Proceedings (1913), pp. 311-7.

Stuart, Elizabeth G. "The Power of Thought." In International Council of Women, 1888. Report, p. 420.

Stuckert, Mary Coleman. "Cooperative Housekeeping." In World's Congress of Representative Women, Chicago, 1893. A Historical Resume, pp. 625-6.

Sturges, Vera L. "The Progress of Adjustment in Mexican and United States Life." In National Conference of Social Work. Proceedings (1920), pp. 481-6.

Sturtevant, Sarah M. "Change and the Student." Vital Speeches, 2 (November 18, 1935), 112-4.

Sudarkasa, Niara. "Women and Migration in Contemporary West Africa." In Conference on Women and Development. "Women and National Development: The Complexities of Change." Signs, 3 (Autumn, 1977), 178-89.

Sullivan, Leonor Kretzer. "The Citizen's Role in Furthering Consumer Interests: Stop Being Cheated." Vital Speeches, 32 (June 1, 1966), 498-501.

________. "Controversy over Enactment of Standby Wage and Price Controls." Congressional Digest, 49 (October, 1970), 246-50.

________. "Lack of Leadership in Washington. A Congresswoman Looks at Congress." Vital Speeches, 23 (June 1, 1957), 489-92.

________. "Statement." In U. S. Congress. Committee on Education and Labor. Select Subcommittee on Labor. Equal Pay for Equal Work, pp. 129-31.

Sunderland, Eliza Read. "Higher Education and the Home." In World's Congress of Representative Women, Chicago, 1893. Congress of Women, pp. 318-22.

Susan, Barbara. "Public Testimony." In New York (City). Commission on Human Rights. Women's Role in Contemporary Society, pp. 448-9.

Swanker, Esther M. "Controversy over Federal Experimentation with Education Vouchers." Congressional Digest, 51 (August-September, 1972), 220-2.

Swanson, Pearl. "Physiological Changes and Adjustments: From the Standpoint of a Nutritionist." In Michigan State University, East Lansing, School of Home Economics. Potentialities of Women in the Middle Years, pp. 59-85.

Swartz, Maud. "Statement." In U.S. Women's Bureau. Proceedings of the Women's Industrial Conference, pp. 156-7.

________. "Trade Union Organisation Among Women Workers." Industrial and Labor Information, 7 (October, 1923), 12.

________. "Women's Wages." In U.S. Women's Bureau. Proceedings of the Women's Industrial Conference, pp. 78-85.

Swayze, Minnie. "Ethics and Aesthetics of Dress." In Association for the Advancement of Women. Congress of Women, 3rd. Papers, pp. 59-62.

Swerdlow, Amy. "Introduction to Conference." In Conference on Feminist Perspectives on Housework and Child Care. Feminist Perspectives on Housework and Child Care, pp. 5-6.

Swing, Betty Gram. "Statement." In U.S. Congress. House. Committee on the Judiciary. Subcommittee No. 1. Equal Rights Amendment (1948), pp. 28-30.

Switton, Florence W. "Meeting the Needs of the Aged Through Private Institutional Care." In National Conference of Social Work. Proceedings (1938), pp. 606-16.

Sytz, Florence. "Professional Relations: The School of Social Work and the Agency." In National Conference of Social Work. Proceedings (1942), pp. 541-52.

________. "Relation of a Standard of Education and Training to Professional Practice." In National Conference of Social Work. Proceedings (1936), pp. 100-7.

________. "Social Service Supervision of the Feebleminded." In National Conference of Social Work. Proceedings (1928), pp. 373-7.

Taft, Jessie. "The Function of a Mental Hygienist in a Children's Agency." In National Conference of Social Work. Proceedings (1927), pp. 392-9.

________. "Mental Hygiene of Childhood: The Social Workers Opportunity." In National Conference of Social Work. Proceedings (1922), pp. 371-5.

________. "Mental Hygiene Problems of Normal Adolescence." In National Conference of Social Work. Proceedings (1921), pp. 355-9.

________. "Problems of Social Case Work with Children." In National Conference of Social Work. Proceedings (1920), pp. 377-85.

_______. "Progress in Social Case Work: In Mental Hygiene." In National Conference of Social Work. Proceedings (1923), pp. 338-9.

_______. "Qualifications of the Psychiatric Social Worker." In National Conference of Social Work. Proceedings (1919), pp. 593-9.

_______. "Relation of Personality Study to Child Placing." In National Conference of Social Work. Proceedings (1919), pp. 63-7.

_______. "The Relation of the School to the Mental Health of the Average Child." In National Conference of Social Work. Proceedings (1923), pp. 394-8.

_______. "The Time Element in Mental Hygiene Therapy as Applied to Social Case Work." In National Conference of Social Work. Proceedings (1932), pp. 368-81.

_______. "The Use of the Transfer Within the Limits of the Office Interview." In National Conference of Social Work. Proceedings (1924), pp. 307-11.

Taft, Martha Wheaton Bowers. "The Woman Voter." In New York Herald Tribune. Report of the 10th Annual Forum on Current Problems, pp. 163-7.

Taggart, Alice D. "Case Work and Community Change." In National Conference of Social Work. Proceedings (1939), pp. 326-33.

Talbot, Marion. "The History, Aims, and Methods of the Association of Collegiate Alumnae." In World's Congress of Representative Women, Chicago, 1893. A Historical Resume, pp. 784-96.

Tanner, Nancy. "Matrifocality in Indonesia and Africa and Among Black Americans." In Rosaldo, M. Women, Culture, and Society, pp. 129-56.

Taunton, Ruth. "Statement." In U. S. Congress. Senate. Committee on the Judiciary. Subcommittee on Constitutional Amendments. Equal Rights for Men and Women (1933), pp. 14-5.

Taussig, Frances. "The Place of Psychiatric Social Work: In a Family Case Work Organization." In National Conference of Social Work. Proceedings (1924), pp. 442-7.

Taylor, Ethel. "What Kind of Mental Hygiene Service Do Children's Agencies Need?" In National Conference of Social Work. Proceedings (1926), pp. 412-9.

Taylor, Lea D. "Seeing the Problem Whole." In International Congress of Women, Chicago, 1933. Our Common Cause, Civilization, pp. 844-50.

Taylor, Mary Waldo. "Applying a Maternity and Infancy Program to Rural Sections." In National Conference of Social Work. Proceedings (1928), pp. 208-13.

Taylor, Mildred D. "Newbery Award Acceptance, 1977." Horn Book Magazine, 53 (August, 1977), 401-9.

Taylor, Ruth. "The Care of Children in Foster Homes." In National Conference of Social Work. Proceedings (1924), pp. 125-7.

________. "Child Welfare in Westchester County." In National Conference of Social Work. Proceedings (1919), 36-41.

________. "The Integration of Effort in Theory and Practice by Private and Public Agencies for the Common Good." In National Conference of Social Work. Proceedings (1927), pp. 246-52.

________. "Problems Created by Assistance Categories." In National Conference of Social Work. Proceedings (1940), pp. 199-205.

Temple, Shirley see Black, Shirley Temple

Tenner, Hallie. "Statement." In U.S. Congress. House. Committee on Education and Labor. Subcommittee on Equal Opportunities. Equal Opportunity for Displaced Homemakers Act, pp. 20-1.

Terp, Barbara. "Testimony." In U.S. Congress. House. Select Committee on Crime. Drugs in Our Schools, p. 593.

Terrell, Mary Church. "Frederick Douglass." In Douglass, F. Frederick Douglass on Women's Rights, pp. 176-81.

________. "The Justice of Woman Suffrage. Address to the National American Woman Suffrage Association Convention of 1900." In Stanton, E. History of Woman Suffrage, 4, 358-9.

________. "Statement." In U.S. Congress. House. Committee on the Judiciary. Subcommittee No. 1. Equal Rights Amendment (1948), pp. 38-9.

________. "Statement." In U.S. Congress. Senate. Committee on the Judiciary. Subcommittee on Constitutional Amendments. Equal Rights Amendment (1945), p. 40.

Thayer, Eliva Anne. "The Light in the East." In World's Congress of Representative Women, Chicago, 1893. A Historical Resume, pp. 286-8.

Theis, Sophie Van Senden. "Case Work in the Process of Adoption." In National Conference of Social Work. Proceedings (1942), pp. 405-15.

________. "How Foster Children Turn Out." In National Conference of Social Work. Proceedings (1924), pp. 121-4.

________. "Minimum Qualifications for a Good Child Placing Agency." In National Conference of Social Work. Proceedings (1922), pp. 121-4.

Thibeault, Mary Lou. "The Hazards of Equality: Awareness of Self." Vital Speeches, 40 (July 15, 1974), 588-91.

Thoma, Marilynn. "Women into Management: Vignettes." In Gordon, F. Bringing Women into Management, pp. 136-9.

Thomas, Caroline S. "The National Young Ladies' Mutual Improvement Association." In National Council of Women of the U. S. Washington, 1891. Transactions, pp. 256-8.

Thomas, Dorothy. "Public Testimony." In New York (City). Commission on Human Rights. Women's Role in Contemporary Society, pp. 164-6.

Thomas, Dorothy V. "The Return of the Serviceman to His Family and Community: As Seen in a Private Family Case Work Agency." In National Conference of Social Work. Proceedings (1945), pp. 109-15.

Thomas, Harriet Park. "The Five Cent Theatre." In National Conference of Charities and Correction. Proceedings (1910), pp. 145-9.

Thomas, Martha Cary. "Address at the College Evening of the 38th Annual Convention of the National American Woman Suffrage Association, February 8, 1906." In Harper, I. The Life and Work of Susan B. Anthony, 3, 1393-5.

_______. "Address at the National American Woman Suffrage Association Convention of 1906." In Stanton, E. History of Woman Suffrage, 5, 171-3.

_______. "Address of President Thomas." In Bryn Mawr College. Carola Woerishoffer, Her Life and Work. pp. 40-9.

_______. "The Bryn Mawr Woman." In Cross, B. The Educated Woman in America, pp. 139-44.

_______. "Marriage and the Woman Scholar." In Cross, B. The Educated Woman in America, pp. 170-5.

_______. "Present Tendencies in Women's College and University Education." In Kraditor, A. Up from the Pedestal, pp. 90-8.

_______. "The Purpose of the College." In Cross, B. The Educated Woman in America, pp. 155-7.

_______. "Story of the Lowell Offering." In International Council of Women, 1888. Report, pp. 161-2.

_______. "The Work of Sorosis." In International Council of Women, 1888. Report, pp. 215-7.

Thompson, Clara Mildred. "Women in the American Culture." In Fremon, S. Women and Men, pp. 10-22. Also in Psychiatry, 4 (1941), 1-8.

_______. "Women's Status--Yesterday, Today, Tomorrow: A Chapter in the History of Freedom, 1848-1948." In U. S. Women's Bureau. American Woman--Her Changing Role, pp. 42-51.

Thompson, Dorothy. "America Facing Tomorrow's World." In New York Herald Tribune. Report of the 8th Annual Forum on Current Problems, pp. 228-33.

________. "Axioms of Global Policy. The Security of the Nation." Vital Speeches, 15 (May 1, 1949), 433-8.

________. "The Changing Status of Women." In New York Herald Tribune. Report of the 4th Annual Women's Conference on Current Problems, pp. 190-8.

________. "The Death of Democracies. How to Avoid It: By Facing Realities." Vital Speeches, 3 (April 1, 1937), 354-8.

________. "Freedom's Back Is Against the Wall. Making Our Own Beds and Lying in Them." Vital Speeches, 3 (June 1, 1937), 546-51.

________. "The Future World Order. The Ideal of the United Nations." Vital Speeches, 8 (June 15, 1942), 533-6.

________. "Government by Propaganda." In New York Herald Tribune. Report of the 5th Annual Forum on Current Problems, pp. 260-7.

________. "Greece Today. A Miracle of Survival." Vital Speeches, 16 (January 15, 1950), 200-5.

________. "Let's Face the Facts. There Are No Neutral Hearts." Vital Speeches, 7 (March 15, 1941), 345-7.

________. "The Liberal Spirit." Vital Speeches, 4 (December 1, 1937), 98-103.

________. "The Middle East Problem. Results of U.S. Aid to Israel." Vital Speeches, 20 (March 1, 1954), 295-300.

________. "Nation of Speculators." Vital Speeches, 3 (May 15, 1937), 450-4.

________. "Nazi Foreign Missions. German Propaganda in the United States and the World." Vital Speeches, 3 (September 15, 1937), 712-4.

________. "The Power to Maintain Peace. Responsibilities Must Be Accepted." Vital Speeches, 10 (November 15, 1943), 81-3.

________. "Propaganda in the Modern World." Vital Speeches, 2 (November 4, 1935), 66-8.

________. "Saving Democracy." In New York Herald Tribune. Report of the 10th Annual Forum on Current Problems, pp. 198-204.

________. "Sino-Japanese Dossier: Background and Personalities." Vital Speeches, 3 (September 1, 1937), 698-700.

________. "The State in a Democracy. The State, the Negation of Anarchy." Vital Speeches, 14 (April 15, 1948), 394-9.

________. "Stopping Propaganda. The Democracies Have the Jitters." Vital Speeches, 5 (June 1, 1939), 494-5.

________. "The War's Challenge to the United States." In New York Herald Tribune. Report of the 9th Annual Forum on Current Problems, pp. 206-10.

________. "Which Way America? The Progressive Decay of Standards." Vital Speeches, 16 (July 1, 1950), 548-52.

________. "Woman and Freedom in Our Society." Vital Speeches, 2 (December 16, 1935), 154-5.

Thompson, Ellen Powell. "Tribute to Susan B. Anthony at Her 80th Birthday Celebration, February 15, 1900." In Harper, I. The Life and Work of Susan B. Anthony, 3, 1183-4. Also in Stanton, E. History of Woman Suffrage, 4, 399.

Thompson, Melissa A. "The Question of the Ratification of the Equal Rights Amendment." Congressional Digest, 56 (June-July, 1977), 182-8.

Thomson, Ruth. "Statement." In U.S. Congress. House. Committee on Education and Labor. Select Subcommittee on Labor. Equal Pay for Equal Work, pt. 2, 245-9.

Thorne, Barrie. "The Modern Family: Sticky Myths, Diverse Realities, and the Problem of Isolation." In Hammond, N. Women and Children in Contemporary Society, pp. 81-9.

Thorne, Julia. "Forestry." In General Federation of Women's Clubs. Biennial Convention, 16 (1922), 558-60.

Thornton, Janet. "Social Case Work Method in Health Work." In National Conference of Social Work. Proceedings (1923), pp. 23-7.

Thringold, Faye. "Public Testimony." In New York (City). Commission on Human Rights. Women's Role in Contemporary Society, pp. 769-72.

Tillett, Gladys A. "Statement." In U.S. Congress. House. Committee on Education and Labor. Select Subcommittee on Labor. Equal Pay for Equal Work, pp. 87-91.

________. "Statement." In U.S. Congress. House. Committee on Education and Labor. Select Subcommittee on Labor. Equal Pay for Equal Work, pt. 2, 227-30.

Tillinghast, Elizabeth Sheldon. "The Economic Basis of Woman Suffrage. Address to the House Judiciary Committee, 1900." In Stanton, E. History of Woman Suffrage, 4, 377-8. Also in Tanner, L. Voices from Women's Liberation, pp. 94-5.

Tillman, Randy. "Approaches to Correct the Underrepresentation of Women in the Health Professions. A U.S. Response to the Scandinavian Experience." In International Conference on Women in Health. Proceedings, pp. 53-5.

Tillmon, Johnnie. "Testimony on Sex Discrimination in Unemployment Insurance, Veterans Programs, and Public Assistance." In U.S. Congress. House. Joint Economic Committee. Economic Problems of Women, pt. 2, 390-3.

Tilton, Elizabeth. "What Makes Men Stop Drinking?" In National Conference of Charities and Correction. Proceedings (1916), pp. 112-6.

________. "The Whence and Whither of Prohibition." In National Conference of Social Work. Proceedings (1919), pp. 767-73.

Timberlake, Josephine B. "The Deaf Child and the Hard-of-Hearing Child." In National Conference of Social Work. Proceedings (1923), pp. 390-3.

Tinsley, Willa Vaughn. "Changes in the University Scene: Their Effect on Home Economics." In American Home Economics Association. The Adventure of Change, pp. 58-65.

Titcomb, Mary L. "Report-Library Extension." In General Federation of Women's Clubs. Biennial Convention, 16 (1922), 164-7.

Tobias, Sheila. "Educating Women for Leadership: A Program for the Future." In McGuigan, D. A Sampler of Women's Studies, pp. 109-14.

Todd, Hannah M. "Report of the Committee on the Organization of Charities." In National Conference of Charities and Correction. Proceedings (1890), pp. 36-43.

Todd, Mary C. McCabe. "Education of Indian Girls in the West." In World's Congress of Representative Women, Chicago, 1893. Congress of Women, pp. 39-40.

Tompkins, Pauline. "American Association of University Women Educational Foundation, College Faculty Program." In Itasca Conference on the Continuing Education of Women, Itasca State Park, Minnesota, 1962. Education and a Woman's Life, pp. 116-9.

Toombs, Elizabeth. "Publicity." In General Federation of Women's Clubs. Biennial Convention, 16 (1922), 134-7.

Toomy, Alice Timmons. "Discussion of the Effects of Modern Changes in Industrial and Social Life on Woman's Marriage Prospects." In World's Congress of Representative Women, Chicago, 1893. A Historical Resume, pp. 598-9.

________. "The Ethics of Dress." In World's Congress of Representative Women, Chicago, 1893. A Historical Resume, pp. 339-44.

Toomy, Lily Alice. "The Organized Work of Catholic Women." In World's Congress of Representative Women, Chicago, 1893. A Historical Resume, pp. 260-7.

Topping, Ruth. "A Study of the Morals Court in Three Large Cities: Social Aspects." In National Conference of Social Work. Proceedings (1921), pp. 150-55.

Torton, Ina. "Public Testimony." In New York (City). Commission on Human Rights. Women's Role in Contemporary Society, pp. 389-92.

________. "Testimony." In U. S. Congress. Joint Economic Committee. Economic Problems of Women, pt. 4, pp. 588-92.

Tousley, Clare M. "Cooperative Interpretation." In National Conference of Social Work. Proceedings (1946), pp. 159-64.

________. "Focused Publicity." In National Conference of Social Work. Proceedings (1931), pp. 592-6.

________. "Support and Interpretation of Professional Requirements in Social Work: Who Are Our Interpreters?" In National Conference of Social Work. Proceedings (1925), pp. 668-72.

Towle, Charlotte. "Factors in Treatment." In National Conference of Social Work. Proceedings (1936), pp. 179-91.

________. "Helping the Client to Use His Capacities and Resources." In National Conference of Social Work. Proceedings (1948), pp. 259-70.

________. "The Underlying Skills of Case Work Today." In National Conference of Social Work. Proceedings (1941), pp. 254-66.

Travilla, Mary. "Our Divine Possibilities." In National Purity Congress, 1st, Baltimore, 1895. National Purity Congress, pp. 294-8.

Traxler, Margaret Ellen. "Statement." In U. S. Congress. Senate. Committee on the Judiciary. Equal Rights 1970, pp. 349-52.

de Trevino, Elizabeth Borton. "Newbery Award Acceptance--1966." In Kingman, L. Newbery and Caldecott Medal Books, 1966-1975, pp. 5-11.

Trimble, Augusta. "An Opportunity for Youth in the Present Crisis." In New York Herald Tribune. Report of the 3rd Women's Conference on Current Problems, pp. 75-7.

Trotter, Virginia Yarp. "Women in Leadership and Decision Making: A Shift in Balance." Vital Speeches, 41 (April 1, 1975), 373-5.

Troxell, Margaret M. "Changing Status of Women." Washington, U. S. Apprenticeship & Training Bureau, 1963, 12 p.

Truax, Anne Thorsen. "Maternity Leave Policies." In Furniss, W. Women in Higher Education, pp. 137-9.

Trumbull, Grace. "The Role of Commercial Organizations in Social Welfare on the Pacific Coast." In National Conference of Charities and Correction. Proceedings (1913), pp. 95-100.

Trumbull, Millie R. "The Honor System of Prison Labor." In National Conference of Charities and Correction. Proceedings (1913), pp. 116-20.

Truth, Sojourner. "Address at Women Suffrage Convention in New York, 1867." In Beard, M. America Through Women's Eyes, pp. 231-2.

________. "Address to the 1st Annual Meeting of the American Equal Rights Association, May, 1867." In Stanton, E. History of Woman Suffrage, 2, 193-4. (Same as "Address at Women Suffrage Convention in New York, 1867.")

________. "Address to the Woman's Rights Convention in New York, September 1853." In Stanton, E. History of Woman Suffrage, 1, 567-8.

________. "Ain't I a Woman?" In Loewenberg, B. Black Women in Nineteenth-century American Life, pp. 235-6. Also in Schneir, M. Feminism, pp. 93-5.

________. "Frances D. Gage's Reminiscences of Speech by Sojourner Truth." In Irwin, I. Angels and Amazons, pp. 99-101. (Same as "Ain't I a Woman?")

________. "Gage's Reminiscences of Sojourner Truth." In Papachristou, J. Women Together, pp. 35-6. (Same as "Ain't I a Woman?")

________. "I Suppose I Am About the Only Colored Woman That Goes About to Speak for the Rights of Colored Women." In Lerner, G. Black Women in White America, pp. 566-8. (Same as "Address to the Women's Rights Convention in New York, September 1853.")

________. "Keeping the Thing Going While Things Are Stirring." In Loewenberg, B. Black Women in Nineteenth-century American Life, pp. 238-9. Also in Schneir, M. Feminism, pp. 128-31. (Same as "Address to the 1st Annual Meeting of the American Equal Rights Association, May, 1867.")

________. "Mrs. Gage's Reminiscences of Sojourner Truth." In Salper, R. Female Liberation, pp. 78-9. (Same as "Ain't I a Woman?")

________. "The Narrative of Sojourner Truth, 1878." In Martin, W. The American Sisterhood, pp. 101-5.

________. "Remarks at the 1st Annual Meeting of the American Equal Rights Association, May, 1867." In Stanton, E. History of Woman Suffrage, 2, 224-5.

________. "Reminiscences by Frances D. Gage." In Rossi, A. The Feminist Papers, pp. 416-9. Also in Stanton, E. History of Woman Suffrage, 1, 115-7. Also in Tanner, L. Voices from Women's Liberation, pp. 60-2. (Same as "Ain't I a Woman?")

________. "Second Address to the 1st Annual Meeting of the American Equal Rights Association, May, 1867." In Stanton, E. History of Woman Suffrage, 2, 222. (Same as "Remarks at the First Annual Meeting of the American Equal Rights Association, May, 1867.")

________. "Sojourner Truth Speaks Before a Woman's Rights Convention." In Millstein, B. We, the American Women, pp. 116-7.

________. "Speech at the Convention of the American Equal Rights Association, New York, 1867." In Lerner, G. Black Women in White America, pp. 568-72. (Same as "Keeping the Thing Going While Things Are Stirring.")

________. "Speech to a Boston Audience on New Year's Day, 1871." In Loewenberg, B. Black Women in Nineteenth-century American Life, pp. 240-2.

________. "What Time of Night It Is." In Schneir, M. Feminism, pp. 96-8. (Same as "Address to the Woman's Rights Convention in New York, September 1853.")

________. "While the Water Is Stirring I Will Step Into the Pool." In Lerner, G. The Female Experience, pp. 487-9. (Same as "Remarks at the 1st Annual Meeting of the American Equal Rights Association, May 1867.")

________. "The Women Want Their Rights." In Tanner, L. Voices from Women's Liberation, p. 73.

Tsianina (Princess). "Minority Needs--the Indian." In International Congress of Women, Chicago, 1933. Our Common Cause, Civilization, pp. 794-7.

Tucker, Katherine. "Community Relationships Involved in 100 per cent Registration in Social Service Exchange: From the Standpoint of Nursing Organizations." In National Conference of Social Work. Proceedings (1932), pp. 193-7.

________. "The Growth of the Social Point of View: In Nursing." In National Conference of Social Work. Proceedings (1923), pp. 61-4.

Tupper, Mila Frances. "Discussion of Paper on Kindergarten." In World's Congress of Representative Women, Chicago, 1893. A Historical Resume, pp. 99-103.

________. "Present Status of Women in the Church." In National Council of Women of the U. S., Washington, 1891. Transactions, pp. 98-107.

Turner, Mary O'Donnell. "Community Programs and Cooperation in Americanization." In National Conference of Social Work. Proceedings (1926), pp. 582-6.

Tutwiler, Julia Strudwick. "Our Brother in Stripes, in the Schoolroom." In National Education Association. Journal of Proceedings & Addresses (1890), pp. 601-8.

________. "Poor Houses and Jails of the Southwest." In National Conference of Charities and Correction. Proceedings (Special Meeting, 1897), pp. 30-5.

________. "A Self Support Problem." In World's Congress of Representative Women, Chicago, 1893. Congress of Women, pp. 36-8.

Twente, Esther E. "Social Case-work Practice in Rural Communities." In National Conference of Social Work. Proceedings (1938), pp. 122-32.

Twitchell, Eliza Stowe. "Industrial Revolution of the Last Century." In World's Congress of Representative Women, Chicago, 1893. Congress of Women, pp. 495-9.

Tynes, Harriet L. "Administrative Practices for Conserving Human Values in the Public Assistance Program." In National Conference of Social Work. Proceedings (1941), pp. 320-31.

Tyson, Helen Glenn. "Measuring Our Results in Securing the Essentials of Family Life: Some Suggestions Based on a Review of Mothers' Assistance in Pennsylvania." In National Conference of Social Work. Proceedings (1926), pp. 295-300.

Ueland, Elsa. "The Care of Children in Institutions." In National Conference of Social Work. Proceedings (1924), pp. 128-30.

Upton, Harriet Taylor. "Address." In U.S. Women's Bureau. Proceedings of the Women's Industrial Conference, pp. 11-3.

________. "Treasurer's Report for 1906." In National American Woman Suffrage Association. Proceedings of the 39th Annual Convention, pp. 16-21.

Urquhart, Kate. "Impressionist Painting and Painters." In International Congress of Women, Toronto, 1909. Report, 1, 233-40.

Vaile, Gertrude. "The Contribution of Social Case Work to Democracy." In National Conference of Social Work. Proceedings (1918), pp. 283-7.

________. "The Cost of Maintaining Good Case Work in a Public Agency." In National Conference of Social Work. Proceedings (1925), pp. 238-42.

________. "An Experiment in Trying to Grade District Visitors." In National Conference of Charities and Correction. Proceedings (1915), pp. 88-91.

________. "Introductory Remarks by the Vice Chairman (On State Public Welfare)." In National Conference of Social Work. Proceedings (1917), pp. 333-4.

________. "Principles and Methods of Outdoor Relief." In National Conference of Charities and Correction. Proceedings (1915), pp. 479-84.

________. "Public Administration of Charity in Denver." In National Conference of Charities and Correction. Proceedings (1916), pp. 415-8.

________. "Some Organization Problems of Public Welfare Departments." In National Conference of Social Work. Proceedings (1922), pp. 432-7.

________. "Some Significant Trends Since Cleveland, 1912 (Presidential Address)." In National Conference of Social Work. Proceedings (1926), pp. 3-11.

Valentine, Helen. "How to Keep More of the Money You Earn. The Status of Women in Industry." Vital Speeches, 10 (June 1, 1954), 506-8.

Van Allen, Judith. "Memsahib, Militante, Femme Libre: Political and Apolitical Styles of Modern African Women." In Jaquette, J. Women in Politics, pp. 304-21.

Van Blarcom, Carolyn Conant. "A Possible Solution of the Midwife Problem." In National Conference of Charities and Correction. Proceedings (1910), pp. 350-6.

Van de Carr, Katharine. "The Aged Person in the Family Setting." In National Conference of Social Work. Proceedings (1939), pp. 401-8.

Van Doren, Irita. "Books for Leisure Time." In New York Herald Tribune. Report of the 2nd Women's Conference on Current Problems, pp. 29-34.

________. "Some of the New Fall Books." In New York Herald Tribune. Report of the 5th Annual Forum on Current Problems, pp. 175-6.

________. "Taste and Custom as Reflected in Our Literature." In New York Herald Tribune. Report of the 4th Annual Women's Conference on Current Problems, pp. 70-3.

Van Driel, Agnes. "In-service Training." In National Conference of Social Work. Proceedings (1937), pp. 426-31.

________. "Training the Paid, Untrained Worker." In National Conference of Social Work. Proceedings (1943), pp. 331-9.

Van Dusseldorp, Wilma. "The Use of Committees and Volunteers in Rural Social Work." In National Conference of Social Work. Proceedings (1927), pp. 272-6.

Van Dyke, Mabel. "Statement." In U.S. Congress. House. Committee on the Judiciary. Equal Rights Amendment to the Constitution (1932), pp. 16-7.

Van Etten, Ida M. "The Condition of Women Workers Under the Present Industrial System." In Lerner, G. The Female Experience, pp. 302-5.

________. "The Sweating System, Charity, and Organization." In Cott, E. Root of Bitterness, pp. 327-32.

Van Kleeck, Mary. "The Common Goals of Labor and Social Work." In National Conference of Social Work. Proceedings (1934), pp. 284-303.

________. "The Effect of the N.R.A. on Labor." In National Conference of Social Work. Proceedings (1934), pp. 428-36.

________. "Governmental Intervention in the Labor Movement." In National Conference of Social Work. Proceedings (1935), pp. 512-24.

________. "Introductory Statement (On Sources of Power for Industrial Freedom)." In National Conference of Social Work. Proceedings (1924), pp. 370-3.

________. "Our Illusions Regarding Government (Pugsley Award)." In National Conference of Social Work. Proceedings (1934), pp. 473-85.

________. "The Social Consequences of Changing Methods of Production." In National Conference of Social Work. Proceedings (1940), pp. 297-311.

________. "Social Program of the Labor Movement." In National Conference of Social Work. Proceedings (1937), pp. 388-98.

________. "Social Services for Industrial Workers." In National Conference of Social Work. Proceedings (1946), pp. 122-8.

________. "Social Work in the Economic Crisis." In National Conference of Social Work. Proceedings (1935), pp. 64-77.

________. "What Industry Means to Women Workers." In U. S. Women's Bureau. Proceedings of the Women's Industrial Conference, pp. 24-34.

________. "The Working Woman and the New Social Vision." Life and Labor, 9 (December, 1919), 320-3.

Van Slyck, Katharine R. "The Awakened Volunteer Interest." In National Conference of Social Work. Proceedings (1942), pp. 246-54.

Van Waters, Miriam. "Delinquency and the School." In National Conference of Social Work. Proceedings (1925), pp. 435-40.

________. "The Delinquent Attitude--A Study of Juvenile Delinquency from the Standpoint of Human Relationship." In National Conference of Social Work. Proceedings (1924), pp. 160-5.

________. "Institutions for Delinquent Children: What Is the Test of Success?" In National Conference of Social Work. Proceedings (1925), pp. 117-20.

________. "Is the Agency or the Individual Primarily Responsible for the Professional Development of the Social Worker?" In National Conference of Social Work. Proceedings (1925), pp. 696-700.

________. "The New Morality and the Social Worker." In National Conference of Social Work. Proceedings (1929), pp. 65-79.

________. "Philosophical Trends in Modern Social Work (Presidential Address)." In National Conference of Social Work. Proceedings (1930), pp. 3-19.

Van Winkel, Mina C. "The Policewoman." In National Conference of Social Work. Proceedings (1924), pp. 187-92.

________. "Standardization of the Aims and Methods of the Work of Policewomen." In National Conference of Social Work. Proceedings (1920), pp. 151-4.

Vanderbilt, Amy. "Bad Manners in America." Annals. "The Changing American People: Are We Deteriorating or Improving?" 378 (July, 1968), 90-8.

Vaughan, Mary C. "President's Address at a Mass Meeting of "The Daughters of Temperance" on January 28, 1852." In Stanton, E. History of Woman Suffrage, 1, 476-8.

Vernon, Mabel. "Address at the Columbia Theatre in Washington, D. C., November 15, 1914." In Irwin, I. The Story of the Woman's Party, pp. 85-6.

Verry, Ethel. "Meeting Challenge of Today's Needs in Working with Unmarried Mothers Through Use of Institution (Maternity Home)." Washington, U. S. Children's Bureau, 1945, 10 p.

________. "Problems Facing Children with Relatively Long Period of Institutional Care." In National Conference of Social Work. Proceedings (1938), pp. 684-95.

Vetter, Betty M. "Analysis of the Role of Women in Health Care Decisionmaking. A U. S. Response to a Look at the Philippines." In International Conference on Women in Health. Proceedings, pp. 159-61.

Vining, Elizabeth Gray. "The Educated Heart. The Heart, Informed with Love, Will Never Be in Conflict with the Enlightened Mind." Vital Speeches, 20 (July 15, 1954), 600-2.

________. "Young People in New Japan." In New York Herald Tribune. Report of the 16th Annual Forum on Current Problems, pp. 36-41.

Vittum, Harriet E. "Culture of Family Life from the Social Settlement Standpoint." In National Conference of Charities and Correction. Proceedings (1914), pp. 111-4.

________. "Politics from the Social Point of View." In National Conference of Social Work. Proceedings (1924), pp. 422-8.

________. "The Use of Leisure." In National Conference of Charities and Correction. Proceedings (1914), pp. 367-70.

Vlachos, Anna. "Social Treatment Through the Interview: Opening the Way." In National Conference of Social Work. Proceedings (1924), pp. 295-9.

Vogel, Lise. "Hearts to Feel and Tongues to Speak: New England Mill Women in the Early Nineteenth Century." In Cantor, M. Class, Sex, and the Woman Worker, pp. 64-82.

Voutsis, Marina. "Public Testimony." In New York (City). Commission on Human Rights. Women's Role in Contemporary Society, pp. 303-4.

Vredenburgh, Dorothy. "What's New in the '52 Campaign?" In New York Herald Tribune. Report of the 21st Annual Forum on Current Problems, pp. 198-202.

Wadley, Susan S. "Women and the Hindu Tradition." In Conference on Women and Development. "Women and National Development: The Complexities of Change." Signs, 3 (Autumn, 1977), 113-25.

Wadsworth, Emily Marshall. "Discussion of the Effects of Modern Changes in Industrial and Social Life on Woman's Marriage Prospects." In World's Congress of Representative Women, Chicago, 1893. A Historical Resume, pp. 603-4.

Waight, Lavinia. "Remarks of the Secretary, Lavinia Waight." In Lerner, G. The Female Experience, pp. 278-9.

Waite, Jessie T. "Testimony at a Hearing of the House Committee on the Judiciary, January 24, 1880." In Stanton, E. History of Woman Suffrage, 3, 161-2.

Wakeman, Antoinette Van Housen. "What Do the Signs of the Times Signify?" In National Council of Women of the U.S., Washington, 1891. Transactions, pp. 270-8.

Wald, Lillian D. "Address at Conference Dinner." In National Conference of Social Work. Proceedings (1932), pp. 33-40.

________. "The Immigrant Young Girl." In National Conference of Charities and Correction. Proceedings (1909), pp. 261-5.

________. "Nurses in Settlement Work." In National Conference of Charities and Correction. Proceedings (1895), pp. 264-7.

Waldo, Alice. "Legal Aid Service and Social Work: The Social Point of View." In National Conference of Social Work. Proceedings (1923), pp. 188-92.

Walker, Alice H. "The Use of Central Clinics for Child Caring Agencies." In National Conference of Social Work. Proceedings (1925), pp. 127-8.

Walker, Mabel L. "The American City Is Obsolescent. Factors Affecting Municipal Revenues." Vital Speeches, 13 (September 1, 1947), 697-9.

Walker, Margaret. "Religion, Poetry, and History: Foundations for a New Educational System." In Barbour, F. The Black Seventies, pp. 284-95.

Wallace, Phyllis A. "Employment Opportunities for Minorities in New York City: An Introduction." In U.S. Equal Employment Opportunity Commission. Hearings on Discrimination in White Collar Employment, pp. 4-13.

________. "'Restricted Membership' at the Management Level: Exclusion of Jews from the Executive Suite." In U.S. Equal Employment Opportunity Commission. Hearing on Discrimination in White Collar Employment, pp. 443-8.

________. "Sex Discrimination: Some Societal Constraints on Upward Mobility for Women Executives." In Conference on Women's Challenge to Management, Arden House, 1971. Corporate Lib, pp. 69-84.

Wallace, Zerelda Gray Sanders. "I Am A Home-Loving, Law-Abiding, Tax-Paying Woman...." In Scott, A. One Half the People, pp. 96-9. Also in U.S. Congress. Senate. Committee on the Judiciary. Appendix to the Report on Suffrage, 49th Congress, 1st session, S. Report, 70, pp. 21-2.

________. "The Moral Power of the Ballot." In International Council of Women, 1888. Report, pp. 428-31.

________. "Testimony at a Hearing of the U.S. Senate, Committee on the January 23, 1880." In Stanton, E. History of Woman Suffrage, 3, 155-6. (Same as "I Am A Home-Loving, Law-Abiding, Tax-Paying Woman....")

________. "A Whole Humanity. Address to the National American Woman Suffrage Association Convention, 1890." In Stanton, E. History of Woman Suffrage, 4, 171-3.

Waller, Helen Hiett. "Introduction to Panel Discussion." In New York Herald Tribune. Report of the 18th Annual Forum on Current Problems, pp. 133-6.

Wallerstein, Helen. "Community Relationships Involved in 100 Per Cent Registration in Social Service Exchange: From the Standpoint of Family Welfare Organizations." In National Conference of Social Work. Proceedings (1932), pp. 198-203.

Walsh, Ethel Bent. "Statement." In U.S. Congress. House. Committee on Education and Labor. Subcommittee on Employment Opportunities. Legislation to Prohibit Sex Discrimination on the Basis of Pregnancy, pp. 121-4.

________. "Statement." In U.S. Senate. Committee on Human Resources. Subcommittee on Labor. Discrimination on the Basis of Pregnancy, 1977, pp. 31-3.

Walters, Barbara. "Address." In Conference on Women in the War on Poverty, 1967. Proceedings, pp. 37-8.

Walton, Genevieve. "The Lost Librarian." NYPL Bulletin, 29 (1925), 529-39.

Wanamaker, Claudia. "The Integration of Group Work and Case Work." In National Conference of Social Work. Proceedings (1935), pp. 300-10.

Ward, Genevieve. "The Drama as a Field for Women." In International Congress of Women, London, 1899, 3, 189-94.

Ward, May Alden. "Address of Welcome to the 9th Biennial Convention of the General Federation of Women's Clubs." In General Federation of Women's Clubs. Biennial Convention, 9 (1908), 23-5.

________. "Report of the Inter-Federation Committee." In General Federation of Women's Clubs. Biennial Convention, 9 (1908), 397-9.

Wardner, Louise Rockwood. "The Care of Girls in Reformatories." In Conference on Charities. Proceedings (1879), pp. 178-89.
________. "Reform Schools for Girls." In Conference of Charities. Proceedings (1878), pp. 189-93.

Ware, Caroline F. "Should It Be Safe to Save?" In International Congress of Women, Chicago, 1933. Our Common Cause, Civilization, pp. 433-40.
________. "Wartime Consumer Activities." In National Conference of Social Work. Proceedings (1944), pp. 374-81.

Ware, Jeannette P. Huntington. "What the Women of Kansas Are Doing Today." In World's Congress of Representative Women, Chicago, 1893. Congress of Women, pp. 277-80.

Warner, Carolyn. "The Taxpayer Needs to Know--Schools Can't Do Everything. Parents Can Make a Difference in Education Today." Vital Speeches, 44 (September 15, 1978), 708-12.

Warner, Esther L. "Women as Farmers." In International Council of Women, 1888. Report, pp. 156-61.

Warren, Althea H. "Salute to the Dawn." ALA Bulletin, 37 (September, 1943), 243-8.

Warren, Constance. "For What Are We Educating Women?" In Institute of Women's Professional Relations. War and Post-War Employment and Its Demands for Educational Adjustments, pp. 191-7.

Warren, Marjory C. "Methods Used by Social Case Workers in the Development of Personality: One of the Processes Used by Caseworkers in Developing Personality." In National Conference of Social Work. Proceedings (1924), pp. 299-303.

Warshay, Diana Wortman. "Women and Their Work Roles." In Hammond, N. Women and Children in Contemporary Society, pp. 12-6.

Warwick, Maya. "Public Testimony." In New York (City). Commission on Human Rights. Women's Role in Contemporary Society, pp. 778-85.

Washington, Bennetta B. "Address." In Conference on Women in the War on Poverty, 2nd, 1968. Proceedings, p. 27.
________. "Statement." In Conference on Women in the War on Poverty, 1967. Proceedings, pp. 31-2.

Watkins, Jacqueline Adele. "What About Youth?" In New York Herald Tribune. Report of the 3rd Women's Conference on Current Problems, pp. 73-4.

________. "Youth Plans for a Civilized World: Forum on the College Generation." In International Congress of Women, Chicago, 1933. Our Common Cause, Civilization, pp. 188-90.

Watson, Amey Brown Eaton. "The Attitude of Married Parents and Social Workers Toward Unmarried Parrents." In National Conference of Social Work. Proceedings (1918), pp. 102-9.

Watson, Barbara M. "International Travel: Consular Operations." Vital Speeches, 37 (May 15, 1971), 463-5.

________. "Providing Consular Services to the American Public Abroad: Statement Before the Subcommittee on International Operations, House. International Relations Committee." Washington, U. S. Department of State, Bureau of Public Affairs, Office of Media Services, 1977, 8 p.

Watson, Margaret H. "Environmental Conflicts in the Family and Social Life of the Modern Child." In National Conference of Social Work. Proceedings (1927), pp. 287-90.

Waxman, Ruth. "Public Testimony." In New York (City). Commission on Human Rights. Women's Role in Contemporary Society, pp. 701-3.

Weaver, Adele T. "Statement." In U. S. Congress. House. Committee on the Judiciary. Subcommittee No. 4. Equal Rights for Men and Women 1971, pp. 290-307.

________. "Statement." In U. S. Congress. Senate. Committee on the Judiciary. Subcommittee on Constitutional Amendments. Women and the "Equal Rights" Amendment, pp. 164-72.

Webb, Dora. "Organized Prostitution. How to Deal with It." In National Purity Congress, 1st, Baltimore, 1895. National Purity Congress, pp. 118-23.

Webb, Susan Bantecou. "Community Relationships Involved in 100 Per Cent Registration in Social Service Exchange: From the Standpoint of Hospital Social Service." In National Conference of Social Work. Proceedings (1932), pp. 186-92.

Weber, Edith. "Statement." In U. S. Congress. House. Committee on the Judiciary. Equal Rights Amendment to the Constitution (1932), pp. 18-9.

Webster, Eleanor. "Retraining for Employment." In M. I. T. Symposium on American Women in Science and Engineering, 1964. Women and the Scientific Professions, pp. 201-5.

Webster, Helen L. "Discussion of Woman's Dress from the Standpoint of Sociology." In World's Congress of Representative Women, Chicago, 1893. _A Historical Resume_, pp. 365-7.

________. "Our Debt to Zurich." In World's Congress of Representative Women, Chicago, 1893. _A Historical Resume_, pp. 692-5.

________. "Woman's Progress in Higher Education." In National Council of Women of the U. S., Washington, 1891. _Transactions_, pp. 192-9.

Weddingson, Sara. "Statement." In U. S. Congress. Senate. Committee on the Judiciary. Subcommittee on Constitutional Amendments. _Abortion_, pt. 4, pp. 297-304.

Weed, Helena Hill. "Address at the Columbia Theatre in Washington, D. C., November 15, 1914." In Irwin, I. _The Story of the Woman's Party_, pp. 84-5.

________. "Statement." In U. S. Congress. Senate. Committee on the Judiciary. Subcommittee on Constitutional Amendments. _Equal Rights for Men and Women_ (1938), pp. 166-9.

Wegny, Lily. "The Role of Women in the World of Today. No Longer Necessary to Try to Emulate Men." _Vital Speeches_, 27 (December 15, 1960), 143-6.

Weidensall, Jean. "The Mentality of the Unmarried Mother." In National Conference of Social Work. _Proceedings_ (1917), pp. 287-94.

Weil, Helen Kahn. "Jewish Women of Modern Days." In Jewish Women's Congress. _Papers_, pp. 26-42.

Weiss, Kay. "Biological and Cultural Determinants of the Division of Labor by Sex." In McGuigan, D. _New Research on Women at the University of Michigan_, pp. 199-212.

Weisstein, Naomi. "Kinder, Kuche, Kirche as Scientific Law: Psychology Constructs the Female." In Morgan, R. _Sisterhood Is Powerful_, pp. 205-20.

Welch, Jane Meade. "The Finding of the New World." In World's Congress of Representative Women, Chicago, 1893. _Congress of Women_, pp. 30-1.

Welcher, Gayle Gordon. "Statement." In U. S. Congress. Senate. Select Committee on Small Business. _The Effects of Government Regulations_, pp. 156-9.

Wellborn, Mary Moss. "Statement." In U. S. Congress. Senate. Committee on the Judiciary. Subcommittee on Constitutional Amendments. _Equal Rights Amendment_ (1929), p. 25.

Wells, Agnes E. "Statement." In U. S. Congress. Senate. Committee on the Judiciary. Subcommittee on Constitutional Amendments. Equal Rights Amendment (1945), pp. 13-5.

Wells, Alice Stebbins. "Policewomen." In National Conference of Charities and Correction. Proceedings (1915), pp. 411-8.

________. "The Policewomen Movement, Present Status and Future Needs." In National Conference of Charities and Correction. Proceedings (1916), pp. 547-52.

Wells, Emmeline B. "The National Woman's Relief Society." In National Council of Women of the U. S., Washington, 1891. Transactions, pp. 258-60.

________. "Western Women Authors and Journalists." In World's Congress of Representative Women, Chicago, 1893. A Historical Resume, pp. 800-2.

Wells, Jean A. "Women and Girls in Labor Market Today and Tomorrow." Washington, U. S. Women's Bureau, 1963, 13 p.

Wells, Kate Garrett. "State Regulation of Marriage." In National Conference of Charities and Correction. Proceedings (1897), pp. 302-8.

Wells, Rollene S. "Statement." In U. S. Congress. House. Committee on the Judiciary. Subcommittee No. 4. Equal Rights for Men and Women 1971, pp. 430-7.

Wells-Barnett, Ida. "Lynching Our National Crime." In National Negro Conference, New York, 1909. Proceedings, pp. 174-9.

Werner, Ella C. "Statement." In U. S. Congress. Senate. Committee on the Judiciary. Subcommittee on Constitutional Amendments. Equal Rights (1956), pp. 23-4.

West, Helen Hunt. "Statement." In U. S. Congress. Senate. Committee on the Judiciary. Subcommittee on Constitutional Amendments. Equal Rights Amendment (1945), pp. 45-6.

West, Mary Allen. "The Woman's Temperance Publishing Association." In National Council of Women of the U. S., Washington, 1891. Transactions, pp. 160-4.

West, Roberta B. "Identifying and Training the Gifted. Need for a Universal Approach." Vital Speeches, 26 (April 1, 1960), 379-82.

Wetherby, Phyllis. "Librarianship: Opportunity for Women?" In Conference of Professional and Academic Women. Sixteen Reports on the Status of Women in the Professions, 4 p.

Weyand, Ruth. "Statement." In U.S. Congress. House. Committee on Education and Labor. Subcommittee on Employment Opportunities. Legislation to Prohibit Sex Discrimination on the Basis of Pregnancy, pp. 199-200.

_______. "Statement." In U.S. Congress. Senate. Committee on Human Resources. Subcommittee on Labor. Discrimination on the Basis of Pregnancy, pp. 293-4.

Wheeler, Candace. "Congratulations on the Possession of Mrs. Palmer's Portrait." In World's Congress of Representative Women, Chicago, 1893. Congress of Women, pp. 818-9.

Wheeler, Mary P. "Some Test for the Evaluation of Case Work Methods." In National Conference of Social Work. Proceedings (1925), pp. 252-8.

Wheelock, Lucy. "The Children of the Other Half." In World's Congress of Representative Women, Chicago, 1893. Congress of Women, pp. 323-5.

White, Armenia S. "President's Address to the 7th Meeting of the New Hampshire Woman Suffrage Association, November 5, 1879." In Stanton, E. History of Woman Suffrage, 3, 376-8.

White, Elizabeth. "Statement." In U.S. Congress. Senate. Committee on the Judiciary. Subcommittee on Constitutional Amendments. Equal Rights for Men and Women (1933), p. 13.

White, Eva Whiting. "Community Centers in School Buildings." In National Conference of Social Work. Proceedings (1923), pp. 440-4.

_______. "How the Agencies and the Schools May Cooperate in the Development of the Curriculum." In National Conference of Social Work. Proceedings (1925), pp. 692-6.

_______. "Local Responsibility for Community Development." In National Conference of Social Work. Proceedings (1929), pp. 377-87.

_______. "War Activities as They Have Affected Housing, Health, and Recreation." In National Conference of Social Work. Proceedings (1919), pp. 496-502.

White, Helen C. "Activity in the Case-Work Relationship." In National Conference of Social Work. Proceedings (1933), pp. 280-7.

White, Jennie F. "Development in Eastern Washington." In World's Congress of Representative Women, Chicago, 1893. Congress of Women, pp. 123-6.

White, Lois A. "Discussion of Woman as a Religious Teacher." In World's Congress of Representative Women, Chicago, 1893. A Historical Resume, pp. 283-4.

Whiting, Marguerite. "Detroit's Experience with Job Classification." In National Conference of Social Work. Proceedings (1946), pp. 289-96.

Whitman, Marina Van Neumann. "From Farm Policy to Food Policy: Satisfying Multiple and Conflicting Goals." Vital Speeches, 39 (August 15, 1973), 656-8.

________. "Testimony on the Economics of Sex Discrimination in Employment." In U.S. Congress. Joint Economic Committee. Economic Problems of Women, pt. 1, p. 3, 33-8.

Whitney, Jessamine A. "The Indigent Migratory Tuberculous: The Facts of the Case." In National Conference of Social Work. Proceedings (1925), pp. 189-94.

________. "Social Research Program of the National Tuberculosis Association." In National Conference of Social Work. Proceedings (1927), pp. 192-3.

________. "The Tuberculous Migrant, a Family Problem: The Magnitude of the Problem." In National Conference of Social Work. Proceedings (1929), pp. 249-57.

Whitney, Mary T. "The Laws of Parentage and Heredity." In National Purity Congress, 1st, Baltimore, 1895. National Purity Congress, pp. 106-8.

Whitney, Mary Watson. "Life and Work of Maria Mitchell, LL.D." In Association for the Advancement of Women. Congress of Women (1890), pp. 12-28.

Whitton, Charlotte. "Juvenile Immigration." In National Conference of Social Work. Proceedings (1924), pp. 609-13.

Wickens, Margaret. "Address on National Relief Corps." In National Conference of Charities and Correction. Proceedings (1894), pp. 342-3.

Wiggin, Kate Douglas. "The Relation of the Kindergarten to Social Reform." In National Conference of Charities and Correction. Proceedings (1888), pp. 247-58.

Wilbour, Charlotte B. "Debate at the 2nd Woman's Suffrage Convention in Washington, D.C., January 1870." In Stanton, E. History of Woman Suffrage, 2, 424.

________. "The Inviolable Home." In Association for the Advancement of Women. Congress of Women, 1st. Papers, pp. 67-74.

Wildy, Lois. "Current Trends in Foster Parent Education." In National Conference of Social Work. Proceedings (1942), pp. 385-95.

Wiles, Alice Bradford. "National Society U.S. Daughters of 1812." In General Federation of Women's Clubs. Biennial Convention, 16 (1922), 94-5.

Wiley, Anna Campbell Kelton. "Statement." In U.S. Congress. House. Committee on the Judiciary. Equal Rights Amendment to the Constitution (1932), pp. 19-20.

________. "Statement." In U.S. Congress. Senate. Committee on the Judiciary. Subcommittee on Constitutional Amendments. Equal Rights Amendment (1945), pp. 6-7.

Wilkins, Josephine. "Facts Versus Folklore." In National Conference of Social Work. Proceedings (1939), pp. 461-72.

Wilkinson, Laura. "The Columbia Association of Housekeepers and Bureau of Information, with Plans for the Work Outlined in the National Columbian Household Economic Association, Which Was Incorporated March 15, 1893." In World's Congress of Representative Women, Chicago, 1893. A Historical Resume, pp. 887-91.

________. "Household Economics." In World's Congress of Representative Women, Chicago, 1893. Congress of Women, pp. 233-6.

Willard, Alice C. "Reinstatement of Vagrants Through Municipal Lodging Houses." In National Conference of Charities and Correction. Proceedings (1903), pp. 404-11.

Willard, Frances Elizabeth Caroline. "Address." In International Council of Women, 1888. Report, pp. 286-9, 319-21, 422-4.

________. "Address." In National Purity Congress, 1st, Baltimore, 1895. National Purity Congress, pp. 124-7.

________. "Address at Convention Hall, Washington, D.C. February 15, 1895." In Gordon, A. The Life of Frances E. Willard, pp. 159-65.

________. "Address at Exeter Hall, London, 1893." In Gordon, A. The Beautiful Life of Frances E. Willard, pp. 223-6.

________. "Address to the Senate Committee on Woman Suffrage, April 2, 1888." In Stanton, E. History of Woman Suffrage, 4, 141-2.

________. "Address at the 12th Annual Meeting of the Chicago W.C.T.U. in 1886." In Willard, F. Glimpses of Fifty Years, p. 422.

________. "Address at Welcome Meeting at Exeter Hall, London, 1892." In Gordon, A. The Life of Frances E. Willard, pp. 197-201.

________. "Address Before the Women's Congress, Des Moines, Iowa, 1885." In Willard, F. Glimpses of Fifty Years, pp. 475-8.

________. "Address on Organization." In International Council of Women, 1888. Report, pp. 222-5.

________. "Address to the Annual Convention of the National Woman's Christian Temperance Union, Philadelphia, 1885." In Willard, F. Glimpses of Fifty Years, pp. 419-21.

________. "Address to the Committee on Resolutions of the Republican National Convention in 1884." In Willard, F. Glimpses of Fifty Years, pp. 392-4.

________. "Address to the National Convention of the Woman's Christian Temperance Union, St. Louis, November, 1896." In Gordon, A. The Life of Frances E. Willard, pp. 241-3.

________. "Annual Address at the National Convention of the National Woman's Christian Temperance Union, Detroit, 1883." In Willard, F. Glimpses of Fifty Years, pp. 386-8.

________. "Annual Address at the National Convention of the National Woman's Christian Temperance Union, New York, 1888." In Willard, F. Glimpses of Fifty Years, pp. 463-8.

________. "Annual Address Before the National Convention of the Woman's Christian Temperance Union." In Gordon, A. The Life of Frances E. Willard, pp. 139-47.

________. "Annual Address to National Convention, W. C. T. U. . . . " In Gordon, A. The Beautiful Life of Frances E. Willard, pp. 129-34.

________. "Decoration Day Speech at a Prohibition Party Convention, 1888." In Willard, F. Glimpses of Fifty Years, pp. 447-52.

________. "Extracts from Addresses at International Council of Women in Washington, March 25 to April 1, 1888." In Willard, F. Glimpses of Fifty Years, pp. 592-6.

________. "Gospel Politics. Annual Address to the National Convention of the National Woman's Christian Temperance Union, St. Louis, 1884." In Willard, F. Glimpses of Fifty Years, pp. 403-5.

________. "The "Home Protection" Address." In Gordon, A. The Beautiful Life of Frances E. Willard, pp. 116-25. Also in Gordon, A. The Life of Frances E. Willard, pp. 118-33. Also in Papachristou, J. Women Together, p. 91.

________. "A New Departure in Normal Higher Education." In Association for the Advancement of Women. Congress of Women, 1st. Papers, pp. 94-9.

________. "President's Address." In Papachristou, J. Women Together, p. 92. (Same as "Annual Address at the National Convention of the National Woman's Christian Temperance Union, Detroit, 1883.")

________. "Speech Seconding the Nomination of John P. St. John for President at the Prohibition Party National Convention, Pittsburgh, 1884." In Willard, F. Glimpses of Fifty Years, pp. 397-400.

________. "The Summing-up of the Whole Matter." In Gordon, A. The Beautiful Life of Frances E. Willard, pp. 159-63.

________. "White-Cross Movement in Education." In National Education Association. Journal of Proceedings & Addresses (1890), pp. 159-78.

________. "Willard's Broad View of Temperance." In Papachristou, J. Women Together, p. 97.

________. "Woman's Work in Education." In National Education Association. Journal of Proceedings & Addresses (1884), pp. 161-8.

________. "Women and Organization. (President's Address)." In National Council of Women of the U. S., Washington, 1891. Transactions, pp. 23-57.

________. "Women in Temperance." In International Council of Women, 1888. Report, pp. 110-4.

Willebrandt, Mabel Walker. "The Club Woman and Law Enforcement." In General Federation of Women's Clubs. Biennial Convention, 16 (1922), 619-30.

________. "The Department of Justice and Some Problems of Enforcement." In Smith, F. Law vs. Lawlessness, pp. 78-93.

________. "Prohibition--The Problem of Enforcement from the Federal Standpoint." In National Conference of Social Work. Proceedings (1924), pp. 54-61.

Willen, Pearl. "Address." In Conference on Women in the War on Poverty, 1967. Proceedings, pp. 29-30.

Williams, Ethel James. "Statement." In U.S. Congress. House. Committee on Education and Labor. Select Subcommittee on Labor. Equal Pay for Equal Work, pp. 155-7.

________. "Statement." In U.S. Congress. House. Committee on Government Operations. Subcommittee. National Women's Conference, pp. 35-6.

Williams, Faith M. "Social and Economic Factors Conditioning Food Expenditures." In National Conference of Social Work. Proceedings (1937), pp. 536-41.

Williams, Fannie Barrier. "Address." In World's Parliament of Religions. World's Congress of Religions (Chicago, 1894), 2, 1114-5.

________. "The Intellectual Progress of the Colored Women of the United States Since the Emancipation Proclamation." In Loewenberg, B. Black Women in Nineteenth-century American Life, pp. 270-9. Also in World's Congress of Representative Women, Chicago, 1893. A Historical Resume, pp. 696-711.

________. "Religious Duty to the Negro." In Loewenberg, B. Black Women in Nineteenth-century American Life, pp. 265-70. Also in World's Parliament of Religions, Chicago, 1893. The World's Congress of Religions, pp. 893-7.

Williams, Lucille. "Statement." In U.S. Congress. Joint Economic Committee. Economic Problems of Women, pt. 4, 625-6.

Williams, Maud. "Statement." In U.S. Congress. Senate. Committee on the Judiciary. Subcommittee on Constitutional Amendments. Equal Rights (1931), pp. 3-5.

________. "Statement." In U.S. Congress. Senate. Committee on the Judiciary. Subcommittee on Constitutional Amendments. Equal Rights for Men and Women (1938), pp. 104-8.

Williams, Wendy W. "Statement." In U.S. Congress. House. Committee on Education and Labor. Subcommittee on Employment Opportunities. Legislation to Prohibit Sex Discrimination on the Basis of Pregnancy, pp. 43-7.

________. "Statement." In U. S. Congress. Senate. Committee on Human Resources. Subcommittee on Labor. Discrimination on the Basis of Pregnancy, pp. 113-7.

Williamson, Emily E. "The Children's Age." In National Conference of Charities and Correction. Proceedings (1903), pp. 192-6.

________. "Dwellings of the Poor in the Smaller Cities." In National Conference of Charities and Correction. Proceedings (1900), pp. 159-66.

________. "The Relation of Municipal and County Charities to the Commonwealth." In National Conference of Charities and Correction. Proceedings (1896), pp. 272-5.

________. "The Street Arab." In National Conference of Charities and Correction. Proceedings (1898), pp. 358-61.

Williamson, M. Lillian. "Committee on Industrial and Business Relations." In General Federation of Women's Clubs. Biennial Convention, 16 (1922), 501-3.

________. "Industrial and Business Relations." In General Federation of Women's Clubs. Biennial Convention, 16 (1922), 418-20.

Williston, Anne S. "Waterways and Water." In General Federation of Women's Clubs. Biennial Convention, 16 (1922), 555-8.

Wilson, Alisan. "From Signs of the Times." In World's Congress of Representative Women, Chicago, 1893. Congress of Women, pp. 488-90.

Wilson, Elizabeth Miller. "Pioneer Woman of Oregon." In World's Congress of Representative Women, Chicago, 1893. Congress of Women, pp. 203-4.

Wilson, Gertrude. "Human Needs Pertinent to Group Work Services." In National Conference of Social Work. Proceedings (1942), pp. 338-60.

________. "Interplay of the Insights of Case Work and Group Work." In National Conference of Social Work. Proceedings (1937), pp. 150-62.

________. "Methods of Record-keeping of Group Behavior and Individual Contacts." In National Conference of Social Work. Proceedings (1936), pp. 212-8.

Wilson, Marjorie P. "Career Patterns of Women in Medicine." In Spieler, C. Women in Medicine--1976, pp. 89-104.

Wing, Virginia R. "Arousing Voters to Action: A Story of a City Campaign." In National Conference of Social Work. Proceedings (1929), pp. 620-7.

________. "Making Human Geography Talk." In National Conference of Social Work. Proceedings (1928), pp. 633-4.

Wing, Virginia R.

________. "Some Psychological Experiments in Health Publicity." In National Conference of Social Work. Proceedings (1929), pp. 258-63.

________. "The Use of Volunteers in Rural Social Work: In Scioto County, Ohio." In National Conference of Social Work. Proceedings (1922), pp. 270-4.

Winn, Agnes. "Statement." In U.S. Congress. Senate. Committee on the Judiciary. Subcommittee on Constitutional Amendments. Equal Rights Amendment (1945), p. 13.

Winslow, Caroline B. "The Starting Point." In International Council of Women, 1888. Report, pp. 272-5.

Winslow, Helen M. "Strikes and Their Causes." In O'Neill, W. The Woman Movement, pp. 136-41.

Winslow, Mary N. "The Effect of Labor Laws on Women Workers." In National Conference of Social Work. Proceedings (1927), pp. 312-25.

________. "Married Women in Industry." In National Conference of Social Work. Proceedings (1923), pp. 321-6.

________. "Statement." In U.S. Congress. Senate. Committee on the Judiciary. Subcommittee on Constitutional Amendments. Equal Rights Amendment (1929), pp. 47-50.

________. "Statement." In U.S. Congress. Senate. Committee on the Judiciary. Subcommittee on Constitutional Amendments. Equal Rights for Men and Women (1933), pp. 17-22.

________. "Statement." In U.S. Congress. Senate. Committee on the Judiciary. Subcommittee on Constitutional Amendments. Equal Rights for Men and Women (1938), p. 83.

Winston, Ellen. "Women's Role in Bringing Peace Through Understanding." Washington, U.S. Welfare Administration, 1964, 11 p.

Winter, Alice Ames. "The Movies and Public Opinion." In New York Herald Tribune. Report of the 5th Annual Forum on Current Problems, pp. 255-9.

________. "President's Report, 1920-1922." In General Federation of Women's Clubs. Biennial Convention, 16 (1922), 74-81.

Wirtz, Jane. "Address." In Conference on Women in the War on Poverty, 1967. Proceedings, pp. 42-3.

Wise, Louise Waterman. "The Economy of Nursing the Sick Poor in Their Homes." In National Conference of Charities and Correction. Proceedings (1905), pp. 226-8.

Wiseman, Jacqueline P. "Case History I: Social Forces and the Politics of Research Approaches--Studying the Wives of Alcoholics." In U.S. National Center for Health Services Research. Women and Their Health, pp. 22-7.

Wisner, Elizabeth. "Professional Training in the Light of Wartime Shortages." In National Conference of Social Work. Proceedings (1943), pp. 319-30.

________. "War and the Social Services." In National Conference of Social Work. Proceedings (1944), pp. 1-15.

Witherspoon, Pauline. "Progress in Louisville Social Centers." In National Conference of Charities and Correction. Proceedings (1914), pp. 395-7.

Withrow, Kathryne B. "Statement." In U.S. Congress. Senate. Committee on the Judiciary. Subcommittee on Constitutional Amendments. Equal Rights Amendment (1945), p. 47.

Witkowsky, Esther. "Influence of the Discovery of America on the Jews." In Jewish Women's Congress. Papers, pp. 74-6.

Witmer, Helen Leland. "Some Underlying Principles of Research in Social Case Work." In National Conference of Social Work. Proceedings (1942), pp. 563-73.

Wittenmyer, Annie. "President's Address." In Papachristou, J. Women Together, pp. 90-1.

Witter, Jean. "Should Congress Approve the "Equal Rights Amendment"?" Congressional Digest, 50 (January, 1971), 24-30.

________. "Statement at the Senate Hearings on the Equal Rights Amendment." In Bosmajian, H. This Great Argument, pp. 203-14. Also in U.S. Congress. Senate. Committee on the Judiciary. Subcommittee on Constitutional Amendments. Women and the "Equal Rights" Amendment, pp. 39-41. (Same as "Should Congress Approve the "Equal Rights Amendment"?")

Wittich, Jean. "Squaring Income and Outgo." In International Congress of Women, Chicago, 1933. Our Common Cause, Civilization, pp. 541-6.

Wojciechowska, Maia. "Acceptance Paper--1965: Shadow of a Kid." In Kingman, L. Newbery and Caldecott Medal Books, 1956-1965, pp. 142-6.

Wolcott, Henrietta L. T. "Legislation to Prevent Cruelty to Children." In Association for the Advancement of Women. "Truth, Justice, and Honor," pp. 81-92.

Wolcott, Louise. "Treatment of Poor Widows with Dependent Children." In National Conference of Charities and Correction. Proceedings (1888), pp. 137-40.

Wold, Emma. "Statement." In U.S. Congress. Senate. Committee on the Judiciary. Subcommittee on Constitutional Amendments. Equal Rights Amendment (1929), pp. 11-6.

Wolf, Margery. "Chinese Women: Old Skills in a New Context." In Rosaldo, M. Woman, Culture, and Society, pp. 157-72.

Wolfe, Helen B. "The Backlash Phenomenon: The Equal Rights Amendment." Vital Speeches, 42 (August 15, 1976), 669-72.

Wolfgang, Myra K. "Should Congress Approve the "Equal Rights Amendment"?" Congressional Digest, 50 (January, 1971), 19-23.

________. "Statement." In U.S. Congress. House. Committee on the Judiciary. Equal Rights for Men and Women 1971, pp. 211-30.

________. "Statement." In U.S. Congress. Senate. Committee on the Judiciary. Subcommittee on Constitutional Amendments. Equal Rights 1970, pp. 28-45.

________. "Statement." In U.S. Congress. Senate. Committee on the Judiciary. Subcommittee on Constitutional Amendments. Women and the "Equal Rights" Amendment, pp. 91-102.

________. "Statement Before the Senate Committee on the Judiciary Hearings on the Equal-Rights Amendment, May 6, 1970." In Baxandall, R. America's Working Women, pp. 376-9.

Wolkoff, Regina L. "Men and Women in the Family: History of the Idea of Family in America's Depression Generation." In McGuigan, D. New Research on Women at the University of Michigan, pp. 132-5.

Wood, Edith Elmer. "Must Working People Live in Frayed-out Houses?" In National Conference of Social Work. Proceedings (1923), pp. 349-52.

Wood, Martha C. "The Effective Organization of Social Forces in Small Towns and Rural Communities." In National Conference of Social Work. Proceedings (1941), pp. 565-76.

Wood, Mary I. "Report of Bureau of Information." In General Federation of Women's Clubs. Biennial Convention, 9 (1908), 77-86.

Wood-Allen, Mary. "Moral Education of the Young." In National Purity Congress, 1st, Baltimore, 1895. National Purity Congress, pp. 244-38.

Woodhouse, Chase Going. "Chairman's Introduction. The Direct Impact of the Depression." In International Congress of Women, Chicago, 1933. Our Common Cause, Civilization, p. 279.

________. "Training on the Job While in College." In Institute of Women's Professional Relations. War and Post-war Employment and Its Demands for Educational Adjustments, pp. 205-9.

________. "Why the Conference." In Institute of Women's Professional Relations. War and Post-war Employment and Its Demands for Educational Adjustments, p. 104.

Woodhull, Victoria Claflin. "Address at the 20th Annual Meeting of the American Association of Spiritualists, Chicago, 1873." In Sachs, E. The Terrible Siren, pp. 222-4.

________. "Address of Victoria C. Woodhull, January 11, 1871, to the Honorable the Judiciary Committee of the House of Representatives of the Congress of the United States." In Stanton, E. History of Woman Suffrage, 2, 444-8.

________. "Address to National Woman Suffrage Association Convention, January 11, 1972, Washington." In Sachs, E. The Terrible Siren, p. 147.

________. "Address to the Organization Meeting of the People's Party, 1872." In Sachs, E. The Terrible Siren, pp. 157-8.

________. "Are Women Enfranchised by the 14th & 15th Amendments. Address of Victoria Claflin Woodhull to the House Judiciary Committee." In Scott, A. One Half the People, pp. 75-76. (Same as "Address of Victoria C. Woodhull, January 11, 1871, to the Honorable the Judiciary Committee of the House of Representatives of the Congress of the United States").

________. "The Elixir of Life." In Scheir, M. Feminism, pp. 152-4. (Same as "Address at the 20th Annual Meeting of the American Association of Spiritualists, Chicago, 1873".)

________. "Free Love Speech at Steinway Hall, New York, November 10, 1871." In Sachs, E. The Terrible Siren, pp. 131-7.

________. "From Woodhull's Speech on Social Freedom." In Papachristou, J. Women Together, p. 76.

________. "From Woodhull's Speech to the National Convention." In Papachristou, J. Women Together, p. 75. (Same as "Address to National Woman Suffrage Association Convention.")

________. "The Impending Revolution. Lectures at New York Academy of Music, February 20, 1872." In Sachs, E. The Terrible Siren, pp. 151-2.

________. "A Lecture on Constitutional Equality, Delivered at Lincoln Hall, Washington, D.C., Thursday, February 16, 1871." In Davis, P. A History of the National Woman's Rights Movement, Supplement, pp. 3-28. Also in Lerner, G. The Female Experience, pp. 351-4.

________. "A New Political Party and a New Party Platform." In Davis, P. A History of the National Woman's Rights Movement, Supplement, pp. 40F-40J.

________. "The New Rebellion. The Great Secession Speech of Victoria C. Woodhull Before the National Woman's Suffrage Convention, at the Apollo Hall, May 11, 1871." In Davis, P. A History of the National Woman's Rights Movement, pp. 112-9. (Same as "From Woodhull's Speech to the National Convention.")

________. "The Scare-crows of Sexual Freedom." In Sachs, E. The Terrible Siren, pp. 218-9.

Woods, Amy. "Consumer Organization." In International Congress of Women, Chicago, 1933. Our Common Cause, Civilization, pp. 461-6.

________. "Family Life and Alcoholism." In National Conference of Social Work. Proceedings (1917), pp. 491-4.

Woods, Elizabeth L. "The School and Delinquency: Every School a Clinic." In National Conference of Social Work. Proceedings (1929), pp. 213-21.

Woods, Kate Tannatt. "Women in the Pulpit." In National Council of Women of the U. S., Washington, 1891. Transactions, pp. 286-93.

Woods, Roberta. "Statement." In U. S. Congress. Senate. Committee on Human Resources. Subcommittee on Labor. Discrimination on the Basis of Pregnancy, pp. 301-2.

Woodside, Nina B. "Analysis of the Role of Women in Health Care Decisionmaking. A U. S. Response to a Look at Poland." In International Conference on Women in Health. Proceedings, pp. 145-9.

Woodward, Ellen S. "Womanpower." Washington, U. S. Federal Security Agency, Social Security Board, 1942, 6 p.

Woodward, Josephine. "Woman's Clubs from a Reporter's Point of View." In O'Neill, W. The Woman Movement, pp. 142-7.

Woolley, Celia Parker. "Race Reconciliation." In National Negro Conference, New York, 1909. Proceedings, pp. 74-88.

________. "Synopsis of Lecture on Margaret Fuller." In World's Congress of Representative Women, Chicago, 1893. Congress of Women, p. 763.

Woolley, Helen Thompson. "The Future Responsibility of the School Toward Children Under Five Years, Both Directly and Through Training for Parenthood." In National Conference of Social Work. Proceedings (1923), pp. 459-64.

________. "Mental and Physical Diagnosis of School Children (Report of a Subcommittee)." In National Conference of Social Work. Proceedings (1918), pp. 109-11.

________. "Social Consequences of the Neglect of Mental Hygiene in Young Childhood." In National Conference of Social Work. Proceedings (1924), pp. 459-64.

________. "The Supervision of Working Children Under the Ohio Law." In National Conference of Charities and Correction. Proceedings (1915), pp. 526-8.

Woolley, Mary Emma. "Address at the College Evening of the 38th Annual Convention of the National American Woman Suffrage Association, February 8, 1906." In Harper, I. The Life and Work of Susan B. Anthony, 3, 1390.

________. "The Crisis and Our Responsibility. Common Sense Is Lacking." Vital Speeches, 6 (January 15, 1940), 205-8.

________. "Progress, Man's Distinctive Mark Alone. Brute Force Shall Give Way--." Vital Speeches, 4 (August 15, 1938), 656-7.

________. "The Relation of Educated Women to the Peace Movement." In American Peace Congress, 1st, New York, 1907. Proceedings, pp. 97-100.

________. "Woman's Part and Power in the Peace Movement." In New York Herald Tribune. Report of the 2nd Women's Conference on Current Problems, pp. 67-70.

Woolson, Abba G. "The Relation of Woman to Her Dress." In Association for the Advancement of Women. Congress of Women, 1st. Papers, pp. 109-20.

Worcester, Daisy Lee Worthington. "The Standard of Living." In National Conference of Social Work. Proceedings (1929), pp. 337-53.

Worden, Anna M. "Women in the Grange." In International Council of Women, 1888. Report, pp. 137-42.

Workum, Ruth I. "The Relationship Between the Functions of the Juvenile Court and Those of the General Child-caring Agencies." In National Conference of Social Work. Proceedings (1922), pp. 141-5.

Wright, Alice Morgan. "Statement." In U.S. Congress. Senate. Committee on the Judiciary. Subcommittee on Constitutional Amendment. Equal Rights Amendment (1945), pp. 11-2.

Wright, Frances. "Address, Containing a Review of the Times, as First Delivered in the Hall of Science, New-York on Sunday May 9, 1830." In Wright, F. Course of Popular Lectures, Supplement, pp. 3-20.

________. "Address on the State of the Public Mind, and the Measures Which It Calls For. As Delivered in New-York and Philadelphia, in the Autumn of 1829." In Wright, F. Course of Popular Lectures, Supplement, pp. 3-21.

________. "Address I.--Delivered in the New Harmony Hall, on the Fourth of July, 1828." In Wright, F. Course of Popular Lectures, pp. 171-82.

________. "Address II.--Delivered in the Walnut-Street Theatre, Philadelphia, on the Fourth of July, 1829." In Wright F. Course of Popular Lectures, pp. 183-202.

________. "Address III.--Delivered at the Opening of the Hall of Science, New-York, Sunday, April 26, 1829." In Wright, F. Course of Popular Lectures, pp. 203-26.

________. "An Address to Young Mechanics. As Delivered in the Hall of Science, June 13, 1830." In Wright F. Course of Popular Lectures, Supplement, pp. 3-13.

________. "Course of Popular Lectures, (Excerpts from "Introductory Address" and "Lecture I, On the Nature of Knowledge" and "Lecture II, Free Enquiry.")" In Schneir, M. Feminism, pp. 18-24.

________. "Free Enquiry, 1829." In Martin, W. The American Sisterhood, pp. 197-202. (Same as "Lecture II.")

________. "In a Daughter They Have a Human Being: In a Son the Same." In Lerner, G. The Female Experience, pp. 223-9. (Same as "Address I.--Delivered in the New Harmony Hall, on the Fourth of July, 1828.")

________. "Introductory Address to the Course, as Delivered for the Second Time in New-York." In Wright, F. Course of Popular Lectures, pp. 13-6.

________. "Lecture I.--On the Nature of Knowledge." In Wright, F. Course of Popular Lectures, pp. 17-40.

________. "Lecture II.--Of Free Enquiry, Considered as a Means of Obtaining Just Knowledge." In Wright, F. Course of Popular Lectures, pp. 41-62.

________. "Lecture III.--Of the More Important Divisions and Essential Parts of Knowledge." In Wright, F. Course of Popular Lectures, pp. 63-84.

________. "Lecture IV.--Religion." In Wright, F. Course of Popular Lectures, pp. 85-105.

________. "Lecture V.--Morals." In Wright, F. Course of Popular Lectures, pp. 106-26.

________. "Lecture VI.--Opinions." In Wright, F. Course of Popular Lectures, pp. 127-49.

________. "Lecture VII.--On Existing Evils and Their Remedy, as Delivered in Philadelphia, on June 2nd, 1829." In Wright, F. Course of Popular Lectures, pp. 150-70.

________. "Of Free Enquiry Considered as a Means for Obtaining Just Knowledge." In Rossi, A. The Feminist Papers, pp. 108-17. Also in Tanner, L. Voices from Women's Liberation, pp. 34-5. (Same as "Lecture II.")

________. "On Free Enquiry." In Cott, N. Root of Bitterness, pp. 219-22. (Same as "Lecture II.")

________. "Parting Address, as Delivered in the Bowery Theatre, to the People of New-York, in June, 1830." In Wright, F. Course of Popular Lectures, Supplement, pp. 3-22.

________. "Reply to the Traducers of the French Reformers of the Year 1789." In Wright, F. Course of Popular Lectures, pp. 227-32.

Wright, Helen. "Why Unemployment?" In International Congress of Women, Chicago, 1933. Our Common Cause, Civilization, pp. 280-5.

Wright, Leslie. "Statement." In U.S. Congress. House. Committee on the Judiciary. Subcommittee No. 1. Equal Rights Amendment (1948), pp. 69-70.

Wright, Lucy. "The Creative Use of Leisure." In International Congress of Women, Chicago, 1933. Our Common Cause, Civilization, pp. 936-43.

________. "Prevention of Blindness from Opthalmia Neonatorum." In National Conference of Charities and Correction. Proceedings (1919), pp. 357-64.

________. "The Worker's Attitude as an Element in Social Case Work." In National Conference of Social Work. Proceedings (1924), pp. 303-6.

Wright, Martha Coffin. "President's Address at the 10th National Woman's Rights Convention, New York, May 10-11, 1860." In Stanton, E. History of Woman Suffrage, 1, 689.

Wright, Mary Page. "Woman's Life in Asiatic Turkey." In World's Congress of Representative Women, Chicago, 1893. Congress of Women, p. 305.

Wu, Chien-Shiung. "Panelist Statement." In M. I. T. Symposium on American Women in Science and Engineering, 1964. Women and the Scientific Professions, pp. 44-8.

Wubnig, Sylvia. "Statement." In U. S. Congress. House. Committee on the Judiciary. Subcommittee No. 1. Equal Rights Amendment (1948), pp. 181-2.

Wyman, Marian M. "What Is Basic in Case-work Practice." In National Conference of Social Work. Proceedings (1938), pp. 112-21.

Yalof, Helen. "Public Testimony." In New York (City). Commission on Human Rights. Women's Role in Contemporary Society, pp. 796-7.

Yalow, Rosalyn S. "Radio Immunoassay: A Probe for the Fine Structure of Biologic Systems." Science, 200 (June 16, 1978), 1236-45.

Yans-McLaughlin, Virginia. "Italian Women and Work: Experience and Perception." In Cantor, M. Class, Sex, and the Woman Worker, pp. 101-19.

Yarrows, Rachelle S. "Community Organization for Health-Discussion." In International Congress of Women, Chicago, 1933. Our Common Cause, Civilization, pp. 620-2.

________. "The Prostitute as a Health and Social Problem." In National Conference of Social Work. Proceedings (1919), pp. 220-4.

Yates, Elizabeth. "Acceptance Paper--Newbery Medal 1951. Climbing Some Mountain in the Mind." In Miller, B. Newbery Medal Books, 1922-1955, pp. 361-71.

Yerxa, Elizabeth. "The Modern Program of Rural Social Work as It Affects Children." In National Conference of Social Work. Proceedings (1924), pp. 116-70.

Yocum, Susan. "The Use of Current Case-work Concepts Where There Is Physical Illness: From the Experience of the Case Worker in the Social Agency." In National Conference of Social Work. Proceedings (1939), pp. 314-25.

Young, Imogene Stokes. "The Responsibility of the Psychiatric Social Worker in Civilian Life." In National Conference of Social Work. Proceedings (1946), pp. 319-24.

Young, Mary A. "Re-examination of Child-care Functions in Family Agencies." In National Conference of Social Work. Proceedings (1935), pp. 187-99.

Young, Virginia D. "Testimony to the Senate." In Scott, A. One Half the People, pp. 104-5.

Young, Zina D. H. "Discussion of Woman as a Religious Teacher." In World's Congress of Representative Women, Chicago, 1893. A Historical Resume, p. 284.

Younger, Maud. "Address to the Rules Committee of the House on a Hearing on the Question of the Creation of a Suffrage Committee, May, 1917." In Irwin, I. The Story of the Woman's Party, pp. 303-5.

________. "Memorial Address for Inez Milholland Boissevain." In Stevens, D. Jailed for Freedom, pp. 49-51.

________. "Statement." In U.S. Congress. Senate. Committee on the Judiciary. Subcommittee on Constitutional Amendments. Equal Rights Amendment (1929), pp. 102.

________. "Statement." In U.S. Congress. Senate. Committee on the Judiciary. Subcommittee on Constitutional Amendments. Equal Rights (1931), pp. 2-3, 65-6.

________. "Statement." In U.S. Congress. Senate. Committee on the Judiciary. Subcommittee on Constitutional Amendments. Equal Rights for Men and Women (1933), pp. 3-4.

Zapoleon, Marguerite W. "College Women and Employment." In Conference on the Present Status and Prospective Trends of Research on the Education of Women, Rye, N.Y., 1957. The Education of Women, pp. 56-63.

Zemach, Margot. "Caldecott Award Acceptance--1974." In Kingman, L. Newbery and Caldecott Medal Books, 1966-1975, pp. 257-9.

Ziegler, Susan. "Self-perception of Athletes and Coaches." In Harris, D. Women and Sports, pp. 293-305.

Zimmerman, Cynthia. "The Citizen's Responsibility; A Panel Discussion." In New York Herald Tribune. Report of the 18th Annual Forum on Current Problems, pp. 160-2.

Zizzmia, Alba I. "The Career Woman." In Bier, W. Woman in Modern Life, pp. 194-209.

Zoble, Judith. "Femininity and Achievement in Sports." In Harris, D. Women and Sports, pp. 203-23.

Zuill, Frances. "How Home Economics Can Contribute to Meeting These Problems." In Michigan State University, East Lansing, School of Home Economics. Potentialities of Women in the Middle Years, pp. 169-81.

SUBJECT INDEX

ABANDONED CHILDREN

Lesley, S.	"Foundlings and Deserted Children."

ABOLITIONISTS

Anthony, S.	"Abolitionist Speech."
________.	"Speech of Susan B. Anthony."
Blackwell, A.	"Address at the Woman's National Loyal League Convention, May 14, 1863."
Diaz, A.	"Address of Mrs. Abby M. Diaz."
Foster, A.	"Address at Philadelphia Anti-slavery Meeting, 1855."
________.	"Speech of Abby Kelley Foster."
Gage, F.	"Speech of Mrs. Frances D. Gage."
Grew, M.	"Annals of Women's Anti-slavery Societies."
Grimke, A.	"Address at the Woman's National Loyal League Convention, May 14, 1863."
________.	"Angelina Grimke's Address."
________.	"The Sufferings of the Slaves."
Mott, L.	"Speech of Lucretia Mott."
Remond, S.	"Miss Remond's First Lecture in Dublin."
Rose, E.	"Address at the Woman's National Loyal League Convention, May 14, 1863."
Staley, S.	"Address of the Ladies' Anti-slavery Society of Delaware, Ohio to the Convention of Disfranchised Citizens of Ohio."
Stewart, M.	"An Address, Delivered at the African Masonic Hall, Boston, 27 February 1833."
________.	"Lecture, Delivered at the Franklin Hall, Boston, 21 September 1832."
________.	"Mrs. Stewart's Farewell Address to Her Friends in the City of Boston, 21 September 1833."
________.	"Throw Off Your Fearfulness and Come Forth!"
Stone, L.	"Address of Mrs. Lucy Stone."
________.	"Concluding Remarks at the Woman's National Loyal League Convention, May 14, 1863."
________.	"Debate at the Woman's National Loyal League Convention, May 14, 1863."
________.	"Speech of Lucy Stone."

ABORTION

Abzug, B.	"The Abortion Rights Act."
________.	"Statement."
Barry, M.	"Statement."
Chisholm, S.	"Abortion."
________.	"Abortion and Population Control."
Colom, A.	"Statement."
Corin, L.	"Public Testimony."
Czarnecki, D.	"Statement."
Engle, R.	"Statement."
Friedan, B.	"Abortion: A Woman's Civil Right."
________.	"Statement."
Fruchter, R.	"Public Testimony."
Furlong-Cahill, J.	"Statement."
Garton, J.	"Statement."
Goldenberg, S.	"Public Testimony."
Goltz, P.	"Statement."
Hartle, M.	"Statement."
Hatcher, S.	"The Adolescent Experience of Pregnancy and Abortion."
Horrobin, M.	"Statement."
Hunt, M.	"Statement."
Jefferson, M.	"Statement."
Katz, K.	"Statement."
Kenyon, D.	"Public Testimony."
Lancione, I.	"Statement."
Lowry, P.	"Statement."
Mayer, S.	"Public Testimony."
Mears, J.	"Statement."
Mecklenburg, M.	"Statement."
Pilpel, H.	"Statement."
Roudebush, D.	"Statement."
Schiffer, L.	"Statement."
Shoup, J.	"Statement."
Stearns, N.	"Access to Abortion and Family Planning."
Stitt, J.	"Statement."
Weddingson, S.	"Statement."

ACTRESSES

Gayvan, G.	"The Stage and Its Women."
Marlowe, J.	"Woman's Work Upon the Stage."
Morris, C.	"Woman in the Emotional Drama."
Ward, G.	"The Drama as a Field for Women."

ADDAMS, JANE

Abbott, E.	"Remarks at Jane Addams Memorial Service."
Lenroot, K.	"Remarks at Jane Addams Memorial Service."

Perkins, F.	"Remarks at Jane Addams Memorial Service."
Simkhovitch, M.	"Remarks at Jane Addams Memorial Service."

ADOPTION

Aleshire, R.	"Problems of Adoption in Rural Areas."
Colby, M.	"Protection of Children in Adoption."
Foster, S.	"Fees for Adoption Service."
Gordon, H.	"Current Trends in Adoption."
Harral, E.	"The Foster Parent and the Agency in the Adoption Process."
Ray, A.	"A Good Adoption Program: Can Standards Be Maintained Without Sacrificing Flexibility?"
Theis, S.	"Case Work in the Process of Adoption."

ADULT EDUCATION

American, S.	"Vacation Schools."
Bane, G.	"The Home Teacher Experiment in Springfield, Illinois."
Roche, J.	"The Place of the Foreign Language Press in an Educational Program."
Woolley, H.	"The Future Responsibility of the School Toward Children Under Five Years, Both Directly and Through Training for Parenthood."

ADULTHOOD

Foxwroth, J.	"Our Creeping Idiot Savantism: Maturity Can Be Magnificent."

ADVERTISING

Stephenson, M.	"Blind People Do Not Fear Snakes. Advertising: Is It Legal, Moral & Ethical?"

AERONAUTICS--U. S. --SAFETY MEASURES

Bailey, K.	"Remarks Before the Air Transport Association, 1977 Airlines Operations Forum, Tampa, Florida, October 19, 1977."

AEROPLANE AMBULANCES

Richardson, H.	"Ambulances of the Air."

AESTHETICS

Baird, P.	"Aesthetic Culture."
Howe, J.	"The Halfness of Nature."

AFFIRMATIVE ACTION PROGRAMS--U. S.

Klotzburger, K.	"Advisory Committee Role In Constructing Affirmative Action Programs."
Rumbarger, M.	"The Great Quota Debate and Other Issues in Affirmative Action."
Sandler, B.	"Affirmative Action on the Campus: Like It Or Not, Uncle Sam Is Here to Stay."

AFRICA

Barnes, S.	"Political Transition in Urban Africa."
Morgenthau, R.	"From European Colonies to the Third World--The Developing States of Africa."
Sheldon, M.	"An African Expedition."

AFRO-AMERICAN WOMEN

Bethune, M.	"A Century of Progress of Negro Women."
Brown, H.	"Discussion of the Organized Efforts of the Colored Women of the South to Improve Their Condition."
Cade, T.	"On the Issues of Roles."
Cooper, A.	"The Colored Woman Should Not Be Ignored."
________.	"Discussion of the Intellectual Progress of the Colored Women of the United States Since the Emancipation Proclamation."
Davidson, O.	"How Shall We Make the Women of Our Race Stronger?"
Early, S.	"The Organized Efforts of the Colored Women of the South to Improve Their Condition."
French-Sheldon, M.	"Practical Issues of an African Experience."
Hamer, F.	"The Special Plight and the Role of Black Women."
Harper, F.	"The Afro-American Mother."
Height, D.	"To Be Black and a Woman."
Irwin, H.	"Conditions in Industry as They Affect Negro Women."
Kennedy, F.	"To Be Black and a Woman."

Keyserling, M.	"Negro Woman in United States, New Roles, New Challenges."
Laney, L.	"Address Before the Women's Meeting."
________.	"The Burden of the Educated Colored Woman."
Parker, J.	"The Duty of the American White Woman to the American Black Woman."
Ruffin, J.	"The Beginnings of the National Club Movement."
________.	"From Josephine St. Pierre Ruffin's Speech."
Truth, S.	"Address to the Woman's Rights Convention in New York, September 1853."
________.	"I Suppose I Am About the Only Colored Woman that Goes About to Speak for the Rights of Colored Women."
Williams, F.	"The Intellectual Progress of the Colored Women of the United States Since the Emancipation Proclamation."

AFRO-AMERICANS

Beatty, B.	"Negro Child Life in Rural Communities."
Cooley, R.	"The Regeneration of the Colored Population in the Rural South."
Eliot, M.	"Health of Our Negro Children."
Fisher, A.	"Equal Educational Opportunities."
Foster, A.	"Remarks at the 1st Annual Meeting of the American Equal Rights Association, May, 1867."
Griffing, J.	"Address to the 1st Annual Meeting of the American Equal Rights Association, May, 1867."
Guzman, J.	"The Southern Race Problem in Retrospect. South Unable Psychologically to Solve Its Problem Alone."
Harper, F.	"A Black Woman Appeals to White Women for Justice for Her Race."
________.	"Duty to Dependent Races."
Hurst, F.	"The Submerged Race."
Jones, F.	"The Effects on Case Work Services of Social Factors in the Negro's Life: From the Point of View of Economic Factors."
Laney, L.	"General Conditions of Mortality."
Lyells, R.	"New Emancipation. Responsibilities of the Negro."
________.	"A Look Ahead. What the Negro Wants."
Remond, S.	"The Negroes in the United States of America."
Smith, L.	"Ten Years from Today. We Are Changing Rapidly, Without Violence.

Stewart, M.	"Sufferings During the War."
Williams, F.	"Address."
________.	"Religious Duty to the Negro."

AGED

Brungardt, T.	"Fun for the Older Person in the Country."
Grasso, E.	"The Handicapped and Older Americans."
Mead, M.	"Aging Differently in the Space Age; Excerpts from Address."
Spohn, R.	"Public Testimony."

ALASKA

Gruber, R.	"Alaska--The New Crossroads."
________.	"Rediscovery of Alaska. Crossroads of America."

ALCOHOLISM

Amigh, O.	"Alcoholism as a Case of Degeneracy."
Anthony, S. B.	"Statement."
Baker, S.	"Alcoholism."
Clayton, J.	"Statement."
D'Angelo, A.	"Statement."
Higgins, A.	"Alcohol Problems."
King, G.	"Intemperance as a Cause of Mortality."
Mann, M.	"What Shall We Do About Alcoholism? Alcoholics Anonymous."
Tilton, E.	"What Makes Men Stop Drinking?"
Woods, A.	"Family Life and Alcoholism."

ALMSHOUSES

Clark, M.	"The Almshouse."
Clark, S.	"Almshouse Property: The Ideal in Amount and Upkeep."
Hinrichsen, A.	"The District Almshouse for Illinois."
Potter, E.	"The Future Development of the Almshouse."
Randall, E.	"Admissions and Records in an Almshouse."

AMERICA--DISCOVERY AND EXPLORATION

Welch, J.	"The Finding of the New World."

AMNESTY

Abzug, B.	"Should "Conditional Amnesty" Be Granted to Vietnam War Draft Evaders?"

ANARCHISM AND ANARCHISTS

Smith, M.	"U. S. Faces Choice Between Anarchy and Repression. Address, June 1, 1970."

ANTHONY, MARY S.

Gannett, M.	"Eulogy for Mary S. Anthony's Funeral, February 7, 1907."
Greenleaf, J.	"Tribute to Mary S. Anthony, at Her Funeral, February 7, 1907."
Montgomery, H.	"Eulogy at Mary S. Anthony's Funeral, February 7, 1907."
Shaw, A.	"Eulogy for Mary S. Anthony, at Her Funeral, February 7, 1907."

ANTHONY, SUSAN BROWNELL

Avery, R.	"Reminiscence of Susan B. Anthony at Berkshire Historical Society Meeting, July 1897."
Blatch, H.	"Tribute to Susan B. Anthony at Her 80th Birthday Celebration, February 15, 1900."
Catt, C.	"Address at the Annual Meeting of the Historical and Scientific Society of Berkshire, July, 1897."
________.	"Eulogy at Susan B. Anthony's Funeral, March 15, 1906."
Colby, C.	"Tribute to Susan B. Anthony at Berkshire Historical Society Meeting, July, 1897."
Cook, C.	"Tribute to Susan B. Anthony at Her 80th Birthday Celebration, February 15, 1900."
Gaffney, F.	"Tribute to Susan B. Anthony at Her 80th Birthday Celebration, February 15, 1900."
Greenleaf, J.	"What Woman's New Social Service Owes. Address at Susan B. Anthony's 85th Birthday Celebration."
Hultin, I.	"Tribute to Susan B. Anthony at Her 80th Birthday Celebration, February 15, 1900."
Jordan, M.	"Address at the College Evening of the 38th Annual Convention of the National American Woman Suffrage Association, February 8, 1906."
Moore, E.	"Address at the College Evening of the 38th Annual Convention of the National American Woman Suffrage Association, February 8, 1906."
Park, M.	"Address at the College Evening of the 38th Annual Convention of the National American Woman Suffrage Association, February 8, 1906."

Anthony, Susan Brownell 332

Salmon, L.	"Address at the College Evening of the 38th Annual Convention of the National American Woman Suffrage Association, February 8, 1906."
Sewall, M.	"Tribute to Susan B. Anthony at Berkshire Historical Society Meeting, July, 1897."
________.	"Tribute to Susan B. Anthony at Her 80th Birthday Celebration, February 15, 1900."
Shaw, A.	"Anecdote of Susan B. Anthony, 32nd Annual Convention of the National American Woman Suffrage Association, February 1900."
________.	"Final Tribute at Susan B. Anthony's Funeral, March 15, 1906."
________.	"Tribute to Susan B. Anthony at Berkshire Historical Society Meeting, July, 1897."
________.	"Tribute to Susan B. Anthony at Her 80th Birthday Celebration, February 15, 1900."
Stanton, E.	"The Friendships of Women."
Thompson, E.	"Tribute to Susan B. Anthony at Her 80th Birthday Celebration, February 15, 1900."
Woolley, M.	"Address at the College Evening of the 38th Annual Convention of the National American Woman Suffrage Association, February 8, 1906."

ANTHROPO-GEOGRAPHY

Howell, B.	"Making Human Geography Talk."
Renard, B.	"Making Human Geography Talk."
Wing, V.	"Making Human Geography Talk."

ANTHROPOLOGY

Bamberger, J.	"The Myth of Matriarchy: Why Men Rule in Primitive Society."
Danaraj, S.	"Son Preference in Taiwan: Verbal Preference and Demographic Behavior."
Denich, B.	"Sex and Power in the Balkans."
Diamond, N.	"Toward an Anthropology of Women."
Gonzalez, N.	"Women and the Jural Domain: An Evolutionary Perspective."
Hoffer, C.	"Madam Yoko: Ruler of the Kpa Mende Confederacy."
Jay, P.	"The Female Primate."
Lamphere, L.	"Strategies, Cooperation, and Conflict Among Women in Domestic Groups."
Leis, N.	"Women in Groups: Ijaw Women's Associations."
O'Laughlin, B.	"Mediation of Contradiction: Why Mbum Women Do Not Eat Chicken."

Ortner, S.	"Is Female to Male as Nature Is to Culture?"
Paul, L.	"The Mastery of Work and the Mystery of Sex in a Guatemalan Village."
Rosaldo, M.	"Woman, Culture, and Society: A Theoretical Overview."
Sanday, P.	"Female Status in the Public Domain."
Stack, C.	"Sex Roles and Survival Strategies in an Urban Black Community."
Tanner, N.	"Matrifocality in Indonesia and Africa and Among Black Americans."

ANTIMISSILE MISSILES

Smith, M.	"Senate Speech on Safeguard ABM System."

ANTISEMITISM

Hirshfield, L.	"How Can Nations Be Influenced to Protest or Interfere in Cases of Persecution?"
Jacobson, L.	"How Can Nations Be Influenced to Protest or Interfere in Cases of Persecution?"

ARBITRATION, INTERNATIONAL

Lord, E.	"International Arbitration."

ARISTOPHANES

Howe, J.	"Aristophanes."

ART

Bagg, M.	"Historic Art."
Berry, R.	"Address. The Needs of Art To-day."
________.	"The Gift of the Fine Arts Department to the General Federation of Women's Clubs."
Bibb, G.	"Art as a Medium of Civilization."
Cole, A.	"Art-isms."
Cohen, K.	"Life of Artists."
Doggett, K.	"Art for Women."
Hinds, I.	"Harmonious Culture."
Howe, J.	"On the Formation of Art Groups."
Mason, F.	"Address: Art and the Next Generation."
Morey, A.	"Fine Arts Slides."
Norris, M.	"An Appeal of Art to the Lovers of Art."
Sartain, E.	"Discussion of the Contribution of Women to the Applied Arts."

Scull, S. — "Study of Greek Art."
Sheldon, E. — "The Educational Value of Applied Arts."

ASTRONOMERS

Leavitt, H. — "The Work of Women in Modern Astronomy."

ATHEISM

Goldman, E. — "The Philosophy of Atheism."

ATOMIC ENERGY

Ray, D. — "General Conference of the International Atomic Energy Agency Holds 17th Session at Vienna; Statement, September 18, 1973."

ATOMIC WARFARE

Smith, M. — "Address on Nuclear Credibility to Senate and President, September 21, 1961."
________. — "2nd Address of Nuclear Credibility, Senate, September 21, 1962."

ATOMIC WEAPONS

Smith, M. — "Nuclear Credibility."

AUTOMOBILE INDUSTRY AND TRADE

Maltese, F. — "Notes for a Study of the Automobile Industry."

BARNETT, SAMUEL A.

Addams, J. — "Canon Samuel A. Barnett. Memorial Address Given to the American Federation of Settlements."

BEAUTY, PERSONAL

Gage, M. — "Intelligent Treatment of the Body."

BEVERAGE CONTAINERS--LAWS AND LEGISLATION

Anderson, J.	"Should Congress Enact Proposed Legislation to Require Mandatory Deposits on Beverage Containers?"

BIRTH CONTROL

Cisler, L.	"Public Testimony."
Gaylord, G.	"Restrictions in Regard to Regulation of Birth Imposed by Laws of the Various Civilized Nations."
Hoffman, C.	"Address."
Moque, A.	"Reproduction and Natural Law."
Sanger, M.	"Speech at Dinner Given in Her Honor, January 23, 1916."
________.	"Speech at 6th International Neo-Malthusian and Birth Control Conference, March, 1925."
________.	"Speech Before Senate Sub-committee, February 13, 1931."
Stone, H.	"Family Limitation and Family Health."

BLENNERHASSETT, MARGARET AGNEW

Curwen, M.	"The Wife of Blennerhassett."

BLIND

Hayden, A.	"Organization of Social Forces for Prevention of Blindness."
Keller, H.	"Social Causes of Blindness. Speech in Behalf of the Massachusetts Association for Promoting the Interests of the Blind, Boston, February 14, 1911."
La Barraque, C.	"What the Seeing Woman Can Do for the Blind Woman in a Business-like Way."

BOOKBINDING

Preston, E.	"Artistic Book Binding."

BOWEN, JOSEPH TILTON

Addams, J.	"Joseph Tilton Bowen. At the Opening of the Joseph Tilton Bowen Country Club."

BRAIN

Gardner, H. "Sex in Brain."

BUDGETS, PERSONAL

Hanchette, H. "Family Budget Planning."
Nathan, M. "The Ethics of Spending."
Wittich, J. "Squaring Income and Outgo."

BUSINESS EDUCATION

Crain, L. "What Are Our Schools Teaching About Business? Responsibility Lies with the Taxpayers."

BUSINESS TAX

Graves, J. "Impact of Taxation on Small Business. Lack of Working Capital Prohibits Expansion."

CAMPS

Rippin, J. "Specific Problems in Camp Communities."

CARVER, GEORGE WASHINGTON

Luce, C. "Saintly Scientist. George Washington Carver."

CARY, ALICE

Anthony, S. "Homes of Single Women."

CATHOLIC CHURCH

Meyers, B. "Raise Your Voice: Cast Your Vote."
Onahan, M. "Catholic Women's Part in Philanthropy."

CERAMICS

Braumuller, L. "Art in Ceramics."

CHARACTER

Richardson, E.	"Character Building in Education."

CHARITIES

Acton, A.	"Chartering and Supervision by State Authority."
Addams, J.	"Charitable Effort."
________.	"Charity and Social Justice."
Barrett, K.	"The Need for State Supervision for Both Public and Private Charities."
Barrows, I.	"What Unitarian Women Are Doing."
Belmont, A.	"Co-ordinating Relief."
Bemis, A.	"Human Relations in Public Charity."
Bidwell, A.	"Address on Presenting a Gift of Land for a Park to Chico, California, 1905."
Breckinridge, S.	"Public Charitable Service as a Profession."
Brown, C.	"The Protective Agency for Women and Children."
Buffington, A.	"Co-ordinating as Done by Charity Organization Societies."
Cheney, E.	"Boston Charities--New England Hospital."
Colcord, J.	"Training for the Work of Civilian Relief."
Curry, H.	"The County as a Unit in Charity Administration--Roundtable."
Curtis, F.	"What Had the Public a Right to Know About Public and Private Charities and How Shall It Learn About Them."
Deardorff, N.	"Joint Financing of Private Social Work: Enter New York."
Duryea, F.	"Near East Relief."
Evans, E.	"Scientific Charity."
Felton, K.	"Status of Organized Charity in the West."
________.	"The Charities Endorsement Committee."
Gardiner, E.	"Municipal Organization of Social Service in the Proposed New Charter of Grand Rapids."
Genger, M.	"The Financial History of the Newark Bureau of Associated Charities."
Glenn, M.	"Report of the Committee: The Working Force of Organized Charity."
Godman, H.	"Argument Against Public Outdoor Relief."
Hoffman, C.	"Organization Among Women Considered with Respect to Philanthropy--Continued."
Lowell, J.	"A Better System of Public Charities and Correction for Cities."
________.	"How to Adapt Charity Organization Methods to Small Communities."
________.	"Scientific Charity."
McNeier, L.	"Ladies of the Grand Army of the Republic."
Morse, F.	"How Can We Further the Organization of Charities?"

Newman, A.	"Report on Jail Work of the W. C. T. U. in Nebraska."
Prier, M.	"Charity Organization in the Smaller Cities."
Putnam, E.	"Paper on the System of Visiting the Girls and Small Boys Who Are Wards of the State in Massachusetts."
Reed, A.	"Public Charities in Washington."
Richards, E.	"Women's Relief Associations."
Richards, J.	"The National Woman's Relief Society."
Richardson, A.	"The Cooperation of Women in Philanthropy."
Richardson, V.	"Report of Western Women's Unitarian Conference."
Richmond, M.	"Charitable Co-operation."
________.	"The Message of the Associated Charities."
________.	"The Need of a Training-school in Applied Philanthropy."
________.	"Organization Among Women Considered with Respect to Philanthropy."
Rowe, L.	"Municipalization of Charitable and Correctional Work in Chicago."
Shattuck, H.	"Remarks on Philanthropy."
Sherwood, E.	"Modern Charities and Church Work."
Smith, V.	"The Co-operation of Women in Philanthropic and Reformatory Work."
Smith, Z.	"Report of the Committee on the Organization of Charity."
Spencer, A.	"State Control and Social Care of the Vicious and Dependent Classes: Woman's Share in the Work."
Stewart, J.	"The Needlework Guild of America."
Stern, E.	"Charity as Taught by the Mosaic Law."
Todd, H.	"Report of the Committee on the Organization of Charities."
________.	"The Utility of Organized Charity in an Emergency."
Vaile, G.	"Introductory Remarks by the Vice Chairman (On State Public Welfare)."
________.	"Public Administration of Charity in Denver."
Wells, E.	"The National Woman's Relief Society."
Williamson, E.	"The Relation of Municipal and County Charities to the Commonwealth."

CHILD STUDY

Clifton, E.	"What We Learn from the Child's Own Psychology to Guide Treatment."
Johnson, L.	"What We Learn from the Child's Own Psychology to Guide Treatment in a Small Institution."

CHILD WELFARE

Abbott, G.	"Developing Standards of Rural Child Welfare."
________.	"The Government and Youth in a Troubled World."
________.	"Neglected Fundamentals in Children's Work: Fundamental Question Now Before Us."
________.	"The Public Protection of Children a First Part of the Public Welfare Program."
________.	"Public Protection of Children. (Presidential Address)."
________.	"The Responsibility of Club Women in Promoting the Welfare of Children."
Addams, J.	"Child at the Point of Greatest Pressure."
________.	"Modern Devices for Minimizing Dependencies."
Ames, F.	"Care of Dependent Children."
Arnold, M.	"The Growth of Child Welfare Services in Rural Areas."
________.	"The Specialized Consultant in Child Welfare Services."
Atkinson, M.	"Administration of Child Welfare Services from the Federal Level."
Aves, G.	"Potentialities of Social Service to Children."
Bailey, E.	"Country Homes for Dependent Children."
Baskett, J.	"Undifferentiated Case Work Through the Medium of Rural Schools."
Binford, J.	"Making the Community Safe for the Child."
Bolotin, A.	"Outside Activities of Children's Institutions."
Bowen, J.	"Responsibilities in Placement of Children."
Bradley, F.	"Remedial Work for Rural Children."
Bragdon, I.	"A Plea for Migrant Children: Lift the Marks from Their Faces."
Breckinridge, S.	"Children and the Depression."
Buxenbaum, A.	"Public Testimony."
Calkins, A.	"Boarding-out of Dependent Children in Massachusetts."
Chisholm, S.	"Aid to Dependent Children."
Cowan, L.	"Environmental Conflicts in the Family and Social Life of the Modern Child."
Curry, H.	"County Programs of Child Care: What Should a County Program Undertake?"
Curtis, F.	"Report of the Committee (on Children)."
Deardorff, N.	"Philadelphia as a Provider for Dependent Children."
Easley, L.	"Community Organizations and Child-care Arrangements."
Embry, M.	"The Role of the Private Agency: Children's Institutions and Agencies."
Evans, E.	"What Do You Know of Children After They Leave Your Institution? Do You Supervise Them?"

Evans, S.	"Public Testimony."
Fitz-Simons, L.	"Undifferentiated Case Work, as Illustrated by the Preliminary Report of the Georgia Study of Negro Child Welfare."
Foster, S.	"Co-ordination of Institution Care of Children with Other Services in the Community."
Gane, E.	"Discussion of the Responsibility of Juvenile Court and Public Agency in Child Welfare."
________.	"A Program for the Protection of Children."
Gerard, M.	"Learning to Know the Child Through the Everyday Contacts of the Case Worker."
Gibson, K.	"County Programs of Child Care: The Relation of Probation to Other County Social Work."
Greve, B.	"Opportunities for Developing Better Children's Work Throughout a State: Examples of Activities of State Departments."
Guggenheimer, E.	"Child Care and Family Services."
Handley, V.	"The Interpretation to the Community of a Public Agency."
Harding, M.	"Individualization of the Child."
Haskins, A.	"Progress in Social Case Work: In Child Welfare."
Johnson, L.	"Case Work with Children in Institutions."
Kelley, F.	"How Can Social Agencies Promote the Effectiveness of the Public Schools?"
Kirwan, K.	"Rural Case Work--Progress of Undifferentiated Case Work Made in the Children's Aid Society of Baltimore County."
Lansburg, T.	"Statement."
Lash, T.	"Child Care and Family Services."
Lathrop, J.	"Child Welfare Standards a Test of Democracy."
________.	"The Imperatives of International Relations: Social Implications."
________.	"Introductory Statement (on Public Schools and Social Service)."
________.	"Our Nation's Obligation to Her Children."
________.	"Participation in International Child Welfare Work."
________.	"Uniform Legislation."
Lenroot, K.	"American Childhood Challenges American Democracy."
________.	"Current National Developments and Problems in Public Welfare, Children's Services."
________.	"Trends in Public Services for Children."
Lothrop, A.	"Helping Widows to Bring Up Citizens."
McCoy, H.	"The Philadelphia Plan of a Central Bureau of Inquiry and Specialized Care."
McHugh, R.	"Some Conclusions from a Series of Studies by the National Catholic Welfare Conference."

Meigs, G. "Infant Welfare Work in War Time."
Mendum, G. "Child Welfare Work in a Rural Community."
Mitchell, D. "The Place of Mothers' Aid in a State Program of Child Welfare."
Montgomery, A. "The Reaction of Children's Case Work in the Development of the Constructive and Preventive Work of a Community: In the Removal of Degrading Causes."
Moore, M. "Research in the Child Welfare Field: A Study of Intake in Westchester County."
Newmann, F. "The Effects on the Child of an Unstable Home Situation."
Nutt, A. "The Responsibility of Juvenile Court and Public Agency in Child Welfare."
Putnam, E. "The Work of the Auxiliary Visitors Appointed to Assist the Department of the Massachusetts State Board in Charge of the Visitation of Dependent and Delinquent Children."
Reynolds, B. "Environmental Handicaps of Four Hundred Habit Clinic Children."
Schulze, S. "Group Living and the Dependent Child."
Smalley, R. "The School Social Worker and the Social Development of the Child."
Smith, V. "The Economy of the State in the Care of Dependent and Neglected Children."
________. "Report of the Committee on Preventive Work Among Children."
Stevens, M. "Necessary Modifications of Child Welfare Services to Meet the Needs of Dependent Negro Children."
Strong, A. "The Child Welfare Exhibit as a Means of Child Helping."
Taft, J. "Problems of Social Case Work with Children."
Taylor, R. "Child Welfare in Westchester County."
Watson, M. "Environmental Conflicts in the Family and Social Life of the Modern Child."
Williamson, E. "The Children's Age."
Young, M. "Re-examination of Child-care Functions in Family Agencies."

CHILDBIRTH

Jordan, B. "The Cultural Production of Childbirth."
Mulligan, J. "Public Policy and Childbearing."

CHILDREN--CARE AND HYGIENE.

Bauer, A. "Health Activities of Child Caring Agencies: Examinations on Admission."

Bradley, F.	"Suggestions for the Teaching of Child Hygiene."
Culbert, J.	"Health Activities of Child Caring Agencies: The School and Social Problems."
DuBois, M.	"Thirty Years Experience in Nursery and Child Hospital Work."
Gruenberg, S.	"Health Training of the Preschool Child."
Hathaway, W.	"Some Needed Readjustments in Special Fields of Child Welfare: The Extension of Non-Institutional Care of Children with Seriously Defective Vision."
Hooper, E.	"The Health of the Child."
Hutchinson, D.	"Therapy with Older Children as Seen by the Psychiatrist."
Lattimore, F.	"Children's Institutions and the Accident Problem."
McCord, E.	"Child Guidance Clinics and Child Caring Agencies: The Value of the Psychiatric Approach for All Children's Case Workers."
Murphy, M.	"Health Activities of Child Caring Agencies: Continuous Health Supervision."
Schweitzer, A.	"What State Divisions of Child Hygiene Are Doing to Promote Child Health."
Solenberger, E.	"Some Needed Readjustments in Special Fields of Child Welfare: The Extension of Non-Institutional Care for Crippled Children."
Walker, A.	"The Use of Central Clinics for Child Caring Agencies."

CHILDREN--DISEASES

Gawin, L.	"Preventive and Public Health Aspects of Rheumatic Fever in Children."

CHILDREN--EMPLOYMENT

Abbott, G.	"Social Standards in Industry: Child Labor."
Addams, J.	"Child Labor and Education."
________.	"Child Labor and Pauperism."
________.	"Child Labor Legislation: A Requisite for Industrial Efficiency."
________.	"Child Labor on the Stage."
________.	"National Protection for Children."
________.	"Operation of the Illinois Child Labor Law."
________.	"Street Trading."
________.	"Ten Years Experience in Child Labor Legislation in Illinois."
Griebel, H.	"Youth in Industry."
Johnston, L.	"Street Trades and Their Regulation."
Kelley, F.	"Child Labor in Illinois."

________.	"Child Labor Laws."
________.	"Evolution of the Illinois Child Labor Law."
________.	"Kelley on Child Labor and Woman Suffrage."
________.	"The Moral Dangers of Premature Employment."
________.	"The Working Child."
Lunde, L.	"Children at Work."
McConnell, B.	"The Employment of Minors in Wartime."
Matthews, E.	"Work Opportunities and School Training for Coal-Miners' Children."
Perkins, F.	"Miss Perkins Asks Child Labor Ban. Abandon's Prepared Address to Urge Professional Women to Support Amendment."
Stewart, M.	"Junior Employment Problems."
Woolley, H.	"The Supervision of Working Children Under the Ohio Law."

CHILDREN'S LIBRARIANS

Plummer, M.	"Training for Librarianship and the Work of Children's Libraries."

CHILDREN'S LITERATURE

Armer, L.	"Acceptance Paper--Newbery Medal 1931."
Bailey, C.	"Acceptance Paper--Newbery Medal 1947."
Becker, M.	"Directed Reading for Children."
Brink, C.	"Acceptance Paper--Newbery Medal 1936. Caddie Woodlawn."
Brown, M.	"Acceptance Paper (Caldecott Award 1955) Integrity and Intuition."
________.	"Caldecott Award Acceptance: Big and Little."
Burton, V.	"Acceptance Paper (Caldecott Awards 1943). Making Picture Books."
Byars, B.	"Newbery Award Acceptance--1971."
Clark, A.	"Acceptance Paper--Newbery Medal 1953."
Cooney, B.	"Caldecott Award Acceptance."
Cooper, S.	"Newbery Award Acceptance, 1976."
D'Aulaire, I.	"Acceptance Paper (Caldecott Award 1940). Working Together on Books for Children."
DeAngeli, M.	"Acceptance Paper--Newbery Medal 1950."
Enright, E.	"Acceptance Paper--Newbery Medal 1939."
Estes, E.	"Acceptance Paper--Newbery Medal 1952."
Ets, M.	"Caldecott Award Acceptance--1960."
Field, R.	"Acceptance Paper--Newbery Medal 1930."
Forbes, E.	"Acceptance Paper--Newbery Medal 1944."
Fox, P.	"Newbery Award Acceptance--1974."
George, J.	"Newbery Award Acceptance--1973."
Gray, E.	"Acceptance Paper--Newbery Medal 1943. History Is People."

Haley, G. "Caldecott Award Acceptance--1971."
Hamilton, V. "Newbery Award Acceptance--1975."
Henry, M. "Acceptance Paper--Newbery Medal 1949."
Hogrogian, N. "Caldecott Award Acceptance--1966."
________. "Caldecott Award Acceptance: How the Caldecott Changed My Life--Twice (1972)."
Hunt, I. "Books and the Learning Process. Newbery Award Acceptance--1967."
Jones, E. "Acceptance Paper (Caldecott Award 1945). Every Child and His Hilltop."
Konigsburg, E. "Newbery Award Acceptance--1968."
Latham, J. "Newbery Acceptance Speech--1956."
Lathrop, D. "Acceptance Paper (The Caldecott Award 1938)."
L'Engle, M. "Newbery Award Acceptance: The Expanding Universe."
Lenski, L. "Acceptance Paper--Newbery Medal 1946. Seeing Others as Ourselves."
Lewis, E. "Acceptance Paper--Newbery Medal 1933."
McDonald, C. "Literature for Young People."
Meigs, C. "Acceptance Paper--Newbery Medal 1934."
Milhous, K. "Acceptance Paper (Caldecott Award 1951). The Egg Tree and How It Grew."
Ness, E. "Caldecott Acceptance Speech--1967."
Neville, E. "Newbery Award Acceptance: Out Where the Real People Are."
Paterson, K. "Newbery Award Acceptance--1978."
Petersham, M. "Acceptance Paper (Caldecott Award 1946). A Short Tale of the Depressions and the Peaks that Occur in the Making of the Little Pretty Picture Book."
Sawyer, R. "Acceptance Paper--Newbery Medal 1937."
Seredy, K. "Acceptance Paper--Newbery Medal 1938."
Shannon, M. "Acceptance Paper--Newbery Medal 1935. Bewitched Mountains."
Sorensen, V. "Newbery Award Acceptance--1957."
Speare, E. "Newbery Award Acceptance--1959."
________. "Newbery Award Acceptance--1962: Report of a Journey."
Taylor, M. "Newbery Award Acceptance, 1977."
de Trevino, E. "Newbery Award Acceptance--1966."
Wojciechowska, M. "Acceptance Paper--1965: Shadow of a Kid."
Yates, E. "Acceptance Paper--Newbery Medal 1951. Climbing Some Mountain in the Mind."
Zemach, M. "Caldecott Award Acceptance--1974."

CHINA--POLITICS AND GOVERNMENT

Luce, C. "China's Government. Federal Union Offers Real Solution."

CHINESE LITERATURE

Buck, P. "The Chinese Novel." (Nobel Lecture)

________. "Nobel Lecture on the Chinese Novel."

CHRISTIAN SCIENCE

Eddy, M. "Address Before the Alumni of the Massachusetts Metaphysical College, 1895."

________. "Address Before the Christian Scientist Association of the Massachusetts Metaphysical College in 1893. Subject: Obedience."

________. "Address on the Fourth of July at Pleasant View, Concord, N.H., Before 2,500 Members of the Mother Church, 1897."

________. "Bible Lessons."

________. "Christian Healing; A Sermon Delivered at Boston."

________. "Christian Science in Tremont Temple."

________. "A Christmas Sermon; Delivered in Chickering Hall, Boston, Mass., on the Sunday Before Christmas, 1888. Subject: The Corporeal and the Incorporeal Savior."

________. "Communion Address, January, 1896."

________. "Message to the Annual Meeting of the Mother Church, Boston, 1896."

________. "Science and the Senses: Substance of My Address at the National Convention in Chicago, June 13, 1888."

________. "Sunday Services on July Fourth: Extempore Remarks."

CHRISTIANITY

Clymer, E. "The Light in the East."

Cratty, M. "On Being a Christian."

________. "Ourselves and Our Religion."

Goldman, E. "The Failure of Christianity."

Thayer, E. "The Light in the East."

CHRISTMAS

Green, E. "Christmas Gifts."

CITIES & TOWNS--PLANNING

James, H. "Planning the Urban Community."

CITIZENSHIP

Brown, V.	"Building Leadership for Peace ... New Ideas from New Voters: Panel Discussion."
Buck, D.	"The Citizen's Responsibility; A Panel Discussion."
Dickinson, L.	"The Citizen's Responsibility; A Panel Discussion."
Dunbar, S.	"The Importance of Keeping Informed."
Dunne, I.	"Freedom Is Responsibility. The Family's Responsibility to the Community."
Edwards, I.	"The Citizen's Responsibility; A Panel Discussion."
Farrington, M.	"The Citizen's Responsibility; A Panel Discussion."
Gaffrey, F.	"Responsibility of Women as Citizens."
Gunderson, B.	"Building Leadership for Peace ... New Ideas from New Voters: Panel Discussion."
Heffelfinger, E.	"The Citizen's Responsibility; A Panel Discussion."
Hobby, O.	"Citizen Responsibilities. "They" Is "We"."
Hottel, A.	"The Citizen's Responsibility; A Panel Discussion."
Hughes, S.	"Building Leadership for Peace ... New Ideas from New Voters: Panel Discussion."
Lord, M.	"Building Leadership for Peace ... New Ideas from New Voters: Panel Discussion."
________.	"The Citizen's Responsibility; A Panel Discussion."
Monroe, H.	"Synopsis of the Making of Citizens."
Ozbirn, C.	"From Where I Stand. Responsible, Responsive Citizenship Program."
Parisi, A.	"Building Leadership for Peace ... New Ideas from New Voters; Panel Discussion."
Poletti, J.	"The Woman Voter."
Schisby, M.	"Hindus and American Citizenship."
Scott, K.	"The Citizen's Responsibility; A Panel Discussion."
Stevens, D.	"Nationality Rights."
Strauss, A.	"The Citizen's Responsibility; A Panel Discussion."
Taft, M.	"The Woman Voter."
Waller, H.	"Introduction to Panel Discussion."
Zimmerman, C.	"The Citizen's Responsibility; A Panel Discussion."

CIVICS

Moore, S.	"Labor Camp Schools." (abstract)

CIVIL DEFENSE

Leopold, A. "Civil Defense Begins at Home."
Luce, C. "Unpreparedness of the Individual."

CIVIL RIGHTS

Boggs, G. "The Black Revolution in America."
Brown, C. "Speaking Up for the Race at Memphis, Tennessee, October 8, 1920."
Buck, P. "Commencement Speech on Equality, Delivered at Howard University in Washington, D. C., on June 5, 1942."
Freeman, F. "Something Is Wrong. Civil Rights: A Source of Irritation."
Harris, P. "U. N. Adopts International Covenants on Human Rights; Statement, December 12, 1966."
King, C. "Speech at Memphis City Hall."
Lord, M. "Forced Labor. The Wholesale Suppression of Human Rights by Government."
Rose, E. "Speech of Ernestine L. Rose at the Infidel Convention, N. Y., May 4, 1845."
Sampson, E. "Equal Opportunity & Equal Responsibility. These Are Two Sides of the Same Single Coin."
Truth, S. "Speech to a Boston Audience on New Year's Day, 1871."

CIVIL SERVICE

Clark, A. "Report of Civil Service Reform Committee."
Flower, L. "The Merit System in Public Institutions."
Holtzman, E. "Should Congress Enact H. R. 10 to Permit Greater Political Activity by Federal Employees?"
Lowell, J. "Civil Service Reform."
Main, C. "Patriotism in Civil Service Reform."
Mitchell, E. "Certification and Reclassification in the Civil Service."
Oakley, I. "Report--Civil Service Conference."
Perkins, F. "Address to a Group of Government Personnel Workers."

CIVILIZATION

Beard, M. "Struggling Towards Civilization."
Cooley, C. "Greeting from Honorary Vice-President."
Meloney, M. "What Man Cannot Destroy."
Poole, G. "Chairman's Introduction. The World as It Could Be."

Sternberger, E. "Report of the Committee on Plan of Action."
Woolley, M. "Progress, Man's Distinctive Mark Alone. Brute Force Shall Give Way--."

CLINICS

Barrows, E. "The Social Worker and Habit Clinics."

CLOTHING AND DRESS

Bates, O. "Discussion of the Ethics of Dress."
Hayes, E. "Woman's Dress from the Standpoint of Sociology."
Krecker, E. "Discussion of the Ethics of Dress."
Miller, A. "Dress Improvement."
Swayze, M. "Ethics and Aesthetics of Dress."
Toomy, A. "The Ethics of Dress."
Webster, H. "Discussion of Woman's Dress from the Standpoint of Sociology."
Woolson, A. "The Relation of Woman to Her Dress."

COAL MINES AND MINING

Lewis, H. "Should the Federal Government Assume a Direct Role in the Regulation of Surface Mining of Coal in the States?"
Matisoff, N. "Should the Federal Government Assume a Direct Role in the Regulation of Surface Mining of Coal in the States?"
Russell, L. "Should the Federal Government Assume a Direct Role in the Regulation of Surface Mining of Coal in the States?"

COLLEGE STUDENTS

Chambers, E. "Forum on the College Generation."
Douglas, E. "Forum on the College Generation."
Drake, J. "Forum on the College Generation."
Holcomb, M. "Forum on the College Generation."
Kelly, A. "Forum on the College Generation."
McNary, J. "Forum on the College Generation."
Morrison, J. "Forum on the College Generation."
Olmstead, C. "Forum on the College Generation."
Schleman, H. "Student Government: Human Trust."
Shambaugh, J. "Forum on the College Generation."
Spiegel, M. "Forum on the College Generation."
Steinbrecher, A. "Forum on the College Generation."
Watkins, J. "Forum on the College Generation."

COMMERCE

Anderson, B.	"Customs Reorganization and Modernization: The Procedures Which Affect International Trade."

COMMUNICATION

Bailey, M.	"Communication: Alternative Points of View."
Efron, E.	"The Free Mind and the Free Market."
Livingson, L.	"Communecology: A Concept for More Effective Communication."

COMMUNISM

Dean, V.	"The United States and the Communist Threat."
Karsner, R.	"Remarks at a Banquet in Los Angeles Celebrating the Publication of the First Ten Years of American Communism, December 15, 1962."
Lamb, M.	"The Communist Apparatus in Canada Today: Respectability and Acceptance."
Luce, C.	"American and World Communism. Shall It Be One World?"
________.	"Chamber of Commerce and Communism. The Devil's Cleverist Trick."

COMMUNIST COUNTRIES

Beck, M.	"Captive Nations: Lest We Forget."
Brandon, D.	"Asia's Red Riddle."
Leith, S.	"Chinese Women in the Early Communist Movement."

COMMUNITY LIFE

McDowell, M.	"The Significance to the City of Its Local Community Life."
White, E.	"Community Centers in School Buildings."

COMMUNITY ORGANIZATION

Powell, S.	"A Plan of County Co-operation."
Preston, J.	"Report of Community Service Division."

CONFLICT OF GENERATIONS

Mead, M.	"Generation Gap; Adaptation of Address."

CONNECTICUT--INDUSTRIES

Grasso, E.	"Imports Continue to Threaten U. S. Ball and Roller Bearing Industries."

CONSERVATION OF NATURAL RESOURCES

Myers, H.	"Birds and Flowers."
Smith, M.	"The Voice of the Forest."

CONSERVATISM

Alexander, R.	"Formula for Freedom. Attack Subversives Wherever Found."
Douglas, H.	"Freedom Cannot Be Inherited. We Are the Conservative Party."

CONSUMER PROTECTION

Austin, J.	"Alone Together."
Bostick, M.	"Consumerism: A Three-toed Sloth."
Coles, J.	"Getting What We Want."
Daniels, K.	"Consumers' Interests in the National Recovery Act."
Furness, B.	"Betty Furness Speaks for Consumers."
Kelley, F.	"The Right to Know the Truth."
Mason, L.	"Government Lends a Hand."
May, C.	"The American Farmer: The Consumers' Real Protector."
Peterson, E.	"Should the Congress Approve the Proposed "Fair Packaging and Labeling Act"?"
Phelps, E.	"The Clothing Program for Federated Clubs."
Sullivan, L.	"The Citizen's Role in Furthering Consumer Interests: Stop Being Cheated."
Ware, C.	"Wartime Consumer Activities."
Woods, A.	"Consumer Organization."

COOKERY

Johnson, H.	"Cooking as an Art."
Lincoln, M.	"Cookery."

COONLEY-WARD, LYDIA AVERY

Addams, J. "Lydia Avery Coonley-Ward."

COPYRIGHT

Sherwood, K. "Insurance Against Piracy of Brains."

CORPORATIONS, INTERNATIONAL

Sindona, M. "From Multi-nationals to Cosmo-corporations: The World Economic Welfare."

CORRECTIONS

Potter, E. "An Institutional Program in the Field of Corrections."

COST AND STANDARD OF LIVING

Costigan, M. "Public Control of the Packing Industry. A Factor in Reducing the Cost of Living."
Van Kleech, M. "Introductory Statement (on Sources of Power for Industrial Freedom)."
Worcester, D. "The Standard of Living."

COUNTRY LIFE

Dingman, H. "Enriching the Rural Community."
Roosevelt, A. "Greetings Delivered at Constitution Hall, June 1, 1936."

CREDIT

Sheffield, A. "Introductory Remarks (On Co-operative Credit)."

CRIME AND CRIMINALS

Additon, H. "Community Responsibility for Preventing Crime."
________. "The Responsibility of the Police for Preventing Crime."
Hawthone, J. "Crime: An Address."

CRIMINAL JUSTICE, ADMINISTRATION OF

Murphy, E.	"The Administration of Criminal Justice in Canada."

CRUELTY TO CHILDREN

Welcott, H.	"Legislation to Prevent Cruelty to Children."

DANCING

Chorpenning, C.	"Contrasting Values of the Drama and Festival in Group Work."
Cohen, S.	"Woman as Artistic Innovator: The Case of the Choreographer."
Moskowitz, B.	"The Dance Problem."
St. Denis, R.	"Creative Uses of the Arts--The Dance."

DANTE ALIGHIERI, 1265-1321

Howe, J.	"Dante and Beatrice."

DAY NURSERIES

Atkinson, M.	"The Relation of State Institutions and Agencies to Private Institutions: The Ohio Plan."
Bainbridge, L.	"Mothers of the Submerged World. Day Nurseries."
Bushong, R.	"Public Testimony."
Butler, S.	"Need of Day Nurseries."
Caldwell, G.	"Standards of Admission to Day Nurseries."
Dewey, M.	"The Scope of Day Nursery Work."
Dodge, J.	"Neighborhood Work and Day Nurseries."
Gillam, M.	"Some Needed Readjustments in Special Fields of Child Welfare: A Net Interpretation of the Task of Day Nurseries. How Large a Part Should They Play in Children's Work?"
Guyler, C.	"Social Work Responsibility for the Development of Day Care."
Hedger, C.	"Standards of Hygiene and Equipment of Day Nurseries."
Hodges, G.	"Statement."
Murphy, I.	"Detroit's Experience with the Wartime Care of Children."
Radcliff, D.	"Statement."
Torton, I.	"Testimony."
William, L.	"Statement."

DEACONESSES

Robinson, J.	"The Modern Deaconess Movement."

DEAF--EDUCATION

Garrett, E.	"Address to the Convention of the American Instructors of the Deaf and Dumb, 1882."
Garrett, M.	"The Next Step in the Education of the Deaf."
Keller, H.	"Address of Helen Keller at Mt. Airy, (July 8, 1896)."
Timberlake, J.	"The Deaf Child and the Hard-of-Hearing Child."

DECENTRALIZATION IN GOVERNMENT

Bushnell, L.	"New Lamps for Old? Centralism."

DELINQUENT GIRLS

Francis, V.	"The Delinquent Girl."
Hall, E.	"Reformation of Criminal Girls."
Keeley, S.	"Reform Work for Girls."
Morse, F.	"The Methods Most Helpful to Girls."
Murray, V.	"The Runaway and the Stranded Girl."
Smith, C.	"Can the Institution Equip the Girl for Normal Social Relationships?"
________.	"The Unadjusted Girl."

DEMOCRACY

Gambrell, M.	"Old Wine in New Bottles. The Democratic Way of Life."
Meyer, A.	"British Home Front Compared with Ours. If Democracy Is Worth Fighting For, It Is Worth Fighting With."
Perkins, F.	"What Is Worth Working for in America?"
Roosevelt, A.	"Humanistic Democracy--The American Ideal."
Thompson, D.	"The Death of Democracies. How to Avoid It: By Facing Realities."
________.	"Saving Democracy."

DENTAL HEALTH EDUCATION

Gallinger, E.	"The New Dental Program."

DEPORTATION

Clark, J.	"American Deportation Procedure: An International Social Problem."
________.	"Detention of Deporteds."
Rom, G.	"Family Problems Resulting from the Present Deportation System."

DEPRESSION--1929--U. S.

Woodhouse, C.	"Chairman's Introduction. The Direct Impact of the Depression."

DEWEY, GORDON

Addams, J.	"Gordon Dewey."

DISARMAMENT

Newcomer, M.	"Economics of Disarmament. Expansion in Civilian Markets at Home and Abroad."

DISCRIMINATION IN EMPLOYMENT

Abzug, B.	"Statement."
Bellamy, C.	"Statement."
Bergmann, B.	"Testimony on the Economics of Sex Discrimination in Employment."
Bernard, J.	"Historical and Structural Barriers to Occupational Desegregation."
Blau, F.	"Sex Segregation of Workers by Enterprise in Clerical Occupations."
Boyer, E.	"Statement."
Czarnecki, D.	"Statement."
Dall, C.	"Woman's Right to Labor; Or, Low Wages and Hard Work."
Davies, M.	"Woman's Place Is at the Typewriter: The Feminization of the Clerical Labor Force."
Fasteau, B.	"Statement."
Fields, D.	"Statement."
Freeman, F.	"Statement."
Griffiths, M.	"Can We Still Afford Occupational Segregation? Some Remarks."
________.	"Opening Statement on Federal Efforts to End Sex Discrimination in Employment."
________.	"Opening Statement on the Economics of Sex Discrimination in Employment."
________.	"Women Are Being Deprived of Legal Rights by the Equal Employment Opportunity Commission."

Groneman, C.	"She Earns as a Child; She Pays as a Man: Women Workers in a Mid-nineteenth-century New York City Community."
Hartmann, H.	"Capitalism, Patriarchy, and Job Segregation By Sex."
Heide, W.	"Statement."
Herman, A.	"Statement."
________.	"Statement."
Hernandez, A.	"Testimony on Federal Efforts to End Sex Discrimination in Employment."
Kessler-Harris, A.	"Stratifying by Sex: Understanding the History of Working Women."
Komisar, L.	"Statement."
Koontz, E.	"Statement."
________.	"Testimony on Federal Efforts to End Sex Discrimination in Employment."
Lapidus, G.	"Occupational Segregation and Public Policy: A Comparative Analysis of American and Soviet Patterns."
Nolan-Haley, J.	"Statement."
Norton, E.	"Statement."
O'Steen, S.	"Statement."
Peratis, K.	"Statement."
Pressmen, S.	"Job Equality for Women."
Putnam, P.	"Statement."
Roberts, S.	"Statement."
Ross, S.	"Statement."
Rossi, A.	"Women in the Seventies: Problems and Possibilities."
Rubin, E.	"Statement."
Sandler, B.	"Testimony on Federal Efforts to End Sex Discrimination in Employment."
Sawhill, I.	"Discrimination and Poverty Among Women Who Head Families."
Scott, T.	"Statement."
Springen, P.	"The Dimensions of the Oppression of Women: Unequal Pay for Equal Work."
Sterling, T.	"Statement."
Stevenson, M.	"Women's Wages and Job Segregation."
Strober, M.	"Toward Dimorphics: A Summary Statement to the Conference on Occupational Segregation."
Voutsis, M.	"Public Testimony."
Walsh, E.	"Statement."
________.	"Statement."
Weiss, K.	"Biological and Cultural Determinants of the Division of Labor by Sex."
Weyand, R.	"Statement."
________.	"Statement."
Whitman, M.	"Testimony on the Economics of Sex Discrimination in Employment."
Williams, W.	"Statement."
________.	"Statement."
Woods, R.	"Statement."

DISCRIMINATION IN HOUSING

Betanzos, A. "Statement."

DIVORCE

Anthony, S. "Comments on Divorce Resolutions at 10th National Woman's Rights Convention, May 11, 1860."

________. "Remarks on Divorce at the 1905 Meeting of the National Council of Women."

Blackwell, A. "Debate on the Divorce Resolution at the 10th National Woman's Rights Convention, N. Y., May 10-11, 1860."

Bloomer, A. "Debate on Divorce at Daughters of Temperance Meeting, Rochester, N. Y., 1852."

Friedan, B. "The Crises of Divorce."

Nichols, C. "Address on Divorce at Woman's Rights Convention, Syracuse, N. Y., September 8, 1852."

Rose, E. "Debate on the Divorce Resolutions at the 10th National Woman's Rights Convention, N. Y., May 10-11, 1860."

Stanton, E. "Address at the Decade Meeting, on Marriage and Divorce."

________. "Address at the 10th National Woman's Rights Convention in Cooper Institute, N. Y., May 10, 1860."

________. "Address on Divorce Resolutions at the 10th National Woman's Rights Convention, N. Y., May 10-11, 1860."

________. "Address on Divorce at 10th National Woman's Rights Convention, May 11, 1860."

________. "On Marriage and Divorce." (Private Club, 1870)

DODGE, GRACE HOADLEY

Cratty, M. "Miss Dodge."

________. "The Qualities of Leadership as Revealed in Miss Dodge."

DOUGLASS, FREDERICK

Hazel, R. "Mrs. Rosa H. Hazel at Douglass Memorial Meeting, St. Paul, Minnesota."

Terrell, M. "Frederick Douglass."

EAST (FAR EAST)

Buck, P. "Like and Unlike in East and West."

ECONOMIC ASSISTANCE

Smith, M. "Impatience and Generosity. Comments on European and Asian Trips."

ECONOMIC SECURITY

Bowman, G. "Chairman's Introduction. Economic Security Through Government."
Sporborg, C. "The Struggle for Security."

ECONOMICS

Brainerd, H. "Opening Remarks."
Porter, S. "Are We a Nation of Economic Illiterates? Make Peace Synonymous with Prosperity."
________. "Charter of Economic Human Rights. Economic and Human Rights Tied Into One Package."

EDUCATION

Addams, J. "The Public School and the Immigrant Child."
Alexander, M. "Religion, Poetry, and History: Foundations for a New Educational System."
Anerdson, E. "Teacher on a Tightrope. Whither Your Goal?"
Cabell, M. "Discussion of Paper on Ethical Influence of Woman in Education."
Cheney, E. "Place of Women in Our Public Schools."
Crain, L. "Dissent in Education."
Dulles, E. "Education, Communist Style, American Style. The Students of Today Are the Leaders of Tomorrow."
Eastman, M. "Woman in Education."
Gildersleeve, V. "Education for a New Day."
Gill, L. "Co-operation of the National Women's Organizations for Good Schools."
Goldman, E. "The Child and Its Enemies."
________. "The Social Importance of the Modern School."
Gruenberg, S. "Where Security Begins."
Hanna, R. "Schools and the Rulers of Mankind--Discussion."
Hefferan, M. "What Can the Educator Do?"

Hopkins, L.	"Woman's Work in Education."
Houghton, D.	"World Challenges American Educators. The Opportunity to Build New Frontiers of Understanding and Peace."
Kellogg, E.	"Needs in American Education."
Leonard, A.	"Discussion of Paper on the Ethical Influence of Woman in Education."
Lichtman, S.	"Motifs for Living."
McIntosh, M.	"Education for What? A Challenge to Teaching."
________.	"Goals of Progressive Education Not Sufficient Today. Educators Must Provide Moral Synthesis."
Marwedel, E.	"Practical Culture."
Meyer, A.	"Freedom of the Mind."
________.	"A New Phase of Woman's Education in America."
Milledge, L.	"To Speak of Eagles. Education: The Expression of the Individual."
Mills, H.	"The Winning of Educational Freedom. Address to the National American Woman Suffrage Association Convention of 1900."
Mosher, F.	"Discussion of Paper on the Ethical Influence Of Woman in Education."
Pierce, B.	"Schools and the Rulers of Mankind--Discussion."
Roosevelt, E.	"American Education and the Child. Philosophical Ideas Old and New."
Sampson, E.	"Choose One of Five: Its Your Life."
Sewall, M.	"Woman's Work in Education."
Swanker, E.	"Controversy Over Federal Experimentation with 'Education Vouchers'."
Tutwiler, J.	"Our Brother in Stripes, in the Schoolroom."
Vining, E.	"The Educated Heart. The Heart, Informed with Love, Will Never Be in Conflict with the Enlightened Mind."
Walker, M.	"Religion, Poetry, and History: Foundations for a New Educational System."
Warner, C.	"The Taxpayer Needs to Know--Schools Can't Do Everything. Parents Can Make a Difference in Education Today."
White, J.	"Development in Eastern Washington."
Willard, F.	"Woman's Work in Education."

EDUCATION, ELEMENTARY

Addams, J.	"Foreign-born Children in the Primary Grades."
________.	"Italian Children in the Primary Grades."
Blatch, H.	"Manual Training in Primary Schools."
Foley, A.	"The Quality Elementary School. Problems Facing Elementary Education."

EDUCATION, HIGHER

Apter, J.	"Increasing the Professional Visibility of Women in Academe: A Case Study."
Astin, H.	"Where Are All the Talented Women?"
Babey-Brooke, A.	"Patterns of Discrimination and Discouragement in Higher Education."
Bell, C.	"Women in Higher Education: An Unsatisfactory Accounting."
Fuller, A.	"Liberating the Administrator's Wife."
Griffiths, M.	"It Is a National Calamity ... Remarks."
Harris, A.	"Patterns of Discrimination and Discouragement in Higher Education."
________.	"Statement."
Harris, P.	"Problems and Solutions in Achieving Equality for Women."
Horton, M.	"Presidential Address."
Kreps, J.	"The Woman Professional in Higher Education."
Mattfeld, J.	"Many Are Called, But Few Are Chosen."
Murray, P.	"Statement."
Peterson, M.	"Women, Autonomy, and Accountability in Higher Education."
Richter, M.	"Patterns of Discrimination and Discouragement in Higher Education."
Roberts, J.	"Women's Right to Choose, or Men's Right to Dominate."
Rogers, M.	"The Role of the Equal Employment Opportunity Commission."
Sandler, B.	"Academic Women Attack Institutional Discrimination--1970."
Schmalzried, B.	"Day Care Services for Children of Campus Employees."
Sigworth, H.	"Issues in Nepotism Rules."
Smythe, M.	"Feminism and Black Liberation."
Stimpson, C.	"Conflict, Probable; Coalition, Possible; Feminism and the Black Movement."
Sunderland, E.	"Higher Education and the Home."
Truax, A.	"Maternity Leave Policies."
Waxman, R.	"Public Testimony."
Webster, H.	"Woman's Progress in Higher Education."

EDUCATION OF WOMEN

Adickes, S.	"Public Testimony."
Alschuler, R.	"Chairman's Introduction. Foundations of Education."
Banning, M.	"The Facts, The Hopes, and the Possibilities."
________.	"Points of General Agreement."
________.	"Today's Woman--Her Future Role in a Changing Society."

Beard, M.	"Society's Interest in Human Resources."
Beecher, C.	"The Education of Female Teachers."
Berry, J.	"University of Kansas City Project for Continuing Education of Women."
Bragdon, H.	"Comment on Pressures and Opportunities That Face the Educated Woman."
Breckinridge, D.	"The Educational Work of the Kentucky Federation of Women's Clubs."
Brown, M.	"Institutive Power."
Boyer, L.	"A Case History. (Pilot Projects for Continuing Education for Women)"
Bunting, M.	"Today's Woman Prepares for Tomorrow's World. Introduction to Panel Discussion."
Cahill, J.	"A Catholic View of the Education of Women."
Clapp, M.	"Comment on Current Trends in the Education of Women."
Conway, C.	"The Needs of Southern Women."
Cotton, S.	"A National Training School for Women."
Davis, M.	"Education--New Currents."
Dickinson, M.	"The Next Thing in Education."
Donlon, M.	"Greetings from the Executive Committee."
________.	"The Scope of the Problem."
Douvan, E.	"Adolescent Girls: Their Attitude Toward Education."
Eastman, M.	"Remarks."
Fitzgerald, L.	"Statement."
Flowers, A.	"A Matter of Degree: Education of Women."
Gage, M.	"Decade Speech, on the Progress of Education and Industrial Avocations for Women."
Galpin, K.	"The Ethical Influence of Woman in Education."
Goodman, J.	"Public Testimony."
Havens, R.	"The Girl of the Future. Address to the National American Woman Suffrage Association, Convention of 1893."
Heide, W.	"Statement."
Hottel, A.	"Women's Education: New Needs in Our Time."
Joachim, M.	"So Let Your Light Shine. The Role of the Educated Woman in the Modern World."
Knapp, P.	"Comment on Background and Purpose of the Conference on the Present Status and Prospective Trends of Research on the Education of Women."
Littleton, B.	"Women's Education: To Discover Ourselves As Women."
Lease, M.	"Women in the Farmers' Alliance."
Leopold, A.	"Search for Skills."
Lord, E.	"Educated Women as Factors in Industrial Competition."
McGee, L.	"The Home of the Future."
Manor, S.	"Planning Training for Future Womanpower."

Marston, H.	"Rutgers--The State University, Ford Foundation Program for the Retraining in Mathematics of College Graduate Women."
Michaels, R.	"Co-education."
________.	"Women as Educators."
Mueller, K.	"The Cultural Pressures on Women."
O'Connor, L.	"Let's Keep One Stake In Tomorrow: Women of Today."
Palmer, A.	"Women's Education at the World's Fair."
________.	"Women's Education in the Nineteenth Century."
Peck, M.	"Education as a Preparation for Life."
Peterson, E.	"The Impact of Education."
________.	"The Need for Educated Womanpower."
________.	"Needs and Opportunities in Our Society for the Educated Woman."
Pettigrew, L.	"Education and Socialization."
Raushenbush, E.	"Sarah Lawrence College, The Center for Continuing Education."
Robinson, E.	"Report on Education."
Rose, E.	"Remarks on Women's Condition at the 7th National Convention, N.Y., November 25, 1856."
Ross, D.	"A Modest Beginning and a Modest Proposal."
Schuck, V.	"Statement."
Shaw, D.	"Statement."
Simmons, A.	"Education and Ideology in Nineteenth-century America: The Response of Educational Institutions to the Changing Role of Women."
Spencer, S.	"Co-education of the Sexes, Based upon the Law of Sex."
Stanton, E.	"The Co-education of the Sexes."
Stowell, L.	"Retrospection."
Strommen, E.	"Learning Not To: It Takes a Long Time."
Thomas, C.	"The National Young Ladies' Mutual Improvement Association."
Thomas, M.	"Marriage and the Woman Scholar."
Tobias, S.	"Educating Women for Leadership: A Program for the Future."
Tutwiler, J.	"A Self Support Problem."
Webster, H.	"Our Debt to Zurich."
Willard, F.	"A New Departure in Normal Higher Education."
Yalof, H.	"Public Testimony."

EDUCATIONAL SOCIOLOGY

Campbell, M.	"The School's Responsibility for the Leisure Time of the Child: In Relation to Its Effect on the Conduct and Efficiency of the Child and His Family."

Deardorff, N. "The School's Responsibility for the Leisure Time of the Child: In Relation to the Services of the School."

DeLong, E. "The School as a Community Center."

Simkhovitch, M. "The Enlarged Function of the Public School."

EFFICIENCY, INDUSTRIAL

Gilbreth, L. "The Newer Efficiency."

ELECTIONS--CAMPAIGN FUNDS

Abzug, B. "Should Federal Subsidies Be Provided for Congressional Election Campaigns?"

ELIOT, GEORGE

Street, I. "George Eliot."

ELOCUTION

Morgan, A. "The Art of Elocution."

EMERSON, ELLEN LOUISA TUCKER

Shaw, A. "Memorial Tributes to Mrs. Ralph Waldo Emerson and Anna Oliver at the National American Woman Suffrage Association Convention, 1893."

EMIGRATION AND IMMIGRATION

Abbott, E. "Discussion of Immigration Under the Per-centum Limit Law."

________. "Immigration Legislation and the Problems of Assimilation."

Addams, J. "The Immigrant and Social Unrest."

________. "The Immigrant Woman as She Adjusts Herself to American Life."

________. "Immigrants."

________. "Report of the Committee on Immigrants."

________. "Social Consequences of the Immigration Law."

Alsberg, E. "The Immigrant. Means of Using National and Racial Customs and Organizations in Relating Isolated Groups to General Community Movements."

American, S.	"The Child or Girl Without a Mother and Mother Without a Child."
Bird, E.	"Social Attitudes Conditioning Immigrant Maladjustments: Twofold Problem of Immigration."
Bowler, A.	"Recent Statistics on Crime and the Foreign Born."
Burnett, M.	"Adult Immigration Education: In the United States."
Claghorn, K.	"The Law's Delay: Lower Court Justice and the Immigrant."
________.	"The Work of Voluntary Immigrant Protective Agencies."
Clark, J.	"Immigrant Populations."
Crawford, R.	"Port Problems in Europe and the United States."
Frasca, M.	"Democracy in Immigrant Neighborhood Life."
Hull, I.	"The Immigrant as a Factor in Social Case Work: In the Family Welfare Field."
Hurlbutt, M.	"International Aspects of the Migration Problem: Development of International Case Work."
________.	"The Invisible Environment of an Immigrant."
Ledbetter, E.	"Recent Development in Library Work with Immigrants."
McDowell, M.	"The Quota Law and the Family."
Mitchell, R.	"The New Quota Law in the United States."
Murray, V.	"Training for Successful Work with Immigrants: Training and Use of Nationality Workers."
Pagan de Colon, P.	"The Status of the Migrant. People with the Same Aspirations."
Razovsky, C.	"Humanitarian Effects of the Immigration Law."
________.	"The Quota Law and the Effect of Its Administration in Contiguous Territory."
________.	"The Visa and Quota Laws as They Affect the Clients of Social Agencies."
Schisby, M.	"Emigration Conditions in European Ports of Embarkation."
________.	"Pending Immigration Legislation."
Sears, A.	"Training for Successful Work with Immigrants: Training of American Workers."
Sturges, V.	"The Progress of Adjustment in Mexican and United States Life."
Turner, M.	"Community Programs and Cooperation in Americanization."
Wald, L.	"The Immigrant Young Girl." (abstract)
Whitton, C.	"Juvenile Immigration."
Williamson, E.	"The Street Arab."

EMPLOYEE COUNSELING

McGowan, C.	"Counseling in Industry."
Van Kleech, M.	"Social Services for Industrial Workers."

ENERGY CONSERVATION

MacDonald, R.	"Human Values and Energy Conservation: Our Common Concern."

ENGELS, FREDERICK

Lane, A.	"Women in Society: A Critique of Frederick Engels."
Sacks, K.	"Engels Revisited: Women, the Organization of Production, and Private Property."

ENGINEERING AS A PROFESSION

Bernard, J.	"The Present Situation in the Academic World of Women Trained in Engineering."
Cavanagh, A.	"Official Opening of Conference."
French, I.	"Spotlight on Engineers and Scientists."
Gilbreth, L.	"Closing the Gap."
________.	"Focus on the Future."
Hicks, B.	"Welcome and Introduction of Keynote Speaker."
Shafer, R.	"Welcome and Opening Message."

ENGLISH DRAMA

Casey, L.	"Madame Vestris in America."

EQUAL PAY FOR EQUAL WORK

Bosone, R.	"Statement."
Boyle, D.	"Statement."
Brady, D.	"Equal Pay, What Are the Facts?"
Breckinridge, S.	"The Equal Wage."
Cunningham, S.	"Statement."
Davis, B.	"Statement."
Dwyer, F.	"Statement."
Gierke, T.	"Statement."
Gilman, C.	"Equal Pay for Equal Work."
Griffiths, M.	"Statement."
Gross, G.	"Statement."
Haener, D.	"Statement."
________.	"Statement."

Higgins, L.	"Statement."
Holt, L.	"Statement."
Johnson, E.	"Statement."
________.	"Statement."
Kelly, E.	"Statement."
Kenyon, D.	"Statement."
Kopelov, C.	"Statement."
Miles, M.	"Statement."
Miller, E.	"Statement."
Neuberger, M.	"Statement."
Peden, K.	"Statement."
Peterson, E.	"Statement."
________.	"Statement."
________.	"Statement."
Pollitzer, A.	"Statement."
Pressman, S.	"Statement."
________.	"Statement."
Roosevelt, A.	"Statement."
Ross, J.	"Statement."
Sullivan, L.	"Statement."
Thomson, R.	"Statement."
Tillett, G.	"Statement."
________.	"Statement."
Williams, E.	"Statement."

EQUALITY

Buck, P.	"Heart of Democracy. Equality for All."
Bushnell, L.	"What Is America?: Think About Equality."

ETCHING

Dillays, B.	"Etching."

ETHICS

Mannes, M.	"The Exercise of Conscience. "Is It Good?" Not "Will It Sell?" Should Be the Criterion."
Slaughter-Morton, R.	"A Higher Standard of Morality."
Wright, F.	"Lecture V. --Morals."

ETIQUETTE

Vanderbilt, A.	"Bad Manners in America."

EUROPEAN WAR, 1914-1918

Rankin, J.	"First Speech in Congress to Offer an Amendment to the Lever Bill, May 28, 1917."
________.	"Speech at Joint Session of Congress to Declare War Against Austria--Hungary, December 1917."
White, E.	"War Activities as They Have Affected Housing, Health, and Recreation."

EXCEPTIONAL CHILDREN--EDUCATION

Addams, J.	"The Home and the Special Child."
Janvier, C.	"The School Program in Case Work with Exceptional Children."
Richman, J.	"Special Classes and Special Schools for Delinquent and Backward Children."

EXPLORERS

French-Sheldon, M.	"Woman as an Explorer."

FACTORY INSPECTION

Anderson, M.	"Recent Industrial Investigations: Recent Investigations by Government Bureaus."
DeGraffenried, M.	"Testimony on Work as a Labor Department Investigator."
Kelley, F.	"Factory Legislation in Illinois."
________.	"Use and Abuse of Factory Inspection."
Perkins, F.	"Improving Working Conditions in Industry."
________.	"Testimony Before Factory Investigating Commission, December 1912."
________.	"Testimony Before the Factory Investigating Commission."
________.	"Testimony on Cellar Bakeries in N. Y."

FACTORY LAWS & LEGISLATION

Blatch, H.	"Factory Legislation."

FAITH

Cheney, E.	"Address."
Willard, F.	"Address."

FAMILY

Addams, J.	"Family Affection."
________.	"Filial Relations, 1902."
________.	"Household Adjustment."
Banning, M.	"War and the Family. The Unit for "A Better World"."
Brandt, L.	"Statistics of Dependent Families."
Breckinridge, S.	"The Family and the Law."
________	"The Family in the Community, but Not Yet of the Community."
________.	"The Scope and Place of Research in the Program of the Family Society."
Brisley, M.	"Family Achievement."
Byington, M.	"The Scope and Limitations of Family Rehabilitation: Due to Mental Conditions."
Chodorow, N.	"Family Structure and Feminine Personality."
Cohen, M.	"The Influence of the Jewish Religion in the Home."
Colcord, J.	"Chairman's Report on What of the Immediate Future of the Family?"
________.	"Strengths of Family Life."
________.	"What Has Social Work to Do with the Founding of New Families?"
Corson, J.	"The Evolution of Home."
Eastman, A.	"The Home and Its Foundations."
Falconer, M.	"The Culture of Family Life Versus Reformatory Treatment."
Felsenthal, J.	"The Influence of the Jewish Religion in the Home."
Goodwillie, M.	"Family Readjustment After the War."
Haefner, R.	"Family Life in the Rural Community."
Hood, L.	"Foreign Organizations and Family Welfare."
Hull, I.	"Special Problems in Italian Families."
Hutchinson, H.	"What Irregular Employment Means to Household and Community."
Johnesse, A.	"Helping the Client to Deal with His Reactions to Restraints Governing Intrafamily Relationships."
Kelley, F.	"The Family and the Woman's Wage."
Kellogg, A.	"What Educational Psychology Can Contribute to Case Work with the Normal Family."
Kohut, R.	"Parental Reverence as Taught in the Hebrew Home."
Levinson, F.	"Counseling in the Family Agency."
McDowell, M.	"How Casual Work Undermines Family and Neighborhood Life."
________.	"The Relation of Community Work to Family Life."
McIntosh, M.	"New Horizons for Women." The Modern Home Is a Cooperative Venture."
McLemore, E.	"Restoring Stability to the Family. Emotional Disturbances Brought on by the Demands of Business."

Mead, M.	"Future Family; Adaptation of Address. February 12, 1970."
________.	"How Fares the American Family? Address."
________.	"What Is Happening to the American Family?"
Moloney, E.	"Massachusetts. The Family Budget and the Adequacy of Relief."
Mudgett, M.	"The Development of Greater Sympathy and Understanding Between Parents and Children."
Nesbitt, F.	"The Family Budget and Its Supervision."
Neustaedter, E.	"The Integration of Economic and Psychological Factors in Family Case Work."
Pannell, A.	"A Nation's Strength Begins in the Home. Parents Are the Real Molders of Character."
Parker, V.	"The Family Keystone."
Powers, E.	"Rural Conditions in Pennsylvania."
Richmond, M.	"The Family and the Social Worker."
________.	"Report of the Committee (on Families and Neighborhoods); the Inter-Relation of Social Movements."
________.	"Some Next Steps in Social Treatment."
________.	"War and Family Solidarity."
Roebling, M.	"Power and Influence of Women. Dedication to Family and Nation."
Sears, A.	"The Psychology of Co-operation."
Smith, C.	"Home Side of Progress."
Smith, F.	"Continued Care of Families."
Thorne, B.	"The Modern Family: Sticky Myths, Diverse Realities, and the Problem of Isolation."
Tyson, H.	"Measuring Our Results in Securing the Essentials of Family Life: Some Suggestions Based on a Review of Mothers' Assistance in Pennsylvania."
Van de Carr, K.	"The Aged Person in the Family Setting."
Vittum, H.	"Culture of Family Life from the Social Settlement Standpoint."
Wolkoff, R.	"Men and Women in the Family: History of the Idea of Family in America's Depression Generation."

FARM INCOME

Rowe, B.	"The Farm Family and Buying Power."
Sherman, C.	"Which Way Agriculture?"

FARRAGUT, DAVID

Hoxie, V.	"Lincoln and Farragut."

FEDERAL AID TO COMMUNITY DEVELOPMENT--U. S.

Harris, P.	"Statement Before the Senate Committee on Banking, Housing and Urban Affairs: April 19, 1977."

FEDERAL AID TO EDUCATION

Green, E.	"Should Congress Establish A Major Federal Role in General Financing of U. S. Education?"
Meyer, A.	"Federal Aid to Education."
Smith, M.	"How Much Should Government Do--On Health, Education, and Housing? Panel Discussion."

FEMALE OFFENDERS

Chace, E.	"Relation of Women to Crime and Criminals."
Davis, K.	"Outdoor Work for Women Prisoners."
Gold, S.	"Women, the Criminal Code, and the Correction System."
Hodder, J.	"Disciplinary Measures in the Management of the Psychopathic Delinquent Women."
________.	"The Next Step in the Treatment of Girls and Women Offenders."
Johnson, E.	"The Treatment of Women in Prison."
Lynde, M.	"The Treatment of Criminal and Erring Women."
Miner, M.	"Treatment of Women Offenders."

FEMINISM

Atkinson, T.	"Catholic University."
________.	"The Equality Issue."
________.	"Individual Responsibility and Human Oppression (Including Some Notes on Prostitution and Pornography)."
________.	"Lesbianism and Feminism."
________.	"Metaphysical Cannibalism or Self-Creativity."
________.	"Movement Politics and Other Slights of Hand."
________.	"On "Violence in the Women's Movement": Collaborators."
________.	"The Political Woman."
________.	"The Sacrificial Lambs."
________.	"Strategy and Tactics: A Presentation of Political Lesbianism."
________.	"Vaginal Orgasm as a Mass Hysterical Survival Response."

Beard, M.	"The College and Alumnae in Contemporary Life."
Bushnell, L.	"What's Happened to Eve? The Women's Liberation Movement."
De Crow, K.	"Address to 1974 NOW National Conference."
________.	"Keynote Address at 1975 NOW National Conference."
Dworkin, A.	"Feminism, Art, and My Mother Sylvia."
________.	"Our Blood: The Slavery of Women in America."
________.	"Remembering the Witches."
________.	"Renouncing Sexual Equality."
________.	"The Root Cause."
________.	"The Sexual Politics of Fear and Courage."
East, C.	"What Do Women Want?"
Eastman, C.	"Statement to the First Feminist Congress, 1919."
Estrada, C.	"Uncontained, Undefined, Unafraid."
Fasteau, B.	"Public Testimony."
Friedan, B.	"Address at Founder's Reception--5th Annual Conference, Los Angeles, September 1971."
________.	"Address at NOW's 6th National Conference."
________.	"Beyond the Feminine Mystique--A New Image of Woman." (excerpts)
________.	"The First Year: President's Report to NOW, 1967."
________.	"The Next Step: Opening Remarks to the Organizing Conference of The National Women's Political Caucus."
________.	"Our Revolution Is Unique."
________.	"Strike Day, August 26th, 1970."
________.	"Tokenism and the Pseudo-Radical Cop-Out: Ideological Traps for New Feminists to Avoid."
Fritz, A.	"The Novel Women: Origins of the Feminist Literary Tradition in England and France."
Gunn, B.	"And They Came Out of Their Cotton-Batting World: Enjoy, Enjoy."
Haener, D.	"Address at the Founder's Reception--5th Annual Meeting of NOW, September 1971."
Heide, W.	"Address to 1974 NOW National Conference."
________.	"Feminism; The Sine Qua Non for a Just Society."
________.	"Revolution: Tomorrow Is NOW. Keynote Address--Opening Session of NOW's 6th National Conference."
________.	"Women's Liberation Means Putting Sex in Its Place."
Hernandez, A.	"Address August 26, 1970--Los Angeles Rally."
________.	"Address to 1974 NOW National Conference."

________.	"Introduction at Founder's Reception."
________.	"Introduction to Keynote Address."
________.	"Revolution: From the Doll's House to the White House!"
Lyon, P.	"Keynote Address at the 1974 NOW National Conference."
Renner, A.	"Public Testimony."
Rose, E.	"Equal Rights for Women; Speeches by Ernestine L. Rose at the Third National Woman's Rights Convention, Syracuse, N.Y., September 8-10, 1852."
Schiller, L.	"Feminist Culture from 1790 to 1850: A Trans-Atlantic Community."

FERTILITY

Manis, J.	"Fertility Motivations and Career Conflicts in Educated Women."

FICTION

Rogers, M.	"The Novel as the Educator of the Imagination."

FIREARMS--LAWS AND REGULATIONS

Holt, M.	"Should Manufacture and Sale of Handguns for Private Use Be Prohibited in the United States."

FOLK-LORE, AFRO-AMERICAN

Bacon, A.	"The Study of Folk-lore."

FOOD CONTAMINATION

Abel, M.	"Clean Food."
Richards, E.	"Clean Food."

FOOD PRICES

Grasso, E.	"Food Price Hearing."
________.	"Price of Meat."

FOOD RELIEF

Abzug, B.	"Should Congress Limit the Present Scope of the Federal Food Stamps Program?"
Chisholm, S.	"Should Congress Limit the Present Scope of the Federal Food Stamp Program?"

FOOD SUPPLY

Addams, J.	"World's Food Supply and Woman's Obligation."
Jacobson, D.	"The War on Hunger: Temptation or Challenge."
Kelley, F.	"Address of the Chairman (On Industrial and Economic Problems.)"
Pope, J.	"Hunger in the United States: Women and Children First."
Prewett, V.	"World Population and Food Problems: The Need for Awareness."
Whitman, M.	"From Farm Policy to Food Policy: Satisfying Multiple and Conflicting Goals."

FORESTS AND FORESTRY

Dock, M.	"Forestry and Village Improvement."
Thorne, J.	"Forestry."

FOSTER HOME CARE

Baylor, E.	"Establishing Foster Parental Relationships."
________.	"When Should the Foster Home Be Prescribed for the Problem Child?"
Bissell, E.	"The Effects of Foster Home Placements."
Bullock, K.	"Developing Community Interest in Foster Homes."
Clarke, E.	"A Re-examination of Child-Welfare Functions in Foster-Care Agencies."
Fairbank, M.	"Visitation of Children Placed with Families."
Falconer, M.	"Work of the Girl's Department, Home of Refuge, Philadelphia."
Fenske, V.	"Supervision and Licensing of Institutions and Homes for Children."
Hutchinson, D.	"Foster Home Care in Wartime."
Johnston, R.	"The Case Worker in Foster Families for Day Care."
Leonard, C.	"Family Homes for Pauper and Dependent Children."
Lincoln, A.	"The Fixvale-Union Cottage Homes, and Classification of Public Dependents."

Richardson, A.	"The Massachusetts System of Placing and Visiting Children."
Smith, V.	"The Work of Temporary Homes and of Finding Homes for Children in Connecticut."
Taft, J.	"Relation of Personality Study to Child Placing."
Taylor, R.	"The Care of Children in Foster Homes."
Theis, S.	"How Foster Children Turn Out."
________.	"Minimum Qualifications for a Good Child Placing Agency."
Ueland, E.	"The Care of Children in Institutions."
Wildy, L.	"Current Trends in Foster Parent Education."

FREE LOVE

Rose, E.	"Debate at the 3rd Annual Meeting of the American Equal Rights Association, N. Y., May, 1869."
Stone, L.	"Debate at the 3rd Annual Meeting of the American Equal Rights Association, N. Y., May, 1869."
Woodhull, V.	"Address at the 10th Annual Meeting of the American Association of Spiritualists, Chicago, 1873."
________.	"Free Love Speech at Steinway Hall, N. Y., November 10, 1871."
________.	"The Impending Revolution. Lectures at New York Academy of Music, February 20, 1872."
________.	"The Scare-crows of Sexual Freedom."

FREEDMEN

Gage, F.	"Address to the 1st Annual Meeting of the American Equal Rights Association, May, 1867."
Rose, E.	"Address to the 1st Annual Meeting of the American Equal Rights Association, May, 1867."

FRIENDS, SOCIETY OF

Mott, L.	"Discourse at Friends' Meeting, Fifteenth Street, New York. Delivered Eleventh Month 11th, 1866."
________.	"Extracts from Address by Lucretia Mott at the Anti-sabbath Convention, Held in Boston, Massachusetts, March 23rd and 24th, 1848."

________.	"Extracts from Reports of Lucretia Mott's Addresses at the Annual Meetings of the Free Religious Association, in Boston."
________.	"Sermon, Delivered at Bristol, Pennsylvania, 6th month, 6th, 1860."
________.	"Sermon on the Religious Aspect of the Age. Delivered at Friends' Meeting, Race Street, Philadelphia, First Month 3rd, 1869, on her 76th Birthday."

GERMAN DRAMA

Butler, M.	"Hrotsvitha of Gandersheim: The Playable Dramas of a Woman Playwright of the Tenth Century."

GERMANY--HISTORY

Hackett, A.	"Feminism and Liberalism in Wilhelmine Germany, 1890-1918."

GIFTED CHILDREN--EDUCATION

West, R.	"Identifying and Training the Gifted. Need for a Universal Approach."

GIRL SCOUTS

Bacon, J.	"Girl Scouts."
Brady, G.	"Scouts and the New Frontier."

GOETHE, JOHANN WOLFGANG VON

Keene, M.	"Goethe and Schiller."
Peabody, M.	"A Study in Goethe's Faust."

GREAT BRITAIN--HISTORY

Judd, E.	"Influential Women in Anglo-Saxon England."

GREECE

Howe, J.	"Greece Revisited."
Thompson, D.	"Greece Today. A Miracle of Survival."

GREEK DRAMA

Howe, J.	"Women in the Greek Drama. Extracts from Julia Ward Howe's Lecture."

GROUP COUNSELING

Adkins, F.	"Reporting Activities of Group-Work Agencies."
Boyd, N.	"Group Work Experiments in State Institutions in Illinois."
Coyle, G.	"The Contribution of Group Experience to the Development of Older Children."
________.	"Group Work and Social Change (Pugsley Award)."
Elliott, G.	"Importance of Maturity and a Social Philosophy for Group Leaders and Supervisors."
Hall, H.	"The Consequences of Social Action for the Group-Work Agency."

GYNECOLOGY

Rugek, S.	"Emergent Modes of Utilization: Gynecological Self Help."

HALFWAY HOUSES

D'Arcambel, A.	"An Ideal Home for Discharged Prisoners."

HANDICAPPED CHILDREN

Huse, B.	"Care and Treatment of Crippled Children."
Neil, J.	"Public School Classes for Crippled Children."

HANDICRAFT

Albee, H.	"Value of Encouraging Handicrafts and Home Industries."

HARVEY, JENNY DOW

Addams, J.	"Jenny Dow Harvey."

HEALTH EDUCATION

Mohr, J. "Educating Women for Safety and Health."

HELLMAN, LILLIAN

Patrika, V. "Lillian Hellman: Dramatist of the Second Sex."

HEREDITY

Blackwell, A. "Heredity."
Gardener, H. "Heredity and Ethics."
________. "Heredity in Its Relation to a Double Standard of Morals."
________. "The Moral Responsibility of Women in Heredity."
Logan, A. "Prenatal and Hereditary Influences."
Whitney, M. "The Laws of Parentage and Heredity."

HIGHER EDUCATION OF WOMEN

Allan, V. "Statement."
Allen, L. "The Council's Interest."
Beard, M. "The Direction of Women's Education."
________. "University Discipline for Women--Asset or Handicap?"
Bell, D. "Junior College Programs."
Brownell, L. "Co-Education in Universities."
Bunting, M. "Adapting the Four-Year College to New Patterns."
Campbell, J. "The Nontraditional Student in Academe."
Chapin, A. "University Extension."
Conway, C. "Need of a Great College in the South."
Cross, K. "The Woman Student."
Getman, L. "From Conestoga to Career."
Goodman, J. "Status of Women Students."
Green, E. "Campus Issues in 1980."
Gulick, A. "A Woman's College in Spain."
Habein, M. "The Liberal Arts Program."
Harbert, L. "Higher Education for Women."
Hawkes, A. "Factors Affecting College Attendance."
Jelly, K. "Coeducation: One Student's View."
Loring, R. "Expanding Opportunities Through Continuing Education."
Mitchell, M. "The Higher Education of Woman."
Morrow, E. "College Women and the New Leisure."
Palmer, A. "Three Types of Women's Colleges."
________. "Why Go to College."
Perkins, F. "Address at a Meeting of the Board of Trustees of Mount Holyoke, May, 1944."

Perkins, S.	"The Higher Education of Women."
Reinhardt, A.	"Women in the American University of the Future."
Roberts, E.	"Comment on Patterns of Higher Education for Women."
Rodriguez, G.	"Coeds View an Undergraduate Campus."
Sandler, B.	"Patterns of Discrimination and Discouragement in Higher Education."
________.	"Statement."
________.	"Women in Higher Education: What Constitutes Equality?"
Schletzer, V.	"University of Minnesota, the Minnesota Plan."
Sewall, M.	"Higher Education for Women in the United States."
Smith, C.	"Radcliffe Institute for Independent Study."
Soule, C.	"A Collegiate Education for Woman, and the Necessity of a Woman-Professor in the Mixed College."
Stone, L.	"A Demand for Women in the Faculties of Co-Educational Colleges and Universities."
Thomas, M.	"The Bryn Mawr Woman."
________.	"Present Tendencies in Women's College and University Education."
________.	"The Purpose of the College."
Tompkins, P.	"American Association of University Women Educational Foundation, College Faculty Program."

HOME

Bronson, L.	"No Home, and the No Home Influences."
Howes, E.	"Social Progress Within the Home."
Miller, K.	"An Ideal Home for Children."
Paradise, V.	"Industry and the Home: Behind the Statistic."
Wilbour, C.	"The Inviolable Home."

HOME ECONOMICS

Barry, M.	"Home Economics."
Blair, M.	"Report of Household Economics Committee."
Brady, D.	"The City Worker's Family Budget."
Calvin, H.	"What the Club Woman Can Do for Home Economics Education."
Davison, E.	"Racing with Science."
Gilbreth, L.	"A Challenge to Women."
________.	"The Home--A Major Industry."
Goessmann, H.	"Discussion of the Trades and Professions Underlying the Home."
Hall, O.	"Facilitating Change."

Jennings, M.	"The Half of the Nation Outside of the Cities."
Jones, A.	"The Woman's Canning and Preserving Company."
Jones, N.	"Then and Now."
King, G.	"Mothers Meetings."
Le Baron, H.	"An Evaluation of Home Economics Training."
Miller, A.	"Science in the Kitchen."
Morgan, R.	"What Robin Morgan Said at Denver."
Richards, E.	"How Can the Increased Cost of Living Be Regulated to Meet the Decrease in the Salaries of Clerks and Professional Men?"
Shepperd, J.	"How Shall We Teach the Mother to Recognize the Necessity of a Sanitary Home?"
Stuckert, M.	"Cooperative Housekeeping."
Tinsley, W.	"Changes in the University Scene: Their Effect on Home Economics."
Wilkinson, L.	"The Columbian Association of Housekeepers and Bureau of Information, with Plans for the Work Outlined in the National Columbian Household Economic Association, Which Was Incorporated March 15, 1893."
________.	"Household Economics."

HOMER

Cohen, N.	"Homer and His Poems."

HOMOSEXUALITY

Fee, E.	"Science and Homosexuality."
Gittings, B.	"Keynote Address."

HOUSEWIVES

Ayala, A.	"Statement."
Bellamy, C.	"Remarks."
Blackwell, A.	"Relations of Woman's Work in the Household to the Work Outside."
Burke, Y.	"Statement."
Chacon, E.	"Statement."
Chen, L.	"Statement."
Cohan, E.	"Statement."
Cole, M.	"Statement."
Frances, L.	"Statement."
Grannis, E.	"Woman as Wife, Mother and Home Builder."
Haggarty, R.	"Statement."
Hicky, A.	"Statement."
Hull, M.	"Woman and Household Labor."
James, W.	"Statement."

Jones, P. "Women in Household Employment."

Kelly, J. "Housewife-Mother: The Institution and the Experience."

Kessler-Harris, A. "Statement."

Krupsak, M. "Remarks."

Lerner, G. "The American Housewife: A Historical Perspective."

Martinez, S. "Statement."

Miller, M. "Statement."

Moore, G. "Statement."

Peterson, E. "Importance of the Home-maker."

Pogrebin, L. "Rethinking Housework."

Reed, C. "Statement."

Sanders, I. "Statement."

Schleman, H. "Women Might Have Helped: Some Problems Ahead."

Seifer, N. "Statement."

Shields, L. "Statement."

Skelsey, A. "Mrs. Homemaker--Mrs. Wonderful: The Myths from Women's Lib."

Sommer, T. "Statement."

Swerdlow, M. "Introduction to Conference."

Tenner, H. "Statement."

HOUSING

Addams, J. "The Housing Problem in Chicago."

Bacon, A. "Housing: Its Relation to Social Work."

________. "How to Get Housing Reform."

Bailey, E. "The Management of Tenement-houses."

Coman, J. "What Does the Group Work Process Have to Contribute to a Housing Program?"

Daniel, A. "Testimony on Housing and Tenement Homework."

Fulmer, H. "The Housing Problem, and Its Relation to Other Social Problems."

Greitzer, C. "Discrimination in Housing, Public Accommodations, and Employment."

Hauser, C. "The Essence of Shelter."

Lincoln, A. "Housing Reform in Boston."

Lumsden, M. "Health and the New Housing."

Richmond, M. "How Social Workers Can Aid Housing Reform."

Roosevelt, A. "Better Housing."

Williamson, E. "Dwellings of the Poor in the Smaller Cities."

Wood, E. "Must Working People Live in Frayed-out Houses?"

HUMANITIES

Meyer, A.	"Do We Need Emerson Today? New Theories of Living Are Being Forced Upon Us."

HUMANITY

Hoppock, A.	"No Time for Panic. We Must Not Lose Our Humanness."

HUNGARY

Grasso, E.	"The Crown of St. Stephen."

HYGIENE, PUBLIC

Bishop, F.	"Committee on Social Hygiene."
Bolton, F.	"Presentation of the 1949 Award of the Snow Medal (With Her Reply)."
Brophy, F.	"A Combination Heart and Tuberculosis Program."
Cannon, M.	"Hospital Work in Relation to Public Health."
Dingman, M.	"Chairman's Introduction. Security Against Disease."
Gardiner, E.	"Health Security for Mother and Child."
Goodrich, A.	"Community Organization for Health."
Hamilton, A.	"The Work of the Health Committee of the League of Nations."
Hamilton, E.	"Health Programs for Use of Lone Workers in Rural Areas."
Jean, S.	"Creating a Demand for Health."
________.	"Instruction of School Children in Health Habits and Ideals."
McFarland, C.	"How Lay Citizens Can Influence the Local Administration of Health."
Parker, V.	"The Social Worker in a Sound Social Hygiene Program."
Roche, J.	"Health Ahead."
________.	"Report on the Washington Health Conference."
Yarros, R.	"Community Organization for Health--Discussion."

HYMNS

Smith, E.	"Woman in Sacred Song."

IDEALISM

Parson, M.	"Idealism: What's Wrong with It? A Declaration of Independence for Broadcasters."

ILLITERACY

Brothers, J.	"Meet the MS READ-a-thon: The Written Word."

IMPRESSIONISM (ART)

Urquhart, K.	"Impressionist Painting and Painters."

INDIANS OF NORTH AMERICA

Bronson, R.	"Shall We Repeat Indian History in Alaska."
Fletcher, A.	"Allotment of Land to Indians."
________.	"Legal Conditions of Indian Women."
________.	"Our Duty to Dependent Races."
________.	"The Preparation of the Indian for Citizenship."
Hiles, O.	"The Mission Indians of California."
James, S.	"Public Responsibility for the American Indians."
La Du, B.	"What Minnesota Is Doing for the Indians."
Lathrop, J.	"What the Indian Service Needs."
Lund, H.	"Progress in Social Case Work: Among the Indians."
McDiarmid, C.	"Our Neighbors, the Alaskan Women."
Mark, M.	"The Needs in Human Relationships."
Quinton, A.	"The Woman's National Indian Association."
________.	"The Work and Objects of the Woman's National Indian Association."
Stevenson, M.	"From the Zuni Scalp Ceremonial."
Todd, M.	"Education of Indian Girls in the West."
Tsianina (Princess)	"Minority Needs--the Indian."

INDUSTRIAL ACCIDENTS

Eastman, C.	"Work Accidents and Employer's Liability."
Lathrop, J.	"Institutional Records and Industrial Causes of Dependency."

INDUSTRIAL ARTS

Cory, F.	"The Contribution of Women to the Applied Arts."

INDUSTRIAL LAWS AND LEGISLATION

Abbott, E.	"The Social Case Worker and the Enforcement of Industrial Legislation."

INDUSTRIAL ORGANIZATION

Kelley, F.	"Introductory Statement (on Industrial Reorganization After the War)."

INDUSTRIAL RELATIONS

Frost, W.	"Exploiting the Employed--Discussion."

INDUSTRIAL SAFETY

Perkins, F.	"Worker's Stake in Safety."
Schneiderman, R.	"Triangle Fire Speech."
________.	"Triangle Memorial Speech."
________.	"We Have Found You Wanting."

INDUSTRIAL SOCIOLOGY

Stone, K.	"The Origins of Job Structures in the Steel Industry."

INDUSTRY--HISTORY

Twitchell, E.	"Industrial Revolution of the Last Century."

INDUSTRY--SOCIAL ASPECTS

Addams, J.	"Industrial Amelioration."

INDUSTRY AND STATE

Grasso, E.	"Emergency Loan Guarantee Act of 1971 to Lockheed Corp."
Kreps, J.	"Thoughts About Government and Business: Changing Public Habits and Attitudes."
________.	"Who is Responsible for the Quality of Life?"
Perkins, F.	"Governments' Share in the Solution of Modern Work Problems."
________.	"My Job."

INFANTS--MORTALITY

Rochester, A. — "Infant Mortality as an Economic Problem."

INHERITANCE AND TRANSFER TAX

Barton, B. — "Testimony on Features of Federal Income, Estate, and Gift Tax Law Which Have a Disparate Impact on Women."

Blumberg, G. — "Testimony on Features of Federal Income, Estate and Gift Tax Law Which Have a Disparate Impact on Women."

Griffiths, M. — "Opening Statement on Features of Federal Income, Estate, and Gift Tax Law Which Have a Disparate Impact on Women."

INSTITUTION LIBRARIES

Curtis, F. — "A Survey of Institution Libraries."

Jones, E. — "Importance of Organized Libraries in Institutions."

INSURANCE, HEALTH

Abbott, G. — "Toward Health Security: Economic Security Against Illness."

Griffiths, M. — "Excerpt from Statement on Pending Health Security Act, April 23, 1974."

INSURANCE, LIFE

Grady, A. — "A Massachusetts Experiment in Savings Bank Life Insurance."

Slocum, F. — "Life Insurance in Dependent Families."

INSURANCE, SOCIAL

Abbott, G. — "Testimony Before the United States Senate Committee During the "Hearing" on the Economic Security Bill."

Abzug, B. — "Statement."

Arnold, M. — "Statement."

Barrett, M. — "Public Assistance Features of the Social Security Act."

Bell, C. — "Testimony on the Treatment of Women Under Social Security and Private Pension Plans."

Burns, E. — "Income Security for the Aged."

Carroll, M.	"Social Insurance."
Fraser, A.	"Statement."
________.	"Statement."
Griffiths, M.	"Excerpt from Testimony Before Committee on Finance of the U. S. Senate, September 22, 1967."
________.	"Opening Statement on the Treatment of Women Under Social Security and Private Pension Plans."
________.	"Statement."
McCamman, D.	"Statement."
Perkins, F.	"Address Before New York Board of Trade."
________.	"Miss Perkins Asks Social Insurance."
________.	"The Outlook for Economic and Social Security in America."
________.	"The Significance of Social Security."
________.	"The Social Security Act."
Sommer, T.	"Statement."
________.	"Statement."

INSURANCE, UNEMPLOYMENT

Carroll, M.	"Controlling Labor Reduction."
________.	"Unemployment Insurance by Industry: Some Suggestions from Germany."
Colcord, J.	"Necessary Supplement to Unemployment Insurance."
Dahm, M.	"Testimony on Sex Discrimination in Unemployment Insurance, Veterans Programs, and Public Assistance."
Engle, L.	"Unemployment Insurance."
Griffiths, M.	"Opening Statement on Sex Discrimination in Unemployment Insurance. Veterans Programs, and Public Assistance."
Magee, E.	"Unemployment Insurance: Ohio Takes Stock."
Perkins, F.	"Federal Unemployment Insurance."

INTELLECTUALS

Goldman, E.	"Intellectual Proletarians."
McIntosh, M.	"Can the Intellect Survive? Meeting the Circumstances of Living."
Stricker, M.	"The Intellectual. His Journey and His Home."

INTELLIGENCE LEVELS

Bronner, A.	"Individual Variations in Mental Equipment."
Maccoby, E.	"Women's Intellect."

INTERGOVERNMENTAL FISCAL RELATIONS

Mink, P. — "Should Congress Adopt the Nixon Administration's Program for 'Revenue Sharing' ?"

INTERIOR DECORATION

MacDonald, F. — "Interior Decorator."
Meloney, M. — "Twenty Years of Pioneering."
Rogers, A. — "Elegance Is Not Undemocratic. Stop the Search for the Lowest Common Denominator."

INTERNATIONAL FINANCE

Sindona, M. — "The Phantom Petrodollar: A Deposit Withdrawal Program."

INTERNATIONAL LAW

Kelly, E. — "Principles of International Law Concerning Friendly Relations Among States: Sovereign Equality of States."
________. — "Principles of International Law Concerning Friendly Relations and Cooperation Among States: Peaceful Settlement of Disputes."

INTERNATIONAL RELATIONS

Addams, J. — "Labor as a Factor in the Newer Conception of International Relationships."
Frederick, P. — "View from the World Bridge."
Norrell, C. — "Roads to International Understanding."
Peterson, E. — "The Contribution of American Women to National and International Affairs. Achievements and Goals of American Women."
Thompson, D. — "Axioms of Global Policy. The Security of the Nation."

INTERNATIONAL WOMEN'S YEAR, 1975

Hutar, P. — "Statement Before the Social Committee of the U. N. Economic and Social Council, May 7, 1974 Supporting Holding Conference During International Women's Year."
Maymi, C. — "Explanation of Vote on Draft Resolution on World Conference of the International Women's Year."

________.	"Statement of December 3, 1976 on the Fulfillment of Goals of International Women's Year in the U. S."

INTERNATIONALISM

Addams, J.	"New Internationalism."

INTERVIEWING

Sears, A.	"Outline of the First Interview."
Taft, J.	"The Use of the Transfer Within the Limits of the Office Interview."
Vlachos, A.	"Social Treatment Through the Interview: Opening the Way."

ISABELLA OF CASTILE, 1451-1504

Bucklin, L.	"Life and Times of Isabella of Castile."

ISLAM

Clark, L.	"The Faith of Islam."

ISRAEL

Paul, N.	"Costumes and Customs from the Holy Land."

ITALY

Luce, C.	"Italy in 1955. Problems Which Italy Confronts Today."

JAPAN

Hitchcock, E.	"The Japanese."

JEALOUSY

Goldman, E.	"Jealousy: Causes and a Possible Cure."

JEWISH FAMILIES

Kahn, D.	"Special Problems in Jewish Families."

JEWS IN RUSSIA

Grasso, E.	"Remarks on House Concurrent Resolution 471 on the Status of Soviet Jews."

JEWS IN THE UNITED STATES

Adams, M.	"The Influence of the Discovery of America on the Jews."
Rosenberg, P.	"Influence of the Discovery of America on the Jews."
Witkowsky, E.	"Influence of the Discovery of America on the Jews."

JOURNALISM

Alden, M.	"The Responsibility of Women to the Press."
Graham, L.	"Justice in Journalism."
Lincoln, M.	"The Press--Its Powers and Possibilities."
Wakeman, A.	"What Do the Signs of the Times Signify?"

JURY

Aronoff, R.	"Public Testimony."

JUVENILE COURTS

Abbott, G.	"Case Work Responsibility of Juvenile Courts."
Lenroot, K.	"Progressive Methods of Care for Children Pending Juvenile Court Hearings."
Montgomery, A.	"The Child of the Juvenile Court."
Nutt, A.	"The Future of the Juvenile Court as a Case-Work Agency."
Rippin, J.	"The Co-Ordination of the Juvenile Court with Other Courts."
Workum, R.	"The Relationship Between the Functions of the Juvenile Court and Those of the General Child-Caring Agencies."

JUVENILE DELINQUENCY

Alexander, R.	"What Price the Fatted Calf? Juvenile Delinquency Approaching Epidemic Proportions."
Bowen, L.	"The Delinquent Child of Immigrant Parents." (abstract)

________. "The Treatment of Juvenile Offenders Against the Law."

Bowler, A. "Experiments in Preventing Juvenile Delinquency."

Brannick, C. "Schools and Delinquency."

Cobb, M. "Paper on Preventive Work Among Children."

Gibbons, M. "The Prevention and Treatment of Juvenile Delinquency in Wartime."

Glueck, E. "Family, the School, and Crime."

Goldsmith, E. "Psychiatry and the Offender in the Community: The Juvenile Offender."

Hoey, J. "Division on Delinquents and Correction."

________. "Understanding the Delinquent: Society in Relation to the Child."

Jaffray, J. "Preventing the First Offender."

Johnson, G. "The Boy and Girl Out on Furlough."

Kelley, F. "Industrial Causes of Juvenile Delinquency."

Labares, M. "The Purpose of Statewide Statistics in Building the Foundation for the Prevention of Delinquency."

Lenroot, K. "Statement at Public Hearings on Juvenile Delinquency Before Subcommittee on Wartime Health and Education of Committee on Education and Labor, Senate, November 30, 1943."

Lewis, O. "Medical Social Service as a Factor in Protective Work."

Lovell, M. "Preventive Work as Carried on in the Public Schools of America."

Lundberg, E. "The Child-Mother as a Delinquency Problem."

________. "The Juvenile Court as a Constructive Social Agency."

Lynde, M. "Prevention in Some of Its Aspects and Woman's Part in It."

McGuire, L. "Social-Work Basis for Prevention and Treatment of Delinquency and Crime: Community Factors."

Mendum, G. "Conditions Breeding Delinquency in Rural Communities."

Miner, M. "A Community Program for Protective Work."

Osborn, H. "Problems in Teen-Age Hangouts."

Putnam, E. "Dependent and Delinquent Children in This Country and Abroad."

________. "The Work of the Auxiliary Visitors Appointed to Assist the Department of the Massachusetts State Board in Charge of the Visitation of Dependent and Delinquent Children."

Richardson, A. "Massachusetts Institutions: Supplementary Work in the Care of Dependent and Delinquent Children."

Van Waters, M.	"Delinquency and the School."
________.	"The Delinquent Attitude--A Study of Juvenile Delinquency from the Standpoint of Human Relationship."
________.	"Institutions for Delinquent Children: What Is the Test of Success?"
Woods, E.	"The School and Delinquency: Every School a Clinic."

KELLEY, FLORENCE

Perkins, F.	"Eulogy for Florence Kelley, March, 1932."

KENNEDY, JOHN FITZGERALD

Smith, M.	"The Kennedy Twist."

KINDERGARTEN

Bass, R.	"Need of Kindergartens."
Bryan, A.	"The Letter Killeth."
Cooper, S.	"The Kindergarten as a Character Builder."
________.	"The Kindergarten as a Child-Saving Work."
________.	"The Kindergarten as an Educational Agency and the Relation of the Kindergarten to Manual Training."
________.	"Practical Results of Ten Years' Work."
Cropsey, N.	"The Kindergarten and the Primary School."
Harding, E.	"The Place of the Kindergarten in Child-Saving."
Hofer, A.	"What the Kindergarten Means to Mothers."
Kraus-Boelte, M.	"The Kindergarten and the Mission of Woman."
Mackenzie, C.	"Free Kindergartens."
Murray, M.	"International Kindergarten Union."
Severance, C.	"Discussion of Paper on Kindergarten."
Smith, V.	"The Kindergarten."
Stewart, S.	"The International Kindergarten Union."
Tupper, M.	"Discussion of Paper on Kindergarten."
Wheelock, L.	"The Children of the Other Half."
Wiggin, K.	"The Relation of the Kindergarten to Social Reform."

KNIGHT, HOWARD R.

Kahn, D.	"Howard R. Knight and the International Conference of Social Work."

KOREAN WAR, 1950-1953

Higgins, M. "Report from Korea."

LABOR AND LABORING CLASSES

Bristol, A. "Labor and Capital."
Perkins, F. "The Nation's Workers."
Van Kleeck, M. "Our Illusions Regarding Government (Pugsley Award)."
________. "The Social Consequences of Changing Methods of Production."
________. "Social Program of the Labor Movement."

LABOR DISPUTES

Perkins, F. "The Labor Question."

LABOR LAWS AND LEGISLATION

Ackroyd, M. "Remarks on Hours Limitation Law, Administrative and Technical Problems."
Herrick, E. "Federal Wage and Hour Regulation."
Kelley, F. "The Need of Uniformity in Labor Legislation."
Krupsak, M. "Woman and the New York Labor Laws."
Norton, M. "Wage and Hour Legislation, the Object of the Law."
Stitt, L. "Government Regulation of Wages and Hours: Progress Under the Federal Fair Labor Standards Act."

LABOR SUPPLY

Nestor, A. "Exploiting the Employed."

LATIN AMERICA

Dodd, A. "Our Spanish-American Neighbors."

LAW

Donlon, M. "Law and Government. The Underlying Concept or Philosophy of Our Law."
Hufstedler, S. "Courtship and Other Legal Arts: The Appellate System."

________.	"In the Name of Justice: The Unending Rush to the Courts."
Prewitt, A.	"Bar vs. Bench: New Fears in an Old Relationship."
Robins, M.	"The Social Perils of Lawlessness."

LAW ENFORCEMENT

Willebrandt, M.	"The Club Woman and Law Enforcement."
________.	"The Department of Justice and Some Problems of Enforcement."

LEADERSHIP

Cratty, M.	"On Being a Builder."
________.	"On Being a Leader."
________.	"The Qualities of Leadership."
Fowdick, D.	"The World Is Our Framework."

LEGAL AID

Philbrook, M.	"Legal Aid."
Waldo, A.	"Legal Aid Service and Social Work: The Social Point of View."

LEGISLATORS--U. S.

O'Day, C.	"Congresswoman."

LEISURE

Aronovici, C.	"Organized Leisure as a Factor in Conservation."
Hall, H.	"When Leisure Palls."
Robnett, F.	"A Look at the Problem."
Taylor, L.	"Seeing the Problem Whole."
Vittum, H.	"The Use of Leisure."
Wright, L.	"The Creative Use of Leisure."

LESBIANISM

Cooper, J.	"Coming Out."
Dworkin, A.	"Lesbian Pride."
Eisenbud, R.	"Female Homosexuality: A Sweet Enfranchisement."
Harris, B.	"The Lesbian in Literature: Or, Is There Life on Mars?"

Stanley, J. "Coming Out."
Susan, B. "Public Testimony."

LIBERALISM

Thompson, D. "The Liberal Spirit."

LIBERTY

Bolton, F. "Wanted: Women to Defend Freedom."
Flynn, E. "Elizabeth Gurley Flynn's Defense."
________. "Miss Flynn Continues Defense."
Kaiser, C. "Has Group Work a Part to Play in the Preservation and Extension of Civil Liberties?"
Luce, C. "Permanent Revolution. The Concept of Liberty Under Law Is Universal."
Rose, E. "Speech of Ernestine L. Rose at the Thomas Paine Anniversary Celebration, New York, January 29, 1852."
Sampson, E. "Show the East How the Freedom Revolution Works. Industrial Civilizations Are Built from the Bottom Up."
Thompson, D. "Woman and Freedom in Our Society."

LIBERTY OF SPEECH

Anthony, S. "Debate on the Bible Resolution at the National Convention of the National American Woman Suffrage Association, November 1895."
________. "Plea on Behalf of Elizabeth Stanton at the Convention of the National American Woman Suffrage Association, January 1896."
Gordon, D. "Youth's Right to Knowledge and Free Speech. The Challenge of Youth Forum Discussions."
Hoeber, S. "Academic Freedom. Panel Discussion."
May, C. "Every Man Should Have His Say: Free Discussion."
Pilpel, H. "Libraries and the First Amendment."

LIBERTY OF THE PRESS

Grasso, E. "Newspersons' Information and Source Protection Act."

LIBRARIES

Bradshaw, L.	"Library Response to a Restive World."
Countryman, G.	"Building for the Future."
Culver, E.	"A Call to Action."
Eastman, L.	"Presidential Address at Washington Conference."
Fyan, L.	"Presidential Address."
________.	"Strength, Conviction and Unity."
Gaver, M.	"Masters of the Raging Book?"
Laich, K.	"Our Highest Common Denominator."
Lowrie, J.	"Inaugural Address--What Is Librarianship?"
Ludington, F.	"Taproot, Trunk and Branches."
________.	"Report to Council, June 25, 1954, Minneapolis."
Martin, A.	"ALA's New Goal and Greatest Challenge: From "The Inaugural Address"."
Molz, R.	"Libraries and the Development and Future of Tax Support."
Morsch, L.	"Promoting Library Interests Throughout the World."
Morton, F.	"United by Common Interests and Common Purposes."
Ovitz, D.	"The Library's Relation to Neighborhood and Community Work."
Paul, H.	"Regional Coordination."
Rathbone, J.	"Creative Librarianship."
Rothrock, M.	"Libraries in a New Era."
Spain, F.	"Upon the Shining Mountains."
Titcomb, M.	"Report Library Extension."
Walton, G.	"The Lost Librarian."
Warren, A.	"Salute to the Dawn."

LITERATURE

Bates, J.	"Address."
Berry, R.	"Life and the Literature of To-morrow."
Brown, C.	"Organization as a Means of Literary Culture."
Poppenheim, M.	"Report of Literature Committee."

LITERATURE, IMMORAL

Holme, P.	"Address to the National Purity Congress, Baltimore Yearly Meeting Committee."

LLOYD, HENRY DEMAREST

Addams, J.	"At a Memorial Meeting for Henry Demarest Lloyd Held Under the Auspices of United Mine Workers of America...."

LOCAL GOVERNMENT

Lee, D. "Local Government and World Affairs."

LOCAL TRANSIT

Christensen, D. "Autos and Mass Transit: Paradox and Confusion."

LYNCHING

Wells-Barnett, I. "Lynching Our National Crime."

MCCARTHY, JOSEPH

Smith, M. "A Declaration of Conscience: June 1, 1950."

MCCULLOCH, OSCAR C.

Barrows, K. "Address: Tribute to Oscar C. McCulloch."

MARKETING RESEARCH

Angell, B. "Why Do New Products Fail: Mini-Market Tests."

MARRIAGE

Anthony, S. "Marriage Has Ever Been a One-Sided Affair."
Blackwell, A. "Address at the 10th National Woman's Rights Convention, N.Y., May 10-11, 1860."
_______. "On Marriage and Work."
Colby, C. "Woman in Marriage. Address to the National American Woman Suffrage Association Convention of 1889."
Goldman, E. "Marriage and Love."
Grannis, E. "Marriage and Divorce."
Hollis, F. "The Impact of the War on Marriage Relationships."
Shaw, A. "Discussion of the Effects of Modern Changes in Industrial and Social Life on Woman's Marriage Prospects."
Toomy, A. "Discussion of the Effects of Modern Changes in Industrial and Social Life on Woman's Marriage Prospects."

Wadsworth, E.	"Discussion of the Effects of Modern Changes in Industrial and Social Life on Woman's Marriage Prospects."

MARRIAGE COUNSELING

Hanford, J.	"Family Case Work with Marital Difficulties."
Martens, E.	"Case Work Treatment of Emotional Maladjustment in Marriage."

MARRIAGE LAW

Brown, S.	"Administration of Marriage Laws in Michigan."
Mudgett, M.	"When People Apply at a Marriage License Bureau."
Wells, K.	"State Regulation of Marriage."

MATERNAL AND INFANT WELFARE

Corbin, H.	"An Adequate Local Maternity Program."
Gardiner, E.	"A Maternity and Infancy Program for Rural and Semirural Communities."
Hedley, C.	"Public Testimony."
Lathrop, J.	"State Care for Mothers and Infants."
Perkins, F.	"Remarks on Maternity Care for Foreign-Born Women."
Sloane, M.	"Health Security for Mother and Child--Discussion."
Taylor, M.	"Applying a Maternity and Infancy Program to Rural Sections."

MATRIARCHY

Pomeroy, S.	"A Classical Scholar's Perspective on Matriarchy."

MEDICAL CARE, COST OF

Chisholm, S.	"The Cost of Care."

MEDICAL RESEARCH

Lape, E.	"Report on Research Among 5,000 Doctors."
Smith, M.	"Senate Speech on Support for Medical Research, January 12, 1956."

MEDICAL SOCIAL WORK

Baker, E.	"The Contribution of Hospital Social Service to Health Conservation."
Bartlett, H.	"Influence of the Medical Setting on Social Case Work Services."
Cannon, I.	"Community Relationships Involved in 100 Per Cent Registration in Social Service Exchange: From the Standpoint of Hospital Social Service."
________.	"Social Work at Massachusetts General Hospital."
Cannon, M.	"Case Work in the Hospital."
________.	"Equipment Needed by the Medical Social Worker."
________.	"Health Problems of the Foreign Born from the Point of View of the Hospital Social Worker."
Cockerill, E.	"Casework and the New Emphasis on an Old Concept in Medicine."
________.	"The Use of Current Case-Work Concepts Where There Is Physical Illness: From the Experience of the Case Worker in the Medical Agency."
Donahoe, M.	"Next Steps in State Hospital Social Service."
Eliot, M.	"The Work of the Interdepartmental Committee to Coordinate Health and Welfare Activities."
Foster, E.	"Is an Independent Administration of Health and Social Work Desirable?"
Hall, H.	"When Sickness Strikes."
Harper, G.	"Some Uses of Social Case Work in Medical Training."
Hedger, C.	"Medical Inspection in the Schools--Its Technique and Its Results."
Henry, E.	"Bridging the Chasm."
Lothrop, A.	"The Responsibility of Medical Social Workers."
Pelton, G.	"The History and Status of Hospital Social Work."
Post, K.	"The Use of Available Resources."
Potter, E.	"Resources for Care of the Chronically Ill: Maintenance."
Richmond, M.	"Medical and Social Co-operation."
Smith, A.	"Group Play in a Hospital Environment."
Webb, S.	"Community Relationships Involved in 100 Per Cent Registration in Social Service Exchange; From the Standpoint of Hospital Social Service."
Yocum, S.	"The Use of Current Case-Work Concepts Where There Is Physical Illness: From the Experience of the Case Worker in the Social Agency."

MEDICINE, PREVENTIVE

Donohue, M.	"Preventive Medicine."

MENTAL DEFICIENCY

Anderson, M.	"Community Control of the Feeble-minded--Instruction."
Bancroft, M.	"Classification of the Mentally Deficient."
Barrows, I.	"Manual Training for the Feeble-minded."
Brown, C.	"Public Aid for the Feeble-minded."
Chace, L.	"Public School Classes for Mentally Deficient Children."
Davis, K.	"Introductory Remarks on Defective Delinquents."
Dunlap, M.	"Progress in the Care of the Feeble-minded and Epileptics."
Dutcher, E.	"Possibilities of Home Supervision of Moron Women."
Fitts, A.	"How to Fill the Gap Between the Special Class and the Institution."
MacMurchy, H.	"The Relation of Feeble-mindedness to Other Social Problems."
Mott, A.	"The Education and Custody of the Imbecile."
Streeter, L.	"The Relation of Mental Defect to the Neglected, Dependent and Delinquent Children of New Hampshire."
Sytz, F.	"Social Service Supervision of the Feeble-minded."

MENTAL HYGIENE

Anderson, M.	"Mental Hygiene Problems of Subnormal Children: In the Public Schools."
Bache, L.	"The Value of Parades in an Educational Program."
Bingham, A.	"The Personal Problems of a Group of Workers."
Crutcher, H.	"The Problems of a Permanent Child Guidance Clinic."
Dawley, A.	"Coordination of Effort in Mental Hygiene in the Community."
________.	"The Essential Similarities in All Fields of Case Work."
Dearborn, J.	"The Prevention of Nervous Strain by Home and School Training."
Dexter, E.	"Mental Hygiene in Our Schools: Attitudes of Teachers Toward Problem Behavior."
Foster, S.	"Mental-Health Needs in Children's Institutions."
________.	"Personality Deviations and Their Relation to the Home."

Jarrett, M.	"Educational Value to the Community of Mental Hygiene Agencies: Psychiatric Social Work."
________.	"The Mental Hygiene of Industry: Repeat of Progress on Work Undertaken Under Engineering Foundation."
Johnson, E.	"How Mental Hygiene May Help in the Solution of School Problems."
Johnson, H.	"Mental Hygiene of Younger Children."
Johnson, L.	"Use of a Small Institution in Treatment of Personality Problems."
Lyday, J.	"The Place of the Mobile Clinic in a Rural Community."
Macdonald, V.	"Social Work and the National Committee for Mental Hygiene."
Marcus, G.	"Community Organization for Child Guidance Clinic Work."
________.	"How Case Work Training May Be Adapted to Meet the Worker's Personal Problems."
Mead, M.	"Mental Health in Our Changing Culture; Excerpts from Address."
Nickel, L.	"The Role and Aims of the Social Worker in Treatment."
Overholser, W.	"The Problem of Mental Disease in an Aging Population."
Regensburg, J.	"The Place of the Home in Treatment."
Reynolds, B.	"The Mental Hygiene of Young Children: From the Point of View of a Psychiatric Social Worker in a Habit Clinic."
________.	"Treatment Processes as Developed by the Social Worker."
Richards, E.	"The Elementary School and the Individual Child."
________.	"Formulating the Problem in Social Case Work with Children."
Robb, C.	"The Problem of Meeting the Needs of the Social Worker Who Refers Cases to a Psychiatric Clinic."
Ryther, M.	"Place and Scope of Psychiatric Social Work in Mental Hygiene."
Taft, J.	"The Function of a Mental Hygienist in a Children's Agency."
________.	"Mental Hygiene Problems of Normal Adolescence."
________.	"Progress in Social Case Work: In Mental Hygiene."
________.	"The Relation of the School to the Mental Health of the Average Child."
________.	"The Time Element in Mental Hygiene Therapy as Applied to Social Case Work."
Taylor, E.	"What Kind of Mental Hygiene Service Do Children's Agencies Need?"
Woolley, H.	"Social Consequences of the Neglect of Mental Hygiene in Young Childhood."

MENTAL ILLNESS

Furbush, E.	"Summary of Present Legislation on Insanity in Various States, with Program for Meeting the Present Situation."
Horten, E.	"Instances of After Care of the Insane."
Jarrett, M.	"War Neuroses (Shell Shock) After the War--Extra-Institutional Preparation."
Lathrop, J.	"Village Care for the Insane."
McCowen, J.	"The Prevention of Insanity."
Powers, M.	"The Industrial Cost of the Psychopathic Employee."

MERCHANT MARINE

Bentley, H.	"The Impediments to Rapid Regulatory Action: The Bureaucratic Red Tape."
________.	"Merchant Marine! Stepchild of the Economy."
________.	"Russian Merchant Marine and Naval Supremacy: Awake Before It's Too Late!"
________.	"Shipping: The Conference System."

MEXICANS IN THE U.S.

Alvarado, E.	"Mexican Immigration to the United States."

MEXICO

Romney, C.	"Four Months in Old Mexico."

MIDDLE AGE

Knapp, P.	"Research in Progress at the Merrill-Palmer School."
Kyrk, H.	"The Economic Role of Women, Forty-five to Sixty-five."
LaFollette, I.	"Employment Opportunities in the Woman's Service Exchange Program of Madison, Wisconsin."
Lloyd-Jones, E.	"Progress Report of Pertinent Research."
Macfarlane, C.	"Physiological Changes and Adjustments: From the Standpoint of a Physician."
Meyer, A.	"The Middle-Aged Woman in Contemporary Society."
Neugarten, B.	"Kansas City Study of Adult Life."
Swanson, P.	"Physiological Changes and Adjustments: From the Standpoint of a Nutritionist."
Zuill, F.	"How Home Economics Can Contribute to Meeting These Problems."

MIDWIVES

Van Blaroom, C.	"A Possible Solution of the Midwife Problem."

MIGRANT LABOR

Abbott, G.	"The Tragedy of Transients; A Statement Before a United States Senate Committee."
Buffington, A.	"Automobile Migrants."
Hanna, A.	"Social Services on the Mexican Border."
Higgins, A.	"Comparative Advantages of Municipal and C. O. S. Lodging Houses."
Hill, R.	"Goals for Wanderers."
Hoey, J.	"Adequate Public Social Services for Migrants."
Hutchinson, W.	"Citizenship and Domicile Versus Social Considerations in Problems of Migrated Families."
Larned, R.	"The Tangled Threads of Migrant Family Problems."
McCall, B.	"Migration Problems and the Federal Government."
O'Connor, A.	"Citizenship and Domicile Versus Social Considerations in Problems of Migrated Families."
Parker, L.	"Migratory Children."
Shields, L.	"Migratory Workers in Agriculture."
Willard, A.	"Reinstatement of Vagrants Through Municipal Lodging Houses."

MIGRATION, INTERNAL

Blakeslee, R.	"Law and Administrative Practices as Barriers to Mobility: Remedies in Relation to Human Welfare."

MILITARISM

Keller, H.	"Menace of the Militarist Program. Speech at the Labor Forum, Washington Irving High School, New York City, December 19, 1915."

MILITARY ASSISTANCE

Bird, D.	"Should Present Military Assistance Programs of U. S. Foreign Aid Be Substantially Curtailed?"

MILITARY SERVICE, COMPULSORY

Bacon, S.	"Military Service--Bridge or Gap? Panel Discussion."
Chisholm, S.	"Is Proposed Conversion of U.S. Armed Forces to an All-Volunteer Basis a Sound National Policy?"
Goldman, E.	"Address to the Jury."
Hallaren, M.	"Military Service--Bridge or Gap? Panel Discussion."
Hobby, O.	"The Draft: Education for Citizenship."
Holder, E.	"Military Service--Bridge or Gap? Panel Discussion."
Rosenberg, A.	"Mobilization in Action."

MINORITIES--EMPLOYMENT

Herman, J.	"Public Testimony."
McWilliams, M.	"Testimony of American Broadcasting Company."
Norton, E.	"Statement."
Wallace, P.	"Employment Opportunities for Minorities in New York City: An Introduction."
________.	"Restricted Membership at the Management Level: Exclusion of Jews from the Executive Suite."

MINORITY BUSINESS ENTERPRISES

Kreps, J.	"Remarks Before the Opportunities Industrialization Centers of America, Detroit, Michigan, June 8, 1977."

MISSIONS

Andrews, J.	"The Ramabai Association."
Bailey, H.	"The Woman's Foreign Missionary Union of Friends."
Blackall, E.	"Baptist Home Mission Society."
Burlingame, E.	"National Free-Will Baptist Woman's Missionary Society."
Cook, G.	"The Brahmo Somaj and What It Is Doing for the Women of India."
Grannis, E.	"Church Union."
Haynes, L.	"The Relation of Young Women to Church Missions."
Hills, M.	"Report of Free Baptist Missionary Society."
Isaacs, M.	"Christ on the Avenue."
Jones, S.	"Post Office Missions."
Morris, H.	"Missionary Work."

Scudder, A.	"Woman's Work in the Society of Christian Endeavor."

MITCHELL, MARIA

Whitney, M.	"Life and Work of Maria Mitchell, LL.D."

MONOLOGUES

Potter, J.	"The Monologue as an Entertainment."

MORTGAGES

Birtwell, M.	"Chattel Mortgages."

MOTHERS

Birney, A.	"Address of Welcome."
Blatch, H.	"Voluntary Motherhood."
________.	"Voluntary Motherhood."
Bogue, M.	"Problems in the Administration of Mothers' Aid."
Booth, M.	"Mothers to the Motherless."
Bram, S.	"To Have or Have Not: The Social Psychology of the Decision to Have or Not Have Children."
Bristol, A.	"Enlightened Motherhood."
Chandler, L.	"Enlightened Motherhood--How Attainable."
Corbally, M.	"From This Mother: The Old Brick Wall Theory."
Corbin, C.	"Enlightened Motherhood."
Cutler, H.	"Enlightened Motherhood."
Dickinson, M.	"Response to Address of Welcome."
Lovering, E.	"Enlightened Motherhood."
Meriweather, L.	"Organized Motherhood."
Milner, E.	"The Mother's Role."
Newton, F.	"The Mother's Greatest Needs."
Sangster, M.	"Reading Courses for Mothers."

MOTHERS' PENSIONS

Abbott, E.	"The Experimental Period of Widows' Pension Legislation."
Lundberg, E.	"The Present Status of Mothers' Pensions Administration."

MOTOR VEHICLES--POLLUTION CONTROL DEVICES

Abzug, B.	"Should Auto Emission Controls Be Removed in Low-Pollution Areas to Help Conserve the U. S. Supply of Motor Fuels?"

MOURNING ETIQUETTE

Smith, J.	"The Mourning Garb."

MOVING-PICTURES

Garson, G.	"Education for the Millions Through Pictures."
Hepburn, K.	"Keeping the Mind of the Nation Young Through Motion Pictures."
Stecker, H.	"Some Desirable Goals for Motion Pictures."
Temple, S.	"Responsibility of the Movies."
Winter, A.	"The Movies and Public Opinion."

MOTT, LUCRETIA COFFIN

Stanton, E.	"Eulogy for Lucretia Mott--Memorial Service in 1881."
________.	"Lucretia Mott: Eulogy at the Memorial Services Held In Washington by the National Woman Suffrage Association, January 19, 1881."

MUNICIPAL FINANCE

Walker, M.	"The American City Is Obsolescent. Factors Affecting Municipal Revenues."

MUSIC

Oberndorfer, M.	"Introductory Remarks--Music in Your Community."

MYTHOLOGY

Lefkowitz, M.	"Classical Mythology and the Role of Women in Modern Literature."
Reed, E.	"Assyrian Mythology."

NARCOTICS

Beneby, P. "Testimony."
Blanchette, D. "Testimony."
Causey, R. "Testimony."
Fletcher, S. "Testimony."
King, E. "Tell Us the Truth!"
MacDonald, L. "Testimony."
Miller, P. "Testimony."
Mock, J. "Testimony."
Pace, S. "Testimony."
Siegel, M. "Testimony."
Sommer, A. "Testimony."
Sporborg, C. "How Can Women Fight Marijuana?"
Terp, B. "Testimony."

NATIONAL CHARACTERISTICS, AMERICAN

Dibble, M. "The Nervous American."

NATIONAL INCOME

Hohman, H. "Proposals for Distribution."
Kyrk, H. "Who Gets It? Who Spends It?"

NATIONALISM

Bay, L. "Nationalism."
Manus, R. "Excessive Nationalism--Discussion."

NATURALIZATION

Minick, C. "The Naturalization Law and Its Administration."
Roche, J. "The Effect of the Cable Law on the Citizenship Status of Foreign Women."

NATURE (THEOLOGY)

Carson, R. "A Statement of Relief: Speech to Theta Sigma Phi, April 21, 1954."

NATURE STUDY

Schryver, A. "Nature Studies in the Home."

NEIGHBORHOOD

Addams, J.	"Neighborhood Improvement."
Breckinridge, D.	"The Story of Irishtown."
Falconer, M.	"Neighborhood Development in Philadelphia."
Farra, K.	"Neighborhood Councils."
Moore, D.	"The Saving of Telegraph Hill."
Neufeld, E.	"The Development of Existing Neighborhood Activities."
Robbins, J.	"Bureau and Political Influences in Neighborhood Civic Problems."
White, E.	"Local Responsibility for Community Development."
Witherspoon, P.	"Progress in Louisville Social Centers."

NEUTRALITY

Rankin, J.	"Testimony on Neutrality Act Before House Foreign Affairs Committee, February 16, 1937."
Thompson, D.	"Let's Face the Facts. There Are No Neutral Hearts."

NEWSPAPERS

Bentley, H.	"American Press. A Product of the Time?"
Graham, K.	"Press and Its Responsibilities: Finance and Government Security."
________.	"A Vigilant Press: Its Job to Inform."
Griffiths, M.	"Life Without a Newspaper, from an Address to Congress."
Luce, C.	"What's Wrong with the American Press? The Debasement of Popular Taste."

NOBEL PRIZES

Buck, P.	"Acceptance Speech for the Nobel Prize, December, 1938."
________.	"Nobel Acceptance Speech."
Mayer, M.	"Shell Model: Address, December 12, 1963."
Yalow, R.	"Radio Immunoassay: A Probe for the Fine Structure of Biologic Systems."

NON-WAGE PAYMENTS

Haener, D.	"Women and Employment Benefits: Maternity and Other Fringe Benefits."

NORTHWEST, PACIFIC

Duniway, A.	"The Pacific Northwest."

NUCLEAR TEST BAN TREATY, 1963

Smith, M.	"Senate Speech on Ratification of the Nuclear Test Ban Treaty."
________.	"Speech on the Nuclear Test Ban Treaty."

NURSES AND NURSING

Collins, V.	"1977--The Year of the Nurse: We Are Professionally Competent."
Daiche, L.	"Blackwell's Island Hospitals."
Fescher, L.	"The Visiting Nurse as an Economic Factor."
Fullerton, A.	"The Science of Nursing: A Plea."
Hitchcock, J.	"Report of the Sub-Committee on Visiting Nursing."
Kimber, D.	"District Nursing in London."
Lincoln, A.	"The Almshouse Hospital."
Nutting, M.	"Address of the President."
________.	"Address of the President."
________.	"Address of the President."
________.	"Graduating Address."
Palmer, S.	"The Trained Nurse."
Richards, L.	"The Moral Influence of Trained Nurses In Hospitals."
Robb, I.	"The Organization of Trained Nurses' Alumnae Associations."
Robinson, M.	"A Floating Hospital."
Rogers, L.	"The Physician and the Nurse in the Public School."
Tucker, K.	"Community Relationships Involved in 100 Per Cent Registration in Social Service Exchange: From the Standpoint of Nursing Organizations."
________.	"The Growth of the Social Point of View: In Nursing."
Wise, L.	"The Economy of Nursing the Sick Poor in Their Homes."

NURSING SCHOOLS

Brennan, A.	"Training Schools for Nurses--Theory and Practice."
Brent, E.	"Training Schools for Nurses--District Nurses."
Brown, C.	"A Bureau of Information: The Need of a Post-Graduate School for Nurses."

Hampton, I.	"Training Schools for Nurses."
Lathrop, J.	"Training Schools for Nurses--District Nurses."
Richards, L.	"Training Schools for Nurses--Mission Training Schools."
Roberts, A.	"Nursing Education and Opportunities for the Colored Nurse."
Smith, M.	"Training Schools for Nurses--Trained Nurses in Hospitals for the Insane."

NUTRITION

Gillett, L.	"Education in Food Values as a Preventive of Dietary Deficiencies."
________.	"The Relation of Food Economics to the Nutritive Value of the Diet."
Hogan, L.	"Dietetics."
Jean, S.	"The Educational Opportunities Presented by the School Luncheon."
Richards, E.	"Food for Students."
Spohn, A.	"To What Shall We Hold Fast in Nutrition During Periods of Lower Income?"
Williams, F.	"Social and Economic Factors Conditioning Food Expenditures."

OCCUPATIONAL DISEASES

Hamilton, A.	"Occupational Diseases."

OCCUPATIONAL THERAPY

Biggerstaff, M.	"Occupational Therapy."
Slagle, E.	"Occupational Therapy."

OCCUPATIONAL TRAINING

Addams, J.	"Address."
________.	"How Shall We Approach Industrial Education?"
________.	"Standards of Education for Industrial Life."
Adler, H.	"Working Man's School of New York City."
Arnold, S.	"Industrial Education."
Cobb, M.	"Scholastic and Industrial Education."
Kirkwood, L.	"Methods of Industrial Training for Girls."
McDouglad, E.	"The School and Its Relation to the Vocational Life of the Negro."
Nestor, A.	"Workers' Education for Women in Industry."
Paddock, S.	"Industrial and Technological Training."
Potter, H.	"Woman in the Industrial Arts."

Sickels, L. "Industrial Training in Girls' Schools."
Spencer, A. "What Machine Dominated Industry Means in Relation to Women's Work: The Need of New Training of Apprenticeship for Girls."

OCEANOGRAPHY

Mink, P. "Oceans: Antarctic Resource and Environmental Concerns."
________. "Visions of the Future."

OLD AGE

Nairne, L. "Private Living Arrangements for Elderly People."
Nicholson, E. "Private Living Arrangements for Elderly People."

OLD AGE ASSISTANCE

Grasso, E. "Action to Help Older Americans."
________. "A More Realistic and Comprehensive National Policy for Older Americans."
Guiney, M. "Planning Services for the Aged in the Local Community."
Gunn, B. "Toward a National Policy on Aging: Every Person Counts."
Hill, R. "Old and the Needy."
Long, E. "Old Age Assistance Administration: Varieties of Practice in the United States."
McHugh, R. "A Constructive Program for the Aged."
Smith, G. "What Are the Case-Work Needs of the Aged?"

OLD AGE HOMES

Hill, R. "Group Living for the Elderly."
Switton, F. "Meeting the Needs of the Aged Through Private Institutional Care."

ORGANIZATION

American, S. "Organization."
Anthony, S. "Organization Among Women as an Instrument in Promoting the Interests of Political Liberty."
Avery, R. "Organization and Its Relation to the International and National Councils of Women."

Blake, L.	"Organization Among Women as an Instrument in Promoting the Interests of Political Liberty."
Brackett, A.	"Organization as Related to Civilization."
Brown, C.	"The Moral Influence of Women's Associations."
Clymer, E.	"The National Value of Women's Clubs."
Dickinson, M.	"Organization Among Women as an Instrument in Promoting Religion."
Eastman, M.	"Address on Organization."
Fields, A.	"Constitution of a District Conference."
Gage, M.	"Remarks on Organization."
Henrotin, E.	"Organization."
Hollister, L.	"Fraternal Benefit Associations: Their Origin, Scope and Value."
Howe, J.	"How Can Women Best Associate?"
________.	"The Power of Organization."
Hultin, I.	"Address on Organization Among Women as an Instrument in Promoting Religion."
Sewall, M.	"Address on Organization."
________.	"The Economy of Woman's Forces Through Organization."
________.	"Organization as a Factor in the Development of Modern Social Life."
Spencer, A.	"Advantages and Dangers of Organization."
Willard, F.	"Address on Organization."
________.	"Woman and Organization. President's Address."

ORPHANS AND ORPHAN--ASYLUMS

Verry, E.	"Problems Facing Children with Relatively Long Period of Institutional Care."

OSSOLI, MARGARET FULLER

Woolley, C.	"Synopsis of Lecture on Margaret Fuller."

PALMER, BERTHA HONORE

Eagle, M.	"Unveiling of the Portrait."
Lockwood, M.	"Presentation of Portrait."
Wheeler, C.	"Congratulation on the Possession of Mrs. Palmer's Portrait."

PANAMA CANAL

Boswell, H.	"Conditions in the Canal Zone."

PARENT AND CHILD

Laws, G. "Can Parental Education be Applied?"

PARIS

Howe, J. "Paris."

PAROLE

Burleigh, E. "Some Principles of Parole for Girls."

PATERNITY

Marsh, M. "Common Attitudes Toward the Unmarried Father."
Morlock, M. "Establishment of Paternity."

PATRIOTISM

Barnes, E. "Patriotic Principles of Americanism. Freedom Must be Earned."
Bushnell, L. "Pride in America: Lets' Start a Renaissance."
Catt, C. "Practical Points in Patriotism."
Gaddess, M. "The Land We Love."
Shaw, A. "What Is Americanism? Address at the National American Woman Suffrage Association Convention of 1916."

PEACE

Addams, J. "Address, City Club, 1926."
________. "Address of Miss Jane Addams, Delivered at Carnegie Hall, Friday, July 9, 1915."
________. "Address WILPF, Washington 1924."
________. "The Attack on War."
________. "Count Tolstoy."
________. "Disarmament and Life."
________. "The Interest of Labor in International Peace."
________. "Maturing Concepts of Peace."
________. "New Ideals of Peace."
________. "The New Internationalism."
________. "New Methods of Procedure."
________. "The Newer Ideals of Peace."
________. "Patriotism and Pacifists in War Time."

________. "Presidential Address."

________. "Presidential Address, International Congress, The Hague."

________. "Presidential Address, International Congress of Women, Zurich."

________. "Presidential Address, Women of the Pacific."

________. "The Responsibilities and Duties of Women Toward the Peace Movement."

________. "The Revolt Against War."

________. "Speech at the Abraham Lincoln Center."

________. "Speech at the Civic Dedication of the Abraham Lincoln Center."

________. "Statement."

________. "Statement."

________. "Testimony."

________. "Testimony."

________. "Testimony."

________. "Testimony Before Committee on Military Affairs."

________. "Tolstoy's Theory of Life."

________. "Three Addresses, Thirteenth Universal Peace Congress."

________. "What Peace Means."

________. "What War Is Destroying."

________. "Woman's Peace Meeting--Jane Addams's Address."

________. "Woman's Special Training for Peacemaking."

________. "The World Court."

Ahlgren, M. "Challenge of Democracy. Build World Peace in Your Own Community."

Allen, F. "Adventures in Understanding."

Andrews, F. "The American School Peace League."

________. "Education and International Peace."

Bailey, H. "Woman's Place in the Peace Reform Movement."

Boeckel, F. "Civilization or War?"

Bond, E. "Friends as Promoters of Peace."

Catt, C. "Address Delivered at the Banquet, June 4, 1936."

________. "American Leadership."

Dean, V. "The Implications of the Peace."

Detzer, D. "Vested Interest in War."

Deyo, A. "Woman's War for Peace."

Eckstein, A. "A World Petition to the Third Hague Conference."

Hastings, C. "Peace in the Public Schools."

Henrotin, E. "Address on Woman's Work for Peace."

________. "The Home and the Economic Waste of War."

Hall, F. "Message of Julia Ward Howe to the National Arbitration and Peace Congress."

Huck, W. "Universal Peace Among the Nations of the World."

Ilma, V.	"What the Colleges Can Do for Peace."
Keller, H.	"Strike Against War. Speech at Carnegie Hall, New York City, January 5, 1916, Under the Auspices of the Women's Peace Party and the Labor Forum."
Lease, M.	"Synopsis of Peace."
Lockwood, B.	"Remarks at the Conference of Delegates."
________.	"What Are the Activities, the Object and Aims of the National Arbitration Society."
Lord, E.	"War from the Standpoint of Eugenics."
McDowell, M.	"Woman's Industrial and International Interests."
Mead, L.	"America's Danger and Opportunity."
________.	"History of the Peace Movement."
________.	"Remarks at the Conference of Delegates."
________.	"Report of Committee on Peace and Arbitration."
________.	"Some Common Fallacies."
Moore, E.	"Address to Peace Congress."
Nathan, M.	"Industry and Its Relation to Peace."
O'Reilly, L.	"The Cry of Humanity."
Phillips, L.	"Why Call It Peace?"
Pierson, M.	"Peace Work in the Schools."
________.	"The Young People's International Federation League."
Sewall, M.	"Address at the Conference for Peace Workers."
________.	"The International Council of Women."
________.	"Woman's Part in the Promotion of Internationalism."
Shaw, A.	"Women's Responsibility in the Peace Movement."
Shontz, E.	"A Call of Old Glory for Heroism."
Spencer, A.	"Remarks at the Conference of Delegates."
Thompson, D.	"The Power to Maintain Peace. Responsibilities Must Be Accepted."
Winston, E.	"Women's Role in Bringing Peace Through Understanding."
Woolley, M.	"The Relation of Educated Women to the Peace Movement."
________.	"Woman's Part and Power in the Peace Movement."

PENSIONS

Chisholm, S.	"Pension Legislation for Women."
Folsom, M.	"Pension Drive. Social and Economic Implications."

de PERON, MARIA EVA DUARTE

Navarro, M.	"The Case of Eva Peron."

PESTICIDES

Carson, R.	"Address to a Conference Sponsored by the National Council of Women of the United States, October 11, 1962."
________.	"Testimony Before a Senate Committee on Environmental Hazards, June 4, 1963."

PETROLEUM PRODUCTS--PRICES

Grasso, E.	"Oil Price Statement."

PHILOSOPHY

Adams, M.	"The Struggle and Reconciliation of the Ideal and the Practical in America."
Fisher, K.	"Solving the Conflict."
Hansen, N.	"Even Sea Shells Sing When You Listen: Let Us Not Waste Precious Time Asking Who We Are."
Hiett, H.	"Spiritual Contributions to the Strength of Man."
Horton, M.	"Predictions for the Unpredictable Future. Every Big Accomplishment Involves Many Small Ones."
Rich, E.	"The Art of Living."
St. Denis, R.	"Winging One's Own Way."
Skinner, C.	"Life Is Simple. Find the Courage to Maximize Your Lives."
Smith, I.	"Chairman's Introduction. Joy in Living."
Smith, M.	"The Square."
________.	"This I Believe."
Wright, F.	"Address, Containing a Review of the Times, As First Delivered in the Hall of Science, New-York on Sunday, May 9, 1830."
________.	"Address on the State of the Public Mind, and the Measures Which It Calls For. As Delivered in New-York and Philadelphia, in the Autumn of 1829."
________.	"Address I. --Delivered in the New Harmony Hall, on the Fourth of July, 1828."
________.	"Address II. --Delivered in the Walnut-Street Theatre, Philadelphia, on the Fourth of July, 1829."
________.	"Address III. --Delivered at the Opening of the Hall of Science, New-York, Sunday April 26, 1829."

________.	"An Address to Young Mechanics. As Delivered in the Hall of Science, June 13, 1830."
________.	"Course of Popular Lectures."
________.	"Free Enquiry, 1829."
________.	"Introductory Address to the Course, As Delivered for the Second Time in New-York."
________.	"Lecture I. --On the Nature of Knowledge."
________.	"Lectures II. --Of Free Enquiry, Considered As a Means of Obtaining Just Knowledge."
________.	"Lecture III. --Of the More Important Divisions and Essential Parts of Knowledge."
________.	"Lecture IV. --Religion."
________.	"Lecture VI. --Opinions."
________.	"Lecture VII. --On Existing Evils and Their Remedy, As Delivered in Philadelphia, On June 2nd, 1829."
________.	"Of Free Enquiry Considered as a Means for Obtaining Just Knowledge."
________.	"On Free Enquiry."
________.	"Parting Address, As Delivered in the Bowery Theatre, to the People of New-York, in June, 1830."
________.	"Reply to the Traducers of the French Reformers of the Year 1789."

PHYSICAL FITNESS FOR WOMEN

Gould, M.	"Harmonious Adjustment Through Exercise."
King, J.	"Physical Culture."
Leiter, F.	"Physical Education for Women."

PIANO--PRACTICING

Hayes, M.	"Piano Playing Without Piano Practicing."

PLAYGROUNDS

Addams, J.	"Address."
American, S.	"Play and Playgrounds."
Mackenzie, C.	"Playgrounds in Cities."
Meade, M.	"Playgrounds."

POETRY

Sibley, A.	"Paradox and Poetic Truth: The Beauty of Life."

POLICE

Higgins, L.	"Law Enforcement Responsibility. What Can Police Do?"
Schpritzer, F.	"Public Testimony."

POLICEWOMEN

Barney, S.	"Police Matrons."
Beveridge, E.	"Establishing Policewomen in Maryland in 1912."
Blake, L.	"Women as Police Matrons."
Brown, C.	"The Policewoman; Discussion."
Devall, S.	"The Results of the Employment of a Police Matron in the City of Portland, Maine."
Miner, M.	"The Policewoman and the Girl Problem."
Van Winkel, M.	"The Policewoman."
________.	"Standardization of the Aims and Methods of the Work of Policewomen."
Wells, A.	"Policewomen."
________.	"The Policewomen Movement, Present Status and Future Needs."

POLITICAL SCIENCE

Rooney, M.	"Kinds of Government and the Growth of Isms. Property and Force vs. Personality and Reason."
Smith, M.	"Second Declaration of Conscience."

POLITICS, PRACTICAL

Stevenson, M.	"We, the Public. Our Responsibility in Politics."
Chisholm, S.	"Vote for the Individual, Not the Political Party. Whatever Is Given to Us Is Almost Always a Trap."

POSTAGE-STAMPS

Brooks, M.	"Remarks at Ceremonies Issuing the 1973 Philatelic-Numismatic Commemorative at Faneuil Hall, Boston, Massachusetts, 11:30 A.M., July 4, 1973."

POTTERY

McLaughlin, M.	"Pottery in the Household."

POVERTY

Addams, J.	"Struggle for Life Above the Poverty Line."
Atkins, R.	"Address."
Bass, R.	"Poverty as a Cause of Mortality."
Blatt, G.	"Speech."
Burke, Y.	"Is the Administration Plan to Terminate the Federal Anti-Poverty Agency Now A Sound National Policy?"
Carpenter, E.	"Address."
Chisholm, S.	"Debate on Office of Economic Opportunity."
Furness, B.	"Statement."
Garcia, C.	"Statement."
George, Z.	"Speech."
Gilman, C.	"Poverty and Woman."
Griffiths, M.	"Statement."
Height, D.	"Address."
________.	"Summing Up."
Hultin, I.	"Treatment of the Destitute Classes in the United States."
Keyseling, M.	"Address."
Lerrigo, E.	"Address."
Lincoln, A.	"Classification of Paupers. Is It Practicable in the U. S. to Classify Almshouse Inmates According to Character & Conduct?"
Lowell, J.	"One Means of Preventing Pauperism."
________.	"Poverty and Its Relief: Methods Possible in the City of New York."
Mink, P.	"Statement."
Orshansky, M.	"Speech."
Peterson, E.	"The War on Poverty--What is the Federal Government Doing?"
Schorr, L.	"Address."
Sheenan, P.	"Remarks."
Smith, M.	"Public Testimony."
________.	"Public Testimony."
Smith, Z.	"Introduction to Discussion on Needy Families in Their Homes."
Walters, B.	"Address."
Washington, B.	"Address."
________.	"Statement."
Willen, P.	"Address."
Wirtz, J.	"Address."

POWER RESOURCES

Ray, D.	"Biologist Looks at the Energy Crisis; Address June 17, 1974."

PRENATAL CARE

Putnam, E. — "Pre-natal Care."

PRESIDENTS--U.S. ELECTION

Benson, L. — "Should the President Be Chosen by Direct Popular Vote?"

Cowles, F. — "Does the Health of Our Democracy Require A Change of Party in November." (panel)

Douglas, H. — "The Campaign Issue."

Heckler, M. — "Should the "District" Method of Electing the President Be Adopted?"

Howard, K. — "What's New in the '52 Campaign?"

Luce, C. — "Waging the Peace."

Schiff, D. — "Does the Health of Our Democracy Require a Change of Party in November: Panel Discussion."

Smith, M. — "Final Statement at End of Television Debate with Eleanor Roosevelt, November 4, 1956."

________. — "Presidential Candidacy Announcement."

Vredenburgh, D. — "What's New in the '52 Campaign?"

Woodhull, V. — "Address to the Organization Meeting of the People's Party, 1872."

PRICE REGULATION

Knauer, V. — "Price Controls and Revenues: Federal Regulations."

PRISONERS

Fairbanks, C. — "Address on Convicts."

Fernald, M. — "Practical Applications of Psychology to the Problems of a Clearing House."

Keeley, S. — "Address."

Kinsella, N. — "The Arrested Offender."

Spaulding, E. — "The Short-Term Offender."

PROBATION

Friday, L. — "Work of the Probation Officer in Court."

Ramsey, A. — "Work of the Probation Officer Preliminary to the Trial."

Rogers, H. — "The Probation System of the Juvenile Court of Indianapolis."

PROFESSIONAL EDUCATION OF WOMEN

Blank, D.	"Statement."
King, E.	"The Admission of Women to the Medical School of the Johns Hopkins University."
Lavine, T.	"The Motive to Achieve Limited Success: The New Woman Law School Applicant."
Rees, M.	"The Graduate Education of Women."

PROGRAM BUDGETING

Gillett, L.	"Basis for Estimating Budgets."

PROGRESS

O'Connor, L.	"Progress of Humanity. What You Can Contribute to Man's Progress."

PROHIBITION

Tilton, E.	"The Whence and Whither of Prohibition."
Willebrandt, M.	"Prohibition--The Problem of Enforcement from the Federal Standpoint."

PROMISCUITY

Bergman, M.	"A Psychoanalytic Approach to the Genesis of Promiscuity."

PROPAGANDA

Bonny, D.	"Women's Heritage. Beware of Propaganda."
Knaust, E.	"Nazi Propaganda in the United States."
Poole, G.	"Propaganda and Organized Women."
Sporborg, C.	"Public Forums and Public Opinion."
Thompson, D.	"Government by Propaganda."
________.	"Nazi Foreign Missions. German Propaganda in the United States and the World."
________.	"Propaganda in the Modern World."
________.	"Stopping Propaganda. The Democracies Have the Jitters."

PROSTITUTION

Blackwell, A.	"Immorality of the Regulation System."
Blackwell, E.	"The Responsibility of Women in Regard to Questions Concerning Public Morality."

Breckinridge, D.	"A New Hope."
Brownmiller, S.	"Speaking Out on Prostitution, A Victimless Crime."
D'Arcambal, A.	"How Can We Aid?"
Edholm, M.	"The Traffic in Girls and Florence Crittenton Missions."
Falconer, M.	"Report of the Committee (on Social Hygiene)."
Glenn, M.	"Some Social Causes of Prostitution."
Goldman, E.	"The Traffic in Women."
Grannis, E.	"The Christian League for the Promotion of Social Purity."
Lake, I.	"Graded Homes."
________.	"The Tempted Woman."
Miner, M.	"The Girls' Protective League."
________.	"Protective Work for Girls in War Time."
________.	"Report of the Committee (on Social Hygiene)."
Powell, A.	"The International Federation for the Abolition of State Regulation of Vice."
Satterthwaite, L.	"The Great Need of the Moral Crusade."
Spaulding, E.	"Mental and Physical Factors in Prostitution."
Webb, D.	"Organized Prostitution. How to Deal with It."
Yarros, R.	"The Prostitute as a Health and Social Problem."

PSYCHIATRIC HOSPITALS

Estes, B.	"The Mental Hospital as a Teaching Center."
Spink, M.	"Psychopathic Hospitals."

PSYCHIATRIC SOCIAL WORK

Allen, E.	"Discussion (of the Evolution of Psychiatric Social Work)--From the Viewpoint of the Psychiatric Social Worker."
Jarrett, M.	"The Psychiatric Thread Running Through All Social Case Work."
Lloyd, R.	"Psychiatric Social Work in Relation to a State Mental Hygiene Program."
Lyons, S.	"The Training of Social Service Workers in Psychiatric Field Work."
MacDonald, V.	"Function of the Social Worker in Relation to the Community."
Mallory, C.	"Psychiatry, Social Service, and Society."
Marcus, G.	"The Responsibility of the Psychiatric Social Worker: A Further Consideration of Psychiatric Social Work."

Moore, K.	"The Evolution of Psychiatric Social Work (Shown by Use of a Case Presentation)."
Neumann, F.	"The Use of Psychiatric Consultation by a Case Work Agency."
Spaulding, E.	"The Training School of Psychiatric Social Work at Smith College."
Taft, J.	"Qualifications of the Psychiatric Social Worker."
Taussig, F.	"The Place of Psychiatric Social Work In a Family Case Work Organization."
Young, I.	"The Responsibility of the Psychiatric Social Worker in Civilian Life."

PSYCHOLOGY

Mead, M.	"Crisis of Self: America's Secret War; Remarks at the 1973 Congress for Recreation and Parks."
________.	"Public Policy and Behavioral Science; Excerpt from Testimony Before the U. S. Senate Foreign Relations Committee, June 20, 1969."
Parr, M.	"The Personalising Process: Union Differentiates."
Rand, A.	"Faith and Force, the Destroyers of the Modern World. The Age of Guilt."

PUBLIC HEALTH NURSING

Aikers, C.	"The Educational Opportunity of the Visiting Nurse in the Prevention of Disease."
Beard, M.	"Family Health Teaching, or the Public Health Nurse."
Clement, F.	"The District Nurse in Rural Work."
Fox, E.	"The Public Health Nursing Program of the American Red Cross."
Fulmer, H.	"The Work of the Visiting or District Nurse."
Haasis, B.	"War Time Developments in Public Health Nursing."
Janime, M.	"The District Nurse in Co-operative Work."
Lent, M.	"Public Health Nursing and the War."
________.	"Sanitary Conditions About Military Camps, and Parts Played by the Public Health Nursing."
Marriner, J.	"The Co-ordination of Public and Private Agencies in a State Program of Public Health Nursing."
Quaife, F.	"District Nursing."
Roberts, A.	"National Organization for Public Health Nursing."
Stewart, A.	"Public Health Nursing and Tuberculosis."

Wald, L. "Nurses in Settlement Work."

PUBLIC OPINION

Meloney, M. "The New World Power--Mass Opinion."

Moskowitz, B. "How Far Have Social Welfare Considerations Entered into State, National, and Local Elections."

PUBLIC UTILITIES

Bursch, A. "Electric Power and the Public Welfare. Address to 1926 National Convention of the League of Women Voters."

PUBLIC WELFARE

Abbott, E. "Public Assistance--Wither Bound? (Presidential Address)."

________. "Public Welfare and Politics."

________. "Relief, the No Man's Land, and How to Reclaim It."

________. "Work or Maintenance?"

Abbott, G. "The County Versus the Community as an Administrative Unit."

________. "How Secure Administrative Skill with Professional Competence for State and Local Public Welfare Service?"

________. "The Need of Federal Aid for Relief in the Winter 1932-33. Testimony Before a United States Senate Committee."

________. "The Public Welfare Administrator and Civil Service in State and Local Services."

Atkinson, M. "The Rural Community Program of Relief."

Bogue, M. "Pennsylvania. The Greater Economy of Adequate Grants."

Breckinridge, S. "What We Have Learned About Emergency Training for Public Relief Administration."

Brown, J. "Present Relief Situation in the United States."

________. "What We Have Learned About Emergency Training for Public Relief Administration."

Carr, C. "Public Relief--Its Relation to Higher Labor Standards and Social Security."

Choate, R. "Two Types of Public Welfare Administration."

Clevenger, L. "How Can We Interpret More Effectively to the Public the Role Played in the Community's Welfare Program by Social Settlement, Recreations Agencies, and National Program Agencies?"

Colby, M. "What Is Happening in County Organization?"

Colcord, J. "The Impact of the War Upon Community Welfare Organization."

________. "Relief, Style 1936."

________. "Report of Committee on Current Relief Program."

________. "Social Work and the First Federal Relief Programs."

Cottrell, L. "The Iowa Plan of Cooperation in County Welfare Work."

Curry, H. "Co-operation of Obstruction in Determining Fields of Activity."

________. "Development of County or Town Boards."

________. "The Extra-Institutional Services of County Institutions."

Dexter, E. "Has Case Work a Place in the Administration of Public Relief?"

Foreman, C. "Controversy Over the Carter Administration Proposals for Welfare Reform."

Grasso, E. "Welfare Reform Needed."

Hayden, H. "Case Work Possibilities in a Public Assistance Program."

Hoey, J. "The Federal Government and Desirable Standards of State and Local Government."

________. "Next Steps in Public Assistance."

Johnson, K. "The Relation of a Board of Public Welfare to the Public."

________. "The Work of a Commission of Public Welfare."

Kahn, D. "Conserving Human Values in Public Welfare Programs."

________. "Democratic Principles in Public Assistance."

________. "The Use of Cash, Orders for Goods, or Relief in Kind, in a Mass Program."

Kuhn, M. "Controversy Over the Carter Administration Proposals for Welfare Reform."

LaDu, B. "Co-ordination of State and Local Units for Welfare Administration."

Liveright, A. "The Growing Importance of State Welfare Work--in Financial Support for Local Welfare Services."

Lowell, J. "The Economic and Moral Effects of Public Outdoor Relief."

McClenahan, B. "County Organization of Welfare Agencies."

McCormick, R. "Welfare Work."

Marcus, G. "Changes in the Theory of Relief Giving."

Merrill, M. "Lessons Learned in Personnel Selection and Management in Emergency Relief Administration."

Perlman, H. "Casework Services in Public Welfare."

Potter, E. "Coordination and Development of Welfare Service in the County."

________. "Recent Developments in the Organization and Operation of Public Welfare Departments: The Bureau System."

Sanders, B.	"Multiple Jeopardies of the Welfare Mother."
Sheffield, A.	"Public Relief Officials."
Stevenson, M.	"The Expanding Role of Government--Discussion."
________.	"The States and a Federal Department of Welfare."
Taylor, R.	"Problems Created by Assistance Categories."
Tousley, C.	"Cooperative Interpretation."
Tynes, H.	"Administrative Practices for Conserving Human Values in the Public Assistance Program."
Vaile, G.	"Principles and Methods of Outdoor Relief."
________.	"Some Organization Problems of Public Welfare Departments."
Wallerstein, H.	"Community Relationships Involved in 100 Per Cent Registration in Social Service Exchange: From the Standpoint of Family Welfare Organizations."

PUBLICITY

Dodson, M.	"Publicity."
Ellis, M.	"How Can Social Information Be Obtained and Made Available for Publicity Purposes?"
Read, L.	"Report--Mrs. Leslie Stringfellow Read, Chairman Publicity."
Toombs, E.	"Publicity."
Tousley, C.	"Focused Publicity."
Wing, V.	"Some Psychological Experiments in Health Publicity."

PUBLISHERS AND PUBLISHING

Lippincott, S.	"A Statement of Facts."

PUERTO RICO

Bolton, F.	"Nature of U.S. Puerto Rican Relations." Texts of Statements Made in Committee IV (Trusteeship)

PULLMAN, GEORGE MORTIMER

Addams, J.	"A Modern Lear."

RACE PROBLEMS

Buck, P.	"An Address to Graduates."
________.	"Asiatic Problem. The Colored People Are Still Waiting, Still Watchful."
Chisholm, S.	"Progress Through Understanding."
Luce, C.	"Racial Cooperation."
Mead, M.	"Symposium on Knowledge and Problems of Race: Introductory Remarks; Excerpts from Science and the Concept of Race."
Smith, L.	"The Race Question: A Problem Above Politics."
Woolley, C.	"Race Reconciliation."

RADICALISM

Davis, A.	"Statement to the Court."

RAILROADS

Bailey, K.	"Remarks Before the 1977 National Conference on Railroad-Highway Crossing Safety, Salt Lake City, Utah, August 23, 1977."
________.	"Remarks Before the Association of American Railroads Annual Safety Section Meeting, Duluth, Minn., June 22, 1977."
Grasso, E.	"Rail Passenger Service."
Dworkin, A.	"The Rape Atrocity and the Boy Next Door."

READING

Plummer, M.	"The Seven Joys of Reading."
Van Doren, I.	"Books for Leisure Time."
________.	"Some of the New Fall Books."
________.	"Taste and Custom as Reflected in Our Literature."

RECONSTRUCTION (1914-1939)

Addams, J.	"Testimony."

RECONSTRUCTION (1939-1951)

Alexander, R.	"Post-War America That America Does Not Want. A Fair Trade Act Needed for Ideas."
________.	"Which Way America? What Businessmen Can Do About It."

Allen, F.	"Bridge to the Future. Have We Here and Now the Intelligence and Devotion to Cross Over?"
Burns, E.	"The Security Report of the National Resources Planning Board."
Dean, V.	"After Victory--What?"
Dickinson, L.	"Leadership Through Young Minds."
Luce, C.	"Greater and Freer America. G. I. Joe's Future."
________.	"Waging the Peace. Blueprints of Past Lacked Courage and Loyalty."
Mead, M.	"What Kind of World Do We Want? Contributions by Social Science and by Women."
Rosenberg, A.	"What the Community Can Do."

RECREATION

Addams, J.	"Some Reflections of the Failure of the Modern City to Provide Recreation for Young Girls."
Binford, J.	"Community Responsibility for Recreation Facilities."
Bowen, L.	"The Need of Recreation."
Boyd, N.	"Chairman's Introduction--Release from Labor--The Problem."
Coyle, G.	"Social Group Work in Recreation."
Enderis, D.	"The Milwaukee Recreation System."
Ingram, F.	"The Public Dance Hall."
Ingram, H.	"The Value of the Fresh Air Movement."
Monahan, F.	"Community Responsibility for Recreation Facilities--Discussion."
Moskowitz, B.	"Recreation in Rural Communities."
Simkhovitch, M.	"The Place of Recreation in the Settlement Program."

RED CROSS

Barton, C.	"Address."
________.	"Address by Clara Barton."
________.	"The Red Cross."
________.	"What Is the Significance of the Red Cross in Its Relation to Philanthropy?"
________.	"Work of the Red Cross."
Dinwiddie, E.	"Illustrations from the Annals of the Gulf Division--American Red Cross."

REFORMATORIES

Davis, K.	"Report of the Committee (on Law Breakers): The Reformatory Method."

Falconer, M.	"Work of the Section on Reformatories and Houses of Detention."
Jaffray, J.	"Committee on Institutional Relations."
Kelley, F.	"Prison Labor."
Kinsella, N.	"County Jails."
Sickels, L.	"Woman's Influence in Juvenile Reformatories."
Smith, C.	"The Elimination of the Reformatory."
Trumbull, M.	"The Honor System of Prison Labor."
Tutwiler, J.	"Poorhouses and Jails of the Southwest."

REFORMATORIES FOR WOMEN

Boyd, M.	"Industrial Training School for Girls."
Falconer, M.	"Reformatory Treatment of Women."
Montgomery, S.	"Discipline and Training of Girls in Industrial Schools."
Peterson, A.	"The Administrative Problems of a Woman's Reformatory."
Rippir, J.	"Municipal Detention for Women."
Wardner, L.	"The Care of Girls in Reformatories."
________.	"Reform Schools for Girls."

REFUGEES

Biehle, M.	"The International Refugee Organization and Social Welfare."
Derian, P.	"Indochinese Refugees."
Goldman, E.	"The Refugee Alien."
Hoey, J.	"Mass Relocation of Aliens."
Houghton, D.	"Report from Europe."
Hurlbutt, M.	"The United Nations Relief and Rehabilitation Administration's Task for Displaced Persons."
Kraus, H.	"The Plight of Refugees in a Preoccupied World."
Lenroot, K.	"The United States Program for the Care of Refugee Children."

REGISTERS OF BIRTHS, ETC.

Huffman, H.	"The Importance of Birth Records."

RELIGION

Blackwell, A.	"What Religious Truths Can Be Established by Science and Philosophy."
Cratty, M.	"Giving and Receiving."
________.	"Unity with the Creation."

Harbert, E.	"God Is Love."
Palmer, A.	"Prophets, Old and New."
Stuart, E.	"The Power of Thought."

RELIGIOUS EDUCATION

Adams, M.	"The Highest Education."
Cabot, E.	"The Religious Life of the Child."
Cooper, S.	"Discussion of Woman as a Religious Teacher."
Gestefeld, U.	"Woman as a Religious Teacher."
Grannis, E.	"Discussion of Woman as a Religious Teacher."
Harley, F.	"Discussion of Woman as a Religious Teacher."
Maher, M.	"The Catholic Woman as an Educator."
Rollins, M.	"The Place of Religion in a Liberal Arts Curriculum. The Academic Study of Religion."
Scudder, A.	"Discussion of Woman as a Religious Teacher."
White, L.	"Discussion of Woman as a Religious Teacher."
Young, Z.	"Discussion of Woman as a Religious Teacher."

RESEARCH, INDUSTRIAL

Blodgett, K.	"Miracles in Glass."

REWARDS (PRIZES, ETC.)

Benedict, R.	"Achievement Award to Ruth Fulton Benedict. Dr. Benedict's Speech of Acceptance."
Buck, P.	"Acceptance Speech for the Howells Medal."
Carson, R.	"Acceptance Speech for the Schweitzer Medal of the Animal Welfare Institute, January 7, 1963."
________.	"National Book Award Acceptance Speech."
________.	"Rachel Carson Receives Audubon Medal; With Acceptance Address."

RICHMOND, MARY E.

Perkins, F.	"Social Seer."

ROOSEVELT, ANNA ELEANOR

Perkins, F.	"Tribute to Eleanor Roosevelt at Breakfast Rally for Women Delegates to the 1936 Democratic Convention."

ROOSEVELT, THEODORE

Addams, J.	"Speech Seconding Theodore Roosevelt's Nomination for President at the Progressive Convention."

RUSSIA

Antin, M.	"Russia."
Dickinson, L.	"What I Saw in the U. S. S. R."
Hanna, R.	"Economic Security Under Communism."
Luce, C.	"Crisis in Soviet-Chinese Relations: The Two Red Giants."
Scott, M.	"Russian-American Life."

SAMOA

Ormsbee, F.	"Samoa--Its People and Their Customs."

SAVING AND THRIFT

Fairbank, M.	"Habits of Thrift."
Oberholtzer, S.	"The Popular Inculcation of Economy."
________.	"School Savings-Banks."
Scribner, A.	"The Savings Society."
Ware, C.	"Should It Be Safe to Save?"

SCHOLARSHIPS

Benneson, C.	"College Fellowships for Women."

SCHOOL ATTENDANCE

O'Reilly, M.	"The Problem of Truancy."

SCHOOL CHILDREN--TRANSPORTATION

Green, E.	"School Busing: Are We Hurting the People We Want to Help?"
Ruffra, J.	"Should Congress Curtail the Use of "Busing" for School Desegregation?"

SCHOOLS--PRAYERS

Grasso, E.	"House Joint Resolution 191 on School Prayers."

SCIENCE

Mead, M.	"Towards a Human Science; Adaptation of Address."
Mink, P.	"Science and Its Interrelationship with Foreign Policy: Speech."

SCIENCE AS A PROFESSION

Mead, M.	"Wanted: Young Scientists; Summary of Address."

SECURITY, INTERNATIONAL

Benson, L.	"Security Assistance: Conventional Arms Transfer Policy."

SELF-RESPECT

Bushnell, L.	"Integrity: What and How."

SERVANTS

Addams, J.	"Domestic Service and the Family Claim."
Gates, S.	"General Conditions of Domestic Service."
Koontz, E.	"Household Employment, Quiet Revolution."

SEX CRIMES

Topping, R.	"A Study of the Morals Court in Three Large Cities: Social Aspects."

SEX DISCRIMINATION AGAINST WOMEN

Griffiths, M.	"Statement During Debate on Bill to Extend Civil Rights Act of 1964 to Prohibit Discrimination on the Basis of Sex."
Lipman-Blumen, J.	"Toward a Homosocial Theory of Sex Roles: An Explanation of the Sex Segregation of Social Institutions."
Mannes, M.	"The Problems of Creative Women."

SEX DISCRIMINATION AGAINST WOMEN--LAWS AND LEGISLATION--U. S.

Abzug, B.	"The Equal Rights Amendment."
________.	"Statement."
Allan, V.	"Statement."
________.	"Statement."
Anderson, M.	"Statement."
Armstrong, F.	"Statement."
Avery, N.	"Statement."
________.	"Statement."
Barney, N.	"Statement."
Basto, E.	"Statement."
Berrien, L.	"Statement."
________.	"Statement."
Bingman, O.	"Statement."
Bird, C.	"Statement."
Bittermann, H.	"Statement."
Borchardt, S.	"Statement."
________.	"Statement."
________.	"Statement."
________.	"Statement."
Bostanian, A.	"Statement."
Boyer, E.	"Statement."
Bresette, L.	"Statement."
________.	"Statement."
Brown, H.	"Statement."
________.	"What Is the Constitution of the United States Worth to American Women?"
Brunswick, R.	"Statement."
Butler, S.	"Statement."
Carpenter, C.	"Statement."
Casey, J.	"Statement."
Chisholm, S.	"Equal Rights Amendment."
________.	"Equal Rights Amendment."
________.	"Equal Rights for Women."
________.	"The 51% Minority."
________.	"Representative Shirley Chisholm Speaks in Support of the Equal Rights Amendment."
________.	"Should Congress Approve the "Equal Rights Amendment"?"
________.	"Statement."
________.	"Statement."
Cook, E.	"Statement."
Crawford, M.	"Statement."
Crocker, G.	"Statement."
Cummings, S.	"Statement."
Debman, M.	"Statement."
Dent, M.	"Statement."
Dock, L.	"Statement."
Dolan, E.	"Statement."
Downey, M.	"Statement."
Dwyer, F.	"Statement."

Eastman, E.	"Statement."
Edwards, A.	"Statement."
Ellickson, K.	"Statement."
Farians, E.	"Statement."
________.	"Statement."
________.	"Statement."
Fasteau, B.	"Statement."
Faust, J.	"Statement."
Ferguson, A.	"Statement."
Fields, D.	"Statement."
Finegan, B.	"Statement."
Fisse, E.	"Statement."
Forbes, C.	"Statement."
Franklin, B.	"Statement."
Freedom, V.	"Statement."
Freedman, B.	"Statement."
Friedan, B.	"Statement."
Frohman, P.	"Statement."
Gage, O.	"Statement."
Grace, L.	"Statement."
Granger, D.	"Statement."
Grasso, E.	"Equal Rights Amendment."
Greathouse, R.	"Statement."
________.	"Statement."
________.	"Statement."
Green, E.	"Representative Edith Green Speaks in Support of the Equal Rights Amendment."
Griffiths, M.	"Equal Rights Amendment."
________.	"Excerpt from Testimony Before the Subcommittee on Constitutional Amendments, May 5, 1970."
________.	"Should Congress Approve the "Equal Rights Amendment"?"
________.	"Statement."
________.	"Statement."
________.	"Statement."
Gutwillig, J.	"Statement."
Hadley, L.	"Statement."
Hales, E.	"Statement."
Hall, S.	"Statement."
Hankin, C.	"Statement."
Harmon, M.	"Statement."
Harrington, K.	"Statement."
Heckler, M.	"Statement."
Heide, W.	"Equal Rights Amendment."
________.	"Statement."
________.	"Statement."
Hellinger, J.	"Statement."
Hernandez, A.	"Statement."
________.	"Statement."
Hilgert, B.	"Statement."
Hilles, F.	"Statement."
Hodnett, I.	"Statement."
Hogan, A.	"Statement."

Howard, C. "Statement."
Katzenstein, C. "Statement."
Kearon, P. "Public Testimony."
Kefauver, C. "Statement."
Kelley, F. "Statement."
Kennedy, M. "Statement."
Kenyon, D. "Statement."
Keyserling, M. "Should Congress Approve the "Equal Rights Amendment"?"
________. "Statement."
________. "Statement."
Kingsbury, S. "Statement."
Kitchelt, F. "Is the Equal-Rights Amendment Equitable to Women."
Lauder, A. "Statement."
Laws, J. "Statement."
Leonard, M. "Should Congress Approve the "Equal Rights Amendment"?"
________. "Statement."
Liggett, C. "Statement."
Lindsey, M. "Statement."
Low, R. "Statement."
Luers, M. "Statement."
McDoal, M. "Statement."
McGerr, H. "Statement."
McNally, G. "Statement."
Madar, O. "Statement."
________. "Statement."
Magee, E. "Statement."
Maloney, M. "Statement."
Markajani, M. "Statement."
Matthews, B. "Statement."
________. "Statement."
________. "Statement."
________. "Statement."
________. "Statement."
________. "Statement."
________. "Statement Before the Senate Hearing on the Equal-Rights Amendment, 1931."
________. "Statement."
Miller, E. "The Equal Rights Amendment."
________. "Statement."
________. "Statement."
________. "Statement."
________. "Statement."
________. "Statement."
________. "Statement."
________. "Statement Against the Equal-Rights Amendment at the Senate Committee Hearings, 1931."
________. "Statement."
Miller, R. "Statement."
________. "Statement."

Moncure, D. "Statement."

Morgan, L. "Statement."

Moynahan, R. "Statement."

Murphy, A. "Statement."

Murray, M. "Statement."

________. "Statement."

________. "Statement."

Murray, P. "Equal Rights Amendment."

Neill, E. "Statement."

Nelson, L. "Public Testimony."

Newman, P. "Statement."

Oatman, M. "Statement."

O'Donnell, G. "Statement."

Ogle, D. "Statement."

Osland, G. "Statement."

Park, M. "Statement."

Peipho, I. "Statement."

Pell, S. "Statement."

Perkins, F. "Comments to Judiciary Committee of House of Representatives on Equal Rights Amendment, 1945."

Philbrook, M. "Statement."

Piepho, I. "Statement."

Pinchot, C. "Statement."

Pollitzer, A. "Statement."

________. "Statement."

________. "Statement."

________. "Statement."

________. "Statement."

________. "Statement Before the Senate Committee on the Equal-Rights Amendment, 1931."

Ramey, M. "Statement."

Rawalt, M. "Statement."

________. "Statement."

________. "Statement."

Regan, A. "Statement."

________. "Statement."

________. "Statement."

Relich, M. "Statement."

Robey, G. "Statement."

Rose, D. "Statement."

St. George, K. "The Equal Rights Amendment."

________. "Statement."

________. "Statement."

St. John, J. "Reflections and Perspectives on the Women's Movement in 1976: The Equal Rights Amendment."

Samuels, L. "Statement."

Sandler, B. "Statement."

________. "Statement."

Schneiderman, R. "Statement."

________. "Statement."

________.	"Statement Against the Equal-Rights Amendment at the Senate Committee Hearings, 1931."
Schurr, C.	"Statement."
Scott, A.	"Statement."
Sellers, G.	"Statement."
________.	"Statement."
________.	"Statement Before the Senate Judiciary Committee Hearings on the Equal-Rights Amendment, May 6, 1970."
Servis, M.	"Statement."
Sherwin, E.	"Statement."
Shriver, L.	"Statement."
________.	"Statement."
Smith, J.	"Statement."
________.	"Statement."
Sollars, S.	"Statement."
Spinks, D.	"Statement."
Springer, M.	"Statement."
Steinem, G.	"Statement."
Stevens, D.	"Statement."
Stitt, L.	"Statement."
Stone, K.	"Statement."
Stone, M.	"Statement."
Straus, D.	"Statement."
Strauss, A.	"Statement."
Swing, B.	"Statement."
Taunton, R.	"Statement."
Terrell, M.	"Statement."
________.	"Statement."
Thompson, M.	"The Question of the Ratification of the Equal Rights Amendment."
Traxler, M.	"Statement."
Van Dyke, M.	"Statement."
Weaver, A.	"Statement."
________.	"Statement."
Weber, E.	"Statement."
Weed, H.	"Statement."
Wellborn, M.	"Statement."
Wells, A.	"Statement."
Wells, R.	"Statement."
Werner, E.	"Statement."
West, H.	"Statement."
White, E.	"Statement."
Wiley, A.	"Statement."
________.	"Statement."
Williams, M.	"Statement."
________.	"Statement."
Winn, A.	"Statement."
Winslow, M.	"Statement."
________.	"Statement."
________.	"Statement."

Withrow, K.	"Statement."
Witter, J.	"Should Congress Approve the "Equal Rights Amendment"?"
________.	"Statement."
________.	"Statement."
Wold, E.	"Statement."
Wolfe, H.	"The Backlash Phenomenon: The Equal Rights Amendment."
Wolfgang, M.	"Should Congress Approve the "Equal Rights Amendment"?"
________.	"Statement."
________.	"Statement."
________.	"Statement."
________.	"Statement."
Wright, A.	"Statement."
Wright, L.	"Statement."
Wubnig, S.	"Statement."
Younger, M.	"Statement."
________.	"Statement."
________.	"Statement."

SEX DISCRIMINATION IN EDUCATION

Polowy, C.	"Sex Discrimination: The Legal Obligations of Educational Institutions."

SEX DISCRIMINATION IN INSURANCE

Bernstein, B.	"Testimony on Sex Discrimination in Unemployment Insurance, Veterans Programs, and Public Assistance."
Tillmon, J.	"Testimony on Sex Discrimination in Unemployment Insurance, Veterans Programs, and Public Assistance."

SEX INSTRUCTION

Richards, F.	"Methods of Instruction in Sex Education."
Saxon, E.	"The Truth Shall Make You Free."
Wood-Allen, M.	"Moral Education of the Young."

SEX ROLE

Albert, E.	"The Roles of Women: A Question of Values."
Faust, J.	"Public Testimony."
Friedan, B.	"The Crisis in Women's Identity."
Gordon, L.	"Woman's Sphere from a Woman's Standpoint."

SEXUAL ETHICS

Ackerman, J.	"Plan of Work Along Social Purity Lines."
Barrett, K.	"The Nation's Peril--A Double Standard of Morals."
Blackwell, A.	"Discussion of the Moral Initiative as Related to Women."
________.	"Response to Address of Welcome."
Castendyck, E.	"Helping to Prevent Sex Delinquency."
Clothier, H.	"The Pure in Heart."
Davis, K.	"Equal Moral Standards."
Goldman, E.	"Victims of Morality."
Grannis, E.	"The National Christian League for the Promotion of Social Purity."
Harbert, E.	"Address on Social Purity."
Harper, F.	"Social Purity: Its Relation to the Dependent Classes."
Howe, J.	"Moral Equality Between the Sexes."
________.	"The Moral Initiative as Related to Woman."
Kellogg, E.	"Purity and Parental Responsibility."
Livermore, M.	"Address."
Locke, J.	"Concludes Discussion of the Moral Initiative as Related to Woman."
Lozier, J.	"Educational Training in Its Bearing Upon the Promotion of Social Purity."
Owings, C.	"The Trail of Social Hygiene in Social Work: Prevention Versus Salvage."
Powell, A.	"The American Purity Alliance and Its Work."
Robinson, A.	"Address of Welcome."
Roundtree, M.	"Crusade for Morality: Women Power."
Schofield, M.	"Slavery's Legacy of Impurity."
Shattuck, H.	"Address, Social Purity."
Travilla, M.	"Our Divine Possibilities."
Van Waters, M.	"The New Morality and the Social Worker."
Willard, F.	"Address."
________.	"Address."
Winslow, C.	"The Starting Point."

SHAKESPEARE, WILLIAM

Mott, E.	"Katharina in the Taming of the Shrew."

SICKLE CELL ANEMIA

Grasso, E.	"Priority Status Needed for Sickle Cell Anemia."

SIN, ORIGINAL

Foster, A.	"Remarks During Debate at 4th National Convention, Cleveland, Ohio, in October 1853."

Rose, E. "Remarks During Debate at the 4th National Convention, October 1853 in Cleveland, Ohio."

SINGING

Bjorn, T. "Vocal Art."
Brown, M. "Extracts from Vocal Art."

SINGLE WOMEN

Moon, M. "The Unattached Woman."

SINO-JAPANESE CONFLICT, 1937-1945

Roosevelt, E. "Sino-Japanese Dossier: Eye-witness."
Thompson, D. "Sino-Japanese Dossier: Background and Personalities."

SMALLPOX

Humphrey, E. "The Smallpox Problem in the West."

SMITH, SARAH ROZET

Addams, J. "Sarah Rozet Smith. At the Dedication of the Hull-House Organ."

SOCIAL ACTION

Hayden, A. "Organizing the Community for Social Action."
Wing, V. "Arousing Voters to Action: A Story of a City Campaign."

SOCIAL CASE WORK

Aronovici, C. "Wider Use of Case Records."
Austin, L. "Evolution of Our Case-Work Concepts."
________. "Trends in Differential Treatment in Casework."
Baker, E. "How Social Case Work Meets Individual Problems of Public Relief Clients from the Point of View of Medical Social Case Work."
Bedford, C. "Methods of Assembling Material."
Blackman, E. "Some Tests for the Evaluation of Case Work Methods."

Boie, M.	"The Case Worker's Need for Orientation to the Culture of the Client."
Dawley, A.	"Professional Skills Requisite to a Good Intake Service."
Day, F.	"Social Case Work and Social Adjustment."
Dietzel, L.	"Activity in the Case-Work Relationship."
Dresden, M.	"The Case Worker as an Interpreter of Case Work."
Everett, E.	"Case Work in School Counseling."
Gane, E.	"Case Work in Protective Agencies."
Glenn, M.	"Case Work Disciplines and Ideals."
Goodwillie, M.	"Case Work as a Factor."
Jennrich, L.	"Some Experiments in Case Work in Motherless Families."
Kraus, H.	"Contribution of Case Work to the Administration of Social Insurance--A Critical Analysis of European Experience."
Libbey, B.	"Case Work in a Family Agency."
________.	"The Philadelphia Experiment."
Lowry, F.	"A Philosophy of Supervision in Social Case Work."
Marcus, G.	"Application of Psychology to Case Work."
________.	"The Case Worker's Problem in Interpretation."
________.	"Helping the Client to Use His Capacities and Resources."
________.	"The Responsibility of the Case Worker in the Conflict Between the Interests of the Individual and the Interests of Society."
________.	"The Status of Social Case Work Today."
Moore, M.	"Case Work and Credit System Problems."
Murray, A.	"Case Work Above the Poverty Line."
Nathan, C.	"Needs for Social Case Work as Revealed in Groups."
Nesbitt, F.	"The Significance of the Rise in Relief-Giving During the Past Five Years: Its Relation to Standards of Case Work."
Neustaedter, E.	"The Case Worker's Role in Treatment."
Odencrantz, L.	"Social Case Work in Industry: Personnel Work in Factories."
Paige, C.	"Case-Work Objectives--Achieved in Volume."
Porter, R.	"The Cost of Maintaining Good Case Work in a Public Agency."
Reynolds, B.	"The Status of Social Case Work Today."
Reynolds, R.	"Need of Case Work in a Public Relief Agency."
Rich, M.	"The Effect of Joint Administration on Case Work Practices."
Richmond, M.	"The Social Case Worker in a Changing World."
________.	"The Social Case Worker's Task."
Robinson, V.	"Analysis of Processes in the Records of Family Case Working Agencies."

________.	"Psychoanalytic Contributions to Social Case Work Treatment."
Sanders, C.	"The Relationship Between Children and Family Case Working Agencies: Relationships in Technique."
Sheffield, A.	"Identifying Clue-Aspects in Social Case Work."
Simkhovitch, M.	"The Case Work Plane."
Taft, J.	"Mental Hygiene of Childhood: The Social Workers Opportunity."
Taggart, A.	"Case Work and Community Change."
Thornton, J.	"Social Case Work Method in Health Work."
Towle, C.	"Helping the Client to Use His Capacities and Resources."
________.	"The Underlying Skills of Case Work Today."
Twente, E.	"Social Case-Work Practice in Rural Communities."
Vaile, G.	"The Contribution of Social Case Work to Democracy."
________.	"The Cost of Maintaining Good Case Work in a Public Agency."
Warren, M.	"Methods Used by Social Case Workers in the Development of Personality: One of the Processes Used by Case Workers in Developing Personality."
Wheeler, M.	"Some Tests for the Evaluation of Case Work Methods."
White, H.	"Activity in the Case-Work Relationship."
Wilson, G.	"Interplay of the Insights of Case Work and Group Work."
Witmer, H.	"Some Underlying Principles of Research in Social Case Work."
Wright, L.	"The Worker's Attitude as an Element in Social Case Work."
Wyman, M.	"What Is Basic in Case-Work Practice."

SOCIAL CHANGE

Hilton, A.	"Of Worth and Value: The Human Spirit and the Cybercultural Revolution."

SOCIAL CONFLICT

Addams, J.	"Class Conflict in America."

SOCIAL GROUP WORK

Kaiser, C.	"Current Frontiers in Social Group Work."
Konopka, G.	"Therapy Through Social Group Work."
Wanamaker, C.	"The Integration of Group Work and Case Work."

Wilson, G.	"Human Needs Pertinent to Group Work Services."
________.	"Methods of Record-keeping of Group Behavior and Individual Contacts."

SOCIAL LEGISLATION

Breckinridge, S.	"Promotion of National and State Social Legislation by Social Workers."
Chickering, M.	"The Part Social Workers Have Taken in Promoting Social Legislation in California."
Johnson, L.	"The Case Worker Looks at Legislative Planning."
Magee, E.	"Opportunities for Social Workers to Participate in Social Legislation."
Rockwood, E.	"Organizing the Community for Legislative Reform."
Thomas, D.	"Public Testimony."

SOCIAL POLICY

Johnson, A.	"The Obstacle of Limited Participation in Local Social Planning."
Kimball, N.	"Participants and Policy Making."
van Kleeck, M.	"Social Planning and Social Work."

SOCIAL ROLE

Komarovsky, M.	"Presidential Address: Some Problems in Role Analysis."

SOCIAL SCIENCE RESEARCH

Davis, K.	"Discussion of Social Research in Public Institutions."
Deardorff, N.	"Fact Finding and Research as a Basis of Program Making in Social Work."
________.	"Sociological Research Studies--What Are the Values for the Social Worker of the More Recent Sociological Type of Community Study?"
Hewins, K.	"Shaping the Record to Facilitate Research."
Hill, R.	"Some Community Values in a Social Survey."
Loomis, A.	"Some Experiments in Research in Social Behavior."
Mudgett, M.	"Research as a Method of Training for Social Work."

SOCIAL SERVICE

Addams, J.	"Breadgivers."
________.	"The Call of the Social Field."
________.	"Education."
________.	"Educational Methods."
________.	"How Much Social Work Can a Community Afford? From the Ethical Point of View."
________.	"International Co-operation for Social Welfare."
________.	"The Philosophy of a New Day."
________.	"Political Reform."
________.	"Remarks as Chairman of Discussion."
________.	"The Spirit of Social Service."
Anderson, H.	"Cooperation of the Home Service Department of the American Red Cross with Other Social Agencies."
Barnard, K.	"Shaping the Destinies of a New State."
Beveridge, H.	"Reformatory and Preventive Work in Illinois."
Binford, J.	"Community Protective Social Measures."
Bing, L.	"What the Public Thinks of Social Work."
Blakeslee, R.	"Regional and State-wide Exchanges."
Bowen, G.	"Interpretative Publicity as a Function of Social Work: What Part Can the Federation Take in Its Development?"
Bremer, E.	"The Foreign Language Worker in the Fusion Process, as Indispensable Asset to Social Work in America."
________.	"Our International Communities and the War."
Brisley, M.	"An Attempt to Articulate Processes."
Brown, S.	"A County Unit for Social Service."
Burnett, M.	"Community Councils in Pittsburgh."
________.	"The Role of the Social Worker in Agency-Community Relationships."
Byington, M.	"The Confidential Exchange in the Small City."
________.	"Co-ordination of Civil Effort in Small Communities."
________.	"The Future of Home Service."
________.	"Leadership."
Campbell, M.	"The Strategic Position of the School in Programs of Social Work: From the Point of View of the Social Worker."
Cannon, I.	"How Can We Vitalize the Relationship of Our Public and Private Social Work?"
Cannon, M.	"Recent Changes in the Philosophy of Social Workers."
________.	"Underlying Principles and Common Practice in Social Work."
________.	"The Unknown Future."
Chickering, M.	"Official Recognition and Status of the Social Worker."

________.	"What a Visitor in a Public Agency Should Know."
Claghorn, K.	"Some New Developments in Social Statistics."
________.	"The Use and Misuse of Statistics in Social Work."
Clarke, H.	"Uniform Area Plan for Chicago City-Wide Social Agencies."
Clevenger, L.	"The Influence of Publicity in Developing Community Organization."
Clifton, E.	"The Role of Personalities in the Treatment of Problem Children in an Institution."
Clow, L.	"The Art of Helping Through the Interview: A Study of Two Interviews."
Conner, L.	"The Effects on Case Work Services of Social Factors in the Negro's Life: From the Point of View of Socio-political Factors."
Conrad, I.	"Professional Standards for Council and Chest Executives."
Cooley, E.	"West Palm Beach County, Florida: A Unit for Social Work."
Copp, T.	"Need of State Legislation to Supplement and Follow Up the N. R. A."
Corbett, L.	"The Background of a Family's Religious Life as Social Data."
Coyle, G.	"Social Work at the Turn of the Decade."
Crosby, H.	"Business as an Ally."
Curry, H.	"The Status of Social Work in Rural Communities."
Davis, K.	"How the Public May Help."
Deardorff, N.	"Next Steps in Job Analysis (Pugsley Award)."
Dexter, E.	"The Social Case Worker's Attitudes and Problems as They Affect Her Work."
Dickey, G.	"The Social Service Exchange."
Eggleston, M.	"Relation of Case-Work Staffs to Interpretation, Officials, Governing Boards, Volunteers, and the Public."
Faatz, A.	"Interpretation in the Public Agency."
Foster, E.	"Constructive Federal-State Relationships: From the Federal Viewpoint."
Foster, M.	"Legislation, Cooperation, and the Board."
Glenn, H.	"The Value of Analyzing One's Job."
Glenn, M.	"The Background of a Family's Religious Life as Social Data."
________.	"Personal and Professional Sources of Inspiration for Social Workers: Roots of Courage."
________.	"President's Address: A Prelude to Peace."
________.	"Service."
Gottemoller, R.	"Implications in the Broader Use of Budgets."
Hall, B.	"The Social Service Exchange: Is It a Mechanical Overhead, or a Case Work Stimulant?"

Hanford, J. "Standards of Measurement Used in Staff Evaluations in a Private Agency."

Hanson, E. "Forty-three Families Treated by Friendly Visiting."

Hoey, J. "The Contribution of Social Work to Government."

________. "Social Work Concepts and Methods in the Postwar World."

Holbrook, E. "A Survey of a Month's Work Made Six Months Afterward."

Hosch, F. "The Determination of Social Work Salaries."

Howlett, V. "Relation of Case-Work Staffs to Interpretation, Officials, Governing Boards, Volunteers, and the Public."

Jacobs, B. "The Work of One State."

Johnson, A. "The Administrative Process in Social Work."

________. "The County as a Unit for Co-Ordinate Planning and Service in Public and Private Social Work (Point of View of Public Officials)."

________. "Science and Social Work."

Kahn, D. "The Need for Interpretation of Trends and Accomplishments in Family Social Work."

Kauffman, M. "Supervision of Case-Work Staffs."

Kelley, F. "What Our Official Statistics Do Not Tell Us."

King, A. "The Present Opportunity of the City Home Service Section."

Kohut, R. "Mission-work Among the Unenlightened Jews."

Lally, D. "The Interrelationships of Merit Systems and the Quality of Public Welfare Personnel."

Lathrop, J. "Report of the Committee on State Supervision and Administration."

________. "The Transition from Charities and Correction to Social Work--1873 to 1923--Then?"

Lazarus, E. "Integration of Supervision with the Total Program of the Agency."

Lenroot, K. "The Federal Government and Desirable Standards of State and Local Administration."

________. "Government Provision for Social Work Statistic: On a National Scale from the Point of View of the Registration of Social Statistics."

________. "Social Work and the Social Order (Presidential Address)."

Lewelling, A. "Report of Iowa."

Libbey, B. "The Art of Helping by Changing Habit."

Lincoln, L. "Report of the Standing Committee--State Boards and Commissions."

Louis, M. "Mission-Work Among the Unenlightened Jews."

Low, M.	"Co-operation Between Courts and Voluntary Public Agencies, (Abstract)."
________.	"The Wider Use of Registration."
Lundberg, E.	"Interpretation and Support of Public Welfare Work: Publications and Uniform Social Data."
McCord, E.	"A Cooperative Experiment Between Public and Private Agencies."
McCowen, J.	"Report from Iowa."
McHugh, R.	"The Background of a Family's Religious Life as Social Data."
________.	"The Organization of Social Service in Connection with State Institutions."
McMurray, G.	"Social Work."
Marcus, G.	"The Effects of Financial Dependency and Relief Giving upon Social Attitudes."
________.	"Worker and Client Relationships."
Marshall, S.	"Bringing People and Services Together."
Millar, M.	"Modern Use of Older Treatment Methods."
Miller, P.	"The Confidential Relationship in Social Work Administration."
Minton, E.	"Changing the Program of a Public Welfare Agency."
Odencrantz, L.	"Social Work Jobs Analyzed."
Paradise, V.	"Creative Writing for Social Work."
Parker, I.	"The Study of Agency Interrelationships."
Patten, M.	"Social Work Under Church Auspices, and Social Work Under Community Auspices: From the Standpoint of the Rural Community."
Perry, M.	"Values and Limitations of the Evaluation Process as Seen by the Worker."
Potter, E.	"Co-Ordination of State and Local Units for Welfare Administration."
________.	"How to Secure a Continuing and Progressive Policy in Public Social Work and Institutions."
________.	"Personnel in the Public Service from the Administrator's Point of View."
________.	"The Year of Decision for Social Work."
Pratt, L.	"The Philosophy and Use of Budget Standards."
Putnam, E.	"Auxiliary Visitors. Volunteer Visiting of State Wards in Connection with Official Work."
Putnam, M.	"Friendly Visiting."
Quinn, L.	"How to Establish a Community Service."
Renard, B.	"Uniform Districting in a Large City for Social and Civic Purposes."
Routzahn, M.	"Available Channels of Publicity."
________.	"Interpreting the Social Worker to the Public."
Saloman, A.	"The Relation of the Church to Social Work."
Schmidt, F.	"Values and Limitations of the Evaluation Process: As Seen by the Supervisor."

Seymour, G.	"The Relation of Health Officers and Social Work."
Shaw, T.	"Community Representation and Participation in Community Organization."
Sheffield, A.	"Public Agencies as Public Carriers of Ideas."
Smith, Z.	"Field Work."
Spencer, A.	"Social Work Under Church Auspices, and Social Work Under Community Auspices: From the Standpoint of the Urban Community."
Spencer, S.	"Report from the District of Columbia."
________.	"Report of District of Columbia."
Springer, G.	"The Responsibility of the Social Worker in a Democracy."
Stabler, D.	"The Effect of Staff Turnover on Families Under Care, as Demonstrated in Changes of Plan and Treatment and General Tempo of Work."
Stewart, H.	"Co-Ordinating as Done by the Public Health Nurse."
Taylor, R.	"The Integration of Effort in Theory and Practice by Private and Public Agencies for the Common Good."
Towle, C.	"Factors in Treatment."
Trumbull, G.	"The Role of Commercial Organizations in Social Welfare on the Pacific Coast."
Vaile, G.	"Some Significant Trends Since Cleveland, 1912 (Presidential Address)."
Van Kleeck, M.	"Social Work in the Economic Crisis."
Van Waters, M.	"Philosophical Trends in Modern Social Work (Presidential Address)."
Vittum, H.	"Politics from the Social Point of View."
Vaile, G.	"An Experiment in Trying to Grade District Visitors."
Whiting, M.	"Detroit's Experience with Job Classification."
Wilkins, J.	"Facts Versus Folklore."
Wood, M.	"The Effective Organization of Social Forces in Small Towns and Rural Communities."

SOCIAL SERVICE, RURAL

Baskett, J.	"Undifferentiated Case Work the Surest Approach to Rural Social Work: Its Challenge and Its Opportunity: From the School."
Brown, J.	"The Use of Volunteers in Rural Social Work: In Dakota County, Minnesota."
Cottrell, L.	"Organization Needed to Support and Free the Local Worker for Undifferentiated Case Work."

Eicher, L.	"Undifferentiated Case Work the Surest Approach to Rural Social Work: Its Challenge and Its Opportunity: From the Public Department of Welfare."
Hagood, B.	"Sod Busting for Social Work: Children with Plenty o'Nothin'."
Hastings, C.	"Undifferentiated Case Work the Surest Approach to Rural Social Work: Its Challenge and Its Opportunity: From the Private Agency."
Lund, H.	"Case Work as Applied to Rural Communities."
McLennan, H.	"Sod Busting for Social Work in Rural Michigan."
Mills, E.	"Co-Operative Case-Work Services to Sick People in Rural Areas."
Reeves, M.	"Community Planning in Rural Communities."
Starkweather, V.	"Sod Busting for Social Work in White Pine County, Nevada."
Wing, V.	"The Use of Volunteers in Rural Social Work: In Scioto County, Ohio."
Yerxa, E.	"The Modern Program of Rural Social Work as It Affects Children."

SOCIAL SETTLEMENTS

Addams, J.	"A Function of the Social Settlement."
________.	"The Objective Value of a Social Settlement."
________.	"Social Settlements."
________.	"The Subjective Necessity for Social Settlements."
________.	"Summary of an Address on Settlements."
Davis, K.	"Civic Efforts of Social Settlements."
Hart, H.	"The Changing Function of the Settlement Under Changing Conditions."
Ingram, F.	"A Community Kitchen in a Neighborhood House."
Lathrop, J.	"What the Settlement Work Stands For."
McDowell, M.	"The Settlement and Organized Charity."
Simkhovitch, M.	"Standards and Tests of Efficiency in Settlement Work."

SOCIAL SURVEYS

Atkinson, M.	"Demonstration as Part of the Survey Process."

SOCIAL WORK AS A PROFESSION

Abbott, G.	"Developing and Protecting Professional Standards in Public Welfare Work."

447 Social Work as a Profession

Addams, J.	"Social Workers and the Other Professions."
Breckinridge, S.	"Report of the Committee (on Securing and Training Social Workers)."
Brown, E.	"Social Work Against a Background of the Other Professions."
Deardorff, N.	"The Objectives of the Professional Organization."
Eliel, H.	"The California Plan for the State Certification of Social Workers."
Fairchild, M.	"The Study of Industrial Processes as a Tool for Professional Standards and Education."
Kahn, D.	"Social Action from the Viewpoint of Professional Organizations."
Kingsbury, S.	"The Study of Industrial Processes as a Tool for Professional Standards and Education."
Linderholm, N.	"The Social Worker's Responsibility for the Reputation of the Profession."
Richmond, M.	"The Art of Beginning in Social Work."
Rowe, C.	"Interpreting Professional Standards of Social Work to the Public: From the Viewpoint of a National Agency."
Smith, Z.	"Possibilities of the Social Workers' Club."
Tousley, C.	"Support and Interpretation of Professional Requirements in Social Work: Who Are Our Interpreters?"

SOCIAL WORK EDUCATION

Abbott, E.	"Field Work and the Training of the Social Worker."
Alper, M.	"Supervision as One Method of Staff Development: In a Rural Setting."
Anderson, H.	"Training."
Berry, M.	"Professional Standards in Social Agencies: The Value to the Agency of Students in Training."
Blackey, E.	"Training the Rural Relief Worker on the Job."
Breckinridge, S.	"The New Horizons of Professional Education for Social Work."
Brown, J.	"Principles, Content, and Objectives of Supervision."
Browning, G.	"The Responsibility of the Schools of Social Work for Training for the Public Welfare Services."
Burnett, M.	"Recruiting of Students by Schools and of Apprentices by Agencies."
Byington, M.	"The Possibilities of Centralized Supervision."
Cannon, A.	"The Philosophy of Social Work and Its Place in the Professional Curriculum."
Clemence, E.	"Changing Trends in the Education of Caseworkers."

Conrad, I. "The Need of a Few Fundamental Courses."

Cosgrove, E. "Use of Service Ratings in the Evaluation of Performance."

Engel, D. "Supervision as One Method of Staff Development: In the Urban Agency."

Farnham, B. "Interpretation of Social Work in the School Curriculum--How Detroit Lays the Foundation."

Feder, L. "Changing Emphasis in Professional Education."

FitzSimons, R. "Preparation and Direction of Case-Work Personnel: The Washington Training Plan."

Gartland, R. "Generic Aspects of Professional Training for Case Work and Group Work: From the Point of View of a Teacher of Case Work."

Glenn, M. "The History of Social Work and Its Place in the Professional Curriculum."

Hardwick, K. "Minimum Educational Requirements Which Should Be Demanded of Those Beginning Family Case Work."

Hathway, M. "Education for Public Social Services."

________. "Gaps in Education and Training."

________. "Social Action and Professional Education."

Hendricks, T. "The Learning Process in Agency Settings."

Hollis, F. "Emotional Growth of the Worker Through Supervision."

James, S. "Field Supervision--Unilateral or Integrated?"

Kaiser, C. "Generic Aspects of Professional Training for Case Work and Group Work: From the Point of View of a Teacher of Group Work."

Kempshall, A. "Tentative Observations on Basic Training."

Mudgett, M. "The Place of Field Work in Training for Social Work: Its Educational Content."

Rich, M. "Professional Training from the Point of View of the Family Field."

Schindler, A. "Professional and In-Service Training for Group Work."

Sheibley, E. "Professional Education in the Agency Setting."

Smith, Z. "The Education of the Friendly Visitor."

Spencer, S. "Major Issues in Social Work Education."

Sytz, F. "Professional Relations: The School of Social Work and the Agency."

________. "Relation of a Standard of Education and Training to Professional Practice."

Van Driel, A. "In-Service Training."

________. "Training the Paid, Untrained Worker."

Van Waters, M. "Is the Agency or the Individual Primarily Responsible for the Professional Development of the Social Worker?"

White, E.	"How the Agencies and the Schools May Cooperate in the Development of the Curriculum."
Wisner, E.	"Professional Training in the Light of Wartime Shortages."

SOCIAL WORK WITH THE AGED

Dexter, E.	"New Concepts and Old People."

SOCIALISM

Keller, H.	"A New Light Is Coming. Address at the Sociological Conference, Sagamore Beach, Massachusetts."
________.	"Onward, Comrades! An Address at the Rand School New Year's Eve Ball, December 31, 1920."

SOCIALLY HANDICAPPED CHILDREN

Culbert, J.	"The Public School as a Little-Used Agency: As a Factor in the Treatment of the Socially Handicapped Child."

SOCIOLOGY

Spencer, A.	"The Sociological and Practical Value of Our Accumulated Knowledge."

SOLDIERS

Roosevelt, A.	"Responsibility to Our Men and Women in the Services."

SOUTH AFRICA

Bolton, F.	"Treatment of Indians in South Africa."

SOUTHERN STATES

George, J.	"Who Are the Builders?"
Herring, H.	"The Southern Industrial Problem, as the Social Worker Sees It."
Roman, S.	"Extracts from Possibilities of the Southern States."

SPAIN

Bell, L.	"A Glimpse of Modern Spain."
Cantrell, E.	"The Moors of Spain."
Goldman, E.	"Address to the International Working Men's Association Congress (Paris, 1937)."

SPIRITUALISM

Woodhull, V.	"The Elixir of Life."

SPORTS FOR WOMEN

Adrian, M.	"Sex Differences in Biomechanics."
Allen, D.	"Self Concept and the Female Participant."
Drinkwater, B.	"Maximal Oxygen Uptake of Females."
Graber, P.	"Public Testimony."
Green, E.	"The Road Is Paved with Good Intentions: Title IX and What It Is Not."
Harris, D.	"Dimensions of Physical Activity."
________.	"Needed Approaches for a Better Understanding of Behavior and Performance."
________.	"Stress Seeking and Sport Involvement."
Kennicke, L.	"Masks of Identity."
Moody, H.	"Maintaining the Balance Between Life and Play."
Phillips, M.	"Sociological Considerations of the Female Participant."
Portz, E.	"Influence of Birth Order and Sibling Sex on Sports Participation."
Sherif, C.	"Females in the Competitive Process."
Strati, J.	"Body Image and Performance."
Ziegler, S.	"Self-Perception of Athletes and Coaches."
Zogle, J.	"Femininity and Achievement in Sports."

STAEL-HOLSTEIN, ANNE LOUISE GERMAINE (HECKER) BARONNE DE

Jenkins, H.	"Madame de Stael."

STATE, THE

Thompson, D.	"The State in a Democracy. The State, the Negation of Anarchy."

STERILIZATION

Perry, M.	"Minority Report of the Report of Committee on Colonies for Segregation of Defectives."

Rothman, E.	"Public Testimony."
Rothstein, A.	"Public Testimony."

STOCK AND STOCK BREEDING

Meredith, V.	"Stock Breeding."

STONE, LUCY

Howe, J.	"Address at Memorial Service for Lucy Stone During the National-American Woman Suffrage Association Convention of 1894."

STRIKES AND LOCKOUTS--COPPER MINING

Rankin, J.	"Debate on Resolution Authorizing the President to Requisition the Copper Mines of Montana During Labor Unrest."

STUDENTS

Sturtevant, S.	"Change and the Student."

STUDENTS' SOCIETIES

Pearson, L.	"Student Fellowship."

SWEATING SYSTEM

Kelley, F.	"Insanitary Conditions Amongst Home Workers."
________.	"The Sweating System."

TAXATION

Abzug, B.	"Nixon and Welfare for the Rich."
Grasso, E.	"Tax Credit for Parents of Students Attending Nonpublic Elementary and Secondary School."
Kellems, V.	"Taxes. Is It Not Time That the Women of America Make Themselves Heard?"
McCaffrey, C.	"Statement."
Platt, M.	"Statement."

TEACHERS

Mead, M.	"Revise Role of Teacher; Summary of Address."

TEACHERS, TRAINING OF

Prewitt, L.	"The Need for Quality Instruction: To the Teacher."

TEACHING, FREEDOM OF

Fields, J.	"Academic Freedom: Panel Discussion."

TECHNOLOGY

Gilbreth, L.	"Can the Machine Pull Us Out?"
________.	"Safeguarding Machine Development."
Grasso, E.	"Office of Technology Assessment."

TEMPERANCE

Andrew, E.	"The Origin, History and Development of the World's Woman's Christian Temperance Union."
Anthony, S.	"First Address at a Daughters of Temperance Supper, March, 1, 1849."
Blackwell, A.	"Remarks on the World's Temperance Convention."
Bloomer, A.	"Address at the 2nd Annual Meeting of the Woman's Temperance Society, Utica, N. Y., June 7, 1854."
________.	"Debate on Divorce Resolution at the N. Y. State Temperance Convention, Rochester, N. Y., 1852."
________.	"Mrs. Bloomer's Address. Presentation to Flag to Local Regiment, Council Bluffs, Iowa, 1861."
________.	"Mrs. Bloomer's Speech, at a Temperance Meeting in Metropolitan Hall, New York City, February, 1853."
Burnett, M.	"National Temperance Hospital."
Burt, M.	"Address."
Carse, M.	"The Temperance Temple."
Foster, J.	"Non-Partisan National Woman's Christian Temperance Union."
Goff, H.	"Temperance."
Gordon, A.	"How to Reach the Children."

________.	"World Prohibition, World Purity, World Peace: Our International Goal. Address to the Annual Convention of the National Woman's Christian Temperance Union. Philadelphia, Pennsylvania, November 17, 1922."
Harper, F.	"The Neglected Rich."
Hoffman, C.	"A Bird's-Eye View of the National Woman's Christian Temperance Union."
Hunt, M.	"Our Reasons."
________.	"Temperance Education."
Lathrap, M.	"The National Woman's Christian Temperance Union."
Lease, M.	"Women in the Farmers' Alliance."
Leavitt, M.	"Temperance and Purity."
Pollard, M.	"Foot Free in God's Country."
Shaw, A.	"The Temperance Problem."
Smith, H.	"World's Woman's Temperance Union."
Stanton, E.	"Address at the 1st Annual Meeting of the Woman's State Temperance Society, Rochester, June 1, 1853."
________.	"Mrs. Stanton's Address at the 1st Annual Meeting of the Woman's State Temperance Society, Rochester, 1853."
________.	"President's Address at New York State Temperance Convention, Rochester, N. Y., April 20, 1852."
________.	"Stanton's Address."
________.	"Statement at the 1st Woman's State Temperance Convention in Corinthian Hall, Rochester, on April 20, 1852."
Vaughan, M.	"President's Address at a Mass Meeting of "The Daughters of Temperance" on January 28, 1852."
West, M.	"The Woman's Temperance Publishing Association."
Willard, F.	"Address at Convention Hall, Washington, D. C. February 15, 1895."
________.	"Address at Exeter Hall, London, 1893."
________.	"Address at the 12th Annual Meeting of the Chicago W. C. T. U., in 1886."
________.	"Address at Welcome Meeting at Exeter Hall, London, 1892."
________.	"Address Before the Women's Congress, Des Moines, Iowa, 1885."
________.	"Address to the Annual Convention of the National Woman's Christian Temperance Union, Philadelphia, 1885."
________.	"Address to the Committee on Resolutions of the Republican National Convention in 1884."
________.	"Address to the National Convention of the Woman's Christian Temperance Union, St. Louis, November, 1896."

________.	"Annual Address at the National Convention of the National Woman's Christian Temperance Union, Detroit, 1883."
________.	"Annual Address at the National Convention of the National Woman's Christian Temperance Union, New York, 1888."
________.	"Annual Address Before the National Convention of the Woman's Christian Temperance Union."
________.	"Annual Address to National Convention, W. C. T. U."
________.	"Decoration Day Speech at a Prohibition Party Convention, 1888."
________.	"Extracts from Addresses at International Council of Women in Washington, March 25 to April 1, 1888."
________.	"Gospel Politics. Annual Address to the National Convention of the National Woman's Christian Temperance Union, St. Louis, 1884."
________.	"The "Home Protection" Address."
________.	"President's Address." WCTU 1883.
________.	"Speech Seconding the Nomination of John P. St. John for President at the Prohibition Party National Convention, Pittsburgh, 1884."
________.	"The Summing-Up of the Whole Matter."
________.	"White-Cross Movement in Education."
________.	"Willard's Broad View of Temperance."
________.	"Women in Temperance."
Wittenmyer, A.	"President's Address."

THEATER--U. S.

Hayes, H.	"The American Theatre Comes of Age."
Thomas, H.	"The Five Cent Theatre."

TRADE-UNIONS

Etheridge, F.	"Trade Unions in Federal Service."
Fairchild, M.	"Educational Methods in Teaching Workers."
Flynn, E.	"The Truth About the Paterson Strike."
Keller, H.	"What Is the IWW? Speech at the New York City Civic Club, January 1918."
Kyle, C.	"Case Work in Unions."
Martin, E.	"Statement Concerning Her Abduction Before the Senate Committee on Labor and Public Welfare, November 17, 1947."
Perkins, F.	"Address at Twenty-first Annual Convention of International Association of Governmental Labor Officials."

________.	"Address Before the Annual Convention of the American Federation of Labor, October 8, 1941."
________.	"Address to Annual Convention of American Federation of Labor, New Orleans, La., November 20, 1944."
Robinson, C.	"Trade Unions and the Labour Problem."
Sayles, L.	"Co-Operation, the Law of the New Civilization."
Scott, N.	"Social Workers and Labor Unions: Social Work Touches an Organized Industry."
Van Kleeck, M.	"The Common Goals of Labor and Social Work."
________.	"The Effect of the N. R. A. on Labor."
________.	"Governmental Intervention in the Labor Movement."
Winslow, H.	"Strikes and Their Causes."

TRAFFIC ACCIDENTS

Rogers, E.	"Tragedy of the Highways."

TRAFFIC ENGINEERING

Jacobs, J.	"Downtown Planning. Solving Traffic Problems."

TRANSPORTATION--SAFETY MEASURES

Bailey, K.	"Remarks, First Houston Regional Transportation Conference, Whitehall Hotel, September 23, 1976, Houston, Texas."

TUBERCULOSIS

Lummis, J.	"The Responsibility of State and Municipal Authorities to the Migrant Consumptive."
Radebaugh, K.	"Rehabilitation Work."
Whitney, J.	"The Indigent Migratory Tuberculosis: The Facts of the Case."
________.	"Social Research Program of the National Tuberculosis Association."
________.	"The Tuberculosis Migrant, a Family Problem: The Magnitude of the Problem."

TULEY, MURRAY F.

Addams, J.	"Judge Murray F. Tuley."

TWENTIETH CENTURY

Howell, M.	"The Dawning of the Twentieth Century."

TYLER, ALICE KELLOGG

Addams, J.	"Alice Kellogg Tyler."

UNEMPLOYED

Bedford, C.	"The Effect of an Unemployment Situation in Family Societies."
Bell, C.	"Women and Unemployment."
Breckinridge, S.	"What the Schools Are Doing."
Carr, C.	"What One Family Agency Is Doing."
Grasso, E.	"The Emergency Employment Bill."
Hall, H.	"Report of a Survey of the Effect of Unemployment."
Nelson, A.	"Youth and the Industrial Slack."
Nestor, A.	"What Labor Is Doing."
Perkins, F.	"The Outlook in Unemployment Relief."
Scott, N.	"Some New Problems for the Family Agency Arising Out of Industry."
Wright, H.	"Why Unemployment?"

UNITED NATIONS

Black, S.	"United Nations Conference on the Human Environments; Statement, December 15, 1969."
________.	"United States Comments on Work of UNICEF; Statement, December 2, 1969."
________.	"U. S. Discusses Priorities for the 1972 UN Conference on the Human Environment; Statement, September 20, 1971."
________.	"Youth-Related Activities of the United Nations; Statement, September 30, 1969."
Bolton, F.	"U. N.: A Family of Nations."
Hahn, L.	"United Nations Commission on the Status of Women."
Luce, C.	"Crisis in the United Nations: American Public Opinion."
Miller, F.	"Report Before Conference of Women's Organizations, March 14, 1946 on United Nations Sessions in London."
Reid, H.	"An American Newspaper and the United Nations."
Roosevelt, E.	"United Nations and You. Language Difficulties Are Barriers to Confidence."
Thompson, D.	"The Future World Order. The Ideal of the United Nations."

U.S. AIR FORCE

Luce, C.	"America in the Post-War Air World. Be Practical--Ration Globaloney."
Smith, M.	"Campaign Speech on U.S. Air Force, September 12, 1954."
________.	"Statement at the Senate Armed Forces Hearing on the Promotion of Jimmy Stewart to Brigadier General, May 2, 1957."

U.S. ARMY, 5TH

Luce, C.	"Newsblackout of the Fifth Army. Fixed Tour of Duty for Infantry."

U.S. CHILDREN'S BUREAU

Abbott, G.	"Address at Conference Dinner."
________.	"The Children's Bureau."
Addams, J.	"The Federal Children's Bureau--A Symposium."
Lathrop, J.	"The Children's Bureau."
Rude, A.	"The Federal Children's Bureau."
Wald, L.	"Address at Conference Dinner."

U.S.--CIVILIZATION

Alexander, R.	"Mid-Century World. Whose World Has It Turned Out To Be?"
Allen, F.	"Address."
Buck, P.	"What I See Happening in America."
Davies, E.	"Learning America's Meaning."
Hurst, F.	"Are We Coming Or Going?"
Mead, M.	"Changing World of Living; Address."
Millay, E.	"Termites in America."
Thompson, D.	"America Facing Tomorrow's World."
________.	"Nation of Speculators."
________.	"Which Way America? The Progressive Decay of Standards."

U.S. CONGRESS

Bennett, M.	"Congress in 1943 and 1944. Procedure Must Be Brought Up to Date."
Smith, M.	"Election Eve Campaign Speech, 1st Senate Campaign, November 1948."
________.	"Margaret Smith's Answer to a Smear."
________.	"Opening and Closing Statements at a Debate with Lucia Cormier, WCSH-TV, Portland, Maine, November 6, 1960."

Sullivan, L.	"Lack of Leadership in Washington. A Congresswoman Looks at Congress."

U. S. CONSTITUTION. 1ST-10TH AMENDMENTS

Allen, F.	"How Can We Put Our Living Traditions to Work?"

U. S. --DEFENSES

Elliott, H.	"Women's Part in Defense Plans."

U. S. --DIPLOMATIC AND CONSULAR SERVICE

Watson, B.	"International Travel: Consular Operations."
________.	"Providing Consular Services to the American Public Abroad: Statement."

U. S. --ECONOMIC CONDITIONS

Bernstein, P.	"The Danger Line in Public Economy."
Breckinridge, S.	"Industrial and Economic Problems--Introductory Statement."
Newcomer, M.	"How Are We Going to Pay for Defense? There Is a Possibility of Marked Inflation."

U. S. --FOREIGN RELATIONS

Cannon, M.	"International Relations, Distaff Side."
Dulles, E.	"The Challenge to the Western Policy for Germany. The Threat to Berlin."
Frederick, P.	"What Are Your Intentions? Peace-Making Requires Dedication."
Harris, P.	"View from the Otherside; Address, November 23, 1965."
Keller, H.	"A Plea for Recognition of Soviet Russia. Statement at a Hearing on Russian Free Trade Before the U. S. Senate Foreign Relations Committee."
Lamb, M.	"Cold War Thaw. An Asset or a Liability."
Luce, C.	"American Morality and Nuclear Diplomacy. The Force of Our Free Spirits."
________.	"Search for an American Foreign Policy. Yardsticks to Measure Our Objectives."
________.	"The Seventeen Year Trend to Castro: The Art of Economic Brinkmanship."
________.	"U. S. Foreign Policy and Italy: The Community and Detente."

________.	"U. S. Foreign Policy and World Communism. The Jungle World of Sovereign States."
McCormick, A.	"United States as World Leader. Don't Limit Our Aims."
Thompson, D.	"The Middle East Problem. Results of U. S. Aid to Israel."

U. S. --HISTORY

Armstrong, A.	"America's Bicentennial: Crisis and Challenge."
Smith, M.	"Growing Confusion. Need for Patriotic Thinking."
Thompson, D.	"Freedom's Back Is Against the Wall. Making Our Own Beds and Lying in Them."

U. S. --HISTORY--CIVIL WAR, 1861-1865--PUBLIC OPINION

Anthony, S.	"Address to President Lincoln. Adopted by the Women's National Loyal League, May 14, 1863."
________.	"Address to the Women's National Loyal League Convention, May 14, 1863."
________.	"The Loyal Women of the Country to Abraham Lincoln, President of the United States. Address Read at the Woman's National Loyal League Convention, May 14, 1863."
________.	"Report on Year's Activities of the Woman's National Loyal League at the Anniversary Meeting, May 12, 1864."
Stanton, E.	"Concluding Remarks at the Anniversary Meeting of the Woman's National Loyal League, May 12, 1864."

U. S. --HISTORY--WAR OF 1898

Anthony, S.	"Remarks at a Meeting of the Cuban League in Rochester, N. Y., February 1897."

U. S. NAVY

Smith, M.	"Closure of Kittery-Portsmouth Naval Shipyard."
________.	"Speech on Closure of Kittery-Portsmouth Naval Shipyard."

U. S. --POLITICS AND GOVERNMENT

Jordan, B.	"Democratic Convention Keynote Address: Who Then Will Speak for the Common Good?"
Kenyon, D.	"Technique of Utilizing American Political Machinery to Secure Social Action."

U. S. --SOCIAL CONDITIONS

Rose, F.	"Maintaining Standards of Living in the New Day."

U. S. --SOCIAL LIFE & CUSTOMS

Howe, J.	"Is Polite Society Polite?"
________.	"The Salon in America."

UNMARRIED MOTHERS

Barrett, K.	"The Unmarried Mother and Child."
Block, B.	"The Unmarried Mother: Is She Different?"
Bosworth, A.	"Factors Affecting Decision on Unmarried Mother to Give Up or Keep Her Child, Environmental Factors."
Brenner, R.	"What Facilities Are Essential to the Adequate Care of the Unmarried Mother?"
Brisley, M.	"Parent-Child Relationships in Unmarried Parenthood."
Chenet, W.	"Public Testimony."
Curry, H.	"A Girl with a Second or Third Illegitimate Child."
Donahue, A.	"The Case of an Unmarried Mother Who Has Cared for Her Child, and Succeeded."
________.	"A Case of Illegitimacy When Mother and Baby Have Been Dealt with Separately."
Labaree, M.	"Unmarried Parenthood Under the Social Security Act."
Lee, E.	"Court Procedure in Securing Support for a Child of Illegitimate Birth."
Lundberg, E.	"Illegitimacy in Europe as Affected by the War."
________.	"Progress in Legal Protection for Children Born Out of Wedlock."
________.	"Progress Toward Better Laws for the Protection of Children Born Out of Wedlock."
Parmenter, L.	"The Case of an Unmarried Mother Who Has Cared for Her Child, and Failed."
Sheffield, A.	"The Nature of the Stigma upon the Unmarried Mother and Her Child."

________.	"Program of the Committee on Illegitimacy--Committee Report."
Shuman, C.	"The Girl with a First Baby, Who Is Not Feeble-Minded."
Verry, E.	"Meeting Challenge of Today's Needs in Working with Unmarried Mothers Through Use of Institution (Maternity Home)."
Watson, A.	"The Attitude of Married Parents and Social Workers Toward Unmarried Parents."
Weidensall, J.	"The Mentality of the Unmarried Mother."

URBAN ECONOMICS

Kreps, J.	"Remarks at the U. S. Conference of Mayors, Tucson, Arizona, June 14, 1977."

URBAN RENEWAL

Kreps, J.	"Address Before the National League of Cities; Congressional City Conference, Washington Hilton Hotel, Washington, D. C., March 6, 1977."

URBANIZATION

McLean, E.	"Urbanization for the Future."

VENEREAL DISEASES

Buffington, A.	"Seamen with Venereal Disease in the Port of New York."
Corrigan, H.	"Social Casework in a Social Protection Program."
Doyle, A.	"Venereal Disease and Clinics for Civilians Near Military Camps."
Hamilton, A.	"Venereal Diseases in Institutions for Women and Girls."
Hearsey, M.	"The Control of Syphilis, from the Viewpoint of Medical Social Service."
King, E.	"Relations and Duties of Public Health Nurses and Social Workers in the Diagnosis, Treatment, and Control of Syphilis."
Parker, V.	"Hidden Problems in Hard Times."
Rappaport, M.	"Casework in Social Protection."
Robinson, D.	"Social Hygiene. The Responsibility of Women's Organizations in the Social Hygiene Movement."
Smith, C.	"Venereal Disease Problems in Institutions."

VETERANS

Craddock, C. "The Return of the Serviceman to His Family and Community: As Seen in Home Service, American National Red Cross."
Davis, D. "The Return of the Serviceman to His Family and Community: As Seen in a Military Hospital at the Point of Discharge."
Ginsbury, E. "The Case Worker in a Veteran Service Center."
Gutwillig, J. "Testimony on Sex Discrimination in Unemployment Insurance, Veterans Programs, and Public Assistance."
Jeter, H. "Separation Allowances for Service Men's Families."
Ross, E. "Social Work's Responsibilities for Veterans."
Thomas, D. "The Return of the Serviceman to His Family and Community: As Seen in a Private Family Case Work Agency."

VICE-PRESIDENTS--U.S.

Abzug, B. "The Vice-Presidency and the Order of Succession."

VIETNAMESE CONFLICT, 1961-1975

Abzug, B. "Speech by Congresswoman Bella S. Abzug at Inaugural Day Peace Demonstration in Washington--January 20, 1973."
Grasso, E. "Aid to North Vietnam."
________. "A Full Accounting of All MIA's."

VIOLENCE

Griffiths, M. "The Rising Tide of Violence. Maintaining Order in a Nation."

VISITING HOUSEKEEPERS

Goodwin, M. "Housekeeper Service in Family Welfare."

VISITING TEACHERS

Case, E. "A Day with the Visiting Teacher."
Culbert, J. "Visiting Teachers and Their Activities."
Pratt, A. "Courses of Training for Visiting Teachers."

VOCATIONAL GUIDANCE

Alexander, E.	"Reflections for a Graduate: Dare to Be Your Creative Self."
Banning, M.	"Test of an Education."
Campbell, M.	"Vocational Guidance."
Chasan, E.	"Public Testimony."
Dowding, N.	"Statement."
Keyserling, M.	"Summary of Speech on Guidance Counselors Needed for Career and Employment Decisions."
Lewis, H.	"Vocational and Employment Guidance of Older Children."
Reed, A.	"Is Guidance a Racket? The Ultimate of Confusion."

VOCATIONAL REHABILITATION

Cobb, M.	"Instructive and Productive Employments. Their Suitability for Industrial Schools and Houses of Refuge."

VOLUNTEER WORKERS IN SOCIAL SERVICE

Cahn, G.	"The Volunteer Gives--and Receives."
Curry, H.	"The Use of Committees and Volunteers in Rural Social Work."
Deardorff, N.	"Areas of Responsibility of Voluntary Social Work During Period of Changing Local and National Governmental Programs."
Frank, M.	"Volunteers in Mental Hospitals."
Godman, H.	"Auxiliary Visitors."
Goodwillie, M.	"Efficiency in the Use of Volunteers."
________.	"Volunteers in Family Work."
Houghteling, L.	"War Time Volunteers in Chicago."
Indritz, R.	"Volunteer Women Spark ORT, the Charity to End Charity, Through Vocational Education."
Kelley, F.	"Voluntary Agencies."
Keyserling, M.	"Address on Exploring Diversity of Opportunities for Citizenship Action."
King, M.	"Statement."
Kraus, H.	"Lay Participation in Social Work as It Affects the Public Agency."
Liveright, A.	"Possibilities of Volunteer Service in Public Agencies."
Newbold, F.	"A Community-Wide Volunteer Placement Bureau."
McDowell, M.	"Friendly Visiting."
Price, M.	"Friendly Visiting."
Richmond, M.	"Friendly Visiting."

Sears, A.	"Introductory Statement by the Chairman (On the Role of the Volunteer in Social Work)."
Smith, Z.	"How to Get and Keep Visitors."
________.	"Volunteer Visiting."
Stern, B.	"Tribute to the Important Contribution of the Woman Volunteer in a Democratic Society."
Van Dusseldorp, W.	"The Use of Committees and Volunteers in Rural Social Work."
Van Slyck, K.	"The Awakened Volunteer Interest."

VOTING

Clusen, R.	"Should the Expiring "Special Provision" of the Voting Rights Act Be Further Extended?"
Engle, L.	"The Voter's Part."
Grasso, E.	"Debate on Constitutional Amendment to Lower Voting Age to 18."
Lord, M.	"Non-Partisan Appeal for a Full Vote."
Strohm, E.	"The Voter's Part."

WAGE-PRICE POLICY

Sullivan, L.	"Controversy over Enactment of Standby Wage and Price Controls."

WAGES--MINIMUM WAGE

Burris, C.	"Should Congress Provide for Automatic Adjustments in the Federal Minimum Wage?"
Herrick, E.	"Renewing the Battle for Minimum Wage Legislation."
Kelley, F.	"Minimum Wage Board."
________.	"The Present Status of Minimum Wage Legislation."
________.	"Report of the Committee (on Standards of Living and Labor): Minimum Wage Boards."
Mason, L.	"Progress and Administration of Minimum Wage Laws in 1933."
Miller, F.	"Government Regulation of Wages and Hours: The States and Their Opportunity."
Mortenson, C.	"The Minimum Wage at Work in the District of Columbia."
Sells, D.	"Minimum Wage; Home Worker and Union Worker."

WAGES--WOMEN

Robins, M.	"Standard of Payment for Women and Girls. (Abstract)."
Swartz, M.	"Women's Wages."

WATER

Ray, D.	"Miracle of Water: Excerpts from Address, April, 1968."
Williston, A.	"Waterways and Water."

WATERGATE AFFAIR, 1972-74

Abzug, B.	"The Conduct of the President."

WEBB, WALTER PRESCOTT

Fried, L.	"This I Remember."

WELFARE STATE

Alexander, R.	"What Price the Welfare State? Government--The Guardian or Master?"

WIDOWS

Wolcott, L.	"Treatment of Poor Widows with Dependent Children."

WILMARTH, MARY HAWES

Addams, J.	"Mary Hawes Wilmarth."

WOERISHOFFER, CAROLA

Kelley, F.	"Address of Mrs. Kelley."
Marot, H.	"Address of Miss Marot."
Simkhovitch, M.	"Address of Mrs. Simkhovitch."
Thomas, M.	"Address of President Thomas."

WOMAN (THEOLOGY)

Cary, E.	"The Elevation of Womanhood Wrought Through the Veneration of the Blessed Virgin."

Cass, R.	"The Career Wife."
Clemens, L.	"Members One of Another."
________.	"The Problem of Roles."
________.	"Using All Gifts Creatively."
________.	"Who Is Woman?"
________.	"Woman's Natural Strengths."
________.	"Women Functioning Under God."
Engel, M.	"The Widow."
Gardner, H.	"Historical Facts and Theological Fictions."
________.	"Vicarious Atonement."
Hooker, I.	"Address."
Ostazeski, A.	"The Childless Married Woman."
Riggs, A.	"God's Thought of Women."
Sexton, V.	"Psychological Fulfillment for the Woman."
Shaw, A.	"God's Women."
Zizzmia, A.	"The Career Woman."

WOMAN (THEOLOGY)--BIBLICAL TEACHING

Blackwell, A.	"Resolution and Bible Argument at the Syracuse National Convention, September 1852."
Davis, P.	"Comments at the Syracuse National Convention, September 1852."
Mott, L.	"Debate During the 4th National Convention, Cleveland, Ohio, October 1853."
________.	"Discourse in the Assembly Buildings in Philadelphia on Woman and the Bible, and Women's Rights."
Rose, E.	"Comments on the Bible Issue at the Syracuse National Convention, September 1852."
________.	"Remarks at Woman's Rights Convention, Syracuse, N.Y., September 8, 1852."
Stone, L.	"Debate at the 4th National Convention, Cleveland, Ohio, October 1853."

WOMEN--AFRICA

Clignet, R.	"Social Change and Sexual Differentiation in the Cameroun and the Ivory Coast."
Mueller, M.	"Women and Men, Power and Powerlessness in Lesotho."
Sudarkasa, N.	"Women and Migration in Contemporary West Africa."

WOMEN--ALGERIA

Boals, K.	"The Politics of Cultural Liberation: Male-Female Relations in Algeria."

WOMEN--BIOGRAPHY

Adams, M.	"Influence of Great Women."

WOMEN--CHICAGO

Stevenson, S.	"Chicago Women."

WOMEN--CONDUCT OF LIFE

Fisher, E.	"Action Scale to Finer Womanhood. Make a Better Person of Yourself."
Palffy, E.	"Act of Living for Women Today. Be Stingy with Time."

WOMEN--CONGRESSES

Abbott, A.	"Compensation."
Abzug, B.	"Opening Statement."
Addams, J.	"Response."
Fields, D.	"Statement."
Heckler, M.	"Statement."
Henrotin, E.	"The Board of Lady Managers of the Columbian Exposition."
________.	"Opening Address."
Jenkins, S.	"Statement."
Meredith, V.	"The Columbian Exposition."
Mink, P.	"Statement."
Palmer, B.	"Address Delivered by Mrs. Potter Palmer, President of the Board of Lady Managers, on the Occasion of the Opening of the Woman's Building, May 1st, 1893."
________.	"The Board of Lady Managers of the Columbian Exposition."
________.	"Closing Address."
________.	"Welcoming Address."
Park, M.	"Mrs. Park's Greetings for the National League of Women Voters to the Pan-American Conference of Women."
Pena, A.	"Statement."
Phillips, L.	"Chairman's Introduction."
________.	"Chairman's Introduction. Working Session."
Reid, H.	"Introduction to the Forum."
________.	"Introduction to the Forum."
________.	"Opening the Forum."
________.	"Opening the Forum."
________.	"Opening the Forum."
________.	"Welcome to the Delegates."
________.	"Welcome to the Delegates."
Roosevelt, A.	"Opening Address."

Ruckelshaus, J.	"Statement."
Sewall, M.	"Opening Address."
Shaw, A.	"Opening Remarks."
Solomon, H.	"Address."
Stevenson, L.	"Response to an Address of Welcome."
Stone, L.	"Higher Lessons of the World's Fair."
Williams, E.	"Statement."
Wilson, A.	"From Signs of the Times."

WOMEN--ECONOMIC CONDITIONS

Blatch, H.	"Woman as an Economic Factor."
Bristol, A.	"Woman, the New Factor in Economics."
Chisholm, S.	"Economic Justice for Women."
Cleveland, C.	"What Practical Measures Will Promote the Financial Independence of Women."
Cunningham, E.	"Statement."
DeSarem, C.	"Statement."
Elliott, C.	"Theories of Development: An Assessment."
Epstein, C.	"Testimony."
Green, E.	"Statement."
Griffiths, M.	"Opening Statement on Women's Access to Credit and Insurance."
Harmon, M.	"Statement."
Henrotin, E.	"The Financial Independence of Women."
Keyserling, M.	"International Cooperation and Economic Advance of Women."
Kreps, J.	"The Status of Women. The Economic Change."
Miller, F.	"Role of Women in National Economy."
Perkins, S.	"Uses of Money."
Prescott, L.	"The Economic Independence of Women."
Scott, A.	"Public Testimony."
Shack, B.	"Statement."
Stevens, V.	"Public Testimony."

WOMEN--EGYPT

Reed, C.	"Historic Women of Egypt."

WOMEN--EMPLOYMENT

Abbott, G.	"Address at the Women's Industrial Conference."
Anderson, M.	"Closing Statement at the Women's Industrial Conference."
________.	"Post-War Role of American Women."
________.	"Welcoming Address."
________.	"The Women's Bureau and Standards of Women's Work."

Anthony, S.	"Remarks on Women in Industry."
Barrows, A.	"New Professions for Women Centering in the Home. Address to the National-American Woman Suffrage Association Convention of 1900."
Bell, C.	"Alternatives for Social Change: The Future Status of Women."
Berry, B.	"Public Testimony."
Bloodworth, B.	"American Women on the Job."
Bolton, E.	"Have It Your Way: Mid-Career Women and Their Options."
Boulding, E.	"Familial Constraints on Women's Work Roles."
Bowman, G.	"The Trained Women Survives the Depression."
Brady, A.	"Changing Ideals in Southern Women."
________.	"Public Testimony."
Bresette, L.	"Statement."
Bullock, E.	"Industrial Women."
Bushnell, L.	"Would You Believe ... the Secretary of Tomorrow? She Can Reach the Top."
Carroll, M.	"Report of the Findings Committee."
Ceballos, J.	"Public Testimony."
Church, R.	"Keynote Speech for Workshop Session of Labor and Industry Committee of National Council of Negro Women, Washington, D.C., November 10, 1954."
Commander, L.	"The Social Value of the Professional Woman."
Copp, T.	"The Need for Women to Enforce Women's Labor Law."
Cowles, B.	"Report on Labor."
Cox, L.	"Statement."
Dall, C.	"Address at the New England Convention, May, 1859."
Davis, M.	"Public Testimony."
De Fazio, M.	"Public Statement."
Dennett, J.	"Federal Women's Program."
Dickason, G.	"Gains and Goals of Women Workers."
Douty, A.	"Address on Job Opportunities in the Labor Market."
Dunlap, F.	"The Social Result of Legislation Affecting Women Workers."
East, C.	"The Current Status of the Employment of Women."
Epstein, C.	"Closing Remarks to the Conference of Professional and Academic Women."
________.	"Public Testimony."
________.	"Success Motivation and Social Structure; Comments on Women and Achievement."
Field, M.	"Come South, Young Woman."
Gardner, J.	"Breaking Down the Barriers."
Gilson, M.	"What Women Workers Mean to Industry."

Gordon, J.	"Protective Standards for Women Wage Earners."
Graddick, L.	"Statement."
Graves, E.	"Will Women Stay in Industry?"
Gray, V.	"Female Status: A New Population Policy."
Green, I.	"Public Statement."
Greenberg, G.	"Public Testimony."
Hahn, P.	"Public Testimony."
Hansl, E.	"Utilization of Womanpower. An Unnecessary Waste of Human Resources."
Haring, A.	"Public Testimony."
Herberg, D.	"Social Research on Women's Professional Careers."
Hickey, M.	"What's Ahead for Woman Who Earns."
Hilton, M.	"Entry and Reentry of Older Women into Labor Market: Older Women in Labor Force."
________.	"Working Women: Their Home Obligations."
Hoagland, M.	"Labor Legislation for Women."
Howe, F.	"Public Testimony."
________.	"Status of Women in the Academic Profession--Another Perspective."
Hull, J.	"Public Testimony."
Jacobson, C.	"Public Testimony."
Jahoda, M.	"Women in Transition, Social Psychologists' Approach, Summary."
Johns, L.	"Remarks on Women in Industry."
Kanter, R.	"The Policy Issues: Presentation VI."
Katzell, M.	"Opening Remarks (Conference on Women in the Work Force)."
Kelley, F.	"Florence Kelley on Working Girls."
________.	"Home Work."
________.	"Social Standards in Industry: Progress of Labor Legislation for Women."
Keyserling, M.	"American Women at Work, New Challenges and New Responsibilities."
________.	"Challenges Ahead."
________.	"Employment Opportunities for Women."
________.	"Facing Facts About Women's Lives Today."
________.	"New Horizons for Women, Talk."
________.	"New Opportunities and Responsibilities for Women, Convocation Address."
________.	"Recent Federal Employment Policy Developments, New Progress for Women."
________.	"Remarks on Labor Standard Improvement and Greater Employment Opportunity."
________.	"Research and Your Job."
________.	"The Socioeconomic Waste: Underutilization of Women."
________.	"Womanpower Needed."
________.	"Women Wage Earners, New Challenges and Opportunities."
________.	"Your Talents, Let's Not Waste Them."

Klotzburger, K.	"The Position of Women in Their Professional Associations."
________.	"Public Testimony."
Kluckhohn, F.	"Horizons for Women, American Woman's Role."
Koester, M.	"Statement."
Koontz, E.	"American Women at Crossroads."
________.	"Speech at Windham College."
________.	"Women in the Labor Force."
Kreps, J.	"Six Cliches in Search of a Woman; Happily Ever After."
________.	"Women in Academia: Today Is Different."
Kyrk, H.	"Family Responsibilities of Earning Women."
Lake, L.	"Is Labor Dignified?"
Laughlin, G.	"Conditions of Wage-Earning Women."
Laws, J.	"Work Aspiration of Women: False Leads and New Starts."
Leach, R.	"Training on the Job After College."
________.	"Women and the Top Jobs."
Leopold, A.	"The Challenge of Tomorrow. Womanpower."
________.	"Role of Mature Woman in Economy."
________.	"Welcome Address at Conference on Effective Use of Womanpower, March 10-11, 1955."
________.	"Womanpower in Changing World."
________.	"Women's New Role on International Scene."
Leopold, S.	"Women Wage-Workers: With Reference to Directing Immigrants."
Lervold, L.	"Public Testimony."
Livermore, M.	"Industrial Gains of Women During the Last Half-Century."
Long, N.	"The Policy Issues: Presentation II."
Lowther, D.	"Summary of February 17 Evening Session."
McDowell, M.	"The Need for Women to Enforce Women's Labor Laws."
________.	"Work for Normal Young Working Women."
MacLean, A.	"Abstract of an Address on Industrial Conditions for Women."
Magee, E.	"Role of Women's Legislation in Meeting Basic Problems of Working Conditions."
________.	"The Role of Women's Legislation in Meeting Basic Problems of Working Conditions."
Maguire, M.	"Public Testimony."
Manning, C.	"The Industrial Woman Looks at the Problems."
Margolin, O.	"Working Women: Their Citizenship Responsibilities."
Matthews, E.	"Employment Implications of Psychological Characteristics of Men and Women."
Miller, F.	"Older Women Workers, Statement at Public Hearing of New York State Joint Legislative Committee on Problems of the Aging, December 14, 1950, in New York City."
________.	"Patterns of Women in Industry."

________.	"War and Postwar Adjustments of Women Workers."
________.	"Where Do We Stand on Minimum Wage."
________.	"Who Works, Where and Why."
Millett, K.	"The Status of Women in the Academic Profession."
Mills, T.	"Summary of February 17 Morning Session."
Milner, E.	"Public Testimony."
Molamphy, T.	"Statement."
Myerson, B.	"Women and the Employment Agencies."
Nestor, A.	"The Need for Women to Enforce Women's Labor Laws."
________.	"Statement."
Norton, E.	"The Challenge to Women--Organizing Around an Issue."
Norwood, J.	"The Policy Issues: Presentation V."
Odencrantz, L.	"Statement."
Penna, Z.	"Public Testimony."
Perkins, F.	"The Future of the Woman Who Works for Wages."
________.	"Labor Day Address Over Columbia Broadcasting System Network, September 6, 1943."
________.	"Labor Day Address Over Columbia Broadcasting System Network, September 4, 1944."
________.	"Women Workers."
Peterson, E.	"Address on Modern American Woman, Status and Opportunity."
________.	"Address on Woman's Status in Industry, Business, Society, Etc."
________.	"Address on Work Opportunities Through Education."
________.	"Let's Look Ahead."
Phillips, L.	"Will the Professional Woman Progress or Perish?"
Phillips, M.	"Public Testimony."
Plebanek, T.	"Youth in Industry."
Potts, E.	"Woman's Work in Kentucky."
Prewitt, L.	"The Employment Rights of the Female: The Present Challenge."
Ravner, P.	"Entry and Reentry of Older Women into Labor Market: Psychological Barriers to Employment of Mature Women."
Richman, J.	"Women Wage-Workers: With Reference to Directing Immigrants."
Ripley, M.	"Employment of Married Women in the Public Schools."
Rittenhouse, I.	"Commentary on the Role of Women's Legislation in Meeting Basic Problems of Working Conditions."
Robertson, A.	"Remarks."
Robins, M.	"What Industry Means to Women Workers."

Robinson, M.	"Peculiar Insecurities of Women as Workers."
Sandler, B.	"The Policy Issues: Presentation IV."
Sands, S.	"Public Testimony."
Saporta, S.	"The Status of Women in Art."
Sassower, D.	"Women in the Professions."
Schepps, M.	"Senators vs. Working Women."
Schneiderman, R.	"Remarks."
Scott, M.	"Labor Legislation for Women."
Segal, T.	"Public Testimony."
Seymour, M.	"Occupations of Women to Date."
Shaeffer, R.	"The Policy Issues: Presentation I."
Sherman, J.	"A New Field for Women."
Silva, V.	"Public Testimony."
Spain, J.	"Job-Stereotyping: A Time for Change."
Stanton, E.	"On Labor." (Summer, 1868) Edited by Ellen DuBois.
Stanton, H.	"Public Testimony."
Stead, B.	"Why Help Women Into Careers? A Look at Today's Reality."
Stone, L.	"Comments at the Syracuse National Convention, September 1852."
Stooms, L.	"Opportunities for Women in the Food Industries."
Swartz, M.	"Statement."
Torton, I.	"Public Testimony."
Troxell, M.	"Changing Status of Women."
Upton, H.	"Address."
Valentine, H.	"How to Keep More of the Money You Earn. The Status of Women in Industry."
Van Kleeck, M.	"What Industry Means to Women Workers."
________.	"The Working Woman and the New Social Vision."
Warren, C.	"For What Are We Educating Women?"
Warshay, D.	"Women and Their Work Roles."
Wells, J.	"Woman and Girls in Labor Market Today and Tomorrow."
Williamson, M.	"Industrial and Business Relations."
Winslow, M.	"The Effect of Labor Laws on Women Workers."
________.	"Married Women in Industry."
Woodhouse, C.	"Training on the Job While in College."
________.	"Why the Conference."
Woodward, E.	"Womanpower."
Zapoleon, M.	"College Women and Employment."

WOMEN--EUROPE

Schoonmaker, N.	"The New Woman in the New Europe."

WOMEN--FRANCE

Davis, N. "City Women and Religious Change in Sixteenth-Century France."

WOMEN--GREAT BRITAIN

Fairbanks, C. "Some English Women of the Eighteenth Century."

WOMEN--GUATEMALA

Chinchilla, N. "Industrialization, Monopoly Capitalism, and Women's Work in Guatemala."

WOMEN--HEALTH AND HYGIENE

Holcombe, E. "Physical Decline of Leisure-class American Women. A Paper Read Before the Woman's Alliance of Syracuse and Other Clubs, and Published by Request."

WOMEN--HISTORIOGRAPHY

Johaneson, S. "Herstory as History: A New Field or Another Fad?"

Lerner, G. "Placing Women in History: A 1975 Perspective."

Rossi, A. "Feminist History in Perspective: Sociological Contributions to Biographic Analysis."

Sklar, K. "Four Levels of Women's History."

WOMEN--HISTORY

Anthony, S. "Address to the National Delegates Before the First Joint Convention with the American Woman Suffrage Association, 1890."

Beard, M. "What Nobody Seems to Know About Woman. Radio Address, 1950."

________. "Woman--the Pioneer. Radio Address, 1939."

Beecher, C. "The Evils Suffered by American Women and American Children: The Causes and the Remedy, Presented in an Address by Miss C. E. Beecher, to Meetings of Ladies in Cincinnati, Washington, Baltimore, Philadelphia, New York, and Other Cities."

Blake, L. "Our Forgotten Foremothers."

Catt, C.	"Forward or Backward?"
Corbin, C.	"The Higher Womanhood."
Denison, D.	"The Long Path."
Du Mars, M.	"No Rocking Chair Age. A Challenge to American Women of Today."
Gardener, H.	"Woman as an Annex."
Green, A.	"Woman's Awakenment."
Grinnell, K.	"Woman in an Ideal Government."
Hauser, R.	"The Challenge to Women Today."
Hickey, M.	"Bound for the Future. Women's Responsibility for the Future."
Horton, M.	"Woman's Responsibility Today. An American Woman's Viewpoint."
Howe, J.	"Address by the President."
Howell, M.	"Gains of the Last Three Years."
Hurst, F.	"Crisis in the History of Women. Let Us Have Action Instead of Lip-Service."
Keller, S.	"The Future Role of Women."
Kessler-Harris, A.	"Women, Work, and the Social Order."
Kleinberg, S.	"The Systematic Study of Urban Women."
Leopold, A.	"Speech Before Girl's Nation, August 3, 1954."
________.	"Welcome."
Livermore, M.	"Superfluous Women."
Meyering, A.	"Women in Families and History."
Mitchell, M.	"Address of the President."
Owen, R.	"Place of Women in the Present Crisis."
Porter, F.	"The Power of Womanliness in Dealing with Stern Problems."
Robinson, L.	"Chairman's Introduction. Women in a Changing World."
Sewall, M.	"Culture--Its Fruit and Its Price."
Sherman, C.	"Characteristics of the Modern Woman."
Smith, M.	"Woman, the Key Individual of Our Democracy. Think Well, Then Speak Your Mind."
Stanton, E.	"Closing Address."
Thompson, C.	"Women's Status--Yesterday, Today, Tomorrow. A Chapter in the History of Freedom, 1848-1948."
Wegny, L.	"The Role of Women in the World of Today. No Longer Necessary to Try to Emulate Men."

WOMEN--INDONESIA

Stoler, A.	"Class Structure and Female Autonomy in Rural Java."
Vogel, L.	"Hearts to Feel and Tongues to Speak: New England Mill Women in the Early Nineteenth Century."

WOMEN--ITALY

Di Brazza Savorghan, C.	"The Italian Woman in the Country."
Yans-McLaughlin, V.	"Italian Women and Work: Experience and Perception."

WOMEN--KANSAS

Ware, J.	"What the Women of Kansas Are Doing Today."

WOMEN--LEGAL STATUS, LAWS, ETC.

Beard, M.	"Report of the Manifesto Committee."
Blake, L.	"Legal Disabilities."
Caplan, S.	"Public Testimony."
Conlin, R.	"Government Policy and the Legal Status of Women."
Everett, G.	"Civil and Political Rights--Where Are We Now?"
Gage, F.	"Address at the Woman's Rights Convention, in New York, September 1853."
________.	"3rd Address to the 1st Annual Meeting of the American Equal Rights Association, May 1867."
Gage, M.	"Remarks on Legal Disabilities at the Woman's Rights State Convention, Rochester, N. Y., November 30, 1853."
Giddings, M.	"Report on the Common Law."
Gillett, E.	"Legal Rights of a Married Woman in Her Husband's Property."
Greene, M.	"Legal Condition of Woman in 1492-1892."
Hooker, I.	"The Constitutional Rights of Women in the United States."
Hunt, H.	"Reprint of Remarks by Dr. Hunt in the Tribune, September 12, 1853 (New York)."
Jones, E.	"Remarks at the 10th National Woman's Rights Convention, N. Y., 1860."
Meacham, C.	"The Law: Where It Is and Where It's Going."
Mott, L.	"Comments on Women's Property Rights at Westchester (Penn.) Convention, June, 1852."
Nichols, C.	"Comments at the Syracuse National Convention, September 1852."
Peck, M.	"Law and Women."
Rose, E.	"Remarks at the Woman's Rights Convention in New York, September 1853."
________.	"Remarks on Wills at the Woman's Rights Convention, in New York, September 1853."

________.	"Remove the Legal Shackles from Women."
________.	"Reprint of Remarks by Mrs. Rose in the Tribune, September 12, 1853."
Seidenberg, F.	"Family, Property, and Domicile Law in the State of New York."
Stanton, E.	"The Matriarchate, or Mother-Age."
Stone, L.	"Address."
________.	"Remarks on the Case of Mrs. Norton at the Woman's Rights Convention in N. Y., September 1853."
________.	"Reprint of Remarks in the (New York) Tribune, September 12, 1853."
Strickland, M.	"Woman's Position and Influence in the Civil Law."

WOMEN--OREGON

Duniway, A.	"Women in Oregon History. Address at the Celebration of Oregon's Fortieth Anniversary, January 14, 1899."
Wilson, E.	"Pioneer Woman of Oregon."

WOMEN--PSYCHOLOGY

Anastasi, A.	"Psychological Differences Between Men and Women."
Bardwick, J.	"The Dynamics of Successful People."
Fried, E.	"The Fear of Loving."
Gardner, J.	"The Psychology and the Psychological Effects of Discrimination."
Grimm, E.	"Women's Attitudes and Reactions to Childbearing."
Guber, S.	"Sex Role and the Feminine Personality."
Hoffman, L.	"Psychology Looks at the Female."
________.	"A Re-Examination of the Fear of Success."
Kennard, B.	"Emotional Life of Girls."
Riger, S.	"The Effects of Participation in Women's Consciousness-Raising Groups."
Sachs, B.	"Discussion of the Psychological and Physiological Aspects of Woman and the Role They Play in Her Destiny."
Schaefer, L.	"Frigidity."
Shainess, N.	"A Psychiatrist's View: Images of Woman--Past and Present, Overt and Obscured."
Spiegel, R.	"Depressions and the Feminine Situation."
Steinmann, A.	"Public Testimony."
Thompson, C.	"Women in the American Culture."
Weisstein, N.	"Kinder, Kuche, Kirche as Scientific Law: Psychology Constructs the Female."

WOMEN--RUSSIA

Atkinson, D.	"Society and the Sexes in the Russian Past."
Chapman, J.	"Equal Pay for Equal Work?"
Dunn, E.	"Russian Rural Women."
Farnsworth, B.	"Bolshevik Alternatives and the Soviet Family: The 1926 Marriage Law Debate."
Glickman, R.	"The Russian Factory Woman, 1880-1914."
Lapidus, G.	"Sexual Equality in Soviet Policy: A Developmental Perspective."
Madison, B.	"Social Services for Women: Problems and Priorities."
Rosenhan, M.	"Images of Male and Female in Children's Readers."
Shulman, C.	"The Individual and the Collective."

WOMEN--SOCIAL CONDITIONS

Louchheim, K.	"Citizen in a Changing World: Women of Today."
Louis, M.	"Woman--The Inciter to Reform."
Lyells, R.	"Woman-Power for a Better World. Civilizing Influence in a Man's World."
Norton, E.	"A Strategy for Change."
Palmer, S.	"Is Woman the Weaker Vessel?"
Parr, M.	"World Harvest: Woman's Talent, Woman's Role in the Changing World."
Roosevelt, A.	"The American Woman's Place in the World Today."
Thompson, D.	"The Changing Status of Women."

WOMEN--SOCIAL LIFE & CUSTOMS

Hanna, I.	"Ethics of Social Life."

WOMEN--SOCIETIES AND CLUBS

Addams, J.	"Women's Clubs and Public Policies."
Bacon, G.	"Report of the Local Biennial Board."
Brown, C.	"The Illinois Woman's Alliance."
Cole, I.	"Address of Welcome."
Croly, J.	"Women's Clubs."
Davis, I.	"The King's Daughters."
Decker, S.	"Report of the President."
________.	"Response to Addresses of Welcome."
Denison, D.	"Report of Foreign Correspondent."
Diaz, A.	"Work of Women's Educational and Industrial Union."
Dibert, F.	"Building Junior Membership."
Dickinson, L.	"Greetings from the General Federation of Women's Clubs."

Dickinson, M.	"The King's Daughters."
Edison, M.	"Address of Welcome."
Flint, M.	"The Value of the Eastern Star as a Factor in Giving Women a Better Understanding of Business Affairs, and Especially Those Relating to Legislative Matters."
Frazar, C.	"The Moral Education Society of Boston."
Gaffney, F.	"Report of the National Council of the United States."
Hafford, L.	"Legislative Councils."
Homes, E.	"The Working Girl's or Working Women's Club in the United States."
Hooker, I.	"The Queen Isabella Association."
Howe, J.	"Greeting to the 9th Biennial Convention of the General Federation of Women's Clubs, June 23, 1908."
Jennings, M.	"Report of the First Vice President."
Lake, H.	"Report of Outlook Committee."
Learned, L.	"Results of Club Life Among Women Upon the Home."
Mac Quillin, L.	"Club House Manager."
O'Leary, H.	"The Ladies' Physiological Institute of Boston."
Park, M.	"Address of the President."
________.	"Address of the President."
________.	"Greetings from National League of Women Voters."
________.	"President's Address."
________.	"President's Address."
Parker, V.	"The Yesterday, Today and Tomorrow of the National Council of Women."
Peterson, E.	"Address of Women & Their Accomplishments Through National and International Women's Organizations."
Plummer, M.	"Report of Corresponding Secretary, General Federation of Women's Clubs."
Poole, H.	"Difficulties and Delights of Women's Clubs."
Ruhl, J.	"Report of Mrs. Julia A. Ruhl, Chairman Membership Committee."
Sherwin, B.	"Address of the President. The Way of the League."
________.	"Among the Pillars of Society."
________.	"Facing the Future."
________.	"Pointing the Way in 1933. Address of the President."
________.	"Ten Years of Growth."
Snedden, M.	"The Eastern Star, Its Origin, Progress, and Development."
Talbot, M.	"The History, Aims, and Methods of the Association of Collegiate Alumnae."
Thomas, M.	"The Work of Sorosis."
Ward, M.	"Address of Welcome to the 9th Biennial Convention of the General Federation of Women's Clubs."

________. "Report of Inter Federation Committee."
Wiles, A. "National Society U. S. Daughters of 1812."
Williamson, M. "Committee on Industrial and Business Relations."
Winter, A. "President's Report 1920-1922."
Wood, M. "Report of Bureau of Information."
Woodward, J. "Woman's Clubs from a Reporter's Point of View."

WOMEN--SOUTHERN STATES

Douglass, J. "The Young Woman of the South."
Kearney, B. "Kearney's Speech on the South."

WOMEN--SUFFRAGE

Addams, J. "The Modern City and the Municipal Franchise for Women."
________. "Remarks."
________. "Speech."
________. "Testimony."
Allen, N. "Testimony at a Hearing of the U. S. Senate, Committee on the Judiciary, January 23, 1880."
Anthony, S. "Address."
________. "Address on the Amendment of the Rochester, N. Y. City Charter, December 12, 1892."
________. "Address to a Congressional Hearing, March, 1884."
________. "Address to a Convention in Hartford, Connecticut, October 1869."
________. "Address to a Convention of Bricklayers' and Masons' International Union, Rochester, N. Y., January 13, 1900."
________. "Address to a Hearing of the Congressional Committee on the District of Columbia, 1870."
________. "Address to a Hearing of the Joint Committee of Congress of the District of Columbia, January 22, 1870."
________. "Address to a Senate Committee, February 1900."
________. "Address to an Equal Rights Meeting, Albany, November 21, 1866."
________. "Address to Congress, Adopted by the Eleventh National Woman's Rights Convention, Held in New York City, Thursday, May 10, 1866."
________. "Address to Congress, Read at the 1866 Woman's Rights Convention."
________. "Address to Her 80th Birthday Celebration, February 15, 1900."

________. "Address to the Judiciary Committee of the House, March 8, 1884."

________. "Address to the National Woman Suffrage Convention, May 10, 1870."

________. "Address to the Second National Woman Suffrage Association Convention, January 19, 1870."

________. "Address to the Senate Committee on Woman Suffrage, March 7, 1884."

________. "Address to the Senate Judiciary Committee, January 12, 1872."

________. "Address to the Senate Judiciary Committee, January 17, 1872."

________. "Address to the 3rd Anniversary Meeting of the Equal Rights Association, May 12, 1869."

________. "Address to the 31st Annual Convention of the National American Woman Suffrage Association, April 27, 1899."

________. "Address to the 33rd Annual Convention of the National American Woman Suffrage Association, May 30, 1901."

________. "Address to the Woman's Rights Convention, N. Y., May 10, 1866."

________. "Anthony Explains the National's Strategy."

________. "Anthony on the Ballot and Women's Wages."

________. "Anthony's Remarks."

________. "Anthony's Speech."

________. "Closing Address at the 16th Annual Convention of the National Woman Suffrage Association, March, 1884."

________. "Constitutional Argument. Delivered in Twenty-nine of the Post-Office Districts of Monroe, and Twenty-one of Ontario, in Miss Anthony's Canvass of Those Counties Prior to Her Trial in June 1873."

________. "Debate at the 1893 Convention of the National American Woman Suffrage Association."

________. "Debate with Judge Hunt at Her Trial for Voting, June 1873."

________. "Demand for Party Recognition. Delivered in Kansas City at the Opening of the Campaign, May 4, 1894."

________. "Discussion of Resolutions at the 11th National Woman's Rights Convention, May 10, 1866."

________. "1873 Trial for Voting, Rochester, N. Y."

________. "Failure Is Impossible, Last Public Speech at Her 86th Birthday Celebration, February 15, 1906."

________. "History of the Fourteenth Amendment. Address to the National Suffrage Convention of 1889."

______. "Is It a Crime for a United States Citizen to Vote?"

______. "Last Address to the 1906 National American Woman Suffrage Association Convention."

______. "Opening Address at the National-American Woman Suffrage Association Convention of 1900."

______. "Opening Address at the National Woman Suffrage Association Convention, January 16, 1873."

______. "Political Enfranchisement of Women."

______. "Position of Women in the Political Life of the United States. Address to the International Council of Women in London, 1899."

______. "Presentation of Carrie Chapman Catt as Her Successor as President of the National American Woman Suffrage Association, 1900."

______. "President's Address at the National-American Woman Suffrage Association Convention of 1896."

______. "President's Address to the 5th Annual Convention National Woman's Suffrage Association, Washington, D. C., January 16, 1873."

______. "President's Address to the National-American Woman Suffrage Association Convention of 1897."

______. "President's Address to the National-American Woman Suffrage Association Convention of 1899."

______. "Public Address, 1894 on Political Parties Support for Suffrage."

______. "Reconstruction. Address Delivered at Ottumwa, Kansas, July 4, 1865."

______. "Remarks at a W. C. T. U. National Convention in Cleveland, November 1895."

______. "Remarks at the 1894 Convention of the National American Woman Suffrage Association."

______. "Remarks at Her 70th Birthday Celebration, February 15, 1890."

______. "Remarks Before a Senate Committee, 1902."

______. "Remarks During Debate on Resolution Denouncing Dogmas and Creeds at the 17th National Convention of the National Woman Suffrage Association, January 1885."

______. "Report on the International Council of Women in London to the 32nd Annual Convention of the National American Woman Suffrage Association, February 1900."

________. "Resignation Speech at the 32nd Annual Convention of the National American Woman Suffrage Association, Washington, D. C., February 1900."

________. "Resolution for a Federal Amendment at May 1863 Meeting of the Women's Loyal League."

________. "Response to Greeting of South Carolina at the National-American Woman Suffrage Association Convention of 1894."

________. "Response to Tribune at Reception in Honor of Her 63rd Birthday, Philadelphia, February 15, 1883."

________. "Secretary's Report at the 1st Annual Meeting of the American Equal Rights Association, May 1867."

________. "Social Purity. First Delivered at Chicago in the Spring of 1875, in the Sunday Afternoon Dime Lecture Course."

________. "Statement of Support for the Populists at Their 1894 Convention."

________. "Woman Wants Bread, Not the Ballot!"

________. "Women's Declaration of Rights."

Arnold, B. "Appeal to Lafayette at a Demonstration at the Lafayette Monument, September 16, 1918."

Barton, C. "Address at the National American Woman Suffrage Convention of 1902."

Bass, Z. "Address at a Hearing of the Senate Committee on Woman Suffrage, December 15, 1915."

Bates, O. "Municipal Suffrage for Women in Michigan."

Beard, M. "Address at a Hearing of the House Committee on Rules, December 3, 1913."

________. "Address at a Hearing of the House Judiciary Committee, March 3, 1914."

________. "Statement to the House Committee on Woman Suffrage."

Blackwell, A. "Address at a Hearing of the House Committee on Rules, December 1913."

________. "Address at the 7th Annual Meeting of the American Woman Suffrage Association, 1875."

________. "Address to the House Judiciary Committee, February 17, 1892."

________. "The Indifference of Women. Address to the House Judiciary Committee, February 15, 1898."

Blake, L. "Address to the New York City Suffrage Society, Union League Theatre, April 19, 1876."

________. "The Constitutional Argument. Address to the House Judiciary Committee, 1900."

________.	"Satire on the Rights of Men, Presented to the National Suffrage Convention, January 1887."
________.	"Testimony at a Hearing of the House Committee on the Judiciary, January 24, 1880."
Blatch, H.	"Address at a Protest Meeting--Headquarters of the National Women's Party, 1917."
Blount, A.	"Address to the Senate Committee, April 19, 1910."
Bones, M.	"Address to the Constitutional Convention of the Dakota Territory, September 1883."
Branham, L.	"Speech While Burning President Wilson's Message at Demonstration at Lafayette Monument, September 16, 1918."
Breckinridge, D.	"Address at a Hearing of the House Committee on Rules, December 3, 1913."
Brown, O.	"Address to a Hearing of the Congressional Committee on Privileges and Elections, January 1878."
________.	"Debate at the 2nd Annual Meeting of the American Equal Rights Association, May 14, 1868."
________.	"Foreign Rule. Address to the National Woman Suffrage Association Convention of 1889."
________.	"Olympia Brown's Attack on Immigrants, Given at the National Woman Suffrage Association's Convention in 1889."
________.	"On the Foreign Menace."
Burleigh, C.	"Woman's Rights to Be a Woman. Address at the American Woman Suffrage Association Convention, 1870."
Burns, L.	"Speech Summing Up Case for Suffragists Arrested for Picketing the White House, July 4, 1917."
________.	"Speech to the National American Woman Suffrage Association Convention, December 1913."
Calkins, M.	"Address at the College Evening of the 38th Annual Convention of the National American Woman Suffrage Association, February 8, 1906."
Cannon, M.	"Woman Suffrage in Utah. Address to the House Judiciary Committee February 15, 1898."
Catt, C.	"Acceptance Speech on Being Elected President of the National American Woman Suffrage Association, February 1900."
________.	"Address at a Hearing of the House Committee on Rules, December 3, 1913."
________.	"Address at a Hearing of the House Judiciary Committee, December 16, 1915."

________. "Address at the Last or Victory Convention of the National American Woman Suffrage Association, February 1920."

________. "Address Before a House Committee, 1904."

________. "Address of Mrs. Carrie Chapman Catt at Senate Hearing, December 15, 1915."

________. "Address to the Executive Council of the National American Woman Suffrage Association, at the 1916 Convention."

________. "Address to the Kiwanis Club of Nashville, Tennessee, 1920."

________. "Address to the National American Woman Suffrage Association Convention of 1897."

________. "Address to the 1916 Convention of the National Woman Suffrage Association Convention."

________. "Address to the National American Woman Suffrage Association Convention of 1920."

________. "Carrie Chapman Catt Addresses Congress."

________. "Carrie Chapman Catt Describes the Opposition."

________. "Danger to Our Government."

________. "For the Sake of Liberty."

________. "Only Yesterday."

________. "Presentation of Gift to Miss Anthony, at the National American Woman Suffrage Association Convention of 1900."

________. "President's Annual Address."

________. "Report on Work in Arizona to the National-American Woman Suffrage Association Convention of 1899."

________. "Report on Work in Oklahoma at the National-American Woman Suffrage Association Convention of 1899."

________. "Report to the National-American Woman Suffrage Association Convention of 1916."

________. "Statement by Mrs. Carrie Chapman Catt at Senate Hearings of 1910."

________. "Suffrage Militancy."

________. "Why We Ask for the Submission of an Amendment. Address to the National-American Woman Suffrage Association Convention of 1900."

________. "The World Movement for Woman Suffrage 1904 to 1911: Is Woman Suffrage Progressing?"

Chace, E. "Report to the American Woman Suffrage Association on the Work of the Rhode Island Association, Philadelphia, 1876."

Chapman, M. "Equal Suffrage as Related to the Purity Movement."

________. "Women as Capitalists and Taxpayers."

Churchill, E. "Remarks at the Semi-Annual Meeting of the American Woman Suffrage Association, N. Y., May 1871."

Clarke, H. "Remarks at the 1st Annual Meeting of the American Woman Suffrage Association, Cleveland, Ohio, November 1870."

Clay, L. "Address of Greeting to the National American Convention of 1911."

________. "Fitness of Women to Become Citizens from the Standpoint of Physical Development."

Clay, M. "Address to the Judiciary Committee of the House, March 8, 1884."

Colby, C. "Address to the House Judiciary Committee, February 20, 1886."

________. "Resolutions at the Memorial Services of the National-American Woman Suffrage Association Convention of 1898."

Conine, M. "Address to the National-American Woman Suffrage Association Convention of 1898 from Colorado."

Couzins, P. "Address on the Fifteenth Amendment to a Meeting of the St. Louis Woman Suffrage Association."

________. "Address to the National Woman Suffrage Association Convention, January 1882."

________. "Address to the 3rd Annual Meeting of the American Equal Rights Association, N. Y., May 1869."

________. "Testimony at a Hearing of the House Committee on the Judiciary, January 24, 1880."

________. "Welcoming Address at the Annual Convention of the National Woman Suffrage Association, St. Louis, Missouri, May 1879."

Curtis, E. "Are Women Represented in Our Government?"

________. "Universal Suffrage. Address to the National-American Woman Suffrage Association Convention of 1896."

Cutler, H. "Address to the Convention of the American Woman Suffrage Association, N. Y., May 1870."

________. "Remarks at the 4th Annual Meeting of the American Woman Suffrage Association, 1872."

________. "Reply to the Paper of Catherine E. Beecher, Convention of the American Woman Suffrage Association, N. Y., May 1870."

________. "Speech at the National Convention at Cincinnati, Ohio, October 1855."

Darwin, M. "Woman's Right to Serve Her Country."

Davis, P. "President's Address at the 20th Anniversary Convention, N. Y., October 1870."

Dennett, M.	"Report of the Corresponding Secretary to the National-American Woman Suffrage Association Convention of 1913."
Dickinson, A.	"Address to the Chicago Woman Suffrage Convention, 1869."
Dietrick, E.	"The Best Methods of Interesting Woman in Suffrage, Address to the National-American Convention of 1893."
Duffy, M.	"Address Before State Suffrage Hearing, Albany, N.Y., February 1907."
________.	"Mary Duffy Speaks Before the Legislature."
Duniway, A.	"Address to the National-American Woman Suffrage Association Convention of 1895."
________.	"Address to the State Constitutional Convention, Boise, Idaho, July 16, 1889."
________.	"Ballots and Bullets."
________.	"How to Win the Ballot."
________.	"Success in Sight."
Eastman, C.	"Address at a Hearing of the House Judiciary Committee, March 3, 1914."
Eastman, M.	"Speech at the 7th Annual Meeting of the American Woman Suffrage Association, 1875."
________.	"Speech at the 9th Annual Meeting of the American Woman Suffrage Association, 1878."
Everett, M.	"School Suffrage in Massachusetts."
Field, K.	"A Talk."
Field, S.	"Speech Representing a Deputation of 300 Women to President Wilson, January 9, 1917."
Fisher, K.	"Speech at Dinner in Honor of Released Prisoners, 1917."
Funk, A.	"Presentation of the Shafroth-Palmer Amendment to the National American Woman Suffrage Association Convention of 1914."
________.	"Report of Campaign Work to the National American Woman Suffrage Association Convention of 1914."
________.	"Report of the Congressional Committee to the National American Woman Suffrage Association Convention of 1915."
Gage, F.	"Second Address to the 1st Annual Meeting of the American Equal Rights Association, May 1867."
Gage, M.	"Address at a Hearing of the Congressional Committee on Privileges and Elections, January 1878."
________.	"Address at the National American Woman Suffrage Association in Washington, D.C., 1884."
________.	"Address to the 5th Annual National Woman's Suffrage Association Convention, Washington, D.C., January, 1872."

________.	"Address to the National Woman Suffrage Association Convention of 1887."
________.	"Annual Report to the 5th Annual National Woman Suffrage Association Convention, Washington, D. C., January 1873."
________.	"Argument for Woman's Suffrage, 1886."
________.	"President's Address at the National Woman Suffrage Association Convention, Washington, D. C., January 1876."
________.	"Review of the Decision in Virginia Minor's Court Case at Convention in Washington, 1875."
________.	"Testimony at a Hearing of the House Judiciary Committee, January 24, 1880."
Gano, E.	"Address to the Senate Committee, April 19, 1910."
Gilman, C.	"Duty and Honor. Address to the National-American Woman Suffrage Association Convention of 1897."
Gordon, K.	"Report of Committee on Enrollment."
Gougar, H.	"Address to the Senate Committee on Woman Suffrage, March 7, 1884."
Greenleaf, J.	"Address to the House Judiciary Committee, February 17, 1892."
Grew, M.	"Address to the Semi-Annual Meeting of the American Woman Suffrage Association, N. Y., May 1871."
Griffing, J.	"Mrs. Griffing's Report of 1871 Work to the National Woman Suffrage Association, May 11, 1871."
Haggart, M.	"Address to the House Judiciary Committee, March 8, 1884."
Hansford, P.	"Address to Convention of the American Woman Suffrage Association, N. Y., May 1870."
Harbert, E.	"Address at a Hearing of the Congressional Committee on Privileges and Elections, January 1878."
Harper, I.	"Address at a Hearing of the House Committee on Rules, December 3, 1913."
________.	"Report to the National American Convention of 1918-1919."
Hauser, E.	"Headquarters Report for 1906."
Hay, M.	"Address to the National American Woman Suffrage Association Convention of 1917."
Hazard, R.	"Speech at the 10th Annual Meeting of the American Woman Suffrage Association, 1879."
Henry, J.	"Woman Suffrage in the South. Address to the National-American Woman Suffrage Association Convention of 1895."
Hilles, F.	"Defense Speech at Trial for Picketing White House, 1917."

Hooker, I. "Address of Mrs. Isabella Beecher Hooker."

________. "Address to the Judiciary Committee, U.S. Senate, January 17, 1872."

________. "Message of Thanks to Members of Congressional Committee Supporting Cause."

________. "Mrs. Hooker Presents Thanks to Members of Congress on Behalf of the National Woman Suffrage and Educational Committee, 1871."

________. "Report of the Year's Work to the National Woman's Suffrage Association Convention, January 1872."

Howe, J. "Address at the 2nd Session the American Woman Suffrage Association Convention, N.Y., May 1870."

________. "Address of the American Woman Suffrage Association Convention, N.Y., May 1870."

________. "Annual Address to the 6th Annual Meeting of the American Woman Suffrage Association, October 1874."

________. "Benefits of Suffrage for Women."

________. "Boston a Little Island of Darkness. Speech at a Suffrage Hearing at the State House in Boston, February 4, 1908."

________. "The Chivalry of Reform. Address to the National American Woman Suffrage Association Convention, 1890."

________. "Extemporaneous Speech Made at a Suffrage Hearing, February 1884."

________. "Hearing of Massachusetts Legislature, February 1900."

________. "How to Extend the Sympathies of Women."

________. "Let There Be Light."

________. "The Moral Initiative as Belonging to Women."

________. "The Patience of Faith."

________. "The Position of Women in Plato's Republic."

________. "President's Address to the American Woman Suffrage Association, 6th Annual Meeting, October 1874."

________. "The Relation of the Woman Suffrage Movement to Other Reforms."

________. "Speech at a Suffrage Hearing Before the Massachusetts Legislature."

________. "Speech at Legislative Hearing."

________. "Speech at Meeting of the American Woman Suffrage Association, Philadelphia, July 1876."

________. "Speech at the Annual Meeting of an Equal Suffrage Association, 1895."

________. "Speech on Equal Rights."

________. "Why Are Women the Natural Guardians of Social Morals."

Hunt, H. "Annual Protest on Taxation Read at the Woman's Rights Convention in N. Y., September 1853."

Jacobs, P. "Address at a Hearing of the Senate Committee on Woman Suffrage, December 15, 1915."

Johns, L. "Municipal Suffrage."

Jones, J. "Report of May 16th, 1861 to the National Convention."

Kearney, B. "The South and Woman Suffrage."

Kelley, F. "Address to the House Judiciary Committee, April 19, 1910."

________. "Working Woman's Need of the Ballot."

________. "The Young Breadwinners' Need of Women's Enfranchisement."

Ketcham, E. "Are Women Citizens and People?"

Langhorne, O. "Testimony to the Senate."

Latimer, E. "Address at the Columbia Theatre in Washington, November 15, 1914."

Laughlin, G. "Address at a Procession of Suffragists, at the Panama-Pacific Exposition of 1915."

Lewis, H. "Testimony to the Senate."

Lippincott, S. "Tribute to Pioneers of Suffrage Movement."

Livermore, M. "Address to the Convention of the American Woman Suffrage Association, N. Y., May 1870."

________. "Debate at the 3rd Annual Meeting of the American Equal Rights Association, N. Y., May 1869."

Lockwood, B. "Annual Report to the 8th Annual Convention of the National Woman Suffrage Association, Washington, D. C., January 1876."

Longley, M. "Remarks at the 4th Annual Meeting of the American Woman Suffrage Association, 1872."

Lowe, C. "Address to a Joint Hearing of the Senate Judiciary Committee and the Senate Committee on Woman Suffrage, March 13, 1912."

________. "On Behalf of 7,000,000 Wage-Earning Women...."

Ludington, K. "Address Before Annual Convention." (Connecticut Woman Suffrage Convention).

________. "Address for a Deputation of Connecticut Women to the Chairman of the Republican Party, Will Hays, August, 1920."

McCormick, R. "Report of Special Campaign Committee to the National American Woman Suffrage Association Convention of 1914."

________. "Report of the Campaign Committee to the National American Woman Suffrage Association Convention of 1914."

McCulloch, C.	"The Protective Power of the Ballot. Address to the House Judiciary Committee, 1900."
McRae, E.	"Testimony at a Hearing of the House Committee on the Judiciary, January 24, 1880."
Marble, E.	"Address."
Meriwether, L.	"Address to the House Judiciary Committee, February 17, 1892."
Minor, V.	"Opening Address to the Convention of the Woman Suffrage Association of Missouri, St. Louis, October, 1869."
Mott, L.	"Remarks at the 1st Annual Meeting of the American Equal Rights Association, May 1867."
Nelson, J.	"Address to the House Judiciary Committee, February 20, 1886."
Neymann, C.	"German and American Independence Contrasted. Address to the National Woman Suffrage Association Convention of February 1886."
Nolan, M.	"Statement on Release from Prison."
O'Reilly, L.	"Testimony to the Senate."
Park, M.	"Report of the Congressional Committee to the National American Woman Suffrage Association Convention of 1917."
Patridge, L.	"Speech at the 9th Annual Meeting of the American Woman Suffrage Association, 1878."
Paul, A.	"Address at a Meeting of the Advisory Council (Congressional Union) in New York City on March 31, 1915."
________.	"Address at the Organizational Convention of the National Woman's Party, March 2, 1917."
________.	"Address Before the Advisory Council of the Congressional Union Conference, August 29 and 30, 1914."
________.	"Comment After Defeat in House Judiciary Committee, March 1916."
________.	"Speech at a Suffrage Hearing Before the (House) Judiciary Committee, December 16, 1915."
________.	"Speech Before the 3rd Conference of the Congressional Union's Advisory Council, April 8, 1916."
________.	"Statement on Leaving Prison."
Penfield, J.	"Address at a Joint Hearing of the Senate Judiciary Committee and the Senate Committee on Woman Suffrage, March 13, 1912."
Phillips, E.	"Address to a Joint Hearing of the Senate Judiciary Committee and Senate Committee on Woman Suffrage, March 13, 1912."

Pincus, J. "Address at the Columbia Theatre in Washington, November 15, 1914."

Rankin, J. "Address on Raker Resolution to Establish a House Committee on Woman Suffrage, September 24, 1917."

Reel, E. "Address to the National-American Woman Suffrage Convention of 1898."

Reynolds, M. "Address to the Senate Committee, April 19, 1910."

Robinson, H. "Political Parties and Woman Suffrage."

Roessing, J. "Report of the National Congressional Committee to the National American Woman Suffrage Association Convention of 1916."

Rogers, C. "Address to the Senate Committee on Woman Suffrage, March 7, 1884."

Rose, E. "Mrs. Rose Moves Change of Name from Equal Rights Association to Woman's Suffrage Association, at the 3rd Annual Meeting of the American Equal Rights Association, N. Y., May 1869."

________. "Remarks at the 10th National Woman's Rights Convention, N. Y., May 10-11, 1860."

Saxon, E. "Testimony at a Hearing of the U. S. Senate, Committee on the Judiciary, January 23, 1880."

Scott, M. "Address at Mass Meeting Before Calling on President Wilson. (Feb. 1914)."

Sergio, L. "The Idea Takes Root."

Sewall, M. "Address to the Senate Committee on Woman Suffrage, March 7, 1884."

________. "Fitness of Women to Become Citizens from the Standpoint of Education and Mental Development."

Shaw, A. "Address at a Hearing of the Senate Committee on Woman Suffrage, December 15, 1915."

________. "Address at a Reception by President Wilson of a Delegation from the National American Woman Suffrage Association, December 8, 1913."

________. "Address to the House Judiciary Committee, February 17, 1892."

________. "Address to the House Judiciary Committee, 1900."

________. "Address to the National American Woman Suffrage Association Convention of 1913."

________. "Address to the National American Woman Suffrage Association Convention of 1917."

________. "The Fate of Republics."

________. "From Address of Dr. Anna Howard Shaw When Resigning the Presidency of the National American Woman Suffrage Association, December 15, 1915."

________. "Let No Man Take Thy Crown. Sermon in Metzerott's Music Hall During the National-American Woman Suffrage Association Convention of 1894."

________. "Opening Address at the National American Woman Suffrage Association Convention of 1914."

________. "President's Address at the National American Woman Suffrage Association Convention of 1905."

________. "President's Address at the National American Woman Suffrage Association Convention of 1906."

________. "President's Address to the National American Woman Suffrage Association Convention of 1915."

________. "Report of the Vice-President-At-Large to the National American Woman Suffrage Association Convention of 1896."

________. "President's Address to 38th Annual Convention of the National American Woman Suffrage Association, February 1906."

________. "School Suffrage."

Shuler, N. "Report of Campaigns and Surveys Committee to the National American Woman Suffrage Association Convention of 1918-1919."

________. "Report of the Corresponding Secretary to the National American Woman Suffrage Association Convention of 1920."

Silver, C. "Address Before State Suffrage Hearing, Albany, N. Y., February 1907."

Smith, A. "Abby H. Smith's Speech Before the R. I. Suffrage Society at Its Annual Meeting."

________. "Abby Smith's Appeal to Her Townsmen."

________. "Address at the Dayville (Killingly) Fair and Festival August 27, 1875."

________. "Address at the Melrose Convention."

________. "Miss Abby Smith's Address at Hearing Before the Committee on Woman Suffrage, Hartford, Connecticut."

________. "Speech of Abby Smith, July 11, 1874."

________. "Speech of Miss Abby H. Smith, of Glastonbury, Before the Town Meeting of That Place November 5th 1873."

Smith, E. "Report of the Congressional Committee to the National American Woman Suffrage Association Committee of 1915."

Smith, H. "Address at a Meeting of the National Woman Suffrage Association, Philadelphia, 1882."

Smith, J. "Address at the Melrose Convention."

________. "Address to Congressional Committee on Privileges and Elections, January 1878."

________.	"Address--Worchester Convention, February 20, 1874."
________.	"Taxation Without Representation."
________.	"Testimony at a Hearing of the U.S. Senate, Committee on the Judiciary, January 23, 1880."
Spencer, A.	"Duty to the Women of Our New Possessions."
________.	"Fitness of Women to Become Citizens from the Standpoint of Moral Development."
Stanton, E.	"Address."
________.	"Address at a Hearing of the Joint Committee of Congress of the District of Columbia, January 22, 1870."
________.	"Address at Hearings by the Congressional Committee on Privileges and Elections, January 1878."
________.	"Address at the 1st Meeting of the American Equal Rights Association, May 10, 1866."
________.	"Address at the First Suffrage Convention Held in Washington, D.C., 1869."
________.	"Address Before the N.Y. State Legislature, February 1854."
________.	"Address to the National Woman's Rights Convention, Held in Washington, D.C., January 1869."
________.	"Address to the N.Y. State Legislature, January 23, 1867."
________.	"Address to the Senate Judiciary Committee, January 17, 1872."
________.	"Address to the Senate Committee on Woman Suffrage, April 2, 1888."
________.	"Address to the Senate Select Committee on Woman Suffrage, February 8, 1890."
________.	"The Degradation of Disfranchisement. Read to the National American Woman Suffrage Association by Susan B. Anthony, February 26, 1891."
________.	"The Demand for the Vote."
________.	"Elizabeth Cady Stanton on the Politics of Woman Suffrage."
________.	"The Ethics of Suffrage."
________.	"Opening Address to the National American Woman Suffrage Association, February 18, 1890."
________.	"President's Address to the National Woman Suffrage Association Convention, May 10, 1870."
________.	"Remarks on Religion at the National Woman Suffrage Association Convention, January 1885."
________.	"2nd Address to the N.Y. State Legislature, Judiciary Committee, February 18, 1860."

________.	"The Solitude of Self. Address to the Senate Committee on Woman Suffrage, February 20, 1892."
________.	"Speech at the National Woman Suffrage Association Convention, May, 1872."
________.	"Speech Before Congressional Committee on the District of Columbia, 1870."
________.	"This Is the Negro's Hour."
Stebbins, C.	"Testimony at a Hearing of the House Committee on the Judiciary, January 24, 1880."
Stevens, D.	"Summing Up for the Defense of Arrested Pickets."
Stewart, M.	"Testimony at a Hearing of the U. S. Senate, Committee on the Judiciary, January 23, 1880."
Stone, L.	"Address."
________.	"Address to the Semi-Annual Meeting of the American Woman Suffrage Association, N. Y., May 1871."
________.	"Address to the Senate Committee on Woman Suffrage, February 20, 1892."
________.	"Annual Report of the Chairman of the Executive Committee of the American Woman Suffrage Association, at the 1st Annual Meeting, Cleveland, Ohio, November 1870."
________.	"Closing Address of the Annual Meeting of the American Woman Suffrage Association, 1885."
________.	"Debate at the 3rd Annual Meeting of the American Equal Rights Association, N. Y., May, 1869."
________.	"President's Address at the 7th National Convention, New York, November 25 & 26, 1856."
________.	"Speech at the Concord Convention of the Massachusetts Suffrage Association, May, 1875."
Terrell, M.	"The Justice of Woman Suffrage. Address to the National-American Woman Suffrage Association Convention of 1900."
Thomas, M.	"Address at the College Evening of the 38th Annual Convention of the National American Woman Suffrage Association, February 8, 1906."
________.	"Address at the National American Woman Suffrage Association Convention of 1906."
Tillinghast, E.	"The Economic Basis of Woman Suffrage. Address to the House Judiciary Committee, 1900."
Truth, S.	"Remarks at the 1st Annual Meeting of the American Equal Rights Association, May, 1867."

Upton, H.	"Treasurer's Report for 1906."
Vernon, M.	"Address at the Columbia Theatre in Washington, D. C., November 15, 1914."
Waite, J.	"Testimony at a Hearing of the House Committee on the Judiciary, January 24, 1880."
Wallace, Z.	"I Am a Home-Loving, Law-Abiding, Taxpaying Woman...."
________.	"The Moral Power of the Ballot."
________.	"Testimony at a Hearing of the U. S. Senate, Committee on the Judiciary, January 23, 1880."
________.	"A Whole Humanity. Address to the National American Woman Suffrage Association Convention, 1890."
________.	"Woman's Ballot a Necessity for the Permanence of Free Institutions. Address to the National Suffrage Convention of 1887."
Weed, H.	"Address at the Columbia Theatre in Washington, D. C., November 15, 1914."
White, A.	"President's Address to the 7th Meeting of the New Hampshire Woman Suffrage Association, November 5, 1879."
Wilbour, C.	"Debate at the 2nd Woman's Suffrage Convention in Washington, D. C., January 1870."
Willard, F.	"Address to the Senate Committee on Woman Suffrage, April 2, 1888."
Woodhull, V.	"Address of Victoria C. Woodhull January 11, 1871, to the Honorable the Judiciary Committee of the House of Representatives of the Congress of the United States."
________.	"Address to National Woman Suffrage Association Convention, January 11, 1872, Washington."
________.	"Are Women Enfranchised by the 14th and 15th Amendments. Address of Victoria Claflin Woodhull to the House Judiciary Committee."
________.	"A Lecture on Constitutional Equality."
Young, V.	"Testimony to the Senate."
Younger, M.	"Address to the Rules Committee of the House on a Hearing on the Question of a Suffrage Committee, May, 1917."
________.	"Memorial Address for Inez Milholland Boissevain."

WOMEN--TURKEY

Wright, M.	"Woman's Life in Asiatic Turkey."

WOMEN--UTAH

Richard, E.	"The Legal and Political Status of Woman in Utah."

WOMEN--VIRGINIA

Smith, M.	"The Virginia Woman of Today."

WOMEN--WEST INDIES

Moses, Y.	"Female Status, the Family, and Male Dominance in a West Indian Community."

WOMEN, HINDU

Wadley, S.	"Women and the Hindu Tradition."

WOMEN, JEWISH

Frank, H.	"Jewish Women of Modern Days."
Henrotin, E.	"Address."
Louis, M.	"Woman's Place in Hebrew Thought."
Mannheimer, L.	"Jewish Women of Biblical and of Medieval Times."
Solomon, H.	"Address."
Weil, H.	"Jewish Women of Modern Days."

WOMEN, MUSLIM

Howard, A.	"Moorish Women as I Found Them."

WOMEN AND RELIGION

Cheek, A.	"Women and Religion."
Foster, A.	"The Pulpit Has a Bad Influence."
Gage, M.	"Woman in the Early Christian Church."
Gardner, H.	"Men, Women and Gods."
Hultin, I.	"Extracts from Woman and Religion."
Lathrap, M.	"Women in the Methodist Church."
Mott, L.	"Discourse on Women, 1849."
________.	"It Is Not Christianity, but Priestcraft That Has Subjected Women as We Find Her. Debate at the 5th National Convention, Philadelphia, 1854."
Nichols, C.	"Remarks at the Woman's Rights Convention in New York, September 1853."

Price, A.	"Comments at the Syracuse National Convention, September 1852."
Shaw, A.	"Sermon Preached in the Hall of Washington, on Sunday Morning, May 21st, 1893."
Stone, L.	"Address on Women and Religion at the 7th National Convention, N. Y., November 25, 1856."
Tupper, M.	"Present Status of Women in the Church."

WOMEN ARCHITECTS

Cisler, L.	"Status of Women in Architecture."

WOMEN ARTISTS

Kamerick, M.	"The Woman Artist and the Art Academy: A Case Study in Institutional Prejudice."
Millett, K.	"The Image of Women in Arts and Letters."
Sartain, E.	"Art in Its Various Branches as a Profession for Women."
Skiles, J.	"Public Testimony."
Thringold, F.	"Public Testimony."
Warwick, M.	"Public Testimony."

WOMEN AUTHORS

Cummins, E.	"The Women Writers of California."
Lockwood, M.	"The Evolution of Women in Literature."
Lourie, M.	"Literary Women and the Masculated Sensibility."
Meyer, A.	"Woman's Place in Letters."
________.	"Woman's Place in the Republic of Letters."
Rollins, A.	"Woman in the Republic of Letters."
Seton, G.	"Report of the International Women Writers' Concave."
Wells, E.	"Western Women Authors and Journalists."

WOMEN CLERGY

Bartlett, C.	"Woman's Call to the Ministry."
Bowles, A.	"Woman in the Ministry."
Chapin, A.	"Woman's Work in the Pulpit and Church."
Hanaford, P.	"Statistics of the Woman Ministry."
________.	"Woman in the Church and Pulpit."
Kollock, F.	"Woman in the Pulpit."
Moreland, M.	"Discussion on Woman's Call to the Ministry."
Quinton, A.	"Discussion of Woman as a Minister of Religion."

Safford, M.	"Woman as a Minister of Religion."
St. John, E.	"Discussion on Woman's Call to the Ministry."
Wood, K.	"Women in the Pulpit."

WOMEN ENGINEERS

Honigman, R.	"Women in Engineering."

WOMEN EXECUTIVES

Austin, M.	"Women into Management: Vignettes."
Blanchette, E.	"Women into Management: Vignettes."
Epstein, C.	"Institutional Barriers: What Keeps Women Out of the Executive Suite?"
Fasenmyer, M.	"Brainwashed Women."
Gordon, F.	"Bringing Women into Management: The Role of the Senior Executive."
Insel, B.	"Women into Management: Vignettes."
Janeway, E.	"Family Life in Transition."
Kreps, J.	"The Sources of Inequality."
Leopold, A.	"What It Takes to Be Tops as Women Executive, Outline of Address."
Lipscomb, M.	"Woman as a Financier."
Oppenheimer, V.	"A Sociologist's Skepticism."
Park, R.	"Like Their Fathers Instead."
Stead, B.	"Women in Management: Gaining Acceptance on an Equal Basis."
Strober, M.	"Bringing Women into Management: Basic Strategies."
Thoma, M.	"Women into Management: Vignettes."
Trotter, V.	"Women in Leadership and Decision Making: A Shift in Balance."
Wallace, P.	"Sex Discrimination: Some Societal Constraints on Upward Mobility for Women Executives."

WOMEN IN AERONAUTICS

Cochran, J.	"The Future of Women in the Aviation Industry."
Earhart, A.	"New Wings for Mercury."
Love, N.	"Women in Aviation."

WOMEN IN AGRICULTURE

Abzug, B.	"Address to National Farmers Union Women Fly-In."
Edwards, A.	"Agriculture."

Howard, E.	"The Women's Agricultural and Horticultural Union."
Kinney, A.	"Women as Farmers."
Warner, E.	"Women as Farmers."
Worden, A.	"Women in the Grange."

WOMEN IN BANKING

Deane, A.	"Women in Banking."

WOMEN IN BUSINESS

Austin, I.	"Statement."
Barlow, F.	"A Business Woman in Kentucky."
Buerk, S.	"Women's Opportunity ... Starting Your Own Business. Understanding and Overcoming the Obstacles."
Carse, M.	"Woman and Finance."
Cavanaugh, D.	"Statement."
Chapman, J.	"Statement."
Cumming, T.	"Testimony."
DeVore, O.	"Public Testimony."
Freeman, F.	"Testimony."
Gates, M.	"Testimony on Women's Access to Credit and Insurance."
Grover, E.	"Statement."
Hagar, S.	"Statement."
Halliday, V.	"Machinery Broker."
Hayden, I.	"Statement."
Kaiser, I.	"Testimony."
Kreps, J.	"Testimony."
Neal, J.	"A New Avenue of Employment and Investment for Business Women."
O'Bannon, D.	"Testimony."
Persing, B.	"Statement."
Peterson, E.	"Opportunities and Trends in Employment of Women in Business, Summary of Address."
Rivers, D.	"Statement."
Roberts, J.	"Statement."
Salazar, G.	"Statement."
Schoonover, J.	"Why Corporate America Fears Women: Business and the New Woman."
Shack, B.	"Testimony on Women's Access to Credit and Insurance."
Simmons, L.	"Testimony."
Starkweather, L.	"Woman as an Investor."
Welcher, G.	"Statement."

WOMEN IN CHARITABLE WORK

Bamber, G.	"Woman's Place in Charitable Work--What It Is and What It Should Be."
Barker, E.	"The Woman's Relief Corps."
Benjamin, C.	"Woman's Place in Charitable Work--What It Is and What It Should Be."
Sherwood, K.	"The Past, Present, and Future of the Woman's Relief Corps."
_______.	"Woman's Relief Corps."
Wickens, M.	"Address on National Relief Corps."

WOMEN IN JOURNALISM

Alden, C.	"The Economic Position of Women as Journalists."
Armstrong, B.	"The New England Woman's Press Association."
Bayard, M.	"Woman in Journalism."
Brower, M.	"Public Testimony."
Croly, J.	"Women in Journalism."
Field, M.	"Report of Woman's International Press Association."
Harper, I.	"The Training of Women Journalists."
Holloway, L.	"Woman in Journalism."
Kirchway, F.	"Ninety Years Young; Excerpt from Address, June 19, 1955."
MacDougal, S.	"Two Powers--Women and the Press."
Merrill, E.	"The New England Woman's Press Association."
Mohl, A.	"An Idea and Its Results."

WOMEN IN LITERATURE

Black, A.	"Women's Influence in Poetry, Fiction, the Drama and History."
Schmidt, D.	"The Great American Bitch."

WOMEN IN POLITICS

Abzug, B.	"Women in Elective Office."
_______.	"Women's Political Power."
Aviel, J.	"Changing the Political Role of Women: A Costa Rican Case Study."
Bass, C.	"I Accept This Call."
Blake, L.	"Discussion of Women as an Actual Force in Politics."
Boals, K.	"The Politics of Cultural Liberation."
Chaney, E.	"The Mobilization of Women in Allende's Chile."

Chisholm, S.	"Women in Elective Office."
Collier, J.	"Women in Politics."
Donlon, M.	"Get into Politics Up to Your Ears. Women's Political Power Is Not Being Used Effectively."
Eastman, M.	"Woman's Place in Government."
Eldridge, R.	"Statement."
Foster, J.	"Woman as a Political Leader."
________.	"Women in Politics."
________.	"Women in Politics."
Harper, F.	"Woman's Political Future."
Iglitzin, L.	"The Making of the Apolitical Woman: Femininity and Sex-Stereotyping in Girls."
Jaquette, J.	"Women in American Politics."
Kirschbaum, K.	"Statement."
Kovner, S.	"Women's Share in Political and Governmental Decision-Making."
Lansing, M.	"The American Woman: Voter and Activist."
________.	"Women: The New Political Class."
Lapidus, G.	"Modernization Theory and Sex Roles in Critical Perspective: The Case of the Soviet Union."
Lepper, M.	"A Study of Career Structures of Federal Executives: A Focus on Women."
McWilliam, N.	"Contemporary Feminism, Consciousness-Raising, and Changing Views of the Political."
Neymann, C.	"Sentimentalism in Politics."
Ormsby, M.	"Discussion of Woman as a Political Leader."
Peaslie, A.	"The Relation of Woman to Our Present Political Problems."
Prestage, J.	"Black Women Officeholders: The Case of State Legislators."
Rattley, J.	"Statement."
Russell, P.	"Statement."
Schroeder, P.	"You Can Do It."
Sewall, M.	"Remarks on Interest in Political Questions."
Shaw, A.	"Remarks on Emotionalism in Politics Given at the National American Woman Suffrage Association Convention in 1913."
Sherwin, B.	"The President's Address. Taking Part in Government."
Spain, J.	"A Woman Could Be President: It's Getting More Reasonable."
Springer, A.	"Woman's Role in the Machinery of Government. Past, Present and Future."
Van Allen, J.	"Memsahib, Militante, Femme Libre: Political and Apolitical Styles of Modern African Women."
Willard, F.	"Address."

WOMEN IN THE CIVIL SERVICE

Burkholder, M.	"Public Testimony."
Duncanson, L.	"One Phase of Woman's Work for the Municipality."
Gordon, D.	"The Status of Women in Municipal Government."
Hall, S.	"Discussion of One Phase of Woman's Work for the Municipality."
Harper, I.	"Women in Municipal Government."
Layzer, J.	"Public Testimony."
Maymi, C.	"Statement."
Millstein, S.	"Public Testimony."
Poston, E.	"Women in Government Employment."
Pressman, S.	"The Status of Women in the Federal Government."

WOMEN IN THE MASS MEDIA INDUSTRY

Brownmiller, S.	"The Status of Women in Communications."
Hennock, F.	"Women and Future of Broadcasting."
Komisar, L.	"Public Testimony."
________.	"Women in the Media; In Honor of Margaret Fuller, America's First Woman Journalist. Who Would Not Think We Have Come Very Far (Baby)."
Lipton, M.	"Public Testimony."

WOMEN IN TRADE UNIONS

Ackerman, J.	"Our Union Has Kept Faith with Us."
Addams, J.	"Excerpt from Address at the Organizational Meeting of the National Women's Trade Union League, Boston, 1903."
Barry, L.	"A Report of the General Instructor of Woman's Work, 1889."
________.	"What the Knights of Labor Are Doing for Woman."
Bond, K.	"Organization Among Women as an Instrument in Promoting the Interests of Industry."
Cohen, M.	"Role of Women in the Organization of the Men's Garment Industry, Chicago, 1910."
Cohn, F.	"A Union Officer Calls for Idealism."
Dye, N.	"Creating a Feminist Alliance: Sisterhood and Class Conflict in the New York Women's Trade Union League, 1903-1914."
Eastman, M.	"Address to a Meeting of the Manchester Industrial Reform Association (September 1846)."
Harris, A.	"Organizing the Unorganizable: Jewish Women and Their Unions."

Hasner, D.	"What Is Labor Doing About Women in the Work Force."
Jacoby, R.	"Feminism and Class Consciousness in the British and American Women's Trade Union Leagues, 1890-1925."
________.	"The Women's Trade Union League and American Feminism."
Jameson, E.	"Imperfect Unions: Class and Gender in Cripple Creek, 1894-1904."
Kenney, M.	"Organization of Working Women."
Keyser, H.	"Organizing Among Women as an Instrument in Promoting the Interests of Industry."
Loud, H.	"Women in the Knights of Labor."
Mitchell, L.	"An Address Delivered by Louise Mitchell, United Tailoresses Society."
Newman, P.	"We Have Kept the Faith."
Perkins, F.	"Not in Vain."
Rice, F.	"Testimony Concerning Discrimination in the ILGWU at Hearings Held in 1962 by the House Committee on Labor, Education and Welfare."
Roberts, L.	"Union and Blue-Collar Women."
Robins, M.	"The Value of Unions."
Roosevelt, E.	"At Unity House."
Stewart, J.	"National Women's Trade Union League."
Swartz, M.	"Trade Union Organization Among Women Workers."
Van Etten, I.	"The Condition of Women Workers Under the Present Industrial System."
________.	"The Sweating System, Charity and Organization."
Waight, L.	"Remarks of the Secretary, Lavina Waight."

WOMEN LAWYERS

Bates, O.	"The Study of Law for Women."
Bittenbender, A.	"Women in Law."
Kilgore, C.	"The Address ... Before the Legislature of Pennsylvania Delivered in the Hall of the House of Representatives, at Harrisburg, March 23rd, 1881."
Mussey, E.	"The Woman Attorney and Counsellor."
Ross, S.	"Statement."
Sassower, D.	"Women in Law."
Sawyer, W.	"The Legal Profession for Women."

WOMEN LIBRARIANS

Plummer, M.	"The Training of Women as Librarians."
Schiller, A.	"Sex and Library Careers."
Sherif, C.	"Dreams and Dilemmas of Being a Woman Today."

Wetherby, P.	"Librarianship: Opportunity for Women?"

WOMEN PHYSICIANS

Cleaves, M.	"Women as Hospital Physicians."
Jacobi, M.	"Social Aspects of the Readmission of Women into the Medical Profession."
Lankton, F.	"The Medical Profession for Woman."
McAnarney, E.	"The Impact of Medical Women in United States Medical Schools."
Norris, F.	"Statement."
Stevenson, S.	"The Training and Qualification of Women Doctors."
________.	"Women in Medicine."

WOMEN PUBLISHERS

Clark, K.	"Women as Publishers."

WOMEN SCIENTISTS

Bunting, M.	"The Commitment Required of a Women Entering a Scientific Profession."
Edisen, A.	"Women in Science."
Hogan, M.	"Self-Employment."
Jacobi, M.	"Women in Science."
Kerby-Miller, W.	"Academic Employment."
Lewis, G.	"Science for Women."
McCabe, R.	"Panelist Discussion."
Missakian, E.	"Public Testimony."
Nachimias, V.	"Panelist Statement."
Rees, M.	"Panelist Statement."
Rossi, A.	"Barriers to the Career Choice of Engineering, Medicine, or Science Among American Women."
Simon, D.	"Panelist Statement."
Webster, E.	"Retraining for Employment."
Wu, C.	"Panelist Statement."

WOMEN SCULPTORS

Hoxia, V.	"Sculpture for Women."
Johnson, A.	"Sculpture as a Profession for Women."

WOMEN SOLDIERS

Clay, L.	"Can Women Be Fighters?"

WOMEN'S HEALTH SERVICES

Benoliel, J.	"Self as Critical Variable in Sensitive Research in Women's Health."
Brown, C.	"New Roles for Women in Health Care Delivery; A U.S. Response to Conditions in the People's Republic of China."
Campbell, J.	"Approaches to Correct the Under-Representation of Women in the Health Professions: A U.S. Response to a Look at the U.S.S.R. Dentistry as a Career for Women in the United States: A Discussion with Comparisons to the Soviet Union."
Cheney, E.	"Hospitals Managed By and For Women."
Cleaves, M.	"The Medical and Moral Care of Female Patients."
Cleland, V.	"Approaches to the Organization of Nurses, Allied Health and Support Personnel. A U.S. Response to the Australian Experience."
Cosner, R.	"Why Bother? Is Research on Issues of Women's Health Worthwhile?"
Ehrenreich, B.	"The Status of Women as Health Care Providers in the United States."
Fahy, E.	"Innovations in the Utilization of Nurses, Allied Health and Support Personnel. Innovative Functions of Women Health Workers."
Flannigan, J.	"Women in the Professions."
Ford, L.	"How to Improve the Utilization of Women in the Health Occupations in Which They Are Well Represented. A U.S. Response to the Swedish Experience."
Handy, G.	"Questions for the Future. Research."
Harding, E.	"How to Improve the Utilization of Nurses, Allied Health and Support Personnel. A U.S. Response to the Swedish Model."
Height, D.	"Questions for the Future. Action."
Howell, M.	"Highlights of the Conference."
Jackson, J.	"New Roles for Women in Health Care Delivery. A U.S. Response to the Cameroonian Experience."
Keys, M.	"Statement."
Kravits, J.	"Sex Differences in Health Care: Social Survey Research Methods."
Lewis, M.	"New Roles for Women in Health Care Delivery. A U.S. Response to the Cameroon Experience."
Lipman-Blumen, J.	"Overview: Demographic Trends and Issues in Women's Health."
Lockett, B.	"Opening Remarks."
Lubic, R.	"Innovations in the Utilization of Nurses, Allied Health and Support Personnel. A U.S. Response to a Look at Colombia."

Marieskind, H.	"New Roles for Women in Health Care Delivery: A U.S. Response to Conditions in China. The Women's Health Movement: Political, Social and Working Roles for Women in Health Care Delivery."
Meanes, L.	"Co-Operation with the Women's Foundation for Health."
Muller, C.	"Methodological Issues in Health Economics Research Relevant to Women."
Nelson, C.	"New Ways of Viewing Key Questions for Investigation. Cultural: Reconceptualizing Health Care."
Ramey, E.	"Approaches to Correct the Underrepresentation of Women in the Health Professions. A U.S. Response to the Scandinavia Experience."
Ravenhill, M.	"The Woman's Health Protective Association."
Rodgers-Rose, L.	"New Ways of Viewing Key Questions for Investigation. Social Psychological: Relationships Between Black Males and Females--Toward a Definition."
Rodriguez-Trios, H.	"Analysis of the Role of Women in Health Care Decisionmaking. A U.S. Response to a Look at the Philippines."
Roemer, R.	"Innovations in the Utilization of Nurses, Allied Health and Support Personnel. A U.S. Response to a Look at Colombia."
Sechrest, L.	"Ethical Problems in Medical Experimentation Involving Women."
Sidel, R.	"New Roles for Women in Health Care Delivery. Conditions in the People's Republic of China."
Smith-Rosenberg, C.	"New Ways of Viewing Key Questions for Investigation. Historical: Women, History and New Insights."
Spelman, J.	"Analysis of the Role of Women in Health Care Decisionmaking Among Women."
Tillman, R.	"Approaches to Correct the Underrepresentation of Women in the Health Professions. A U.S. Response to the Scandinavian Experience."
Vetter, B.	"Analysis of the Role of Women in Health Care Decisionmaking. A U.S. Response to a Look at the Philippines."
Wilson, M.	"Career Patterns of Women in Medicine."
Wiseman, J.	"Case History I: Social Forces and the Politics of Research Approaches--Studying the Wives of Alcoholics."
Woodside, N.	"Analysis of the Role of Women in Health Care Decisionmaking. A U.S. Response to a Look at Poland."

WOMEN'S PERIODICALS

Thomas, M.	"Story of the Lowell Offering."

WOMEN'S RIGHTS

Anneke, M.	"Address to the 3rd Annual Meeting of the American Equal Rights Association, N. Y., May 1869."
Anthony, S.	"Address to the N. Y. State Assembly, February 1854, As Reported in Newspaper."
________.	"Declaration of Rights for Women, Read at Independence Hall, Philadelphia, July 4, 1876."
________.	"Opening Address."
________.	"Political Economy of Women."
________.	"Remarks at State Teachers' Convention, Rochester, N. Y., August 3, 1853."
________.	"Report to the 10th National Woman's Rights Convention, N. Y., May 10-11, 1860."
Bird, C.	"On Being Born Female: Integration."
________.	"What Do Women Want? An Access to Forums."
Blackwell, A.	"Address."
________.	"Address at Woman's Rights Convention, Syracuse, N. Y., September 8, 1852."
________.	"Comments at the Syracuse National Convention, September 1852."
________.	"The Indifference of Women."
________.	"Landmarks."
________.	"Our Cause Is Progressing Triumphantly. Address to the Woman Rights Convention in N. Y., September 1853."
Blair, E.	"Have Women Contributed to the Crisis?"
Bottome, M.	"Exhortation."
Brooks, R.	"Woman's Place Is in the Wrong. The Loyal Opposition."
Bullock, H.	"Power and Purpose of Women."
Carpenter, M.	"Today's Tensions; Women, the Problem or the Answer."
Coe, E.	"Remarks on the Laws of Ohio, at 4th National Convention, Cleveland Ohio, October 1853."
Coleman, L.	"Debate at the Woman's National Loyal League Convention, May 14, 1863."
Colom, A.	"Statement."
Couzins, P.	"Address to a Convention of the National Woman Suffrage Association, Philadelphia, July 1876."
Davis, P.	"Appeal from Man's Injustice."
________.	"The History of the Woman's Rights Movement, Read in the Meeting Held in Apollo Hall, New York, October 21, 1870."

________.	"The President's Address at the First National Woman's Rights Convention in Worcester, Mass., 1850."
Douty, A.	"Conference Summary."
Fraser, A.	"Women: The New Image."
Friedan, B.	"Judge Carswell and the 'Sex Plus' Doctrine."
________.	"Women's Rights and the Revolution of Rising Expectations."
Gage, F.	"President's Address at the Akron Convention, May 28, 1851."
Gage, M.	"Address."
________.	"Address to the Syracuse National Woman's Rights Convention, September 1852."
________.	"A Plan of Action."
Goldman, E.	"The Tragedy of Woman's Emancipation."
Gooding, M.	"Woman's Need at the Present Day."
Grew, M.	"Address."
________.	"Closing Address at the 10th National Women's Rights Convention, N. Y., May 10-11, 1860."
Grimke, A.	"Angelina Grimke's Speech."
________.	"The Rights of Women and Negroes."
Gunderson, B.	"The Implication of Rivalry."
Haskell, M.	"Remarks on Women's Wrongs at the 2nd Worcester Convention, October 1851."
Hazlett, A.	"Address at the Decade Meeting Held at Apollo Hall, October 20, 1870."
de Hericourt, J.	"Address to the 3rd Annual Meeting of the American Equal Rights Association, N. Y., May 1869."
Holt, C.	"The Woman Who Has Come."
Hutar, P.	"Statement of June 20, 1975 to the U. N. World Conference of the International Women's Year Held at Mexico City."
________.	"Statement of July 2, 1975 to the U. N. World Conference of the International Women's Year Held at Mexico City."
Johnson, M.	"Memorial to the Constitutional Convention. Adopted by the Woman's Rights Convention, Salem, Ohio, April 19th and 20th, 1850."
________.	"President's Address at the Westchester (Pennsylvania) Convention, June 1852."
________.	"A Revolution in Human Society."
Jones, E.	"Address at the 10th National Woman's Rights Convention N. Y., May 10-11, 1860."
Jones, J.	"Comments at the Syracuse National Convention, September 1852."
________.	"Women of Ohio."
Koch, A.	"Two Cheers for Equality."
Komarovsky, M.	"Cultural and Psychohistorical Background of Women's Status in America."

Logan, O. "Address to the 3rd Annual Meeting of the American Equal Rights Association, N. Y., May, 1869."

Manning, A. "Complete Freedom for Women."

Mead, M. "A Cultural Dilemma."

________. "Women's Rights: A Cultural Dilemma."

Morrissy, E. "Status of Women. To Be Equal Does Not Mean to be Identical."

Mott, L. "Address to the 1st Annual Meeting of the American Equal Rights Association, May 1867."

________. "Comments at the Syracuse National Convention, September 1852."

________. "A Demand for the Political Rights of Women."

________. "Discourse on Woman, Delivered Twelfth Month 17th, 1849."

________. "Remarks on a Public Disturbance at the Women's Rights Convention in New York, September 1853."

Nichols, C. "Comments on the Declaration of Sentiments Adopted at the Westchester Convention at the Syracuse National Convention, September 1852."

Papanek, H. "Development Planning for Women."

Peterson, E. "Address on Equality Through Opportunities, Training, Employment, Education, Etc."

Phillips, L. "Shall It Be Progress?"

Potter, F. "In Non-Essentials, Liberty."

Preston, A. "Ann Preston's Address (Westchester, Pennsylvania Convention, June 1852)."

________. "What Does Woman Want?"

Reese, C. "We, the Women."

Rose, E. "Address at the 2nd National Convention at Worcester, October 1851."

________. "Address at the 10th National Woman's Rights Convention, N. Y., May 10-11, 1860."

________. "Address Before a House Committee of the N. Y. State Legislature, February 1854."

________. "Address to the Woman's Rights State Convention, Rochester, N. Y., November 30 and December 1, 1853."

________. "Debate at the Woman's National Loyal League Convention, May 14, 1863."

________. "Ernestine Rose at Worcester."

________. "On Legal Discrimination."

________. "Petitions Were Circulated."

________. "President's Address at the 5th National Convention in Philadelphia, October 1854."

________. "Remarks at the 7th National Convention, N. Y., November 25, 1856."

________. "Speech of Ernestine L. Rose at the Second National Woman's Rights Convention, Worcester, Mass., October 15, 1851."

________. "Speech of Ernestine L. Rose at the Thomas Paine Anniversary Celebration, New York, January 29, 1850."

St. John, J. "Women's Legislative Issues: Today and Tomorrow."

Severance, C. "Argument and Appeal at the Woman's Rights Convention in N.Y., September 1853."

________. "President's Address at the New England Convention of 1859."

Shaw, A. "The Heavenly Vision. Sermon Preached March 24, 1888, at International Council of Women, Washington, D.C."

________. "Sermon, the Heavenly Vision."

Smith, E. "Comments at the Syracuse National Convention, September 1852."

________. "A Dissolution of the Existing Social Compact."

________. "Public Testimony."

Smith, M. "In Pursuit of the Golden Age for Women."

Spencer, A. "Women of Our New Possessions. Speech Delivered in 1898."

Stanton, E. "Address to the New York State Legislature, 1854."

________. "The Civil and Social Evolution of Woman."

________. "Excerpt from 2nd Address to the N.Y. Legislature, March 19, 1860."

________. "Address to the New York State Legislature, 1860."

________. "Mrs. Stanton's Address to the Legislature of the State of New York Read at the Albany, N.Y., Convention, February 1854."

________. "Our Young Girls."

________. "President's Address at the Eleventh National Woman's Rights Convention, May 10, 1866."

________. "Solitude of Self."

________. "Speech Before the Legislature, 1860."

________. "Stanton Defends Woodhull."

________. "Toast to the Women of Nebraska, at Celebration in Lincoln, Nebraska, 1875."

________. "Welcoming Address."

________. "Welcoming Address at the International Council of Women, March 25, 1888."

________. "Womanliness."

Steinem, G. "Woman and Attitudes Toward War, National Priorities, and Values."

Stewart, M. "What if I Am A Woman?"

Stone, L. "Address at Woman's Rights Convention, Syracuse, N.Y., September 8, 1852."

________.	"Address at the Woman's Rights Convention, in New York, September 1853."
________.	"Comments at the Syracuse National Convention, September 1852."
________.	"Debate on the Elevation of Women at the 2nd Worcester Convention, October 1851."
________.	"Disappointment Is the Lot of Woman."
________.	"Extemporaneous Speech at a National Woman's Rights Convention in Cincinnati in October 1855."
________.	"I Have Been a Disappointed Woman."
________.	"Lucy Stone's Speech."
________.	"President's Closing Remarks at the 7th National Convention, N. Y., November 25 & 26, 1853."
________.	"The Progress of Fifty Years."
________.	"Speech Before the National Woman's Rights Convention of 1855."
Thibeault, M.	"The Hazards of Equality: Awareness of Self."
Thomas, M.	"Discussion of the Civil and Social Evolution of Woman."
Truth, S.	"Address at Women Suffrage Convention in New York, 1867."
________.	"Address to the 1st Annual Meeting of the American Equal Rights Association, May 1867."
________.	"Ain't I a Woman?"
________.	"Frances D. Gage's Reminiscences of Speech by Sojourner Truth."
________.	"Gage's Reminiscences of Sojourner Truth."
________.	"Keeping the Thing Going While Things Are Stirring."
________.	"Mrs. Gage's Reminiscences of Sojourner Truth."
________.	"The Narrative of Sojourner Truth, 1878."
________.	"Reminiscences by Frances D. Gage."
________.	"2nd Address to the 1st Annual Meeting of the American Equal Rights Association, May 1867."
________.	"Sojourner Truth Speaks Before a Woman's Rights Convention."
________.	"Speech at the Convention of the American Equal Rights Association, N. Y., 1867."
________.	"What Time of Night It Is."
________.	"While the Water Is Stirring I Will Step Into the Pool."
________.	"The Women Want Their Rights."
Woodhull, V.	"From Woodhull's Speech to the National Convention."
________.	"A New Political Party and a New Party Platform."

________.	"A Lecture on Constitutional Equality, Delivered at Lincoln Hall, Washington, D.C., Thursday, February 16, 1871."
________.	"From Woodhull's Speech on Social Freedom."
________.	"The New Rebellion. The Great Secession Speech of Victoria C. Woodhull Before the National Woman's Suffrage Convention, at Apollo Hall, May 11, 1871."
Wright, F.	"In a Daughter They Have a Human Being; In a Son the Same."
Wright, M.	"President's Address at the 10th National Woman's Rights Convention, N.Y., May 10-11, 1860."

WOMEN'S STUDIES

Sicherman, B.	"The Invisible Woman: The Case for Women's Studies."

WORKMEN'S COMPENSATION

Perkins, F.	"After-Care for Industrial Compensation Cases."

WORLD POLITICS

Sampson, E.	"How Can We Go Forward? Panel Discussion."

WORLD WAR II, 1939-1945

Clifton, E.	"Some Psychological Effects of the War as Seen by the Social Worker."
Dean, V.	"Implications of the European Situation for the United States."
Hurlbutt, M.	"The Postwar Role of Social Workers."
Meloney, M.	"You Have Been Warned."
Morrow, E.	"Lasting Effects of Women's War Activities."
Prosser, L.	"Universal Service for America."
Roosevelt, A.	"The Backlog of Preparedness."
Thompson, D.	"The War's Challenge to the United States."
Wisner, E.	"War and the Social Services."
Woolley, M.	"The Crisis and Our Responsibility. Common-Sense Is Lacking."

YOUNG WOMEN'S CHRISTIAN ASSOCIATION

Boyd, C.	"The Young Women's Christian Association: Its Aims and Methods."

Cratty, M.	"At the Close of a National Convention."
________.	"The Christian Ideal for Women as Interpreted by the Young Women's Christian Association."
________.	"The Goal of Our Calling."
________.	"Our Motives and Methods."
________.	"Some Administrative Problems in the Young Women's Christian Association."
________.	"This Day We Sailed West."

YOUTH

Addams, J.	"Introduction to Forum."
Balkany, C.	"Statement."
Brady, G.	"New Importance of Old Youth Movements."
Bridges, B.	"The Choice for American Youth."
________.	"Teen-Age Centers."
Carner, L.	"Place of Private Group-Work Agency in Program of Youth."
Clifton, R.	"The Moline Plan."
Close, M.	"New Frontiers."
Fleischauer, B.	"Statement."
Garcia, C.	"Statement."
Harpole, M.	"Statement."
Hatcher, O.	"Chairman's Introduction. Youth Plans for a Civilized World."
Hayes, M.	"Job Preparation and Juvenile Guidance on a National Front."
________.	"A Program for Unemployed Youth."
Lyells, R.	"Accent on Youth. Tomorrow's Hope; Or Despair."
Macy, H.	"Youth in Industry."
Roche, J.	"Youth Opportunities Today and Social Security Safeguards."
Roosevelt, A.	"Young America."
________.	"Youth's Contribution."
Sandmann, R.	"Youth of All Nations."
Sclair, V.	"Leadership Through Young Minds."
Trimble, A.	"An Opportunity for Youth in the Present Crisis."
Vining, E.	"Young People in New Japan."
Watkins, J.	"What About Youth?"

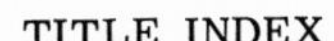

TITLE INDEX

Title	Author
"Abby H. Smith's Speech Before the R.I. Suffrage Society at Its Annual Meeting."	Smith, A.
"Abby Smith's Appeal to Her Townsmen."	Smith, A.
"Abolitionist Speech."	Anthony, S.
"Abortion."	Chisholm, S.
"Abortion: A Woman's Civil Right."	Friedan, B.
"Abortion and Population Control."	Chisholm, S.
"Abstract of an Address on Industrial Conditions for Women."	MacLean, A.
"Academic Employment."	Kerby-Miller, W.
"Academic Freedom: Panel Discussion."	Fields, J.
"Academic Freedom: Panel Discussion."	Hoeber, S.
"Academic Women Attack Institutional Discrimination--1970."	Sandler, B.
"Accent on Youth. Tomorrow's Hope; Or Despair."	Lyells, R.
"Acceptance Paper (The Caldecott Award 1938)."	Lathrop, D.
"Acceptance Paper (Caldecott Award 1940). Working Together on Books for Children."	D'Aulaire, I.
"Acceptance Paper (Caldecott Award, 1943). Making Picture Books."	Burton, V.
"Acceptance Paper (Caldecott Award 1945). Every Child and His Hilltop."	Jones, E.
"Acceptance Paper (Caldecott Award 1946). A Short Tale of the Depressions and the Peaks That Occur in the Making of the Little Pretty Picture Book."	Petersham, M.
"Acceptance Paper (Caldecott Award 1951). The Egg Tree and How It Grew."	Milhous, K.
"Acceptance Paper (Caldecott Award 1955). Integrity and Intuition."	Brown, M.
"Acceptance Paper--Newbery Medal 1930."	Field, R.
"Acceptance Paper--Newbery Medal 1931."	Armer, L.
"Acceptance Paper--Newbery Medal 1933."	Lewis, E.
"Acceptance Paper--Newbery Medal 1934."	Meigs, C.
"Acceptance Paper--Newbery Medal 1935. Bewitched Mountains."	Shannon, M.
"Acceptance Paper--Newbery Medal 1936. Caddie Woodlawn."	Brink, C.
"Acceptance Paper--Newbery Medal 1937."	Sawyer, R.
"Acceptance Paper--Newbery Medal 1938."	Seredy, K.
"Acceptance Paper--Newbery Medal 1939."	Enright, E.

"Acceptance Paper--Newbery Medal 1943. History Is People."	Gray, E.
"Acceptance Paper--Newbery Medal 1944."	Forbes, E.
"Acceptance Paper--Newbery Medal 1946. Seeing Others As Ourselves."	Lenski, L.
"Acceptance Paper--Newbery Medal 1947. Miss Hickory: Her Genealogy."	Bailey, C.
"Acceptance Paper--Newbery Medal 1949."	Henry, M.
"Acceptance Paper--Newbery Medal 1950."	De Angeli, M.
"Acceptance Paper--Newbery Medal 1951. Climbing Some Mountain in the Mind."	Yates, E.
"Acceptance Paper--Newbery Medal 1952."	Estes, E.
"Acceptance Paper--Newbery Medal 1953."	Clark, A.
"Acceptance Paper--1965: Shadow of a Kid."	Wojciechowska, M.
"Acceptance Speech for the Howells Medal."	Buck, P.
"Acceptance Speech for the Nobel Prize, December, 1938."	Buck, P.
"Acceptance Speech for the Schweitzer Medal of the Animal Welfare Institute, January 6, 1963."	Carson, R.
"Acceptance Speech on Being Selected President of the National American Woman Suffrage Association, February 1900."	Catt, C.
"Access to Abortion and Family Planning."	Stearns, N.
"Achievement Award to Ruth Fulton Benedict. Dr. Benedict's Speech of Acceptance."	Benedict, R.
"Action Scale to Finer Womanhood. Make a Better Person of Yourself."	Fisher, E.
"Action to Help Older Americans."	Grasso, E.
"Activity in the Case-Work Relationship."	Dietzel, L.
"Activity in the Case-Work Relationship."	White, H.
"Adapting the Four-Year College to New Patterns."	Bunting, M.
"Address."	Addams, J.
"Address."	Addams, J.
"Address."	Allen, F.
"Address."	Anthony, S.
"Address."	Atkins, R.
"Address."	Barton, C.
"Address."	Bates, J.
"Address."	Blackwell, A.
"Address."	Burt, M.
"Address."	Carpenter, E.
"Address."	Cheney, E.
"Address."	Gage, M.
"Address."	Grew, M.
"Address."	Height, D.
"Address."	Henrotin, E.
"Address."	Hoffman, C.
"Address."	Hooker, I.

"Address."	Keeley, S.
"Address."	Keyserling, M.
"Address."	Lerrigo, E.
"Address."	Livermore, M.
"Address."	Marble, E.
"Address."	Schorr, L.
"Address."	Solomon, H.
"Address."	Solomon, H.
"Address."	Stanton, E.
"Address."	Stone, L.
"Address."	Stone, L.
"Address."	Willard, F.
"Address."	Williams, F.
"Address."	Upton, H.
"Address."	Walters, B.
"Address."	Washington, B.
"Address."	Willard, F.
"Address."	Willard, F.
"Address."	Willard, F.
"Address."	Willen, P.
"Address."	Wirtz, J.
"Address: Art and the Next Generation."	Mason, F.
"Address at a Hearing of the Congressional Committee on Privileges and Elections, January, 1878."	Gage, M.
"Address at a Hearing of the Congressional Committee on Privileges and Elections, January, 1878."	Harbert, E.
"Address at a Hearing of the House Committee on Rules, December 3, 1913."	Beard, M.
"Address at a Hearing of the House Committee on Rules, December 1913."	Blackwell, A.
"Address at a Hearing of the House Committee on Rules, December 3, 1913."	Breckinridge, D.
"Address at a Hearing of the House Committee on Rules, December 3, 1913."	Catt, C.
"Address at a Hearing of the House Committee on Rules, December 3, 1913."	Harper, I.
"Address at a Hearing of the House Judiciary Committee, March 3, 1914."	Beard, M.
"Address at a Hearing of the House Judiciary Committee, March 3, 1914."	Eastman, C.
"Address at a Hearing of the House Judiciary Committee, December 16, 1915."	Catt, C.
"Address at a Hearing of the Joint Committee of Congress of the District of Columbia, January 22, 1870."	Stanton, E.
"Address at a Hearing of the Senate Committee on Woman Suffrage, December 15, 1915."	Bass, Z.
"Address at a Hearing of the Senate Committee on Woman Suffrage, December 15, 1951."	Jacobs, P.

"Address at a Hearing of the Senate Committee on Woman Suffrage, December 15, 1915." Shaw, A.
"Address at a Joint Hearing of the Senate Judiciary Committee and the Senate Committee on Woman Suffrage, March 13, 1912." Penfield, J.
"Address at a Meeting of the Advisory Council (Congressional Union) in New York City on March 31, 1915." Paul, A.
"Address at a Meeting of the Board of Trustees of Mount Holyoke, May 1944." Perkins, F.
"Address at a Meeting of the National Woman Suffrage Association, Philadelphia, 1882." Smith, H.
"Address at a Procession of Suffragists, at the Panama-Pacific Exposition of 1915." Laughlin, G.
"Address at a Protest Meeting--Headquarters of the National Woman's Party, 1917." Blatch, H.
"Address at a Reception by President Wilson of a Delegation from the National American Woman Suffrage Association, December 8, 1913." Shaw, A.
"Address at Conference Dinner." Abbott, G.
"Address at Conference Dinner." Wald, L.
"Address at Convention Hall, Washington, D.C., February 15, 1895." Willard, F.
"Address at Exeter Hall, London, 1893." Willard, F.
"Address at Founder's Reception--5th Annual Conference, Los Angeles, September 1971." Friedan, B.
"Address at Hearings by the Congressional Committee on Privileges and Elections, January 1878." Stanton, E.
"Address at Mass Meeting Before Calling on President Wilson. (Feb. 1914)." Scott, M.
"Address at Memorial Service for Lucy Stone During the National-American Woman Suffrage Association Convention of 1894." Howe, J.
"Address at NOW's 6th National Conference." Friedan, B.
"Address at Philadelphia Anti-slavery Meeting, 1855." Foster, A.
"Address at the Annual Meeting of the Historical and Scientific Society of Berkshire, July 1897." Catt, C.
"Address at the College Evening of the 38th Annual Convention of the National American Woman Suffrage Association, February 8, 1906." Calkins, M.

"Address at the College Evening of the 38th Annual Convention of the National American Woman Suffrage Association, February 8, 1906." Jordan, M.
"Address at the College Evening of the 38th Annual Convention of the National American Woman Suffrage Association, February 8, 1906." Moore, E.
"Address at the College Evening of the 38th Annual Convention of the National American Woman Suffrage Association, February 8, 1906." Park, M.
"Address at the College Evening of the 38th Annual Convention of the National American Woman Suffrage Association, February 8, 1906." Salmon, L.
"Address at the College Evening of the 38th Annual Convention of the National American Woman Suffrage Association, February 8, 1906." Thomas, M.
"Address at the College Evening of the 38th Annual Convention of the National American Woman Suffrage Association, February 8, 1906." Woolley, M.
"Address at the Columbia Theatre in Washington, November 15, 1914." Latimer, E.
"Address at the Columbia Theatre in Washington, November 15, 1914." Pincus, J.
"Address at the Columbia Theatre in Washington, D. C., November 15, 1914." Vernon, M.
"Address at the Columbia Theatre in Washington, D. C., November 15, 1914." Weed, H.
"Address at the Conference for Peace Worker." Sewall, M.
"Address at the Dayville (Killingly) Fair and Festival, August 27, 1875." Smith, A.
"Address at the Decade Meeting Held at Apollo Hall, October 20, 1870." Hazlett, A.
"Address at the Decade Meeting on Marriage and Divorce." Stanton, E.
"Address at the 1st Annual Meeting of the Woman's State Temperance Society, Rochester, June 1, 1853." Stanton, E.
"Address at the 1st Meeting of the American Equal Rights Association, May 10, 1866." Stanton, E.
"Address at the First Suffrage Convention Held in Washington, D. C., 1869." Stanton, E.
"Address at the Founder's Reception--5th Annual Meeting of NOW, September 1971." Haener, D.

"Address at the Last or Victory Convention of the National American Woman Suffrage Association, February 1920." Catt, C.
"Address at the Melrose Convention." Smith, A.
"Address at the Melrose Convention." Smith, J.
"Address at the National American Woman Suffrage Association Convention of 1906." Thomas, M.
"Address at the National American Woman Suffrage Association in Washington, D. C., 1884." Gage, M.
"Address at the National American Woman Suffrage Convention of 1902." Barton, C.
"Address at the New England Convention, May, 1859." Dall, C.
"Address at the Organizational Convention of the National Woman's Party, March 2, 1917." Paul, A.
"Address at the 2nd Annual Meeting of the Woman's Temperance Society, Utica, N. Y., June 7, 1854." Bloomer, A.
"Address at the 2nd National Convention at Worcester, October 1851." Rose, E.
"Address at the 2nd Session of the American Woman Suffrage Association Convention, N. Y., May 1870." Howe, J.
"Address at the 7th Annual Meeting of the American Woman Suffrage Association, 1875." Blackwell, A.
"Address of the 10th Annual Meeting of the American Association of Spiritualists, Chicago, 1873." Woodhull, V.
"Address at the 10th National Woman's Rights Convention in Cooper Institute, N. Y., May 10, 1860." Stanton, E.
"Address at the 10th National Woman's Rights Convention, N. Y., May 10-11, 1860." Blackwell, A.
"Address at the 10th National Woman's Rights Convention N. Y., May 10-11, 1860." Jones, E.
"Address at the 10th National Woman's Rights Convention, N. Y., May 10-11, 1860." Rose, E.
"Address at the 12th Annual Meeting of the Chicago, W. C. T. U. in 1886." Willard, F.
"Address at the Woman's National Loyal League Convention, May 14, 1863." Blackwell, A.
"Address at the Woman's National Loyal League Convention, May 14, 1863." Grimke, A.
"Address at the Woman's National Loyal League Convention, May 14, 1863." Rose, E.

"Address at the Woman's Rights Convention in New York, September 1853." Gage, F.
"Address at the Woman's Rights Convention, in N. Y., September 1853." Stone, L.
"Address at the Women's Industrial Conference." Abbott, G.
"Address at Twenty-first Annual Convention of International Association of Governmental Labor Officials." Perkins, F.
"Address at Welcome Meeting at Exeter Hall, London, 1892." Willard, F.
"Address at Woman's Rights Convention, Syracuse, N. Y., September 8, 1852." Blackwell, A.
"Address at Woman's Rights Convention, Syracuse, N. Y., September 8, 1852." Stone, L.
"Address at Woman Suffrage Convention in New York, 1867." Truth, S.
"Address August 26, 1970--Los Angeles Rally." Hernandez, A.
"Address Before a House Committee, 1904." Catt, C.
"Address Before a House Committee of the N. Y. State Legislature, February 1854." Rose, E.
"Address Before Annual Convention." Ludington, K.
"Address Before New York Board of Trade." Perkins, F.
"Address Before State Suffrage Hearing, Albany, N. Y., February 1907." Duffy, M.
"Address Before State Suffrage Hearing, Albany, N. Y., February 1907." Silver, C.
"Address Before the Advisory Council of the Congressional Union Conference, August 29 and 30, 1914." Paul, A.
"Address Before the Alumni of the Massachusetts Metaphysical College, 1895." Eddy, M.
"Address Before the Annual Convention of the American Federation of Labor, October 8, 1941." Perkins, F.
"Address Before the Christian Scientist Association of the Massachusetts Metaphysical College in 1893. Subject: Obedience." Eddy, M.
"The Address ... Before the Legislature of Pennsylvania Delivered in the Hall of the House of Representatives, at Harrisburg, March 23rd, 1881." Kilgore, C.
"Address Before the National League of Cities' Congressional City Conference, Washington Hilton Hotel, Washington, D. C., March 6, 1977." Kreps, J.
"Address Before the N. Y. State Legislature, February 1854." Stanton, E.

"Address Before the Women's Congress, Des Moines, Iowa, 1885."	Willard, F.
"Address Before the Women's Meeting."	Laney, L.
"Address by Clara Barton."	Barton, C.
"Address by the President."	Howe, J.
"Address, City Club, 1926."	Addams, J.
"Address, Containing a Review of the Times, as First Delivered in the Hall of Science, New-York on Sunday, May 9, 1830."	Wright, F.
"An Address, Delivered at the African Masonic Hall, Boston, 27 February 1833."	Stewart, M.
"Address Delivered at the Banquet, June 4, 1936."	Catt, C.
"An Address Delivered by Louise Mitchell, United Tailoresses Society."	Mitchell, L.
"Address Delivered by Mrs. Potter Palmer, President of the Board of Lady Managers, on the Occasion of the Opening of the Woman's Building, May 1st, 1893."	Palmer, B.
"Address for a Deputation of Connecticut Women to the Chairman of the Republican Party, Will Hays, August, 1920."	Ludington, K.
"Address of Greeting to the National American Convention of 1911."	Clay, L.
"Address of Helen Keller at Mt. Airy, (July 8, 1896)."	Keller, H.
"Address of Miss Jane Addams, Delivered at Carnegie Hall, Friday, July 9, 1915."	Addams, J.
"Address of Miss Marot."	Marot, H.
"Address of Mrs. Abby M. Diaz."	Diaz, A.
"Address of Mrs. Carrie Chapman Catt at Senate Hearing, December 15, 1915."	Catt, C.
"Address of Mrs. Isabella Beecher Hooker."	Hooker, I.
"Address of Mrs. Kelley."	Kelley, F.
"Address of Mrs. Lucy Stone."	Stone, L.
"Address of Mrs. Simkhovitch."	Simkhovitch, M.
"Address of President Thomas."	Thomas, M.
"Address of the American Woman Suffrage Association Convention, N. Y., May 1870."	Howe, J.
"Address of the Chairman (On Industrial and Economic Problems)."	Kelley, F.
"Address of the Ladies' Anti-slavery Society of Delaware, Ohio to the Convention of Disfranchised Citizens of Ohio."	Staley, S.
"Address of the President."	Mitchell, M.
"Address of the President."	Nutting, M.
"Address of the President."	Nutting, M.

"Address of the President." Nutting, M.
"Address of the President." Park, M.
"Address of the President." Park, M.
"Address of the President. The Way of the League." Sherwin, B.
"Address of Victoria C. Woodhull, January 11, 1871, to the Honorable the Judiciary Committee of the House of Representatives of the Congress of the United States." Woodhull, V.
"Address of Welcome." Birney, A.
"Address of Welcome." Cole, I.
"Address of Welcome." Edison, M.
"Address of Welcome." Robinson, A.
"Address of Welcome to the 9th Biennial Convention of the General Federation of Women's Clubs." Ward, M.
"Address on Convicts." Fairbanks, C.
"Address on Divorce at 10 National Woman's Rights Convention, May 11, 1860." Stanton, E.
"Address on Divorce at Woman's Rights Convention Syracuse, N. Y., Sept. 8, 1852." Nichols, C.
"Address on Divorce Resolutions at the 10th National Woman's Rights Convention, N. Y., May 10-11, 1860." Stanton, E.
"Address on Equality Through Opportunities, Training, Employment, Education, Etc." Peterson, E.
"Address on Exploring Diversity of Opportunities for Citizenship Action." Keyserling, M.
"Address on Job Opportunities in the Labor Market." Douty, A.
"Address on Modern American Woman, Status and Opportunity." Peterson, E.
"Address on National Relief Corps." Wickens, M.
"Address on Nuclear Credibility to Senate, and President, September 21, 1961." Smith, M.
"Address on Organization." Willard, F.
"Address on Organization Among Women as an Instrument in Promoting Religion." Hultin, I.
"Address on Organizations." Eastman, M.
"Address on Organizations." Sewall, M.
"Address on Presenting a Gift of Land for a Park to Chico, California, 1905." Bidwell, A.
"Address on Raker Resolution to Establish a House Committee on Woman Suffrage, September 24, 1917." Rankin, J.
"Address on Social Purity." Harbert, E.
"Address on the Amendment of the Rochester, N. Y. City Charter, December 12, 1892." Anthony, S.

"Address on the Fifteenth Amendment to a Meeting of the St. Louis Woman Suffrage Association." Cousins, P.
"Address on the Fourth of July at Pleasant View, Concord, N.H., Before 2,500 Members of the Mother Church, 1897." Eddy, M.
"Address on the State of the Public Mind, and the Measures Which It Calls For. As Delivered in New-York and Philadelphia, in the Autumn of 1829." Wright, F.
"Address on Woman's Status in Industry, Business, Society, Etc." Peterson, E.
"Address on Woman's Work for Peace." Henrotin, E.
"Address on Women and Religion at the 7th National Convention, N.Y., November 25, 1856." Stone, L.
"Address on Women & Their Accomplishments Through National and International Women's Organizations." Peterson, E.
"Address on Work Opportunities Through Education." Peterson, E.
"Address I.--Delivered in the New Harmony Hall, on the Fourth of July, 1828." Wright, F.
"Address, Social Purity." Shattuck, H.
"Address to a Conference Sponsored by the National Council of Women of the United States, October 11, 1962." Carson, R.
"Address to a Congressional Hearing, March, 1884." Anthony, S.
"Address to a Convention in Hartford, Conn., October 1869." Anthony, S.
"Address to a Convention of Bricklayers' and Masons' International Union, Rochester, N.Y., January 13, 1900." Anthony, S.
"Address to a Convention of the National Woman Suffrage Association, Philadelphia, July 1876." Couzins, P.
"Address to a Group of Government Personnel Workers." Perkins, F.
"Address to a Hearing of the Congressional Committee on Privileges and Elections, January 1878." Brown, O.
"Address to a Hearing of the Congressional Committee on the District of Columbia, 1870." Anthony, S.
"Address to a Hearing of the Joint Committee of Congress of the District of Columbia, January 22, 1870." Anthony, S.
"Address to a Joint Hearing of the Senate

Judiciary Committee and the Senate Committee on Woman Suffrage, March 13, 1912."	Lowe, C.
"Address to a Joint Hearing of the Senate Judiciary Committee and Senate Committee on Woman Suffrage, March 13, 1912."	Phillips, E.
"Address to a Meeting of the Manchester Industrial Reform Association (September 1846)."	Eastman, M.
"Address to a Senate Committee, February 1900."	Anthony, S.
"Address to an Equal Rights Meeting, Albany, November 21, 1866."	Anthony, S.
"Address to Annual Convention of American Federation of Labor, New Orleans, La., November 20, 1944."	Perkins, F.
"Address to Congress, Adopted by the Eleventh National Woman's Rights Convention, Held in New York City, Thursday, May 10, 1866."	Anthony, S.
"Address to Congress, Read at the 1866 Woman's Rights Convention."	Anthony, S.
"Address to Congressional Committee on Privileges and Elections, January, 1878."	Smith, J.
"Address to Convention of the American Woman Suffrage Association, N. Y., May 1870."	Hanaford, P.
"An Address to Graduates."	Buck, P.
"Address to Her 80th Birthday Celebration, February 15, 1900."	Anthony, S.
"Address to 1974 NOW National Conference."	De Crow, K.
"Address to 1974 NOW National Conference."	Heide, W.
"Address to 1974 NOW National Conference."	Hernandez, A.
"Address to Peace Congress."	Moore, E.
"Address to President Lincoln. Adopted by the Women's National Loyal League, May 14, 1863."	Anthony, S.
"Address to the Annual Convention of the National Woman's Christian Temperance Union, Philadelphia, 1885."	Willard, F.
"Address to the Chicago Woman Suffrage Convention, 1869."	Dickinson, A.
"Address to the Committee on Resolutions of the Republican National Convention in 1884."	Willard, F.
"Address to the Constitutional Convention of the Dakota Territory, Sept. 1883."	Bones, M.

"Address to the Convention of the American Instructors of the Deaf and Dumb, 1882."	Garrett, E.
"Address to the Convention of the American Woman Suffrage Association, N. Y., May, 1870."	Cutler, H.
"Address to the Convention of the American Woman Suffrage Association, N. Y., May, 1870."	Livermore, M.
"Address to the Executive Council of the National American Woman Suffrage Association, at the 1916 Convention."	Catt, C.
"Address to the 5th Annual National Woman's Suffrage Association Convention, Washington, D. C., January 1872."	Gage, M.
"Address to the 1st Annual Meeting of the American Equal Rights Association, May, 1867."	Gage, F.
"Address to the 1st Annual Meeting of the American Equal Rights Association, May, 1867."	Griffing, J.
"Address to the 1st Annual Meeting of the American Equal Rights Association, May, 1867."	Mott, L.
"Address to the 1st Annual Meeting of the American Equal Rights Association, May, 1867."	Rose, E.
"Address to the 1st Annual Meeting of the American Equal Rights Association, May, 1867."	Truth, S.
"Address to the House Judiciary Committee, April 19, 1910."	Kelley, F.
"Address to the House Judiciary Committee, February 17, 1892."	Blackwell, A.
"Address to the House Judiciary Committee, February 17, 1892."	Greenlead, J.
"Address to the House Judiciary Committee, February 17, 1892."	Meriwether, L.
"Address to the House Judiciary Committee, February 17, 1892."	Shaw, A.
"Address to the House Judiciary Committee, February 20, 1886."	Colby, C.
"Address to the House Judiciary Committee, February 20, 1886."	Nelson, J.
"Address to the House Judiciary Committee, March 8, 1884."	Haggart, M.
"Address to the House Judiciary Committee, 1900."	Shaw, A.
"Address to the International Working Men's Association Congress (Paris, 1937)."	Goldman, E.
"Address to the Judiciary Committee of the House, March 8, 1884."	Anthony, S.
"Address to the Judiciary Committee of the House, March 8, 1884."	Clay, M.

"Address to the Judiciary Committee, U. S. Senate, January 17, 1872." Hooker, I.
"Address to the Jury." Goldman, E.
"Address to the Kiwanis Club of Nashville, Tennessee, 1920." Catt, C.
"Address to the National-American Woman Suffrage Association Convention of 1895." Duniway, A.
"Address to the National-American Woman Suffrage Association Convention of 1897." Catt, C.
"Address to the National-American Woman Suffrage Association Convention of 1898." Reel, E.
"Address to the National American Woman Suffrage Association Convention of 1913." Shaw, A.
"Address to the National American Woman Suffrage Association Convention of 1917." Hay, M.
"Address to the National American Woman Suffrage Association Convention of 1917." Shaw, A.
"Address to the National American Woman Suffrage Association Convention of 1920." Catt, C.
"Address to the National-American Woman Suffrage Convention of 1898 from Colorado." Conine, M.
"Address to the National Convention of the Woman's Christian Temperance Union, St. Louis, November, 1896." Willard, F.
"Address to the National Delegates Before the First Joint Convention with the American Woman Suffrage Association, 1890." Anthony, S.
"Address to the National Farmers Union Women Fly-In. Abzug, B.
"Address to the National Purity Congress, Baltimore Yearly Meeting Committee." Holme, P.
"Address to the National Woman Suffrage Association Convention, January 11 1872, Washington." Woodhull, V.
"Address to the National Woman Suffrage Association Convention, January 1882." Couzins, P.
"Address to the National Woman Suffrage Association Convention of 1887." Gage, M.
"Address to the National Woman Suffrage Convention, May 10, 1870." Anthony, S.
"Address to the National Woman's Rights Convention, Held in Washington, D. C., January 1869." Stanton, E.
"Address to the New York City Suffrage Society, Union League Theatre, April 19, 1876." Blake, L.

"Address to the N. Y. State Assembly, February 1854, as Reported in Newspaper." Anthony, S.
"Address to the New York State Legislature, 1854." Stanton, E.
"Address to the New York State Legislature, 1860." Stanton, E.
"Address to the N. Y. State Legislature, January 23, 1867." Stanton, E.
"Address to the 1916 Convention of the National Woman Suffrage Convention." Catt, C.
"Address to the Organization Meeting of the People's Party, 1872." Woodhull, V.
"Address to the Rules Committee of the House on a Hearing on the Question of the Creation of a Suffrage Committee, May, 1917." Younger, M.
"Address to the Second National Woman Suffrage Association Convention, January 19, 1870." Anthony, S.
"Address to the Semi-Annual Meeting of the American Woman Suffrage Association, N. Y., May, 1871." Grew, M.
"Address to the Semi-Annual Meeting of the Woman Suffrage Association, N. Y., May, 1871." Stone, L.
"Address to the Senate Committee, April 19, 1910." Blount, A.
"Address to the Senate Committee, April 19, 1910." Gano, E.
"Address to the Senate Committee, April 19, 1910." Reynolds, M.
"Address to the Senate Committee on Woman Suffrage, April 2, 1888." Stanton, E.
"Address to the Senate Committee on Woman Suffrage, April 2, 1888." Willard, F.
"Address to the Senate Committee on Woman Suffrage, February 10, 1892." Stone, L.
"Address to the Senate Committee on Woman Suffrage, March 7, 1884." Anthony, S.
"Address to the Senate Committee on Woman Suffrage, March 7, 1884." Gougar, H.
"Address to the Senate Committee on Woman Suffrage, March 7, 1884." Rogers, C.
"Address to the Senate Committee on Woman Suffrage, March 7, 1884." Sewall, M.
"Address to the Senate Judiciary Committee, January 12, 1872." Anthony, S.
"Address to the Senate Judiciary Committee, January 17, 1872." Anthony, S.
"Address to the Senate Judiciary Committee, January 17, 1872." Stanton, E.

"Address to the Senate Select Committee on Woman Suffrage, February 8, 1890." Stanton, E.
"Address to the State Constitutional Convention, Boise, Idaho, July 16, 1889." Duniway, A.
"Address to the Syracuse National Woman's Rights Convention, Sept. 1852." Gage, M.
"Address to the 3rd Anniversary Meeting of the Equal Rights Association, May 12, 1869." Anthony, S.
"Address to the 3rd Annual Meeting of the American Equal Rights Association, N. Y., May, 1869." Anneke, M.
"Address to the 3rd Annual Meeting of the American Equal Rights Association, N. Y., May, 1869." Couzins, P.
"Address to the 3rd Annual Meeting of the American Equal Rights Association, N. Y., May, 1869." de Hericourt, J.
"Address to the 3rd Annual Meeting of the American Equal Rights Association, N. Y., May, 1869." Logan, O.
"Address to the 31st Annual Convention of the National American Woman Suffrage Association, April 27, 1899." Anthony, S.
"Address to the 33rd Annual Convention of the National American Woman Suffrage Association, May 30, 1901." Anthony, S.
"Address to the Woman's Rights Convention in N. Y., Sept. 1853." Truth, S.
"Address to the Woman's Rights Convention, N. Y., May 10, 1866." Anthony, S.
"Address to the Woman's Rights State Convention, Rochester, N. Y., November 30 and December 1, 1853." Rose, E.
"Address to the Women's National Loyal League Convention, May 14, 1863." Anthony, S.
"An Address to Young Mechanics, as Delivered in the Hall of Science, June 13, 1830." Wright, F.
"Address. The Needs of Art To-day." Berry, R.
"Address III. --Delivered at the Opening of the Hall of Science, New-York, Sunday, April 26, 1829." Wright, F.
"Address: Tribute to Oscar C. McCulloch." Barrows, K.
"Address II. --Delivered in the Walnut-Street Theatre, Philadelphia, on the Fourth of July, 1829." Wright, F.
"Address WILPF, Washington 1924." Addams, J.
"Address--Worchester Convention, February 10, 1874." Smith, J.
"An Adequate Local Maternity Program." Corbin, H.
"Adequate Public Social Services for Migrants." Hoey, J.

"Administration of Child Welfare Services from the Federal Level."	Atkinson, M.
"The Administration of Criminal Justice in Canada."	Murphy, E.
"Administration of Marriage Laws in Michigan."	Brown, S.
"Administration Practices for Conserving Human Values in the Public Assistance Program."	Tynes, H.
"The Administrative Problems of a Woman's Reformatory."	Petersen, A.
"The Administrative Process in Social Work."	Johnson, A.
"The Admission of Women to the Medical School of the Johns Hopkins University."	King, E.
"Admissions and Records in an Almshouse."	Randall, E.
"The Adolescent Experience of Pregnancy and Abortion."	Hatcher, S.
"Adolescent Girls: Their Attitude Toward Education."	Douvan, E.
"Adult Immigration Education: In the United States."	Burnett, M.
"Advantages and Dangers of Organization."	Spencer, A.
"Adventures in Understanding."	Allen, F.
"Advisory Committee Role in Constructing Affirmative Action Programs."	Klotzburger, K.
"Aesthetic Culture."	Baird, P.
"Affirmative Action on the Campus: Like It or Not, Uncle Sam Is Here to Stay."	Sandler, B.
"An African Expedition."	Sheldon, M.
"The Afro-American Mother."	Harper, F.
"After Victory--What?"	Dean, V.
"After-care for Industrial Compensation Cases."	Perkins, F.
"The Aged Person in the Family Setting."	Van de Carr, K.
"Aging Differently in the Space Age; Excerpts from Address."	Mead, M.
"Agriculture."	Edwards, A.
"Aid to Dependent Children."	Chisholm, S.
"Aid to North Vietnam."	Grasso, E.
"Ain't I a Woman?"	Truth, S.
"ALA's New Goal and Greatest Challenge: From "The Inaugural Address."	Martin, A.
"Alaska--The New Crossroads."	Gruber, R.
"Alcohol Problems."	Higgins, A.
"Alcoholism."	Baker, S.
"Alcoholism as a Case of Degeneracy."	Amigh, O.
"Alice Kellogg Tyler."	Addams, J.
"Allotment of Land to Indians."	Fletcher, A.
"The Almshouse."	Clark, M.
"The Almshouse Hospital."	Lincoln, A.

"Almshouse Property: The Ideal in Amount and Upkeep."	Clark, S.
"Alone Together."	Austin, J.
"Alternatives for Social Change: The Future Status of Women."	Bell, C.
"Ambulances of the Air."	Richardson, H.
"America and World Communism. Shall It Be One World?"	Luce, C.
"America Facing Tomorrow's World."	Thompson, D.
"America in the Post-War Air World. Be Practical--Ration Globaloney."	Luce, C.
"American Association of University Women Educational Foundation, College Faculty Program."	Tompkins, P.
"American Childhood Challenges American Democracy."	Lenroot, K.
"The American City in Obsolescent. Factors Affecting Municipal Revenues."	Walker, M.
"American Deportation Procedure: An International Social Problem."	Clark, J.
"American Education and the Child. Philosophical Ideas Old and New."	Roosevelt, E.
"The American Farmer: The Consumers' Real Protector."	May, C.
"The American Housewife: A Historical Perspective."	Lerner, G.
"American Leadership."	Catt, C.
"American Morality and Nuclear Diplomacy, the Force of Our Free Spirits."	Luce, C.
"An American Newspaper and the United Nations."	Reid, H.
"American Press. A Product of the Time?"	Bentley, H.
"The American Purity Alliance and Its Work."	Powell, A.
"The American School Peace League."	Andrews, F.
"The American Theatre Comes of Age."	Hayes, H.
"The American Woman: Voter and Activist."	Lansing, M.
"The American Woman's Place in the World Today."	Roosevelt, A.
"American Women at Crossroads."	Koontz, E.
"American Women at Work, New Challenges and New Responsibilities."	Keyserling, M.
"American Women on the Job."	Bloodworth, B.
"America's Bicentennial: Crisis and Challenge."	Armstrong, A.
"America's Danger and Opportunity."	Mead, L.
"Among the Pillars of Society."	Sherwin, B.
"Analysis of Processes in the Records of Family Case Working Agencies."	Robinson, V.
"Analysis of the Role of Women in Health Care Decisionmaking. A U.S. Response to a Look at the Philippines."	Rodriguez-Trios, H.

"Analysis of the Role of Women in Health Care Decisionmaking. A U. S. Response to a Look at the Philippines." Vetter, B.
"Analysis of the Role of Women in Health Care Decisionmaking. A U. S. Response to a Look at Poland." Woodside, N.
"Analysis of the Role of Women in Health Care Decisionmaking. A U. S. Response to a Look at Poland. The Class Nature of Decisionmaking Among Women." Spelman, J.
"And They Came Out of Their Cotton-batting World: Enjoy, Enjoy." Gunn, B.
"Anecdote of Susan B. Anthony, 32nd Annual Convention of the National American Woman Suffrage Association, Feb., 1900." Shaw, A.
"Angelina Grimke's Address." Grimke, A.
"Angelina Grimke's Speech." Grimke, A.
"Ann Preston's Address (Westchester, Penn. Convention, June, 1852)." Preston, A.
"Annals of Women's Anti-slavery Societies." Grew, M.
"Annual Address at the National Convention of the National Woman's Christian Temperance Union, Detroit, 1883." Willard, F.
"Annual Address at the National Convention of the National Woman's Christian Temperance Union, New York, 1888." Willard, F.
"Annual Address Before the National Convention of the Woman's Christian Temperance Union." Willard, F.
"Annual Address to National Convention, W. C. T. U." Willard, F.
"Annual Address to the 6th Annual Meeting of the American Woman Suffrage Association, October 1874." Howe, J.
"Annual Protest on Taxation Read at the Woman's Rights Convention in N. Y., September 1853." Hunt, H.
"Annual Report of the Chairman of the Executive Committee of the American Woman Suffrage Association, at the 1st Annual Meeting, Cleveland, Ohio, November 1870." Stone, L.
"Annual Report to the 5th Annual National Woman Suffrage Association Convention, Washington, D. C., January 1873." Gage, M.
"Annual Report to the 8th Annual Convention of the National Woman Suffrage Association, Washington, D. C., January 1876." Lockwood, B.

"Anthony Explains the National's Strategy."	Anthony, S.
"Anthony on the Ballot and Women's Wages."	Anthony, S.
"Anthony's Remarks."	Anthony, S.
"Anthony's Speech."	Anthony, S.
"Appeal from Man's Injustice."	Davis, P.
"An Appeal of Art to the Lovers of Art."	Norris, M.
"Appeal to Lafayette at a Demonstration at the Lafayette Monument, Sept. 16, 1918."	Arnold, B.
"Application of Psychology to Case Work."	Marcus, G.
"Applying a Maternity and Infancy Program to Rural Sections."	Taylor, M.
"Approaches to Correct the Under-representation of Women in the Health Professions: A U. S. Response to a Look at the USSR. Dentistry as a Career for Women in the United States: A Discussion with Comparisons to the Soviet Union."	Campbell, J.
"Approaches to Correct the Underrepresentation of Women in the Health Professions. A U. S. Response to the Scandinavian Experience."	Ramey, E.
"Approaches to Correct the Underrepresentation of Women in the Health Professions. A U. S. Response to the Scandinavian Experience."	Tillman, N.
"Approaches to the Organization of Nurses, Allied Health and Support Personnel. A U. S. Response to the Australian Experience."	Cleland, V.
"Are We a Nation of Economic Illiterates? Make Peace Synonymous with Prosperity."	Porter, S.
"Are We Coming or Going?"	Hurst, F.
"Are Women Citizens and People?"	Ketcham, E.
"Are Women Enfranchised by the 14th & 15th Amendments. Address of Victoria Claflin Woodhull to the House Judiciary Committee."	Woodhull, V.
"Are Women Represented in Our Government?"	Curtis, E.
"Areas of Responsibility of Voluntary Social Work During Period of Changing Local and National Governmental Programs."	Deardorff, N.
"Argument Against Public Outdoor Relief."	Godman, H.
"Argument and Appeal at the Woman's Rights Convention in N. Y., Sept. 1853."	Severance, C.
"Argument for Woman's Suffrage, 1886."	Gage, M.
"Aristophanes."	Howe, J.
"Arousing Voters to Action: A Story of a City Campaign."	Wing, V.

"The Arrested Offender." Kinsella, N.
"Art as a Medium of Civilization." Bibb, G.
"Art for Women." Doggett, K.
"Art in Ceramics." Braumuller, L.
"Art in Its Various Branches as a Profession for Women." Sartain, E.
"The Art of Beginning in Social Work." Richmond, M.
"The Art of Elocution." Morgan, A.
"The Art of Helping by Changing Habit." Libbey, B.
"The Art of Helping Through the Interview: A Study of Two Interviews." Clow, L.
"The Art of Living." Rich, E.
"Art of Living for Woman Today. Be Stingy with Time." Palffy, E.
"Art-isms." Cole, A.
"Artistic Book Binding." Preston, E.
"Asia's Red Riddle." Brandon, D.
"Asiatic Problem. The Colored People Are Still Waiting, Still Watchful." Buck, P.
"Assyrian Mythology." Reed, E.
"At a Memorial Meeting for Henry Demarest Lloyd Held Under the Auspices of United Mine Workers of America...." Addams, J.
"At the Close of a National Convention." Cratty, M.
"At Unity House." Roosevelt, E.
"The Attack on War." Addams, J.
"An Attempt to Articulate Processes." Brisley, M.
"The Attitude of Married Parents and Social Workers Toward Unmarried Parents." Watson, A.
"Automobile Migrants." Buffington, A.
"Autos and Mass Transit: Paradox and Confusion." Christensen, D.
"Auxiliary Visitors." Godman, H.
"Auxiliary Visitors. Volunteer Visiting of State Wards in Connecticut with Official Work." Putnam, E.
"Available Channels of Publicity." Routzahn, M.
"The Awakened Volunteer Interest." Van Slyck, K.
"Axioms of Global Policy. The Security of the Nation." Thompson, D.

"The Background of a Family's Religious Life as Social Data." Corbett, L.
"The Background of a Family's Religious Life as Social Data." Glenn, M.
"The Background of a Family's Religious Life as Social Data." McHugh, R.
"The Backlash Phenomenon: The Equal Rights Amendment." Wolfe, H.

Title	Author
"The Backlog of Preparedness."	Roosevelt, A.
"Bad Manners in America."	Vanderbilt, A.
"Ballots and Bullets."	Duniway, A.
"Baptist Home Mission Society."	Blackall, E.
"Bar vs. Bench: New Fears in an Old Relationship."	Prewitt, A.
"Barriers to the Career Choice of Engineering, Medicine, or Science Among American Women."	Rossi, A.
"Basis for Estimating Budgets."	Gillett, L.
"The Beginnings of the National Club Movement."	Ruffin, J.
"Benefits of Suffrage for Women."	Howe, J.
"The Best Methods of Interesting Women in Suffrage, Address to the National American Convention of 1893."	Dietrick, E.
"Better Housing."	Roosevelt, A.
"A Better System of Public Charities and Correction for Cities."	Lowell, J.
"Betty Furness Speaks for Consumers."	Furness, B.
"Beyond the Feminine Mystique--A New Image of Woman." (excerpts)	Friedan, B.
"Bible Lessons."	Eddy, M.
"Biological and Cultural Determinants of the Division of Labor by Sex."	Weiss, K.
"Biologist Looks at the Energy Crisis; Address June 17, 1974."	Ray, D.
"Birds and Flowers."	Myers, H.
"A Bird's-eye View of the National Woman's Christian Temperance Union."	Hoffman, C.
"The Black Revolution in America."	Boggs, G.
"A Black Woman Appeals to White Women for Justice for Her Race."	Harper, F.
"Black Women Officeholders: The Case of State Legislators."	Prestage, J.
"Blackwell's Island Hospitals."	Daiche, L.
"Blind People Do Not Fear Snakes. Advertising: Is It Legal, Moral & Ethical?"	Stephenson, M.
"The Board of Lady Managers of the Columbian Exposition."	Henrotin, E.
"The Board of Lady Managers of the Columbian Exposition."	Palmer, B.
"Boarding-out of Dependent Children in Massachusetts."	Calkins, A.
"Body Image and Performance."	Strati, J.
"Bolshevik Alternatives and the Soviet Family: The 1926 Marriage Law Debate."	Farnsworth, B.
"Books and the Learning Process. Newbery Award Acceptance--1967."	Hunt, I.
"Books for Leisure Time."	Van Doren, I.

"Boston a Little Island of Darkness. Speech at a Suffrage Hearing at the Senate House in Boston, February 4, 1908."	Howe, J.
"Boston Charities--New England Hospital."	Cheney, E.
"Bound for the Future. Women's Responsibility for the Future."	Hickey, M.
"The Boy and Girl Out on Furlough."	Johnson, G.
"The Brahmo Somaj and What It Is Doing for the Women of India."	Cook, G.
"Brainwashed Women."	Fasenmyer, M.
"Breadgivers."	Addams, J.
"Breaking Down the Barriers."	Gardner, J.
"Bridge to the Future. Have We Here and Now the Intelligence and Devotion to Cross Over?"	Allen, F.
"Bridging the Chasm."	Henry, E.
"Bringing People and Services Together."	Marshall, S.
"Bringing Women into Management: Basic Strategies."	Strober, M.
"Bringing Women into Management: The Role of the Senior Executive."	Gordon, F.
"British Home Front Compared with Ours. If Democracy Is Worth Fighting for, It Is Worth Fighting With."	Meyer, A.
"The Bryn Mawr Woman."	Thomas, M.
"Building for the Future."	Countryman, G.
"Building Junior Membership."	Dibert, F.
"Building Leadership for Peace ... New Ideas from New Voters: Panel Discussion."	Brown, V.
"Building Leadership for Peace ... New Ideas from New Voters: Panel Discussion."	Gunderson, B.
"Building Leadership for Peace ... New Ideas from New Voters: Panel Discussion."	Hughes, S.
"Building Leadership for Peace ... New Ideas from New Voters: Panel Discussion."	Lord, M.
"Building Leadership for Peace ... New Ideas from New Voters: Panel Discussion."	Parisi, A.
"The Burden of the Educated Colored Woman."	Laney, L.
"Bureau and Political Influence in Neighborhood Civic Problems."	Robbins, J.
"A Bureau of Information: The Need of a Post-Graduate School for Nurses."	Brown, C.
"Business as an Ally."	Crosby, H.
"A Business Woman in Kentucky."	Barlow, F.

"Caldecott Acceptance Speech--1967."	Ness, E.
"Caldecott Award Acceptance."	Cooney, B.
"Caldecott Award Acceptance: Big and Little."	Brown, M.
"Caldecott Award Acceptance: How the Caldecott Changed My Life--Twice (1972)."	Hogrogian, N.
"Caldecott Award Acceptance--1960."	Ets, M.
"Caldecott Award Acceptance--1966."	Hogrogian, N.
"Caldecott Award Acceptance--1971."	Haley, G.
"Caldecott Award Acceptance--1974."	Zemach, M.
"The California Plan for the State Certification of Social Workers."	Eliel, H.
"A Call of Old Glory for Heroism."	Shontz, E.
"The Call of the Social Field."	Addams, J.
"A Call to Action."	Culver, E.
"The Campaign Issue."	Douglas, H.
"Campaign Speech on U. S. Air Force, September 12, 1954."	Smith, M.
"Campus Issues in 1980."	Green, E.
"Can Parental Education Be Applied?"	Laws, G.
"Can the Institution Equip the Girl for Normal Social Relationships?"	Smith, C.
"Can the Intellect Survive? Meeting the Circumstances of Living."	McIntosh, M.
"Can the Machine Pull Us Out?"	Gilbreth, L.
"Can We Still Afford Occupational Segregation? Some Remarks."	Griffiths, M.
"Can Women Be Fighters?"	Clay, L.
"Canon Samuel A. Barnett. Memorial Address Given to the American Federation of Settlement."	Addams, J.
"Capitalism, Patriarchy, and Job Segregation by Sex."	Hartmann, H.
"Captive Nations: Lest We Forget."	Beck, M.
"Care and Treatment of Crippled Children."	Huse, B.
"The Care of Children in Foster Homes."	Taylor, R.
"The Care of Children in Institutions."	Ueland, E.
"Care of Dependent Children."	Ames, F.
"The Care of Girls in Reformatories."	Wardner, L.
"Career Patterns of Women in Medicine."	Wilson, M.
"The Career Wife."	Cass, R.
"The Career Woman."	Zizzmia, A.
"Carrie Chapman Catt Addresses Congress."	Catt, C.
"Carrie Chapman Catt Describes the Opposition."	Catt, C.
"Case History I: Social Forces and the Politics of Research Approaches--Studying the Wives of Alcoholics."	Wiseman, J.
"A Case History (Pilot Projects for Continuing Education for Women)."	Boyer, L.

"The Case of an Unmarried Mother Who Has Cared for Her Child, and Failed."	Parmenter, L.
"The Case of an Unmarried Mother Who Has Cared for Her Child, and Succeeded."	Donahue, A.
"The Case of Eva Peron."	Navarro, M.
"A Case of Illegitimacy When Mother and Baby Have Been Dealt with Separately."	Donahue, A.
"Case Work "Above the Poverty Line."	Murray, A.
"Case Work and Community Change."	Taggart, A.
"Case Work and Credit System Problems."	Moore, M.
"Casework and the New Emphasis on an Old Concept in Medicine."	Cockerill, E.
"Case Work as a Factor."	Goodwillie, M.
"Case Work as Applied to Rural Communities."	Lund, H.
"Case Work Disciplines and Ideals."	Glenn, M.
"Case Work in a Family Agency."	Libbey, B.
"Case Work in Protective Agencies."	Gane, E.
"Case Work in School Counseling."	Everett, E.
"Casework in Social Protection."	Rappaport, M.
"Case Work in the Hospital."	Cannon, M.
"Case Work in the Process of Adoption."	Theis, S.
"Case Work in Unions."	Kyle, C.
"Case-Work Objectives--Achieved in Volume."	Paige, C.
"The Case Work Plane."	Simkhovitch, M.
"Case Work Possibilities in a Public Assistance Program."	Hayden, H.
"Case Work Responsibility of Juvenile Courts."	Abbott, G.
"Casework Services in Public Welfare."	Perlman, H.
"Case Work Treatment of Emotional Maladjustment in Marriage."	Martens, E.
"Case Work with Children in Institutions."	Johnson, L.
"The Case Worker as an Interpreter of Case Work."	Dresden, M.
"The Case Worker in a Veteran Service Center."	Ginsbury, E.
"The Case Worker in Foster Families for Day Care."	Johnston, R.
"The Case Worker Looks at Legislative Planning."	Johnson, L.
"The Case Worker's Need for Orientation to the Culture of the Client."	Boie, M.
"The Case Worker's Problem in Interpretation."	Marcus, G.
"The Case Worker's Role in Treatment."	Neustaedter, E.
"Catholic University."	Atkinson, T.
"A Catholic View of the Education of Women."	Cahill, J.
"The Catholic Woman as an Educator."	Maher, M.
"Catholic Women's Part in Philanthropy."	Onahan, M.

"A Century of Progress of Negro Women."	Bethune, M.
"Certification and Reclassification in the Civil Service."	Mitchell, E.
"Chairman's Introduction."	Phillips, L.
"Chairman's Introduction. Economic Security Through Government."	Bowman, G.
"Chairman's Introduction. Foundations of Education."	Alschuler, R.
"Chairman's Introduction. Joy in Living."	Smith, I.
"Chairman's Introduction--Release from Labor--The Problem."	Boyd, N.
"Chairman's Introduction. Security Against Disease."	Dingman, M.
"Chairman's Introduction. The Direct Impact of the Depression."	Woodhouse, C.
"Chairman's Introduction. The World As It Could Be."	Poole, G.
"Chairman's Introduction. Women in a Changing World."	Robison, L.
"Chairman's Introduction. Working Session."	Phillips, L.
"Chairman's Introduction. Youth Plans for a Civilized World."	Hatcher, O.
"Chairman's Report on What of the Immediate Future of the Family?"	Colcord, J.
"Challenge of Democracy. Build World Peace in Your Own Community."	Ahlgren, M.
"The Challenge of Tomorrow. Womanpower."	Leopold, A.
"The Challenge to the Western Policy for Germany. The Threat to Berlin."	Dulles, E.
"A Challenge to Women."	Gilbreth, L.
"The Challenge to Women--Organizing Around an Issue."	Norton, E.
"The Challenge to Women Today."	Hauser, R.
"Challenges Ahead."	Keyserling, M.
"Chamber of Commerce and Communism. The Devil's Cleverist Trick."	Luce, C.
"Change and the Student."	Sturtevant, S.
"Changes in the Theory of Relief Giving."	Marcus, G.
"Changes in the University Scene: Their Effect on Home Economics."	Tinsley, W.
"Changing Emphasis in Professional Education."	Feder, L.
"The Changing Function of the Settlement Under Changing Conditions."	Hart, H.
"Changing Ideals in Southern Women."	Brady, S.
"The Changing Status of Women."	Thompson, D.
"Changing Status of Women."	Troxell, M.
"Changing the Political Role of Women: A Costa Rican Case Study."	Aviel, J.
"Changing the Program of a Public Welfare Agency."	Minton, E.

"Changing Trends in the Education of Caseworkers."	Clemence, E.
"Changing World of Living; Address."	Mead, M.
"Character Building in Education."	Richardson, E.
"Characteristics of the Modern Women."	Sherman, C.
"Charitable Co-operation."	Richmond, M.
"Charitable Effort."	Addams, J.
"The Charities Endorsement Committee."	Felton, K.
"Charity and Social Justice."	Addams, J.
"Charity as Taught by the Mosaic Law."	Stern, E.
"Charity Organization in the Smaller Cities."	Prier, M.
"Charter of Economic Human Rights. Economic and Human Rights Tied Into One Package."	Porter, S.
"Chartering and Supervision by State Authority."	Acton, A.
"Chattel Mortgages."	Birtwell, M.
"Chicago Women."	Stevenson, S.
"The Child and Its Enemies."	Goldman, E.
"Child at the Point of Greatest Pressure."	Addams, J.
"Child Care and Family Services."	Guggenheimer, E.
"Child Care and Family Services."	Lash, T.
"Child Guidance Clinics and Child Caring Agencies: The Value of the Psychiatric Approach for All Children's Case Workers."	McCord, E.
"Child Labor and Education."	Addams, J.
"Child Labor and Pauperism."	Addams, J.
"Child Labor in Illinois."	Kelley, F.
"Child Labor Laws."	Kelley, F.
"Child Labor Legislation: A Requisite for Industrial Efficiency."	Addams, J.
"Child Labor on the Stage."	Addams, J.
"The Child-Mother as a Delinquency Problem."	Lundberg, E.
"The Child of the Juvenile Court."	Montgomery, A.
"The Child or Girl Without a Mother and Mother Without a Child."	American, S.
"The Child Welfare Exhibit as a Means of Child Helping."	Strong, A.
"Child Welfare in Westchester County."	Taylor, R.
"Child Welfare Standards a Test of Democracy."	Lathrop, J.
"Child Welfare Work in a Rural Community."	Mendum, G.
"The Childless Married Woman."	Ostazeski, A.
"Children and the Depression."	Breckinridge, S.
"Children at Work."	Lunde, L.
"The Children of the Other Half."	Wheelock, L.
"The Children's Age."	Williamson, E.
"The Children's Bureau."	Abbott, G.
"The Children's Bureau."	Lathrop, J.

"Children's Institutions and the Accident Problem." Lattimore, F.
"China's Government. Federal Union Offers Real Solution." Luce, C.
"The Chinese Novel." Novel Lecture. Buck, P.
"Chinese Women in the Early Communist Movement." Leith, S.
"Chinese Women: Old Skills in a New Context." Wolf, M.
"The Chivalry of Reform. Address to the National American Woman Suffrage Association Convention, 1890." Howe, J.
"The Choice for American Youth." Bridges, B.
"Choose One of Five: Its Your Life." Sampson, E.
"Christ on the Avenue." Isaacs, M.
"Christian Healing; A Sermon Delivered at Boston." Eddy, M.
"The Christian Ideal for Woman as Interpreted by the Young Women's Christian Association." Cratty, M.
"The Christian League for the Promotion of Social Purity." Grannis, E.
"Christian Science in Tremont Temple." Eddy, M.
"Christmas Gifts." Green, E.
"A Christmas Sermon; Delivered in Chickering Hall, Boston, Mass., on the Sunday Before Christmas, 1888. Subject: The Corporeal and Incorporeal Savior." Eddy, M.
"Church Union." Grannis, E.
"Citizen in a Changing World: Women of Today." Louchheim, K.
"Citizen Responsibilities. 'They' Is 'We'." Hobby, O.
"The Citizen's Responsibility; A Panel Discussion." Buck, D.
"The Citizen's Responsibility; A Panel Discussion." Dickinson, L.
"The Citizen's Responsibility; A Panel Discussion." Edwards, I.
"The Citizen's Responsibility; A Panel Discussion." Farrington, M.
"The Citizen's Responsibility; A Panel Discussion." Heffelfinger, E.
"The Citizen's Responsibility; A Panel Discussion." Hottel, A.
"The Citizen's Responsibility; A Panel Discussion." Lord, M.
"The Citizen's Responsibility; A Panel Discussion." Scott, K.
"The Citizen's Responsibility; A Panel Discussion." Strauss, A.
"The Citizen's Responsibility; A Panel Discussion." Zimmerman, C.

"The Citizen's Role in Furthering Consumer Interests: Stop Being Cheated." Sullivan, L.
"Citizenship and Domicile Versus Social Considerations in Problems of Migrated Families." Hutchinson, W.
"Citizenship and Domicile Versus Social Considerations in Problems of Migrated Families." O'Connor, A.
"City Women and Religious Change in Sixteenth-century France." Davis, N.
"The City Worker's Family Budget." Brady, D.
"Civic Efforts of Social Settlements." Davis, K.
"Civil and Political Rights--Where Are We Now?" Everett, G.
"The Civil and Social Evolution of Woman." Stanton, E.
"Civil Defense Begins at Home." Leopold, A.
"Civil Service Reform." Lowell, J.
"Civilization or War?" Boeckel, F.
"Class Conflict in America." Addams, J.
"Class Structure and Female Autonomy in Rural Java." Stoler, A.
"Classical Mythology and the Role of Women in Modern Literature." Lefkowitz, M.
"A Classical Scholar's Perspective on Matriarchy." Pomeroy, S.
"Classification of Paupers. Is It Practicable in the U. S. to Classify Almshouse Inmates According to Character & Conduct?" Lincoln, A.
"Classification of the Mentally Deficient." Bancroft, M.
"Clean Food." Abel, M.
"Clean Food." Richards, E.
"Closing Address." Palmer, B.
"Closing Address." Stanton, E.
"Closing Address at the 16th Annual Convention of the National Woman Suffrage Association, March, 1884." Anthony, S.
"Closing Address at the 10th National Woman's Rights Convention, N. Y., May 10-11, 1860." Grew, M.
"Closing Address of the Annual Meeting of the American Woman Suffrage Association, 1885." Stone, L.
"Closing Remarks to the Conference of Professional and Academic Women." Epstein, C.
"Closing Statement at the Women's Industrial Conference." Anderson, M.
"Closing the Gap." Gilbreth, L.
"Closure of Kittery-Portsmouth Naval Shipyard." Smith, M.
"The Clothing Program for Federated Clubs." Phelps, E.

Title	Author
"Club House Manager."	Mac Quillin, L.
"The Club Woman and Law Enforcement."	Willebrandt, M.
"Coeds View an Undergraduate Campus."	Rodriguez, G.
"Co-education."	Michaels, R.
"Co-education in Universities."	Brownell, L.
"The Co-education of the Sexes."	Stanton, E.
"Co-education of the Sexes, Based Upon the Law of Sex."	Spencer, S.
"Coeducation: One Student's View."	Jelly, K.
"Cold War Thaw. An Asset or a Liability."	Lamb, M.
"The College and Alumnae in Contemporary Life."	Beard, M.
"College Fellowships for Women."	Benneson, C.
"College Women and Employment."	Zapoleon, M.
"College Women and the New Leisure."	Morrow, E.
"A Collegiate Education for Woman, and the Necessity of a Woman-Professor in the Mixed College."	Soule, C.
"The Colored Woman Should Not Be Ignored."	Cooper, A.
"The Columbian Association of Housekeepers and Bureau of Information, with Plans for the Work Outlined in the National Columbian Household Economic Association, Which Was Incorporated March 15, 1893."	Wilkinson, L.
"The Columbian Exposition."	Meredith, V.
"A Combination Heart and Tuberculosis Program."	Brophy, F.
"Come South, Young Woman."	Field, M.
"Coming Out."	Cooper, J.
"Coming Out."	Stanley, J.
"Commencement Speech on Equality, Delivered at Howard University in Washington, D. C., on June 5, 1942."	Buck, P.
"Comment After Defeat in House Judiciary Committee, March, 1916."	Paul, A.
"Comment on Background and Purpose of the Conference on the Present Status and Prospective Trends of Research on the Education of Women."	Knapp, P.
"Comment on Current Trends in the Education of Women."	Clapp, M.
"Comment on Patterns of Higher Education for Women."	Roberts, E.
"Comment on Pressures and Opportunities That Face the Educated Woman."	Bragdon, H.
"Commentary on the Role of Women's Legislation in Meeting Basic Problems of Working Conditions."	Rittenhouse, I.
"Comments at the Syracuse National Convention, Sept. 1852."	Blackwell, A.

"Comments at the Syracuse National Convention, Sept. 1852."	Davis, P.
"Comments at the Syracuse National Convention, Sept. 1852."	Jones, J.
"Comments at the Syracuse National Convention, Sept. 1852."	Mott, L.
"Comments at the Syracuse National Convention, Sept. 1852."	Nichols, C.
"Comments at the Syracuse National Convention, Sept. 1852."	Price, A.
"Comments at the Syracuse National Convention, Sept. 1852."	Smith, E.
"Comments at the Syracuse National Convention, Sept. 1852."	Stone, L.
"Comments at the Syracuse National Convention, Sept. 1852."	Stone, L.
"Comments on Divorce Resolutions at 10th National Woman's Rights Convention, May 11, 1860."	Anthony, S.
"Comments on the Bible Issue at the Syracuse National Convention, Sept. 1852."	Rose, E.
"Comments on the Declaration of Sentiments Adopted at the Westchester Convention at the Syracuse National Convention, Sept. 1852."	Nichols, C.
"Comments on Women's Property Rights at Westchester (Penn.) Convention, June, 1852."	Mott, L.
"Comments to Judiciary Committee of House of Representatives on Equal Rights Amendment, 1945."	Perkins, F.
"The Commitment Required of a Woman Entering a Scientific Profession."	Bunting, M.
"Committee on Industrial and Business Relations. Scientific Profession."	Williamson, M.
"Committee on Institutional Relations."	Jaffray, J.
"Committee on Social Hygiene."	Bishop, F.
"Common Attitudes Toward the Unmarried Father."	Marsh, M.
"The Common Goals of Labor and Social Work."	Van Kleeck, M.
"Communecology: A Concept for More Effective Communication."	Livingston, L.
"Communication: Alternative Points of View."	Bailey, M.
"Communion Address, January, 1896."	Eddy, M.
"The Communist Apparatus in Canada Today: Respectability and Acceptance."	Lamb, M.
"Community Centers in School Buildings."	White, E.

"Community Control of the Feeble-minded Instruction."	Anderson, M.
"Community Councils in Pittsburgh."	Burnett, M.
"A Community Kitchen in a Neighborhood House."	Ingram, F.
"Community Organization for Child Guidance Clinic Work."	Marcus, G.
"Community Organization for Health."	Goodrich, A.
"Community Organization for Health--Discussion."	Yarros, R.
"Community Organizations and Child-care Arrangements."	Easley, L.
"Community Planning in Rural Communities."	Reeves, M.
"A Community Program for Protective Work."	Miner, M.
"Community Programs and Cooperation in Americanization."	Turner, M.
"Community Protective Social Measures."	Binford, J.
"Community Relationships Involved in 100 Per Cent Registration in Social Service Exchange: From the Standpoint of Family Welfare Organizations."	Wallerstein, H.
"Community Relationships Involved in 100 Per Cent Registration in Social Service Exchange: From the Standpoint of Hospital Social Service."	Cannon, I.
"Community Relationships Involved in 100 Per Cent Registration in Social Service Exchange: From the Standpoint of Hospital Social Service."	Webb, S.
"Community Relationships Involved in 100 Per Cent Registration in Social Service Exchange: From the Standpoint of Nursing Organizations."	Tucker, K.
"Community Representation and Participation in Community Organization."	Shaw, T.
"Community Responsibility for Preventing Crime."	Additon, H.
"Community Responsibility for Recreation Facilities."	Binford, J.
"Community Responsibility for Recreation Facilities--Discussion."	Monahan, F.
"A Community-Wide Volunteer Placement Bureau."	Newbold, F.
"Comparative Advantages of Municipal and C. O. S. Lodging Houses."	Higgins, A.
"Compensation."	Abbott, A.

"Complete Freedom for Women."	Manning, A.
"Concludes Discussion of the Moral Initiative as Related to Woman."	Locke, J.
"Concluding Remarks at the Anniversary Meeting of the Woman's National Loyal League, May 12, 1864."	Stanton, E.
"Concluding Remarks at the Woman's National Loyal League Convention, May 14, 1863."	Stone, L.
"The Condition of Women Workers Under the Present Industrial System."	Van Etten, I.
"Conditions Breeding Delinquency in Rural Communities."	Mendum, G.
"Conditions in Industry as They Affect Negro Women."	Irwin, H.
"Conditions in the Canal Zone."	Boswell, H.
"Conditions of Wage-Earning Women."	Laughlin, G.
"The Conduct of the President."	Abzug, B.
"Conference Summary."	Douty, A.
"The Confidential Exchange in the Small City."	Byington, M.
"The Confidential Relationship in Social Work Administration."	Miller, P.
"Conflict, Probable; Coalition, Possible; Feminism and the Black Movement."	Stimpson, C.
"Congratulation on the Possession of Mrs. Palmer's Portrait."	Wheeler, C.
"Congress in 1943 and 1944, Procedure Must Be Brought Up to Date."	Bennett, M.
"Congresswoman."	O'Day, C.
"The Consequences of Social Action for the Group-Work Agency."	Hall, H.
"Conserving Human Values in Public Welfare Programs."	Kahn, D.
"Constitution of a District Conference."	Fields, A.
"The Constitutional Argument. Address to the House Judiciary Committee, 1900."	Blake, L.
"Constitutional Argument. Delivered in Twenty-nine of the Post-Office Districts of Monroe, and Twenty-one of Ontario, in Miss Anthony's Canvass of Those Counties Prior to Her Trial in June, 1873."	Anthony, S.
"The Constitutional Rights of Women in the United States."	Hooker, I.
"Constructive Federal-State Relationships: From the Federal Viewpoint."	Foster, E.
"A Constructive Program for the Aged."	McHugh, R.
"Consumer Organization."	Woods, A.
"Consumerism: A Three-toed Sloth."	Bostick, M.
"Consumers' Interests in the National Recovery Act."	Daniels, K.

"Contemporary Feminism, Consciousness-raising, and Changing Views of the Political." McWilliam, N.
"Continued Care of Families." Smith, F.
"Contrasting Values of the Drama and Festival in Group Work." Chorpenning, C.
"The Contribution of American Women to National and International Affairs. Achievements and Goals of American Women." Peterson, E.
"Contribution of Case Work to the Administration of Social Insurance--A Critical Analysis of European Experience." Kraus, H.
"The Contribution of Group Experience to the Development of Older Children." Coyle, G.
"The Contribution of Hospital Social Service to Health Conservation." Baker, E.
"The Contribution of Social Case Work to Democracy." Vaile, G.
"The Contribution of Social Work to Government." Hoey, J.
"The Contribution of Women to the Applied Arts." Cory, F.
"The Control of Syphilis, from the Viewpoint of Medical Social Service." Hearsey, M.
"Controlling Labor Reduction." Carroll, M.
"Controversy Over Enactment of Standby Wage and Price Controls." Sullivan, L.
"Controversy Over Federal Experimentation with Education Vouchers." Swanker, E.
"Controversy Over the Carter Administration Proposals for Welfare Reform." Foreman, C.
"Controversy Over the Carter Administration Proposals for Welfare Reform." Kuhn, M.
"Cookery." Lincoln, M.
"Cooking as an Art." Johnson, H.
"Cooperation Between Courts and Voluntary Public Agencies (Abstract)." Low, M.
"Cooperation of the Home Service Department of the American Red Cross with Other Social Agencies." Anderson, H.
"Co-operation of the National Women's Organizations for Good Schools." Gill, L.
"The Co-operation of Women in Philanthropic and Reformatory Work." Smith, V.
"The Cooperation of Women in Philanthropy." Richardson, A.
"Co-operation or Obstruction in Determining Fields of Activity." Curry, H.
"Co-operation, the Law of the New Civilization." Sayles, L.
"Co-operation with the Women's Foundation for Health." Meanes, L.

"Co-operative Case-Work Services to Sick People in Rural Areas."	Mills, E.
"A Cooperative Experiment Between Public and Private Agencies."	McCord, E.
"Cooperative Housekeeping."	Stuckert, M.
"Cooperative Interpretation."	Tousley, C.
"Co-ordinating as Done by Charity Organization Societies."	Buffington, A.
"Co-ordinating as Done by the Public Health Nurse."	Stewart, H.
"Co-ordinating Relief."	Belmont, A.
"Coordination and Development of Welfare Services in the County."	Potter, E.
"Co-ordination of Civil Effort in Small Communities."	Byington, M.
"Coordination of Effort in Mental Hygiene in the Community."	Dawley, A.
"Coordination of Institution Care of Children with Other Services in the Community."	Foster, S.
"The Co-ordination of Public and Private Agencies in a State Program of Public Health Nursing."	Marriner, J.
"Co-ordination of State and Local Units for Welfare Administration."	LaDu, B.
"Co-ordination of State and Local Units for Welfare Administration."	Potter, E.
"The Co-ordination of the Juvenile Court with Other Courts."	Rippin, J.
"The Cost of Care."	Chisholm, S.
"The Cost of Maintaining Good Case Work in a Public Agency."	Porter, R.
"The Cost of Maintaining Good Case Work in a Public Agency."	Vaile, G.
"Costumes and Customs from the Holy Land."	Paul, N.
"The Council's Interest."	Allen, L.
"Counseling in Industry."	McGowan, C.
"Counseling in the Family Agency."	Levinson, F.
"Count Tolstoy."	Addams, J.
"Country Homes for Dependent Children."	Bailey, E.
"The County as a Unit for Co-ordinate Planning and Service in Public and Private Social Work (Point of View of Public Officials)."	Johnson, A.
"The County as a Unit in Charity Administration--Roundtable."	Curry, H.
"County Jails."	Kinsella, N.
"County Organization of Welfare Agencies."	McClenahan, B.
"County Programs of Child Care: The Relation of Probation to Other County Social Work."	Gibson, K.
"County Programs of Child Care: What Should a County Program Undertake?"	Curry, H.

"A County Unit for Social Service."	Brown, S.
"The County Versus the Community as an Administrative Unit."	Abbott, G.
"Course of Popular Lectures."	Wright, F.
"Courses of Training for Visiting Teachers."	Pratt, A.
"Court Procedure in Securing Support for a Child of Illegitimate Birth."	Lee, E.
"Courtship and Other Legal Arts: The Appellate System."	Hufstedler, S.
"Creating a Demand for Health."	Jean, S.
"Creating a Feminist Alliance: Sisterhood and Class Conflict in the New York Women's Trade Union League, 1903-1914."	Dye, N.
"Creative Librarianship."	Rathbone, J.
"The Creative Use of Leisure."	Wright, L.
"Creative Uses of the Arts--the Dance."	St. Denis, R.
"Creative Writing for Social Work."	Paradise, V.
"Crime: An Address."	Hawthone, J.
"The Crises of Divorce."	Friedan, B.
"The Crisis and Our Responsibility. Commonsense Is Lacking."	Woolley, M.
"Crisis in Soviet-Chinese Relations: The Two Red Giants."	Luce, C.
"Crisis in the History of Women. Let Us Have Action Instead of Lip-Service."	Hurst, F.
"Crisis in the United Nations: American Public Opinion."	Luce, C.
"The Crisis in Women's Identity."	Friedan, B.
"Crisis of Self: America's Secret War; Remarks at the 1973 Congress for Recreation and Parks."	Mead, M.
"The Crown of St. Stephen."	Grasso, E.
"Crusade for Morality. Women Power."	Roundtree, M.
"The Cry of Humanity."	O'Reilly, L.
"Cultural and Psychohistorical Background of Women's Status in America."	Komarovsky, M.
"A Cultural Dilemma."	Mead, M.
"The Cultural Pressures on Women."	Mueller, K.
"The Cultural Production of Childbirth."	Jordan, B.
"Culture--Its Fruit and Its Price."	Sewall, M.
"Culture in Family Life from the Social Settlement Standpoint."	Vittum, H.
"The Culture of Family Life Versus Reformatory Treatment."	Falconer, M.
"Current Frontiers in Social Group Work."	Kaiser, C.
"Current National Developments and Problems in Public Welfare, Children's Services."	Lenroot, K.
"The Current Status of the Employment of Women."	East, C.

"Current Trends in Adoption."	Gordon, H.
"Current Trends in Foster Parent Education."	Wildy, L.
"Customs Reorganization and Modernization: The Procedures Which Affect International Trade."	Anderson, B.
"The Dance Problem."	Moskowitz, B.
"The Danger Line in Public Economy."	Bernstein, P.
"Danger to Our Government."	Catt, C.
"Dante and Beatrice."	Howe, J.
"The Dawning of the Twentieth Century."	Howell, M.
"Day Care Services for Children of Campus Employees."	Schmalzried, B.
"A Day with the Visiting Teacher."	Case, E.
"The Deaf Child and the Hard-of-Hearing Child."	Timberlake, J.
"The Death of Democracies. How to Avoid It: By Facing Realities."	Thompson, D.
"Debate at the 1893 Convention of the National American Woman Suffrage Association."	Anthony, S.
"Debate at the 4th National Convention, Cleveland, Ohio, October 1853."	Stone, L.
"Debate at the 2nd Annual Meeting of the American Equal Rights Association, May 14, 1868."	Brown, O.
"Debate at the 2nd Woman's Suffrage Convention in Washington, D. C., January 1870."	Wilbour, C.
"Debate at the 3rd Annual Meeting of the American Equal Rights Association, N. Y., May, 1869."	Livermore, M.
"Debate at the 3rd Annual Meeting of the American Equal Rights Association, N. Y., May, 1869."	Rose, E.
"Debate at the 3rd Annual Meeting of the American Equal Rights Association, N. Y., May, 1869."	Stone, L.
"Debate at the 3rd Annual Meeting of the American Equal Rights Association, N. Y., May, 1869."	Stone, L.
"Debate at the Woman's National Loyal League Convention, May 14, 1863."	Coleman, L.
"Debate at the Woman's National Loyal League Convention, May 14, 1863."	Rose, E.
"Debate at the Woman's National Loyal League Convention, May 14, 1863. '	Stone, L.
"Debate During the 4th National Convention, Cleveland, Ohio, Oct. 1853."	Mott, L.
"Debate on Constitutional Amendment to Lower Voting Age to 18."	Grasso, E.

"Debate on Divorce at Daughters of Temperance Meeting, Rochester, N. Y., 1852." Bloomer, A.
"Debate on Divorce Resolution at the N. Y. State Temperance Convention, Rochester, N. Y., 1852." Bloomer, A.
"Debate on Office of Economic Opportunity." Chisholm, S.
"Debate on Resolution Authorizing the President to Requisition the Copper Mines of Montana During Labor Unrest." Rankin, J.
"Debate on the Bible Resolution at the National Convention of the National American Woman Suffrage Association, November 1895." Anthony, S.
"Debate on the Divorce Resolution at the 10th National Woman's Rights Convention, N. Y., May 10-11, 1860." Blackwell, A.
"Debate on the Divorce Resolutions at the 10th National Woman's Rights Convention, N. Y., May 10-11, 1860." Rose, E.
"Debate on the Elevation of Women at the 2nd Worcester Convention, Oct. 1851." Stone, L.
"Debate with Judge Hunt at Her Trial for Voting, June, 1873." Anthony, S.
"Decade Speech, on the Progress of Education and Industrial Avocations for Women." Gage, M.
"A Declaration of Conscience: June 1, 1950." Smith, M.
"Declaration of Rights for Women, Read at Independence Hall, Philadelphia, July 4, 1876." Anthony, S.
"Decoration Day Speech at a Prohibition Party Convention, 1888." Willard, F.
"Defense Speech at Trial for Picketing White House, 1917." Hilles, F.
"The Degradation of Disfranchisement. Read to the National American Woman Suffrage Association by Susan B. Anthony, Feb. 16, 1891." Stanton, E.
"Delinquency and the School." Van Waters, M.
"The Delinquent Attitude--A Study of Juvenile Delinquency from the Standpoint of Human Relationship." Van Waters, M.
"The Delinquent Child of Immigrant Parents." Bowen, L.
"The Delinquent Girl." Francis, V.
"Demand for Party Recognition. Delivered in Kansas City at the Opening of the Campaign, May 4, 1894." Anthony, S.

"A Demand for the Political Rights of Women." Mott, L.
"The Demand for the Vote." Stanton, E.
"A Demand for Women in the Faculties of Co-Educational Colleges and Universities." Stone, L.
"Democracy in Immigrant Neighborhood Life." Frasca, M.
"Democratic Convention Keynote Address: Who Then Will Speak for the Common Good?" Jordan, B.
"Democratic Principles in Public Assistance." Kahn, D.
"Demonstration as Part of the Survey Process." Atkinson, M.
"The Department of Justice and Some Problems of Enforcement." Willebrandt, M.
"Dependent and Delinquent Children in This Country and Abroad." Putnam, E.
"Depressions and the Feminine Situation." Spiegel, R.
"The Determination of Social Work Salaries." Hosch, F.
"Detroit's Experience with Job Classification." Whiting, M.
"Detroit's Experience with the Wartime Care of Children." Murphy, I.
"Developing and Protecting Professional Standards in Public Welfare Work." Abbott, G.
"Developing Community Interest in Foster Homes." Bullock, K.
"Developing Standards of Rural Child Welfare." Abbott, G.
"Development in Eastern Washington." White, J.
"Development of County or Town Boards." Curry, H.
"The Development of Existing Neighborhood Activities." Neufeld, E.
"The Development of Greater Sympathy and Understanding Between Parents and Children." Mudgett, M.
"Development Planning for Women." Papanek, H.
"Detention of Deportees." Clark, J.
"Dietetics." Hogan, L.
"Difficulties and Delights of Women's Clubs." Poole, H.
"Dimensions of Physical Activity." Harris, D.
"The Dimensions of the Oppression of Women: Unequal Pay for Equal Work." Springen, P.
"Directed Reading for Children." Becker, M.
"The Direction of Women's Education." Beard, M.
"Disappointment Is the Lot of Woman." Stone, L.
"Disarmament and Life." Addams, J.
"Disciplinary Measures in the Management of the Psychopathic Delinquent Women." Hodder, J.

Title	Author
"Discipline and Training of Girls in Industrial Schools."	Montgomery, S.
"Discourse at Friends' Meeting, Fifteenth Street, New York. Delivered Eleventh Month 11th, 1866."	Mott, L.
"Discourse in the Assembly Buildings in Philadelphia on Woman and the Bible, and Women's Rights."	Mott, L.
"Discourse on Woman, Delivered Twelfth Month 17th, 1849."	Mott, L.
"Discourse on Women, 1849."	Mott, L.
"Discrimination and Poverty Among Women Who Head Families."	Sawhill, I.
"Discrimination in Housing, Public Accommodations, and Employment."	Greitzer, C.
"Discussion of Immigration Under the Percentum Limit Law."	Abbott, E.
"Discussion of One Phase of Woman's Work for the Municipality."	Hall, S.
"Discussion of Paper on Kindergarten."	Severance, C.
"Discussion of Paper on Kindergarten."	Tupper, M.
"Discussion of Paper on the Ethical Influence of Woman in Education."	Cabell, M.
"Discussion of Paper on the Ethical Influence of Woman in Education."	Leonard, A.
"Discussion of Paper on the Ethical Influence of Woman in Education."	Mosher, F.
"Discussion of Resolutions at the 11th National Woman's Rights Convention, May 10, 1866."	Anthony, S.
"Discussion of Social Research in Public Institutions."	Davis, K.
"Discussion of the Civil and Social Evolution of Woman."	Thomas, M.
"Discussion of the Contribution of Women to the Applied Arts."	Sartain, E.
"Discussion of the Effects of Modern Changes in Industrial and Social Life on Woman's Marriage Prospects."	Shaw, A.
"Discussion of the Effects of Modern Changes in Industrial and Social Life on Woman's Marriage Prospects."	Toomy, A.
"Discussion of the Effects of Modern Changes in Industrial and Social Life on Woman's Marriage Prospects."	Wadsworth, E.
"Discussion of the Ethics of Dress."	Bates, O.
"Discussion of the Ethics of Dress."	Krecker, E.
"Discussion (of the Evolution of Psychiatric Social Work)--From the Viewpoint of the Psychiatric Social Worker."	Allen, E.

"Discussion of the Intellectual Progress of the Colored Women of the United States Since the Emancipation Proclamation." Cooper, A.
"Discussion of the Moral Initiative as Related to Women." Blackwell, A.
"Discussion of the Organized Efforts of the Colored Women of the South to Improve Their Condition." Brown, H.
"Discussion of the Psychological and Physiological Aspects of Woman and the Role They Play in Her Destiny." Sachs, B.
"Discussion of the Responsibility of Juvenile Court and Public Agency in Child Welfare." Gane, E.
"Discussion of the Trades and Professions Underlying the Home." Goessmann, H.
"Discussion of Woman as a Minister of Religion." Quinton, A.
"Discussion of Woman as a Political Leader." Ormsby, M.
"Discussion of Woman as a Religious Teacher." Cooper, S.
"Discussion of Woman as a Religious Teacher." Grannis, E.
"Discussion of Woman as a Religious Teacher." Harley, F.
"Discussion of Woman as a Religious Teacher." Scudder, A.
"Discussion of Woman as a Religious Teacher." White, L.
"Discussion of Woman as a Religious Teacher." Young, Z.
"Discussion of Woman's Dress from the Standpoint of Sociology." Webster, H.
"Discussion of Women as an Actual Force in Politics." Blake, L.
"Discussion on Woman's Call to the Ministry." Moreland, M.
"Discussion on Woman's Call to the Ministry." St. John, E.
"Dissent in Education." Crain, L.
"A Dissolution of the Existing Social Compact." Smith, E.
"The District Almshouse for Illinois." Hinrichsen, A.
"The District Nurse in Co-operative Work." Janime, M.
"The District Nurse in Rural Work." Clement, F.
"District Nursing." Quaife, F.
"District Nursing in London." Kimber, D.
"Division on Delinquents and Correction." Hoey, J.
"Do We Need Emerson Today? New Theories of Living Are Being Forced Upon Us." Meyer, A.

"Does the Health of Our Democracy Require a Change of Party in November." Cowles, F.
"Does the Health of Our Democracy Require a Change of Party in November: Panel Discussion." Schiff, D.
"Domestic Service and the Family Claim." Addams, J.
"Downtown Planning. Solving Traffic Problems." Jacobs, J.
"The Draft: Education for Citizenship." Hobby, O.
"The Drama as a Field for Women." Ward, G.
"Dreams and Dilemmas of Being a Woman Today." Sherif, C.
"Dress Improvement." Miller, A.
"Duty and Honor. Address to the National-American Woman Suffrage Association Convention of 1897." Gilman, C.
"The Duty of the American White Woman to the American Black Woman." Parker, J.
"Duty to Dependent Races." Harper, F.
"Duty to the Women of Our New Possessions." Spencer, A.
"Dwellings of the Poor in the Smaller Cities." Williamson, E.
"The Dynamics of Successful People." Bardwick, J.

"The Eastern Star, Its Origin, Progress, and Development." Snedden, M.
"The Economic and Moral Effects of Public Outdoor Relief." Lowell, J.
"The Economic Basis of Woman Suffrage. Address to the House Judiciary Committee, 1900." Tillinghast, E.
"The Economic Independence of Women." Prescott, L.
"Economic Justice for Women." Chisholm, S.
"The Economic Position of Women as Journalists." Alden, C.
"The Economic Role of Women, Forty-five to Sixty-five." Kyrk, H.
"Economic Security Under Communism." Hanna, R.
"Economics of Disarmament. Expansion in Civilian Markets at Home and Abroad." Newcomer, M.
"The Economy of Nursing the Sick Poor in Their Homes." Wise, L.
"The Economy of the State in the Care of Dependent and Neglected Children." Smith, V.
"The Economy of Woman's Forces Through Organization." Sewall, M.
"The Educated Heart. The Heart, Informed with Love, Will Never Be

in Conflict with the Enlightened Mind." Vining, E.
"Educated Women as Factors in Industrial Competition." Lord, E.
"Educating Women for Leadership: A Program for the Future." Tobias, S.
"Educating Women for Safety and Health." Mohr, J.
"Education." Addams, J.
"The Education and Custody of the Imbecile." Mott, A.
"Education and Ideology in Nineteenth-Century America: The Response of Educational Institutions to the Changing Role of Women." Simmons, A.
"Education and International Peace." Andrews, F.
"Education and Socialization." Pettigrew, L.
"Education as a Preparation for Life." Peck, M.
"Education, Communist Style, American Style. The Students of Today Are the Leaders of Tomorrow." Dulles, E.
"Education for a New Day." Gildersleeve, V.
"Education for Public Social Services." Hathway, M.
"Education for the Millions Through Pictures." Garson, G.
"Education for What? A Challenge to Teaching." McIntosh, M.
"Education in Food Values as a Preventive of Dietary Deficiencies." Gillett, L.
"Education--New Currents." Davis, M.
"The Education of Female Teachers." Beecher, C.
"Education of Indian Girls in the West." Todd, M.
"The Education of the Friendly Visitor." Smith, Z.
"Educational Methods." Addams, J.
"Educational Methods in Teaching Workers." Fairchild, M.
"The Educational Opportunities Presented by the School Luncheon." Jean, S.
"The Educational Opportunity of the Visiting Nurse in the Prevention of Disease." Aikers, C.
"Educational Training in Its Bearing Upon the Promotion of Social Purity." Lozier, J.
"The Educational Value of Applied Arts." Sheldon, E.
"Educational Value to the Community of Mental Hygiene Agencies: Psychiatric Social Work." Jarrett, M.
"The Educational Work of the Kentucky Federation of Women's Clubs." Breckinridge, D.
"The Effect of an Unemployment Situation in Family Societies." Bedford, C.
"The Effect of Joint Administration on Case Work Practices." Rich, M.

"The Effect of Labor Laws on Women Workers."	Winslow, M.
"The Effect of Staff Turnover on Families Under Care, as Demonstrated in Changes of Plan and Treatment and General Tempo of Work."	Stabler, D.
"The Effect of the Cable Law on the Citizenship Status of Foreign Women."	Roche, J.
"The Effect of the N. R. A. on Labor."	Van Kleeck, M.
"The Effective Organization of Social Forces in Small Towns and Rural Communities."	Wood, M.
"The Effects of Financial Dependency and Relief Giving Upon Social Attitudes."	Marcus, G.
"The Effects of Foster Home Placements."	Bissell, E.
"The Effects of Participation in Woman's Consciousness-Raising Groups."	Riger, S.
"The Effects on Case Work Services of Social Factors in the Negro's Life: From the Point of View of Economic Factors."	Jones, F.
"The Effects on Case Work Services of Social Factors in the Negro's Life: From the Point of View of Socio-Political Factors."	Conner, L.
"The Effects on the Child of an Unstable Home Situation."	Newmann, F.
"Efficiency in the Use of Volunteers."	Goodwillie, M.
"1873 Trial for Voting, Rochester, N. Y."	Anthony, S.
"Election Eve Campaign Speech, 1st Senate Campaign, Nov. 1948."	Smith, M.
"Electric Power and the Public Welfare. Address to 1926 National Convention of the League of Women Voters."	Bursch, A.
"Elegance Is Not Undemocratic, Stop the Search for the Lowest Common Denominator."	Rogers, A.
"Elementary Adult Education for Native--and Foreign-Born."	Baughman, R.
"The Elementary School and the Individual Child."	Richards, E.
"The Elevation of Womanhood Wrought Through the Veneration of the Blessed Virgin."	Cary, E.
"The Elimination of the Reformatory."	Smith, C.
"The Elixir of Life."	Woodhull, V.
"Elizabeth Cady Stanton on the Politics of Woman Suffrage."	Stanton, E.
"Elizabeth Gurley Flynn's Defense."	Flynn, E.
"The Emergency Employment Bill."	Grasso, E.
"Emergency Loan Guarantee Act of 1971 to Lockheed Corp."	Grasso, E.

"Emergent Modes of Utilization: Gynecological Self Help."	Rugek, S.
"Emigration Conditions in European Ports of Embarkation."	Schisby, M.
"Emotional Growth of the Worker Through Supervision."	Hollis, F.
"Emotional Life of Girls."	Kennard, B.
"Employment Implications of Psychological Characteristics of Men and Women."	Matthews, E.
"Employment of Married Women in the Public Schools."	Ripley, M.
"The Employment of Minors in Wartime."	McConnell, B.
"Employment Opportunities for Minorities in New York City: An Introduction."	Wallace, P.
"Employment Opportunities for Women."	Keyserling, M.
"Employment Opportunities in the Woman's Service Exchange Program of Madison, Wisconsin."	La Follette, I.
"The Employment Rights of the Female: The Present Challenge."	Prewitt, L.
"Engels Revisited: Women, the Organization of Production, and Private Property."	Sacks, K.
"The Enlarged Function of the Public School."	Simkhovitch, M.
"Enlightened Motherhood."	Bristol, A.
"Enlightened Motherhood."	Corbin, C.
"Enlightened Motherhood."	Cutler, H.
"Enlightened Motherhood."	Lovering, E.
"Enlightened Motherhood--How Attainable."	Chandler, L.
"Enriching the Rural Community."	Dingman, H.
"Entry and Reentry of Older Women into Labor Market: Older Women in Labor Force."	Hilton, M.
"Entry and Reentry of Older Women into Labor Market: Psychological Barriers to Employment of Mature Women."	Ravner, P.
"Environmental Conflicts in the Family and Social Life of the Modern Child."	Cowan, L.
"Environmental Conflicts in the Family and Social Life of the Modern Child."	Watson, M.
"Environmental Handicaps of Four Hundred Habit Clinic Children."	Reynolds, B.
"Equal Educational Opportunities."	Fisher, A.
"Equal Opportunity & Equal Responsibility. These Are Two Sides of the Same Single Coin."	Sampson, E.
"Equal Pay for Equal Work?"	Chapman, J.
"Equal Pay for Equal Work."	Gilman, C.
"Equal Pay, What Are the Facts?"	Brady, D.

"Equal Moral Standards."	Davis, K.
"The Equal Rights Amendment."	Abzug, B.
"Equal Rights Amendment."	Chisholm, S.
"Equal Rights Amendment."	Chisholm, S.
"Equal Rights Amendment."	Grasso, E.
"Equal Rights Amendment."	Griffiths, M.
"Equal Rights Amendment."	Heide, W.
"The Equal Rights Amendment."	Miller, E.
"Equal Rights Amendment."	Murray, P.
"The Equal Rights Amendment."	St. George, K.
"Equal Rights for Women."	Chisholm, S.
"Equal Rights for Women; Speeches by Ernestine L. Rose at the Third National Woman's Rights Convention, Syracuse, N. Y., September 8-10, 1852."	Rose, E.
"Equal Suffrage as Related to the Purity Movement."	Chapman, M.
"The Equal Wage."	Breckinridge, S.
"The Equality Issue."	Atkinson, T.
"Equipment Needed by the Medical Social Worker."	Cannon, M.
"Ernestine Rose at Worcester."	Rose, E.
"The Essence of Shelter."	Hauser, C.
"The Essential Similarities in All Fields of Case Work."	Dawley, A.
"Establishing Foster Parental Relationships."	Baylor, E.
"Establishing Policewomen in Maryland in 1912."	Beveridge, E.
"Establishment of Paternity."	Morlock, M.
"Etching."	Dillaye, B.
"The Ethical Influence of Woman in Education."	Galpin, K.
"Ethical Problems in Medical Experimentation Involving Women."	Sechrest, L.
"Ethics and Aesthetics of Dress."	Swayze, M.
"The Ethics of Dress."	Toomy, A.
"Ethics of Social Life."	Hanna, I.
"The Ethics of Spending."	Nathan, M.
"The Ethics of Suffrage."	Stanton, E.
"Eulogy at Mary S. Anthony's Funeral, February 7, 1907."	Montgomery, H.
"Eulogy at Susan B. Anthony's Funeral, March 15, 1906."	Catt, C.
"Eulogy for Florence Kelley, March, 1932."	Perkins, F.
"Eulogy for Lucretia Mott--Memorial Service in 1881."	Stanton, E.
"Eulogy for Mary S. Anthony, at Her Funeral, February 7, 1907."	Shaw, A.
"Eulogy for Mary S. Anthony's Funeral, February 7, 1907."	Gannett, M.

Title	Author
"An Evaluation of Home Economics Training."	LeBaron, H.
"Even Sea Shells Sing When You Listen: Let Us Not Waste Precious Time Asking Who We Are."	Hansen, N.
"Every Man Should Have His Say: Free Discussion."	May, C.
"The Evils Suffered by American Women and American Children: The Causes and the Remedy, Presented in an Address by Miss C. E. Beecher, to Meetings of Ladies in Cincinnati, Washington, Baltimore, Philadelphia, New York, and Other Cities."	Beecher, C.
"The Evolution of Home."	Corson, J.
"Evolution of Our Case-Work Concepts."	Austin, L.
"The Evolution of Psychiatric Social Work (Shown by Use of a Case Presentation)."	Moore, K.
"Evolution of the Illinois Child Labor Law."	Kelley, F.
"The Evolution of Women in Literature."	Lockwood, M.
"Excerpt from Address at the Organizational Meeting of the National Women's Trade Union League, Boston, 1903."	Addams, J.
"Excerpt from 2nd Address to the N. Y. Legislature, March 19, 1860."	Stanton, E.
"Excerpt from Statement on Pending Health Security Act, April 23, 1974."	Griffiths, M.
"Excerpt from Testimony Before Committee on Finance of the U. S. Senate, September 22, 1967."	Griffiths, M.
"Excerpt from Testimony Before the Subcommittee on Constitutional Amendments, May 5, 1970."	Griffiths, M.
"Excessive Nationalism--Discussion."	Manus, R.
"The Exercise of Conscience. "Is It Good?" Not "Will It Sell?" Should Be the Criterion."	Mannes, M.
"Exhortation."	Bottome, M.
"Expanding Opportunities Through Continuing Education."	Loring, R.
"The Expanding Role of Government--Discussion."	Stevenson, M.
"An Experiment in Trying to Grade District Visitors."	Vaile, G.
"The Experimental Period of Widows' Pension Legislation."	Abbott, E.
"Experiments in Preventing Juvenile Delinquency."	Bowler, A.

Title	Author
"Explanation of Vote on Draft Resolution on World Conference of the International Women's Year."	Maymi, C.
"Exploiting the Employed."	Nestor, A.
"Exploiting the Employed--Discussion."	Frost, W.
"Extemporaneous Speech at a National Woman's-Rights Convention in Cincinnati in October 1855."	Stone, L.
"Extemporaneous Speech Made at a Suffrage Hearing, February 1884."	Howe, J.
"Extracts from Address by Lucretia Mott at the Anti-Sabbath Convention, Held in Boston, Mass., March 23rd and 24th, 1848."	Mott, L.
"Extracts from Addresses at International Council of Women in Washington, March 25 to April 1, 1888."	Willard, F.
"Extracts from Possibilities of the Southern States."	Roman, S.
"Extracts from Reports of Lucretia Mott's Addresses at the Annual Meetings of the Free Religious Association, in Boston."	Mott, L.
"Extracts from Vocal Art."	Brown, M.
"Extracts from Woman and Religion."	Hultin, I.
"The Extra-Institutional Services of County Institutions."	Curry, H.
"Facilitating Change."	Hall, O.
"Facing Facts About Women's Lives Today."	Keyserling, M.
"Facing the Future."	Sherwin, B.
"Fact Finding and Research as a Basis of Program Making in Social Work."	Deardorff, N.
"Factors Affecting College Attendance."	Hawkes, A.
"Factors Affecting Decision on Unmarried Mother to Give Up or Keep Her Child, Environmental Factors."	Bosworth, A.
"Factors in Treatment."	Towle, C.
"Factory Legislation."	Blatch, H.
"Factory Legislation in Illinois."	Kelley, F.
"The Facts, the Hopes, and the Possibilities."	Banning, M.
"Facts Versus Folklore."	Wilkins, J.
"Failure Is Impossible, Last Public Speech at Her 86th Birthday Celebration, February 15, 1906."	Anthony, S.
"The Failure of Christianity."	Goldman, E.
"Faith and Force, the Destroyers of the Modern World. The Age of Guilt."	Rand, A.
"The Faith of Islam."	Clark, L.

"Familial Constraints on Women's Work Roles."	Boulding, E.
"Family Achievement."	Brisley, M.
"Family Affection."	Addams, J.
"The Family and the Law."	Breckinridge, S.
"The Family and the Social Worker."	Richmond, M.
"The Family and the Woman's Wage."	Kelley, F.
"The Family Budget and Its Supervision."	Nesbitt, F.
"Family Budget Planning."	Hanchette, H.
"Family Case Work with Marital Difficulties."	Hanford, J.
"Family Health Teaching, or the Public Health Nurse."	Beard, M.
"Family Homes for Pauper and Dependent Children."	Leonard, C.
"The Family in the Community, but Not Yet of the Community."	Breckinridge, S.
"The Family Keystone."	Parker, V.
"Family Life and Alcoholism."	Woods, A.
"Family Life in the Rural Community."	Haefner, R.
"Family Life in Transition."	Janeway, E.
"Family Limitation and Family Health."	Stone, H.
"Family Problems Resulting from the Present Deportation System."	Rom, G.
"Family, Property, and Domicile Law in the State of New York."	Seidenberg, F.
"Family Readjustment After the War."	Goodwillie, M.
"Family Responsibilities of Earning Women."	Kyrk, H.
"Family Structure and Feminine Personality."	Chodorow, N.
"Family, the School, and Crime."	Glueck, E.
"The Farm Family and Buying Power."	Rowe, B.
"The Fate of Republics."	Shaw, A.
"The Fear of Loving."	Fried, E.
"Federal Aid to Education."	Meyer, A.
"The Federal Children's Bureau."	Rude, A.
"The Federal Children's Bureau--A Symposium."	Addams, J.
"The Federal Government and Desirable Standards of State and Local Administration."	Lenroot, K.
"The Federal Government and Desirable Standards of State and Local Government."	Hoey, J.
"Federal Unemployment Insurance."	Perkins, F.
"Federal Wage and Hour Regulation."	Herrick, E.
"Federal Women's Program."	Dennett, J.
"Fees for Adoption Service."	Foster, S.
"Female Homosexuality: A Sweet Enfranchisement."	Eisenbud, R.
"The Female Primate."	Jay, P.

Title	Author
"Female Status: A New Population Policy."	Gray, V.
"Female Status in the Public Domain."	Sanday, P.
"Female Status, the Family and Male Dominance in a West Indian Community."	Moses, Y.
"Females in the Competitive Process."	Sherif, C.
"Femininity and Achievement in Sports."	Zoble, J.
"Feminism and Black Liberation."	Smythe, M.
"Feminism and Class Consciousness in the British and American Women's Trade Union Leagues, 1890-1925."	Jacoby, R.
"Feminism and Liberalism in Wilhelmine Germany, 1890-1918."	Hackett, A.
"Feminism, Art, and My Mother Sylvia."	Dworkin, A.
"Feminism: The Sine Qua Non for a Just Society."	Heide, W.
"Feminist Culture from 1790 to 1850: A Trans-Atlantic Community."	Schiller, L.
"Feminist History in Perspective: Sociological Contributions to Biographic Analysis."	Rossi, A.
"Fertility Motivations and Career Conflicts in Educated Women."	Manis, J.
"Field Supervision--Unilateral or Integrated?"	James, S.
"Field Work."	Smith, Z.
"Field Work and the Training of the Social Worker."	Abbott, E.
"The 51% Minority."	Chisholm, S.
"Filial Relations, 1902."	Addams, J.
"Final Statement at End of Television Debate with Eleanor Roosevelt, November 4, 1956."	Smith, M.
"Final Tribute at Susan B. Anthony's Funeral, March 15, 1906."	Shaw, A.
"The Financial History of the Newark Bureau of Associated Charities."	Genger, M.
"The Financial Independence of Women."	Henrotin, E.
"The Finding of the New World."	Welch, J.
"Fine Arts Slides."	Morey, A.
"First Address at a Daughters of Temperance Supper, March 1, 1849."	Anthony, S.
"First Speech in Congress to Offer an Amendment to the Lever Bill, May 18, 1917."	Rankin, J.
"The First Year: President's Report to NOW, 1967."	Friedan, B.
"Fitness of Women to Become Citizens from the Standpoint of Education and Mental Development."	Sewall, M.
"Fitness of Women to Become Citizens from the Standpoint of Moral Development."	Spencer, A.

Title	Author
"Fitness of Women to Become Citizens from the Standpoint of Physical Development."	Clay, L.
"The Five Cent Theatre."	Thomas, H.
"The Fixvale-Union Cottage Homes, and Classification of Public Dependents."	Lincoln, A.
"A Floating Hospital."	Robinson, M.
"Florence Kelley on Working Girls."	Kelley, F.
"Focus on the Future."	Gilbreth, L.
"Focused Publicity."	Tousley, C.
"Food for Students."	Richards, E.
"Food Price Hearing."	Grasso, E.
"Foot Free in God's Country."	Pollard, M.
"For the Sake of Liberty."	Catt, C.
"For What Are We Educating Women?"	Warren, C.
"Forced Labor. The Wholesale Suppression of Human Rights by Government."	Lord, M.
"Foreign-Born Children in the Primary Grades."	Addams, J.
"The Foreign Language Worker in the Fusion Process, an Indispensable Asset to Social Work in America."	Bremer, E.
"Foreign Organizations and Family Welfare."	Hood, L.
"Foreign Rule. Address to the National Woman Suffrage Association Convention of 1889."	Brown, O.
"Forestry."	Thorne, J.
"Forestry and Village Improvement."	Dock, M.
"Formula for Freedom. Attack Subversives Wherever Found."	Alexander, R.
"Formulating the Problem in Social Case Work with Children."	Richards, E.
"Forty-three Families Treated by Friendly Visiting."	Hanson, E.
"Forum on the College Generation."	Chambers, E.
"Forum on the College Generation."	Douglas, E.
"Forum on the College Generation."	Drake, J.
"Forum on the College Generation."	Holcomb, M.
"Forum on the College Generation."	Kelly, A.
"Forum on the College Generation."	McNary, J.
"Forum on the College Generation."	Morrison, J.
"Forum on the College Generation."	Olmstead, C.
"Forum on the College Generation."	Shambaugh, J.
"Forum on the College Generation."	Spiegel, M.
"Forum on the College Generation."	Steinbrecher, A.
"Forum on the College Generation."	Watkins, J.
"Forward or Backward?"	Catt, C.
"Foster Home Care in Wartime."	Hutchinson, D.
"The Foster Parent and the Agency in the Adoption Process."	Harral, E.
"Foundlings and Deserted Children."	Lesley, S.

"Four Levels of Women's History." Sklar, K.
"Four Months in Old Mexico." Romney, C.
"Frances D. Gage's Reminiscences of Speech by Sojourner Truth." Truth, S.
"Fraternal Benefit Associations: Their Origin, Scope and Value." Hollister, L.
"Frederick Douglass." Terrell, M.
"Free Enquiry, 1829." Wright, F.
"Free Kindergartens." Mackenzie, C.
"Free Love Speech at Steinway Hall, N.Y., November 20, 1871." Woodhull, V.
"The Free Mind and the Free Market." Efron, E.
"Freedom Cannot Be Inherited. We Are the Conservative Party." Douglas, H.
"Freedom Is Responsibility. The Family's Responsibility to the Community." Dunne, I.
"Freedom of the Mind." Meyer, A.
"Freedom's Back Is Against the Wall. Making Our Own Beds and Lying in Them." Thompson, D.
"Friendly Visiting." McDowell, M.
"Friendly Visiting." Price, M.
"Friendly Visiting." Putnam, M.
"Friendly Visiting." Richmond, M.
"Friends as Promoters of Peace." Bond, E.
"The Friendships of Women." Stanton, E.
"Frigidity." Schaefer, L.
"From Address of Dr. Anna Howard Shaw When Resigning the Presidency of the National American Woman Suffrage Association, Dec. 15, 1915." Shaw, A.
"From Conestoga to Career." Getman, L.
"From European Colonies to the Third World--The Developing States of Africa." Morgenthau, R.
"From Farm Policy to Food Policy: Satisfying Multiple and Conflicting Goals." Whitman, M.
"From Josephine St. Pierre Ruffin's Speech." Ruffin, J.
"From Multi-national to Cosmo-corporations: The World Economic Welfare." Sindona, M.
"From Signs of the Times." Wilson, A.
"From the Zuni Scalp Ceremonial." Stevenson, M.
"From This Mother: The Old Brick Wall Theory." Corbally, M.
"From Where I Stand. Responsible, Responsive Citizenship Program." Ozbirn, C.
"From Woodhull's Speech on Social Freedom." Woodhull, V.

"From Woodhull's Speech to the National Convention."	Woodhull, V.
"A Full Accounting of All MIA's."	Grasso, E.
"Fun for the Older Person in the Country."	Brungardt, T.
"The Function of a Mental Hygienist in a Children's Agency."	Taft, J.
"A Function of the Social Settlement."	Addams, J.
"Function of the Social Worker in Relation to the Community."	MacDonald, V.
"The Future Development of the Almshouse."	Potter, E.
"Future Family; Adaptation of Address. February 12, 1970."	Mead, M.
"The Future of Home Service."	Byington, M.
"The Future of the Juvenile Court as a Case-Work Agency."	Nutt, A.
"The Future of the Woman Who Works for Wages."	Perkins, F.
"The Future of Women in the Aviation Industry."	Cochran, J.
"The Future Responsibility of the School Toward Children Under Five Years, Both Directly and Through Training for Parenthood."	Woolley, H.
"The Future Role of Women."	Keller, S.
"The Future World Order. The Ideal of the United Nations."	Thompson, D.
"Gage's Reminiscences of Sojourner Truth."	Truth, S.
"Gains and Goals of Women Workers."	Dickason, G.
"Gains of the Last Three Years."	Howell, M.
"Gaps in Education and Training."	Hathway, M.
"General Conditions of Domestic Service."	Gates, S.
"General Conditions of Mortality."	Laney, L.
"General Conference of the International Atomic Energy Agency Holds 18th Session at Vienna; Statement, September 17, 1974."	Ray, D.
"General Conference of the International Atomic Energy Agency Holds 17th Session at Vienna; Statement, Sept. 18, 1973."	Ray, D.
"Generation Gap; Adaptation of Address."	Mead, M.
"Generic Aspects of Professional Training for Case Work and Group Work: From the Point of View of a Teacher of Case Work."	Gartland, R.
"Generic Aspects of Professional Training for Case Work and Group Work: From the Point of View of a Teacher of Group Work."	Kaiser, C.

"George Eliot." Street, I.
"German and American Independence Contrasted. Address to the National Woman Suffrage Association Convention of February 1886." Neymann, C.
"Get Into Politics Up to Your Ears. Women's Political Power Is Not Being Used Effectively." Donlon, M.
"Getting What We Want." Coles, J.
"The Gift of the Fine Arts Department to the General Federation of Women's Clubs." Berry, R.
"The Girl of the Future. Address to the National American Woman Suffrage Association Convention of 1893." Havens, R.
"Girl Scouts." Bacon, J.
"The Girl with a First Baby, Who Is Not Feeble-minded." Shuman, C.
"A Girl with a Second or Third Illegitimate Child." Curry, H.
"The Girls' Protective League." Miner, M.
"Giving and Receiving." Cratty, M.
"A Glimpse of Modern Spain." Bell, L.
"The Goal of Our Calling." Cratty, M.
"Goals for Wanderers." Hill, R.
"Goals of Progressive Education Not Sufficient Today. Educators Must Provide Moral Synthesis." McIntosh, M.
"God Is Love." Harbert, E.
"God's Thought of Women." Riggs, A.
"God's Women." Shaw, A.
"Goethe and Schiller." Keene, M.
"A Good Adoption Program: Can Standards Be Maintained Without Sacrificing Flexibility?" Ray, A.
"Gordon Dewey." Addams, J.
"Gospel Politics. Annual Address to the National Convention of the National Woman's Christian Temperance Union, St. Louis, 1884." Willard, F.
"The Government and Youth in a Troubled World." Abbott, G.
"Government by Propaganda." Thompson, D.
"Government Lends a Hand." Mason, L.
"Government Policy and the Legal Status of Women." Conlin, R.
"Government Provision for Social Work Statistic on a National Scale from the Point of View of the Registration of Social Statistics." Lenroot, K.
"Government Regulation of Wages and Hours: Progress Under the Federal Fair Labor Standards Act." Stitt, L.

"Government Regulation of Wages and Hours: The States and Their Opportunity."	Miller, F.
"Governmental Intervention in the Labor Movement."	Van Kleeck, M.
"Governments' Share in the Solution of Modern Work Problems."	Perkins, F.
"Graded Homes."	Lake, I.
"The Graduate Education of Women."	Rees, M.
"Graduating Address."	Nutting, M.
"The Great American Bitch."	Schmidt, D.
"The Great Need of the Moral Crusade."	Satterthwaite, L.
"The Great Quota Debate and Other Issues in Affirmative Action."	Rumbarger, M.
"Greater and Freer America. G. I. Joe's Future."	Luce, C.
"Greece Revisited."	Howe, J.
"Greece Today. A Miracle of Survival."	Thompson, D.
"Greeting from Honorary Vice-President."	Cooley, C.
"Greeting to the 9th Biennial Convention of the General Federation of Women's Clubs, June 23, 1908."	Howe, J.
"Greetings Delivered at Constitution Hall, June 1, 1936."	Roosevelt, A.
"Greetings from National League of Women Voters."	Park, M.
"Greetings from the Executive Committee."	Donlon, M.
"Greetings from the General Federation of Women's Clubs."	Dickinson, L.
"Group Living and the Dependent Child."	Schulze, S.
"Group Living for the Elderly."	Hill, R.
"Group Play in a Hospital Environment."	Smith, A.
"Group Work and Social Change (Pugsley Award)."	Coyle, G.
"Group Work Experiments in State Institutions in Illinois."	Boyd, N.
"Growing Confusion. Need for Patriotic Thinking."	Smith, M.
"The Growing Importance of State Welfare Work--In Financial Support for Local Welfare Services."	Liveright, A.
"The Growth of Child Welfare Services in Rural Areas."	Arnold, M.
"The Growth of the Social Point of View: In Nursing."	Tucker, K.
"Habits of Thrift."	Fairbank, M.
"The Half of the Nation Outside of the Cities."	Jennings, M.
"The Halfness of Nature."	Howe, J.
"The Handicapped and Older Americans."	Grasso, E.

"Harmonious Adjustment Through Exercise."	Gould, M.
"Harmonious Culture."	Hinds, I.
"Has Case Work a Place in the Administration of Public Relief?"	Dexter, E.
"Has Group Work a Part to Play in the Preservation and Extension of Civil Liberties?"	Kaiser, C.
"Have It Your Way: Mid-Career Women and Their Options."	Bolton, E.
"Have Women Contributed to the Crisis?"	Blair, E.
"The Hazards of Equality: Awareness of Self."	Thibeault, M.
"Headquarters Report for 1906."	Hauser, E.
"Health Activities of Child Caring Agencies: Continuous Health Supervision."	Murphy, M.
"Health Activities of Child Caring Agencies: Examinations of Admission."	Bauer, A.
"Health Activities of Child Caring Agencies: The School and Social Problems."	Culbert, J.
"Health Ahead."	Roche, J.
"Health and the New Housing."	Lumsden, M.
"Health of Our Negro Children."	Eliot, M.
"The Health of the Child."	Hooper, E.
"Health Problems of the Foreign Born from the Point of View of the Hospital Social Worker."	Cannon, M.
"Health Programs for Use of Lone Workers in Rural Areas."	Hamilton, E.
"Health Security for Mother and Child."	Gardiner, E.
"Health Security for Mother and Child--Discussion."	Sloane, M.
"Health Training of the Preschool Child."	Gruenberg, S.
"Hearing of Massachusetts Legislature, Feb. 1900."	Howe, J.
"Heart of Democracy. Equality for All."	Buck, P.
"Hearts to Feel and Tongues to Speak: New England Mill Women in the Early Nineteenth Century."	Vogel, L.
"The Heavenly Vision. Sermon Preached March 24, 1888, at International Council of Women, Washington, D. C."	Shaw, A.
"Helping the Client to Deal with His Reactions to Restraints Governing Intrafamily Relationships."	Johnesse, A.
"Helping the Client to Use His Capacities and Resources."	Marcus, G.
"Helping the Client to Use His Capacities and Resources."	Towle, C.
"Helping to Prevent Sex Delinquency."	Castendyck, E.
"Helping Widows to Bring Up Citizens."	Lothrop, A.
"Heredity."	Blackwell, A.

"Heredity and Ethics."	Gardener, H.
"Heredity in Its Relation to a Double Standard of Morals."	Gardener, H.
"Herstory as History: A New Field or Another Fad?"	Johansson, S.
"Hidden Problems in Hard Times."	Parker, V.
"Higher Education and the Home."	Sunderland, E.
"Higher Education for Women."	Harbert, L.
"Higher Education for Women in the United States."	Sewall, M.
"The Higher Education of Woman."	Mitchell, M.
"The Higher Education of Women."	Perkins, S.
"Higher Lessons of the World's Fair."	Stone, L.
"A Higher Standard of Morality."	Slaughter-Morton, R.
"The Higher Womanhood."	Corbin, C.
"The Highest Education."	Adams, M.
"Highlights of the Conference."	Howell, M.
"Hindus and American Citizenship."	Schisby, M.
"Historic Art."	Bagg, M.
"Historic Woman of Egypt."	Reed, C.
"Historical and Structural Barriers to Occupational Desegregation."	Bernard, J.
"Historical Facts and Theological Fictions."	Gardener, H.
"The History, Aims, and Methods of the Association of Collegiate Alumnae."	Talbot, M.
"The History and Status of Hospital Social Work."	Pelton, G.
"The History of Social Work and Its Place in the Professional Curriculum."	Glenn, M.
"History of the Fourteenth Amendment. Address to the National Woman Suffrage Association Convention of 1889."	Anthony, S.
"History of the Peace Movement."	Mead, L.
"The History of the Woman's Rights Movement, Read in the Meeting Held in Apollo Hall, New York, October 21, 1870."	Davis, P.
"The Home--A Major Industry."	Gilbreth, L.
"The Home and Its Foundations."	Eastman, A.
"The Home and the Economic Waste of War."	Henrotin, E.
"The Home and the Special Child."	Addams, J.
"Home Economics."	Barry, M.
"The Home of the Future."	McGee, L.
"The "Home Protection" Address."	Willard, F.
"Home Side of Progress."	Smith, C.
"The Home Teacher Experiment in Springfield, Illinois."	Bane, G.
"Home Work."	Kelley, F.
"Homer and His Poems."	Cohen, N.
"Homes of Single Women."	Anthony, S.

"The Honor System of Prison Labor." Trumbull, M.
"Horizons for Women, American Woman's Role." Kluckhohn, F.
"Hospital Work in Relation to Public Health." Cannon, M.
"Hospitals Managed By and For Women." Cheney, E.
"House Joint Resolution 191 on School Prayers." Grasso, E.
"Household Adjustment." Addams, J.
"Household Economics." Wilkinson, L.
"Household Employment, Quiet Revolution." Koontz, E.
"Housekeeper Service in Family Welfare." Goodwin, M.
"Housewife-Mother: The Institution and the Experience." Kelly, J.
"Housing: Its Relation to Social Work." Bacon, A.
"The Housing Problem, and Its Relation to Other Social Problems." Fulmer, H.
"The Housing Problem in Chicago." Addams, J.
"Housing Reform in Boston." Lincoln, A.
"How Alabama Organized Her Work for Children." Bush, L.
"How Are We Going to Pay for Defense? There Is a Possibility of Marked Inflation." Newcomer, M.
"How Can the Increased Cost of Living Be Regulated to Meet the Decrease in the Salaries of Clerks and Professional Men?" Richards, E.
"How Can Nations Be Influenced to Protest or Interfere in Cases of Persecution?" Hirshfield, L.
"How Can Nations Be Influenced to Protest or Interfere in Cases of Persecution?" Jacobson, L.
"How Can Social Agencies Promote the Effectiveness of the Public Schools?" Kelley, F.
"How Can Social Information Be Obtained and Made Available for Publicity Purposes?" Ellis, M.
"How Can We Aid?" D'Arcambal, A.
"How Can We Further the Organization of Charities?" Morse, F.
"How Can We Go Forward? Panel Discussion." Sampson, E.
"How Can We Interpret More Effectively to the Public the Role Played in the Community's Welfare Program by Social Settlement, Recreations Agencies, and National Program Agencies?" Clevenger, L.
"How Can We Put Our Living Traditions to Work?" Allen, F.
"How Can We Vitalize the Relationship of Our Public and Private Social Work?" Cannon, I.

Title	Author
"How Can Women Best Associate?"	Howe, J.
"How Can Women Fight Marijuana?"	Sporborg, C.
"How Case Work Training May be Adapted to Meet the Worker's Personal Problems."	Marcus, G.
"How Casual Work Undermines Family and Neighborhood Life."	McDowell, M.
"How Far Have Social Welfare Considerations Entered into State, National, and Local Elections."	Moskowitz, B.
"How Fares the American Family? Address."	Mead, M.
"How Foster Children Turn Out."	Theis, S.
"How Home Economics Can Contribute to Meeting These Problems."	Zuill, F.
"How Lay Citizens Can Influence the Local Administration of Health."	McFarland, C.
"How Mental Hygiene May Help in the Solution of School Problems."	Johnson, E.
"How Much Should Government Do--On Health, Education, and Housing? Panel Discussion."	Smith, M.
"How Much Social Work Can a Community Afford? From the Ethical Point of View."	Addams, J.
"How Secure Administrative Skill with Professional Competence for State and Local Public Welfare Service?"	Abbott, G.
"How Shall We Approach Industrial Education?"	Addams, J.
"How Shall We Make the Women of Our Race Stronger?"	Davidson, O.
"How Shall We Teach the Mother to Recognize the Necessity of a Sanitary Home?"	Shepperd, J.
"How Social Case Work Meets Individual Problems of Public Relief Clients from the Point of View of Medical Social Case Work."	Baker, E.
"How Social Workers Can Aid Housing Reform."	Richmond, M.
"How the Agencies and the Schools May Cooperate in the Development of the Curriculum."	White, E.
"How the Public May Help."	Davis, K.
"How to Adapt Charity Organization Methods to Small Communities."	Lowell, J.
"How to Establish a Community Service."	Quinn, L.
"How to Extend the Sympathies of Women."	Howe, J.
"How to Fill the Gap Between the Special Class and the Institution."	Fitts, A.
"How to Get and Keep Visitors."	Smith, Z.
"How to Get Housing Reform."	Bacon, A.

"How to Improve the Utilization of Nurses, Allied Health and Support Personnel. A U.S. Response to the Swedish Model."	Harding, E.
"How to Improve the Utilization of Women in the Health Occupations in Which They are Well Represented. A U.S. Response to the Swedish Experience."	Ford, L.
"How to Keep More of the Money You Earn. The Status of Women in Industry."	Valentine, H.
"How to Reach the Children."	Gordon, A.
"How to Secure a Continuing and Progressive Policy in Public Social Work and Institutions."	Potter, E.
"How to Win the Ballot."	Duniway, A.
"Howard R. Knight and the International Conference of Social Work."	Kahn, D.
"Hrotsvitha of Gandersheim: The Playable Dramas of a Woman Playwright of the Tenth Century."	Butler, M.
"Human Needs Pertinent to Group Work Services."	Wilson, G.
"Human Relations in Public Charity."	Bemis, A.
"Human Values and Energy Conservation: Our Common Concern."	MacDonald, R.
"Humanistic Democracy--The American Ideal."	Roosevelt, A.
"Humanitarian Effects of the Immigration Law."	Razovsky, C.
"Hunger in the United States: Women and Children First."	Pope, J.
"I Accept This Call."	Bass, C.
"I Am a Home-Loving, Law-Abiding, Tax-Paying Woman..."	Wallace, Z.
"I Have Been a Disappointed Woman."	Stone, L.
"I Suppose I Am About the Only Colored Woman that Goes About to Speak for the Rights of Colored Women."	Truth, S.
"An Idea and Its Results."	Mohl, A.
"The Idea Takes Root."	Sergio, L.
"An Ideal Home for Children."	Miller, K.
"An Ideal Home for Discharged Prisoners."	D'Arcambel, A.
"Idealism: What's Wrong with It? A Declaration of Independence for Broadcasters."	Parson, M.
"Identifying and Training the Gifted. Need for a Universal Approach."	West, R.
"Identifying Clue-Aspects in Social Case Work."	Sheffield, A.

"Illegitimacy in Europe as Affected by the War." Lundberg, E.
"The Illinois Woman's Alliance." Brown, C.
"Illustrations from the Annals of the Gulf Division--American Red Cross." Dinwiddie, E.
"The Image of Women in Arts and Letters." Millett, K.
"Images of Male and Female in Children's Readers." Rosenhan, M.
"The Immigrant and Social Unrest." Addams, J.
"The Immigrant as a Factor in Social Case Work: In the Family Welfare Field." Hull, I.
"The Immigrant. Means of Using National and Racial Customs and Organizations in Relating Isolated Groups to General Community Movements." Alsberg, E.
"Immigrant Populations." Clark, J.
"The Immigrant Woman as She Adjusts Herself to American Life." Addams, J.
"The Immigrant Young Girl." (Abstract) Wald, L.
"Immigrants." Addams, J.
"Immigration Legislation and the Problems of Assimilation." Abbott, E.
"Immorality of the Regulation System." Blackwell, A.
"The Impact of Education." Peterson, E.
"The Impact of Medical Women in United States Medical Schools." McAnarney, E.
"Impact of Taxation on Small Business. Lack of Working Capital Prohibits Expansion." Graves, J.
"The Impact of the War on Marriage Relationships." Hollis, F.
"The Impact of the War Upon Community Welfare Organization." Colcord, J.
"Impatience and Generosity. Comments on European and Asian Trips." Smith, M.
"The Impediments to Rapid Regulatory Action: The Bureaucratic Red Tape." Bentley, H.
"The Impending Revolution. Lectures at New York Academy of Music, Feb. 20, 1872." Woodhull, V.
"The Imperatives of International Relations: Social Implications." Lathrop, J.
"Imperfect Unions: Class and Gender in Cripple Creek, 1894-1904." Jameson, E.
"The Implication of Rivalry." Gunderson, B.
"Implications in the Broader Use of Budgets." Gottemoller, R.
"Implications of the European Situation for the United States." Dean, V.
"The Implications of the Peace." Dean, V.

"The Importance of Birth Records."	Huffman, H.
"The Importance of Keeping Informed."	Dunbar, S.
"Importance of Maturity and a Social Philosophy for Group Leaders and Supervisors."	Elliott, G.
"Importance of Organized Libraries in Institutions."	Jones, E.
"Importance of the Home-maker."	Peterson, E.
"Imports Continue to Threaten U.S. Ball and Roller Bearing Industries."	Grasso, E.
"Impressionist Painting and Painters."	Urquhart, K.
"Improving Working Conditions in Industry."	Perkins, F.
"In a Daughter They Have a Human Being; In a Son the Same."	Wright, F.
"In Non-essentials, Liberty."	Potter, F.
"In Pursuit of the Golden Age for Women."	Smith, M.
"In the Name of Justice: The Unending Rush to the Courts."	Hufstedler, S.
"Inaugural Address--What Is Librarianship?"	Lowrie, J.
"Income Security for the Aged."	Burns, E.
"Increasing the Professional Visibility of Women in Academe: A Case Study."	Apter, J.
"The Indians' Attitude Toward Cooperation."	Bronson, R.
"The Indifference of Women. Address to the House Judiciary Committee, Feb. 15, 1898."	Blackwell, A.
"The Indigent Migratory Tuberculous: The Facts of the Case."	Whitney, J.
"The Individual and the Collective."	Shulman, C.
"Individual Responsibility and Human Oppression (Including Some Notes on Prostitution and Pornography)."	Atkinson, T.
"Individual Variations in Mental Equipment."	Bronner, A.
"Individualization of the Child."	Harding, M.
"Indochinese Refugees."	Derian, P.
"Industrial Amelioration."	Addams, J.
"Industrial and Business Relations."	Williamson, M.
"Industrial and Economic Problems--Introductory Statement."	Breckinridge, S.
"Industrial and Technological Training."	Paddock, S.
"Industrial Causes of Juvenile Delinquency."	Kelley, F.
"The Industrial Cost of the Psychopathic Employee."	Powers, M.
"Industrial Education."	Arnold, S.
"Industrial Gains of Women During the Last Half-Century."	Livermore, M.
"Industrial Revolution of the Last Century."	Twitchell, E.
"Industrial Training in Girls' Schools."	Sickels, L.

"Industrial Training School for Girls."	Boyd, M.
"The Industrial Woman Looks at the Problems."	Manning, C.
"Industrial Women."	Bullock, E.
"Industrialization, Monopoly Capitalism, and Women's Work in Guatemala."	Chinchilla, N.
"Industry and Its Relation to Peace."	Nathan, M.
"Industry and the Home: Behind the Statistic."	Paradise, V.
"Infant Mortality as an Economic Problem."	Rochester, A.
"Infant Welfare Work in War Time."	Meigs, G.
"Influence of Birth Order and Sibling Sex on Sports Participation."	Portz, E.
"Influence of Great Women."	Adams, M.
"The Influence of Publicity in Developing Community Organization."	Clevenger, L.
"The Influence of the Discovery of America on the Jews."	Adams, M.
"Influence of the Discovery of America on the Jews."	Rosenberg, P.
"Influence of the Discovery of America on the Jews."	Witkowsky, E.
"The Influence of the Jewish Religion in the Home."	Cohen, M.
"The Influence of the Jewish Religion in the Home."	Felsenthal, J.
"Influence of the Medical Setting on Social Case Work Services."	Bartlett, H.
"Influential Women in Anglo-Saxon England."	Judd, E.
"Innovations in the Utilization of Nurses, Allied Health and Support Personnel. A U.S. Response to a Look at Colombia."	Lubic, R.
"Innovations in the Utilization of Nurses, Allied Health and Support Personnel. A U.S. Response to a Look at Colombia."	Roemer, R.
"Innovations in the Utilization of Nurses, Allied Health and Support Personnel. Innovative Functions of Women Health Workers."	Fahy, E.
"Insanitary Conditions Amongst Home Workers."	Kelley, F.
"In-Service Training."	Van Driel, A.
"Instances of After Care of the Insane."	Horten, E.
"Institutional Barriers: What Keeps Women Out of the Executive Suite?"	Epstein, C.
"An Institutional Program in the Field of Corrections."	Potter, E.
"Institutional Records and Industrial Causes of Dependency."	Lathrop, J.
"Institutions for Delinquent Children: What Is the Test of Success?"	Van Waters, M.

"Institutive Power."	Brown, M.
"Instruction of School Children in Health Habits and Ideals."	Jean, S.
"Instructive and Productive Employments. Their Suitability for Industrial Schools and Houses of Refuge."	Cobb, M.
"Insurance Against Piracy of Brains."	Sherwood, K.
"The Integration of Economic and Psychological Factors in Family Case Work."	Neustaedter, E.
"The Integration of Effort in Theory and Practice by Private and Public Agencies for the Common Good."	Taylor, R.
"The Integration of Group Work and Case Work."	Wanamaker, C.
"Integration of Supervision with the Total Program of the Agency."	Lazarus, E.
"Integrity: What and How."	Bushnell, L.
"The Intellectual. His Journey and His Home."	Stricker, M.
"The Intellectual Progress of the Colored Women of the United States Since the Emancipation Proclamation."	Williams, F.
"Intellectual Proletarians."	Goldman, E.
"Intelligent Treatment of the Body."	Gage, M.
"Intemperance as a Cause of Mortality."	King, G.
"The Interest of Labor in International Peace."	Addams, J.
"Interior Decorator."	MacDonald, F.
"International Arbitration."	Lord, E.
"International Aspects of the Migration Problem: Development of International Case Work."	Hurlbutt, M.
"International Cooperation and Economic Advance of Women."	Keyserling, M.
"International Co-operation for Social Welfare."	Addams, J.
"The International Council of Women."	Sewall, M.
"The International Federation for the Abolition of State Regulation of Vice."	Powell, A.
"International Kindergarten Union."	Murray, M.
"The International Kindergarten Union."	Stewart, S.
"The International Refugee Organization and Social Welfare."	Biehle, M.
"International Relations, Distaff Side."	Cannon, M.
"International Travel: Consular Operations."	Watson, B.
"Interplay of the Insights of Case Work and Group Work."	Wilson, G.
"Interpretation and Support of Public Welfare Work: Publications and Uniform Social Data."	Lundberg, E.
"Interpretation in the Public Agency."	Faatz, A.

"Interpretation of Social Work in the School Curriculum--How Detroit Lays the Foundation." Farnham, B.
"The Interpretation to the Community of a Public Agency." Handley, V.
"Interpretative Publicity as a Function of Social Work: What Part Can the Federation Take in Its Development?" Bowen, G.
"Interpreting Professional Standards of Social Work to the Public: From the Viewpoint of a National Agency." Rowe, C.
"Interpreting the Social Worker to the Public." Routzahn, M.
"The Interrelationships of Merit Systems and the Quality of Public Welfare Personnel." Lally, D.
"Introduction to Conference." Swerdlow, A.
"Introduction to Discussion on Needy Families in Their Homes." Smith, Z.
"Introduction to Forum." Addams, J.
"Introduction to Keynote Address." Hernandez, A.
"Introduction to Panel Discussion." Waller, H.
"Introduction to the Forum." Reid, H.
"Introductions at Founder's Reception." Hernandez, A.
"Introductory Address to the Course, As Delivered for the Second Time in New-York." Wright, F.
"Introductory Remarks by the Vice Chairman (On State Public Welfare)." Vaile, G.
"Introductory Remarks--Music in Your Community." Oberndorfer, M.
"Introductory Remarks (On Co-Operative Credit)." Sheffield, A.
"Introductory Remarks on Defective Delinquents." Davis, K.
"Introductory Statement by the Chairman (On the Role of the Volunteer in Social Work)." Sears, A.
"Introductory Statement of Chairman (On Pensions, Insurance and the State)." Abbott, E.
"Introductory Statement (On Industrial Reorganization After the War)." Kelley, F.
"Introductory State (On Public Schools and Social Service)." Lathrop, J.
"Introductory Statement (On Sources of Power for Industrial Freedom)." Van Kleeck, M.
"The Invisible Environment of an Immigrant." Hurlbutt, M.
"The Inviolable Home." Wilbour, C.
"The Invisible Woman: The Case for Women's Studies." Sicherman, B.
"The Iowa Plan of Cooperation in County Welfare Work." Cottrell, L.

Title	Author
"Is an Independent Administration of Health and Social Work Desirable?"	Foster, E.
"Is Female to Male as Nature Is to Culture?"	Ortner, S.
"Is Guidance a Racket? The Ultimate of Confusion."	Reed, A.
"Is Labor Dignified?"	Lake, L.
"Is It a Crime for a United States Citizen to Vote?"	Anthony, S.
"Is Polite Society Polite?"	Howe, J.
"Is Proposed Conversion of U.S. Armed Forces to an All-Volunteer Basis a Sound National Policy?"	Chisholm, S.
"Is the Administration Plan to Terminate the Federal Anti-Poverty Agency Now a Sound National Policy?"	Burke, Y.
"Is the Agency or the Individual Primarily Responsible for the Professional Development of the Social Worker?"	Van Waters, M.
"Is the Equal-Rights Amendment Equitable to Women?"	Kitchelt, F.
"Is Woman the Weaker Vessel?"	Palmer, S.
"Issues in Nepotism Rules."	Sigworth, H.
"It Is a National Calamity ... Remarks."	Griffiths, M.
"It Is Not Christianity, But Priestcraft That Has Subjected Woman as We Find Her. Debate at the 5th National Convention, Philadelphia, 1854."	Mott, L.
"Italian Children in the Primary Grades."	Addams, J.
"The Italian Woman in the Country."	Di Brazza Savorgnan, C.
"Italian Women and Work: Experience and Perception."	Yans-McLaughlin, V.
"Italy in 1955. Problems Which Italy Confronts Today."	Luce, C.
"The Japanese."	Hitchcock, E.
"Jealousy: Causes and a Possible Cure."	Goldman, E.
"Jenny Dow Harvey."	Addams, J.
"Jewish Women of Biblical and of Medieval Times."	Mannheimer, L.
"Jewish Women of Modern Days."	Frank, H.
"Jewish Women of Modern Days."	Weil, H.
"Job Equality for Women."	Pressman, S.
"Job Preparation and Juvenile Guidance on a National Front."	Hayes, M.
"Job-Stereotyping: A Time for Change."	Spain, J.
"Joint Financing of Private Social Work: Enter New York."	Deardorff, N.
"Joseph Tilton Bowen. At the Opening of the Joseph Tilton Bowen Country Club."	Addams, J.

"Judge Carswell and the 'Sex Plus' Doctrine."	Friedan, B.
"Judge Murray F. Tuley."	Addams, J.
"Junior College Programs."	Bell, D.
"Junior Employment Problems."	Stewart, M.
"Justice in Journalism."	Graham, L.
"The Justice of Woman Suffrage. Address to the National American Woman Suffrage Association Convention of 1900."	Terrell, M.
"The Juvenile Court as a Constructive Social Agency."	Lundberg, E.
"Juvenile Immigration."	Whitton, C.

"Kansas City Study of Adult Life."	Neugarten, B.
"Katharina in the Taming of the Shrew."	Mott, E.
"Kearney's Speech on the South."	Kearney, B.
"Keeping the Mind of the Nation Young Through Motion Pictures."	Hepburn, K.
"Keeping the Thing Going While Things Are Stirring."	Truth, S.
"Kelley on Child Labor and Woman Suffrage."	Kelley, F.
"The Kennedy Twist."	Smith, M.
"Keynote Address."	Gittings, B.
"Keynote Address at 1975 NOW National Conference."	De Crow, K.
"Keynote Address at the 1974 NOW National Conference."	Lyon, P.
"Keynote Speech for Workshop Session of Labor and Industry Committee of National Council of Negro Women, Washington, D. C., November 10, 1954."	Church, R.
"Kinder, Kuche, Kirche as Scientific Law: Psychology Constructs the Female."	Weisstein, N.
"The Kindergarten."	Smith, V.
"The Kindergarten and the Mission of Women."	Kraus-Boelte, M.
"The Kindergarten and the Primary School."	Cropsey, N.
"The Kindergarten as a Character Builder."	Cooper, S.
"The Kindergarten as a Child-saving Work."	Cooper, S.
"The Kindergarten as an Educational Agency and the Relation of the Kindergarten to Manual Training."	Cooper, S.
"Kinds of Government and the Growth of Isms. Property and Force vs. Personality and Reason."	Rooney, M.

"The King's Daughters." Davis, I.
"The King's Daughters." Dickinson, M.

"Labor and Capital." Bristol, A.
"Labor as a Factor in the Newer Conception of International Relationships." Addams, J.
"Labor Camp Schools." (abstract) Moore, S.
"Labor Day Address Over Columbia Broadcasting System Network, Sept. 4, 1944." Perkins, F.
"Labor Day Address Over Columbia Broadcasting System Network, Sept. 6, 1943." Perkins, F.
"Labor Legislation for Women." Hoagland, M.
"Labor Legislation for Women." Scott, M.
"The Labor Question." Perkins, F.
"Lack of Leadership in Washington. A Congresswoman Looks at Congress." Sullivan, L.
"Ladies of the Grand Army of the Republic." McNeier, L.
"The Ladies' Physiological Institute of Boston." O'Leary, H.
"The Land We Love." Gaddess, M.
"Landmarks." Blackwell, A.
"Last Address to the 1906 National American Woman Suffrage Association Convention." Anthony, S.
"Lasting Effects of Women's War Activities." Morrow, E.
"Law and Administrative Practices as Barriers to Mobility. Remedies in Relation to Human Welfare." Blakeslee, R.
"Law and Government. The Underlying Concept or Philosophy of Our Law." Donlon, M.
"Law and Women." Peck, M.
"Law Enforcement Responsibility. What Can Police Do?" Higgins, L.
"The Law: Where It Is and Where It's Going." Meacham, C.
"The Law's Delay: Lower Court Justice and the Immigrant." Claghorn, K.
"The Laws of Parentage and Heredity." Whitney, M.
"Lay Participation in Social Work as It Affects the Public Agency." Kraus, H.
"Leadership." Byington, M.
"Leadership Through Young Minds." Dickinson, L.
"Leadership Through Young Minds." Sclair, V.
"Learning America's Meaning." Davies, E.
"Learning Not To: It Takes a Long Time." Strommen, E.
"The Learning Process in Agency Settings." Hendricks, T.

Title	Author
"Learning to Know the Child Through the Everyday Contacts of the Case Worker."	Gerard, M.
"Lecture, Delivered at the Franklin Hall, Boston, 21 September 1832."	Stewart, M.
"Lecture V. --Morals."	Wright, F.
"Lecture IV. --Religion."	Wright, F.
"A Lecture on Constitutional Equality, Delivered at Lincoln Hall, Washington, D. C., Thursday, February 16, 1871."	Woodhull, V.
"Lecture I. --On the Nature of Knowledge."	Wright, F.
"Lecture VII. --On Existing Evils and Their Remedy, as Delivered in Philadelphia, on June 2d, 1829."	Wright, F.
"Lecture VI. --Opinions."	Wright, F.
"Lecture III. --Of the More Important Divisions and Essential Parts of Knowledge."	Wright, F.
"Lecture II. --Of Free Enquiry, Considered as a Means of Obtaining Just Knowledge."	Wright, F.
"Legal Aid."	Philbrook, M.
"Legal Aid Service and Social Work: The Social Point of View."	Waldo, A.
"The Legal and Political Status of Woman in Utah."	Richards, E.
"Legal Condition of Women in 1492-1892."	Greene, M.
"Legal Conditions of Indian Women."	Fletcher, A.
"Legal Disabilities."	Blake, L.
"The Legal Profession for Women."	Sawyer, W.
"Legal Rights of a Married Woman in Her Husband's Property."	Gillett, E.
"Legislation, Cooperation, and the Board."	Foster, M.
"Legislation to Prevent Cruelty to Children."	Wolcott, H.
"Legislative Councils."	Hafford, L.
"The Lesbian in Literature: Or, Is There Life on Mars?"	Harris, B.
"Lesbian Pride."	Dworkin, A.
"Lesbianism and Feminism."	Atkinson, T.
"Lessons Learned in Personnel Selection and Management in Emergency Relief Administration."	Merrill, M.
"Let No Man Take Thy Crown. Sermon in Metzerott's Music Hall During the National-American Woman Suffrage Association Convention of 1894."	Shaw, A.
"Let There Be Light."	Howe, J.
"Let's Face the Facts. There Are No Neutral Hearts."	Thompson, D.
"Let's Keep One Stake in Tomorrow: Women of Today."	O'Connor, L.

"Let's Look Ahead." Peterson, E.
"The Letter Killeth." Bryan, A.
"The Liberal Arts Program." Habein, M.
"The Liberal Spirit." Thompson, D.
"Liberating the Administrator's Wife." Fuller, A.
"Libraries and the Development and Future of Tax Support." Molz, R.
"Libraries and the First Amendment." Pilpel, H.
"Libraries in a New Era." Rothrock, M.
"Librarianship: Opportunity for Women?" Wetherby, P.
"Library Response to a Restive World." Bradshaw, L.
"The Library's Relation to Neighborhood and Community Work." Ovitz, D.
"Life and the Literature of To-morrow." Berry, R.
"Life and Times of Isabella of Castile." Bucklin, L.
"Life and Work of Maria Mitchell, LL.D." Whitney, M.
"Life Insurance in Dependent Families." Slocum, F.
"Life Is Simple. Find the Courage to Maximize Your Lives." Skinner, C.
"Life of Artists." Cohen, K.
"Life Without a Newspaper, from an Address to Congress." Griffiths, M.
"The Light in the East." Clymer, E.
"The Light in the East." Thayer, E.
"Like and Unlike in East and West." Buck, P.
"Like Their Fathers Instead." Park, R.
"Lillian Hellman: Dramatist of the Second Sex." Patraka, V.
"Lincoln and Farragut." Hoxie, V.
"Literature for Young People." McDonald, C.
"Literary Women and the Masculated Sensibility." Lourie, M.
"Local Government and World Affairs." Lee, D.
"Local Responsibility for Community Development." White, E.
"The Long Path." Denison, D.
"A Look Ahead. What the Negro Wants." Lyells, R.
"A Look at the Problem." Robnett, F.
"The Lost Librarian." Walton, G.
"The Loyal Women of the Country to Abraham Lincoln, President of the United States. Address Read at the Woman's National Loyal League Convention, May 14, 1863." Anthony, S.
"Lucretia Mott: Eulogy at the Memorial Services Held in Washington by the National Woman Suffrage Association, January 19, 1881." Stanton, E.
"Lucy Stone's Speech." Stone, L.
"Lydia Avery Coonley-Ward." Addams, J.
"Lynching Our National Crime." Wells-Barnett, I.

"Machinery Broker." Halliday, V.
"Madam Yoko: Ruler of the Kpa Mende Confederacy." Hoffer, C.
"Madame de Stael." Jenkins, H.
"Madame Vestris in America." Casey, L.
"Maintaining Standards of Living in the New Day." Rose, F.
"Maintaining the Balance Between Life and Play." Moody, H.
"Major Issues in Social Work Education." Spencer, S.
"Making Human Geography Talk." Howell, B.
"Making Human Geography Talk." Renard, B.
"Making Human Geography Talk." Wing, V.
"The Making of the Apolitical Woman: Feminity and Sex-stereotyping in Girls." Iglitzin, L.
"Making the Community Safe for the Child." Binford, J.
"The Management of Tenement-houses." Bailey, E.
"Manual Training for the Feeble-minded." Barrows, I.
"Manual Training in Primary Schools." Blatch, H.
"Many Are Called, But Few Are Chosen." Mattfeld, J.
"Margaret Smith's Answer to a Smear." Smith, M.
"Marriage and Divorce." Grannis, E.
"Marriage and Love." Goldman, E.
"Marriage and the Woman Scholar." Thomas, M.
"Marriage Has Ever Been a One-sided Affair." Anthony, S.
"Married Women in Industry." Winslow, M.
"Mary Duffy Speaks Before the Legislature." Duffy, M.
"Mary Hawes Wilmarth." Addams, J.
"Marks of Identity." Kennicke, L.
"Mass Relocation of Aliens." Hoey, J.
"A Massachusetts Experiment in Savings Bank Life Insurance." Grady, A.
"Massachusetts Institutions: Supplementary Work in the Care of Dependent and Delinquent Children." Richardson, A.
"The Massachusetts System of Placing and Visiting Children." Richardson, A.
"Massachusetts. The Family Budget and the Adequacy of Relief." Moloney, E.
"Masters of the Raging Book?" Gaver, M.
"The Mastery of Work and the Mystery of Sex in a Guatemalan Village." Paul, L.
"A Maternity and Infancy Program for Rural and Semirural Communities." Gardiner, E.
"Maternity Leave Policies." Truax, A.
"The Matriarchate, or Mother-Age." Stanton, E.
"Matrifocality in Indonesia and Africa and Among Black Americans." Tanner, N.
"A Matter of Degree: Education of Women." Flowers, A.

"Maturing Concepts of Peace." Addams, J.
"Maximal Oxygen Uptake of Females." Drinkwater, B.
"Measuring Our Results in Securing the Essentials of Family Life: Some Suggestions Based on a Review of Mothers' Assistance in Pennsylvania." Tyson, H.
"Mediation of Contradiction: Why Mbum Women Do Not Eat Chicken." O'Laughlin, B.
"The Medical and Moral Care of Female Patients." Cleaves, M.
"Medical and Social Co-operation." Richmond, M.
"Medical Inspection in the Schools--Its Technique and Its Results." Hedger, C.
"The Medical Profession for Woman." Lankton, F.
"Medical Social Service as a Factor in Protective Work." Lewis, O.
"Meet the MS READ-a-thon: The Written Word." Brothers, J.
"Meeting Challenge of Today's Needs in Working with Unmarried Mothers Through Use of Institution (Maternity Home)." Verry, E.
"Meeting the Needs of the Aged Through Private Institutional Care." Switton, F.
"Members One of Another." Clemens, L.
"Memorial Address for Inez Milholland Boissevain." Younger, M.
"Memorial to the Constitutional Convention. Adopted by the Woman's Rights Convention, Salem, Ohio, April 19th and 20th, 1850." Johnson, M.
"Memorial Tributes to Mrs. Ralph Waldo Emerson and Anna Oliver at the National American Woman Suffrage Association Convention, 1893." Shaw, A.
"Memsahib, Militante, Femme Libre: Political and Apolitical Styles of Modern African Women." Van Allen, J.
"Men and Women in the Family: History of the Idea of Family in America's Depression Generation." Wolkoff, R.
"Men, Women and Gods." Gardner, H.
"Menace of the Militarist Program. Speech at the Labor Forum, Washington Irving High School, New York City, December 19, 1915." Keller, H.
"Mental and Physical Diagnosis of School Children (Report of a Sub-Committee)." Woolley, H.
"Mental and Physical Factors in Prostitution." Spaulding, E.
"Mental Health in Our Changing Culture; Excerpts from Address." Mead, M.

"Mental-Health Needs in Children's Institutions." Foster, S.
"The Mental Hospital as a Teaching Center." Estes, B.
"Mental Hygiene in Our Schools: Attitudes of Teachers Toward Problem Behavior." Dexter, E.
"Mental Hygiene of Childhood: The Social Worker's Opportunity." Taft, J.
"The Mental Hygiene of Industry: Report of Progress on Work Undertaken Under Engineering Foundation." Jarrett, M.
"The Mental Hygiene of Young Children: From the Point of View of a Psychiatric Social Worker in a Habit Clinic." Reynolds, B.
"Mental Hygiene of Younger Children." Johnson, H.
"Mental Hygiene Problems of Normal Adolescence." Taft, J.
"Mental Hygiene Problems of Subnormal Children: In the Public Schools." Anderson, M.
"The Mentality of the Unmarried Mother." Weidensall, J.
"Merchant Marine. Stepchild of the Economy." Bentley, H.
"The Merit System in Public Institutions." Flower, L.
"Message of Julia Ward Howe to the National Arbitration and Peace Congress." Howe, J.
"Message of Thanks to Members of Congressional Committee Supporting Cause." Hooker, I.
"The Message of the Associated Charities." Richmond, M.
"Message to the Annual Meeting of the Mother Church, Boston, 1896." Eddy, M.
"Metaphysical Cannibalism or Self-Creativity." Atkinson, T.
"Methodological Issues in Health Economics Research Relevant to Women." Muller, C.
"The Methods Most Helpful to Girls." Morse, F.
"Methods of Assembling Material." Bedford, C.
"Methods of Industrial Training for Girls." Kirkwood, L.
"Methods of Instruction in Sex Education." Richards, F.
"Methods of Record-keeping of Group Behavior and Individual Contacts." Wilson, G.
"Methods Used by Social Case Workers in the Development of Personality: One of the Processes Used by Case Workers in Developing Personality." Warren, M.
"Mexican Immigration to the United States." Alvarado, E.
"Mid-Century World. Whose World Has It Turned Out To Be?" Alexander, R.
"The Middle-Aged Woman in Contemporary Society." Meyer, A.

"The Middle East Problem. Results of U.S. Aid to Israel." Thompson, D.
"Migration Problems and the Federal Government." McCall, B.
"Migratory Children." Parker, L.
"Migratory Workers in Agriculture." Shields, L.
"Military Service--Bridge or Gap? Panel Discussion." Bacon, S.
"Military Service--Bridge or Gap? Panel Discussion." Hallaren, M.
"Military Service--Bridge or Gap? Panel Discussion." Holder, E.
"The Milwaukee Recreation System." Enderis, D.
"Minimum Educational Requirements Should Be Demanded of Those Beginning Family Case Work." Hardwick, K.
"Minimum Qualifications for a Good Child Placing Agency." Theis, S.
"The Minimum Wage at Work in the District of Columbia." Mortenson, C.
"Minimum Wage Board." Kelley, F.
"Minimum Wage; Home Worker and Union Worker." Sells, D.
"Minority Needs--the Indian." Tsianina (Princess)
"Minority Report of the Report of Committee on Colonies for Segregation of Defectives." Perry, M.
"Miracle of Water: Excerpts from Address, April, 1968." Ray, D.
"Miracles in Glass." Blodgett, K.
"Miss Abby Smith's Address at Hearing Before the Committee on Woman Suffrage, Hartford, Conn." Smith, A.
"Miss Dodge." Cratty, M.
"Miss Flynn Continues Defense." Flynn, E.
"Miss Perkins Asks Child Labor Ban. Abandon's Prepared Address to Urge Professional Woman to Support Amendment." Perkins, F.
"Miss Perkins Asks Social Insurance." Perkins, F.
"Miss Remond's First Lecture in Dublin." Remond, S.
"The Mission Indians of California." Hiles, O.
"Mission-work Among the Unenlightened Jews." Kohut, R.
"Mission-work Among the Unenlightened Jews." Louis, M.
"Missionary Work." Morris, H.
"Mobilization in Action." Rosenberg, A.
"The Mobilization of Women in Allende's Chile." Chaney, E.
"Modern Charities and Church Work." Sherwood, E.
"The Modern City and the Municipal Franchise for Women." Addams, J.

Title	Author
"The Modern Deaconess Movement."	Robinson, J.
"Modern Devices for Minimizing Dependencies."	Addams, J.
"The Modern Family: Sticky Myths, Diverse Realities, and the Problem of Isolation."	Thorne, B.
"A Modern Lear."	Addams, J.
"The Modern Program of Rural Social Work As It Affects Children."	Yerxa, E.
"Modern Use of Older Treatment Methods."	Millar, M.
"Modernization Theory and Sex Roles in Critical Perspective: The Case of the Soviet Union."	Lapidus, G.
"A Modest Beginning and a Modest Proposal."	Ross, D.
"The Moline Plan."	Clifton, R.
"The Monologue as an Entertainment."	Potter, J.
"Moorish Women as I Found Them."	Howard, A.
"The Moors of Spain."	Cantrell, E.
"The Moral Dangers of Premature Employment."	Kelley, F.
"Moral Education of the Young."	Wood-Allen, M.
"The Moral Education Society of Boston."	Frazar, C.
"Moral Equality Between the Sexes."	Howe, J.
"The Moral Influence of Trained Nurses in Hospitals."	Richards, L.
"The Moral Influence of Women's Associations."	Brown, C.
"The Moral Initiative as Belonging to Women."	Howe, J.
"The Moral Initiative as Related to Women."	Howe, J.
"The Moral Power of the Ballot."	Wallace, Z.
"The Moral Responsibility of Women in Heredity."	Gardner, H.
"A More Realistic and Comprehensive National Policy for Older Americans."	Grasso, E.
"Mother of Men?"	Deinhardt, B.
"The Mother's Greatest Needs."	Newton, F.
"Mothers Meetings."	King, G.
"Mothers of the Submerged World. Day Nurseries."	Bainbridge, L.
"The Mother's Role."	Milner, E.
"Mothers to the Motherless."	Booth, M.
"Motifs for Living."	Lichtman, S.
"The Motive to Achieve Limited Success: The New Woman Law School Applicant."	Lavine, T.
"The Mourning Garb."	Smith, J.
"Movement Politics and Other Sleights of Hand?"	Atkinson, T.
"The Movies and Public Opinion."	Winter, A.
"Mrs. Bloomer's Address. Presentation to Flag to Local Regiment, Council Bluffs, Iowa, 1861."	Bloomer, A.

"Mrs. Bloomer's Speech. At a Temperance Meeting in Metropolitan Hall, New York City, February 1853." Bloomer, A.
"Mrs. Gage's Reminiscences of Sojourner Truth." Truth, S.
"Mrs. Griffing's Report of 1871 Work to the National Woman Suffrage Association May 11, 1871." Griffing, J.
"Mrs. Homemaker--Mrs. Wonderful: The Myths from Women's Lib." Skelsey, A.
"Mrs. Hooker Presents Thanks to Members of Congress on Behalf of the National Woman Suffrage and Educational Committee, 1871." Hooker, I.
"Mrs. Parks' Greetings for the National League of Women Voters to the Pan-American Conference of Women." Park, M.
"Mrs. Rosa H. Hazel at Douglass Memorial Meeting, St. Paul, Minnesota." Hazel, R.
"Mrs. Rose Moves Change of Name from Equal Rights Association to Woman's Suffrage Association, at the 3rd Annual Meeting of the American Equal Rights Association, N. Y., May, 1869." Rose, E.
"Mrs. Stanton's Address at the 1st Annual Meeting of the Woman's State Temperance Society, Rochester, 1853." Stanton, E.
"Mrs. Stanton's Address to the Legislature of the State of New York Read at the Albany, N. Y., Convention, Feb., 1854." Stanton, E.
"Mrs. Stewart's Farewell Address to Her Friends in the City of Boston, 21 September 1833." Stewart, M.
"Multiple Jeopardies of the Welfare Mother." Sanders, B.
"Municipal Detention for Women." Rippir, J.
"Municipal Organization of Social Service in the Proposed New Charter of Grand Rapids." Gardiner, E.
"Municipal Suffrage." Johns, L.
"Municipal Suffrage for Women in Michigan." Bates, O.
"Municipalization of Charitable and Correctional Work in Chicago." Rowe, L.
"Must Working People Live in Frayed-Out Houses?" Wood, E.
"My Job." Perkins, F.
"The Myth of Matriarchy: Why Men Rule in Primitive Society." Bamberger, J.

"The Narrative of Sojourner Truth, 1878."	Truth, S.
"Nation of Speculators."	Thompson, D.
"National Book Award Acceptance Speech."	Carson, R.
"The National Christian League for the Promotion of Social Purity."	Grannis, E.
"National Free-Will Baptist Woman's Missionary Society."	Burlingame, E.
"National Organization for Public Health Nursing."	Roberts, A.
"National Protection for Children."	Addams, J.
"National Society U.S. Daughters of 1812."	Wiles, A.
"National Temperance Hospital."	Burnett, M.
"A National Training School for Women."	Cotton, S.
"The National Value of Women's Clubs."	Clymer, E.
"The National Woman's Christian Temperance Union."	Lathrap, M.
"The National Woman's Relief Society."	Richards, J.
"The National Woman's Relief Society."	Wells, E.
"National Women's Trade Union League."	Stewart, J.
"The National Young Ladies' Mutual Improvement Association."	Thomas, C.
"Nationalism."	Bay, L.
"Nationality Rights."	Stevens, D.
"The Nation's Peril--A Double Standard of Morals."	Barrett, K.
"A Nation's Strength Begins in the Home. Parents Are the Real Molders of Character."	Pannell, A.
"The Nation's Workers."	Perkins, F.
"The Naturalization Law and Its Administration."	Minick, C.
"The Nature of the Stigma upon the Unmarried Mother and Her Child."	Sheffield, A.
"Nature of U.S. Puerto Rican Relations." Texts of Statements Made in Committee IV (Trusteeship).	Bolton, F.
"Nature Studies in the Home."	Schryver, A.
"Nazi Foreign Missions. German Propaganda in the United States and the World."	Thompson, D.
"Nazi Propaganda in the United States."	Knaust, E.
"Near East Relief."	Duryea, F.
"Necessary Modifications of Child Welfare Services to Meet the Needs of Dependent Negro Children."	Stevens, M.
"Necessary Supplement to Unemployment Insurance."	Colcord, J.
"The Need for Educated Womanpower."	Peterson, E.
"The Need for Interpretation of Trends and Accomplishments in Family Social Work."	Kahn, D.

"The Need for Quality Instruction: To the Teacher."	Prewitt, L.
"The Need for State Supervision for Both Public and Private Charities."	Barrett, K.
"The Need for Women to Enforce Women's Labor Law."	Copp, T.
"The Need for Women to Enforce Women's Labor Laws."	McDowell, M.
"The Need for Women to Enforce Women's Labor Laws."	Nestor, A.
"The Need of a Few Fundamental Courses."	Conrad, I.
"Need of a Great College in the South."	Conway, C.
"The Need of a Training-school in Applied Philanthropy."	Richmond, M.
"Need of Case Work in a Public Relief Agency."	Reynolds, R.
"Need of Day Nurseries."	Butler, S.
"The Need of Federal Aid for Relief in the Winter 1932-33. Testimony Before a United States Senate Committee."	Abbott, G.
"Need of Kindergartens."	Bass, R.
"The Need of Recreation."	Bowen, L.
"Need of State Legislation to Supplement and Follow Up the N. R. A."	Copp, T.
"The Need of Uniformity in Labor Legislation."	Kelley, F.
"Needed Approaches for a Better Understanding of Behavior and Performance."	Harris, D.
"The Needlework Guild of America."	Stewart, J.
"Needs and Opportunities in Our Society for the Educated Woman."	Peterson, E.
"Needs for Social Case Work as Revealed in Groups."	Nathan, C.
"Needs in American Education."	Kellogg, E.
"The Needs in Human Relationships."	Mark, M.
"The Needs of Southern Women."	Conway, C.
"Neglected Fundamentals in Children's Work: Fundamental Question Now Reform Us."	Abbott, G.
"The Neglected Rich."	Harper, F.
"Negro Child Life in Rural Communities."	Beatty, B.
"Negro Woman in United States, New Roles, New Challenges."	Keyserling, M.
"The Negroes in the United States of America."	Remond, S.
"Neighborhood Councils."	Farra, K.
"Neighborhood Development in Philadelphia."	Falconer, M.
"Neighborhood Improvement."	Addams, J.
"Neighborhood Work and Day Nurseries."	Dodge, J.
"The Nervous American."	Dibble, M.
"A New Avenue of Employment and Investment for Business Women."	Neal, J.

"New Concepts and Old People." Dexter, E.
"The New Dental Program." Gallinger, E.
"A New Departure in Normal Higher Education." Willard, F.
"New Emancipation. Responsibilities of the Negro." Lyells, R.
"The New England Woman's Press Association." Armstrong, B.
"The New England Woman's Press Association." Merrill, E.
"A New Field for Women." Sherman, J.
"New Frontiers." Close, M.
"A New Hope." Breckinridge, D.
"New Horizons for Women." The Modern Home Is a Cooperative Venture." McIntosh, M.
"New Horizons for Women, Talk." Keyserling, M.
"The New Horizons of Professional Education for Social Work." Breckinridge, S.
"New Ideals of Peace." Addams, J.
"New Importance of Old Youth Movements." Brady, G.
"The New Internationalism." Addams, J.
"New Lamps for Old? Centralism." Bushnell, L.
"A New Light Is Coming. Address at the Sociological Conference, Sagamore Beach, Massachusetts." Keller, H.
"New Methods of Procedure." Addams, J.
"The New Morality and the Social Worker." Van Waters, M.
"New Opportunities and Responsibilities for Women, Convocation Address." Keyserling, M.
"A New Phase of Woman's Education in America." Meyer, A.
"A New Political Party and a New Party Platform." Woodhull, V.
"New Professions for Women Centering in the Home. Address to the National-American Woman Suffrage Association Convention of 1900." Barrows, A.
"The New Quota Law in the United States." Mitchell, R.
"The New Rebellion. The Great Secession Speech of Victoria C. Woodhull Before the National Woman's Suffrage Convention, at Apollo Hall, May 11, 1871." Woodhull, V.
"New Roles for Women in Health Care Delivery: A U.S. Response to Conditions in China. The Women's Health Movement: Political, Social and Working Roles for Women in Health Care Delivery." Marieskind, H.
"New Roles for Women in Health Care Delivery; a U.S. Response to Conditions in the People's Republic of China." Brown, C.

"New Roles for Women in Health Care Delivery. A U.S. Response to the Cameroonian Experience."	Jackson, J.
"New Roles for Women in Health Care Delivery. A U.S. Response to the Cameroon Experience."	Lewis, M.
"New Roles for Women in Health Care Delivery. Conditions in the People's Republic of China."	Sidel, R.
"New Ways of Viewing Key Questions for Investigation. Cultural: Reconceptualizing Health Care."	Nelson, C.
"New Way of Viewing Key Questions for Investigation. Historical: Women, History and New Insights."	Smith-Rosenberg, C.
"New Ways of Viewing Key Questions for Investigation. Social Psychological: Relationships Between Black Males and Females--Toward a Definition."	Rodgers-Rose, L.
"New Wings for Mercury."	Earhart, A.
"The New Woman in the New Europe."	Schoonmaker, N.
"The New World Power--Mass Opinion."	Maloney, M.
"Newbery Acceptance Speech--1956."	Latham, J.
"Newbery Award Acceptance--1957."	Sorensen, V.
"Newbery Award Acceptance--1959."	Speare, E.
"Newbery Award Acceptance--1962: Report of a Journey."	Speare, E.
"Newbery Award Acceptance: The Expanding Universe."	L'Engle, M.
"Newbery Award Acceptance: Out Where the Real People Are."	Neville, E.
"Newbery Award Acceptance--1966."	de Trevino, E.
"Newbery Award Acceptance--1968."	Konigsburg, E.
"Newbery Award Acceptance--1971."	Byars, B.
"Newbery Award Acceptance--1973."	George, J.
"Newbery Award Acceptance--1974."	Fox, P.
"Newbery Award Acceptance--1975."	Hamilton, V.
"Newbery Award Acceptance, 1976."	Cooper, S.
"Newbery Award Acceptance, 1977."	Taylor, M.
"Newbery Award Acceptance, 1978."	Paterson, K.
"Newsblackout of the Fifth Army. Fixed Tour of Duty for Infantry."	Luce, C.
"Newspersons' Information and Source Protection Act."	Grasso, E.
"The Newer Efficiency."	Gilbreth, L.
"The Newer Ideals of Peace."	Addams, J.
"The Next Step in the Education of the Deaf."	Garrett, M.
"The Next Step in the Treatment of Girls and Women Offenders."	Hodder, J.
"The Next Step: Opening Remarks to the Organizing Conference of the National Women's Political Caucus."	Friedan, B.

"Next Steps in Job Analysis (Pugsley Award)."	Deardorff, N.
"Next Steps in Public Assistance."	Hoey, J.
"Next Steps in State Hospital Social Service."	Donahoe, M.
"The Next Thing in Education."	Dickinson, M.
"1977--The Year of the Nurse: We Are Professionally Competent."	Collins, V.
"Ninety Years Young; Excerpt from Address, June 19, 1955."	Kirchway, F.
"Nixon and Welfare for the Rich."	Abzug, B.
"No Home, and the No Home Influences."	Bronson, L.
"No Cooking Chair Age. A Challenge to American Women of Today."	Du Mars, M.
"No Time for Panic. We Must Not Lose Our Humanness."	Hoppock, A.
"Nobel Acceptance Speech."	Buck, P.
"Nobel Lecture on The Chinese Novel."	Buck, P.
"Non-partisan Appeal for a Full Vote."	Lord, M.
"Non-partisan National Woman's Christian Temperance Union."	Foster, J.
"The Nontraditional Student in Academe."	Campbell, J.
"Not in Vain."	Perkins, F.
"Notes for a Study of the Automobile Industry."	Maltese, F.
"The Novel as the Educator of the Imagination."	Rogers, M.
"The Novel Women: Origins of the Feminist Literary Tradition in England and France."	Fritz, A.
"Nuclear Credibility."	Smith, M.
"Nurses in Settlement Work."	Weld, L.
"Nursing Education and Opportunities for the Colored Nurse."	Roberts, A.

"The Objective Value of a Social Settlement."	Addams, J.
"The Objectives of the Professional Organization."	Deardorff, N.
"The Obstacle of Limited Participation in Local Social Planning."	Johnson, A.
"Occupational Diseases."	Hamilton, A.
"Occupational Segregation and Public Policy: A Comparative Analysis of American and Soviet Patterns."	Lapidus, G.
"Occupational Therapy."	Biggerstaff, M.
"Occupational Therapy."	Slagle, E.
"Occupations of Women to Date."	Seymour, M.
"Oceans: Antarctic Resource and Environmental Concerns."	Mink, P.
"Of Free Enquiry Considered as a Means for Obtaining Just Knowledge."	Wright, F.

Title	Author
"Of Worth and Value: The Human Spirit and the Cybercultural Revolution."	Hilton, A.
"Official Opening of Conference."	Cavanagh, A.
"Official Recognition and Status of the Social Worker."	Chickering, M.
"Office of Technology Assessment."	Grasso, E.
"Oil Price Statement."	Grasso, E.
"Old Age Assistance Administration: Varieties of Practice in the United States."	Long, E.
"Old and the Needy."	Hill, R.
"Old Wine in New Bottles. The Democratic Way of Life."	Gambrell, M.
"The Older Woman: A Stockpile of Losses."	Atkinson, T.
"Older Women Workers, Statement at Public Hearing of New York State Joint Legislative Committee on Problems of the Aging, Dec. 14, 1950, in New York City."	Miller, F.
"Olympia Brown's Attack on Immigrants, Given at the National Woman Suffrage Association's Convention in 1889."	Brown, O.
"On Behalf of 7,000,000 Wage-earning Women...."	Lowe, C.
"On Being a Builder."	Cratty, M.
"On Being a Christian."	Cratty, M.
"On Being a Leader."	Cratty, M.
"On Being Born Female: Integration."	Bird, C.
"On Free Enquiry."	Wright, F.
"On Labor."	Stanton, E.
"On Legal Discrimination."	Rose, E.
"On Marriage and Divorce."	Stanton, E.
"On Marriage and Work."	Blackwell, A.
"On the Foreign Menace."	Brown, O.
"On the Formation of Art Groups."	Howe, J.
"On the Issues of Roles."	Cade, T.
"On 'Violence in the Women's Movement': Collaborators."	Atkinson, T.
"One Means of Preventing Pauperism."	Lowell, J.
"One Phase of Woman's Work for the Municipality."	Duncanson, L.
"Only Yesterday."	Catt, C.
"Onward, Comrades: An Address at the Rand School New Year's Eve Ball, December 31, 1920."	Keller, H.
"Opening Address."	Anthony, S.
"Opening Address."	Henrotin, E.
"Opening Address."	Roosevelt, A.
"Opening Address."	Sewall, M.
"Opening Address at the National American Convention of 1914."	Shaw, A.

Title	Author
"Opening Address at the National-American Woman Suffrage Association Convention of 1900."	Anthony, S.
"Opening Address at the National Woman Suffrage Association Convention, Jan. 16, 1873."	Anthony, S.
"Opening Address to the Convention of the Woman Suffrage Association of Missouri, St. Louis, October, 1869."	Minor, V.
"Opening Address to the National American Woman Suffrage Association, Feb. 18, 1890."	Stanton, E.
"Opening and Closing Statements at a Debate with Lucia Cormier, WCSH-TV, Portland, Maine, Nov. 6, 1960."	Smith, M.
"Opening Remarks."	Brainerd, H.
"Opening Remarks."	Lockett, B.
"Opening Remarks."	Shaw, A.
"Opening Remarks (Conference on Women in the Work Force)."	Katzell, M.
"Opening Statement."	Abzug, B.
"Opening Statement on Features of Federal Income, Estate, and Gift Tax Law Which Have a Disparate Impact on Women."	Griffiths, M.
"Opening Statement on Federal Efforts to End Sex Discrimination in Employment."	Griffiths, M.
"Opening Statement on Sex Discrimination in Unemployment Insurance, Veterans Programs, and Public Assistance."	Griffiths, M.
"Opening Statement on the Economics of Sex Discrimination in Employment."	Griffiths, M.
"Opening Statement on the Treatment of Women Under Social Security and Private Pension Plans."	Griffiths, M.
"Opening Statement on Women's Access to Credit and Insurance."	Griffiths, M.
"Opening the Forum."	Reid, H.
"Operation of the Illinois Child Labor Law."	Addams, J.
"Opportunities and Trends in Employment of Women in Business, Summary of Address."	Peterson, E.
"Opportunities for Developing Better Children's Work Throughout a State: Examples of Activities of State Departments."	Greve, B.
"Opportunities for Social Workers to Participate in Social Legislation."	Magee, E.
"Opportunities for Women in the Food Industries."	Stooms, L.
"An Opportunity for Youth in the Present Crisis."	Trimble, A.

Title	Author
"Organization."	American, S.
"Organization."	Henrotin, E.
"Organization Among Women as an Instrument in Promoting Religion."	Dickinson, M.
"Organization Among Women as an Instrument in Promoting the Interests of Industry."	Bond, K.
"Organization Among Women as an Instrument in Promoting the Interests of Political Liberty."	Anthony, S.
"Organization Among Women as an Instrument in Promoting the Interests of Political Liberty."	Blake, L.
"Organization Among Women Considered with Respect to Philanthropy."	Richmond, M.
"Organization Among Women Considered with Respect to Philanthropy--Continued."	Hoffman, C.
"Organization and Its Relation to the International and National Councils of Women."	Avery, R.
"Organization as a Factor in the Development of Modern Social Life."	Sewall, M.
"Organization as a Means of Literary Culture."	Brown, C.
"Organization as Related to Civilization."	Brackett, A.
"Organization Needed to Support and Free the Local Worker for Undifferentiated Case Work."	Cottrell, L.
"Organization of Social Forces for Prevention of Blindness."	Hayden, A.
"The Organization of Social Service in Connection with State Institutions."	McHugh, R.
"The Organization of Trained Nurses' Alumnae Associations."	Robb, I.
"Organization of Working Women."	Kenney, M.
"The Organized Efforts of the Colored Women of the South to Improve Their Condition."	Early, S.
"Organized Leisure as a Factor in Conservation."	Aronovici, C.
"Organized Motherhood."	Meriweather, L.
"Organized Prostitution. How to Deal With It."	Webb, D.
"The Organized Work of Catholic Women."	Toomy, L.
"Organizing Among Women as an Instrument in Promoting the Interests of Industry."	Keyser, H.
"Organizing the Community for Legislative Reform."	Rockwood, E.
"Organizing the Community for Social Action."	Hayden, A.
"Organizing the Unorganizable: Jewish Women and Their Unions."	Harris, A.

Title	Author
"The Origin, History and Development of the World's Woman's Christian Temperance Union."	Andrew, E.
"The Origins of Job Structures in the Steel Industry."	Stone, K.
"Our Blood: The Slavery of Women in Amerika."	Dworkin, A.
"Our Brother in Stripes, in the School-room."	Tutwiler, J.
"Our Cause Is Progressing Triumphantly. Address to the Woman Rights Convention in N. Y., Sept. 1853."	Blackwell, A.
"Our Creeping Idiot Savantism: Maturity Can Be Magnificent."	Foxworth, J.
"Our Debt to Zurich."	Webster, H.
"Our Divine Possibilities."	Travilla, M.
"Our Duty to Dependent Races."	Fletcher, A.
"Our Forgotten Foremothers."	Blake, L.
"Our Highest Common Denominator."	Laich, K.
"Our Illusions Regarding Government (Pugsley Award)."	Van Kleeck, M.
"Our International Communities and the War."	Bremer, E.
"Our Motives and Methods."	Cratty, M.
"Our Nation's Obligation to Her Children."	Lathrop, J.
"Our Neighbors, the Alaskan Women."	McDiarmid, C.
"Our Reasons."	Hunt, M.
"Our Revolution Is Unique."	Friedan, B.
"Our Spanish-American Neighbors."	Dodd, A.
"Our Union Has Kept Faith With Us."	Ackerman, J.
"Our Young Girls."	Stanton, E.
"Ourselves and Our Religion."	Cratty, M.
"Outdoor Work for Women Prisoners."	Davis, K.
"Outline of the First Interview."	Sears, A.
"The Outlook for Economic and Social Security in America."	Perkins, F.
"The Outlook in Unemployment Relief."	Perkins, F.
"Outside Activities of Children's Institutions."	Bolotin, A.
"Overview: Demographic Trends and Issues in Women's Health."	Lipman-Blumen, J.
"The Pacific Northwest."	Duniway, A.
"Panelist Discussion."	McCabe, R.
"Panelist Statement."	Nachimias, V.
"Panelist Statement."	Rees, M.
"Panelist Statement."	Simon, D.
"Panelist Statement."	Wu, C.
"Paper on Preventive Work Among Children."	Cobb, M.

"Paper on the System of Visiting the Girls and Small Boys Who Are Wards of the State in Massachusetts."	Putnam, E.
"Paradox and Poetic Truth: The Beauty of Life."	Sibley, A.
"Parent-Child Relationships in Unmarried Parenthood."	Brisley, M.
"Parental Reverence as Taught in the Hebrew Home."	Kohut, R.
"Paris."	Howe, J.
"The Part Social Workers Have Taken in Promoting Social Legislation in California."	Chickering, M.
"Participants and Policy Making."	Kimball, N.
"Participation in International Child Welfare Work."	Lathrop, J.
"Parting Address, As Delivered in the Bowery Theatre, to the People of New-York, in June, 1830."	Wright, F.
"The Past, Present, and Future of the Women's Relief Corps."	Sherwood, K.
"The Patience of Faith."	Howe, J.
"Patriotic Principles of Americanism. Freedom Must Be Earned."	Barnes, E.
"Patriotism and Pacifists in War Time."	Addams, J.
"Patriotism in Civil Service Reform."	Main, C.
"Patterns of Discrimination and Discouragement in Higher Education."	Babey-Brooke, A.
"Patterns of Discrimination and Discouragement in Higher Education."	Harris, A.
"Patterns of Discrimination and Discouragement in Higher Education."	Richter, M.
"Patterns of Discrimination and Discouragement in Higher Education."	Sandler, B.
"Patterns of Women in Industry."	Miller, F.
"Peace in the Public Schools."	Hastings, C.
"Peace Work in the Schools."	Pierson, M.
"Peculiar Insecurities of Women as Workers."	Robinson, M.
"Pending Immigration Legislation."	Schisby, M.
"Pennsylvania. The Greater Economy of Adequate Grants."	Bogue, M.
"Pension Drive, Social and Economic Implications."	Folsom, M.
"Pension Legislation for Women."	Chisholm, S.
"Permanent Revolution. The Concept of Liberty Under Law is Universal."	Luce, C.
"Personal and Professional Sources of Inspiration for Social Workers: Roots of Courage."	Glenn, M.
"The Personal Problems of a Group of Workers."	Bingham, A.
"The Personalising Process: Union Differentiates."	Parr, M.

"Personality Deviations and Their Relation to the Home."	Foster, S.
"Personnel in the Public Service from the Administrator's Point of View."	Potter, E.
"Petitions Were Circulated."	Rose, E.
"The Phanton Petrodollar: A Deposit Withdrawal Program."	Sindona, M.
"Philadelphia as a Provider for Dependent Children."	Deardorff, N.
"The Philadelphia Experiment."	Libbey, B.
"The Philadelphia Plan of a Central Bureau of Inquiry and Specialized Care."	McCoy, H.
"Philosophical Trends in Modern Social Work (Presidential Address)."	Van Waters, M.
"The Philosophy and Use of Budget Standards."	Pratt, L.
"The Philosophy of a New Day."	Addams, J.
"The Philosophy of Atheism."	Goldman, E.
"The Philosophy of Social Work and Its Place in the Professional Curriculum."	Cannon, A.
"A Philosophy of Supervision in Social Case Work."	Lowry, F.
"Physical Culture."	King, J.
"Physical Decline of Leisure-class American Women. A Paper Read Before the Woman's Alliance of Syracuse and Other Clubs, and Published by Request."	Holcombe, E.
"Physical Education for Women."	Leiter, F.
"The Physician and the Nurse in the Public School."	Rogers, L.
"Physiological Changes and Adjustments: From the Standpoint of a Nutritionist."	Swanson, P.
"Physiological Changes and Adjustments: From the Standpoint of a Physician."	Macfarlane, C.
"Piano Playing Without Piano Practicing."	Hayes, M.
"Pioneer Woman of Oregon."	Wilson, E.
"Place and Scope of Psychiatric Social Work in Mental Hygiene."	Ryther, M.
"The Place of Field Work in Training for Social Work: Its Educational Content."	Mudgett, M.
"The Place of Mothers' Aid in a State Program of Child Welfare."	Mitchell, L.
"Place of Private Group-Work Agency in Program of Youth."	Carner, L.
"The Place of Psychiatric Social Work: In a Family Case Work Organization."	Taussig, F.
"The Place of Recreation in the Settlement Program."	Simkhovitch, M.

"The Place of Religion in a Liberal Arts Curriculum. The Academic Study of Religion." Rollins, M.
"The Place of the Foreign Language Press in an Educational Program." Roche, J.
"The Place of the Home in Treatment." Regensburg, J.
"The Place of the Kindergarten in Child-saving." Harding, E.
"The Place of the Mobile Clinic in a Rural Community." Lyday, J.
"Place of Women in Our Public Schools." Cheney, E.
"Place of Women in the Present Crisis." Owen, R.
"Placing Women in History: A 1975 Perspective." Lerner, G.
"A Plan of Action." Gage, M.
"A Plan of County Co-operation." Powell, S.
"Plan of Work Along Social Purity Lines." Ackerman, J.
"Planning Services for the Aged in the Local Community." Guiney, M.
"Planning the Urban Community." James, H.
"Planning Training for Future Woman-power." Manor, S.
"Play and Playgrounds." American, S.
"Playgrounds." Meade, M.
"Playgrounds in Cities." Mackenzie, C.
"A Plea for Migrant Children: Lift the Marks from Their Faces." Bragdon, I.
"A Plea for Recognition of Soviet Russia. Statement at a Hearing on Russian Free Trade Before the U.S. Senate Foreign Relations Committee." Keller, H.
"Plea on Behalf of Elizabeth Stanton at the Convention of the National American Woman Suffrage Association, Jan. 1896." Anthony, S.
"The Plight of Refugees in a Preoccupied World." Kraus, H.
"Pointing the Way in 1933. Address of the President." Sherwin, B.
"Points of General Agreement." Banning, M.
"Police Matrons." Barney, S.
"The Policewoman." Van Winkel, M.
"The Policewoman and the Girl Problem." Miner, M.
"The Policewoman; Discussion." Brown, C.
"Policewomen." Wells, A.
"The Policewomen Movement, Present Status and Future Needs." Wells, A.
"The Policy Issues: Presentation V." Norwood, J.
"The Policy Issues: Presentation IV." Sandler, B.
"The Policy Issues: Presentation I." Shaeffer, R.
"The Policy Issues: Presentation VI." Kanter, R.
"The Policy Issues: Presentation II." Long, N.
"Political Economy of Women." Anthony, S.

"Political Enfranchisement of Women."	Anthony, S.
"Political Parties and Woman Suffrage."	Robinson, H.
"Political Reform."	Addams, J.
"Political Transition in Urban Africa."	Barnes, S.
"The Political Woman."	Atkinson, T.
"Politics from the Social Point of View."	Vittum, H.
"The Politics of Cultural Liberation: Male-Female Relations in Algeria."	Boals, K.
"Poorhouses and Jails of the Southwest."	Tutwiler, J.
"The Popular Inculcation of Economy."	Oberholtzer, S.
"Port Problems in Europe and the United States."	Howe, J.
"The Position of Women in Plato's Republic."	Howe, J.
"Position of Women in the Political Life of the United States. Address to the International Council of Women in London, 1899."	Anthony, S.
"The Position of Women in Their Professional Associations."	Klotzburger, K.
"The Possibilities of Centralized Supervision."	Byington, M.
"Possibilities of Home Supervision of Moron Women."	Dutcher, E.
"Possibilities of Social Workers' Club."	Smith, Z.
"Possibilities of Volunteer Service in Public Agencies."	Liveright, A.
"Possible Solution of the Midwife Problem."	Van Blaroom, C.
"Post Office Missions."	Jones, S.
"Post-War America that America Does Not Want. A Fair Trade Act Needed for Ideas."	Alexander, R.
"Post-War Role of American Women."	Anderson, M.
"The Postwar Role of Social Workers."	Hurlbutt, M.
"Potentialities of Social Service to Children."	Aves, G.
"Pottery in the Household."	McLaughlin, M.
"Poverty and Its Relief: Methods Possible in the City of New York."	Lowell, J.
"Poverty and Woman."	Gilman, C.
"Poverty as a Cause of Mortality."	Bass, R.
"Power and Influence of Women. Dedication to Family and Nation."	Roebling, M.
"Power and Purpose of Women."	Bullock, H.
"The Power of Organization."	Howe, J.
"The Power of Thought."	Stuart, E.
"The Power of Womanliness in Dealing with Stern Problems."	Porter, F.
"The Power to Maintain Peace. Responsibilities Must Be Accepted."	Thompson, D.
"Practical Applications of Psychology to the Problems of a Clearing House."	Fernald, M.
"Practical Culture."	Marwedel, E.

"Practical Issues of an African Experience."	French-Sheldon, M.
"Practical Points in Patriotism."	Catt, C.
"Practical Results of Ten Years' Work."	Cooper, S.
"Predictions for the Unpredictable Future. Every Big Accomplishment Involves Many Small Ones."	Horton, M.
"Prenatal and Hereditary Influences."	Logan, A.
"Pre-natal Care."	Putnam, E.
"Preparation and Direction of Case-Work Personnel: The Washington Training Plan."	FitzSimons, R.
"The Preparation of the Indian for Citizenship."	Fletcher, A.
"The Present Opportunity of the City Home Service Section."	King, A.
"Present Relief Situation in the United States."	Brown, J.
"The Present Situation in the Academic World of Women Trained in Engineering."	Bernard, J.
"The Present Status of Minimum Wage Legislation."	Kelley, F.
"The Present Status of Mothers' Pensions Administration."	Lundberg, E.
"Present Status of Women in the Church."	Tupper, M.
"Present Tendencies in Women's College and University Education."	Thomas, M.
"Presentation of Carrie Chapman Catt as Her Successor as President of the National American Woman Suffrage Association, 1900."	Anthony, S.
"Presentation of Gift to Miss Anthony, at the National-American Woman Suffrage Association Convention of 1900."	Catt, C.
"Presentation of Portrait."	Lockwood, M.
"Presentation of the 1949 Award of the Snow Medal (With Her Reply)."	Bolton, F.
"Presentation of the Shafroth-Palmer Amendment to the National American Woman Suffrage Association Convention of 1914."	Funk, A.
"Presidential Address."	Addams, J.
"Presidential Address."	Fyan, L.
"Presidential Address."	Horton, M.
"Presidential Address at Washington Conference."	Eastman, L.
"Presidential Address. International Congress of Women, Zurich."	Addams, J.
"Presidential Address, International Congress, The Hague."	Addams, J.
"Presidential Address: Some Problems in Role Analysis."	Komarovsky, M.

"Presidential Address, Women of the Pacific." Addams, J.
"Presidential Candidacy Announcement." Smith, M.
"President's Address." Willard, F.
"President's Address." Wittenmyer, A.
"President's Address: A Prelude to Peace." Glenn, M.
"The President's Address at the First National Woman's Rights Convention in Worcester, Mass., 1850." Davis, P.
"President's Address at a Mass Meeting of "The Daughters of Temperance" on Jan. 28, 1852." Vaughan, M.
"President's Address at New York State Temperance Convention, Rochester, N. Y., April 20, 1852." Stanton, E.
"President's Address at the Akron Convention, May 28, 1851." Gage, F.
"President's Address at the Eleventh National Woman's Rights Convention, May 10, 1866." Stanton, E.
"President's Address at the 5th National Convention in Philadelphia, Oct., 1854." Rose, E.
"President's Address at the National-American Woman Suffrage Convention of 1896." Anthony, S.
"President's Address at the National American Woman Suffrage Association Convention of 1905." Shaw, A.
"President's Address at the National American Woman Suffrage Association Convention of 1906." Shaw, A.
"President's Address at the National Woman Suffrage Association Convention, Washington, D. C., Jan. 1876." Gage, M.
"President's Address at the New England Convention of 1859." Severance, C.
"President's Address at the 7th National Convention, New York, Nov. 25 & 26, 1856." Stone, L.
"President's Address at the 10th National Woman's Rights Convention, N. Y., May 10-11, 1860." Wright, M.
"President's Address at the 20th Anniversary Convention, N. Y., October, 1870." Davis, P.
"President's Address at the Westchester (Pennsylvania) Convention, June, 1852." Johnson, M.
"President's Address to the American Woman Suffrage Association, 6th Annual Meeting, Oct. 1874." Howe, J.

"President's Address to the 5th Annual Convention National Woman's Suffrage Association, Washington, D. C., Jan. 16, 1873."	Anthony, S.
"President's Address to the National-American Woman Suffrage Association Convention of 1899."	Anthony, S.
"President's Address to the National-American Woman Suffrage Association Convention of 1897."	Anthony, S.
"President's Address to the National American Woman Suffrage Association Convention of 1915."	Shaw, A.
"President's Address to the National Woman Suffrage Association Convention, May 10, 1870."	Stanton, E.
"President's Address to the 7th Meeting of the New Hampshire Woman Suffrage Association, Nov. 5, 1879."	White, A.
"President's Address to 38th Annual Convention of the National American Woman Suffrage Association, Feb. 1906."	Shaw, A.
"The President's Address. Taking Part in Government."	Sherwin, B.
"President's Annual Address."	Catt, C.
"President's Closing Remarks at the 7th National Convention, N. Y., Nov. 25 & 26, 1853."	Stone, L.
"President's Report 1920-1922."	Winter, A.
"Press and Its Responsibilities: Finance and Government Security."	Graham, K.
"The Press--Its Powers and Possibilities."	Lincoln, M.
"Preventing the First Offender."	Jaffray, J.
"The Prevention and Treatment of Juvenile Delinquency in Wartime."	Gibbons, M.
"Prevention in Some of Its Aspects and Woman's Part in It."	Lynde, M.
"Prevention of Blindness from Opthalmia Neonatorum."	Wright, L.
"The Prevention of Insanity."	McCowen, J.
"The Prevention of Nervous Strain by Home and School Training."	Dearborn, J.
"Preventive and Public Health Aspects of Rheumatic Fever in Children."	Gawin, L.
"Preventive Medicine."	Donohue, M.
"Preventive Work as Carried on in the Public Schools of America."	Lovell, M.
"Price Controls and Revenues: Federal Regulations."	Knauer, V.
"Price of Meat."	Grasso, E.
"Pride in America: Let's Start a Renaissance."	Bushnell, L.
"Principles and Methods of Outdoor Relief."	Vaile, G.

"Principles, Content, and Objectives of Supervision." Brown, J.
"Principles of International Law Concerning Friendly Relations Among States: Sovereign Equality of States." Kelly, E.
"Principles of International Law Concerning Friendly Relations and Cooperation Among States: Peaceful Settlement of Disputes." Kelly, E.
"Priority Status Needed for Sickle Cell Anemia." Grasso, E.
"Prison Labor." Kelley, F.
"Private Living Arrangements for Elderly People." Nairne, L.
"Private Living Arrangements for Elderly People." Nicholson, E.
"The Probation System of the Juvenile Court of Indianapolis." Rogers, H.
"The Problem of Meeting the Needs of the Social Worker Who Refers Cases to a Psychiatric Clinic." Robb, C.
"The Problem of Roles." Clemens, L.
"The Problem of Truancy." O'Reilly, M.
"Problems and Solutions in Achieving Equality for Women." Harris, P.
"Problems Created by Assistance Categories." Taylor, R.
"Problems Facing Children with Relatively Long Period of Institutional Care." Verry, E.
"Problems in Teen-Age Hangouts." Osborn, H.
"Problems in the Administration of Mothers' Aid." Bogue, M.
"The Problems of a Permanent Child Guidance Clinic." Crutcher, H.
"Problems of Adoption in Rural Areas." Aleshire, R.
"The Problems of Creative Women." Mannes, M.
"The Problems of Mental Diseases in an Aging Population." Overholser, W.
"Problem of Social Case Work with Children." Taft, J.
"Professional and In-Service Training for Group Work." Schindler, A.
"Professional Education in the Agency Setting." Sheibley, E.
"Professional Relations: The School of Social Work and the Agency." Sytz, F.
"Professional Skills Requisite to a Good Intake Service." Dawley, A.
"Professional Standards for Council and Chest Executives." Conrad, I.
"Professional Standards in Social Agencies: The Value to the Agency of Students in Training." Berry, M.

"Professional Training from the Point of View of the Family Field." Rich, M.
"Professional Training in the Light of Wartime Shortages." Wisner, E.
"A Program for the Protection of Children." Gane, E.
"A Program for Unemployed Youth." Hayes, M.
"Program of the Committee on Illegitimacy--Committee Report." Sheffield, A.
"Progress and Administration of Minimum Wage Laws in 1933." Mason, L.
"Progress in Legal Protection for Children Born Out of Wedlock." Lundberg, E.
"Progress in Louisville Social Centers." Witherspoon, P.
"Progress in Social Case Work: Among the Indians." Lund, H.
"Progress in Social Case Work: In Child Welfare." Haskins, A.
"Progress in Social Case Work: In Mental Hygiene." Taft, J.
"Progress in the Care of the Feeble-Minded and Epileptics." Dunlap, M.
"Progress, Man's Distinctive Mark Alone. Brute Force Shall Give Way--." Woolley, M.
"The Progress of Adjustment in Mexican and United States Life." Sturges, V.
"The Progress of Fifty Years." Stone, L.
"Progress of Humanity. What You Can Contribute to Man's Progress." O'Connor, L.
"Progress Report at Pertinent Research." Lloyd-Jones, E.
"Progress Through Understanding." Chisholm, S.
"Progress Toward Better Laws for the Protection of Children Born Out of Wedlock." Lundberg, E.
"Progressive Methods of Care for Children Pending Juvenile Court Hearing." Lenroot, K.
"Prohibition--The Problem of Enforcement from the Federal Standpoint." Willebrandt, M.
"Promotion of National and State Social Legislation by Social Workers." Breckinridge, S.
"Promoting Library Interests Throughout the World." Morsch, L.
"Propaganda and Organized Women." Poole, G.
"Propaganda in the Modern World." Thompson, D.
"Prophets, Old and New." Palmer, A.
"Proposals for Distribution." Hohman, H.
"The Prostitute as a Health and Social Problem." Yarros, R.
"Protection of Children in Adoption." Colby, M.
"The Protective Agency for Women and Children." Brown, C.

"The Protective Power of the Ballot. Address to the House Judiciary Committee, 1900." McCulloch, C.
"Protective Standards for Women Wage Earners." Gordon, J.
"Protective Work for Girls in War Time." Miner, M.
"Providing Consular Services to the American Public Abroad: Statement." Watson, B.
"Psychiatric Social Work in Relation to a State Mental Hygiene Program." Lloyd, R.
"The Psychiatric Thread Running Through All Social Case Work." Jarrett, M.
"A Psychiatrist's View: Images of Woman--Past and Present, Overt and Obscured." Shainess, N.
"Psychiatry and the Offender in the Community: The Juvenile Offender." Goldsmith, E.
"Psychiatry, Social Service, and Society." Mallory, C.
"A Psycholanalytic Approach to the Genesis of Promiscuity." Bergman, M.
"Psychoanalytic Contributions to Social Case Work Treatment." Robinson, V.
"Psychological Differences Between Men and Women." Anastasi, A.
"Psychological Fulfillment for the Woman." Sexton, V.
"The Psychology and the Psychological Effects of Discrimination." Gardner, J.
"Psychology Looks at the Female." Hoffman, L.
"The Psychology of Co-Operation." Sears, A.
"Psychopathic Hospitals." Spink, M.
"Public Address, 1894 on Political Parties Support for Suffrage." Anthony, S.
"Public Administration of Charity in Denver." Vaile, G.
"Public Agencies as Public Carriers of Ideas." Sheffield, A.
"Public Aid for the Feeble-minded." Brown, C.
"Public Assistance Features of the Social Security Act." Barrett, M.
"Public Assistance--Wither Bound? (Pres. Address)." Abbott, E.
"Public Charitable Service as a Profession." Breckinridge, S.
"Public Charities in Washington." Reed, A.
"Public Control of the Packing Industry, A Factor in Reducing the Cost of Living." Costigan, M.
"The Public Dance Hall." Ingram, F.
"Public Forums and Public Opinion." Sporborg, C.
"Public Health Nursing and the War." Lent, M.
"Public Health Nursing and Tuberculosis." Stewart, A.

"The Public Health Nursing Program of the American Red Cross."	Fox, E.
"Public Policy and Behavioral Science; Excerpt from Testimony Before the U. S. Senate Foreign Relations Committee, June 20, 1969."	Mead, M.
"Public Policy and Childbearing."	Mulligan, J.
"The Public Protection of Children; A First Part of the Public Welfare Program."	Abbott, G.
"Public Protection of Children. (Presidential Address)."	Abbott, G.
"Public Relief--Its Relation to Higher Labor Standards and Social Security."	Carr, C.
"Public Relief Officials."	Sheffield, A.
"Public Responsibility for the American Indian."	James, S.
"The Public School and the Immigrant Child."	Addams, J.
"The Public School as a Little-Used Agency: As a Factor in the Treatment of the Socially Handicapped Child."	Culbert, J.
"Public School Classes for Crippled Children."	Neil, J.
"Public School Classes for Mentally Deficient Children."	Chace, L.
"Public Statement."	De Fazio, M.
"Public Statement."	Green, I.
"Public Testimony."	Adickes, S.
"Public Testimony."	Aronoff, R.
"Public Testimony."	Berry, B.
"Public Testimony."	Brady, A.
"Public Testimony."	Brower, M.
"Public Testimony."	Burkholder, M.
"Public Testimony."	Bushong, R.
"Public Testimony."	Buxenbaum, A.
"Public Testimony."	Caplan, S.
"Public Testimony."	Ceballos, J.
"Public Testimony."	Chasan, E.
"Public Testimony."	Chenet, W.
"Public Testimony."	Cisler, L.
"Public Testimony."	Corin, L.
"Public Testimony."	Davis, M.
"Public Testimony."	DeVore, O.
"Public Testimony."	Epstein, C.
"Public Testimony."	Evans, S.
"Public Testimony."	Fasteau, B.
"Public Testimony."	Faust, J.
"Public Testimony."	Fruchter, R.
"Public Testimony."	Goldenberg, S.
"Public Testimony."	Goodman, J.
"Public Testimony."	Graber, P.
"Public Testimony."	Greenberg, G.

"Public Testimony." Hahn, P.
"Public Testimony." Haring, A.
"Public Testimony." Hedley, C.
"Public Testimony." Herman, J.
"Public Testimony." Howe, F.
"Public Testimony." Hull, J.
"Public Testimony." Jacobson, C.
"Public Testimony." Kearon, P.
"Public Testimony." Kenyon, D.
"Public Testiomny." Klotzburger, K.
"Public Testimony." Komisar, L.
"Public Testimony." Layzer, J.
"Public Testimony." Lervold, L.
"Public Testimony." Lipton, M.
"Public Testimony." Maguire, M.
"Public Testimony." Mayer, S.
"Public Testimony." Millstein, S.
"Public Testimony." Milner, E.
"Public Testimony." Missakian, E.
"Public Testimony." Nelson, L.
"Public Testimony." Penna, Z.
"Public Testimony." Phillips, M.
"Public Testimony." Renner, A.
"Public Testimony." Rothman, E.
"Public Testimony." Rothstein, A.
"Public Testimony." Sands, S.
"Public Testimony." Schpritzer, F.
"Public Testimony." Scott, A.
"Public Testimony." Segal, T.
"Public Testimony." Silvan, V.
"Public Testimony." Skiles, J.
"Public Testimony." Smith, E.
"Public Testimony." Smith, M.
"Public Testimony." Spohn, R.
"Public Testimony." Stanton, H.
"Public Testimony." Steinmann, A.
"Public Testimony." Stevens, V.
"Public Testimony." Susan, B.
"Public Testimony." Thomas, D.
"Public Testimony." Thringold, F.
"Public Testimony." Torton, I.
"Public Testimony." Voutsis, M.
"Public Testimony." Warwick, M.
"Public Testimony." Waxman, R.
"Public Testimony." Yalof, H.
"The Public Welfare Administrator and Civil Service in State and Local Services." Abbott, G.
"Public Welfare and Politics." Abbott, E.
"Publicity." Dodson, M.
"Publicity." Toombs, E.
"The Pulpit Has a Bad Influence." Foster, A.
"The Pure in Heart." Clothier, H.

"Purity and Parental Responsibility."	Kellogg, E.
"The Purpose of Statewide Statistics in Building the Foundation for the Prevention of Delinquency."	Labaree, M.
"The Purpose of the College."	Thomas, M.
"Qualifications of the Psychiatric Social Worker."	Taft, J.
"The Qualities of Leadership."	Cratty, M.
"The Qualities of Leadership as Revealed in Miss Dodge."	Cratty, M.
"The Quality Elementary School. Problems Facing Elementary Education."	Foley, A.
"The Queen Isabella Association."	Hooker, I.
"The Question of the Ratification of the Equal Rights Amendment."	Thompson, M.
"Questions for the Future. Action."	Height, D.
"Questions for the Future. Research."	Handy, G.
"The Quota Law and the Effect of Its Administration in Contiguous Territory."	Razovsky, C.
"The Quota Law and the Family."	McDowell, M.
"Race Reconciliation."	Woolley, C.
"The Race Question: A Problem Above Politics."	Smith, L.
"Rachel Carson Receives Audubon Medal; With Acceptance Address."	Carson, R.
"Racial Cooperation."	Luce, C.
"Racing with Science."	Davison, E.
"Radcliffe Institute for Independent Study."	Smith, C.
"Radio Immunoassay: A Probe for the Fine Structure of Biologic Systems."	Yalow, R.
"Rail Passenger Service."	Grasso, E.
"Raise Your Voice: Cast Your Vote."	Meyers, B.
"The Ramabai Association."	Andrews, J.
"The Rape Atrocity and the Boy Next Door."	Dworkin, A.
"The Reaction of Children's Case Work in the Development of the Constructive and Preventive Work of a Community: In the Removal of Degrading Causes."	Montgomery, A.
"Reading Courses for Mothers."	Sangster, M.
"Recent Changes in the Philosophy of Social Workers."	Cannon, M.
"Recent Development in Library Work with Immigrants."	Ledbetter, E.
"Recent Developments in the Organization and Operation of Public Welfare Departments; The Bureau System."	Potter, E.

Title	Author
"Recent Federal Employment Policy Developments, New Progress for Women."	Keyserling, M.
"Recent Industrial Investigations: Recent Investigations by Government Bureaus."	Anderson, M.
"Recent Statistics on Crime and the Foreign Born."	Bowler, A.
"Reconstruction. Address Delivered at Ottumwa, Kansas, July 4, 1865."	Anthony, S.
"Recreation in Rural Communities."	Moskowitz, B.
"Recruiting of Students by Schools and of Apprentices by Agencies."	Burnett, M.
"The Red Cross."	Barton, C.
"Redefining Nonviolence."	Dworkin, A.
"Rediscovery of Alaska. Crossroads of America."	Gruber, R.
"Re-examination of Child-care Functions in Family Agencies."	Young, M.
"A Re-examination of Child-Welfare Functions in Foster-Care Agencies."	Clarke, E.
"A Re-examination of the Fear of Success."	Hoffman, L.
"Reflections and Perspectives on the Women's Movement in 1976: The Equal Rights Amendment."	St. John, J.
"Reflections for a Graduate: Dare to be Your Creative Self."	Alexander, E.
"Reform Schools for Girls."	Wardner, L.
"Reform Work for Girls."	Keeley, S.
"Reformation of Criminal Girls."	Hall, E.
"Reformatory and Preventive Work in Illinois."	Beveridge, H.
"Reformatory Treatment of Women."	Falconer, M.
"The Refugee Alien."	Goldman, E.
"The Regeneration of the Colored Population in the Rural South."	Cooley, R.
"Regional and State-wide Exchanges."	Blakeslee, R.
"Regional Coordination."	Paul, H.
"Rehabilitation Work."	Radebaugh, K.
"Reinstatement of Vagrants Through Municipal Lodging Houses."	Willard, A.
"The Relation of a Board of Public Welfare to the Public."	Johnson, K.
"Relation of a Standard of Education and Training to Professional Practice."	Sytz, F.
"Relation of Case-Work Staffs to Interpretation, Officials, Governing Boards, Volunteers, and the Public."	Eggleston, M.
"Relation of Case-Work Staffs to Interpretation, Officials, Governing Boards, Volunteers, and the Public."	Howlett, V.

"The Relation of Community Work to Family Life."	McDowell, M.
"The Relation of Educated Women to the Peace Movement."	Woolley, M.
"The Relation of Feeble-mindedness to Other Social Problems."	MacMurchy, H.
"The Relation of Food Economics to the Nutritive Value of the Diet."	Gillett, L.
"The Relation of Health Officers and Social Work."	Seymour, G.
"The Relation of Hospital Social Service to Child Health Work."	Cannon, I.
"The Relation of Mental Defect to the Neglected, Dependent and Delinquent Children of New Hampshire."	Streeter, L.
"The Relation of Municipal and County Charities to the Commonwealth."	Williamson, E.
"Relation of Personality Study to Child Placing."	Taft, J.
"The Relation of State Institutions and Agencies to Private Institutions: The Ohio Plan."	Atkinson, M.
"The Relation of the Church to Social Work."	Saloman, A.
"Relation of the Curative Workshop to the Rehabilitation of Disabled Persons."	Goodman, H.
"The Relation of the Kindergarten to Social Reform."	Wiggin, K.
"The Relation of the School to the Mental Health of the Average Child."	Taft, J.
"The Relation of the Woman Suffrage Movement to Other Reforms."	Howe, J.
"The Relation of Woman to Her Dress."	Woolson, A.
"The Relation of Woman to Our Present Political Problems."	Peaslie, A.
"Relation of Women to Crime and Criminals."	Chace, E.
"The Relation of Young Women to Church Missions."	Haynes, L.
"Relations and Duties of Public Health Nurses and Social Workers in the Diagnosis, Treatment, and Control of Syphillis."	King, E.
"Relations of Woman's Work in the Household to the Work Outside."	Blackwell, A.
"The Relationship Between Children and Family Case Working Agencies: Relationships in Technique."	Sanders, C.
"The Relationship Between the Functions of the Juvenile Court and Those of the General Child-Caring Agencies."	Workum, R.
"Relief, Style 1936."	Colcord, J.

Title	Author
"Relief, the No Man's Land, and How to Reclaim It."	Abbott, E.
"Religion, Poetry, and History: Foundations for a New Educational System."	Alexander, M.
"Religion, Poetry, and History: Foundations for a New Educational System."	Walker, M.
"Religious Duty to the Negro."	Williams, F.
"The Religious Life of the Child."	Cabot, E.
"Remarks."	Addams, J.
"Remarks."	Bellamy, C.
"Remarks."	Eastman, M.
"Remarks."	Krupsak, M.
"Remarks."	Robertson, A.
"Remarks."	Schneiderman, R.
"Remarks."	Sheenan, P.
"Remarks as Chairman of Discussion."	Addams, J.
"Remarks at a Banquet in Los Angeles Celebrating the Publication of the First Ten Years of American Communism, December 15, 1962."	Karsner, R.
"Remarks at a Meeting of the Cuban League in Rochester, N. Y., Feb., 1897."	Anthony, S.
"Remarks at a W. C. T. U. National Convention in Cleveland, Nov. 1895."	Anthony, S.
"Remarks at Ceremonies Issuing the 1973 Philatelic-Numismatic Commemorative at Faneuil Hall, Boston, Massachusetts, 11:30 a. m., July 4, 1973."	Brooks, M.
"Remarks at Her 70th Birthday Celebration, Feb. 15, 1890."	Anthony, S.
"Remarks at Jane Addams Memorial Service."	Abbott, E.
"Remarks at Jane Addams Memorial Service."	Lenroot, K.
"Remarks at Jane Addams Memorial Service."	Perkins, F.
"Remarks at Jane Addams Memorial Service."	Simkhovitch, M.
"Remarks at State Teachers' Convention Rochester, N. Y., August 3, 1853."	Anthony, S.
"Remarks at the Conference of Delegates."	Lockwood, B.
"Remarks at the Conference of Delegates."	Mead, L.
"Remarks at the Conference of Delegates."	Spencer, A.
"Remarks at the 1894 Convention of the National American Woman Suffrage Association."	Anthony, S.
"Remarks at the 1st Annual Meeting of the American Equal Rights Association, May, 1867."	Foster, A.

"Remarks at the 1st Annual Meeting of the American Equal Rights Association, May 1867." Mott, L.
"Remarks at the 1st Annual Meeting of the American Equal Rights Association, May 1867." Truth, S.
"Remarks at the 1st Annual Meeting of the American Woman Suffrage Association, Cleveland, Ohio, Nov. 1870." Clarke, H.
"Remarks at the 4th Annual Meeting of the American Woman Suffrage Association, 1872." Cutler, H.
"Remarks at the 4th Annual Meeting of the American Woman Suffrage Association, 1872." Longley, M.
"Remarks at the Semi-Annual Meeting of the American Woman Suffrage Association, N. Y., May, 1871." Churchill, E.
"Remarks at the 7th National Convention, N. Y., Nov. 25, 1856." Rose, E.
"Remarks at the 10th National Woman's Rights Convention, N. Y., 1860." Jones, E.
"Remarks at the 10th National Woman's Rights Convention, N. Y., May 10-11, 1860." Rose, E.
"Remarks at the U. S. Conference of Mayors, Tucson, Arizona, June 14, 1977." Kreps, J.
"Remarks at the Woman's Rights Convention in New York, Sept. 1853." Nichols, C.
"Remarks at the Woman's Rights Convention in New York, Sept. 1853." Rose, E.
"Remarks at Woman's Rights Convention, Syracuse, N. Y., Sept. 8, 1852." Rose, E.
"Remarks Before a Senate Committee, 1902." Anthony, S.
"Remarks Before the 1977 National Conference on Railroad-Highway Crossing Safety, Salt Lake City, Utah, August 23, 1977." Bailey, K.
"Remarks Before the Air Transport Association, 1977 Airlines Operations Forum, Tampa, Florida, October 19, 1977." Bailey, K.
"Remarks Before the Association of American Railroads Annual Safety Section Meeting, Duluth, Minn., June 22, 1977." Bailey, K.
"Remarks Before the Opportunities Industrialization Centers of America, Detroit, Michigan, June 8, 1977." Kreps, J.
"Remarks During Debate at 4th National Convention, Cleveland, Ohio, in Oct. 1853." Foster, A.

"Remarks During Debate at the 4th National Convention, Oct. 1853 in Cleveland, Ohio." Rose, E.
"Remarks During Debate on Resolution Denouncing Dogmas and Creeds at the 17th National Convention of the National Woman Suffrage Association, Jan. 1885." Anthony, S.
"Remarks, first Houston Regional Transportation Conference, Whitehall Hotel, September 23, 1976, Houston, Texas." Bailey, K.
"Remarks of the Secretary, Lavinia Waight." Waight, L.
"Remarks on a Public Disturbance at the Women's Rights Convention in New York, Sept. 1853." Mott, L.
"Remarks on Divorce at the 1905 Meeting of the National Council of Women." Anthony, S.
"Remarks on Emotionalism in Politics Given at the National American Woman Suffrage Association Convention in 1913." Shaw, A.
"Remarks on Hours Limitation Law, Administrative and Technical Problems." Ackroyd, M.
"Remarks on House Concurrent Resolution 47: On the Status of Soviet Jews." Grasso, E.
"Remarks on Interest in Political Questions." Sewall, M.
"Remarks on Labor Standard Improvement and Greater Employment Opportunity." Keyserling, M.
"Remarks on Legal Disabilities at the Woman's Rights State Convention, Rochester, N.Y., Nov. 30, 1853." Gage, M.
"Remarks on Maternity Care for Foreign-Born Women." Perkins, F.
"Remarks on Organization." Gage, M.
"Remarks on Philanthropy." Shattuck, H.
"Remarks on Religion at the National Woman Suffrage Association Convention, Jan. 1885." Stanton, E.
"Remarks on the Case of Mrs. Norton at the Woman's Rights Convention in N.Y., Sept. 1853." Stone, L.
"Remarks on the Laws of Ohio, at 4th National Convention, Cleveland, Ohio, Oct. 1853." Coe, E.
"Remarks on the World's Temperance Convention." Blackwell, A.

"Remarks on Wills at the Woman's Rights Convention, in New York, Sept. 1853." Rose, E.
"Remarks on Women in Industry." Anthony, S.
"Remarks on Women in Industry." Johns, L.
"Remarks on Women's Condition at the 7th National Convention, N. Y., Nov. 25, 1856." Rose, E.
"Remarks on Women's Wrongs at the 2nd Worcester Convention, Oct. 1851." Haskell, M.
"Remedial Work for Rural Children." Bradley, F.
"Remembering the Witches." Dworkin, A.
"Reminiscence of Susan B. Anthony at Berkshire Historical Society Meeting, July 1897." Avery, R.
"Reminiscences by Frances D. Gage." Truth, S.
"Remove the Legal Shackles from Women." Rose, E.
"Renewing the Battle for Minimum Wage Legislation." Herrick, E.
"Renouncing Sexual Equality." Dworkin, A.
"Reply to the Paper of Catherine E. Beecher, Convention of the American Woman Suffrage Association N. Y., May 1870." Cutler, H.
"Reply to the Traducers of the French Reformers of the Year 1789." Wright, F.
"Report Before Conference of Women's Organizations, March 14, 1946 on United Nations Sessions in London." Miller, F.
"Report--Civil Service Conference." Oakley, I.
"Report from Europe." Houghton, D.
"Report from Iowa." McCowen, J.
"Report from Korea." Higgins, M.
"Report from the District of Columbia." Spencer, S.
"Report Library Extension." Titcomb, M.
"Report--Mrs. Leslie Stringfellow Read, Chairman Publicity." Read, L.
"Report of a Survey of the Effects of Unemployment." Hall, H.
"Report of Bureau of Information." Wood, M.
"Report of Campaign Work to the National American Woman Suffrage Association Convention of 1914." Funk, A.
"Report of Campaigns and Surveys Committee to the National American Woman Suffrage Association Convention of 1918-1919." Shuler, N.
"Report of Civil Service Reform Committee." Clark, A.
"Report of Committee on Current Relief Program." Colcord, J.
"Report of Committee on Enrollment." Gordon, K.

"Report of Committee on Peace and Arbitration." Mead, L.
"Report of Community Service Division." Preston, J.
"Report of Corresponding Secretary, General Federation of Women's Clubs." Plummer, M.
"Report of District of Columbia." Spencer, S.
"Report of Foreign Correspondent." Denison, D.
"Report of Free Baptist Missionary Society." Hills, M.
"Report of Household Economics Committee." Blair, M.
"Report of Inter Federation Committee." Ward, M.
"Report of Iowa." Lewelling, A.
"Report of Literature Committee." Poppenheim, M.
"Report of May 16th, 1861 to the National Convention." Jones, J.
"Report of Mrs. Julia A. Ruhl, Chairman Membership Committee." Ruhl, J.
"Report of Outlook Committee." Lake, H.
"Report of Special Campaign Committee to the National American Woman Suffrage Association Convention of 1914." McCormick, R.
"Report of the Campaign Committee to the National American Woman Suffrage Association Convention of 1914." McCormick, R.
"Report of the Committee (on Children)." Curtis, F.
"Report of the Committee (on Families and Neighborhoods); the Inter-Relation of Social Movements." Richmond, M.
"Report of the Committee on Immigrants." Addams, J.
"Report of the Committee (on Law Breakers): The Reformatory Method." Davis, K.
"Report of the Committee on Plan of Action." Sternberger, E.
"Report of the Committee on Preventive Work Among Children." Smith, V.
"Report of the Committee (on Securing and Training Social Workers)." Breckinridge, S.
"Report of the Committee (on Social Hygiene)." Falconer, M.
"Report of the Committee (on Social Hygiene)." Miner, M.
"Report of the Committee (on Standards of Living and Labor): Minimum Wage Boards." Kelley, F.
"Report of the Committee on State Supervision and Administration." Lathrop, J.
"Report of the Committee on the Organization of Charities." Todd, H.

"Report of the Committee on the Organization of Charity."	Smith, Z.
"Report of the Committee: The Working Force of Organized Charity."	Glenn, M.
"Report of the Congressional Committee to the National American Woman Suffrage Association Convention of 1915."	Funk, A.
"Report of the Congressional Committee to the National American Woman Suffrage Association Committee of 1915."	Smith, E.
"Report of the Congressional Committee to the National American Woman Suffrage Association Convention of 1917."	Park, M.
"Report of the Corresponding Secretary to the National American Woman Suffrage Association Convention of 1913."	Dennett, M.
"Report of the Corresponding Secretary to the National American Woman Suffrage Association Convention of 1920."	Shuler, N.
"Report of the Findings Committee."	Carroll, M.
"Report of the First Vice President."	Jennings, M.
"A Report of the General Instructor of Woman's Work, 1889."	Barry, L.
"Report of the International Women Writers' Concave."	Seton, G.
"Report of the Local Biennial Board."	Bacon, G.
"Report of the Manifesto Committee."	Beard, M.
"Report of the National Congressional Committee to the National American Woman Suffrage Association Convention of 1916."	Roessing, J.
"Report of the National Council of the United States."	Gaffney, F.
"Report of the President."	Decker, S.
"Report of the Standing Committee-State Boards and Commissions."	Lincoln, L.
"Report of the Sub-Committee on Visiting Nursing."	Hitchcock, J.
"Report of the Vice-President-at-Large to the National-American Woman Suffrage Association Convention of 1896."	Shaw, A.
"Report of the Year's Work to the National Woman's Suffrage Association Convention, Jan. 1872."	Hooker, I.
"Report of Western Women's Unitarian Conference."	Richardson, V.
"Report of Woman's International Press Association."	Field, M.

"Report on Education." Robinson, E.
"Report on Jail Work of the W. C. T. U. in Nebraska." Newman, A.
"Report on Labor." Cowles, B.
"Report on Research Among 5,000 Doctors." Lape, E.
"Report on the Common Law." Giddings, M.
"Report on the International Council of Women in London to the 32nd Annual Convention of the National American Woman Suffrage Association, Feb. 1900." Anthony, S.
"Report on the Washington Health Conference." Roche, J.
"Report on Work in Arizona to the National-American Woman Suffrage Association Convention of 1899." Catt, C.
"Report on Work in Oklahoma at the National-American Woman Suffrage Association Convention of 1899." Catt, C.
"Report of Year's Activities of the Woman's National Loyal League at the Anniversary Meeting, May 12, 1864." Anthony, S.
"Report to Council, June 25, 1954, Minneapolis." Ludington, F.
"Report to the American Woman Suffrage Association on the Work of the Rhode Island Association, Philadelphia, 1876." Chace, E.
"Report to the National American Convention of 1918-1919." Harper, I.
"Report to the National American Woman Suffrage Convention of 1916." Catt, C.
"Report to the 10th National Woman's Rights Convention, N. Y., May 10-11, 1860." Anthony, S.
"Reporting Activities of Group-Work Agencies." Adkins, F.
"Representative Edith Green Speaks in Support of the Equal Rights Amendment." Green, E.
"Representative Shirley Chisholm Speaks in Support of Equal Rights Amendment." Chisholm, S.
"Reprint of Remarks by Dr. Hunt in the Tribune, Sept. 12, 1853 (New York)." Hunt, H.
"Reprint of Remarks by Mrs. Rose in the Tribune, Sept. 12, 1853." Rose, E.
"Reprint of Remarks in the (New York) Tribune, Sept. 12, 1853." Stone, L.

"Reproduction and Natural Law."	Moque, A.
"Research and Your Job."	Keyserling, M.
"Research as a Method of Training for Social Work."	Mudgett, M.
"Research in Progress at The Merrill-Palmer School."	Knapp, P.
"Research in the Child Welfare Field: A Study of Intake in Westchester County."	Moore, M.
"Resignation Speech at the 32nd Annual Convention of the National American Woman Suffrage Association, Washington, D.C., Feb., 1900."	Anthony, S.
"Resolution and Bible Argument at the Syracuse National Convention, Sept. 1852."	Blackwell, A.
"Resolution for a Federal Amendment at May, 1864 Meeting of the Women's Loyal League."	Anthony, S.
"Resolutions at the Memorial Services of the National-American Woman Suffrage Association Convention of 1898."	Colby, C.
"Resources for Care of the Chronically Ill: Maintenance."	Potter, E.
"Response."	Addams, J.
"Response to Address of Welcome."	Blackwell, A.
"Response to Address of Welcome."	Dickinson, M.
"Response to Addresses of Welcome."	Decker, S.
"Response to an Address of Welcome."	Stevenson, L.
"Response to Greeting of South Carolina at the National-American Woman Suffrage Association Convention of 1894."	Anthony, S.
"Response to Tribune at Reception in Honor of Her 63rd Birthday, Philadelphia, Feb. 15, 1883."	Anthony, S.
"The Responsibilities and Duties of Women Toward the Peace Movement."	Addams, J.
"Responsibilities in Placement of Children."	Bowen, J.
"The Responsibility of Club Women in Promoting the Welfare of Children."	Abbott, G.
"The Responsibility of Juvenile Court and Public Agency in Child Welfare."	Nutt, A.
"The Responsibility of Medical Social Workers."	Lothrop, A.
"The Responsibility of the Case Worker in the Conflict Between the Interests of the Individual and the Interests of Society."	Marcus, G.
"Responsibility of the Movies."	Temple, S.
"The Responsibility of the Police for Preventing Crime."	Additon, H.

Title	Author
"The Responsibility of the Psychiatric Social Worker: A Further Consideration of Psychiatric Social Work."	Marcus, G.
"The Responsibility of the Psychiatric Social Worker in Civilian Life."	Young, I.
"The Responsibility of the Social Worker in a Democracy."	Springer, G.
"The Responsibility of State and Municipal Authorities to the Migrant Consumptive."	Lummis, J.
"The Responsibility of the Schools of Social Work for Training for the Public Welfare Services."	Browning, G.
"Responsibility of Women as Citizens."	Gaffrey, F.
"The Responsibility of Women in Regard to Questions Concerning Public Morality."	Blackwell, E.
"The Responsibility of Women to the Press."	Alden, M.
"Responsibility to Our Men and Women in the Services."	Roosevelt, A.
"Restoring Stability to the Family. Emotional Disturbances Brought on by the Demands of Business."	McLemore, E.
" 'Restricted Membership' at the Management Level: Exclusion of Jews from the Executive Suite."	Wallace, P.
"Restrictions in Regard to Regulation of Birth Imposed by Laws of the Various Civilized Nations."	Gaylord, G.
"Results of Club Life Among Women Upon the Home."	Learned, L.
"The Results of the Employment of a Police Matron in the City of Portland, Maine."	Devall, S.
"Rethinking Housework."	Pogrebin, L.
"Retraining for Employment."	Webster, E.
"Retrospection."	Stowell, L.
"The Return of the Serviceman to His Family and Community: As Seen in a Military Hospital at the Point of Discharge."	Davis, D.
"The Return of the Serviceman to His Family and Community: As Seen in a Private Family Case Work Agency."	Thomas, D.
"The Return of the Serviceman to His Family and Community: As Seen in Home Service, American National Red Cross."	Craddock, C.
"Review of the Decision in Virginia Minor's Court Case at Convention in Washington, 1875."	Gage, M.

"Revise Role of Teacher; Summary of Address." Mead, M.
"The Revolt Against War." Addams, J.
"Revolution: From the Doll's House to the White House." Hernandez, A.
"A Revolution in Human Society." Johnson, M.
"Revolution: Tomorrow is NOW. Keynote Address--Opening Session of NOW'S 6th National Conference." Heide, W.
"The Right to Know the Truth." Kelley, F.
"The Rights of Women and Negroes." Weld, A.
"The Rising Tide of Violence. Maintaining Order in a Nation." Griffiths, M.
"The Road Is Paved with Good Intentions: Title IX and What It Is Not." Green, E.
"Roads to International Understanding." Norrell, C.
"The Role and Aims of the Social Worker in Treatment." Nickel, L.
"The Role of Commercial Organizations in Social Welfare on the Pacific Coast." Trumbull, G.
"Role of Mature Woman in Economy." Leopold, A.
"The Role of Personalities in the Treatment of Problem Children in an Institution." Clifton, E.
"The Role of the Equal Employment Opportunity Commission." Rogers, M.
"The Role of the Private Agency: Children's Institutions and Agencies." Embry, M.
"The Role of the Social Worker in Agency-Community Relationships." Burnett, M.
"Role of Women in National Economy." Miller, F.
"Role of Women in the Organization of the Men's Garment Industry, Chicago, 1910." Cohen, M.
"The Role of Women in the World of Today. No Longer Necessary to Try to Emulate Men." Wegny, L.
"The Roles of Women: A Question of Values." Albert, E.
"The Role of Women's Legislation in Meeting Basic Problems of Working Conditions." Magee, E.
"The Root Cause." Dworkin, A.
"The Runaway and the Stranded Girl." Murray, V.
"Rural Case Work--Progress of Undifferentiated Case Work Made in the Children's Aid Society of Baltimore County." Kirwan, K.
"The Rural Community Program of Relief." Atkinson, M.
"Rural Conditions in Pennsylvania." Powers, E.

"Russia."	Antin, M.
"Russian-American Wife."	Scott, M.
"The Russian Factory Woman, 1880-1914."	Glickman, R.
"Russian Merchant Marine and Naval Supremacy: Awake Before It's Too Late!"	Bentley, H.
"Russian Rural Women."	Dunn, E.
"Rutgers--The State University. Ford Foundation Program for the Re-training in Mathematics of College Graduate Women."	Marston, H.
"The Sacrificial Lambs."	Atkinson, T.
"Safeguarding Machine Development."	Gilbreth, L.
"Saintly Scientist. George Washington Carver."	Luce, C.
"The Salon in America."	Howe, J.
"Salute to the Dawn."	Warren, A.
"Samoa--Its People and Their Customs."	Ormsbee, E.
"Sanitary Conditions About Military Camps, and Parts Played by the Public Health Nursing."	Lent, M.
"Sarah Lawrence College, The Center for Continuing Education."	Raushenbush, E.
"Sarah Rozet Smith. At the Dedication of the Hull-House Organ."	Addams, J.
"Satire on the Rights of Men, Presented to the National Suffrage Convention, Jan. 1887."	Blake, L.
"Saving Democracy."	Thompson, D.
"The Saving of Telegraph Hill."	Moore, D.
"The Savings Society."	Scribner, A.
"The Scare-crows of Sexual Freedom."	Woodhull, V.
"Scholastic and Industrial Education."	Cobb, M.
"The School and Delinquency: Every School a Clinic."	Woods, E.
"The School and Its Relation to the Vocational Life of the Negro."	McDougald, E.
"The School as a Community Center."	DeLong, E.
"School Busing: Are We Hurting the People We Want to Help?"	Green, E.
"The School Program in Case Work with Exceptional Children."	Janvier, C.
"School Savings-Banks."	Oberholtzer, S.
"The School Social Worker and the Social Development of the Child."	Smalley, R.
"School Suffrage."	Shaw, A.
"School Suffrage in Massachusetts."	Everett, M.
"Schools and Delinquency."	Brannick, C.
"Schools and the Rulers of Mankind--Discussion."	Hanna, R.

"Schools and the Rulers of Mankind--Discussion." Pierce, B.

"The School's Responsibility for the Leisure Time of the Child: In Relation to Its Effect on the Conduct and Efficiency of the Child and His Family." Campbell, M.

"The School's Responsibility for the Leisure Time of the Child: In Relation to the Services of the School." Deardorff, N.

"Science and Homosexuality." Fee, E.

"Science and Its Interrelationship with Foreign Policy: Speech." Mink, P.

"Science and Social Work." Johnson, A.

"Science and the Senses: Substance of My Address at the National Convention in Chicago, June 13, 1888." Eddy, M.

"Science for Women." Lewis, G.

"Science in the Kitchen." Miller, A.

"The Science of Nursing: A Plea." Fullerton, A.

"Scientific Charity." Evans, E.

"Scientific Charity." Lowell, J.

"The Scope and Limitations of Family Rehabilitation: Due to Mental Conditions." Byington, M.

"The Scope and Place of Research in the Program of the Family Society." Breckinridge, S.

"The Scope of Day Nursery Work." Dewey, M.

"The Scope of the Problem." Donlon, M.

"Scouts and the New Frontier." Brady, G.

"Sculpture as a Profession for Women." Johnson, A.

"Sculpture for Women." Hoxia, V.

"Seamen with Venereal Disease in the Port of New York." Buffington, A.

"Search for an American Foreign Policy. Yardsticks to Measure Our Objectives." Luce, C.

"Search for Skills." Leopold, A.

"2nd Address on Nuclear Credibility, Senate, Sept. 21, 1962." Smith, M.

"Second Address to the 1st Annual Meeting of the American Equal Rights Association, May, 1867." Gage, F.

"2nd Address to the 1st Annual Meeting of the American Equal Rights Association, May, 1867." Truth, S.

"2nd Address to the N. Y. State Legislature, Judiciary Committee, Feb. 18, 1860." Stanton, E.

"Second Declaration of Conscience." Smith, M.

"Secretary's Report at the 1st Annual Meeting of the American Equal Rights Association, May, 1867." Anthony, S.

"Security Assistance: Conventional Arms Transfer Policy."	Benson, L.
"The Security Report of the National Resources Planning Board."	Burns, E.
"Seeing the Problem Whole."	Taylor, L.
"Self as Critical Variable in Sensitive Research in Women's Health."	Benoliel, J.
"Self Concept and the Female Participant."	Allen, D.
"Self-employment."	Hogan, M.
"Self-perception of Athletes and Coaches."	Ziegler, S.
"A Self Support Problem."	Tutwiler, J.
"Senate Speech on Ratification of the Nuclear Test Ban Treaty."	Smith, M.
"Senate Speech on Safeguard ABM System."	Smith, M.
"Senate Speech on Support for Medical Research, Jan. 12, 1956."	Smith, M.
"Senators vs. Working Women."	Schepps, M.
"Sentimentalism in Politics."	Neymann, C.
"Separation Allowances for Service Men's Families."	Jeter, H.
"Sermon, Delivered at Bristol, Pa., 6th mo. 6th, 1860."	Mott, L.
"A Sermon Delivered at Yardleyville, Bucks Co., Pa., Ninth Mo. 26th, 1858."	Mott, L.
"Sermon on the Religious Aspect of the Age. Delivered at Friends' Meeting, Race Street, Philadelphia, First Month 3rd, 1869, on her 76th Birthday."	Mott, L.
"Sermon Preached in the Hall of Washington, on Sunday Morning, May 21st, 1893."	Shaw, A.
"Sermon, The Heavenly Vision."	Shaw, A.
"Service."	Glenn, M.
"The Settlement and Organized Charity."	McDowell, M.
"The Seven Joys of Reading."	Plummer, M.
"The Seventeen Year Trend to Castro: The Art of Economic Brinkmanship."	Luce, C.
"Sex and Library Careers."	Schiller, A.
"Sex and Power in the Balkans."	Denich, B.
"Sex Differences in Biomechanics."	Adrian, M.
"Sex Differences in Health Care: Social Survey Research Methods."	Kravits, J.
"Sex Discrimination: Some Societal Constraints on Upward Mobility for Women Executives."	Wallace, P.
"Sex Discrimination: The Legal Obligations of Educational Institutions."	Polowy, C.
"Sex in Brain."	Gardner, H.
"Sex Role and the Feminine Personality."	Guber, S.

"Sex Roles and Survival Strategies in an Urban Black Community." Stack, C.
"Sex Segregation of Workers by Enterprise in Clerical Occupations." Blau, F.
"Sexual Equality in Soviet Policy: A Developmental Perspective." Lapidus, G.
"The Sexual Politics of Fear and Courage." Dworkin, A.
"Shall It Be Progress?" Phillips, L.
"Shall We Repeat Indian History in Alaska." Bronson, R.
"Shaping the Destinies of a New State." Barnard, K.
"Shaping the Record to Facilitate Research." Hewins, K.
"She Earns as a Child; She Pays as a Man Women Workers in a Mid-nineteenth-century New York City Community." Groneman, C.
"Shell Model: Address, December 12, 1963." Mayer, M.
"Shipping: The Conference System." Bentley, H.
"The Short-Term Offender." Spaulding, E.
"Should Auto Emission Controls Be Removed in Low-Pollution Areas to Help Conserve the U.S. Supply of Motor Fuels?" Abzug, B.
"Should 'Conditional Amnesty' Be Granted to Vietnam War Draft Evaders?" Abzug, B.
"Should Congress Adopt the Nixon Administration's Program for 'Revenue Sharing'?" Mink, P.
"Should Congress Approve the Equal Rights Amendment." Chisholm, S.
"Should Congress Approve the Equal Rights Amendment?" Griffiths, M.
"Should Congress Approve the 'Equal Rights Amendment'?" Keyserling, M.
"Should Congress Approve the 'Equal Rights Amendment'?" Leonard, M.
"Should Congress Approve the 'Equal Rights Amendment'?" Witter, J.
"Should Congress Approve the 'Equal Rights Amendment'?" Wolfgang, M.
"Should Congress Curtail the Use of 'Busing' for School Desegregation?" Ruffra, J.
"Should Congress Enact H.R. 10 to Permit Greater Political Activity by Federal Employees?" Holtzman, E.
"Should Congress Enact Proposed Legislation to Require Mandatory Deposits on Beverage Containers?" Anderson, J.
"Should Congress Establish a Major Federal Role in General Financing of U.S. Education?" Green, E.

"Should Congress Limit the Present Scope of the Federal Food Stamp Program?" Abzug, B.
"Should Congress Limit the Present Scope of the Federal Food Stamp Program?" Chisholm, S.
"Should Congress Provide for Automatic Adjustments in the Federal Minimum Wage?" Burris, C.
"Should Federal Subsidies Be Provided for Congressional Election Campaigns?" Abzug, B.
"Should It Be Safe to Save?" Ware, C.
"Should Manufacture and Sale of Handguns for Private Use Be Prohibited in the United States." Holt, M.
"Should Present Military Assistance Programs of U. S. Foreign Aid Be Substantially Curtailed?" Bird, D.
"Should the Congress Approve the Proposed 'Fair Packaging and Labeling Act' ?" Peterson, E.
"Should the 'District' Method of Electing the President Be Adopted?" Heckler, M.
"Should the Expiring 'Special Provision' of the Voting Rights Act Be Further Extended?" Clusen, R.
"Should the Federal Government Assume a Direct Role in the Regulation of Surface Mining of Coal in the States?" Lewis, H.
"Should the Federal Government Assume a Direct Role in the Regulation of Surface Mining of Coal in the States?" Matisoff, N.
"Should the Federal Government Assume a Direct Role in the Regulation of Surface Mining of Coal in the States?" Russell, L.
"Should the President Be Chosen by Direct Popular Vote?" Benson, L.
"Show the East How the Freedom Revolution Works. Industrial Civilizations Are Built from the Bottom Up." Sampson, E.
"The Significance of Social Security." Perkins, F.
"The Significance to the City of Its Local Community Life." McDowell, M.
"The Significance of the Rise in Relief-Giving During the Past Five Years: Its Relation to Standards of Case Work." Nesbitt, F.
"Sino-Japanese Dossier: Background and Personalities." Thompson, D.
"Sino-Japanese Dossier: Eye-witness." Roosevelt, E.
"Six Cliches in Search of a Woman; Happily Ever After." Kreps, J.

"Slavery's Legacy of Impurity."	Schofield, M.
"The Smallpox Problem in the West."	Humphrey, E.
"So Let Your Light Shine. The Role of the Educated Woman in the Modern World."	Joachim, M.
"Social Action and Professional Education."	Hathway, M.
"Social Action from the Viewpoint of Professional Organizations."	Kahn, D.
"Social and Economic Factors Conditioning Food Expenditures."	Williams, F.
"Social Aspects of the Readmission of Women into the Medical Profession."	Jacobi, M.
"Social Attitudes Conditioning Immigrant Maladjustments: Twofold Problem of Immigration."	Bird, E.
"Social Case Work and Social Adjustment."	Day, F.
"Social Casework in a Social Protection Program."	Corrigan, H.
"Social Case Work in Industry: Personnel Work in Factories."	Odencrantz, L.
"Social Case Work in Public Assistance."	Smith, M.
"Social Case Work Method in Health Work."	Thornton, J.
"Social Case-Work Practice in Rural Communities."	Twente, E.
"The Social Case Worker and the Enforcement of Industrial Legislation."	Abbott, E.
"The Social Case Worker in a Changing World."	Richmond, M.
"The Social Case Worker's Attitudes and Problems as They Affect Her Work."	Dexter, E.
"The Social Case Worker's Task."	Richmond, M.
"Social Causes of Blindness. Speech in Behalf of the Massachusetts Association for Promoting the Interests of the Blind, Boston, February, 14, 1911."	Keller, H.
"Social Change and Sexual Differentiation in the Cameroun and the Ivory Coast."	Clignet, R.
"The Social Consequences of Changing Methods of Production."	Van Kleeck, M.
"Social Consequences of the Immigration Law."	Addams, J.
"Social Consequences of the Neglect of Mental Hygiene in Young Childhood."	Woolley, H.
"Social Group Work in Recreation."	Coyle, G.
"Social Hygiene. The Responsibility of Women's Organizations in the Social Hygiene Movement."	Robinson, D.
"The Social Importance of the Modern School."	Goldman, E.

"Social Insurance." Carroll, M.
"The Social Perils of Lawlessness." Robins, M.
"Social Planning and Social Work." Van Kleeck, M.
"Social Program of the Labor Movement." Van Kleeck, M.
"Social Progress Within the Home." Howe, E.
"Social Purity. First Delivered at Chicago in the Spring of 1875, in the Sunday Afternoon Dime Lecture Course." Anthony, S.
"Social Purity: Its Relation to the Dependent Classes." Harper, F.
"Social Research on Women's Professional Careers." Herberg, D.
"Social Research Program of the National Tuberculosis Association." Whitney, J.
"The Social Result of Legislation Affecting Women Workers." Dunlap, F.
"The Social Security Act." Perkins, F.
"Social Seer." Perkins, F.
"The Social Service Exchange." Dickey, G.
"The Social Service Exchange: Is It a Mechanical Overhead, or a Case Work Stimulant?" Hall, B.
"Social Service Supervision of the Feeble-minded." Sytz, F.
"Social Services for Industrial Workers." Van Kleeck, M.
"Social Services for Women: Problems and Priorities." Madison, B.
"Social Services on the Mexican Border." Hanna, A.
"Social Settlements." Addams, J.
"Social Standards in Industry: Child Labor." Abbott, G.
"Social Standards in Industry: Progress of Labor Legislation for Women." Kelley, F.
"Social Treatment Through the Interview: Opening the Way." Vlachos, A.
"The Social Value of the Professional Woman." Commander, L.
"Social Work." McMurray, G.
"Social Work Against a Background of the Other Professions." Brown, E.
"Social Work and the First Federal Relief Programs." Colcord, J.
"Social Work and the National Committee for Mental Hygiene." Macdonald, V.
"Social Work and the Social Order (Presidential Address)." Lenroot, K.
"Social Work at Massachusetts General Hospital." Cannon, I.
"Social Work at the Turn of the Decade." Coyle, G.
"Social-Work Basis for Prevention and Treatment of Delinquency and Crime: Community Factors." McGuire, L.

"Social Work Concepts and Methods in the Postwar World."	Hoey, J.
"The Social Worker in a Sound Social Hygiene Program."	Parker, V.
"Social Work in the Economic Crisis."	Van Kleeck, M.
"Social Work Jobs Analyzed."	Odencrantz, L.
"Social Work Responsibility for the Development of Day Care."	Guyler, C.
"Social Work Under Church Auspices, and Social Work Under Community Auspices: From the Standpoint of the Rural Community."	Patten, M.
"Social Work Under Church Auspices, and Social Work Under Community Auspices: From the Standpoint of the Urban Community."	Spencer, A.
"The Social Worker and Habit Clinics."	Barrows, E.
"Social Workers and Labor Unions: Social Work Touches an Organized Industry."	Scott, N.
"Social Workers and the Other Professions."	Addams, J.
"The Social Worker's Responsibility for the Reputation of the Profession."	Linderholm, N.
"Social Work's Responsibilities for Veterans."	Ross, E.
"The Socioeconomic Waste: Underutilization of Women."	Keyserling, M.
"Society and the Sexes in the Russian Past."	Atkinson, D.
"Society's Interest in Human Resources."	Beard, M.
"The Sociological and Practical Value of Our Accumulated Knowledge."	Spencer, A.
"Sociological Considerations of the Female Participant."	Phillips, M.
"Sociological Research Studies--What are the Values for the Social Worker of the More Recent Sociological Type of Community Study?"	Deardorff, N.
"A Sociologist's Skepticism."	Oppenheimer, V.
"Sod Busting for Social Work: Children with Plenty O'Nothin'."	Hagood, B.
"Sod Busting for Social Work in Rural Michigan."	McLennan, H.
"Sod Busting for Social Work in White Pine County, Nevada."	Starkweather, V.
"Sojourner Truth Speaks Before a Woman's Rights Convention."	Truth, S.
"The Solitude of Self. Address to the Senate Committee on Woman Suffrage, Feb. 20, 1892."	Stanton, E.
"Solving the Conflict."	Fisher, K.
"Some Administrative Problems in the Young Women's Christian Association."	Cratty, M.

"Some Common Fallacies." Mead, L.
"Some Community Values in a Social Survey." Hill, R.
"Some Conclusions from a Series of Studies by the National Catholic Welfare Conference." McHugh, R.
"Some Desirable Goals for Motion Pictures." Stecker, H.
"Some English Women of the Eighteenth Century." Fairbanks, C.
"Some Experiments in Case Work in Motherless Families." Jennrich, L.
"Some Experiments in Research in Social Behavior." Loomis, A.
"Some Needed Readjustments in Special Fields of Child Welfare: A New Interpretation of the Task of Day Nurseries. How Large a Part Should They Play in Children's Work?" Gillam, M.
"Some Needed Readjustments in Special Fields of Child Welfare: The Extension of Non-Institutional Care of Children with Seriously Defective Vision." Hathaway, W.
"Some Needed Readjustments in Special Fields of Child Welfare: The Extension of Non-Institutional Care for Crippled Children." Solenberger, E.
"Some New Developments in Social Statistics." Claghorn, K.
"Some New Problems for the Family Agency Arising Out of Industry." Scott, N.
"Some Next Steps in Social Treatment." Richmond, M.
"Some of the New Fall Books." Van Doren, I.
"Some Organization Problems of Public Welfare Departments." Vaile, G.
"Some Principles of Parole for Girls." Burleigh, E.
"Some Psychological Experiments in Health Publicity." Wing, V.
"Some Psychological Effects of the War as Seen by the Social Worker." Clifton, E.
"Some Reflections of the Failure of the Modern City to Provide Recreation for Young Girls." Addams, J.
"Some Significant Trends Since Cleveland, 1912 (Presidential Address)." Vaile, G.
"Some Social Causes of Prostitution." Glenn, M.
"Some Tests for the Evaluation of Case Work Methods." Blackman, E.
"Some Tests for the Evaluation of Case Work Methods." Wheeler, M.

"Some Underlying Principles of Research in Social Case Work."	Witmer, H.
"Some Uses of Social Case Work in Medical Training."	Harper, G.
"Something Is Wrong. Civil Rights: A Source of Irritation."	Freeman, F.
"Son Preference in Taiwan: Verbal Preference and Demographic Behavior."	Danaraj, S.
"The Sources of Inequality."	Kreps, J.
"The South and Woman Suffrage."	Kearney, B.
"The Southern Industrial Problem, as the Social Worker See It."	Herring, H.
"The Southern Race Problem in Retrospect. South Unable Psychologically to Solve Its Problem Alone."	Guzman, J.
"Speaking Out on Prostitution, A Victimless Crime."	Brownmiller, S.
"Speaking Up for the Race at Memphis, Tennessee, October 8, 1920."	Brown, C.
"Special Classes and Special Schools for Delinquent and Backward Children."	Richman, J.
"The Special Plight and the Role of Black Women."	Hamer, F.
"Special Problems in Italian Families."	Hull, I.
"Special Problems in Jewish Families."	Kahn, D.
"The Specialized Consultant in Child Welfare Services."	Arnold, M.
"Specific Problems in Camp Communities."	Rippin, J.
"Speech."	Addams, J.
"Speech."	Blatt, G.
"Speech."	George, Z.
"Speech."	Orshansky, M.
"Speech at a Suffrage Hearing Before the (House) Judiciary Committee, Dec. 16, 1915."	Paul, A.
"Speech at a Suffrage Hearing Before the Massachusetts Legislature."	Howe, J.
"Speech at Dinner Given in Her Honor, Jan. 23, 1916."	Sanger, M.
"Speech at Dinner in Honor of Released Prisoners, 1917."	Fisher, K.
"Speech at Joint Session of Congress to Declare War Against Austria-Hungary, Dec. 1917."	Rankin, J.
"Speech at Legislative Hearing."	Howe, J.
"Speech at Memphis City Hall."	King, C.
"Speech at Meeting of the American Woman Suffrage Association, Philadelphia, July, 1876."	Howe, J.
"Speech at the Abraham Lincoln Center."	Addams, J.

"Speech at the Annual Meeting of an Equal Suffrage Association, 1895."	Howe, J.
"Speech at the Civic Dedication of the Abraham Lincoln Center."	Addams, J.
"Speech at the Concord Convention of the Massachusetts Suffrage Association, May, 1875."	Stone, L.
"Speech at the Convention of the American Equal Rights Association, N. Y., 1867."	Truth, S.
"Speech at the National Convention at Cincinnati, Ohio, Oct. 1855."	Cutler, H.
"Speech at the National Woman Suffrage Association Convention, May, 1872."	Stanton, E.
"Speech at the 9th Annual Meeting of the American Woman Suffrage Association, 1878."	Eastman, M.
"Speech at the 9th Annual Meeting of the American Woman Suffrage Association, 1878."	Patridge, L.
"Speech at the 7th Annual Meeting of the American Woman Suffrage Association, 1875."	Eastman, M.
"Speech at 6th International Neo-Malthusian and Birth Control Conference, March, 1925."	Sanger, M.
"Speech at the 10th Annual Meeting of the American Woman Suffrage Association, 1879."	Hazard, R.
"Speech at Windham College."	Koontz, E.
"Speech Before Congressional Committee on the District of Columbia, 1870."	Stanton, E.
"Speech Before Girl's Nation, Aug. 3, 1954."	Leopold, A.
"Speech Before Senate Sub-committee, Feb. 13, 1931."	Sanger, M.
"Speech Before the Legislature, 1860."	Stanton, E.
"Speech Before the National Women's Rights Convention of 1855."	Stone, L.
"Speech Before the 3rd Conference of the Congressional Union's Advisory Council, April 8, 1916."	Paul, A.
"Speech by Congresswoman Bella S. Abzug at Inaugural Day Peace Demonstration in Washington--January 20, 1973."	Abzug, B.
"Speech of Abby Kelley Foster."	Foster, A.
"Speech of Abby Smith, July 11, 1874."	Smith, A.
"Speech of Ernestine L. Rose at the Infidel Convention, N. Y., May 4, 1845."	Rose, E.
"Speech of Ernestine L. Rose at the Second National Woman's Rights Convention, Worcester, Mass., October 15, 1851."	Rose, E.

Title	Author
"Speech of Ernestine L. Rose at the Thomas Paine Anniversary Celebration, New York, January 19, 1850."	Rose, E.
"Speech of Ernestine L. Rose at the Thomas Paine Anniversary Celebration, New York, January 29, 1852."	Rose, E.
"Speech of Lucretia Mott."	Mott, L.
"Speech of Lucy Stone."	Stone, L.
"Speech of Miss Abby H. Smith, of Glastonbury, Before the Town Meeting of That Place November 5th 1873."	Smith, A.
"Speech of Mrs. Frances D. Gage."	Gage, F.
"Speech of Susan B. Anthony."	Anthony, S.
"Speech on Closure of Kittery-Portsmouth Naval Shipyard."	Smith, M.
"Speech on Equal Rights."	Howe, J.
"Speech on the Nuclear Test Ban Treaty."	Smith, M.
"Speech Representing a Reputation of 300 Women to President Wilson, Jan. 9, 1917."	Field, S.
"Speech Seconding the Nomination of John P. St. John for President at the Prohibition Party National Convention, Pittsburgh, 1884."	Willard, F.
"Speech Seconding Theodore Roosevelt's Nomination for President at the Progressive Convention."	Addams, J.
"Speech Summing Up Case for Suffragists Arrested for Picketing the White House, July 4, 1917."	Burns, L.
"Speech to a Boston Audience on New Year's Day, 1871."	Truth, S.
"Speech to the National American Woman Suffrage Association Convention, Dec. 1913."	Burns, L.
"Speech While Burning President Wilson's Message at Demonstration at Lafayette Monument, Sept. 16, 1918."	Branham, L.
"The Spirit of Social Service."	Addams, J.
"Spiritual Contributions to the Strength of Man."	Hiett, H.
"Spotlight on Engineers and Scientists."	French, I.
"The Square."	Smith, M.
"Squaring Income and Outgo."	Wittich, J.
"The Stage and Its Women."	Cayvan, G.
"Standard of Payment for Women and Girls. (Abstract)."	Robins, M.
"Standard Working Hours."	Goldmark, J.
"Standardization of the Aims and Methods of the Work of Policewomen."	Van Winkle, M.

"Standards and Tests of Efficiency in Settlement Work."	Simkhovitch, M.
"Standards of Admission to Day Nurseries."	Caldwell, G.
"Standards of Education for Industrial Life."	Addams, J.
"Standards of Hygiene and Equipment of Day Nurseries."	Hedger, C.
"The Standard of Living."	Worcester, D.
"Standards of Measurement Used in Staff Evaluations in a Private Agency."	Hanford, J.
"Stanton Defends Woodhull."	Stanton, E.
"Stanton's Address."	Stanton, E.
"The Starting Point."	Winslow, C.
"State Care for Mothers and Infants."	Lathrop, J.
"State Control and Social Care of the Vicious and Dependent Classes: Woman's Share in the Work."	Spencer, A.
"The State in a Democracy. The State, the Negation of Anarchy."	Thompson, D.
"State Regulation of Marriage."	Wells, K.
"Statement."	Abzug, B.
"Statement."	Addams, J.
"Statement."	Allan, V.
"Statement."	Anderson, M.
"Statement."	Anthony, S.
"Statement."	Armstrong, F.
"Statement."	Arnold, M.
"Statement."	Austin, I.
"Statement."	Avery, N.
"Statement."	Ayala, A.
"Statement."	Balkany, C.
"Statement."	Barney, N.
"Statement."	Barry, M.
"Statement."	Basto, E.
"Statement."	Bellamy, C.
"Statement."	Berrien, L.
"Statement."	Betanzos, A.
"Statement."	Bingman, O.
"Statement."	Bird, C.
"Statement."	Bittermann, H.
"Statement."	Blank, D.
"Statement."	Borchardt, S.
"Statement."	Bosone, R.
"Statement."	Bostanian, A.
"Statement."	Boyer, E.
"Statement."	Boyle, D.
"Statement."	Bresette, L.
"Statement."	Brown, H.
"Statement."	Brunswick, R.
"Statement."	Burke, Y.
"Statement."	Butler, S.
"Statement."	Carpenter, C.

"Statement."	Casey, J.
"Statement."	Cavanaugh, D.
"Statement."	Chacon, E.
"Statement."	Chapman, J.
"Statement."	Chen, L.
"Statement."	Chisholm, S.
"Statement."	Clayton, J.
"Statement."	Cohan, E.
"Statement."	Cole, M.
"Statement."	Colom, A.
"Statement."	Cook, E.
"Statement."	Cox, L.
"Statement."	Crawford, M.
"Statement."	Crocker, G.
"Statement."	Cummings, S.
"Statement."	Cunningham, E.
"Statement."	Cunningham, S.
"Statement."	Czarnecki, D.
"Statement."	D'Angelo, A.
"Statement."	Davis, B.
"Statement."	Denman, M.
"Statement."	Dent, M.
"Statement."	DeSarem, C.
"Statement."	Dock, L.
"Statement."	Dolan, E.
"Statement."	Dowding, N.
"Statement."	Downey, M.
"Statement."	Dwyer, F.
"Statement."	Eastman, E.
"Statement."	Edwards, A.
"Statement."	Eldridge, R.
"Statement."	Ellickson, K.
"Statement."	Engle, R.
"Statement."	Farians, E.
"Statement."	Fasteau, B.
"Statement."	Faust, J.
"Statement."	Ferguson, A.
"Statement."	Fields, D.
"Statement."	Finegan, B.
"Statement."	Fisse, E.
"Statement."	Fitzgerald, L.
"Statement."	Fleischauer, B.
"Statement."	Forbes, C.
"Statement."	Frances, L.
"Statement."	Franklin, B.
"Statement."	Fraser, A.
"Statement."	Freedman, B.
"Statement."	Freedom, V.
"Statement."	Freeman, F.
"Statement."	Friedan, B.
"Statement."	Frohman, P.
"Statement."	Furlong-Cahill, J.
"Statement."	Furness, B.

"Statement."	Gage, O.
"Statement."	Garcia, C.
"Statement."	Garcia, C.
"Statement."	Garton, J.
"Statement."	Gierke, T.
"Statement."	Goltz, P.
"Statement."	Grace, L.
"Statement."	Graddick, L.
"Statement."	Granger, D.
"Statement."	Greathouse, R.
"Statement."	Green, E.
"Statement."	Griffiths, M.
"Statement."	Gross, G.
"Statement."	Grover, E.
"Statement."	Gutwillig, J.
"Statement."	Hadley, L.
"Statement."	Haener, D.
"Statement."	Hagar, S.
"Statement."	Haggarty, R.
"Statement."	Hales, E.
"Statement."	Hall, S.
"Statement."	Hankin, C.
"Statement."	Harmon, M.
"Statement."	Harpole, M.
"Statement."	Harrington, K.
"Statement."	Harris, A.
"Statement."	Harris, P.
"Statement."	Hartle, M.
"Statement."	Hayden, I.
"Statement."	Heckler, M.
"Statement."	Heide, W.
"Statement."	Hellinger, J.
"Statement."	Herman, A.
"Statement."	Hernandez, A.
"Statement."	Hicky, A.
"Statement."	Higgins, L.
"Statement."	Hilgert, B.
"Statement."	Hilles, F.
"Statement."	Hodges, G.
"Statement."	Hodnett, I.
"Statement."	Hogan, A.
"Statement."	Holt, L.
"Statement."	Horrobin, M.
"Statement."	Howard, C.
"Statement."	Hunt, M.
"Statement."	James, W.
"Statement."	Jefferson, M.
"Statement."	Jenkins, S.
"Statement."	Johnson, E.
"Statement."	Katz, K.
"Statement."	Katzenstein, C.
"Statement."	Kefauver, C.
"Statement."	Kelley, F.

"Statement."	Kelly, E.
"Statement."	Kennedy, M.
"Statement."	Kenyon, D.
"Statement."	Kessler-Harris, A.
"Statement."	Keys, M.
"Statement."	Keyserling, M.
"Statement."	King, M.
"Statement."	Kingsbury, S.
"Statement."	Kirschbaum, K.
"Statement."	Koester, M.
"Statement."	Komisar, L.
"Statement."	Kopelov, C.
"Statement."	Koontz, E.
"Statement."	Lancione, I.
"Statement."	Lansburg, T.
"Statement."	Lauder, A.
"Statement."	Laws, J.
"Statement."	Leonard, M.
"Statement."	Liggett, C.
"Statement."	Lindsey, M.
"Statement."	Low, R.
"Statement."	Lowry, P.
"Statement."	Loers, M.
"Statement."	McCaffrey, C.
"Statement."	McCamman, D.
"Statement."	McDoal, M.
"Statement."	McGerr, H.
"Statement."	McNally, G.
"Statement."	McNeel, B.
"Statement."	Madar, O.
"Statement."	Magee, E.
"Statement."	Maloney, M.
"Statement."	Markajani, M.
"Statement."	Martinez, S.
"Statement."	Matthews, B.
"Statement."	Maymi, C.
"Statement."	Mears, J.
"Statement."	Mecklenburg, M.
"Statement."	Miles, M.
"Statement."	Miller, E.
"Statement."	Miller, F.
"Statement."	Miller, M.
"Statement."	Miller, R.
"Statement."	Mink, P.
"Statement."	Molamphy, T.
"Statement."	Moncure, D.
"Statement."	Moore, G.
"Statement."	Morgan, L.
"Statement."	Moynahan, R.
"Statement."	Murphy, A.
"Statement."	Murray, M.
"Statement."	Murray, P.
"Statement."	Neill, E.

"Statement." Nestor, A.
"Statement." Neuberger, M.
"Statement." Newman, P.
"Statement." Nolan-Haley, J.
"Statement." Norris, F.
"Statement." Norton, E.
"Statement." Oatman, M.
"Statement." Odencrantz, L.
"Statement." O'Donnell, G.
"Statement." Ogle, D.
"Statement." Oslund, G.
"Statement." O'Steen, S.
"Statement." Park, M.
"Statement." Peden, K.
"Statement." Peipho, I.
"Statement." Pell, S.
"Statement." Pena, A.
"Statement." Peratis, K.
"Statement." Persing, B.
"Statement." Peterson, E.
"Statement." Philbrook, M.
"Statement." Pilpel, H.
"Statement." Pinchot, C.
"Statement." Platt, M.
"Statement." Pollitzer, A.
"Statement." Pressman, S.
"Statement." Putnam, P.
"Statement." Radcliff, D.
"Statement." Ramey, M.
"Statement." Rattley, J.
"Statement." Rawalt, M.
"Statement." Reed, C.
"Statement." Regan, A.
"Statement." Relich, M.
"Statement." Rivers, D.
"Statement." Roberts, J.
"Statement." Roberts, S.
"Statement." Robey, G.
"Statement." Roosevelt, A.
"Statement." Rose, D.
"Statement." Ross, J.
"Statement." Ross, S.
"Statement." Roudebush, D.
"Statement." Rubin, E.
"Statement." Ruckelshaus, J.
"Statement." Russell, P.
"Statement." Salazar, G.
"Statement." Samuels, L.
"Statement." Sanders, I.
"Statement." Sandler, B.
"Statement." Schiffer, L.
"Statement." Schneiderman, R.
"Statement." Schuck, V.

"Statement." Schurr, C.
"Statement." Scott, A.
"Statement." Scott, T.
"Statement." Seifer, N.
"Statement." Sellers, G.
"Statement." Servis, M.
"Statement." Shack, B.
"Statement." Shaw, D.
"Statement." Sherwin, E.
"Statement." Shields, L.
"Statement." Shoup, J.
"Statement." Shriver, L.
"Statement." Smith, J.
"Statement." Sollars, S.
"Statement." Sommer, T.
"Statement." Spinks, D.
"Statement." Springer, M.
"Statement." St. George, K.
"Statement." Steinem, G.
"Statement." Sterling, T.
"Statement." Stevens, D.
"Statement." Stitt, J.
"Statement." Stitt, L.
"Statement." Stone, K.
"Statement." Stone, M.
"Statement." Straus, D.
"Statement." Strauss, A.
"Statement." Sullivan, L.
"Statement." Swartz, M.
"Statement." Swing, B.
"Statement." Taunton, R.
"Statement." Tenner, H.
"Statement." Terrell, M.
"Statement." Thomson, R.
"Statement." Tillett, G.
"Statement." Traxler, M.
"Statement." Van Dyke, M.
"Statement." Walsh, E.
"Statement." Washington, B.
"Statement." Weaver, A.
"Statement." Weber, E.
"Statement." Weddingson, S.
"Statement." Weed, H.
"Statement." Welcher, G.
"Statement." Wellborn, M.
"Statement." Wells, A.
"Statement." Wells, R.
"Statement." Werner, E.
"Statement." West, H.
"Statement." Weyand, R.
"Statement." White, E.
"Statement." Wiley, A.
"Statement." Williams, E.

"Statement." Williams, L.
"Statement." Williams, M.
"Statement." Williams, W.
"Statement." Winn, A.
"Statement." Winslow, M.
"Statement." Withrow, K.
"Statement." Witter, J.
"Statement." Wold, E.
"Statement." Wolfgang, M.
"Statement." Woods, R.
"Statement." Wright, A.
"Statement." Wright, L.
"Statement." Wubnig, S.
"Statement." Younger, M.
"Statement Against the Equal Rights Amendment at the Senate Committee Hearings, 1931." Miller, F.
"Statement Against the Equal Rights Amendment at the Senate Committee Hearings, 1931." Schneiderman, R.
"Statement at Public Hearings on Juvenile Delinquency Before Subcommittee on Wartime Health and Education of Committee on Education and Labor, Senate, Nov. 30, 1943." Lenroot, K.
"Statement at the 1st Woman's State Temperance Convention in Corinthian Hall, Rochester, on April 20, 1852." Stanton, E.
"Statement at the Senate Armed Forces Hearings on the Promotion of Jimmy Stewart to Brigadier General, May 2, 1957." Smith, M.
"Statement Before the Senate Committee on the Equal-Rights Amendment, 1931." Pollitzer, A.
"Statement Before the Senate Hearing on the Equal Rights Amendment, 1931." Matthews, B.
"Statement Before the Senate Judiciary Committee Hearings on the Equal Rights Amendment, May 6, 1970." Sellers, G.
"Statement Before the Social Committee of the U. N. Economic and Social Council, May 7, 1974 Supporting Holding Conference During International Women's Year." Hutar, P.
"Statement by Mrs. Carrie Chapman Catt at Senate Hearing of 1910." Catt, C.
"Statement Concerning Her Abduction Before the Senate Committee on Labor and Public Welfare, November 17, 1947." Martin, E.

"Statement During Debate on Bill to Extend Civil Rights Act of 1964 to Prohibit Discrimination on the Basis of Sex." Griffiths, M.
"A Statement of Relief: Speech to Theta Sigma Phi, April 21, 1954." Carson, R.
"Statement of December 3, 1976 on the Fulfillment of Goals of International Women's Year in the U.N." Maymi, C.
"A Statement of Facts." Lippincott, S.
"Statement of July 2, 1975 to the U.N. World Conference of the International Women's Year Held at Mexico City." Hutar, P.
"Statement of June 20, 1975 to the U.N. World Conference of the International Women's Year Held at Mexico City." Hutar, P.
"Statement of Support for the Populists at Their 1894 Convention." Anthony, S.
"Statement on Leaving Prison." Paul, A.
"Statement on Release from Prison." Nolan, M.
"Statement to the Court." Davis, A.
"Statement to the First Feminist Congress, 1919." Eastman, C.
"Statement to the House Committee on Woman Suffrage." Beard, M.
"The States and a Federal Department of Welfare." Stevenson, M.
"Statistics of Dependent Families." Brandt, L.
"Statistics of the Woman Ministry." Hanaford, P.
"Status of Organized Charity in the West." Felton, K.
"The Status of Social Case Work Today." Marcus, G.
"The Status of Social Case Work Today." Reynolds, B.
"The Status of Social Work in Rural Communities." Curry, H.
"The Status of the Migrant. People with the Same Aspirations." Pagan de Colon, P.
"The Status of Women as Health Care Providers in the United States." Ehrenreich, B.
"Status of Women in Architecture." Cisler, L.
"The Status of Women in Art." Saporta, S.
"The Status of Women in Communications." Brownmiller, S.
"The Status of Women in Municipal Government." Gordon, D.
"The Status of Women in the Academic Profession." Millett, K.
"Status of Women in the Academic Profession--Another Perspective." Howe, F.
"The Status of Women in the Federal Government." Pressman, S.
"Status of Women Students." Goodman, J.
"The Status of Women. The Economic Change." Kreps, J.

Title	Author
"Status of Women. To Be Equal Does Not Mean to Be Identical."	Morrissy, E.
"Stock Breeding."	Meredith, V.
"Stopping Propaganda. The Democracies Have the Jitters."	Thompson, D.
"The Story of Irishtown."	Breckinridge, D.
"Story of the Lowell Offering."	Thomas, M.
"The Strategic Position of the School in Programs of Social Work: From the Point of View of the Social Worker."	Campbell, M.
"Strategies, Cooperation, and Conflict Among Women in Domestic Groups."	Lamphere, L.
"Strategy and Tactics: A Presentation of Political Lesbianism."	Atkinson, T.
"A Strategy for Change."	Norton, E.
"Stratifying by Sex: Understanding the History of Working Women."	Kessler-Harris, A.
"The Street Arab."	Williamson, E.
"Street Trades and Their Regulation."	Johnston, L.
"Street Trading."	Addams, J.
"Strength, Conviction and Unity."	Fyan, L.
"Strengths of Family Life."	Colcord, J.
"Stress Seeking and Sport Involvement."	Harris, D.
"Strike Day, August 26th, 1970."	Friedan, B.
"Strike Against War. Speech at Carnegie Hall, New York City, January 5, 1916, Under the Auspices of the Women's Peace Party and the Labor Forum."	Keller, H.
"Strikes and Their Causes."	Winslow, H.
"The Struggle and Reconciliation of the Ideal and the Practical in America."	Adams, M.
"Struggle for Life Above the Poverty Line."	Addams, J.
"The Struggle for Security."	Sporborg, C.
"Struggling Towards Civilization."	Beard, M.
"Student Fellowship."	Pearson, L.
"Student Government: Human Trust."	Schleman, H.
"A Study in Goethe's Faust."	Peabody, M.
"The Study of Agency Interrelationships."	Parker, I.
"A Study of Career Structures of Federal Executives: A Focus on Woman."	Lepper, M.
"The Study of Folk-lore."	Bacon, A.
"Study of Greek Art."	Scull, S.
"The Study of Industrial Processes as a Tool for Professional Standards and Education."	Fairchild, M.
"The Study of Industrial Processes as a Tool for Professional Standards and Education."	Kingsbury, S.
"The Study of Law for Women."	Bates, O.

"A Study of the Morals Court in Three Large Cities: Social Aspects." Topping, R.
"The Subjective Necessity for Social Settlements." Addams, J.
"The Submerged Race." Hurst, F.
"Success in Sight." Duniway, A.
"Success Motivation and Social Structure; Comments on Women and Achievement." Epstein, C.
"Sufferings During the Way." Stewart, M.
"The Sufferings of the Slaves." Grimke, A.
"Suffrage Militancy." Catt, C.
"Suggestions for the Teaching of Child Hygiene." Bradley, F.
"Summary of an Address on Settlements." Addams, J.
"Summary of February 17 Evening Session." Lowther, D.
"Summary of February 17 Morning Session." Mills, T.
"Summary of Present Legislation on Insanity in Various States, with Program for Meeting the Present Situation." Furbush, E.
"Summary of Speech on Guidance Counselors Needed for Career and Employment Decisions." Keyserling, M.
"Summing Up." Height, D.
"Summing Up for the Defense of Arrested Pickets." Stevens, D.
"The Summing-up of the Whole Matter." Willard, F.
"Sunday Services on July Fourth: Extempore Remarks." Eddy, M.
"Superfluous Women." Livermore, M.
"Supervision and Licensing of Institutions and Homes for Children." Fenske, V.
"Supervision as One Method of Staff Development: In a Rural Setting." Alper, M.
"Supervision as One Method of Staff Development: In the Urban Agency." Engel, D.
"Supervision of Case-Work Staffs." Kauffman, M.
"Support and Interpretation of Professional Requirements in Social Work: Who Are Our Interpreters?" Tousley, C.
"A Survey of a Month's Work Made Six Months Afterward." Holbrook, E.
"A Survey of Institution Libraries." Curtis, F.
"The Supervision of Working Children Under the Ohio Law." Woolley, H.
"The Sweating System." Kelley, F.
"The Sweating System, Charity, and Organization." Van Etten, I.

"Symposium on Knowledge and Problems of Race: Introductory Remarks; Excerpts from Science and the Concept of Race."	Mead, M.
"Synopsis of Lecture on Margaret Fuller."	Woolley, C.
"Synopsis on Peace."	Lease, M.
"Synopsis on The Making of Citizens."	Monroe, H.
"The Systematic Study of Urban Women."	Kleinberg, S.

"A Talk."	Field, K.
"The Tangled Threads of Migrant Family Problems."	Larned, R.
"Taproot, Trunk and Branches."	Ludington, F.
"Taste and Custom as Reflected in Our Literature."	Van Doren, I.
"Tax Credit for Parents of Students Attending Nonpublic Elementary and Secondary School."	Grasso, E.
"Taxation Without Representation."	Smith, J.
"Taxes. Is It Not Time That the Women of America Make Themselves Heard?"	Kellems, V.
"The Taxpayer Needs to Know--Schools Can't Do Everything. Parents Can Make a Difference in Education Today."	Warner, C.
"Teacher on a Tightrope. Whither Your Goal?"	Anerdson, E.
"Technique of Utilizing American Political Machinery to Secure Social Action."	Kenyon, D.
"Teen-Age Centers."	Bridges, B.
"Tell Us the Truth!"	King, E.
"Temperance."	Goff, H.
"Temperance and Purity."	Leavitt, M.
"Temperance Education."	Hunt, M.
"The Temperance Problem."	Shaw, A.
"The Temperance Temple."	Carse, M.
"The Tempted Woman."	Lake, I.
"The Time Element in Mental Hygiene Therapy as Applied to Social Case Work."	Taft, J.
"Ten Years Experience in Child Labor Legislation in Illinois."	Addams, J.
"Ten Years from Today. We Are Changing Rapidly, Without Violence."	Smith, L.
"Ten Years of Growth."	Sherwin, B.
"Tentative Observations on Basic Training."	Kempshall, A.
"Termites in America."	Millay, E.
"Test of an Education."	Banning, M.

Title	Author
"Testimony."	Addams, J.
"Testimony."	Beneby, P.
"Testimony."	Blanchette, D.
"Testimony."	Causey, R.
"Testimony."	Cummings, T.
"Testimony."	Epstein, C.
"Testimony."	Fletcher, S.
"Testimony."	Freeman, F.
"Testimony."	Kaiser, I.
"Testimony."	Kreps, J.
"Testimony."	MacDonald, L.
"Testimony."	Miller, P.
"Testimony."	Mock, J.
"Testimony."	O'Bannon, D.
"Testimony."	Pace, S.
"Testimony."	Siegel, M.
"Testimony."	Simmons, L.
"Testimony."	Sommer, A.
"Testimony."	Terp, B.
"Testimony."	Torton, I.
"Testimony at a Hearing of the House Committee on the Judiciary, Jan. 24, 1880."	Blake, L.
"Testimony at a Hearing of the House Committee on the Judiciary, Jan. 24, 1880."	Couzins, P.
"Testimony at a Hearing of the House Committee on the Judiciary, Jan. 24, 1880."	McRae, E.
"Testimony at a Hearing of the House Committee on the Judiciary, Jan. 24, 1880."	Stebbins, C.
"Testimony at a Hearing of the House Committee on the Judiciary, Jan. 24, 1880."	Waite, J.
"Testimony at a Hearing of the House Judiciary Committee, Jan. 24, 1880."	Gage, M.
"Testimony at a Hearing of the U. S. Senate, Committee on the Judiciary, Jan. 23, 1880."	Allan, N.
"Testimony at a Hearing of the U. S. Senate, Committee on the Judiciary, Jan. 23, 1880."	Parker, J.
"Testimony at a Hearing of the U. S. Senate, Committee on the Judiciary, Jan. 23, 1880."	Saxon, E.
"Testimony at a Hearing of the U. S. Senate, Committee on the Judiciary, Jan. 23, 1880."	Stewart, M.
"Testimony at a Hearing of the U. S. Senate, Committee on the Judiciary, Jan. 23, 1880."	Wallace, Z.

"Testimony Before a Senate Committee on Environmental Hazards, June 4, 1963." Carson, R.
"Testimony Before Committee on Military Affairs." Addams, J.
"Testimony Before the Factory Investigating Commission." Perkins, F.
"Testimony Before Factory Investigating Commission, Dec. 1912." Perkins, F.
"Testimony Before the United States Senate Committee During the "Hearing" on the Economic Security Bill." Abbott, G.
"Testimony Concerning Discrimination in the ILGWU at Hearings Held in 1962 by the House Committee on Labor, Education and Welfare." Rice, F.
"Testimony of American Broadcasting Company." McWilliams, M.
"Testimony on Cellar Bakeries in N. Y." Perkins, F.
"Testimony on Features of Federal Income, Estate, and Gift Tax Law Which Have a Disparate Impact on Women." Barton, B.
"Testimony on Features of Federal Income, Estate and Gift Tax Law Which Have a Disparate Impact on Women." Blumberg, G.
"Testimony on Federal Efforts to End Sex Discrimination in Employment." Hernandez, A.
"Testimony on Federal Efforts to End Sex Discrimination in Employment." Koontz, E.
"Testimony on Federal Efforts to End Sex Discrimination in Employment." Sandler, B.
"Testimony on Housing and Tenement Homework." Daniel, A.
"Testimony on Neutrality Act Before House Foreign Affairs Committee, Feb. 16, 1937." Rankin, J.
"Testimony on Sex Discrimination in Unemployment Insurance, Veterans Programs, and Public Assistance." Bernstein, B.
"Testimony on Sex Discrimination in Unemployment Insurance, Veterans Programs, and Public Assistance." Dahm, M.
"Testimony on Sex Discrimination in Unemployment Insurance, Veterans Programs, and Public Assistance." Gutwilling, J.
"Testimony on Sex Discrimination in Unemployment Insurance. Veterans Programs, and Public Assistance." Tillmon, J.
"Testimony on the Economics of Sex Discrimination in Employment." Bergmann, B.

"Testimony on the Economics of Sex Discrimination in Employment."	Whitman, M.
"Testimony on the Treatment of Women Under Social Security and Private Pension Plans."	Bell, C.
"Testimony on Women's Access to Credit and Insurance."	Gates, M.
"Testimony on Women's Access to Credit and Insurance."	Shack, B.
"Testimony on Work as a Labor Department Investigator."	De Graffenried, M.
"Testimony to the Senate."	Langhorne, O.
"Testimony to the Senate."	Lewis, H.
"Testimony to the Senate."	O'Reilly, L.
"Testimony to the Senate."	Young, V.
"Then and Now."	Jones, N.
"Theories of Development: An Assessment."	Elliott, C.
"Therapy Through Social Group Work."	Konopka, G.
"Therapy with Older Children as Seen by the Psychiatrist."	Hutchinson, D.
"3rd Address to the 1st Annual Meeting of the American Equal Rights Association, May 1867."	Gage, F.
"Thirty Years Experience in Nursery and Child Hospital Work."	DuBois, M.
"This Day We Sailed West."	Cratty, M.
"This I Believe."	Smith, M.
"This I Remember."	Fried, L.
"This Is the Negro's Hour."	Stanton, E.
"Thoughts About Government and Business: Changing Public Habits and Attitudes."	Kreps, J.
"Three Addresses, Thirteenth Universal Peace Congress."	Addams, J.
"Three Types of Women's Colleges."	Palmer, A.
"Throw Off Your Fearfulness and Come Forth!"	Stewart, M.
"To Be Black and a Woman."	Height, D.
"To Be Black and a Woman."	Kennedy, F.
"To Have or Have Not: The Social Psychology of the Decision to Have or Not Have Children."	Bram, S.
"To Speak of Eagles. Education: The Expression of the Individual."	Milledge, L.
"To What Shall We Hold Fast in Nutrition During Periods of Lower Income?"	Spohn, A.
"Toast to the Women of Nebraska, at Celebration in Lincoln, Nebraska, 1875."	Stanton, E.
"Today's Tensions; Women, the Problem or the Answer."	Carpenter, M.

"Today's Woman--Her Future Role in a Changing Society."	Banning, M.
"Today's Woman Prepares for Tomorrow's World. Introduction to Panel Discussion."	Bunting, M.
"Tokenism and the Psuedo-radical Cop-out: Ideological Traps for New Feminists to Avoid."	Friedan, B.
"Tolstoy's Theory of Life."	Addams, J.
"Toward a Homosocial Theory of Sex Roles: An Explanation of the Sex Segregation of Social Institutions."	Lipman-Blumen, J.
"Towards a Human Science; Adaptation of Address."	Mead, M.
"Toward a National Policy on Aging: Every Person Counts."	Gunn, B.
"Toward an Anthropology of Women."	Diamond, N.
"Toward Dimorphics: A Summary Statement to the Conference on Occupational Segregation."	Strober, M.
"Toward Health Security: "Economic Security Against Illness."	Abbott, G.
"Trade Union Organization Among Women Workers."	Swartz, M.
"Trade Unions and the Labour Problem."	Robinson, C.
"Trade Unions in Federal Service."	Etheridge, F.
"The Traffic in Girls and Florence Crittenton Missions."	Edholm, M.
"The Traffic in Women."	Goldman, E.
"Tragedy of the Highways."	Rogers, E.
"The Tragedy of Transients; A Statement Before a United States Senate Committee."	Abbott, G.
"The Tragedy of Woman's Emancipation."	Goldman, E.
"The Trail of Social Hygiene in Social Work: Prevention Versus Salvage."	Owings, C.
"The Trained Nurse."	Palmer, S.
"The Trained Woman Survives the Depression."	Bowman, G.
"Training."	Anderson, H.
"The Training and Qualification of Women Doctors."	Stevenson, S.
"Training for Librarianship and the Work of Children's Libraries."	Plummer, M.
"Training for Successful Work with Immigrants: Training and Use of Nationality Workers."	Murray, V.
"Training for Successful Work with Immigrants: Training of American Workers."	Sears, A.

"Training for the Work of Civilian Relief."	Colcord, J.
"The Training of Social Service Workers in Psychiatric Field Work."	Lyons, S.
"The Training of Women as Librarians."	Plummer, M.
"The Training of Women Journalists."	Harper, I.
"Training on the Job After College."	Leace, R.
"Training on the Job While in College."	Woodhouse, C.
"The Training School of Psychiatric Social Work at Smith College."	Spaulding, E.
"Training Schools for Nurses."	Hampton, I.
"Training Schools for Nurses--District Nurses."	Brent, E.
"Training Schools for Nurses--District Nurses."	Lathrop, J.
"Training Schools for Nurses--Mission Training Schools."	Richards, L.
"Training Schools for Nurses--Theory and Practice."	Brennan, A.
"Training Schools for Nurses--Trained Nurses in Hospitals for the Insane."	Smith, M.
"Training the Paid, Untrained Worker."	Van Driel, A.
"Training the Rural Relief Worker on the Job."	Blackey, E.
"The Transition from Charities and Correction to Social Work--1873 to 1923--Then?"	Lathrop, J.
"Treasurer's Report for 1906."	Upton, H.
"The Treatment of Criminal and Erring Women."	Lynde, M.
"Treatment of Indians in South Africa."	Bolton, F.
"The Treatment of Juvenile Offenders Against the Law."	Bowen, L.
"Treatment of Poor Widows with Dependent Children."	Wolcott, L.
"Treatment of the Destitute Classes in the United States."	Hultin, I.
"The Treatment of Women in Prison."	Johnson, E.
"Treatment of Women Offenders."	Miner, M.
"Treatment Processes as Developed by the Social Worker."	Reynolds, B.
"Trends in Differential Treatment in Casework."	Austin, L.
"Trends in Public Services for Children."	Lenroot, K.
"Triangle Fire Speech."	Schneiderman, R.
"Triangle Memorial Speech."	Schneiderman, R.
"Tribute to Eleanor Roosevelt at Breakfast Rally for Women Delegates to the 1936 Democratic Convention."	Perkins, F.
"Tribute to Mary S. Anthony, at Her Funeral, Feb. 7, 1907."	Greenleaf, J.
"Tribute to Pioneers of Suffrage Movement."	Lippincott, S.

"Tribute to Susan B. Anthony at Berkshire Historical Society Meeting, July, 1897." Colby, C.
"Tribute to Susan B. Anthony at Berkshire Historical Society Meeting, July, 1897." Sewall, M.
"Tribute to Susan B. Anthony at Berkshire Historical Society Meeting, July, 1897." Shaw, A.
"Tribute to Susan B. Anthony at Her 80th Birthday Celebration, Feb. 15, 1900." Blatch, H.
"Tribute to Susan B. Anthony at Her 80th Birthday Celebration, Feb. 15, 1900." Cook, C.
"Tribute to Susan B. Anthony at Her 80th Birthday Celebration, Feb. 15, 1900." Gaffney, F.
"Tribute to Susan B. Anthony at Her 80th Birthday Celebration, Feb. 15, 1900." Hultin, I.
"Tribute to Susan B. Anthony at Her 80th Birthday Celebration, Feb. 15, 1900." Sewall, M.
"Tribute to Susan B. Anthony at Her 80th Birthday Celebration, Feb. 15, 1900." Shaw, A.
"Tribute to Susan B. Anthony at Her 80th Birthday Celebration, Feb. 15, 1900." Thompson, E.
"Tribute to the Important Contribution of the Woman Volunteer in a Democratic Society." Stern, B.
"The Truth About the Paterson Strike." Flynn, E.
"The Truth Shall Make You Free." Saxon, E.
"The Tuberculous Migrant, a Family Problem: The Magnitude of the Problem." Whitney, J.
"Twenty Years of Pioneering." Meloney, M.
"Two Cheers for Equality." Koch, A.
"Two Powers--Women and the Press." MacDougal, S.
"Two Types of Public Welfare Administration." Choate, R.

"The Unadjusted Girl." Smith, C.
"The Unattached Woman." Moon, M.
"Uncontained, Undefined, Unafraid." Estrada, C.
"Underlying Principles and Common Practice in Social Work." Cannon, M.
"The Underlying Skills of Case Work Today." Towle, C.

"Understanding the Delinquent: Society in Relation to the Child."	Hoey, J.
"Undifferentiated Case Work, as Illustrated by the Preliminary Report of the Georgia Study of Negro Child Welfare."	Fitz-Simons, L.
"Undifferentiated Case Work the Surest Approach to Rural Social Work: Its Challenge and Its Opportunity: From the Private Agency."	Hastings, C.
"Undifferentiated Case Work the Surest Approach to Rural Social Work: Its Challenge and Its Opportunity: From the Public Department of Welfare."	Eicher, L.
"Undifferentiated Case Work the Surest Approach to Rural Social Work: Its Challenge and Its Opportunity: From the School."	Baskett, J.
"Undifferentiated Case Work Through the Medium of Rural Schools."	Baskett, J.
"Unemployment Insurance."	Engle, L.
"Unemployment Insurance by Industry: Some Suggestions from Germany."	Carroll, M.
"Unemployment Insurance: Ohio Takes Stock."	Magee, E.
"Uniform Area Plan for Chicago City-Wide Social Agencies."	Clarke, H.
"Uniform Districting in a Large City for Social and Civic Purposes."	Renard, B.
"Uniform Legislation."	Lathrop, J.
"Union and Blue-collar Women."	Roberts, L.
"A Union Officer Calls for Idealism."	Cohn, F.
"United by Common Interests and Common Purposes."	Morton, F.
"U. N.: A Family of Nations."	Bolton, F.
"U. N. Adopts International Covenants on Human Rights; Statement, Dec. 12, 1966."	Harris, P.
"United Nations and You. Language Difficulties Are Barriers to Confidence."	Roosevelt, E.
"United Nations Commission on the Status of Women."	Hahn, L.
"United Nations Conference on the Human Environment; Statement, December 15, 1969."	Temple, S.
"The United Nations Relief and Rehabilitation Administration's Task for Displaced Persons."	Hurlbutt, M.
"The United States and the Communist Threat."	Dean, V.

Title	Author
"United States as World Leader. Don't Limit Our Aims."	McCormick, A.
"United States Comments on Work of UNICEF; Statement, December 2, 1969."	Temple, S.
"U. S. Discusses Priorities for the 1972 U. N. Conference on the Human Environment; Statement, Sept. 20, 1971."	Temple, S.
"U. S. Faces Choice Between Anarchy and Repression."	Smith, M.
"U. S. Foreign Policy and Italy: The Communist and Detente."	Luce, C.
"U. S. Foreign Policy and World Communism. The Jungle World of Sovereign States."	Luce, C.
"The United States Program for the Care of Refugee Children."	Lenroot, K.
"Unity with the Creation."	Cratty, M.
"Universal Peace Among the Nations of the World."	Huck, W.
"Universal Service for America."	Prosser, L.
"Universal Suffrage. Address to the National-American Woman Suffrage Association Convention of 1896."	Curtis, E.
"University Discipline for Women--Asset or Handicap?"	Beard, M.
"University Extension."	Chapin, A.
"University of Kansas City Project for Continuing Education of Women."	Berry, J.
"University of Minnesota, The Minnesota Plan."	Schletzer, V.
"The Unknown Future."	Cannon, M.
"The Unmarried Mother and Child."	Barrett, K.
"The Unmarried Mother: Is She Different?"	Block, B.
"Unmarried Parenthood Under the Social Security Act."	Labaree, M.
"Unpreparedness of the Individual."	Luce, C.
"Unveiling of the Portrait."	Eagle, M.
"Upon the Shining Mountains."	Spain, F.
"Urbanization for the Future."	McLean, E.
"Use and Abuse of Factory Inspection."	Kelley, F.
"The Use and Misuse of Statistics in Social Work."	Claghorn, K.
"Use of a Small Institution in Treatment of Personality Problems."	Johnson, L.
"The Use of Available Resources."	Post, K.
"The Use of Cash, Orders for Goods, or Relief in Kind, in a Mass Program."	Kahn, D.
"The Use of Central Clinics for Child Caring Agencies."	Walker, A.
"The Use of Committees and Volunteers in Rural Social Work."	Curry, H.

Title	Author
"The Use of Committees and Volunteers in Rural Social Work."	Van Dusseldorp, W.
"The Use of Current Case-Work Concepts Where There Is Physical Illness: From the Experience of the Case Worker in the Medical Agency."	Cockerill, E.
"The Use of Current Case-Work Concepts Where There Is Physical Illness: From the Experience of the Case Worker in the Social Agency."	Yocum, S.
"The Use of Leisure."	Vittum, H.
"The Use of Psychiatric Consultation by a Case Work Agency."	Neumann, F.
"Use of Service Ratings in the Evaluation of Performance."	Cosgrove, E.
"The Use of the Transfer Within the Limits of the Office Interview."	Taft, J.
"The Use of Volunteers in Rural Social Work: In Dakota County, Minnesota."	Brown, J.
"The Use of Volunteers in Rural Social Work: In Scioto County, Ohio."	Wing, V.
"Uses of Money."	Perkins, S.
"Using All Gifts Creatively."	Clemens, L.
"The Utility of Organized Charity in an Emergency."	Todd, H.
"Utilization of Womanpower. An Unnecessary Waste of Human Resources."	Hansl, E.
"Vacation Schools."	American, S.
"Vaginal Orgasm as a Mass Hysterical Survival Response."	Atkinson, T.
"The Value of Analyzing One's Job."	Glenn, H.
"Value of Encouraging Handicrafts and Home Industries."	Albee, H.
"The Value of Parades in an Educational Program.	Bache, L.
"The Value of the Eastern Star as a Factor in Giving Women a Better Understanding of Business Affairs, and Especially Those Relating to Legislative Matters."	Flint, M.
"The Value of the Fresh Air Movement."	Ingram, H.
"The Value of Unions."	Robins, M.
"Values and Limitations of the Evaluation Process: As Seen by the Supervisor."	Schmidt, F.
"Values and Limitations of the Evaluation Process As Seen by the Worker."	Perry, M.

"Venereal Disease and Clinics for Civilians Near Military Camps." Doyle, A.
"Venereal Disease Problems in Institutions." Smith, C.
"Venereal Diseases in Institutions for Women and Girls." Hamilton, A.
"Vested Interest in War." Detzer, D.
"Vicarious Atonement." Gardner, H.
"The Vice-Presidency and the Order of Succession." Abzug, B.
"Victims of Morality." Goldman, E.
"View from the Otherside; Address, November 23, 1965." Harris, P.
"View from the World Bridge." Frederick, P.
"A Vigilant Press: Its Job to Inform." Graham, K.
"Village Care for the Insane." Lathrop, J.
"The Virginia Woman of Today." Smith, M.
"The Visa and Quota Laws as They Affect the Clients of Social Agencies." Razovsky, C.
"Visions of the Future." Mink, P.
"Visitation of Children Placed with Families." Fairbank, M.
"The Visiting Nurse as an Economic Factor." Fescher, L.
"Visiting Teachers and Their Activities." Culbert, J.
"Vocal Art." Bjorn, T.
"Vocational and Employment Guidance of Older Children." Lewis, H.
"Vocational Guidance." Campbell, M.
"The Voice of the Forest." Smith, M.
"Voluntary Agencies." Kelley, F.
"Voluntary Motherhood." Blatch, H.
"The Volunteer Gives--and Receives." Cahn, G.
"Volunteer Visiting." Smith, Z.
"Volunteer Women Speak ORT, the Charity to End Charity, Through Vocational Education." Indritz, R.
"Volunteers in Family Work." Goodwillie, M.
"Volunteers in Mental Hospitals." Frank, M.
"Vote for the Individual, Not the Political Party. Whatever Is Given to Us Is Almost Always a Trap." Chisholm, S.
"The Voter's Part." Engle, L.
"The Voter's Part." Strohm, E.

"Wage and Hour Legislation, the Object of the Law." Norton, M.
"Waging the Peace." Luce, C.
"Waging the Peace. Blueprints of Past Lacked Courage and Loyalty." Luce, C.
"Wanted: Women to Defend Freedom." Bolton, F.

"Wanted: Young Scientists; Summary of Address." Mean, M.
"War Activities as They Have Affected Housing, Health, and Recreation." White, E.
"War and Family Solidarity." Richmond, M.
"War and Postwar Adjustments of Women Workers." Miller, F.
"War and the Family. The Unit for 'A Better World.' " Banning, M.
"War and the Social Services." Wisnes, E.
"War from the Standpoint of Eugenics." Lord, E.
"War Neuroses (Shell Shock) After the War--Extra-Institutional Preparation." Jarrett, M.
"The War on Hunger: Temptation or Challenge." Jacobson, D.
"The War on Poverty--What is the Federal Government Doing?" Peterson, E.
"War Time Developments in Public Health Nursing." Haasis, B.
"War Time Volunteers in Chicago." Houghteling, L.
"The War's Challenge to the United States." Thompson, D.
"Wartime Consumer Activities." Ware, C.
"Waterways and Water." Williston, A.
"We Have Found You Wanting." Schneiderman, R.
"We Have Kept the Faith." Newman, P.
"We, the Public. Our Responsibility in Politics." Stevenson, M.
"We, the Women." Reese, C.
"Welcome." Leopold, A.
"Welcome Address at Conference on Effective Use of Womanpower, Mar. 10-11, 1955." Leopold, A.
"Welcome and Introduction of Keynote Speaker." Hicks, B.
"Welcome and Opening Message." Shafer, R.
"Welcome to the Delegates." Reid, H.
"Welcoming Address." Anderson, M.
"Welcoming Address." Palmer, B.
"Welcoming Address." Stanton, E.
"Welcoming Address at the Annual Convention of the National Woman Suffrage Association, St. Louis, Missouri, May, 1879." Couzins, P.
"Welcoming Address at the International Council of Women, March 25, 1888." Stanton, E.
"Welfare Reform Needed." Grasso, E.
"Welfare Work." McCormick, R.
"West Palm Beach County, Florida: A Unit for Social Work." Cooley, E.

"Western Women Authors and Journalists." Wells, E.
"What a Visitor in a Public Agency Should Know." Chickering, M.
"What About Youth?" Watkins, J.
"What Are Our Schools Teaching About Business? Responsibility Lies With the Taxpayers." Crain, L.
"What Are the Activities, the Object and Aims of the National Arbitration Society." Lockwood, B.
"What Are the Case-Work Needs of the Aged?" Smith, G.
"What Are Your Intentions? Peace-Making Requires Dedication." Frederick, P.
"What Can the Educator Do?" Hefferan, M.
"What Do the Signs of the Times Signify?" Wakeman, A.
"What Do Women Want?" East, C.
"What Do Women Want? An Access to Forums." Bird, C.
"What Do You Know of Children After They Leave Your Institution? Do You Supervise Them?" Evans, E.
"What Does the Group Work Process Have to Contribute to a Housing Program?" Coman, J.
"What Does Woman Want?" Preston, A.
"What Educational Psychology Can Contribute to Case Work with the Normal Family." Kellogg, A.
"What Facilities are Essential to the Adequate Care of the Unmarried Mother?" Brenner, R.
"What Had the Public a Right to Know About Public and Private Charities and How Shall It Learn About Them." Curtis, F.
"What Has Social Work to Do with the Founding of New Families?" Colcord, J.
"What I Saw in the U. S. S. R." Dickinson, L.
"What I See Happening in America." Buck, P.
"What If I Am A Woman?" Stewart, M.
"What Industry Means to Women Workers." Robins, M.
"What Industry Means to Women Workers." Van Kleeck, M.
"What Irregular Employment Means to Household and Community." Hutchinson, H.
"What Is America? Think About Equality." Bushnell, L.
"What Is Americanism? Address at the National American Woman Suffrage Association Convention of 1916." Shaw, A.
"What Is Basic In Case-Work Practice." Wyman, M.
"What Is Happening in County Organization?" Colby, M.
"What Is Happening to the American Family?" Mead, M.

"What Is Labor Doing About Women in the Work Force." Haener, D.
"What Is the Constitution of the United States Worth to American Women?" Brown, H.
What Is the IWW? Speech at the New York City Civic Club, January 1918." Keller, H.
"What Is the Significance of the Red Cross in Its Relation to Philanthropy?" Barton, C.
"What Is Worth Working for in America?" Perkins, F.
"What It Takes to be Tops as Woman Executive, Outline of Address." Leopold, A.
"What Kind of Mental Hygiene Service Do Children's Agencies Need?" Taylor, E.
"What Kind of World Do We Want? Contributions by Social Science and by Women." Mead, M.
"What Labor Is Doing." Nestor, A.
"What Machine Dominated Industry Means in Relation to Women's Work: The Need of New Training of Apprenticeship for Cities." Spencer, A.
"What Makes Men Stop Drinking." Tilton, E.
"What Man Cannot Destroy." Meloney, M.
"What Minnesota Is Doing for the Indians." La Du, B.
"What Nobody Seems to Know About Woman. Radio Address, 1950." Beard, M.
"What One Family Agency Is Doing." Carr, C.
"What Our Official Statistics Do Not Tell Us." Kelley, F.
"What Peace Means." Addams, J.
"What Practical Measures Will Promote the Financial Independence of Women." Cleveland, C.
"What Price the Fatted Calf? Juvenile Delinquency Approaching Epidemic Proportions." Alexander, R.
"What Price the Welfare State? Government--the Guardian or Master?" Alexander, R.
"What Religious Truths Can Be Established by Science and Philosophy." Blackwell, A.
"What Robin Morgan Said at Denver." Morgan, R.
"What Shall We Do About Alcoholism? Alcoholics Anonymous." Mann, M.
"What State Divisions of Child Hygiene Are Doing to Promote Child Health." Schweitzer, A.
"What the Club Woman Can Do for Home Economics Education." Calvin, H.
"What the Colleges Can Do for Peace." Ilma, V.
"What the Community Can Do." Rosenberg, A.

Title	Author
"What the Indian Service Needs."	Lathrop, J.
"What the Kindergarten Means to Mothers."	Hofer, A.
"What the Knights of Labor Are Doing for Women."	Barry, L.
"What the Public Thinks of Social Work."	Bing, L.
"What the Schools Are Doing."	Breckinridge, S.
"What the Seeing Woman Can Do for the Blind Woman in a Business-like Way."	La Barraque, C.
"What the Settlement Work Stands For."	Lathrop, J.
"What the Women of Kansas Are Doing Today."	Ware, J.
"What Time of Night It Is."	Truth, S.
"What Unitarian Women Are Doing."	Barrows, I.
"What War Is Destroying."	Addams, J.
"What We Have Learned About Emergency Training for Public Relief Administration."	Breckinridge, S.
"What We Have Learned About Emergency Training for Public Relief Administration."	Brown, J.
"What We Learn from the Child's Own Psychology To Guide Treatment."	Clifton, E.
"What We Learn from the Child's Own Psychology to Guide Treatment in a Small Institution."	Johnson, L.
"What Woman's New Social Service Owes. Address at Susan B. Anthony's 85th Birthday Celebration."	Greenleaf, J.
"What Women Workers Mean to Industry."	Gilson, M.
"What's Ahead for Woman Who Earns."	Hickey, M.
"What's Happened to Eve? The Women's Liberation Movement."	Bushnell, L.
"What's New in the '52 Campaign?"	Howard, K.
"What's New in the '52 Campaign?"	Vredenburgh, D.
"What's Wrong with the American Press? The Debasement of Popular Taste."	Luce, C.
"When Leisure Falls."	Hall, H.
"When People Apply at a Marriage License Bureau."	Mudgett, M.
"When Should the Foster Home Be Prescribed for the Problem Child?"	Baylor, E.
"When Sickness Strikes."	Hall, H.
"The Whence and Whither of Prohibition."	Tilton, E.
"Where Are All the Talented Women?"	Astin, H.
"Where Do We Stand On Minimum Wage."	Miller, F.
"Where Security Begins."	Gruenberg, S.
"Which Way Agriculture?"	Sherman, C.
"Which Way America? The Progressive Decay of Standards."	Thompson, D.

"Which Way America? What Businessmen Can Do About It." Alexander, R.
"While the Water Is Stirring I Will Step Into the Pool." Truth, S.
"White-Cross Movement in Education." Willard, F.
"Who Are the Builders?" George, J.
"Who Gets It? Who Spends It?" Kyrk, H.
"Who Is Responsible for the Quality of Life?" Kreps, J.
"Who Is Woman?" Clemens, L.
"Who Works, Where and Why." Miller, F.
"A Whole Humanity. Address to the National American Woman Suffrage Association Convention, 1890." Wallace, Z.
"Why Are the Children in the Factory." Gordon, J.
"Why Are Women the Natural Guardians of Social Morals?" Howe, J.
"Why Bother? Is Research on Issues of Women's Health Worthwhile?" Coser, R.
"Why Call It Peace?" Phillips, L.
"Why Corporate America Fears Women: Business and the New Woman." Schoonover, J.
"Why Do New Products Fail: Mini-Market Tests." Angell, B.
"Why Go To College." Palmer, A.
"Why Help Women Into Careers? A Look at Today's Reality." Stead, B.
"Why the Conference." Woodhouse, C.
"Why Unemployment?" Wright, H.
"Why We Ask for the Submission of an Amendment. Address to the National-American Woman Suffrage Association Convention of 1900." Catt, C.
"Wider Use of Care Records." Aronovici, C.
"The Wider Use of Registration." Low, M.
"The Widow." Engle, M.
"The Wife of Blennerhassett." Curwen, M.
"Will the Professional Woman Progress or Perish?" Phillips, L.
"Will Women Stay in Industry?" Graves, E.
"Willard's Broad View of Temperance." Willard, F.
"Winging One's Own Way." St. Denis, R.
"The Winning of Educational Freedom. Address to the National-American Woman Suffrage Association Convention of 1900." Mills, H.
"Woman and Attitudes Toward War, National Priorities, and Values." Steinem, G.
"Woman and Finance." Carse, M.
"Woman and Freedom In Our Society." Thompson, D.
"Woman and Girls in Labor Market Today and Tomorrow." Wells, J.
"Woman and Household Labor." Hull, M.

"Woman and the New York Labor Laws."	Krupsak, M.
"The Woman Artist and the Art Academy: A Case Study in Institutional Prejudice."	Kamerick, M.
"Woman as a Minister of Religion."	Safford, M.
"Woman as a Political Leader."	Foster, J.
"Woman as a Religious Teacher."	Gestefeld, U.
"Woman as an Annex."	Gardener, H.
"Woman as an Economic Factor."	Blatch, H.
"Woman as an Explorer."	French-Sheldon, M.
"Woman as a Financier."	Lipscomb, M.
"Woman as an Investor."	Starkweather, L.
"Woman as Artistic Innovator: The Case of the Choreographer."	Cohen, S.
"Woman as Wife, Mother and Home Builder."	Grannis, E.
"The Woman Attorney and Counsellor."	Mussey, E.
"A Woman Could Be President: It's Getting More Reasonable."	Spain, J.
"Woman, Culture, and Society: A Theoretical Overview."	Rosaldo, M.
"Woman in an Ideal Government."	Grinnell, K.
"Woman in Education."	Eastman, M.
"Woman in Journalism."	Bayard, M.
"Woman in Journalism."	Holloway, L.
"Woman in Law."	Bittenbender, A.
"Woman in Marriage. Address to the National American Woman Suffrage Association Convention of 1889."	Colby, C.
"Woman in Sacred Song."	Smith, E.
"Woman in the Church and Pulpit."	Hanaford, P.
"Woman in the Early Christian Church."	Gage, M.
"Woman in the Emotional Drama."	Morris, C.
"Woman in the Industrial Arts."	Potter, H.
"Woman in the Ministry."	Bowles, A.
"Woman in the Pulpit."	Kollock, F.
"Woman in the Republic of Letters."	Rollins, A.
"The Woman Professional in Higher Education."	Kreps, J.
"The Woman Student."	Cross, K.
"Woman Suffrage in the South. Address to the National-American Woman Suffrage Association Convention of 1895."	Henry, J.
"Woman Suffrage in Utah. Address to the House Judiciary Comm., Feb. 15, 1898."	Cannon, M.
"Woman--The Inciter to Reform."	Louis, M.
"Woman, the Key Individual of Our Democracy. Think Well, Then Speak Your Mind."	Smith, M.
"Woman, the New Factor in Economics."	Bristol, A.

"Woman--The Pioneer. Radio Address, 1939."	Beard, M.
"The Woman Voter."	Poletti, J.
"The Woman Voter."	Taft, M.
"Woman Wants Bread, Not the Ballot!"	Anthony, S.
"The Woman Who Has Come."	Holt, C.
"Womanliness."	Stanton, E.
"Womanpower."	Woodward, E.
"Woman-power for a Better World. Civilizing Influence in a Man's World."	Lyells, R.
"Womanpower in Changing World."	Leopold, A.
"Womanpower Needed."	Keyserling, M.
"Woman's Awakement."	Green, A.
"Woman's Ballot a Necessity for the Permanence of Free Institutions. Address to the National Suffrage Convention of 1887."	Wallace, Z.
"Woman's Call to the Ministry."	Bartlett, C.
"The Woman's Canning and Preserving Company."	Jones, A.
"Woman's Clubs from a Reporter's Point of View."	Woodward, J.
"A Woman's College in Spain."	Gulick A.
"Woman's Dress from the Standpoint of Sociology."	Hayes, E.
"The Woman's Foreign Missionary Union of Friends."	Bailey, H.
"The Woman's Health Protective Association."	Ravenhill, M.
"Woman's Industrial and International Interests."	McDowell, M.
"Woman's Influence in Juvenile Reformatories."	Sickels, L.
"Woman's Life in Asiatic Turkey."	Wright, M.
"The Woman's National Indian Association."	Quinton, A.
"Woman's Natural Strengths."	Clemens, L.
"Woman's Need at the Present Day."	Gooding, M.
"Woman's Part and Power in the Peace Movement."	Woolley, M.
"Woman's Part in the Promotion of Internationalism."	Sewall, M.
"Woman's Peace Meeting--Jane Addams's Address."	Addams, J.
"Woman's Place in Charitable Work--What It Is and What It Should Be."	Bamber, G.
"Woman's Place in Charitable Work--What It Is and What It Should Be."	Benjamin, C.
"Woman's Place in Government."	Eastman, M.
"Woman's Place in Hebrew Thought."	Louis, M.
"Woman's Place in Letters."	Meyer, A.
"Woman's Place in the Peace Reform Movement."	Bailey, H.

"Woman's Place in the Republic of Letters."	Meyer, A.
"Woman's Place Is at the Typewriter: The Feminization of the Clerical Labor Force."	Davies, M.
"Woman's Place Is In the Wrong, The Loyal Opposition."	Brooks, R.
"Woman's Political Future."	Harper, F.
"Woman's Position and Influence in the Civil Law."	Strickland, M.
"Woman's Progress in Higher Education."	Webster, H.
"The Woman's Relief Corps."	Barker, E.
"Woman's Relief Corps."	Sherwood, K.
"Woman's Responsibility Today. An American Woman's Viewpoint."	Horton, M.
"Woman's Right to be a Woman. Address at the American Woman Suffrage Association Convention, 1870."	Burleigh, C.
"Woman's Right to Labor; or, Low Wages and Hard Work."	Dall, C.
"Woman's Right to Serve Her Country."	Darwin, M.
"Woman's Role in the Machinery of Government. Past, Present and Future."	Springer, A.
"Woman's Special Training for Peacemaking."	Addams, J.
"Woman's Sphere From a Woman's Standpoint."	Gordon, L.
"The Woman's Temperance Publishing Association."	West, M.
"Woman's War for Peace."	Deyo, A.
"Woman's Work in Education."	Hopkins, L.
"Woman's Work in Education."	Sewall, M.
"Woman's Work in Education."	Willard, F.
"Woman's Work in Kentucky."	Potts, E.
"Woman's Work in the Pulpit and Church."	Chapin, A.
"Woman's Work in the Society of Christian Endeavor."	Scudder, A.
"Woman's Work Upon the Stage."	Marlowe, J.
"Women in Academia: Today Is Different."	Kreps, J.
"Women in American Politics. Introduction."	Jaquette, J.
"Women in Aviation."	Love, N.
"Women in Banking."	Deane, A.
"Women in Elective Office."	Abzug, B.
"Women in Elective Office."	Chisholm, S.
"Women in Engineering."	Honigman, R.
"Women in Families and History."	Meyering, A.
"Women in Government Employment."	Poston, E.
"Women in Groups: Ijaw Women's Associations."	Leis, N.

"Women in Higher Education: An Unsatisfactory Accounting."	Bell, C.
"Women in Higher Education: What Constitutes Equality?"	Sandler, B.
"Women in Household Employment."	Jones, P.
"Women in Journalism."	Croly, J.
"Women in Law."	Sassower, D.
"Women in Leadership and Decision Making: A Shift in Balance."	Trotter, V.
"Women in Management: Gaining Acceptance on an Equal Basis."	Stead, B.
"Women in Medicine."	Stevenson, S.
"Women in Municipal Government."	Harper, I.
"Women in Oregon History."	Duniway, A.
"Women in Politics."	Collier, J.
"Women in Politics."	Foster, J.
"Women in Science."	Edisen, A.
"Women and Employment Benefits: Maternity and Other Fringe Benefits."	Haener, D.
"Women and Future of Broadcasting."	Hennock, F.
"Women and Men, Power and Powerlessness in Lesotho."	Mueller, M.
"Women and Migration in Contemporary West Africa."	Sudarkasa, N.
"Women and Organization. President's Address."	Willard, F.
"Women and Religion."	Cheek, A.
"Women and the Employment Agencies."	Myerson, B.
"Women and the Hindu Tradition."	Wadley, S.
"Women and the Jural Domain: An Evolutionary Perspective."	Gonzalez, N.
"Women and the Top Jobs."	Leace, R.
"Women and Their Work Roles."	Warshay, D.
"Women and Unemployment."	Bell, C.
"Women Are Being Deprived of Legal Rights By the Equal Employment Opportunity Commission."	Griffiths, M.
"Women as Capitalists and Taxpayers."	Chapman, M.
"Women as Educators."	Michaels, R.
"Women as Farmers."	Kinney, A.
"Women as Farmers."	Warner, E.
"Women as Hospital Physicians."	Cleaves, M.
"Women as Police Matrons."	Blake, L.
"Women as Publishers."	Clark, K.
"Women, Autonomy, and Accountability in Higher Education."	Peterson, M.
"Women Functioning Under God."	Clemens, L.
"Women in Science."	Jacobi, M.
"Women in Society: A Critique of Frederick Engels."	Lane, A.
"Women in Temperance."	Willard, F.
"Women in the American Culture."	Thompson, C.

Title	Author
"Women in the American University of the Future."	Reinhardt, A.
"Women in the Farmers' Alliance."	Lease, M.
"Women in the Grange."	Worden, A.
"Women in the Greek Drama. Extracts from Julia Ward Howe's Lecture."	Howe, J.
"Women in the Knights of Labor."	Loud, H.
"Women in the Labor Force."	Koontz, E.
"Women in the Media; In Honor of Margaret Fuller, America's First Woman Journalist. Who Would Not Think We Have Come Very Far (Baby)."	Komisar, L.
"Women in the Methodist Church."	Lathrap, M.
"Women in the Professions."	Flannigan, J.
"Women in the Professions."	Sassower, D.
"Women in the Pulpit."	Wood, K.
"Women in the Seventies: Problems and Possibilities."	Rossi, A.
"Women in Transition, Social Psychologists' Approach, Summary."	Jahoda, M.
"Women Into Management: Vignettes."	Austin, M.
"Women Into Management: Vignettes."	Blanchette, E.
"Women Into Management: Vignettes."	Insel, B.
"Women Into Management: Vignettes."	Thoma, M.
"Women Might Have Helped: Some Problems Ahead."	Schleman, H.
"Women of Ohio."	Jones, J.
"Women of Our New Possessions. Speech Delivered in 1898."	Spencer, A.
"Women, the Criminal Code, and the Correction System."	Gold, S.
"Women: The New Image."	Fraser, A.
"Women: The New Political Class."	Lansing, M.
"Women Wage Earners, New Challenges and Opportunities."	Keyserling, M.
"Women Wage-Workers: With Reference to Directing Immigrants."	Leopold, S.
"Women Wage-Workers: With Reference to Directing Immigrants."	Richman, J.
"The Women Want Their Rights."	Truth, S.
"Women, Work, and the Social Order."	Kessler-Harris, A.
"Women Workers."	Perkins, F.
"The Women Writers of California."	Cummins, E.
"The Women's Agricultural and Horticultural Union."	Howard, E.
"Women's Attitudes and Reactions to Childbearing."	Grimm, E.
"The Women's Bureau and Standards of Women's Work."	Anderson, M.
"Women's Clubs."	Croly, J.
"Women's Clubs and Public Policies."	Addams, J.
"Women's Declaration of Rights."	Anthony, S.

Title	Author
"Women's Education at the World's Fair."	Palmer, A.
"Women's Education in the Nineteenth Century."	Palmer, A.
"Women's Education: New Needs in Our Time."	Hottel, A.
"Women's Education: To Discover Ourselves As Women."	Littleton, B.
"Women's Heritage. Beware of Propaganda."	Bonny, D.
"Women's Influence in Poetry, Fiction, the Drama and History."	Black, A.
"Women's Intellect."	Maccoby, E.
"Women's Legislative Issues: Today and Tomorrow."	St. John, J.
"Women's Liberation Means Putting Sex In Its Place."	Heide, W.
"Women's New Role in International Scene."	Leopold, A.
"Women's Opportunity ... Starting Your Own Business. Understanding and Overcoming the Obstacles."	Buerk, S.
"Women's Part in Defense Plans."	Elliott, H.
"Women's Political Power."	Abzug, B.
"Women's Relief Associations."	Richards, E.
"Women's Responsibility in the Peace Movement."	Shaw, A.
"Women's Right to Choose, Or Men's Right to Dominate."	Roberts, J.
"Women's Rights: A Cultural Dilemma."	Mead, M.
"Women's Rights and the Revolution of Rising Expectations."	Friedan, B.
"Women's Role in Bringing Peace Through Understanding."	Winston, E.
"Women's Share in Political and Governmental Decision-making."	Kovner, S.
"Women's Status--Yesterday, Today, Tomorrow. A Chapter in the History of Freedom, 1848-1948."	Thompson, C.
"The Women's Trade Union League and American Feminism."	Jacoby, R.
"Women's Wages."	Swartz, M.
"Women's Wages and Job Segregation."	Stevenson, M.
"Work Accidents and Employer's Liability."	Eastman, C.
"The Work and Objects of the Woman's National Indian Association."	Quinton, A.
"Work Aspiration of Women: False Leads and New Starts."	Laws, J.
"Work for Normal Young Working Women."	McDowell, M.
"The Work of a Commission of Public Welfare."	Johnson, K.
"The Work of One State."	Jacobs, B.
"The Work of Sorosis."	Thomas, M.

"The Work of Temporary Homes and of Finding Homes for Children in Connecticut." Smith, V.
"The Work of the Auxiliary Visitors Appointed to Assist the Department of the Massachusetts State Board in Charge of the Visitation of Dependent and Delinquent Children." Putnam, E.
"Work of the Girl's Department, Home of Refuge, Philadelphia." Falconer, M.
"The Work of the Health Committee of the League of Nations." Hamilton, A.
"The Work of the Interdepartmental Committee to Coordinate Health and Welfare Activities." Eliot, M.
"Work of the Probation Officer in Court." Friday, L.
"Work of the Probation Officer Preliminary to the Trial." Ramsey, A.
"Work of the Red Cross." Barton, C.
"Work of the Section on Reformatories and Houses of Detention." Falconer, M.
"The Work of the Visiting or District Nurse." Fulmer, H.
"The Work of Voluntary Immigrant Protective Agencies." Claghorn, K.
"The Work of Women in Modern Astronomy." Leavitt, H.
"Work of Women's Educational and Industrial Union." Diaz, A.
"Work Opportunities and School Training for Coal-Miners' Children." Matthews, E.
"Work or Maintenance?" Abbott, E.
"Worker and Client Relationships." Marcus, G.
"The Worker's Attitude as an Element in Social Case Work." Wright, L.
"Workers' Education for Women in Industry." Nestor, A.
"Worker's Stake in Safety." Perkins, F.
"The Working Child." Kelley, F.
"The Working Girl's or Working Women's Club in the United States." Homes, E.
"Working Man's School of New York City." Adler, H.
"The Working Woman and the New Social Vision." Van Kleeck, M.
"Working Woman's Need of the Ballot." Kelley, F.
"Working Women: Their Citizenship Responsibilities." Margolin, O.
"Working Women: Their Home Obligations." Hilton, M.
"World Challenges American Educators. The Opportunity to Build New Frontiers of Understanding and Peace." Houghton, D.

"The World Court."	Addams, J.
"World Harvest: Woman's Talent, Woman's Role in the Changing World."	Parr, M.
"The World Is Our Framework."	Fosdick, D.
"The World Movement for Woman Suffrage 1904 to 1911: Is Woman Suffrage Progressing?"	Catt, C.
"A World Petition to the Third Hague Conference."	Eckstein, A.
"World Population and Food Problems: The Need for Awareness."	Prewett, V.
"World Prohibition, World Purity, World Peace: Our International Goal. Address to the Annual Convention of the National Woman's Christian Temperance Union. Philadelphia, Pennsylvania, November 17, 1922."	Gordon, A.
"World's Food Supply and Woman's Obligation."	Addams, J.
"World's Woman's Temperance Union."	Smith, H.
"Would You Believe ... the Secretary of Tomorrow? She Can Reach the Top."	Bushnell, L.

"The Year of Decision for Social Work."	Potter, E.
"The Yesterday, Today and Tomorrow of the National Council of Women."	Parker, V.
"You Can Do It."	Schroeder, P.
"You Have Been Warned."	Meloney, M.
"Young America."	Roosevelt, A.
"The Young Breadwinners' Need of Women's Enfranchisement."	Kelley, F.
"Young People in New Japan."	Vining, E.
"The Young People's International Federation League."	Pierson, M.
"The Young Woman of the South."	Douglass, J.
"The Young Women's Christian Association: Its Aims and Methods."	Boyd, C.
"Your Talents, Let's Not Waste Them."	Keyserling, M.
"Youth and the Industrial Slack."	Nelson, A.
"Youth in Industry."	Greibel, H.
"Youth in Industry."	Macy, H.
"Youth in Industry."	Plebanek, T.
"Youth of All Nations."	Sandmann, R.
"Youth Opportunities Today and Social Security Safeguards."	Roche, J.
"Youth-related Activities of the United Nations; Statement, September 30, 1969."	Temple, S.

"Youth's Contribution."	Roosevelt, A.
"Youth's Right to Knowledge and Free Speech. The Challenge of Youth Forum Discussions."	Gordon, D.